THE NORWICH SCHOOL OF PAINTERS

by

HAROLD A. E. DAY

Incorporating:

EAST ANGLIAN PAINTERS VOLUME II

and

EAST ANGLIAN PAINTERS VOLUME III

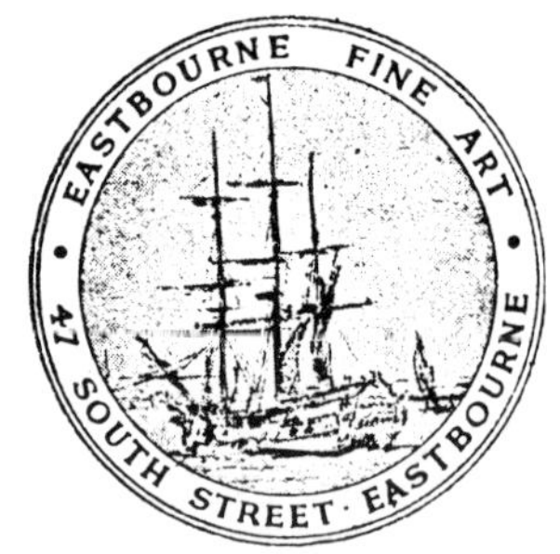

Fine Art Publishers

PUBLISHED BY
EASTBOURNE FINE ART
47, SOUTH STREET, EASTBOURNE, SUSSEX BN21 4UT

1979

SBN 0 902010 10 7

Companion books of East Anglian interest include
'THE SUFFOLK SCHOOL PAINTERS' by H. A. E. DAY
(formerly 'East Anglian Painters' Vol. I)
'CONSTABLE DRAWINGS' by H. A. E. DAY

Other Publications by Eastbourne Fine Art include
DICTIONARY OF BRITISH ARTISTS Working 1900-1950
by Grant M. Waters

PREFACE

THE author would like to thank those people who have contributed information to make this book possible, including the following Fine Art Dealers:

Ackerman & Sons Ltd.; Colnaghi Ltd.; Richard Green (Fine Paintings) Ltd.; Oscar & Peter Johnson; E. D. Levine; Mandell's Gallery; Frank Sabin; Simon Carter; Spink & Sons Ltd.; Marshall Spink Ltd.; The Leger Gallery.

I am indebted to the following Museums for kindly allowing their paintings to be reproduced:-

The Norwich Castle Museum; The Nottingham Art Gallery; The Tate, London; The British Museum, London; Kenwood House, London; and the Yarmouth Museum, Norfolk.

I would like to thank those Collectors who have kindly given permission to have their paintings reproduced.

It is some years since I wrote my small work on Joseph Stannard, followed by the four volumes on the East Anglian Painters. I am pleased to say they have been well received. It is in order that new Collectors will have material on the Norwich School available that the present volume has been formed from East Anglian Painters, volumes II and III.

The Norwich School was one of the first schools of painting to be established in England. The painters with great sincerity endeavoured to depict our beautiful scenery. To Collectors and landscape enthusiasts they represent very often a peak of achievement seldom equalled since their day. To all they offer a life-long interest.

HAROLD DAY

October 1978

INTRODUCTION

THE Norwich School painters represent the most important School of Painting to develop in nineteenth century England. Seen in terms of international Art History, the Norwich School is a connecting link between the Dutch seventeenth century painters and the French Barbizon painters. Whilst having much in common with the Dutch Painters of the seventeenth century, the Norwich School tended to apply themselves more to the study of Nature in the form of landscape and seascape painting. It is interesting to note that they seldom painted Winter scenes or figure subjects.

The Volume opens with John Crome, undoubtedly the most important and influential painter of the School; in fact, it is unlikely that the School would have materialised had it not been for his enthusiasm. His letter to his pupil, James Stark, which concludes with "Pray paint", epitomises his philosophy. That Crome should have been allowed in the nineteenth century to sink at one time into almost oblivion, reflects sadly upon nineteenth century Art Historians and Museum Officials. Even today it is not possible to walk into our National Gallery in London and obtain advice on a Norwich School Painting. However, a chink of light has appeared almost as I pen these words, for I am informed that a John Crome Exhibition is about to be held at the Tate Gallery, London.

Fortunately, the citizens of Norwich have always been loyal to their painters, and a certain Curator, by the name of James Reeve of the Norwich Castle Museum, carefully recorded details of the artists. This he made a life interest. At his death the information was deposited with the British Museum.

The next gentleman to record the School was W. F. Dickes, about whom little is known apart from the fact that he lived in London. His book *Painters of the Norwich School* was published in 1905, price 2 guineas. Such has developed the interest in the School that this volume now attains in auction upwards of £100. It is a very readable book, full of interesting plates and remarkably few errors—a book written by an enthusiast.

To follow such an able volume with the present volume can only be excused by distance of time and to make out of print information again available. I have endeavoured not to repeat any of Dickes' plates and to give added information wherever possible. Certainly there are many more Exhibition records.

In the past, controversy has raged about the authorship of many John Crome paintings. So often John Crome has been studied without reference to the work of his sons, John Berney and William Henry. John Berney certainly worked in his father's studio for many years, and William Henry for possibly one year. In 1821, on the death of Old Crome (as John Crome was later called) his studio contained numerous unfinished works; these were probably worked upon by both sons, the most quoted example being the large *Water Frolic* at Kenwood, which Old Crome commenced a week before his death. At least one work is recorded on which Old Crome and William Henry Crome worked. I think future research will probably reveal numerous joint Crome works. It is these joint efforts that complicate at times the identification of the works of Crome the Elder.

That his son, John Berney Crome, was painter in landscape to the Duke of Sussex and President of the Norwich Society, probably caused his works to be held in higher esteem than those of his father in some circles at the time, hence little effort was made to preserve the identification of the works of Old Crome.

The author remembers meeting, years ago, a Miss Ladbrooke, a niece of Henry Ladbrooke, who passed on a comment made by Henry Ladbrooke to the effect that people at the time of Old Crome considered his work very modern.

From the Cromes we pass to his very able pupil James Stark, a man dogged by ill-health and poverty. The life of his son, Arthur James Stark, is revealed in this volume; that he executed some fine work from Nature in oils and water-colour has been made evident to the writer from his researches.

George Vincent, another Crome pupil, was dealt with by Dickes, but the author feels that there may be a strong case for supporting the year of his death as later than 1831.

The Ladbrookes, like the Cromes, were one of the great Norwich painting families. From Robert, the elder Ladbrooke, who painted partly in the eighteenth century, we pass to his three able sons, Henry, John, and Frederick, the dates of the latter I am pleased to publish for the first time. The Ladbrookes are important, perhaps more so than formerly considered, for they provide such typically Norwich School paintings. By the time the three sons were painting, the Dutch influence (so much seen in many of the works of certain of the painters of the School) had almost disappeared and their work crystallised into something very English. Even the uninitiated would not consider a Ladbrooke to be of the Dutch School

An interesting aspect not over-developed by Dickes, is the fact that many painters of the School sought out distant subjects. Henry Bright travelled extensively in Wales, Scotland and England and on the Continent. Other travellers were Charles and David Hodgson who largely painted architectural subjects. The Ninhams seldom ventured far from Norwich: the same may be observed respecting Obadiah Short. Joseph Paul forsook his native city at an early age and passed most of his life in London. His son, John, became an animal painter and painter of London views. On the reverse of one of his hunting pictures he signs "J. Paul, London". Finally, Edwin Cooper, the animal painter, and Henry Walton the portrait painter, have been included in this volume on account of Cooper's Norwich associations and Walton being a native of Norfolk and an eminent County Portrait Painter.

To the uninitiated, the works of Cotman Senior either make an immediate appeal or are considered to be out of context respecting the other painters of the Norwich School.

In his day Cotman was not accepted; one comes across the phrase "shall not be taught by a Cotman". Today, of course, his work is recognised, hence the £9,000 recently paid for one of his water-colours at auction.

Miles Edmund and John Joseph have formerly received only minimum notice, but they are both illustrious members of the School. John Joseph is particularly original in his approach and probably ranks amongst the foremost water-colourists of the School. The other great painting family introduced in this volume are the Stannards. The earliest Stannard is Joseph, certainly the finest painter of the School in terms of drawing and pencilling, painting sea and river scenes usually of his native Norfolk. Joseph died young and left his brother, Alfred, to maintain the family high standard of painting. Joseph's wife, whose maiden name was Emily Coppin, painted still life in the highly finished Dutch style. Possibly due to the influence of Mrs. Joseph Stannard, Alfred Stannard's daughter, Eloise, took up still life painting and created a peak of achievement in Norwich School painting. The work of Eloise Harriet Stannard is important, for she developed her own realistic style of still life painting, perhaps influenced by earlier painters but sufficiently her own. Many of her works rank as 19th century masterpieces.

Anthony Sandys, the father of the portrait painter Frederick Sandys, is recorded in this volume. Whilst being known as a portrait painter himself, he loved to paint the Yarmouth Marshes at sunset. Another painter discussed is Joseph Clover, primarily a portrait man but known also for his landscapes in oil and water-colour. His work is surprisingly little known. Robert Leman, Thomas Lound and John Middleton were men with other sources of income, but they had a love of Art, which inspired them with a certain dedication which gave rise to the execution of very fine works.

I have included Robert Dixon, whose oils, like those of Robert Ladbrooke, are not the easiest to detect, but we are very conversant with his drawings and water-colours, many of which may be seen in the Castle Museum, Norwich.

Before commencing the record of the Norwich School painters I would like to draw attention to the almost total absence of their presence from our National London Collections. Apart from John Crome our National Gallery seldom, if ever, aspires to have on the walls any works of these painters. Why we choose to exhibit multitudes of continental madonnas (delightful though they may be) and ignore our own painters is surely a matter that deserves attention. The argument that the madonnas cater for the visitors to this country is shallow, for surely they come here to see England and the works of English Artists.

JOHN CROME

(1768-1821)

1768 John Crome was born on 22nd December, 1768, probably in an inn named the "King and Miller", St. George's Tombland, Norwich. His father was John Crome, the landlord of the inn, and in order to avoid impecuniosity, added weaving to his round of employment. Little is known concerning his mother, except her Christian name—Elizabeth. It is just possible that he inherited his artistic streak from his mother. From his father he probably inherited a friendly disposition and integrity.

From letters written in later years it is evident that our painter received education, but we have no details.

1780 About 1780 he followed the custom of numerous Norwich boys and sought a job by "Going on the Palace". This involved presenting himself in the Palace Yard and awaiting the presence of an employer. Dr. Rigby was the gentleman who first hired our future painter, employing him as an errand boy. Presumably he spent most of his time delivering medicines.

Crome, in later days, would jokingly refer to his "bleeding" of patients and throwing skeletons out of the Doctor's window. It is alleged by some writers that Crome was discharged for his activities, but in all probability he took leave of the Doctor to take
1783 up an apprenticeship in 1783 with a certain Francis Whistler, a coach painter. We do know that he later enjoyed a friendly relationship with Dr. Rigby.

At Whistler's he learnt about the grinding and mixing of colours, all of which stood him in good stead for his later paintings. Whilst with Whistler he painted several inn signs and possibly carried on this work for some years after leaving. Several such signs are still in existence. At this time he became friendly with Robert Ladbrooke, who was apprenticed to an engraver and printer. The two of them, in their idealist moments, decided to become painters. They hired a studio; Crome was to paint landscapes, and Ladbrooke portraits, and to their great credit they persevered for several years.

Their pictures did not find a ready sale, but Crome's pictures were noticed by a certain Thomas Harvey, a gentleman of considerable fortune. Crome soon found himself on a friendly footing and was invited to Mr. Harvey's house to view his old Masters. It was whilst enjoying Mr. Harvey's hospitality that Crome really conceived the meaning of great Art. He was able to observe at close hand many of the Dutch Masters, including works by Hobbema. It was probably Mr. Harvey who introduced him to the great portrait painter, Sir William Beechey. This resulted in him visiting Beechey at his London studio.

1790 By the year 1790 Crome's time with Whistler terminated and he was a free agent to garner a livelihood as best he could.

Crome probably continued painting and suffered poverty during the post-Whistler years but gradually, with the aid of some teaching, he made ends meet.

1792 At the age of 24 years he married a Phoebe Berney at St. Mary's, Coslany, his friend, Robert Ladbrooke, marrying Phoebe's sister some twelve months later.

At this juncture I will record Crome's children:

Born 1792	Abigail Crome	30th October (died 31st August, 1794)
1794	John Berney Crome	December (died 1842)
1796	Frederick James Crome	30th September

—	Louisa Crome	(died October, 1800)
1801	Emily Crome	19th April
1803	Susanna Crome	17th June
1804	Hannah Crome	20th September
1806	William Henry Crome	22nd October
1808	Joseph Crome	13th December (died 1809)
1810	Joseph Crome	22nd April
1813	Michael Sharp Crome	27th October

Shortly after his marriage, Dr. Rigby advised him to go into Norwich Hospital, as he was suffering with hydrocela. However, by 1793 he was discharged, cured.

It must have been in Mr. Harvey's house that he observed some of Richard Wilson's work. The effect must have been influential, for he accomplished several paintings at this period in a very Wilson style.

As a teacher, Crome was gradually becoming recognised. He had a splendid character and had the ability to instil enthusiasm. When the Gurney family visited the Lake
1802 District in 1802 they invited Crome to accompany them. Crome's visit to the Lakes
1803 resulted in several paintings. In 1803 it is said that he again set out with the Gurneys and toured part of Wales. In any case, he visited Wales with his friend Robert Ladbrooke about this time.

1805 The year 1805 is important in the history of the Norwich School painters, for it was the first year they banded together and exhibited. The place chosen was Sir Benjamin Wrench's Court; they called themselves the Norwich Art Society, Crome being one of the founders.

1806 In 1806 Crome is recorded as living at 17 Gildersgate, where he lived for the remainder of his life.

This year he joined the Gurneys in a visit northwards to the Lakes. A certain Mr. Buxton, who lived at Weymouth, joined the party. As a result of meeting Mr. Buxton, Crome about this time made a visit to Weymouth, resulting in *View near Weymouth*, exhibited at the Norwich Society in 1806. Also in this year he exhibited at the Royal Academy (two paintings).

1809 An interesting picture *View near Woodbridge* was painted about this time. He executed it for Bernard Barton, the poet and banker, in 1809. I wonder where Thomas Churchyard
1810 was at this time? Did Crome visit Woodbridge again at a later date? By 1810 Crome's pupil Stark was exhibiting at the Norwich Society.

1811 Derbyshire attracted our painter in 1811 and on his return he exhibited several Derbyshire subjects at the Norwich Society. Also included in the Exhibition were works by Crome's three significant pupils—John Berney Crome, George Vincent and James Stark.

Success was beginning now to attend our painter; he was becoming known, not only as a drawing master, but a painter with considerable gifts. It was considered a good thing to buy one of his works. As a result of this new-found prosperity Crome acquired the collector's urge, for he bought pictures and other articles at various sales, until his house in Gildersgate Street, Norwich, became crammed full. Probably his wife's complaints led him to send a lot of his property to Yarmouth for sale. Crome himself is said to have auctioned his own lots. David Hodgson, at a later date, recorded that the sale was unsuccessful and that Crome presented Hanks, the boat owner, who transported the articles, with a painting *A View at the back of the New Mills*.

1812 It was in this year, 1812, that Crome published a prospectus respecting his etchings.

1813 Michael Sharp, a portrait painter, painted Crome's portrait in 1813. He must have been much loved by the Cromes, for they named their youngest son Michael Sharp Crome, who was born the same year. It is said that Michael Sharp painted the figures in the famous *Poringland Oak* painting, now in the Tate Gallery, London.

1814 With the defeat of the French in 1814* Crome decided to visit Paris in order to view the Art treasures. He was accompanied by two other members of the Norwich Society—W. Freeman (father of W. Barnes Freeman) and Daniel Coppin (father of Emily Coppin, wife of Joseph Stannard). Whilst away he wrote the following interesting letter to his wife:

Dear Wife, Paris, October 10th 1814.

After one of the most pleasant journeys of one hundred and seventy miles over one of the most fertile countrys I every saw we arrived in the capital of France. You may imagine how everything struck us with surprise; people of all nations going to and fro—Turks, Jews, &c. I shall not enter into ye particulars in this my letter, but suffice it to say we are all in good health, and in good lodgings—that in Paris is one great difficulty. We have been at St. Cloud and Versailles; I cannot describe it on letter. We have seen there palaces the most magnificent in the world. I shall not trouble you with a long letter this time as the post goes out in an hour that time will not allow me was I so disposed. This morning I am going to see the object of my journey, that is the Thuilleries. I am told here I shall find many English Artists. Glover has been painting. I believe he has not been copying but looking and painting one of his own compositions. Pray let me know how you are going on, giving best respects to all friends. I believe the English may boast of having the start of these foreigners, but a happier race of people there cannot be. I shall make this journey pay. I shall be very careful how I lay out my money. I have seen some shops. They ask treble what they will take, so you may suppose what a set they are. I shall see David to-morrow, and the rest of the artists when I can find time. I write this letter before I know what I am going about at ye Thuilleries as the post compels me.

I am, &c. yours till death,

JOHN CROME.

He returned from Paris by way of Ghent and Ostend. As a result of the visit Crome was pre-occupied with Continental subjects for several years.

For three years James Stark, who was articled to Crome as a pupil, had worked conscientiously by his master's side. In 1815 he left Norwich to become a pupil at the Royal Academy. Also in this year James Sillett became President of the Norwich Society.

1815 Possibly it was the effect of John Crome leaving the Presidency of the Society to Sillett in 1815 that caused the upheaval known as the "Secession" in 1816. Robert Ladbrooke, James Sillett and six other members disagreed with Crome and others concerning the use of the Society funds, so they opened their own exhibition. This rift continued for many years after Crome's death.

Perhaps the most important of Crome's teaching activities was his appointment as Drawing Master at the Grammar School under Dr. Valpy. Crome often painted small cottage scenes during class with his pupils crowded around him. The actual time he spent at the school is not recorded but it was probably very much a part-time post.

At this time it is recorded that he made a weekly visit to Yarmouth where he stayed with a Mr. Paget who lived in a house facing the Quay. With his income from teaching and his paintings now fetching upwards of 50 guineas, our painter was, relatively speaking, enjoying considerable prosperity. It reflects well on Crome that he didn't allow this prosperity to corrupt his Art; indeed his Art improved steadily towards the end of his life. His patrons were not slow at observing this fact and towards the end of his life Crome sold most of the paintings he exhibited.

---

*For further Crome letter, see James Stark, Chapter 4.

1816- From the years 1816 to 1821 Crome is not recorded as making distant trips. He confined
1821 himself to his local views and perhaps the occasional visit to Yarmouth. During his last years he does not appear to have been hampered by ill-health, for not only is he known to have had many commissions but he continued sending a fair number of paintings to the Norwich Society. In 1821 he was working on *A View of the Water Frolic, Wroxham Broad*, when he was taken with fever. He became ill on 14th April, 1821, and a few days later his son, Frederick Crome, was writing to Dawson Turner as follows:

Norwich 21st April 1821.

Dear Sir,

My father's disorder has so much gained ground that there is not the least hope of him. Indeed, I think he is now breathing his last. At the same time he is not aware of his situation; we, of course, are obliged to appear the reverse of our feelings. Mr. J. Gurney was here this morning, but could not see him. Mr. Dalrymple has no hope—what can we have? It is killing to me. He is seldom easy unless I am by his side holding his hands or supporting his head. Excuse what mistakes I may make but you can guess my feelings. All are in tears about me. Should there be the least alteration in the morning I will send you word. Meanwhile,

I am, your obedient Servant,

FREDK. CROME.

(*Reeve Coll., Print Room, B.M.*)

On his last day John Berney Crome, his eldest son, was sitting by his bed when Crome uttered some of his last immortal words, "John, my boy, paint, but paint for fame; and if your subject is only a pig-sty—dignify it." This surely is a moral every painter could carry in his studio.

It was on 22nd April, 1821, that Crome passed away; his last words were "Oh, Hobbema, my dear Hobbema, how I have loved you!"

Crome obviously loved his Art, and on his passing the Norwich School lost one of its pillars.

THE PAINTINGS

John Crome ranks as one of the finest landscape painters of the English School. Even during his early years, when he was feeling his way, his work has an originality and profound strength.

His early Wilson-type pictures are perhaps his least interesting, as they do not carry much observation of Nature. One must suppose that Crome used them for learning the technique of handling paint.

His copying of Rembrandt resulted in him adopting for a period a Rembrandtesque style. This time, however, he applied his study of Rembrandt to Nature. *The View on the Yare—Moonlight*, in the Tate Gallery and *The Old Cart Shed, Melton* exhibited 1806, and the large dark *River Scene in November* are of this period. These Rembrandt Cromes have a quality which gives the viewer a feeling of being "present".

The study of Rembrandt was perhaps the most rewarding aspect of all of Crome's work, for it stood him in good stead in later years. It is not possible to find a Crome which does not reflect his study of this period. After Rembrandt, Crome became interested in Gainsborough; as a result, several copies are recorded.

Crome perhaps studied the Dutch Masters much more than has hitherto been credited. Van Goyen, Ruysdael, Hobbema, and finally Cuyp were his models. The well-known picture entitled *The Beaters* reflects Hobbema, but one would have to look a long way to find a Hobbema to come up to it.

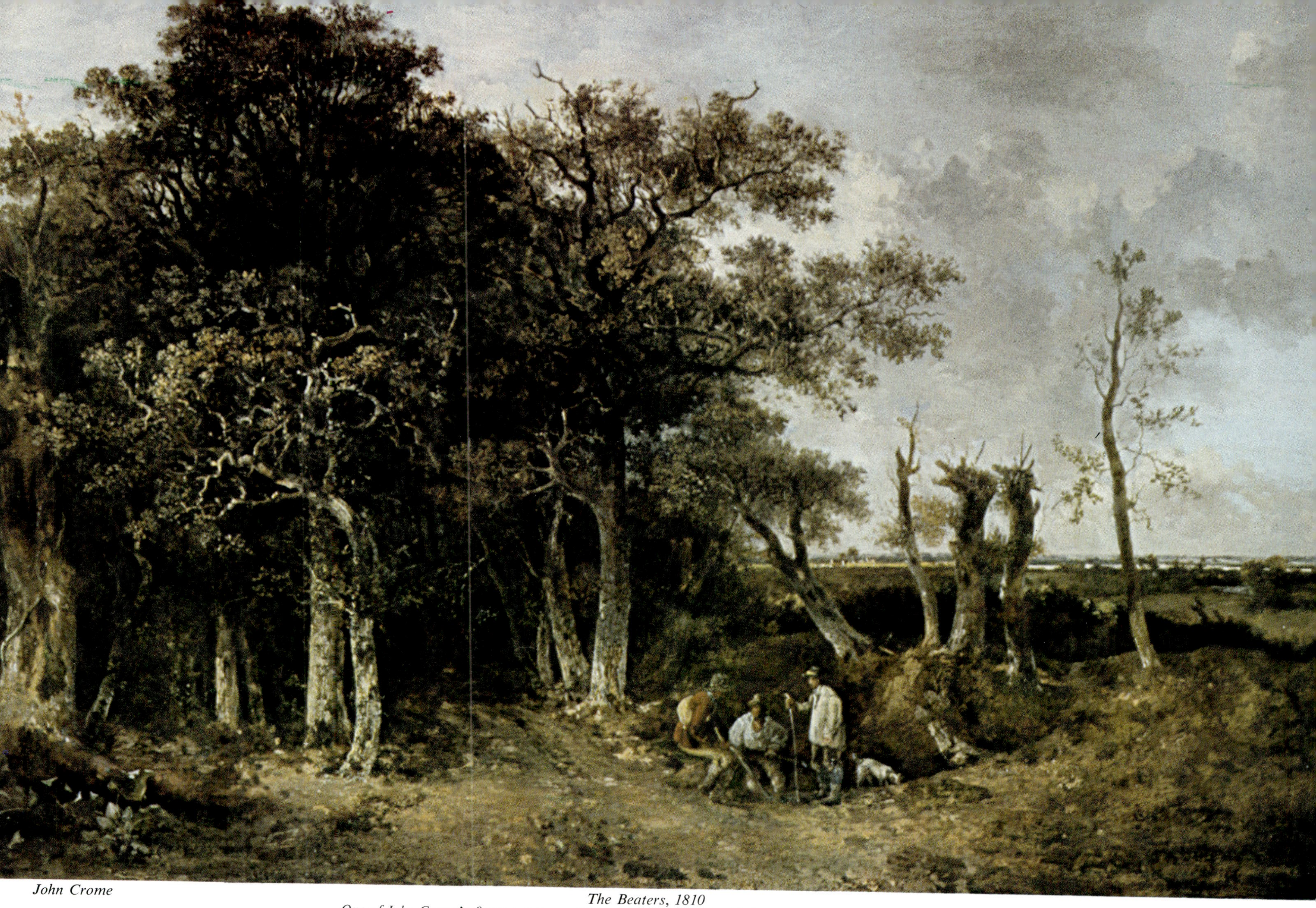

John Crome

The Beaters, 1810

One of John Crome's finest painting. The only signed and dated John Crome oil known to the author

In one respect Crome always differs from the Dutch Masters—his touch. Where they brushed on their paint, Crome almost "placed" on his paint. In most Cromes there are brushwork passages, but the hall-mark of a Crome is the way the paint is placed on the picture. These strong touchings are so characteristic. Besides strong touches, Crome can handle his paint gently; one often sees small darting highlights.

As Colonel Grant has pointed out, Crome has an envelope, *i.e.* the picture glows, the colours being in splendid harmony. Another word that may be used here is "tone". Constable once remarked that tone is the most important aspect in painting.

Undoubtedly in Crome's later years John Berney Crome, his eldest son, assisted in the studio, and there must be certain paintings on which both men have worked. Such a painting is *The Water Frolic* at Kenwood, Hampstead.

In all, Crome exhibited 309 works. There must have been many more, either not exhibited or sold direct. It is not unreasonable to consider that he painted in the region of 500 works. Future research will undoubtedly enable us to identify more of these works.

Whilst Crome will never go down to posterity as a water-colourist, he did employ the medium with considerable success. He tends in his water-colours to use a very close palette, resulting in a very Old Master effect. Possibly in his coloured drawings there appears some influence from William Williams, who worked in Norwich at the end of the eighteenth century. Crome's pencil drawings largely are working drawings. He produced a good line, making the fullest use of accents, leaving much to inference. It is interesting to note that John Crome hardly ever signed his works.

Crome's works are in the following museums: National Gallery, London; Victoria and Albert Museum, London; Tate Gallery, London; National Gallery of Scotland; Norwich Castle, Norwich; Manchester Art Gallery; Wolverhampton Art Gallery; Mellon Collection, U.S.A.; Doncaster Art Gallery; British Museum; Lady Lever Art Gallery; Kenwood House, London; Nottingham Castle; Birmingham City Art Gallery; Leeds City Art Gallery; Nottingham Art Gallery; Philadelphia Museum of Art; Sydney Art Gallery, Australia; Montreal Art Gallery, Canada; Whitworth Art Gallery, Manchester.

NORWICH EXHIBITION EXHIBITS

Year	*Subject*
1805	Moonlight—a sketch in oils.
	A cottage scene.
	Figures—a sketch.
	A marl pit.
	A view on Barford Common.
	A cottage at Harleston.
	A view of Carrow Abbey.
	A view near Yarmouth.
	Bishopsgate Bridge, Norwich.
	View of the fellmongers.
	Sandlings Ferry, Norwich.
	Oulton Church, Suffolk.
	Pigs—a sketch.
1806	View on Thorpe River.
	View on the Thorpe Road.
	Wood scene and moat at Hunstanton.
	Study from Nature in the style of Gainsborough.
	Cart-shed at Melton.
	Brook in Lord Rosebery's grounds at Bixley.
	View on the river at the back of the New Mills, Norwich.

Year	*Subject*
1806	Bloggs' Lime Kiln.
	Lime kiln out of St. Giles' Gates.
	Street scene, St. George's Colegate, near Green Lane.
	Moonlight.
	Moonlight, Sprowston (2½ miles north of Norwich).
	Sketches on the spot—Pigsties.
	The milk pot.
	The windmill.
	View of the lakes in Cumberland.
	Brathey Bridge, Westmoreland.
	Rocks and waterfall.
	Rocks.
	View near Weymouth.
	View in the forest, Hampshire.
	Entrance to Goodwich Castle—morning.
	Evening.
	Trees—a study.
1807	A view in Norwich.
	A view near the Bishop's Gate.
	Broken ground at the back of the barracks, Norwich.
	Landscape and cattle.
	A scene from Nature.
	Sketch from Nature.
	Blacksmith's shop at Hardingham.
	A blacksmith's shop from Nature.
	A cottage near Hunstanton (painted 1806).
	Sketch at Starston (1½ miles from Harleston).
	Landscape at Morton, Norfolk—drawing.
	A cottage, Hingham.
	Trowse—windmill.
	Caistor Castle—three views, coloured on the spot.
	Yarmouth Beach and Jetty.
	Old building at Ambleside.
	Scene in "Goberry" Park, Cumberland—seat of the Duke of Norfolk.
	Scene in Gowbarrow, Westmoreland—a beautiful view of Ulleswater Lake.
	Scene on the Wye.
	Tintern Abbey.
	A Wood Scene.
1808	Yarmouth Beach and Jetty.
	Fishermen in boats.
	A sketch from Nature.
	A sketch from Nature.
	A sketch in water-colours.
	Old stables—a sketch in oils on the spot.
	A landscape.
	A landscape.
	A painting in oils—evening.
	Wood's End, Bramerton.
	Scene near Breydon.
	Scene at Yarmouth—boats and figures.
	Cottage at Hingham—painted on the spot.
	Walnut grove.
	View near St. Martin's-at-Oak—looking down the river.
	Moonlight scene on the river between Beccles and Yarmouth.
1809	A landscape—Barford Common.
	A scene on Yarmouth Quay.
	A landscape in water-colours.
	Cromer Beach—below cliff.
	Old buildings in Norwich.

Year	*Subject*
1809	Grove scene—a drawing in water-colours.
	Yarmouth Beach and Jetty—oils.
	A view in Cumberland looking down from the King of Patterdale's—Ulleswater in the distance.
	Old cottages—painted on the spot.
	A landscape.
	An old house in St. Clement's, Norwich.
	Chepstowe, on the Wye.
1810	A view from Herringfleet.
	A cottage and road scene after rain, near Blundeston.
	Ruins—evening.
	A thistle—painted on the spot.
	A view on St. Martin's River.
	A view from Telegraph Lane, looking towards General Monet's—painted on the spot.
	A cottage.
	An upright landscape—scene from Colney, near Norwich.
	A view looking over Heigham Marshes towards Costessey.
	Trees from Nature.
	A gravel pit.
	An evening landscape.
	Patterdale Church, Westmoreland.
	Scene on Hautbois Common, near Coltishall.
1811	A drawing of rocks at Matlock.
	A waterfall and rocks.
	Landscape of rocks and a waterfall (Derbyshire).
	Windmill at Trowse—evening.
	Woody scene with a public house.
	View in Blundeston Lane (3½ miles from Lowestoft, East Suffolk).
	A lane leading to Mr. William Unthank's.
	The outside view of a blacksmith's shop.
	Public house on a heath.
	Scene near Bawburgh Mill (5 miles north-west of Norwich).
	Moonlight.
	Scene near St. Martin's River—afternoon.
	Cottage on a common.
	Road scene near Heigham.
	Study of trees.
	Mulbarton Green.
	Cottage at Hingham.
	River scene.
	The Temple of Venus—after a sketch by Wilson.
1812	A grove scene.
	View on the Norwich River looking towards the Whitefriars Bridge.
	A river scene in St. Martin-at-Oak.
	Evening—looking down the river from Yarmouth Bridge.
	Cattle crossing a river.
	A cottage scene—three separate pictures so entitled.
	A boy keeping sheep—morning.
	Lane scene at Hingham.
	The blind pensioner.
	View without St. Augustine's Gate.
	A scene on Heigham River.
	Creek scene near the New Mills, Norwich.
	Landscape—a scene near Bawburgh.
	Dutch boars.
	Cottages at Hingham.
1813	Footbridge at Keswick, near Mr. Hudson Gurney's seat.
	Scene at Blofield, on the Yarmouth Road.
	Lane scene near Lord Rosebery's at Bixley.

Year	*Subject*
1813	Scene in Heigham.
	Sketch at Marlingford (on panel).
	Landscape at Hackford.
	Cottage at Deopham.
	Boat-builders' yard near the Cow Tower, on the Yare.
	Scene near Lord Wodehouse's Park, Kimberley.
	A study of docks.
	Scene on St. Martin's River, near Morse & Adams' Brewery.
	Landscape with sheep—evening.
	Lane scene near Cromer.
	Two landscapes.
1815	A composition.
	A landscape.
	A view near Norwich.
	A landscape.
	A landscape.
	Scene on Mousehold.
	A cottage scene.
	A village scene.
	View in Paris—Italian Boulevard.
	Scene in St. Martin's-at-Oak.
1816	Bruges River, Ostend in the distance—moonlight.
	A scene on St. Martin's River.
	A scene on Heigham River.
	A lane scene near Norwich.
	Two scenes from Nature.
	Two landscapes—sketches on the spot.
	A cottage scene.
	A lane scene.
	A cottage at Haddiscoe, on the Waveney.
	A river scene.
	A landscape—autumn.
	A landscape—composition.
	A sketch in oils.
	A study, called "Character of an Oak".
1817	Moon rising.
	Yarmouth Jetty.
	Scene on Mr. Blake's bleaching ground at Heigham.
	Bathing scene.
	Landscape and shore boats.
	Mackerel—shore boats going off—morning.
	Landscape—Raven Craig.
	Hethel Hall, seat of St. Thos. Beevor, Bart.
	Land scene.
	Landscape—sketch from Nature.
	Landscape.
	Sketch in oils.
	Landscape.
1818	Twilight—a sketch in oils.
	Landscape.
	Ruins.
	Scene on the Norwich River.
	A landscape.
	Dogs' heads.
	Moonlight.
	Yarmouth Beach seen from the pier.
1819	Moonlight.
	Landscape.
	Landscape and cattle.

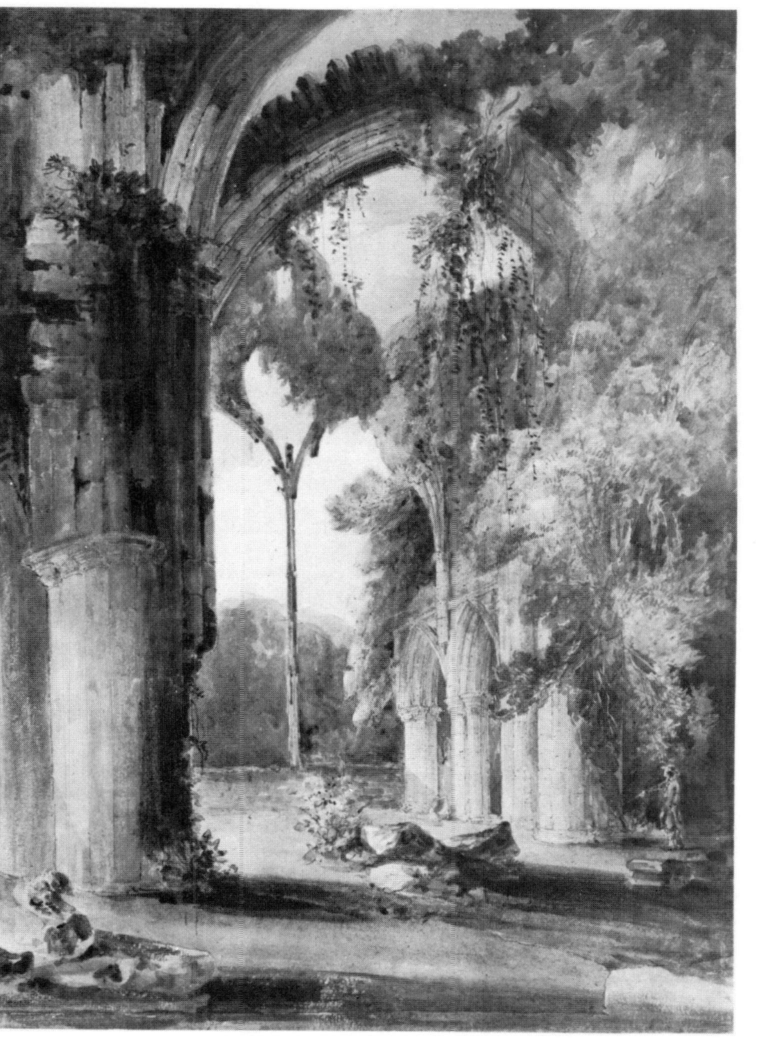

John Crome *Tintern Abbey* *Water-colour* $21\frac{3}{8} \times 16\frac{3}{8}$ *in.*

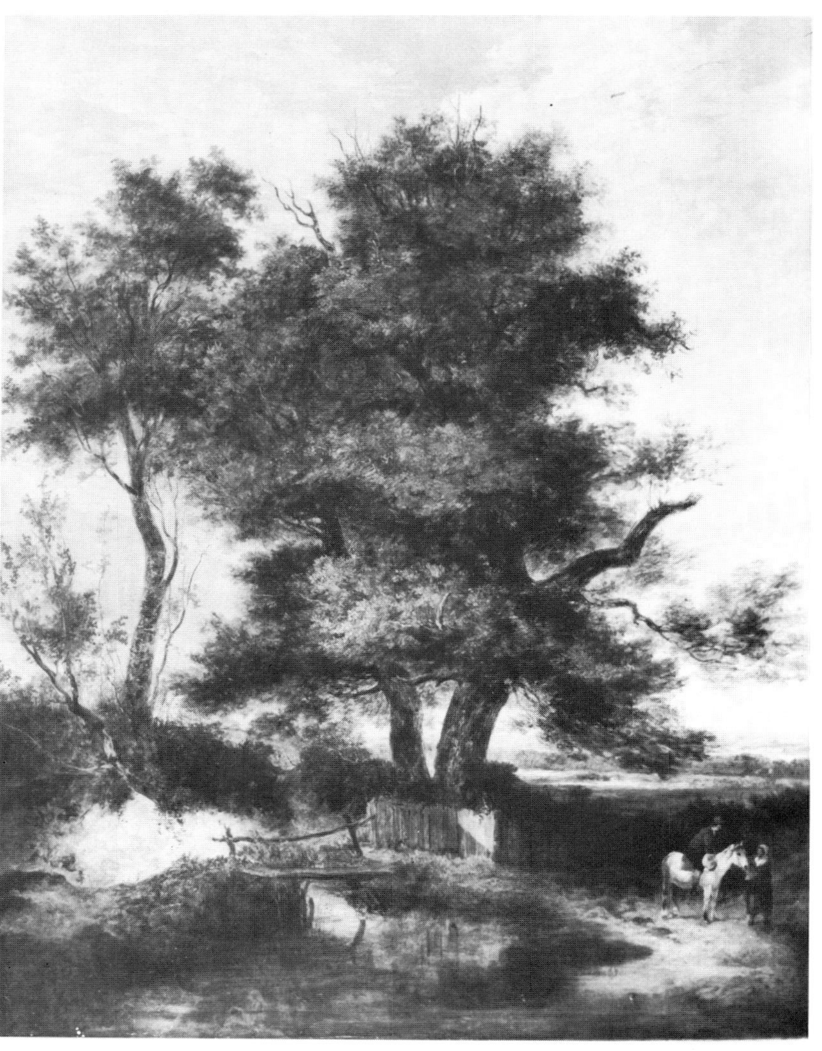

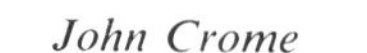

John Crome *The Willow* *(Fairly early work)* *Oil* $49\frac{1}{2} \times 39\frac{1}{2}$ *in.*

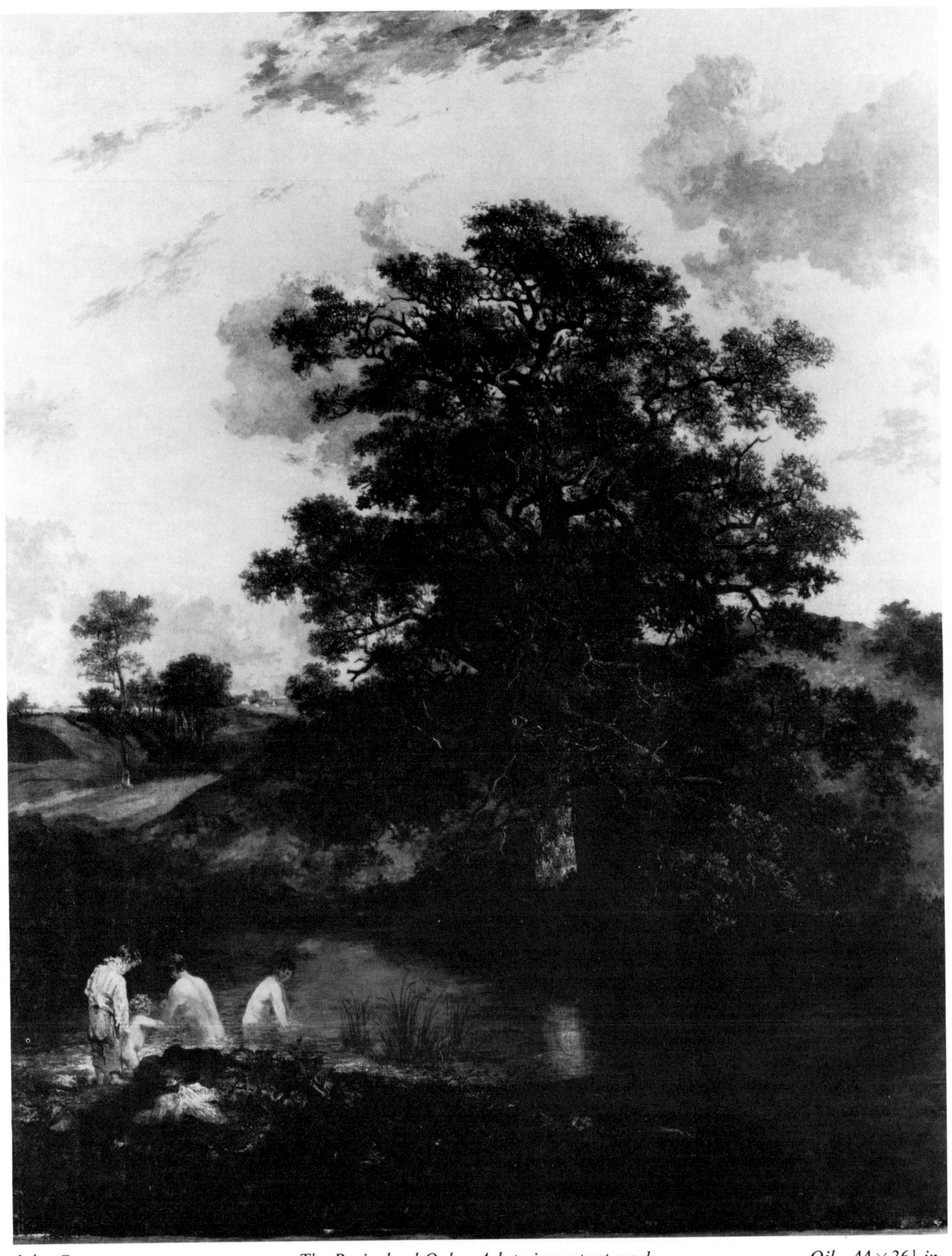

John Crome *The Poringland Oak A late important work* *Oil* 44×36½ *in.*
(One of the figures is said to be Crome's son, Michael Sharp—presumably the youngest)

Year	Subject
1819	Heath scene—sun breaking out after a storm.
	Landscape—mid-day.
	Afternoon scene on the Norwich River.
	Sketch in oils.
	The thorn tree in Hethel Churchyard.
	The moon rising.
	Lane scene.
	Yarmouth Beach, looking north—morning.
	Yarmouth Beach—jetty in distance—evening.
1820	Composition.
	River scene.
	Sketch near Bishop Bridge.
	Group of trees—a sketch.
	The fishmarket at Boulogne—from the sketches made on the spot in 1814.
	Cottage and trees.
	Grove scene—a sketch in oils.
	Evening.
	Moonlight—a sketch.
	Chapel Fields.
	Landscape.
	Cottage and wood scene.
	Cottage on the River Wensum.
1821	Landscape—evening.
	Lane scene.
	Wood scene.
	View looking from the New Mills towards St. Michael's Bridge.

EXHIBITS AT ROYAL ACADEMY

Year	No.	Subject
1806	260	A landscape (Croome).
	285	A landscape.
1807	526	A cottage from Nature, near Lynn, in Norfolk.
1808	591	Blacksmith's shop, near Hingham, Norfolk.
1809	36	A sketch from Nature.
	235	Old building in Norwich.
1811	465	View in Blofield, near Norwich.
1812	11	Landscape.
	84	Landscape.
	132	Landscape.
	384	Landscape.
1816	8	View near Norwich.
1818	218	View near Norwich.

PICTURES EXHIBITED ON LOAN AFTER CROME'S DEATH IN NORWICH, LONDON AND THE PROVINCES

CATALOGUE OF PICTURES IN THE CROME MEMORIAL EXHIBITION 1821

No.	*Subject*	*Owner, 1821*
1	Sketch in oils (first work).	Mr. F. Crome.
2	Composition—style of Wilson.	Mr. W. Spratt.
3	Cumberland scene.	Mr. W. Spratt.
4	Broken ground near St. Augustine's Gates, Norwich.	Mr. W. Spratt.
5	Study near Bishop's Gate.	Mr. W. Spratt.
6	View on the Thames.	Mr. W. Spratt.
7	King St. Meadows—moonlight.	Mr. W. Spratt.
8	Composition—style of Wilson.	C. Higgen, Esq.
9	Road scene and cottages near Bury.	Mr. W. Crome.
10	Landscape composition.	Mr. W. Crome.
11	New Mills, Norwich.	Mrs. Paget.
12	Grove scene near Marlingford.	Saml. Paget.
13	Study at the Duke's Palace.	Saml. Paget.
14	Study of ruins.	Saml. Paget.
15	View at the back of New Mills.	Saml. Paget.
16	Park of Lord Lowther.	Mr. W. Spratt.
17	Trees near Earlham.	Mr. W. Spratt.
18	Trees and broken ground.	Mr. W. Spratt.
19	River Wensum.	J. Brightwen, Esq.
20	Wood and water scene near Bawburgh.	Miss Burroughs.
21	Lane scene near Hingham.	Rev. E. Valpy.
22	Landscape.	Mr. E. Sparshall.
23	Landscape and cattle.	T. Martin, Esq.
24	New Mills.	T. Martin, Esq.
25	View near Yarmouth Bridge.	Rev. E. Valpy.
26	Landscape and cattle.	Mr. Wm. Stark.
27	Cottage and wood scene.	Mr. Wm. Stark.
28	Scene near Dickleborough.	Mr. Wm. Stark.
29	Mulbarton.	Mrs. de Rouillon.
30	Yarmouth Jetty.	Mrs. de Rouillon.
31	Moonlight (Norwich Society, 1818).	Mrs. de Rouillon.
32	View in Postwick Grove.	Mrs. de Rouillon.
33	Beach scene—morning—mackerel boat going off.	Mrs. de Rouillon.
34	Blacksmith's traverse at Hardingham.	Mr. F. Crome.
35	Scene at Woodrising.	—
36	Bawburgh.	—
37	Hautbois Common.	Mr. F. Stone.
38	View from pier head towards Yarmouth Jetty.	Mr. F. Stone.
39	Lane scene near Hingham.	Saml. Paget.
40	Lane scene near Whitlingham.	Mr. Chas. Turner.
41	Yarmouth Jetty.	Mr. Chas. Turner.
42	Near Hardingham.	Mr. Chas. Turner.
43	Lane Scene.	John Bracey, Esq.
44	Boy and sheep—morning.	John Bracey, Esq.
45	Mousehold Heath.	Mr. Wilson.
46	Lane scene at Blofield.	Saml. Paget.
47	Scene at Heigham.	Rev. J. Homfray.
48	Blundeston.	Mr. G. Stacey.
49	View at back of the Mills.	Rev. J. Homfray.
50	Lane scene at Beccles.	Mr. Freeman.
51	Scene in Cumberland.	Mr. D. R. Murphy.
52	Cottages at Barford.	Mr. D. R. Murphy.
53	Lane scene at Catton.	John Bracey, Esq.

No.	Subject	Owner, 1821
54	Marlingford.	Rev. J. H. Browne.
55	Carrow Abbey.	P. M. Martineau.
56	Blundeston—road scene.	T. Brightwell, Esq.
57	Yarmouth Beach.	Mr. P. Barnes.
58	Portrait of the late Mr. Crome, painted by J. J. Wodehouse, Esq., M.D., in 1813.	—
59	Scene at Poringland.	Capt. Steward.
60	Scene between Bruges and Ostend.	Mr. F. Crome.
61	Blacksmith's shop.	Mr. F. Crome.
62	Yarmouth Jetty.	Mr. P. Barnes.
63	Back of New Mills.	Rev. E. Valpy.
64	Scene near Lakenham.	Mr. Wilson.
65	Cottage and wood scene.	Mr. M. Bland.
66	River Wensum.	Mr. Saml. Coleman.
67	Mousehold Heath.	Mr. James Stark.
68	Mill—twilight.	Saml. Paget.
69	Cottage scene near Drayton.	Mr. F. Stone.
70	Cottage at Whitlingham.	Miss Cameron Innes.
71	Landscape—evening.	Mr. J. B. Crome.
72	Sketch of an oak in Kimberley Park.	Mr. J. B. Crome.
73	Trees at Colney.	Mr. F. Crome.
74	Moonlight.	Mr. G. Stacey.
75	Composition in the style of Wilson.	Mr. G. Stacey.
76	Grove scene.	J. Geldart, Junr., Esq.
77	View near Scoulton.	Mr. F. Crome.
78	View on the River Yare.	Mr. F. Crome.
79	Italian Boulevard, Paris.	H. Gurney, Esq.
80	North Elmham.	Mr. F. Stone.
81	New Mills, towards St. Michael's Bridge.	Mr. R. de Carle, Junr.
82	River Wensum.	Mr. J. H. Wright.
83	Scene near Hackford.	Mr. J. H. Wright.
84	Landscape at Whitlingham.	Mr. F. Crome.
85	Trees near Melton.	Mr. R. Steel.
86	Scene near Woodrising.	Mr. W. Freeman.
87	Fish market at Boulogne.	Mr. W. Freeman.
88	View on the River Yare.	Mr. W. Freeman.
89	North Elmham.	Mr. F. Stone.
90	Hethell Hall.	J. H. Gurney, Esq.
91	Keswick—near.	Mr. F. Stone.
92	View on the River Yare.	R. Bygrave, Esq.
93	Thorn tree, Hethell Churchyard.	—
94	Study of plants.	Mr. Crome.
95	View near Wickerwell.	E. Girling, Junr.
96	Norwich—sketch.	E. Girling, June.
97	View of Fritton.	Mr. F. Crome.
98	Marlingford.	Mr. F. Crome.
99	Marlingford—trees and broken ground.	Mr. J. D. Palmer.
100	Lane scene at Mulbarton.	E. Girling, Junr.
101	View near Hellesdon.	Lady Jerningham.
102	View near Honingham.	Lady Jerningham.
103	Hackford Church.	Lady Jerningham.
104	Study at Woodrising.	Miss Paget.
105	View at Bawburgh.	Mr. F. Crome.
106	Cottages at Haddiscoe.	Mr. F. Crome.
107	View at Heigham.	Miss Paget.
108	Cottage scene near Dereham.	Miss Paget.
109	Moonlight sketch.	Miss Paget.
110	Back of New Mills.	Miss Paget.
111	Wood scene (last picture).	Mr. Crome.

NORWICH EXHIBITION OF DECEASED LOCAL ARTISTS 1860

PICTURES BY JOHN CROME EXHIBITED

No.	*Subject*	*Owner, 1860*
1	Landscape and Cottage.	J. J. Colman.
5	Dog's head: Jack.	D. Gurney.
7	Moonlight.	Mr. Boswell.
16	The gate.	Mr. Norgate.
27	Glade Cottage.	J. E. Fordham.
35	Near Harwich.	T. Wells.
40	Catton—road scene.	Rev. J. Gunn.
49	Pollard trees.	J. King.
50	Hethell Old Hall.	J. H. Gurney.
55	Cottage by waterside.	R. N. Bacon.
58	Scene in Wales.	Roe of Cambridge.
62	Cottages and water.	Rev. J. Gunn.
66	Great oak.	R. B. Scott.
67	Sprowston—barn and sheds.	W. Wilde.
68	Sawyers.	Finch Steward.
71	Wood scene.	Norgate.
72	Salhouse—trees.	J. Gunn.
73	Cottage by river.	Mr. Hall.
74	Flints.	T. Brightwell.
79	Trowse—a sketch.	J. Gunn.
87	Sunset.	Norgate.
100	Cottage and water.	Rev. A. T. Paget.
106	Evening—cottage.	J. Wright.
117	On Yare.	D. Gurney.
128	Barn gable.	Rev. A. T. Paget.
130	Cottage in grove.	Rev. A. T. Paget.
129	Cottage.	R. N. Bacon.
139	Old oak.	J. N. Waite.
148	On the Yare.	D. Gurney.
153	Poringland Oak.	C. Steward.
160	The angler.	J. B. Ladbrooke.
164	The willow.	Rev. J. Holmes.
166	Saw pit.	Rev. J. Holmes.
168	Ash pollard.	G. Etheridge.
176	Road scene.	J. H. Gurney.
177	Bury—road scene and cottage.	J. S. Muskett.
179	Hautbois—view.	T. Brightwell.
191	Cottage.	J. N. Waite.
194	Sandbank.	C. Steward.
197	Mousehold Heath.	H. S. Patteson.
202	Norwich River from New Mills.	W. Robinson.
206	Bishop's Bridge.	A. G. Stannard.
233	Landscape (J. B. Crome).	Rev. Fisk.
234	Pencil drawing.	Norgate.
263	Etchings.	J. Reeve.
282	Cottage and river.	W. Wilde.

BRITISH MEDICAL ASSOCIATION LOAN COLLECTION

NORFOLK AND SUFFOLK ARTISTS

(12th August, 1874, Exhibition)

No.	*Subject*	*Owner*
1	Harwich.	T. Wells.
5	Bardock.	R. P. Burcham.
19	Catton—lane scene.	J. Gunn.
36	The willow.	G. Holmes.
52	Roadside and cottages.	Sir Francis Boileau.
48	Cottages.	J. Gunn.
53	Roadside and cottages.	Sir Francis Boileau.
55	Boulevard des Italiens.	Trustees of Hudson Gurney.
59	Yarmouth Jetty.	Miss Martineau.
61	Salhouse—view.	J. Gunn.
62	Bathing house, S. Martin's.	G. Holmes.
63	Fish market, Boulogne.	Trustees of Hudson Gurney.
117	Ketteringham Hall Farm.	Sir Francis Boileau.
146	Dunham—view near (water-colour).	E. Barwell.

PICTURES LOANED—BRITISH INSTITUTION

No.	*Subject*	*Lent by*
142	Mulbarton Gravel Pits.	Bishop of Ely.
51	Trowse Lane, Norwich.	Mrs. Sherrington.
99	Landscape.	W. Smith.
100	Norfolk landscape.	Mrs. Sherrington.
133	Landscape.	William Yetts.
125	The Glade Cottage.	J. E. Fordham.
154	River view near Norwich.	Wynn Ellis.
135	Woody landscape.	E. W. Cooke, R.A.
173	Shepherd boy and sheep.	J. H. Anderdon.
179	Landscape.	Louis Huth.
180	Landscape.	Henry Vaughan.
162	A woody scene.	J. H. Anderdon.
174	Landscape with cottage.	Charles Hancock.
132	Harbour scene with boats.	Wynn Ellis.
147	The old oak.	Wynn Ellis.
172	Coast near Yarmouth.	—
180	Slate quarries.	W. Fuller Maitland.
136	Landscape.	C. H. Gurney.
159	Seashore—boats and figures.	W. Fuller Maitland.
138	Landscape.	Wynn Ellis.
141	A heath near Norwich.	Mrs. Turner.
144	Yarmouth Beach.	W. Fuller Maitland.
161	Yarmouth Beach looking north.	Wynn Ellis.
163	Yarmouth Beach and Jetty.	Wynn Ellis.
182	River scene and boats.	Wynn Ellis.
158	Landscape.	W. Fuller Maitland.

SUFFOLK STREET

Year	*No.*	*Subject*	*Lent by*
1832	51	Scene near Norwich.	J. Stark.
	76	Landscape.	E. W. Cooke.
	116	Scene from Nature.	J. Stark.
1833	82	Grove scene.	J. Stark.

Year	No.	Subject	Lent by
	117	Landscape.	T. Gaskell.
	262	Landscape.	Du Jardin.
1834	70	Hingham, Norfolk.	J. Stark.
	129	Cottage with cattle.	James Wadmore.

MANCHESTER (ART TREASURES)

Year	No.	Subject	Lent by
1857	210	An English homestead.	John Cowes Grundy.

INTERNATIONAL EXHIBITION

Year	No.	Subject	Lent by
1862	125	A clump of trees, Hautbois Common.	Mrs. Ellison.
	126	Landscape.	J. E. Fordham.
	137	Heath scene.	W. H. Hunt.
	138	Carrow Abbey (sky by Opie).	Miss Martineau.
	156	The great oak tree.	R. B. Scott.
	157	On Mousehold Heath.	W. Yetts.
	236	Yarmouth Old Jetty.	Major Marsh.

LEEDS

Year	No.	Subject	Lent by
1868	1072	Slate quarries.	P. Maitland.
	1124	Landscape—evening.	Queen Victoria.
	1146	River scene.	F. Maitland.
	1147	Boats and windmill.	W. R. Drake.
	1197	Tower near Norwich.	Richard Johnson.

ROYAL ACADEMY

Year	No.	Subject	Lent by
1870	32	Landscape and figures. 25×21 in.	J. E. Fordham.
	68	Landscape and figures. 13½×20 in.	C. H. Gurney.
1871	7	The old oak tree. 35×42 in.	Wynn Ellis.
	35	Landscape and figures. 53×38 in.	Louis Huth.
	45	Brathey Bridge. 18×24 in.	Henry Vaughan.
1872	3	Skirts of the forest. 42×31 in.	J. H. Anderdon.
	14	Near Woodbridge, Suffolk. 25×30 in.	Sam Mendel.
	33	Minding sheep, Mousehold Heath. 21¼×32 in.	J. H. Anderdon.
	38	Near Thorpe. 21½×28 in.	T. E. Woolner, A.R.A.
1873	29	River scene—boat-house. 12×18 in.	W. Fuller Maitland.
	42	Yarmouth: water frolic. 41¾×68 in.	Rev. Canon Selwyn.
	47	The slate quarries. 48×62 in.	W. Fuller Maitland.
	94	Edge of a park, with deer. 26×40 in.	W. Fuller Maitland.
	96	Bruges: on Ostend River. 25×31 in.	T. Woolner, A.R.A.
	208	Yarmouth Old Jetty. 35×49½ in.	Col. F. Maitland-Wilson.
1875	4	A thistle. 26×29 in.	W. Fuller Maitland.
	30	The pollard oak. 27½×20 in.	Gen. G. H. Mackinnon.
	41	Group of oaks, white heifer. 30½×47 in.	W. Fuller Maitland.
	51	Old inn, Great Yarmouth. 29½×24½ in.	Rt. Hon. E. P. Bouverie.
	99	Oaks in Kimberley Park. 47×36 in.	W. Fuller Maitland.
	116	Oak in Poringland, boys bathing. 50×39 in.	Rev. C. J. Steward.
	215	Landscape—evening. 26×32 in.	W. H. Haines.

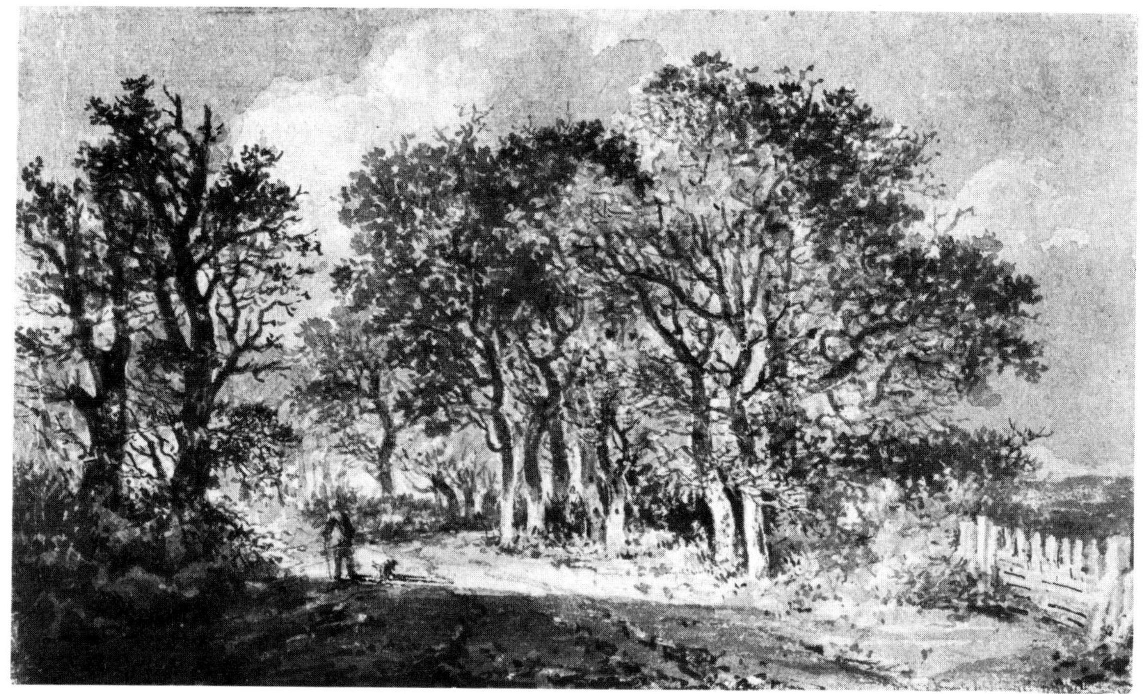

John Crome *Grey Wash on Blue Paper* $8 \times 13\frac{5}{8}$ *in.*

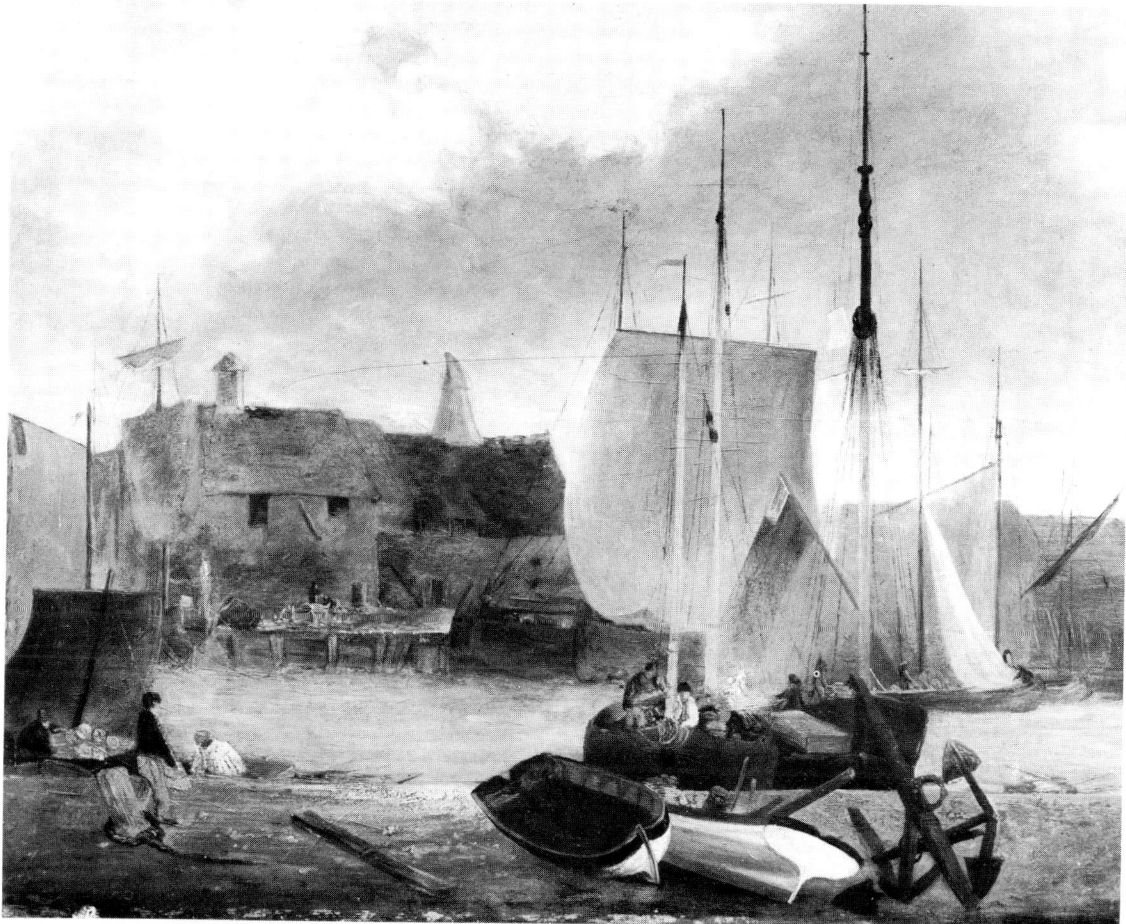

John Crome *Yarmouth Quay* *Oil on Panel* 13×16 *in.*
Crome introduced anchors into several of his works

Year	*No.*	*Subject*	*Lent by*
1876	16	Landscape. 14 × 11 in.	W. R. Fisher.
	17	A Welsh landscape. 15 × 23 in.	Sir Wm. G. Armstrong.
	22	Barge, fishermen, wounded soldiers. 13 × 19½ in.	W. Fuller Maitland.
	30	View of Norwich. 13 × 17½ in.	Louis Huth.
	53	Boat-house, Blunderton. 18½ × 24½ in.	Rev. C. J. Steward.
	89	Whitlingham, near Norwich. 24½ × 24½ in.	J. E. Fordham.
	280	The willow tree. 49½ × 39½ in.	G. Holmes.
1877	14	Moonlight scene. 14½ × 21 in.	J. T. Gibson Craig.
1878	1	Landscape. 15 × 19 in.	C. W. Unthank.
	2	Landscape. 14 × 10 in.	J. E. Fordham.
	8	View at Salhouse. 17½ × 13½ in.	John Gunn.
	13	St. Martin's Gate, Norwich. 19½ × 15 in.	Rev. H. J. Coleman.
	14	Fish market, Boulogne, 1814. 20 × 33 in.	Hudson Gurney.
	15	Lakenham. 14½ × 17½ in.	S. H. de Zoete.
	17	Landscape. 22½ × 30½ in.	J. E. Fordham.
	18	Boulevard des Italiens. 21½ × 34 in.	Hudson Gurney.
	20	On the Back River, Norwich. 19½ × 16 in.	Mrs. T. Temple-Silver.
	23	Study of a burdock. 21 × 16 in.	Robert P. Burcham.
	24	Landscape and figures. 7 × 5¾ in.	Edward Garrett.
	27	Carrow Abbey. 49½ × 37 in.	J. J. Colman.
	28	Yarmouth Jetty. 17¼ × 22¼ in.	S. H. de Zoete.
	32	The shepherd's cottage. 44 × 36 in.	Joseph Parrington.
	34	Near Thorpe, Norwich. 23½ × 19 in.	Edwin Edwards.
	38	Yarmouth Jetty. 17 × 22 in.	J. J. Colman.
	39	Road with pollards. 28 × 42 in.	J. J. Colman.
	40	Yarmouth Harbour. 15¾ × 25½ in.	Edwin H. Lawrence.
	44	Yarmouth: water frolic. 16¼ × 30 in.	Rev. W. H. Stokes.
	46	The lime kiln. 20 × 29½ in.	Mrs. T. Temple-Silver.
	47	On the Wensum, Norwich. 14 × 21 in.	W. H. Robinson.
	48	View of Norwich. 20½ × 29½ in.	Samuel Gurney.
	49	Wood scene, Catton. 27½ × 22¼ in.	John Gunn.
	51	Landscape. 17½ × 14 in.	Rev. W. H. Stokes.
	52	View on river, Norwich. 11 × 13½ in.	Mrs. Hankinson.
	54	On Ostend Canal, Bruges—moonlight. 7½ × 9¾ in.	J. P. Heseltine.
	57	Old bathing house, Norwich. 20¼ × 16 in.	George Holmes.
1880	23	The village glade. 43½ × 35 in.	Cyril Flower.
1881	22	Landscape—sandy bank. 15½ × 20 in.	Lord Wimborne.
1884	13	Landscape. 29 × 24 in.	James Orrock.
1888	3	The old cottage. 29 × 24 in.	Antony Gibbs.
	36	Landscape. 17½ × 26 in.	Lady Jane Swinburne.
1889	138	Landscape and figures. 29 × 23½ in.	Mrs. Owen Roe.
1890	54	Landscape. 10 × 12½ in.	C. T. D. Crews.
1891	9	Grove scene. 18½ × 25½ in.	J. J. Colman.
	29	On the River Yare. 16 × 21½ in.	H. G. Barwell.
	33	The willow tree. 50 × 40 in.	Geo. Holmes.
	39	Poringland Oak. 49 × 39 in.	Rev. C. J. Steward.
1892	28	Landscape. 35 × 54 in.	H. F. Broadwood.
	39	Yarmouth Beach. 14½ × 20 in.	C. S. Roundell.
	42	Yarmouth Harbour. 16 × 26 in.	E. H. Lawrence.
1893	140	The wood cutters. 27½ × 35½ in.	E. L. Raphael.
1894	23	The beaters. 20½ × 33½ in.	S. Montagu.
	27	Heath scene—sun breaking out. 27 × 33½ in.	George Holmes.
1903	19	Landscape. 20½ × 16 in.	Thos. J. Barrett.
	24	Mousehold Heath. 31½ × 44 in.	Hamilton McCormick.
	35	Mousehold Heath. 22 × 28 in.	George Salting.
	68	Sea-piece. 38 × 48½ in.	Lord Hillingdon.
1906	45	Preston Tower, on the Orwell. 37½ × 47½ in.	J. Orrock.
	59	The bathing-place, Norwich. 26½ × 21½ in.	Col. Fairfax Rhodes.
1907	121	The beaters. 20½ × 33½ in.	Sir S. Montagu.

Year	No.	Subject	Lent by
1908	170	Poringland Oak. 49 × 39 in.	Rev. C. J. Steward.
	177	Norwich. $20\frac{1}{2} \times 29\frac{1}{2}$ in.	Eustace Gurney.
1910	136	A Yarmouth water frolic. 42 × 68 in.	Lord Iveagh.

BURLINGTON FINE ARTS CLUB

Year	No.	Subject	Lent by
1871	25	Brathey Bridge, Cumberland.	Henry Vaughan.
	32	The old oak tree.	Wynn Ellis.
	44	Landscape with figures, Marlingford.	Louis Huth.
1910	11	The bathers.	H. Darell Brown.
1912	31	Landscape.	Sir Jos. Beecham.

EDINBURGH

Year	No.	Subject	Lent by
1886	1396	Castle near Norwich.	James Orrock.
	1431	Sheds.	A. Andrews.
	1450	The beaters.	A. Andrews.

NEWCASTLE

Year	No.	Subject	Lent by
1887	728	Bruges—moonlight.	J. J. Colman.
	782	Poringland Oak.	Rev. C. J. Steward.
	789	Old Mill.	A. Fraser.

GLASGOW

Year	No.	Subject	Lent by
1888	246	Landscape.	James Keydon.
1901	59	The road to the farm.	J. P. Forrester Paton.
	206	Landscape with abbey.	Mrs. Keydon.
1902	164	Yarmouth by moonlight.	Arthur Kay.

GUILDHALL

Year	No.	Subject	Lent by
1894	81	Near Hingham.	Henry Tate.
1895	78	A country lane.	—

FRANCO-BRITISH

Year	No.	Subject	Lent by
1908	73	Moonlight.	H. Darell-Brown.

JAPAN EXHIBITION

Year	No.	Subject	Lent by
1910	27	Thistle and water vole.	Arthur Samuel.
	28	Cottage at Trowse.	Arthur Samuel.
	41	Near Old Lakenham Mill.	Arthur Samuel.

LIVERPOOL ART CLUB

Year	*No.*	*Subject*	*Lent by*
1881	98	In port.	Charles Langton.
	120	Norwich—moonlight.	Albert Wood.
	162	Old cottage.	H. Schirmacher.
	200	Woodland glade.	Albert Wood.
	203	Old tree near Bath.	William Bartlett.
	230	A cottage.	H. Schirmacher.
	248	Moonlight.	Peter Stuart.
	273	Landscape.	H. Schirmacher.
	277	The road to the barracks, Norwich.	Gray Hill.
	278	Landscape.	H. Schirmacher.

WHITECHAPEL (ST. JUDE'S)

Year	*No.*	*Subject*	*Lent by*
1883	171	A sea-piece.	W. Graham.
1888	76	Kimberley Oaks.	—
1889	109	Moonlight.	Lewis Fry.
	127	Landscape with old tree.	Col. Hollway.
1891	150	Landscape.	J. Colman.
1893	9	On the Yare.	L. Lesser.

WHITECHAPEL (ART GALLERY)

Year	*No.*	*Subject*	*Lent by*
1901	249	Whitlingham, near Norwich.	H. Darell Brown.

GROSVENOR GALLERY

Year	*No.*	*Subject*	*Lent by*
1888	12	River scene and boat-house. $12\frac{1}{2} \times 17\frac{1}{2}$ in.	W. Fuller Maitland.
	37	Old tanyard, Norwich. $13 \times 10\frac{1}{2}$ in.	A. Andrews.
	53	The beaters. $21\frac{1}{2} \times 34$ in.	A. Andrews.
	76	St. Nicholas' Church, Yarmouth. $10\frac{1}{2} \times 11$ in.	A. Andrews.
	102	Barge and wounded soldier. $13\frac{1}{2} \times 19\frac{1}{2}$ in.	W. Fuller Maitland.
	129	A cottage and trees. $21\frac{1}{2} \times 16\frac{1}{2}$ in.	Duke of Westminster.
	152	Grove scene, Marlingford. 53×38 in.	Louis Huth.
	153	Woody landscape. 24×36 in.	Gray Hill.
	209	River scene. $3 \times 4\frac{1}{2}$ in.	W. S. Hobson.
	214	River scene. $3 \times 4\frac{1}{2}$ in.	W. S. Hobson.
	244	Cottage and waterfall. 12×16 in.	Richard Gibbs.
	259	The oak. $11\frac{1}{2} \times 15$ in.	Albert Wood.
	267	Moonlight. $8\frac{1}{2} \times 10\frac{1}{2}$ in.	S. N. Castle.
	282	Cottages. $11\frac{1}{2} \times 16\frac{1}{2}$ in.	A. Andrews.
	286	Landscape with castle. $12 \times 14\frac{1}{2}$ in.	Richard Gibbs.
	288	The Yare—a river scene. $8\frac{1}{2} \times 10\frac{1}{2}$ in.	A. Andrews.
	295	Barges on the Yare. $18 \times 22\frac{1}{2}$ in.	A. Andrews.
	307	Landscape. 15×22 in.	John Cleland.
	313	Road to barracks, Norwich. $13\frac{1}{2} \times 17\frac{1}{2}$ in.	Gray Hill.
	316	Landscape and cattle. $13\frac{1}{2} \times 11\frac{1}{2}$ in.	Humphrey Roberts.
	331	A flint. 9×12 in.	T. Woolner, R.A.
1889	51	Gibraltar Watering-place, Norwich. $38\frac{1}{2} \times 53\frac{1}{2}$ in.	W. W. Lewis.
	68	The Glade Cottage. $24\frac{1}{2} \times 19$ in.	J. Orrock.
	80	A woody landscape. $21\frac{1}{2} \times 16\frac{1}{2}$ in.	S. S. Joseph.
	82	Hay barges. $15 \times 18\frac{1}{2}$ in.	J. Orrock.
	97	Yarmouth Pier. $17 \times 22\frac{1}{2}$ in.	W. C. Quilter.

Year	No.	Subject	Lent by
	104	Bishop's Bridge, Norwich. 11 × 14 in.	J. W. Knight.
	113	Landscape and sheep. 17 × 21 in.	Wm. Lockwood.
	134	Landscape. 24½ × 25 in.	Lord Wantage.
	136	View on the Yare. 23½ × 19 in.	Mrs. Edwin Edwards.
	145	Sea-piece. 43 × 69½ in.	Lord Wantage.
	160	Landscape. 14½ × 20½ in.	Louis Huth.
	163	A woodland scene. 48 × 65½ in.	Gray Hill.
	188	Moonlight. 9½ × 13 in.	Lewis Fry.

THE BRITISH INSTITUTION

Year	Subject
1818	A blacksmith's traverse. 25 × 22 in.
1821	A heath scene near Norwich. 29 × 38 in.
	A scene in Norwich. 23 × 28 in.

JOHN CROME CENTENARY EXHIBITION, NORWICH CASTLE

(April, 1921)

No.	Subject	Lent by
1	The windmill. Panel, 43 × 36 in.	Trustees of the National Gallery.
2	Slate quarries. 52 × 62 in.	Trustees of the National Gallery.
3	Brathay Bridge, Westmoreland. 18½ × 25¼ in.	Trustees of the National Gallery.
4	On the skirts of the forest. 42 × 30½ in.	Board of Education, Victoria and Albert Museum.
5	View on Mousehold Heath. 21½ × 32 in.	Board of Education, Victoria and Albert Museum.
6	*Bruges River—moonlight. 25 × 31 in.	—
7	*Study of a burdock. 21 × 16 in.	—
8	*Yarmouth Jetty. 17¼ × 22½ in.	—
9	*A view on the Wensum. Panel, 19½ × 16¼ in.	—
10	*Scene near Bury. Panel, 15¼ × 19¾ in.	Mrs. Ashcroft.
11	*View on the Wensum. Panel, 14 × 21 in.	Major Benedict Birkbeck.
12	Carrow Abbey. 50 × 37 in.	Mr. Russell J. Colman.
13	Horses watering. Millboard, 13 × 10 in.	Mr. Russell J. Colman.
14	View of Kirstead Church. 9 × 12 in.	Mr. Russell J. Colman.
15	Early dawn. 12¾ × 11 in.	Mr. Russell J. Colman.
16	The Cow Tower, Norwich. 18 × 24 in.	Mr. Russell J. Colman.
17	A wood scene, Postwick Grove. Millboard, 18¾ × 15½ in.	Mr. Russell J. Colman.
18	Road with pollards. 28 × 42 in.	Mr. Russell J. Colman.
19	Study of flints. Panel, 8 × 12 in.	Mr. Russell J. Colman.
20	Old Trowse Bridge. Panel, 10 × 15 in.	Mr. Russell J. Colman.
21	Grove scene. 18½ × 25½ in.	Mr. Russell J. Colman.
22	On the River Yare. Panel, 16 × 21½ in.	Mr. Russell J. Colman.
23	At Honingham, Norfolk. 14 × 17½ in.	Mr. Russell J. Colman.
24	The gate. 27 × 24½ in.	Mr. Russell J. Colman.
25	Dock leaves. Millboard, 6¼ × 13½ in.	Mr. Russell J. Colman.
26	Harling Gate. 21 × 16¾ in.	Rt. Hon. Earl Curzon, K.G.
27	Yarmouth Harbour. 15½ × 25½ in.	Mr. H. Darell-Brown.
28	A bathing scene. Panel, 18½ × 13 in.	Mr. H. Darell-Brown.
29	Moonlight on the Yare. 37½ × 48 in.	Mr. H. Darell-Brown.
30	Landscape. Panel, 14 × 11 in.	Miss H. M. Fisher.
31	Wood scene at Catton. 27¼ × 22¼ in.	Mr. Frank Gaskell.
32	Norwich Cathedral from Mousehold. Panel, 20½ × 29½ in.	Sir Eustace Gurney.
33	Fishmarket, Boulogne. 20 × 33 in.	Mr. John Henry Gurney.
34	Boulevard des Italiens, Paris. 21½ × 34 in.	Mr. John Henry Gurney.
35	Sheds and old houses. 19 × 24½ in.	Sir Leicester Harmsworth, Bt.
36	View near Woodbridge. 25 × 30 in.	Mr. H. Hirsch.

*From the Collections in the City of Norwich Art Gallery.

No.	*Subject*	*Lent by*
37	Tower near Norwich. $10 \times 8\frac{1}{4}$ in.	Mr. C. J. Holmes.
38	Storm on Mousehold Heath. 8×7 in.	Mr. C. J. Holmes.
39	Coast scene near Yarmouth. $43 \times 69\frac{1}{2}$ in.	Mr. Thomas A. Loyd.
40	Yarmouth Beach. 14×20 in.	Mrs. Geoffrey Lubbock.
41	River scene with boat-house. Panel, $12\frac{1}{4} \times 17\frac{3}{4}$ in.	Mr. W. Fuller Maitland.
42	Barge with wounded soldiers. Panel, $13\frac{1}{4} \times 19\frac{1}{2}$ in.	Mr. W. Fuller Maitland.
43	View of the Solent. $10\frac{1}{2} \times 20\frac{1}{4}$ in.	Mr. W. Fuller Maitland.
44	Tanning mills, Norwich. Panel, 10×13 in.	Mr. E. H. Marsh, C.B.
45	St. Martin's Gate, Norwich. Panel, $19 \times 14\frac{1}{2}$ in.	Miss Faith Moore.
46	View on Mousehold. $12\frac{1}{8} \times 15\frac{1}{8}$ in.	Mr. John R. Nutman.
47	Composition in style of Wilson. $21\frac{7}{8} \times 17\frac{3}{8}$ in.	Mr. John R. Nutman.
48	Castle in ruins. $11\frac{1}{2} \times 13\frac{1}{2}$ in.	Mr. John R. Nutman.
49	Temple of Venus, Balae (after Wilson). $17 \times 27\frac{1}{2}$ in.	Mr. John R. Nutman.
49A	The return of the flock. 18×24 in.	Mrs. E. L. Raphel.
50	View of Norwich. $13\frac{1}{2} \times 18$ in.	Rt. Hon. Viscount Rothermere.
51	Moonlight on the Yare. $10\frac{1}{2} \times 13\frac{1}{2}$ in.	Mr. Walter R. Rudd.
52	Thistle and water vole. $28\frac{3}{4} \times 24$ in.	Mr. Arthur Michael Samuel, M.P.
53	Mill near Lakenham. 11×13 in.	Mr. Arthur Michael Samuel, M.P.
54	Cottage near Lakenham. 11×13 in.	Mr. Arthur Michael Samuel, M.P.
55	The beaters. Panel, $21\frac{1}{4} \times 33\frac{1}{2}$ in.	Rt. Hon. Lord Swaythling.
56	Landscape. $22\frac{1}{2} \times 30$ in.	Mr. J. N. Wiley.
57	Yarmouth Jetty. $17 \times 22\frac{1}{2}$ in.	Mr. W. M. de Zoete.

WATER-COLOUR DRAWINGS, ETC.

58	Castle in hilly landscape (indian-ink wash). $16\frac{3}{4} \times 12$ in.	Professor Bateson.
59	Lane scene near Norwich. $22\frac{1}{2} \times 16\frac{1}{4}$ in.	Mr. Russell J. Colman.
60	Whitlingham. $10\frac{5}{8} \times 17\frac{3}{8}$ in.	Mr. Russell J. Colman.
61	Maltings on the Wensum. $10\frac{3}{8} \times 17\frac{1}{4}$ in.	Mr. Russell J. Colman.
62	Cottage gable in ruins. $9\frac{3}{4} \times 8$ in.	Mr. Russell J. Colman.
63	Farm premises. $7\frac{3}{4} \times 5\frac{7}{8}$ in.	Mr. Russell J. Colman.
64	Road scene with horses and cart. $8\frac{3}{4} \times 7$ in.	Mr. Russell J. Colman.
65	Dolgelly, N. Wales. $6\frac{7}{8} \times 12\frac{1}{4}$ in.	Mr. Russell J. Colman.
66	Landscape. $7\frac{1}{2} \times 6$ in.	Mr. Russell J. Colman.
67	Thatched buildings. $7 \times 9\frac{1}{2}$ in.	Mr. Russell J. Colman.
68	Gabled cottages. $5 \times 7\frac{1}{2}$ in.	Mr. Russell J. Colman.
69	Landscape near Lakenham. $5 \times 10\frac{1}{2}$ in.	Mr. Russell J. Colman.
70	Back River, Norwich. $4\frac{1}{2} \times 10\frac{1}{4}$ in.	Mr. Russell J. Colman.
71	Woodland scene. 13×19 in.	Mr. Russell J. Colman.
72	Thatched buildings. $10 \times 14\frac{1}{4}$ in.	Mr. Russell J. Colman.
73	Thatched cottage (indian ink). $6\frac{3}{8} \times 8\frac{1}{8}$ in.	Mr. Russell J. Colman.
74	Walsingham Priory (indian ink). $12\frac{1}{2} \times 9\frac{1}{2}$ in.	Mr. Russell J. Colman.
75	Figures on the shore (indian ink). $6\frac{3}{8} \times 10\frac{3}{8}$ in.	Mr. Russell J. Colman.
76	Cottage with high gable (indian ink). $5\frac{1}{8} \times 7$ in.	Mr. Russell J. Colman.
77	Church tower (pencil). $4\frac{5}{8} \times 8\frac{1}{8}$ in.	Mr. Russell J. Colman.
78	Trees over stream (pencil). $10 \times 7\frac{3}{4}$ in.	Mr. Russell J. Colman.
79	Tree and cottage (pencil). 3×6 in.	Mr. Russell J. Colman.
79A	River scene. $20 \times 15\frac{1}{2}$ in.	Major S. F. Courtauld.
80	Buildings and barges on the Yare. $16\frac{3}{4} \times 22$ in.	Lt.-Col. J. B. Gaskell.
81	By the roadside. 10×8 in.	Whitworth Institute, Manchester.
82	Pencil study. $7 \times 8\frac{3}{4}$ in.	Mr. Arthur Michael Samuel.
83	Blacksmith's shop at Hingham, Norfolk. $15\frac{1}{2} \times 11\frac{1}{2}$ in.	Mr. W. W. R. Spelman.
84	Hautbois Common.	Mr. W. W. R. Spelman.
85	Roadside with pollards.	Mr. W. W. R. Spelman.
86	The glade.	Mr. W. W. R. Spelman.
87	The shed.	Mr. W. W. R. Spelman.
88	The road.	Mr. W. W. R. Spelman.
89	Lane scene.	Mr. W. W. R. Spelman.
90	The Old North Gate, Yarmouth (pencil).	Mr. W. W. R. Spelman.

PORTRAITS, ETC.

No.	*Subject*	*Lent by*
91	Portrait in oils of John Crome painted by John Opie, R.A. $21\frac{1}{2} \times 16\frac{1}{2}$ in.	Norwich Castle Museum.
91A	Bust of John Crome by Maxotti.	—
92	Portrait in oils of John Crome by J. T. Woodhouse, M.D. $29\frac{1}{4} \times 24\frac{3}{4}$ in.	Guildhall, Norwich.
93	Portrait in oils of John Crome painted by Michael Sharp. $11\frac{3}{4} \times 9\frac{1}{2}$ in.	Mr. Russell J. Colman.
93A	Portrait of John Crome in monochrome by Miss Hannah Gurney (Mrs. Jonathan Backhouse). 15×12 in.	Mr. Charles H. Backhouse.
94	Pencil portrait of John Crome by Miss Jane Gurney (*c.* 1812). 11×9 in.	Mr. Henry Birkbeck.
95	Portrait of Mrs. Crome painted in oils by Michael Sharp. $16\frac{1}{2} \times 13$ in.	Mr. J. P. Heseltine.
96	Portrait of John Crome—water-colour sketch by J. W. Higham. 6×5 in.	Mr. J. P. Heseltine.
97	Landscape. 19×14 in.	Mr. Henry Birkbeck.
98	Landscape in oils. $7\frac{1}{2} \times 6\frac{1}{2}$ in.	H.H. Prince Fred. Duleep Singh.
99	Earlham Hall. Panel, 21×30 in.	Sir Eustace Gurney.
100	Ham House, West Ham. Panel, $5\frac{1}{2} \times 5\frac{1}{2}$ in.	Sir Eustace Gurney.
101	Cottage scene. Millboard, $8\frac{1}{2} \times 10\frac{1}{2}$ in.	Mr. Russell J. Colman.
102	Portrait in oils of Francis Bacon. 20×16 in.	Mr. J. H. Gurney.
103	Portrait of Dr. Richard Lubbock (91808). $8\frac{1}{4} \times 7$ in.	Norfolk and Norwich Hospital.
104	The Sawyers. Panel, 24×29 in.	Messrs. Steward and Patteson.
105	The three cranes.	Lady Hoare.
106	Landscape. Panel, 4×4 in.	Mr. James A. Stark.
107	An original letter, dated January, 1816, from John Crome to James Stark.	Mr. James A. Stark.
108	Fishmarket, Boulogne. $6 \times 9\frac{1}{4}$ in.	Mr. Frank Brown.
109	Palette used for paints by Crome.	Mr. Russell J. Colman.
110	Letter from Crome to his wife, written from Paris and dated 1814.	Mr. Russell J. Colman.
111	Apprenticeship "indenture" of Crome to Whistler, Coach, House and Sign Painter, of 41 Bethel Street, Norwich, dated 15th October, 1783.	Mr. Russell J. Colman.
112	Counterpart on vellum of lease of Crome's house in St. George's, Norwich, dated 5th April, 1806.	Mr. Russell J. Colman.
113	Catalogue of Crome's sale, 25th September, 1821.	Mr. Russell J. Colman.
114	Paint box in which Crome kept his paints in bladders.	The Misses Thirkettle.
115	Probate of Crome's will proved 29th November, 1821.	The Misses Thirkettle.
116	Water-colour drawing. Possibly Crome's sketch for the picture of Wroxham Regatta, which he intended to paint just before his death. $7\frac{3}{8} \times 12\frac{1}{2}$ in.	The Misses Thirkettle.
117	A bill for tuition in drawing by Crome.	Mr. Leonard G. Bolingbroke.
118	Crome's bank book with John Gurney & Co., Norwich.	Mr. Leonard G. Bolingbroke.
119	Framed catalogue of the exhibition of the Norwich Society of Artists, 1814.	Mr. Leonard G. Bolingbroke.
120	Photograph of Crome's house in St. George's, Norwich (now demolished).	Mr. Leonard G. Bolingbroke.
121	Register recording the birth of John Crome on 22nd December, 1768.	The Vicar and Churchwardens of St. George Tombland, Norwich.
122	Register recording the marriage of John Crome and Phoebe Berney on 2nd October, 1792.	The Vicar and Churchwardens of St. Mary Coslany, Norwich.
123	Register recording the burial of John Crome on 27th April, 1821.	The Vicar and Churchwardens of St. George Colegate, Norwich.

JOHN BERNEY CROME

(Moonlight Crome)

(1794-1842)

1794 John Berney Crome was the eldest son of John Crome, being born in the year 1794. He took his mother's maiden name—Berney. This was not an uncommon practice in nineteenth century Norwich families.

At an early age he came under his father's enthusiasm and influence. He must have formed part of many groups of Crome's pupils who took themselves off to the country to study Nature at first hand.

As Crome had teaching associations with Norwich Grammar School it is not surprising to learn that John Berney was educated there. He proved to be a good pupil and acquired a sound education, together with polished manners. Crome the elder was duly proud of his eldest son and had high hopes for his future.

1814 In 1814 John Berney Crome, in company with his father, visited Ipswich and sailed down the River Orwell to Harwich. A letter reproduced in the chapter on James Stark reports this visit.

1816 In 1816 Berney visited the Continent in company with George Vincent. Like his father before him, he visited Paris and beheld the pictorial loot of Napoleon. The extent of his peregrinations on the Continent are not known, but the journey was probably the basis for the large Continental views executed by him (views of Rotterdam, Utrecht, Leyden, Harlem).

After his return he assisted his father in teaching. This probably allowed his father more time for painting in his later period.

1819 By 1819 we find John Berney, known as young Crome, not only a member of the Norwich Society but President—a great honour for one so young. Such became his fame that he was appointed "Painter to the Duke of Sussex".

After the death of his father in 1821 he exercised his diplomacy and brought together the rival factions of the Norwich Society. So we find Robert Ladbrooke, Joseph Stannard, etc., back in the fold. Despite his urbanity and ability, John Berney Crome was endeavouring to do too much and live in too extravagant a manner. True, he sent many important paintings to London Exhibitions, both at the Royal Academy and the British Institution. Alas, it was not enough, for by 1831 he was declared a bankrupt. It has been said that he took to drink, which was his major downfall. Unable to live in style in Norwich, he took up residence in Yarmouth, where he both painted and taught.
1829 In passing, one might add that in 1829 there is evidence of a further trip to the Continent. We have a Continental harbour scene, signed and dated for that year.

1836 Despite financial troubles, he continued to do moonlight scenes, usually on the Yare at Yarmouth or along the Yarmouth waterfront. They are largely moonlights, but early-morning sunrises are also known. In 1836 he recorded the damage done at Yarmouth during the great gale of that year. A further view in Norwich Castle Museum is of Burgh Castle.

1842 In September, 1842, John Berney died at Great Yarmouth after struggling against ill-health for many months. He attended his pupils in the most uncomfortable circumstances right up to the end. Though John Berney Crome married twice, no children are recorded.

John Berney Crome, being a pupil of his father, was very close to that Master. The large *Frolic* at Kenwood House, Hampstead, London, is a masterpiece, not out-distanced by many of the seventeenth century Masters. At his best, John Berney's moonlights can compare with any other moonlight painter of the nineteenth century. They carry beautiful tone, strength and atmosphere. There is a sure touch about his brushwork in his best period which gives his work tremendous conviction. He takes his viewer to the scene and keeps him there. Towards the latter part of his life he tended to paint moonlights without quite the strength of his former years.

J. B. Crome, in his moonlights, has few competitors. One would never confuse him with the Pethers. He tends to use a characteristic type of buoy in his sea pieces—most robust. His figures, like those of his father's, are noted for their short necks. Greys and dark blues seem to predominate in his pictures. Like the rest of the School, he uses plenty of paint in his work. The cottage scene (illustrated) belongs to his early years, the spotty tree work being typical for the period.

John Berney Crome, though not the rarest painter in the School, was not as prolific as we should have liked. His early works are strongly painted with great confidence, whilst his latter works are more gentle, less paint being applied: indeed, some of his passages are extremely thinly painted. Certain of these late pictures have an affinity to those of his brother, William Henry Crome.

The early drawings again exude much confidence. One sees a very firm line, with the use of accents somewhat in his father's style. By 1828 his drawings have become delicate to the extreme, almost feathery. In his last few years, due to ill-health, the quality of his drawings fades—as seen by the drawings in the Coleman Library, Norwich.

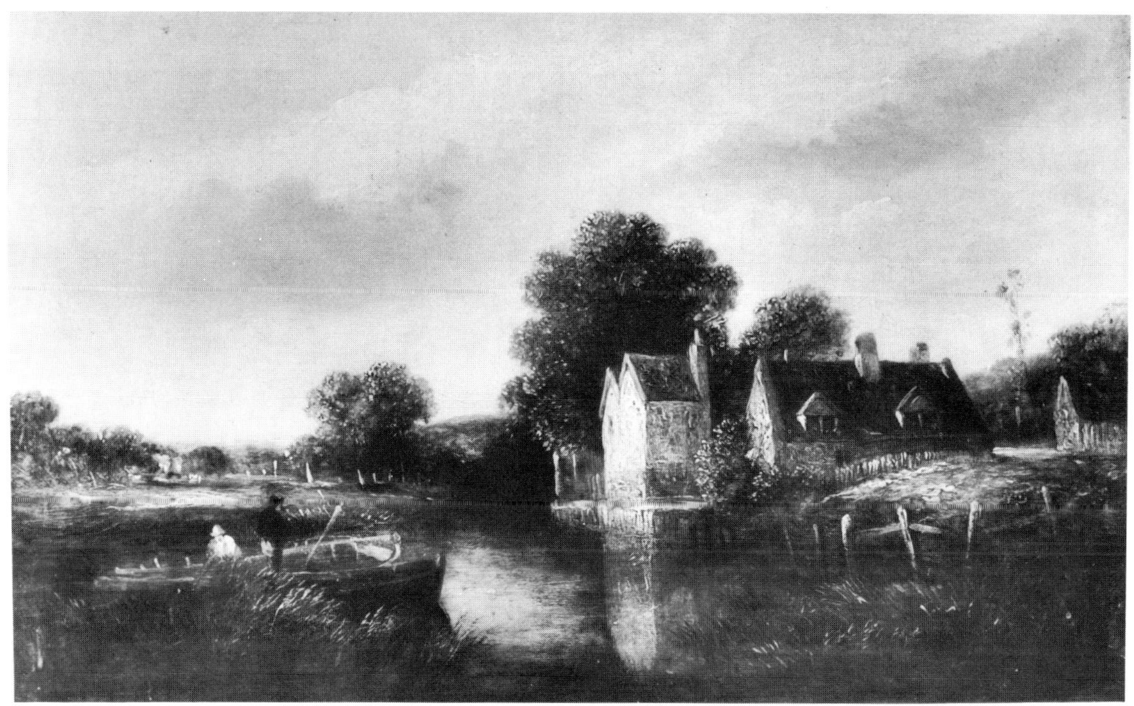

John Berney Crome and John Crome *Thorpe River, Norwich* *Oil on panel* $10\frac{1}{2} \times 17$ *in.*

J. B. Crome did sign occasionally. He letters his name simply, often dark on dark. Most of his works, however, are not signed.

The works of John Berney Crome are to be found at the National Gallery, Ipswich, Norwich, Kenwood House, London, and Yarmouth Museums.

EXHIBITS AT THE ROYAL ACADEMY

Year	*Subject*
1811	A cottage on Hingham Common, Norfolk.
1814	Old building on the Norwich River.
1839	Scene in the Fauxbourg of Rouen.
1840	Near Leyden—moonlight.
1841	Fishing by moonlight at Sanderdorf, near the Brille, Holland.
1842	A drainage mill at Acle, Norfolk, after the gale of Michaelmas morning, 1841—moon rising.
1843	Heath scene near Ipswich.

EXHIBITS AT THE BRITISH INSTITUTION

Year	*Subject*
1820	A view in Rotterdam. 66×81 in.
1821	Rouen, looking from the base of Mount St. Catherine towards the Bridge of Boats. 58×87 in.
1824	Boats at Utrecht. 48×42 in.
	Heath scene near Norwich. 24×30 in.
	A view on the River Maes—the town of Brille in the distance. 34×48 in.
1825	Earlham Bridge, painted from the drawing-room window of Earlham Hall, Norfolk. 34×31 in.
1826	Canal scene between Layden and Haarlem. 65×93 in.
	View at Hingham, Norfolk. 20×17 in.
	Scene on the Norwich River. 27×32 in.
1827	Moonlight. 33×43 in.
1828	View on the River Yare, with Norwich in the distance. 43×48 in.
	St. Benet's Abbey, Norfolk—moonlight. 30×34 in.
1829	Amsterdam—moonlight. 57×72 in.
	Yarmouth fishermen driving their nets along shore—moonlight. 57×72 in.
1830	A view at Heigham, Norwich. 29×20 in.
	Scene on the French coast—moonlight. 38×51 in.
	Scene in Suffolk. 23×26 in.
1831	Moonlight. 48×56 in.
1832	Dutch town—moonlight. 44×55 in.
1833	Heath scene near Norwich—rain coming on. 60×81 in.
1837	View in the neighbourhood of Vlarding, near Rotterdam—moonlight. 27×33 in.
1838	Beach scene—moonlight. 27×33 in.
1839	Scene at Blundestone, Suffolk—moonlight. 16×14 in.
	Scene on the coast of Sussex—moonlight. 19×27 in.
	Moonlight—a sketch. 16×19 in.
1840	Scene on the Old River, Norwich—moonlight—moon rising. 17×25 in.
	Moon—rising. 17×25 in.
	Scene on Breydon Waters: tide out—Yarmouth in the distance—moonlight. 38×39 in.
	View in the neighbourhood of Ipswich—moonlight. 17×25 in.
1841	View from the North River, Great Yarmouth—moonlight. 20×28 in.
	Moon rising. 54×43 in.
1842	Near Maasland Sluys, Holland. 18×22 in.
	At Marlingford, Norfolk—moonlight. 15×16 in.
1843	Dutch church—moonlight. 32×37 in.

He also sent no fewer than fifty-five pieces to Suffolk Street.

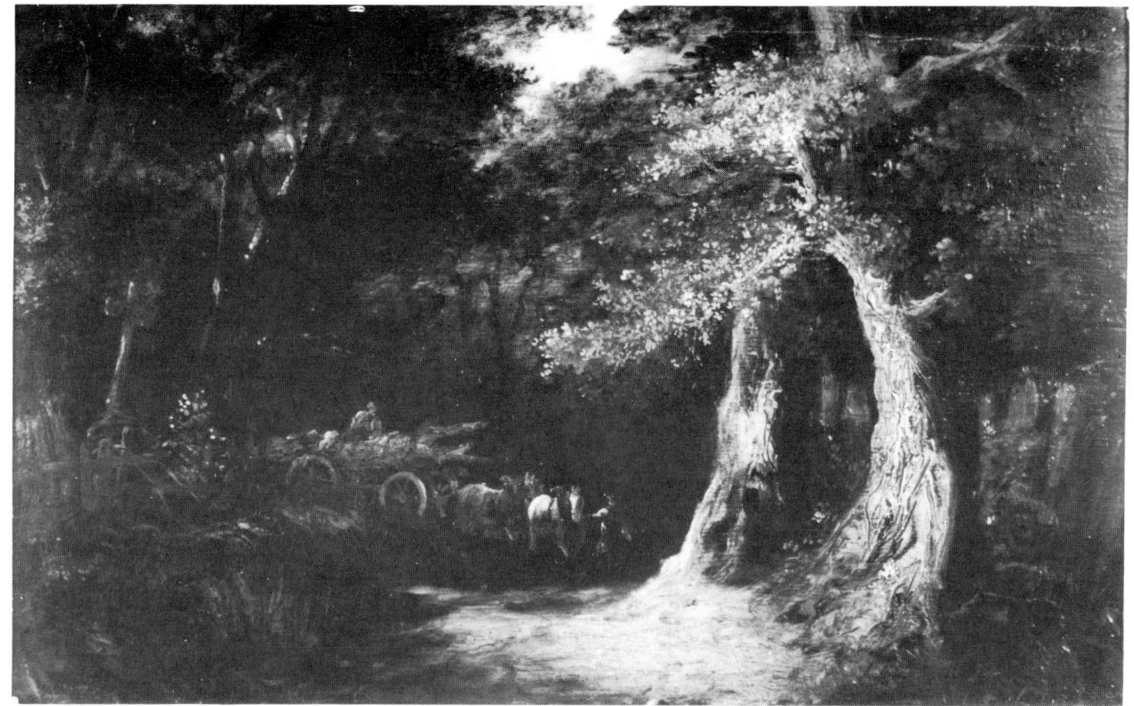

John Berney Crome *The Timber Wimb* *Oil app.* 9 × 15 *in.*
Note use of wooden end of brush on tree bole Mid period

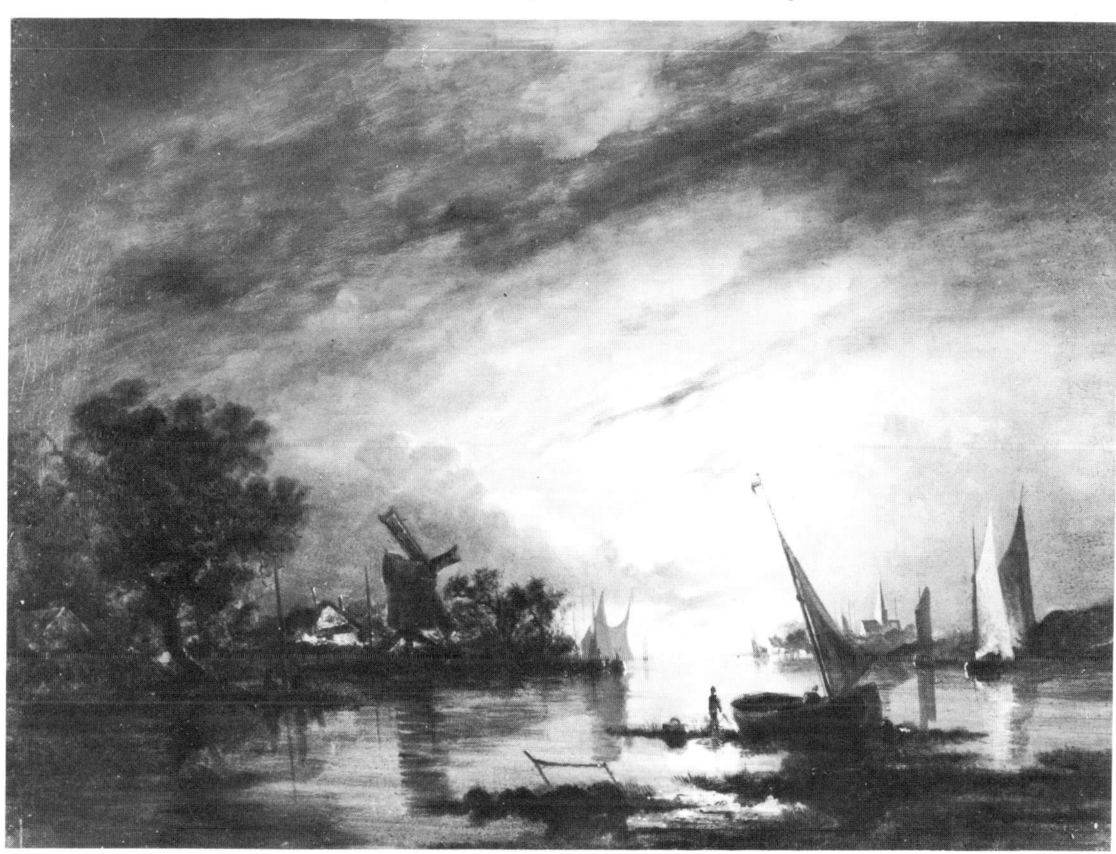

John Berney Crome *Moonlight* *Oil* $13\frac{3}{4} \times 19\frac{1}{2}$ *in.*
(Fairly late work)

John Berney Crome and John Crome

The Water Frolic, Wroxham Broad, Norfolk
(The handling is J. B. Crome, the composition J. Crome)

Oil 41 × 68 *in.*

EXHIBITS AT THE NORWICH SOCIETY

Year	*Subject*
1818	St. Benet's Abbey by moonlight.
	A meadow scene.
	Scene on the Norwich River.
	Boat-houses at Cromer—evening.
	Moonlight effect.
	View looking towards Yarmouth Bridge.
	View of Yarmouth from Gorleston.
	Moonlight.
	Gorleston River.
	Island of Poplars, near Rouen.
1819	The entrance to the port of Rotterdam.
	The Brill.
	Boats—the town of Vlarding in the distance.
	Two drawings in black and white.
1820	View looking from St. Germain-en-Laye towards Paris—Mount Calvaire in the distance—painted on the spot.
1820	Canal scene in the environs of Amsterdam—drawing in black and white.
	Scene in the Bois de Soigne—a sketch.
	Rouen, looking from the base of Mount St. Catherine towards the Bridge of Boats.
	Mount St. Catherine, Rouen, looking from the Boulevard—sketch for large picture painted on the spot.
1829	(1) A moonlight of great beauty and transparency.
	(2) A sea-piece, with a powerful effect of light and shade.

EXHIBITION OF NORWICH SCHOOL PICTURES
NORWICH CASTLE MUSEUM AND ART GALLERIES
October, 1927

OIL PAINTINGS

No.	*Subject*
25	The tower of the castle. $21\frac{3}{4} \times 18\frac{1}{2}$ in.
26	Moonlight scene. $28\frac{1}{2} \times 42$ in.
27	River scene, Great Yarmouth. 44×71 in.
28	The removal of Old Yarmouth Bridge. $29\frac{1}{2} \times 40$ in.
29	Boats—junction of the Yare and Waveney. $19\frac{1}{4} \times 16\frac{1}{4}$ in.
30	Yarmouth Jetty. $20\frac{1}{2} \times 34$ in.

WATER-COLOURS, DRAWINGS, ETC.

No.	*Subject*
157	Interior of a church. $12 \times 8\frac{3}{4}$ in.
158	Interior of a church. $13 \times 8\frac{3}{4}$ in.

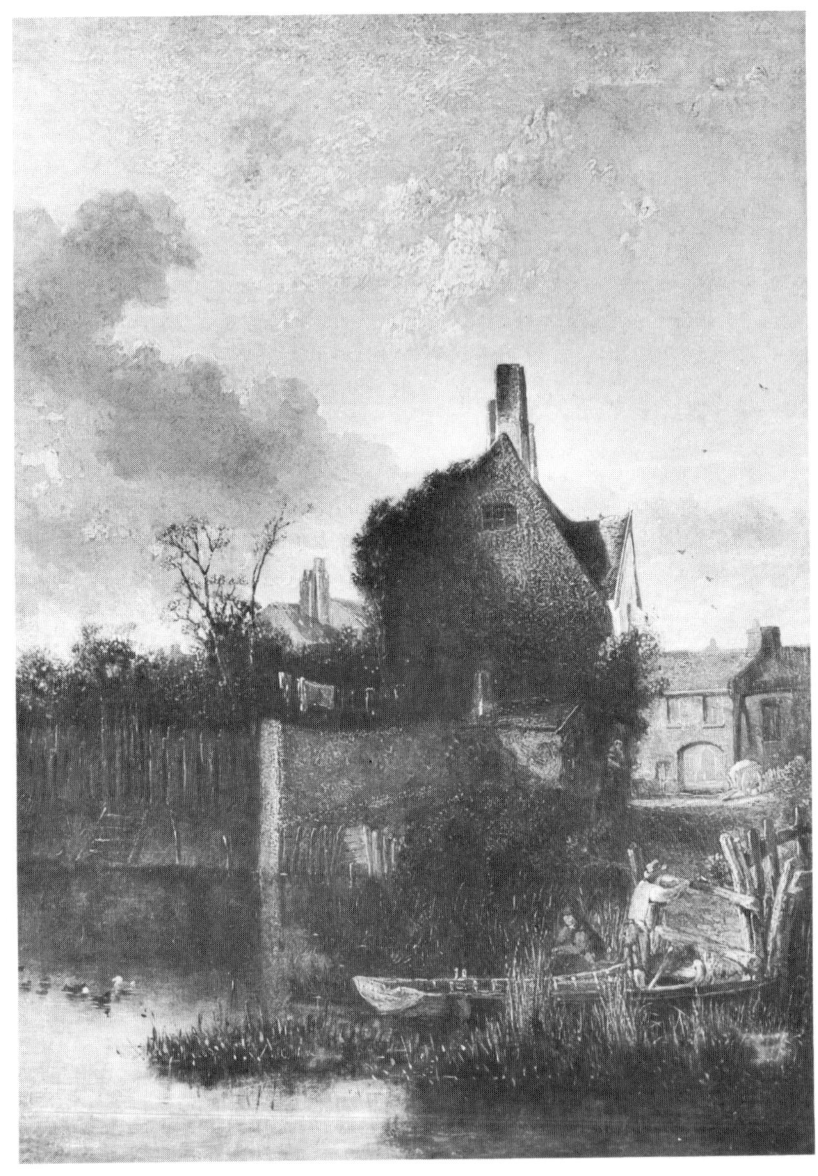

John Berney Crome — *St. Martin's Gate, Norwich* — *Oil on canvas*
A subject also treated by his father — $19\frac{1}{2} \times 14\frac{1}{2}$ *in.*

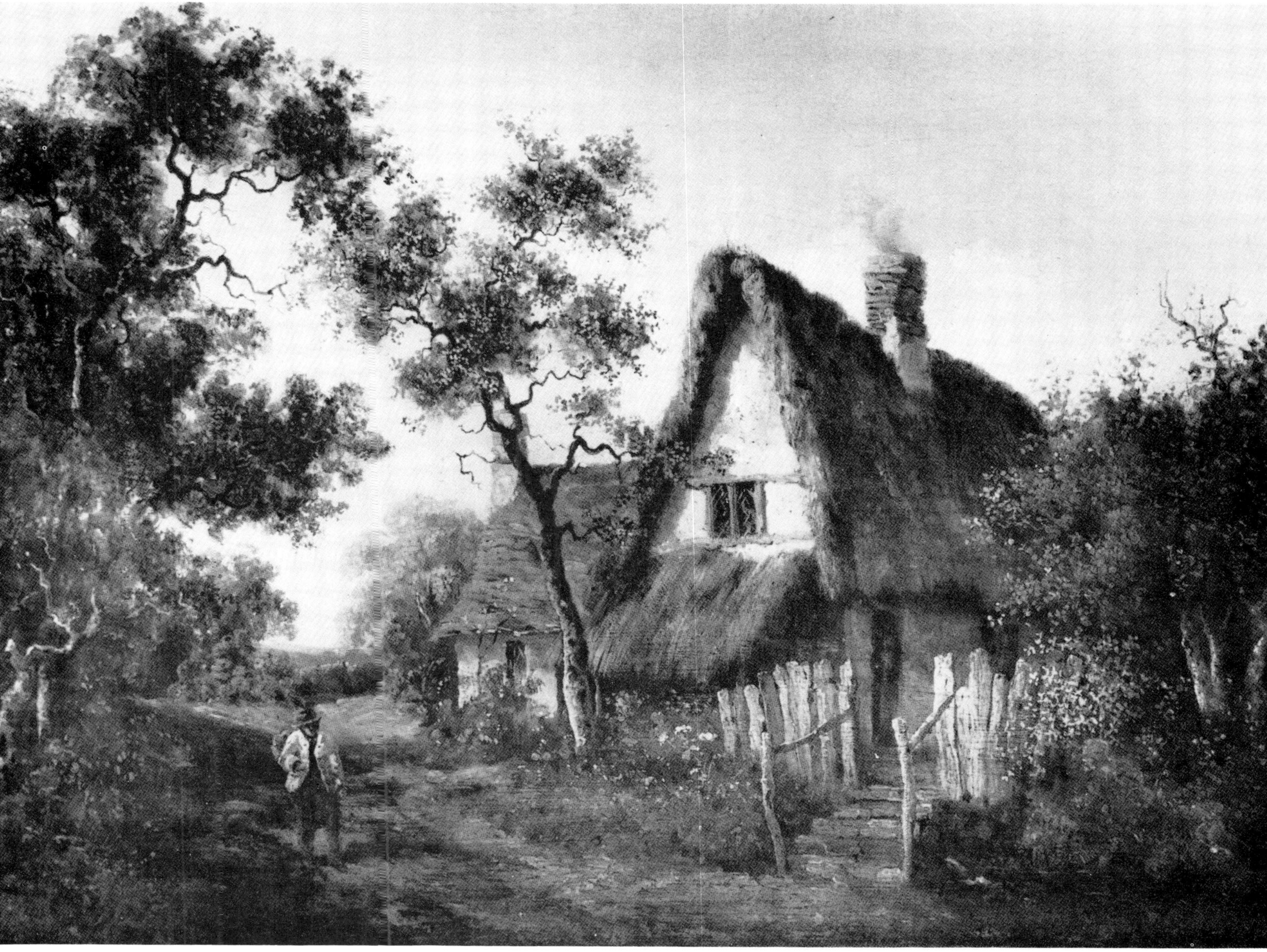

John Berney Crome

Cottage Scene—a fairly early work
(A freely handled work involving the use of the earth colours)

Oil on panel 17½ × 24 *in.*

WILLIAM HENRY CROME

(1806-1867)

1806 William Henry Crome was born in Norwich on 22nd October, 1806, the third son of John Crome, one of the founders of the Norwich School. Later in the same year, 2nd November, he was baptised at St. George's, Colegate. William Henry was very unfortunate in losing his father at the early age of fifteen years; whilst John Berney had sheltered under his father's wing, William had to make his own way, and this he commenced to do with good effect.

1821 Old Crome (John Crome) died in 1821 and in his posthumous Exhibition we read of paintings by him belonging to the young William Henry. Presumably, William had assisted his father in the studio and at the age of fifteen was probably becoming quite competent. John Berney, his elder brother, probably carried on the tuition; indeed, many of William's early works were moonlights, and one can decidedly see the influence of his elder brother.

1826 In 1826 our painter was sufficiently competent to exhibit a painting entitled *A View at Costessy, Norfolk*, at the British Institution. The acceptance of his exhibit must have spurred him on. The portrait by George Clint could have been painted about this time. It shows a man who looks pleasantly on life and who has probably inherited much of his father's idealism. It is interesting to note that George Clint also painted Joseph Stannard, probably on the same visit to Norwich in 1827.

William Henry Crome married Mary Ann Steel (the sister of Steel the surgeon) who married Hannah Crome (William Crome's sister). It is not known how many children William had, but at least one son, Vivian, painted.

At the age of twenty-four William was beginning to look towards one of the Old
1830 Masters—Claude Lorraine, for influence. In the illustrated plate dated 1830 we see a Claudian composition and the use of beautiful Claudian blues. These blues are seen in many of his Scottish views, such as his *Lochleven Castle* and *Pitleven Bridge* which rather suggests that the Scottish visit was during the 1830s. One recalls a George Vincent picture dated 1831: is it possible William Henry accompanied him?

1850 Henry Ladbrooke, in his jottings written about 1850, makes mention of William living in London. It was probably from London that he set out for the Continent. His visit is recorded by an inscription on a painting belonging to Mr. E. Levine, it reads: *Near*
1854 *Aix La Chappelle, Brussels 1854.*

1858 In 1858, the Editor of the *Norwich Mercury* received a communication from Vivian Crome notifying him of the passing of his mother. This was dispatched from Small Heath, Birmingham. As the communication was left to Vivian Crome it would appear that William was not residing at Birmingham at the time, or he may have been ill.
1866 However, he was active in the year 1866, for a painting signed and dated for this year exists. With this last information our knowledge of William Henry Crome terminates—like George Vincent, he just disappeared, at least until further information comes to light.

1867 Died 1867.

William Henry Crome has hitherto been sadly neglected. He had talent, there is little doubt. His early work, executed under the influence of John Berney Crome, consists of moonlight woodland scenes of a rather dark colouring. The distances have an emerald greeny blue appearance, which is often the identification point of a work by William Henry. His palette often includes these greeny blues—one often finds the touches on the tree boles and in the foliage of the trees. Amongst the greens of the trees there is often a tree carrying a deep earth-colour, which gives the picture a rich appeal. From his father he learnt about balancing masses, and one often finds a small mass alongside a larger one. His drawing of figures and animals can, if he wishes, be quite meticulous, but they are never given prominence and used mainly for local colour. Generally the treatment of the figures is slight but effective.

At an early age he came under the influence of his father, painting many moonlights and wooded landscapes of a mellow green colouring.

As a colourist William can be very beautiful. His pictures painted under the influence of Claude, about 1830, have the delightful sylvan distance and exquisite skies. Many of the pictures at this period are prominent in their display of blue tones. An example of this period is illustrated on page 49.

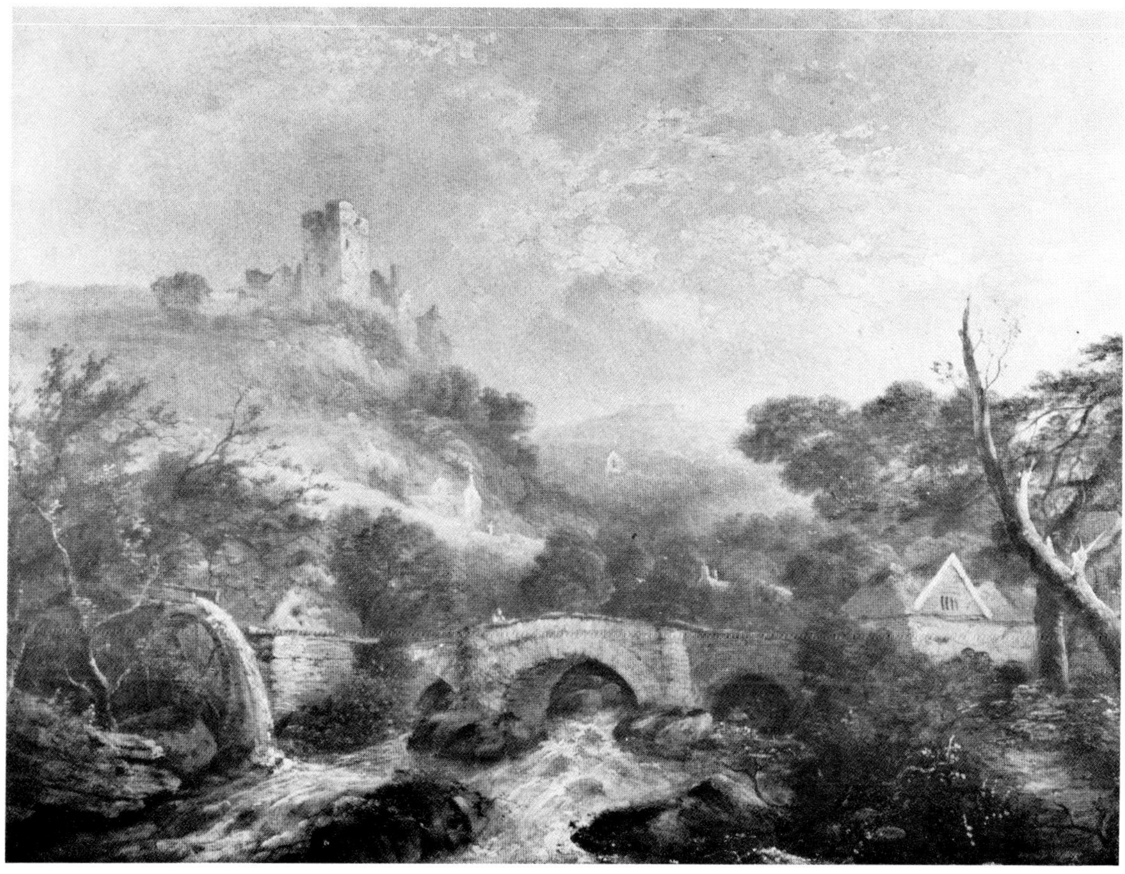

William Henry Crome *Inscribed on reverse — Ludlow Castle* *Oil on canvas* 22 × 30 *in.*

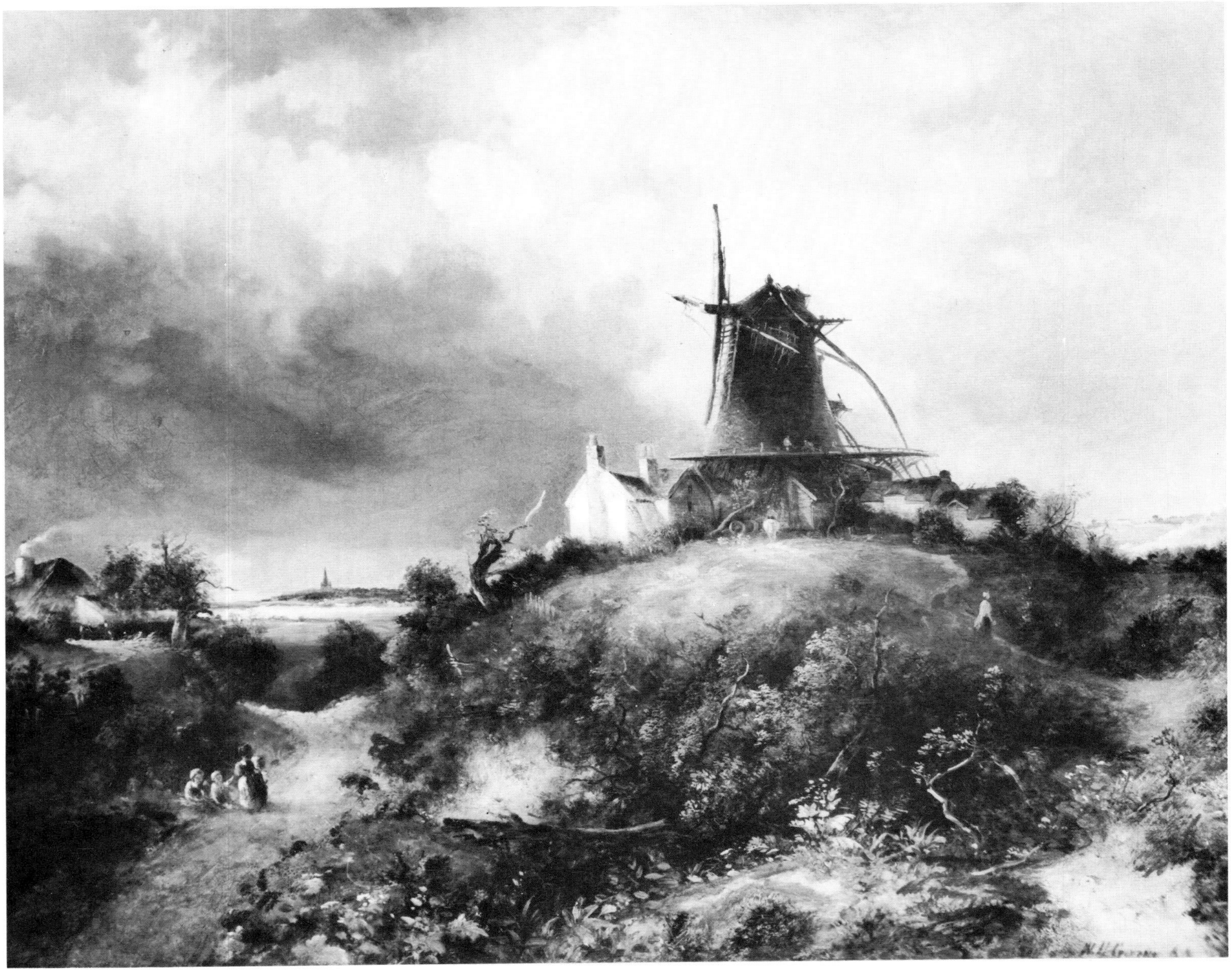

W. H. Crome *View near Norwich* *Oil* 24½ × 29¾ *in.*

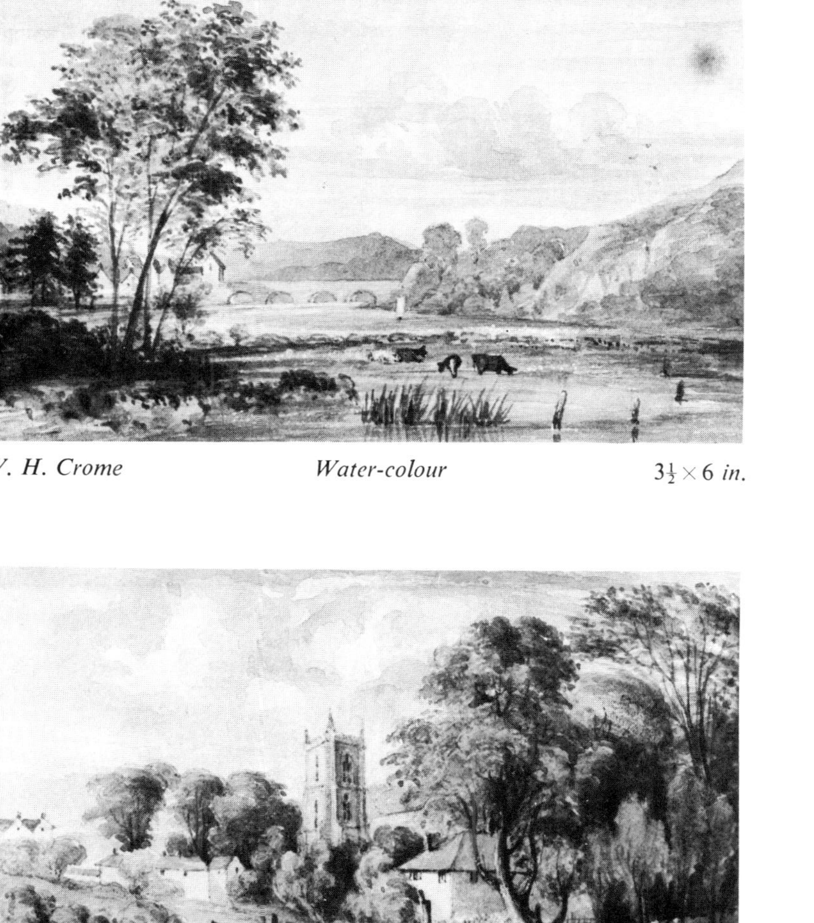

W. H. Crome *Water-colour* $3\frac{1}{2} \times 6$ *in.*

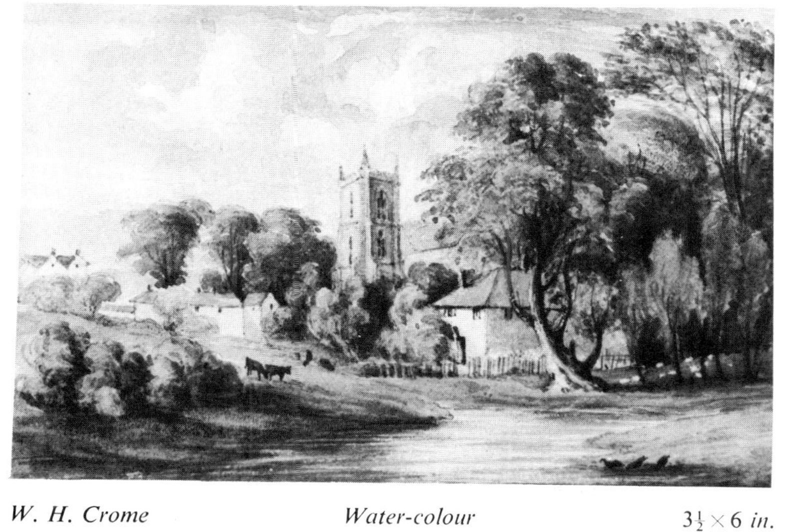

W. H. Crome *Water-colour* $3\frac{1}{2} \times 6$ *in.*

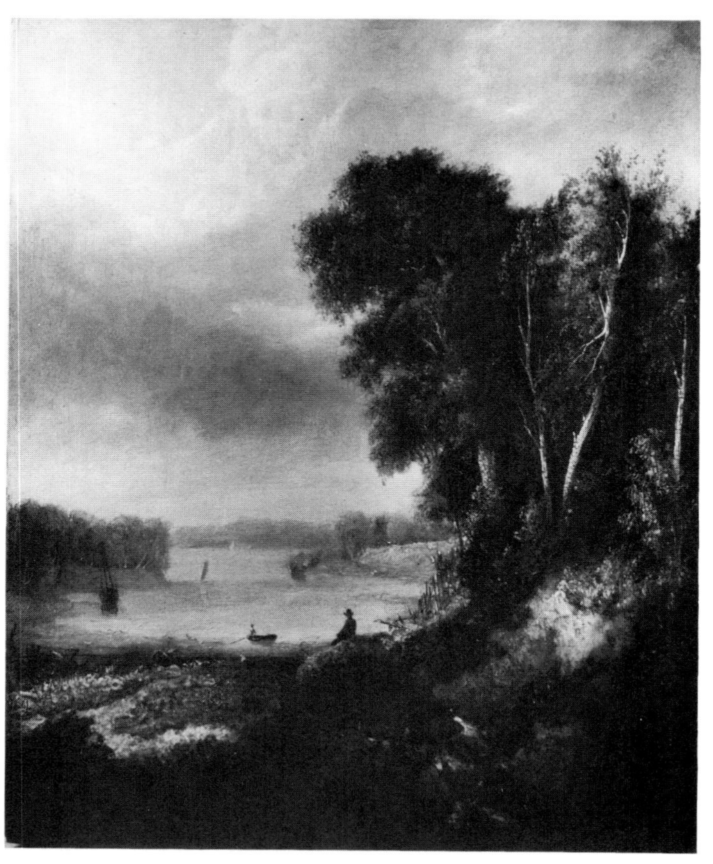

W. H. Crome *View on the Orwell, 1830* *Oil*

The blue period was followed by a number of paintings of very balanced colour, most of them being Norfolk scenes. However, in most of the paintings emerald green, of which he was so fond, is beginning to assert itself. The use of green becomes more and more apparent as time goes by, until he embarks upon his "green" period. The use of predominant colours is a most original trait, resulting in the paintings having a delightfully decorative effect. The illustrated woodland scene belongs to the "green" period. The "green" period commenced about 1840.

In water-colours, William Crome attained great delicacy; though not his usual working medium, several works are recorded, the most interesting being the *View of Windsor*, executed at the early age of fifteen years (see illustration page 54).

The author has seen only one late work from which it would seem that a further colour transition took place, this time to sienna.

Before passing on to the next artist it is interesting to note that in 1867, exhibited at Norwich, was *Norwich from the Hellesdon Road* by John and William Crome, which either suggests that William Henry completed his father's picture, or that they executed a joint work. Possibly other such works exist.

EIGHTEENTH EXHIBITION OF THE NORWICH SOCIETY OF ARTISTS, 1822

No.	*Subject*
28	View at Mistley.
92	View on the river, King Street, Norwich.

TWENTIETH EXHIBITION OF THE NORWICH SOCIETY OF ARTISTS, 1824

No.	*Subject*
26	Bishopsgate Bridge.

TWENTY-FIRST EXHIBITION OF THE NORWICH SOCIETY OF ARTISTS, 1825

No.	*Subject*
80	Landscape, Stratton Strawless.

TWENTY-THIRD EXHIBITION OF THE NORFOLK AND SUFFOLK INSTITUTION FOR THE PROMOTION OF THE FINE ARTS, 1829

No. *Subject*

33 Landscape.

39 Composition from the *Spirit of Solitude.*

"Obedient to the Light
That shone within his soul, he went pursuing
The windings of the dell. The rivulet,
Wanton and wild, through many a green ravine,
Beneath the forest flowed. Some times it fell
Among the moss with hollow harmony,
Dark and profound. Now on the polished stones
It danced; like childhood laughing as it went:
Then through the plain in tranquil wandering crept,
Reflecting every herb and drooping bud
That overhung its quietness."

44 Boats.

57 Landscape.

101 Landscape.

114 Landscape.

TWENTY-FIFTH EXHIBITION OF THE NORFOLK AND SUFFOLK INSTITUTION FOR THE PROMOTION OF THE FINE ARTS, 1831

No.	*Subject*
84	Landscape.
85	Downham Reach on the Orwell—evening.
98	The brig *Eliza*, late in H.M.S.
104	Break water, Harwich.
105	Sun-set.
118	Downham Reach on the Orwell—morning.

TWENTY-SIXTH EXHIBITION OF THE NORFOLK AND SUFFOLK INSTITUTION FOR THE PROMOTION OF THE FINE ARTS, 1832

No.	*Subject*
107	Landscape.
117	Elfin Glen, Cumberland.
123	View on the Orwell—in the possession of the Rev. J. Humfrey.
132	Sketch of a glen.
133	View in Cumberland—from a sketch by Captain Ramsay, R.H.
136	View on the Orwell—in the possession of the Rev. J. Humphrey.
142	Landscape—evening.
148	Dove Cote Grange, Cumberland—morning.
163	Composition from the woods at Malton, the seat of E. Lombe, Esq.

TWENTY-SEVENTH EXHIBITION OF THE NORFOLK AND SUFFOLK INSTITUTION FOR THE PROMOTION OF THE FINE ARTS, 1833

No.	*Subject*
90	Study of an old oak from Nature.
108	Wroxham Church from the seat of the Rev. J. Humfrey.
114	Landscape—morning.
124	The seat of the Rev. John Humfrey, Wroxham, from the east side of the broad.
133	Seat of the Rev. J. Humfrey, Wroxham—south front view.

SECOND EXHIBITION OF THE WORKS OF ANCIENT MASTERS, 1830

No.	*Subject*
96	Composition.

NORFOLK AND NORWICH FINE ART 1860—WORKS OF MODERN ARTISTS

No.	*Subject*
11	A moonlight scene.
62	Near Turnbury Castle.
180	Landscape.

NORWICH AND EASTERN COUNTIES WORKING CLASSES INDUSTRIAL EXHIBITION 1867

No.	*Subject*	*Lent by*
782	Norwich from the Hellesdon Road.	W. Dixon.
811	Landscape—mill, etc.	F. E. Watson.

BRITISH MEDICAL ASSOCIATION LOAN COLLECTION

Works of Norfolk and Suffolk Artists, 1874

No.	*Subject*	*Lent by*
37	Landscape and mill.	F. E. Watson.
72	Small landscape.	W. Boswell.

NORWICH ART LOAN EXHIBITION

in aid of the Fund for the Restoration of the Church of Saint Peter Mancroft, 1878

No.	*Subject*	*Lent by*
80	Moonlight scene.	R. W. Burleigh, Esq.
154	Solitude.	Mr. John Moore*.

FINE ART EXHIBITION

in aid of the new Norfolk and Norwich Hospital, 1883

No.	*Subject*	*Lent by*
41	Lewisham Common.	Mr. J. J. Colman, M.P.

ART LOAN EXHIBITION

in aid of the Fund for the Restoration of St. Peter Mancroft Church, 1885

No.	*Subject*	*Lent by*
33	Woodland scene.	Mrs. Thomas Clabburn.
37	Windmill—with coming storm.	F. E. Watson, Esq.
72	Lewisham.	J. J. Colman, Esq., M.P.

COLLECTION OF PICTURES AND WATER-COLOUR DRAWINGS

Exhibited at the Agricultural Hall Gallery during the Grand Oriental Bazaar, 1894.
Promoted by the C.E.Y.M.S. and the Y.M.C.A. combined

No.	*Subject*	*Lent by*
4	Lewisham.	J. J. Colman, Esq., M.P.

EXHIBITION OF NORWICH SCHOOL PICTURES
NORWICH CASTLE AND ART GALLERIES, OCTOBER 1927

OIL PAINTINGS

No.	*Subject*
32	Landscape and figures. $17 \times 21\frac{3}{4}$ in.
33	Landscape. $29\frac{1}{4} \times 24\frac{1}{4}$ in.
34	Landscape. $29\frac{1}{4} \times 24\frac{1}{4}$ in.

CROME FAMILY NOTES

Frederick James Crome

Born 1796. Exhibited at the Norwich Society from an early age. Later became a bank clerk at Yarmouth. In 1821 he had the sad task of informing Dawson Turner of his father's condition. In his father's will be received £100 and two paintings which were exhibited in the 1821 Exhibition.

Emily Crome

Born in 1800. She painted flower pieces. Examples of her work are in Norwich Castle Museum. Her dictionary is with the Colman family.

Michael Sharp Crome

Born 1813. The last son. He is not known to have painted. Became a dancing master and lived on into the 1880s. In 1878 he offered a John Crome painting to J. J. Colman.

*Possibly the Ipswich artist, see Vol. I.

W. H. Crowe *A work of the Artist's green period c.1840* *Oil on canvas* 26×36 *in.*

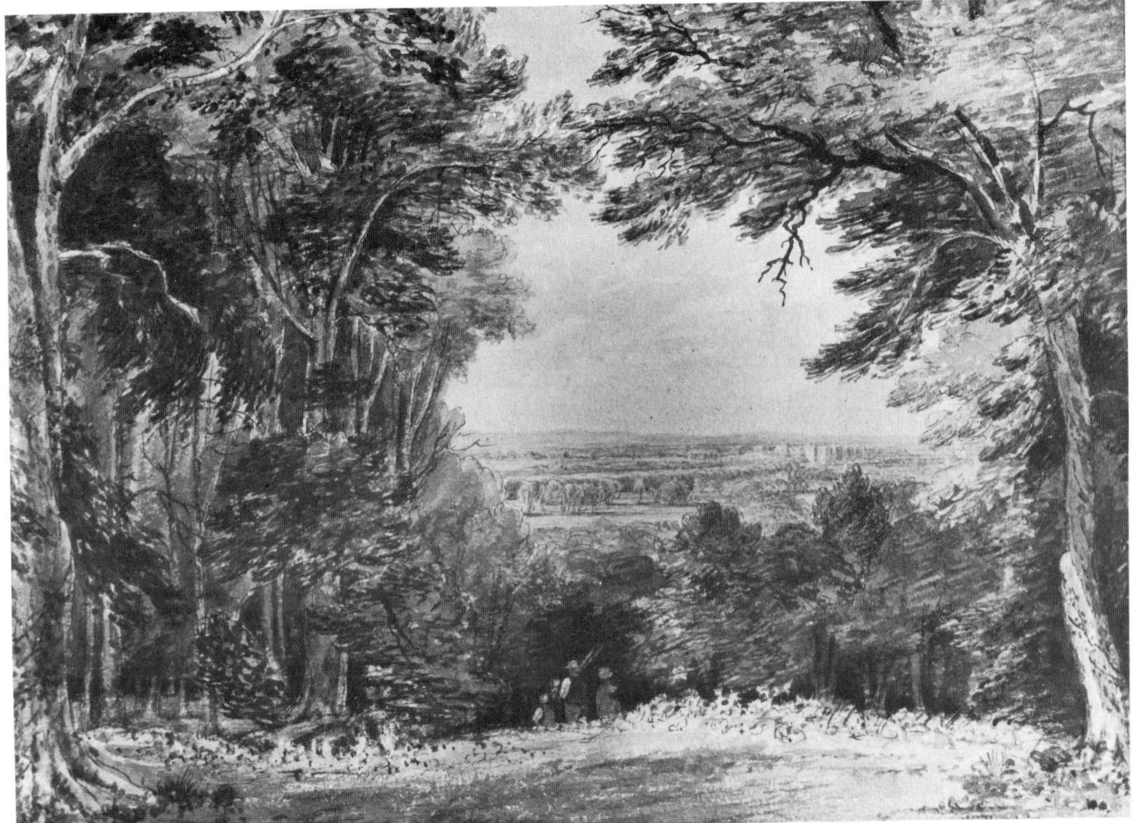

W. H. Crome *View near Windsor, 1821* *Water-colour* $10\frac{3}{4} \times 15$ *in.*

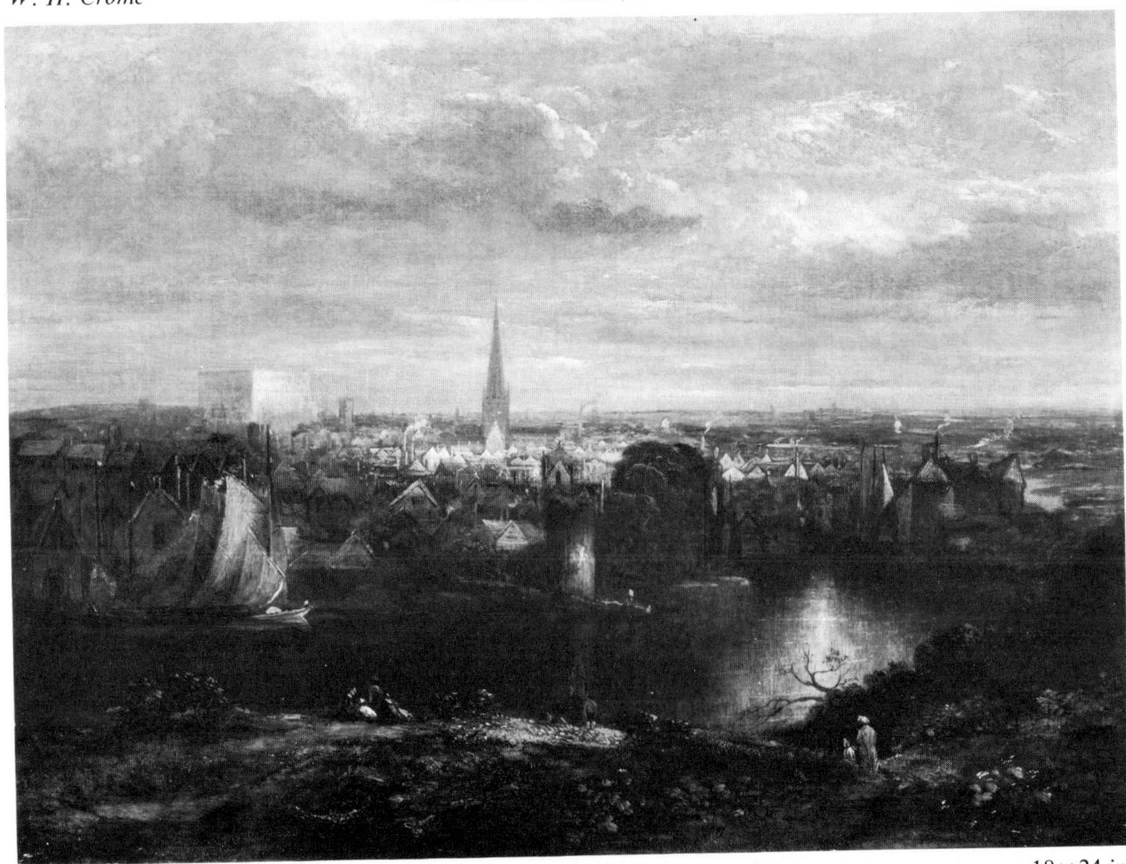

W. H. Crome *An extensive view of Norwich from across the river* 18×24 *in.*

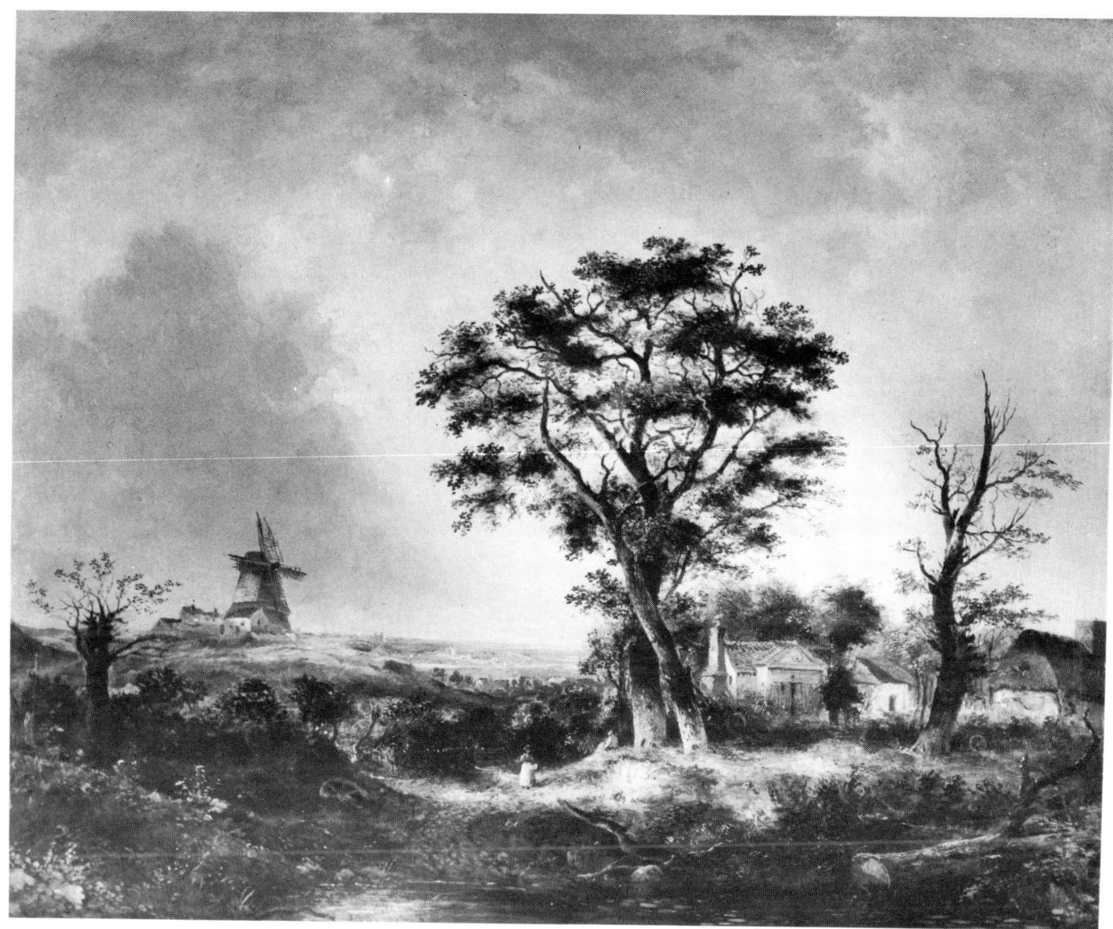

William Henry Crome *View near Cromer* *Oil on canvas* 17 × 21 *in.*

JAMES STARK

(1794-1859)

1794 James Stark was born 19th November, 1794, the son of a successful Scottish dyer named Michael Stark. The family originally came from Fife. James was the youngest son. His brothers were William, born 1788, and Michael, born 1789. He also had a sister.

Early in life, James loved to get outdoors and originally hoped to become a farmer. However, a delicate constitution which troubled him all his life made this impossible.

Again we see Norwich Grammar School as the centre from which emanated much artistic genius. James started there at first under Dr. Forster, and later studied under Dr. Valpy. It was here that he became friendly with John Crome's eldest son, John Berney Crome. It must have been during visits to the Cromes that Stark first kindled
1811 the idea of becoming an artist, for in the year 1811 he was indentured with John Crome
1814 as a pupil. This continued until 1814 when he moved to London. In this year his
Master sent him the following letter:

Norwich, July ye 3d. 1814.

Friend James—After a pleasant ride we arrived in Ipswich at five, we went down by the river-side and made some few sketches. One scene John sketched I think will make a good subject for his large picture. I cannot think the river Orwell will pay you the trouble and expense of a journey. John and myself set off in the vessel with ye tide on the next day morning at half past eleven, reach'd Harwich in the evening at five a river twelve miles long, the first four or five miles both sides were beautifully wooded but not accompanied with shipping as I expected. However when you are at Ipswich it amply repays you the trouble and expense as your fare is only one shilling. The men in the vessel are very civil our crew amounted to about twenty with room enough for a hundred which made it very pleasant. We returned at night at about eleven setting off at about seven so you find our time was but two hours at Harwich, which was dedicated to our mouths and seeing the wall as they call it, it is a sort of round Batterve with a deep fossee in the centre of this vat (for that its like) are all the rooms for the different stores officers etc. etc. so that it is altogether a wonder. I think James if you could study near town it would be much better and less expense. I think you would find some good stuff near Lambeth, I think you may make some good water scenes without going far for them.

My best wishes attend you, *pray paint*.

We are all well I am brewing up something.

Yours etc. etc.,

John Crome.

P.S. Pray don't forget the Norwich Room.

1815 By 1815 he had cast his eyes towards London and became a pupil at the Royal Academy School in that year. By 1818 such was his ability as a landscape painter that the Directors of the British Institution awarded him a prize of £50. It is interesting to note that a similar prize was awarded to Sir Edwin Landseer. A letter written to him by his father and addressed "My dear boy" indicated that John Crome visited him in London in 1818.

Norwich 14th March 1818.

My dear Boy,

I received your very kind and affectionate letter by J. Crome and I believe I shall take your advice with respect to going to the Dyehouse as I am now unable to attend to business as I used to do. I have been very poorly this winter but within a few days I think I am getting better. I write this in our new house which is one of the most clean and comfortable places that can be imagined, the rooms are small but very clean and neat and there is a very good room for you when you come to see us. As soon as I heard you wanted the Color I set about making it. William did not know how to do it the large parcel (?) and

James Stark *Sheep Washing* *Oil* $23\frac{1}{4} \times 31\frac{3}{4}$ *in.*

A further painting of sheep washing is in the Ipswich Art Gallery

small one are made different ways. When you have tried them you will inform me which you like best and if you think they will be of use to you I will make you a large quantity. Let me know as soon as convenient that I may do it while I am able. I have no doubt but I could send you some other colors that might be useful to you and I will send you some soon. I am very happy to hear and see your fame so much sounded abroad, the Examiner have touched you up very high this week and your mother says it is the best newspaper in the world. We have got all our things away from the old house this day and all things go on very well. Michael has got a good room for his organ and has put his new furniture in the drawing room with a fine new Sopha covered with blue silk. It looks very superbe and beautiful. The young folk have got Mr. Sims furniture which is very good and they will cut a fine dash. (Sims has given up house-keeping and furnished two rooms at the Labrotary). I do not know when the honeymoon will be over as they still go on nursing the house for dressing. The Bombazeen is nearly finished and is a very fine building. The trade goes on briskly at present. I know not what you may think but I think I done well, as I have not wrote so much for a long time, and am you most affectionate father,

MICHAEL STARK.

P.S. We are all well.

1821 James Stark married a Miss Elizabeth Dinmore from King's Lynn on 17th July, 1821, and lived in Yarmouth for a short period after his marriage. Later he moved back to Norwich, occupying a small house next door to his father. It was here that his two daughters were born.

1823 It was about 1823 when he became so ill he could not paint for a time. This resulted in only a few paintings of his appearing at the Norwich Exhibition.

1824 By 1824 he had recovered and sent to the British Institution several major paintings. The
1827 year 1827 saw the commencement of the foundation of a volume of etchings; views on Norfolk rivers, which involved the work of several engravers. The publication met with reasonable success and was completed in 1834.

Shortly after the publication of this work he moved to London, his pictures appearing in all the major exhibitions and selling successfully.

Stark was a popular and kindly man and ever concerned for the welfare of his friends. A letter written in the 1820s to Mr. Dan Davey concerns George Vincent:

> . . . do you ever hear anything of Vincent—remember me most kindly to him. Spur him on to something grand, no man is more capable of it. He has talents enough for anything if the poor fellow's spirits will allow of the excercise of it, but in trouble by misfortune everything goes. I must always consider him a good fellow and everyone must. We have a picture of his—a beautiful bit.

The last phrase is interesting—Stark refers to a painting as a "beautiful bit". There is still a London auctioneer who keeps alive this terminology.

1831 On 6th October, 1831, Arthur James Stark, his only son, was born, who later developed into a fine landscape painter. Our artist gave his son much encouragement and later
1834 they worked side by side. It was some three years after the birth of his son that Stark had the misfortune to lose his wife.

1839 In 1839 he moved to Windsor, a place he knew from former visits. Here he painted on for ten years, sending regularly to the London Exhibitions.

When Arthur James Stark reached the age of eighteen, his father thought it would be wise to move back to London in order that his son could attend the Royal Academy School.

The following letter to E. W. Cooke, R.A., is interesting:
[E. W. Cooke was son of George Cooke, who engraved Stark's "Norfolk Rivers."]

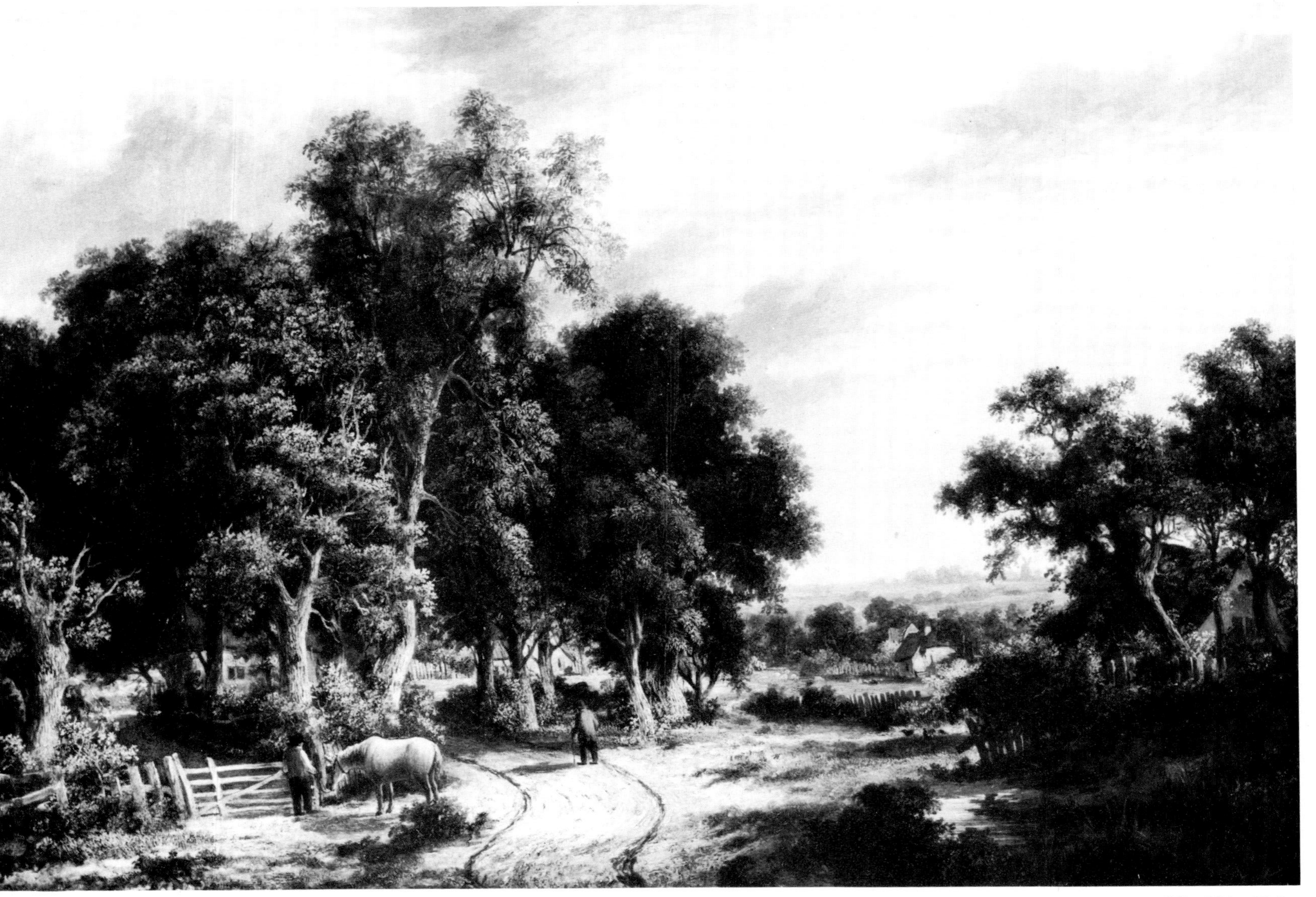

James Stark

The Forest Gate
(Early Norwich Period)

Oil 20¼ × 30 *in.*

16 York Place, Windsor.
Nov. 23rd 1848.

My Dear Cooke,

I am ashamed on looking at your kind letter to find how long it has remained unanswered. I was at Marlborough when it reached me and remained at Windsor for a few days on our return when we started for Norwich. Arthur and myself have been staying there for the last 7 weeks visiting from home to home amongst relatives. We were 3 weeks at Hethnalt your good mother may remember my driving her over there to visit the late Aldmn. Brown. My daughter Julian (Mrs. Back) is now residing in 'a House' directly opposite. We called on the Miss Browns who made kind enquiries about Mrs. Cooke and your family. They are great cultivators of Ferns and have a very interesting collection.

We were at Norwich whilst the Exhibition was open. I was delighted with your little Water Mills and tried to persuade some of the Norwich patrons to purchase it but there was not enough they thought for the money nothing less than a kit kat can be worth 10£. About 700£ has been expended in the purchase of pictures and I would honestly rather have this picture then the whole of them, but gaudy sketchy pictures seems to be the prevailing taste through the country. Should any application be made for a reduction in price pray don't listen to it. It is a little gem and worth any money.

I should have written to you whilst at Norwich but fancied you were from home and as the season is now so far advanced and so much time having been lost in Norfolk, poor me must give up the anticipated pleasure of seeing you at Barnes until the Spring, and should you be there at that time.

We are contemplating a removal but have no final plans unless the determination to give up housekeeping and taking lodging can be called so.

I am most anxious to get to London on Arthur's account, as he is to be an animal painter it is absolutely necessary that he should draw and study in the Academy. He is losing time now. I believe Careys to be the best plan to prepare him. He has painted 2 horses in Norfolk and done them capitally but he wants the stimulus which mixing with lads of his own age and pursuits would give him.

Pray remember me most kindly to your good mother and such members of your family as you may have around you. I saw one marriage announced in the paper, my best wishes attend them.

Believe me my dear Cooke,
Ever Yours,
most faithfully,
J. Stark.

From his studio he continued to produce fine canvases, many of them of considerable size, his son, A. J. Stark, placing in many of the figures and animals. Despite delicate health, Stark lived on for many years after his wife, but finally his health gave way and
1859 he died in lodgings in Norfolk Street, Strand, on 24th March, 1859. At his request he was buried in the Stark enclosure in the Rosary Cemetery, Norwich. Miss Phillipa Stark informs me that A. J. Stark was very close to his father and nursed him during his last illness. So passed one of the most able and delightful painters of the Norwich School.

It is the author's sad part to relate that James Stark, the painter of so many beautiful landscapes, died in abject poverty—his son, Arthur James, having to paint and sell pictures for them to live a hand-to-mouth existence.

THE PAINTINGS

Without doubt James Stark had great gifts. His sensitivity enabled him to achieve delightful colour harmonies and to place the colour in such a manner that accent followed accent with the most able touch. It is the handling which marks Stark's work; so characteristic is his touch that he believed he would be known by this alone, and thus he seldom signed his works.

His early works executed under the strong influence of his master, John Crome, are the most beautiful and the most sought-after by collectors, and it is true to say that Stark maintained a high standard of performance throughout his life-time, though we must bear in mind his ill-health. By and large, his early Norwich works have a greater thickness of paint and a wider use of colour. His later works, often referred to as his "Windsor Period", are often quite thinly painted with a palette largely of the top register.

Stark, in his early work, loves to give impasto touches to his tree boles, often of a grey-green intermingled with Naples yellow. His leaf work is beautifully executed with many touches, often single touches in the case of a willow, and groups of two, three or more strokes placed together to depict the heavy foliage of oaks. Amongst the foliage one sees the winding branches again, often high-lighted with grey-green. This light, watery green foliage is often contrasted with the lovely sienna browns.

The skies are often Crome-like, being placed to balance the landscape masses. In the clouds, freedom of brushwork on the lights and the shadows, often painted with a purple tinge, are characteristic. Pictures of the mid-period and later, often have very large sky masses, particularly over heathland. Stark, in company with most of the other Norwich men, subordinated his figures and animals to the general effect. Often the figures are small but well placed, and the animals strongly executed and well grouped. On his cottages one looks for the warm reds on his chimney stacks, and in the case of his Norfolk views, a very steep roof usually placed in with considerable thickness of paint.

The distances to his heathland scenes often have an uninterrupted sweep—he has sweeping passages complemented with those containing detail. The distant views are often composed of foreground and two or three layers of further distance, shadow being placed against areas of light. The early works in the main contain more detail than his later works, particularly in the foregrounds.

Since James Stark's death, his pictures have sold for high prices. In 1892 his *Fair on the Banks of the Bure* sold for 1,400 guineas, and of recent times his fine medium sized works have sold for upwards of £6,000.

James Stark seldom signed his work.

NORWICH EXHIBITS

Year	*Subject*
1811	A scene on St. Martin's River.
	View on St. Martin's River.
	View on King Street River.
	Two others simply called "Landscapes in oil".
1812	Scene at Heigham.
	Scene at Framlingham.
	Country church—evening.
	Bishopsgate Bridge.
	A lane scene.
	Two scenes at Thorpe.
	View on St. Martin's River.
	A painting in oils.
	Two landscapes.
1813	Scene near the New Mills.
	Scene near Wroxham.
	Scene on Mousehold Heath.
	Scene at Thorpe.
	Scene at Trowse.

Year	*Subject*
1813	View on the river looking towards St. Michael's Bridge.
	Country churchyard—evening.
	Six pieces simply called "Landscapes".
1816	Cattle (after Cuyp).
	Fishing.
	Scene near Windsor (in the style of Paul Potter).
1817	A scene on the Thames.
	A grove scene.
	A sketch from Wilson.
	Lambeth Palace (unfinished).
	Sketch of the Aldieri Claude.
	Sketch from Wilson.
	Sketch from Gainsborough.
	Ulleswater—Morning.
	Evening.
	Lane scene.
	A beach scene.
1818	The interior of a cow-house.
	A lane scene.
1819	Cattle (after Potter).
1821	A scene at Stratton, seven miles on the Cromer Road.
	Two grove scenes.
	Scene on the River Yare.
	Mackerel boat going out.
	A view of Thorpe.
	A scene near the New Mills.
	A sketch in oils.
1822	Sheep washing.
	Lane scene.
	Scene near Caister.
	A grove scene.
	Gipsies encamped.
	Waterfall in Gowbarrow Park, Cumberland.
	Two landscapes.
1823	Two landscapes.
	A study from Nature.
1824	A landscape.
1825	Landscape with Gipsies.
	Scene at Ranworth.
	Scene at Thorpe.
	Two scenes at Trowse.
	Two simply called "Landscapes".
1842	Mill stream near Windsor.
	Trout fishing.
	Landscape with rabbit catchers.
	Returning from gleaning.
	Source of the Ravensbourne, Kent.
	On the Thames.
	Ulleswater.
	Hayes Common.
1848	The Deer Park, Bolton.
	Going for a ride.
	A mountain stream.
	A watermill.
1849	Sheep washing.
	Dead game.
	Gipsies encamped.
1852	Heath scene.
	Landscape.

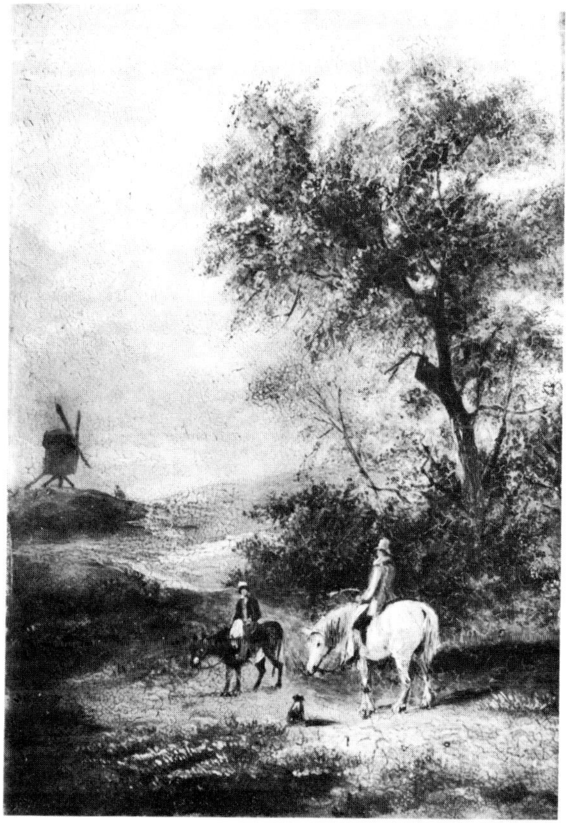

James Stark Windmill on Mousehold Oil $8\frac{1}{2} \times 6\frac{1}{2}$ *in.*
Exhibit No. 44, Stark Exhibition, 1887
Windsor Period

Year	*Subject*
1852	Forest scene.
	Windsor Forest.
1855	Windsor Castle.
	On the wharf.
	Penn Rocks, near Tunbridge Wells.
1856	In Sussex.
	A coast scene.

THE ROYAL ACADEMY EXHIBITS

Year	*Subject*
1811	A view on the King Street River, Norwich.
1812	Cottages.
1814	A road scene.
1815	Landscape.
1821	A view at Thorpe, near Norwich.
1822	A landscape.
1825	A landscape.
1831	Market gardeners at Battersea.
1832	A landscape.
1833	A landscape.
1834	A draining mill.
1835	A scene at Battersea.
1836	A watermill, Norfolk.
1838	Scene near Henley.
1839	Fishing.
	Ferry on the Thames.
1840	On the Medway.
1841	Enlarging the Park, Old Windsor.
	Beech trees near the statue, looking towards Windsor Castle.
	Trout stream.
1842	The village oak (suggested by the *Deserted Village*).
	Taking up eel pots.
1843	In Windsor Great Park.
	The gamekeeper's lodge.
	The forest oak.
1844	Heath scene.
	Stick gatherers.
1845	A road through the forest.
	Milking time.
	A mountain stream.
1846	A roadside cottage.
	A glen.
	On the wharf.
1847	A watermill.
	Environs of the New Forest.
1848	Windsor Great Park.
	A forest pond.
	A lane scene.
1849	Hethersett Church, Norfolk.
	A forest village.
	Beeches in Savernake Forest.
1850	Marlborough Forest.
	Forest scene.
	Windsor.
	Bettws-y-Coed Bridge.
	Donkey and foal.

Year	*Subject*
1851	Windsor—morning.
	A forest farm.
	Bolton Abbey.
1852	On the banks of the Yare.
	Going to market.
	A country churchyard (*vide* Gray's *Elegy*).
1855	Eton College.
	Penn Rocks, near Tunbridge Wells.
1854	Buckhurst Park.
	In Sussex.
	Near Windsor.
1855	A forest brook.
	A farmyard.
1856	Changing pasture.
	On the Mole.
1857	Marlborough Forest.
	In Sussex.
	On the Norfolk coast.
1858	Rokeby Park.
	Entrance to a wood.
	Ruins of a church.
1859	A watermill.

THE BRITISH INSTITUTION

Year	*Subject*
1814	A village scene near Norwich. 20 × 23 in.
1815	A forest scene. 21 × 23 in.
	The bathing place—morning—with boys bathing. 24 × 30 in.
1816	A beach scene. 28 × 30 in.
1817	A lane scene. 21 × 16 in.
	The country churchyard (*vide* Gray's *Elegy*). 36 × 44 in.
	Entrance to a forest. 26 × 28 in.
	Fishing. 51 × 61 in.
1818	Lambeth, looking towards Westminster Bridge. 52 × 70 in. (This gained the British Institution prize of £50 and was bought by the Countess de Grey.)
	Penning the flock. Canvas, 34 × 44 in.
	Landscape and cattle. 22 × 26 in.
	Lake scene. 36 × 46 in.
	Bishop's Bridge, Norwich. 37 × 48 in.
1819	Grove scene. 18 × 22 in.
	Sailing match at Wroxham, near Norwich. 53 × 74 in.
	Interior of a cow-house. 46 × 54 in.
1821	A landscape. 27 × 35 in.
	A grove scene. 26 × 36 in.
	The banks of the Yare. 38 × 85 in.
1822	Scene at Bixley, near Norwich. 27 × 31 in.
	A landscape. 27 × 33 in.
1823	A landscape. 30 × 26 in.
1824	Sheep washing—morning. 57 × 48 in.
	Moonlight on the banks of the Yare. 30 × 36 in.
	A scene near Norwich. 32 × 39 in.
1825	A woody scene.
	Gipsies encamped.
1826	A landscape.
1827	Scene in Gunton Park—Lord Suffield's seat. 28 × 34 in.
	Huntingdon Lock. 45 × 56 in.
	A view on the Yare at Thorpe, looking towards Norwich. 28 × 32 in.

Year	*Subject*
1827	Scene on the banks of the Yare. 20×25 in.
1831	Shipmeadow Lock on the Waveney. 55×72 in.
	Jacques. 46×56 in.
	View in Rydal Park. 21×24 in.
	Scene in Richmond Park, Surrey. 21×25 in.
1832	Going to market. 57×45 in.
	Scene at Battersea. 21×25 in.
	A watermill. 30×26 in.
1833	A scene in Barnes Elm Park. 24×39 in.
	Fishing boats—morning. 72×56 in.
	A landscape. 27×35 in.
1834	Sand-End Common, near Wycombe. 22×38 in.
	Puckaster Bay, Isle of Wight. 48×58 in.
	Scene in the New Forest. 26×28 in.
	Scene in the New Forest, near Lyndhurst. 27×36 in.
1835	Cookham Ferry. 57×72 in.
	Reedham Mill. 38×46 in.
1836	Scene in Westmoreland. 32×40 in.
	Marum Hills, Winterton, Norfolk. 33×43 in.
	Scene near Cromer. 37×42 in.
	Sheringham Heath. 26×30 in.
1837	Scene near Festiniog, North Wales. 30×39 in.
	Cromer, Norfolk. 36×47 in.
	Bird scarers. 41×54 in.
1838	Magpie Island, near Henley. 45×56 in.
	View from Bradeston Cottage, Norfolk. 27×45 in.
	Mile End, near Henley. 32×41 in.
	Scene at Bradeston. 36×40 in.
	Windsor Forest. 22×27 in.
1839	Wood scene. 29×36 in.
	Scene near Bettws, North Wales. 30×36 in.
	Scene at Mottingham, Kent. 27×34 in.
	Going to the fair. 45×57 in.
	Near Guildford. 27×32 in.
	Entrance to a wood. 19×23 in.
1840	Part of Allingdon Castle, Kent.
1841	Removing the park wall, Old Windsor. 27×33 in.
	An avenue of willow pollards. 31×42 in.
	Eton College. 37×50 in.
	In Windsor Great Park. 27×33 in.
	The Ford Farm. 36×50 in.
1842	A forest bourne. 37×33 in.
	Near Windsor. 30×39 in.
	Windsor Castle from Spring Hill. 36×32 in.
	In North Wales. 36×48 in.
1844	Wood scene.
	A watermill.
	A scene in Cumberland.
	Cottage near Windsor.
	Gowbarrow Park. Panel, 9×11 in.
1845	A glen. 64×54 in.
	The Deer Park, Bolton. 32×28 in.
	Near Bolton Abbey, Yorkshire. 35×40 in.
	View of Stourhead—seat of Sir H. R. Hoare, Bt. 37×52 in.
1846	The park stile. 27×22 in.
	Scene from Nature. 28×34 in.
	A roadside inn. 32×28 in.
1847	A forest lane. 38×32 in.
	Morning. 28×34 in.

Year	Subject
1847	Making eel bucks. 36×43 in.
	Returning from pasture. 28×34 in.
	St. Leonard's, Windsor. 41×37 in.
1848	Sheep washing. 23×39 in.
	The Flemish Farm, Windsor. 19×23 in.
1849	Buck shooting in Marlborough Forest. 42×54 in.
	Wood scene. 27×33 in.
1850	Eel fishing on the Thames. 28×34 in.
	A back stream. 27×33 in.
	Marlborough Forest. 32×29 in.
1851	Heath scene. 38×52 in.
	A forest wood yard. 44×53 in.
	On Yarmouth Beach. 16×20 in.
1852	Heath scene. 23×26 in.
	A village timber yard. 25×34 in.
	The sportman's rendezvous. 49×70 in. (The animals by A. J. Stark.)
1853	The Warren, Bridge Park.
	New Tunbridge Wells.
	Eridge Rocks.
1854	Afternoon. (The animals by A. J. Stark.)
	Keston Common.
	Buckhurst Park.
	A trout stream.
1855	Brockham, Surrey.
	The Mole near Dorking.
1856	The Tithe Farm.
	Feeding poultry.
	Northland, Sussex.
	A farm pond.
1857	A farm in Sussex.
	Moorhen shooting.
	On the meadows.
	Passing the lock.
1858	Sheep washing.
	A brook.
	A tributary to the Greta.
	Near Rokeby.
1859	The banks of the Yare.
	Meadows near Norwich.
	Gipsies encamped.

SOCIETY OF PAINTERS IN OIL AND WATER-COLOURS

Year	Subject
1818	Landscape and cattle—spring.
	Scene on the beach at Cromer.
	Lane scene.
	Grove scene near Norwich—autumn.
1819	A cottage scene near Norwich.
	Landscape and cattle.
	A grove scene (two pictures).

SOCIETY OF BRITISH ARTISTS, SUFFOLK STREET

Year	Subject
1824	*The first exhibition.*
	A view on the Yare at Thorpe, near Norwich.
	Gipsies encamped.

Year	*Subject*
1824	Wood cutters.
1825	Three pieces simply called "Landscapes".
1826	Landscape.
1827	Reedham Mill on the Yare.
	Unkennelling at Gunton Park—seat of Lord Suffield.
1831	A landscape with gipsies.
	A landscape.
1832	A landscape with gipsies.
	Elderberry gatherers at Battersea.
	Scene from Nature.
	Scene in Richmond Park.
	A landscape.
	A heath scene (water-colour).
	A scene near Norwich (water-colour).
	A scene near Battersea (water-colour).
	A wild duck decoy (water-colour).
	A wood scene.
	Decoy for wild ducks.
1833	A radical.
	Scene on the River Waveney.
	Scene in Windsor Forest.
	A scene on the Yare.
1834	A scene near Yarmouth, Norfolk.
	A watermill (a water-colour drawing).
1835	A landscape.
	Bird keepers.
	Near Hastings—Beachy Head in the distance.
1836	A grove scene.
	Near Hastings.
	On the Yare.
	Lane scene.
	Cromer Beach.
1837	Stratton Common.
	Mending an eel-pot.
	Pandy Mill, Falls of Machue, North Wales.
	Lloyd's Pulpit, Festiniog, North Wales.
	Wood scene.
1838	Scene near Henley.
	Near Capel Curig, North Wales.
	Scene near Festiniog, North Wales.
	Beach scene.
	Entrance to a wood.
1839	On the Ravensbourne, Kent.
	Hayes Common, Kent.
	Keston Common, Kent (water-colour).
1843	The Lammas Meadow. 29×35 in.
	Going to pasturage. 30×36 in.
	Windsor Castle from the fishery at Black Pots. 35×47 in.
	Penning the flock. 37×50 in.
	One of Her Majesty's green rides in Windsor. 40×30 in.
1848	Peter-boats on the Thames.
	Shower passing off.

James Stark *View at Intwood* $19 \times 15\frac{3}{8}$ *in.*
Oil on canvas
Early Norwich Period

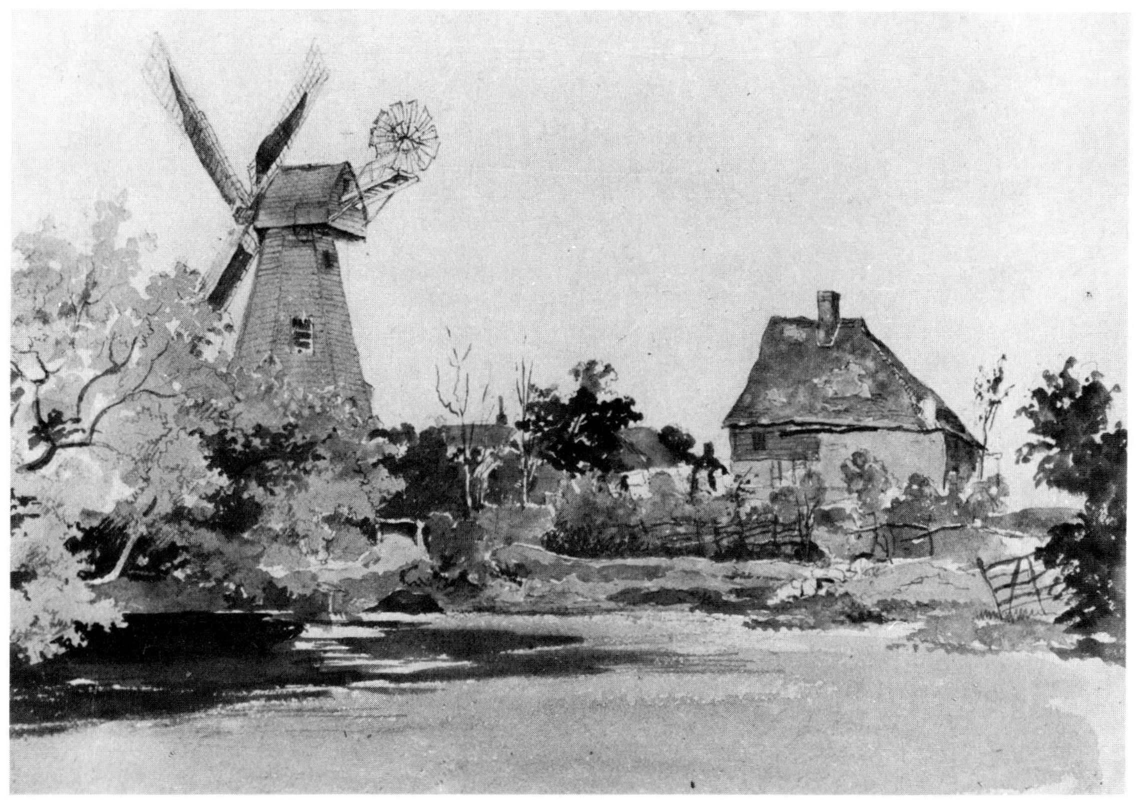

James Stark *Windmill Scene* *Water-colour*

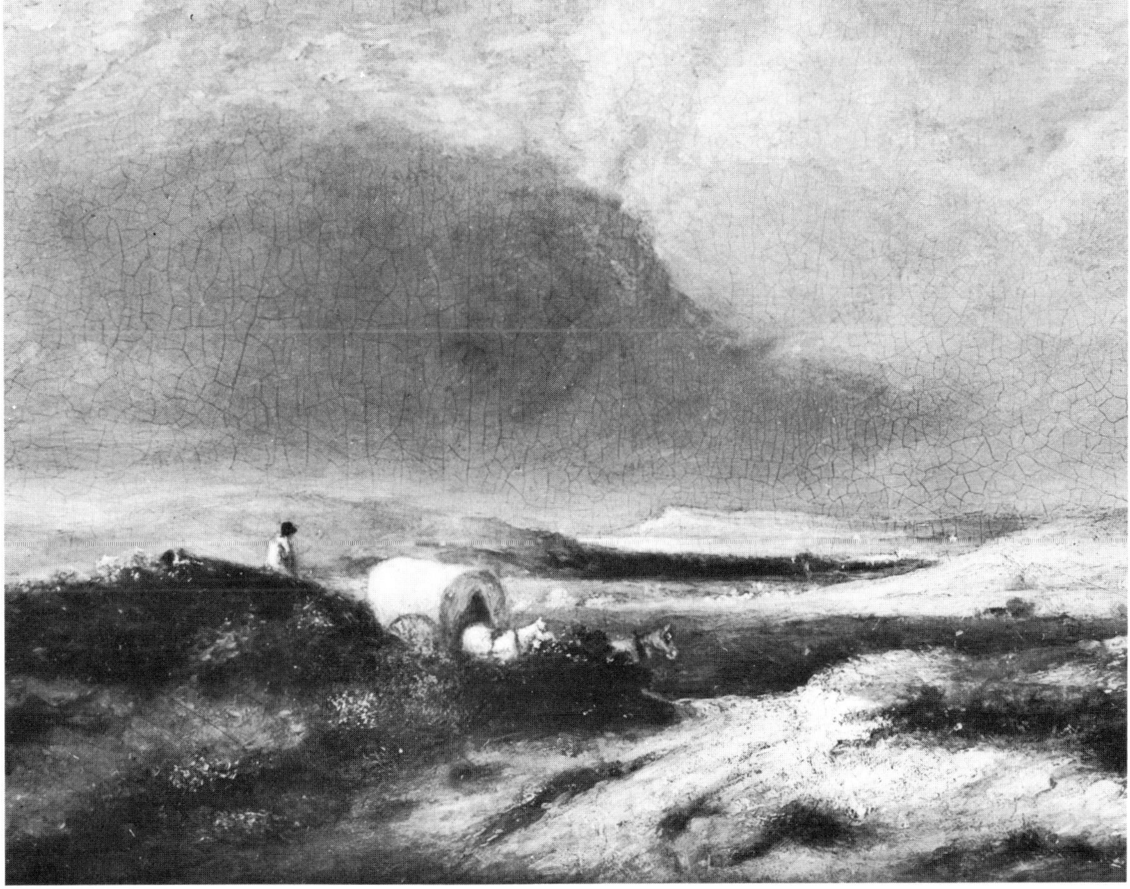

James Stark *Heathland Scene—Mid Period* *Oil on panel* $9\frac{3}{4} \times 12\frac{1}{4}$ *in.*

FIRST EXHIBITION OF THE NORFOLK AND SUFFOLK INSTITUTION

Year	*Subject*
1829	Yarmouth Beach.
	Morning.
	Felbrigg Heath.
	Pilot boats going off early in the morning (unfinished).
	Hardleigh Cross.
	Thorpe Old Hall.
	View from the site of Old Thorpe Grove.
	Harrison's Wharf.
	Hinsby's Gardens, Thorpe.
	A Landscape.
1832	A Landscape.
	Shipmeadow Lock.

1833 was the last exhibition of the Norfolk and Suffolk Institution.

THE NORFOLK AND NORWICH ART UNION EXHIBITION

Year	*Subject*
1831	A wood scene.
	A landscape with cattle.
	A landscape.
1839	Bird scarers—a view in Westmorland.
	Harlech Castle, North Wales.
	Study from Nature.
	Winterton.
	View from Bradeston Cottage.

JAMES STARK EXHIBITION, NORWICH, JUNE, 1887

No.	*Subject*	*Lent by*
1	Marlborough Forest. A dead tree, with other trees behind, in left centre. Sheep on roadway in foreground, with boy on pony beyond. Open country to right, with cottage in middle distance. Exhibited at Royal Academy in 1850. Canvas, $17\frac{1}{4} \times 23\frac{1}{2}$ in.	Joshua Womersley.
2	Landscape and Cattle. Pool of water in left foreground into which cattle and sheep are driven by man with dog; beyond, trees and old thatched cottage. Open country on right, with post windmill and cottage in middle distance. Illustration drawn by R. Bagge Scott. Panel, $19\frac{1}{2} \times 26\frac{1}{2}$ in.	George Holmes.
3	St. Benet's Abbey. Ruins of abbey with windmill to left centre. Cattle and water in foreground; hay-cart in middle distance to right, marshes and wherry sails beyond. Sunset sky. Engraved in *Scenery of the Rivers of Norfolk* by J. Horsburgh. Panel, $8\frac{1}{2} \times 11\frac{3}{4}$ in.	Mrs. Bolingbroke.
4	Lowestoft Beach. Fishing boat and horse and cart on shore to left, sea and cliffs beyond. Fishing boats and look-out to right, with figures and fish-baskets in foreground. Kirkley Church and village on cliff in distance. Engraved in *Scenery of the Rivers of Norfolk* by George Cooke. Panel, $8\frac{3}{4} \times 12\frac{1}{2}$ in.	Mrs. Bolingbroke.
5	Portrait of James Stark by J. Clover. Landscape by J. Stark. The artist seated on bank sketching to right centre. River skirted with trees in middle distance, and mountains beyond. Exhibited at Norwich Society of Artists in 1818. Illustration drawn by W. J. Churchyard. Canvas, $29\frac{1}{2} \times 22$ in.	Mrs. Bolingbroke.
17	The Keeper's Cottage. Bank and trees to right foreground, with cottage beyond. Roadway in centre, with man on pony talking to a woman and child. Trees to left with donkeys. Illustration drawn by Miss H. Wells. Panel, $14\frac{1}{4} \times 18\frac{3}{4}$ in.	Thomas Wells.

No.	*Subject*	*Lent by*
18	Driving Sheep. Roadway in centre. Man driving sheep in foreground. Gravel banks on either side, with trees above. Open country beyond. Panel, $7\frac{1}{4} \times 10$ in.	George Holmes.
19	Burgh Castle. Near the castle, which occupies the centre of picture, are labourers with cart and three horses. Church tower and trees in distance to right. Engraved in *Scenery of the Rivers of Norfolk* by G. Cooke. Panel, $4\frac{3}{4} \times 7\frac{1}{2}$ in.	Mrs. Bolingbroke.
20	Driving Cattle. Roadway to left, with man driving cows. A pool of water in right foreground, palings and trees beyond. Panel, $7\frac{1}{4} \times 10$ in.	George Holmes.
21	Gipsies Encamped. Avenue of beeches. Gipsies' tent, with figures round fire in right foreground, donkey in left. A roadway down the centre with open country beyond. Canvas, $14\frac{1}{2} \times 19\frac{1}{4}$ in.	Mrs. Bolingbroke.
22	Landscape. Roadway through trees to left. Man, woman and boy with donkey, in foreground. Undulating country to right, pool of water in foreground. Canvas, $15\frac{1}{4} \times 23\frac{1}{2}$ in.	R. Wilkinson.
23	Yarmouth Water Frolic. Sailing craft, crowded with spectators and gay with bunting, lining the shore to right. Wherry under sail to left centre, rowboat covered with awning in foreground. Burgh Castle on rising ground in distance. Engraved in *Scenery of the Rivers of Norfolk* by R. Brandard; the steam packet in the engraving having been replaced by the sailing wherry. Panel, $14\frac{1}{4} \times 22\frac{1}{4}$ in.	J. A. Back.
24	Sheep Washing—Morning. A grove of trees to right, with open country to left. A pool of water in foreground, in part of which (staked off with hurdles) men are washing sheep. A flock of sheep to right foreground. Exhibited at the British Institution in 1824. Illustration drawn by J. M. Marshall. Canvas, $32\frac{1}{4} \times 44\frac{1}{2}$ in.	Rev. H. H. Carlisle.
25	An Old Gravel Pit. High gravel bank to left, with trees at top. Donkeys in front with a pool of water in foreground. Cottage in centre. Trees (two dead) with woman between the trunks, to right. Millboard, $13 \times 16\frac{3}{4}$ in.	Rev. C. Turner.
26	Back of Stoke Mills. River and cows in foreground, wooden water-mill with tiled roofs beyond. Meadow and trees to right. A cart shed and meadows in distance to left. Illustration drawn by Charles Clowes. Panel, $16\frac{3}{4} \times 22\frac{3}{4}$ in.	J. J. Colman, M.P.
36	Landscape. Road in foreground, along which cattle are being driven to pool in right corner. By the side of the road, half hidden by trees, is a cottage, near which are two men, one on a donkey. Panel, $19\frac{1}{4} \times 15$ in.	Rev. H. J. Coleman.
37	Near Stratton Strawless Common. A roadway in left centre leading through wood, into which a woman and two children are entering, carrying sheaves. Open country to extreme right. Donkeys in foreground. Panel, $20\frac{1}{4} \times 31\frac{3}{4}$ in.	A. Andrews.
38	Penning the Flock. A flock of sheep driven by two men into a fold on rising ground to right. A river winds in distance to left, past a wooded hill in middle distance. Evening glow in sky. Exhibited in British Institution in 1818. Illustration drawn by J. M. Marshall. Canvas, 34×44 in.	Duke of Sutherland.
39	Road Scene and Cottage. A group of trees divided by roadway. Woman and dog in centre. Thatched cottage to right. Water in foreground. Millboard, $16 \times 12\frac{1}{4}$ in.	Mrs. Noverre.
40	Landscape. Group of trees in right centre, cottage beyond. Pond and two donkeys in right corner. Road in left centre. Two men by side of bushes, and sign post in left foreground. Trees beyond in middle distance. Panel, $8 \times 9\frac{1}{4}$ in.	Rev. H. J. Coleman.
41	The Grove. A roadway through trees on which a woman and child are driving cows to right centre. A fence, behind which are man and cattle in left foreground. Trees and a glimpse of open country beyond. Illustration drawn by Miss F. J. Bayfield. Panel, $19\frac{1}{2} \times 27\frac{1}{2}$ in.	A. Andrews.

No.	*Subject*	*Lent by*
42	River Scene. River bank, rows, and two hay barges, with sails hoisted, to left. River to right, with two men in boat netting. Opposite bank, and post windmill, in distance. Panel, 9×12½ in.	Mrs. Bolingbroke.
43	Wood Scene. A man and dog on road which passes through trees to left centre. To the right of road, cottages are seen between the stems of trees. A footpath leading to open country to right. Panel, 11¾×15¾ in.	H. D. Geldart.
44	The Road to the Mill. Trees to right, with roadway in foreground. Windmill on rising ground in distance to left. Man on a white horse, and boy on donkey in foreground. Panel, 8½×6½ in.	H. G. Barwell.
45	Landscape. Cottages and poplar trees in centre. Rustic bridge in front, from which a man is fishing. Water in foreground. Roadway leading to a gate, and trees to right. Panel, 11½×13½ in.	Charles Thorn.
46	At Lakenham. Thatched cottage and trees to right, with two boys fishing in river in foreground. Cottage and sheep in distance to left. Panel, 14¾×13 in.	Joshua Womersley.
47	Landscape. Group of trees to left, with two donkeys in foreground. Figures and cottage beyond. Roadway to right centre, with cart and two horses, fields and distant landscape to right. Canvas, 17¼×23½ in.	Jacob Mills.
48	The Ferry, Close, Norwich. River in foreground. Old water gate in centre, middle distance. Ferry House and willow tree to left, ferry boat and figures in left foreground. Boat houses and sailing boat with two figures to right. Cathedral in distance. Engraved in *Scenery of the Rivers of Norfolk* by W. R. Smith. Panel, 19½×25½ in.	Mrs. Bolingbroke.
49	The Forest Gate. A road leading to a cottage through group of lofty trees in left centre. Gate with man and white horse in left foreground. In centre, man on roadway. Cottages and open country in right centre. Thatched cottage with trees, enclosed in palings in right foreground. Windmill on rising ground in distance. Illustration drawn by Miss C. M. Nichols. Panel, 19½×29½ in.	J. J. Colman, M.P.
50	A Glen. A mountain torrent rushing between boulders in foreground. High rocks crowned with trees to right and left. Man with fishing rod and dog in right centre. Exhibited at British Institution in 1845. Illustration drawn by S. H. Baldrey. Canvas, 49½×39 in.	J. A. Back.
51	Ferry on the Wye. Trees and horses and cart in ferry boat crossing river to right. Cows in foreground. River in left foreground. Man in a boat in centre, windmill on opposite bank, and range of hills in distance. Canvas, 19×29 in.	Mrs. Bolingbroke.
52	Runton. Undulating country with hill to right, crowned with two windmills, and cottages. Stream of water and foot-bridge, two men (one on a white horse) and cattle and dogs in right centre foreground. Tree and cattle to left. Church, village, and glimpse of sea beyond. Illustration drawn by Miss M. M. Blake. Canvas, 21¼×32 in.	B. E. Fletcher.
53	Yarmouth Bridge. Pencil drawing for the engraving by G. Cooke in the *Rivers of Norfolk*.	A. J. Stark.
54	Yarmouth Quay. Pencil drawing for the engraving by G. Cooke in the *Rivers of Norfolk*.	A. J. Stark.
55	Landscape with River. Water-colour drawing.	A. J. Stark.
56	Dover Castle and Pier. Water-colour drawing.	A. J. Stark.
57	Harvest Field. Water-colour drawing.	A. J. Stark.
58	Cromer, from the North. Water-colour drawing.	A. J. Stark.
59	View looking towards Carrow, with Snuff Tower in the distance. Water-colour drawing.	A. J. Stark.
60	Crome from the Beadon Hill. Water-colour drawing.	A. J. Stark.
61	Old Hulk. Water-colour drawing.	A. J. Stark.
62	Beach Scene with Boats. Water-colour drawing.	A. J. Stark.
63	Back of the New Mills. Water-colour drawing.	A. J. Stark.
64	At Battersea. Water-colour drawing.	A. J. Stark.
65	Water-colour sketch.	A. J. Stark.
66	Old Houses. Water-colour sketch.	A. J. Stark.

No.	Subject	Lent by
67	Hills, with water in distance. Water-colour sketch.	A. J. Stark.
68	Winterton. Water-colour drawing on grey paper.	A. J. Stark.
69	Monochrome drawing.	A. J. Stark.
70	Lake and Mountains. Water-colour sketch.	A. J. Stark.
71	Old Houses, and Wherry on River, Norwich. Water-colour drawing.	A. J. Stark.
72	Windsor Castle. Water-colour drawing.	A. J. Stark.
73	Windmill. Water-colour drawing.	A. J. Stark.
74	Sherringham Gangway. Pencil drawing.	A. J. Stark.
75	Road Scene. Monochrome drawing.	A. J. Stark.
76	Yarmouth Quay. Pencil drawing.	A. J. Stark.
77	Water-colour drawing on grey paper.	A. J. Stark.
78	Markshall. Water-colour drawing.	A. J. Stark.
79	Landscape with Marsh Mill. Water-colour drawing.	A. J. Stark.
80	Cliff near Cromer. Monochrome drawing.	A. J. Stark.
81	Cromer from the North Cliff. Pencil drawing.	A. J. Stark.
82	Heath Scene. Water-colour drawing on tinted paper.	A. J. Stark.
83	Study of Trees. Water-colour drawing.	A. J. Stark.
84	Eton College. Water-colour drawing.	A. J. Stark.
85	Cantley Beck, near Ketteringham. Water-colour drawing.	A. J. Stark.
86	Three Small Landscapes. Water-colour.	Mrs. Bolingbroke.
87	Winterton Beach. Water-colour drawing.	A. J. Stark.
88	Cromer. Water-colour drawing.	Mrs. Bolingbroke.
89	Sand Hills, Winterton. Water-colour drawing.	A. J. Stark.
90	Water Mill. Water-colour drawing.	A. J. Stark.
91	Sharringham Beach. Water-colour drawing.	A. J. Stark.
92	Winterton Sand Hills. Water-colour drawing.	A. J. Stark.
93	Lane Scene. Water-colour drawing.	A. J. Stark.
94	Two etchings.	James Reeve.
95	Two etchings.	James Reeve.
96	Portrait of James Stark by H. B. Love. Tinted pencil drawing. En- in *Art Journal*, 1850.	A. J. Stark.
97	Portrait of James Stark (artist unknown).	Mrs. Bolingbroke.
98	Portrait of James Stark by R. Hollingdale. Crayon drawing. Illustra- tion drawn by E. Elliot.	A. J. Stark.
99	Portrait of James Stark. Pencil sketch by William Collins, R.A.	A. J. Stark.
100	Portrait of James Stark. Silhouette.	Mrs. Bolingbroke.
101	Bust of James Stark by Heffernan. Exhibited at the Royal Academy in 1818.	Mrs. Bolingbroke.

EXHIBITION OF NORWICH SCHOOL PICTURES

Norwich Castle Museum and Art Galleries, October, 1927

OIL-PAINTINGS

No.	Subject
110	St. Benet's Abbey (the original of the engraving in *Rivers of Norfolk*). $8\frac{1}{4}\times 11\frac{3}{4}$ in.
111	Fritton Decoy, Norfolk. $10\frac{1}{4}\times 14\frac{3}{4}$ in.
112	The river at Thorpe. 24×40 in.
113	Windsor Home Park. $24\frac{1}{2}\times 20$ in.
114	Near Cromer (International Fine Arts Exhibition, Rome, 1911). $16\frac{3}{4}\times 24\frac{3}{4}$ in.
115	Two studies of a tree (in one frame). $10\times 7\frac{1}{2}$ in.
116	Beckham Abbey. $23\frac{1}{2}\times 35$ in.
117	Trees with cattle, woman and child. $17\frac{1}{2}\times 25\frac{1}{2}$ in.
118	Cottage and trees—church in background. 11×14 in.
119	Landscape with sheep. $7\frac{1}{2}\times 10$ in.

No.	*Subject*
248	Landscape. $9 \times 12\frac{1}{2}$ in.
249	Old cottage. $9 \times 13\frac{1}{4}$ in.
250	Sand dunes. 9×13 in.
251	Windsor Castle. $9\frac{1}{4} \times 13\frac{1}{4}$ in.
252	Interior. 9×13 in.
253	Cover Castle. $6\frac{3}{4} \times 10\frac{1}{4}$ in.
254	Study of cliffs. $6\frac{3}{4} \times 10\frac{1}{4}$ in.
255	Study of cliffs. $8\frac{1}{2} \times 12\frac{1}{2}$ in.
256	The ruined church. $9\frac{1}{4} \times 13\frac{1}{4}$ in.
257	Cliff scene. 8×12 in.
258	River scene with boats. $5\frac{3}{4} \times 11\frac{1}{4}$ in.

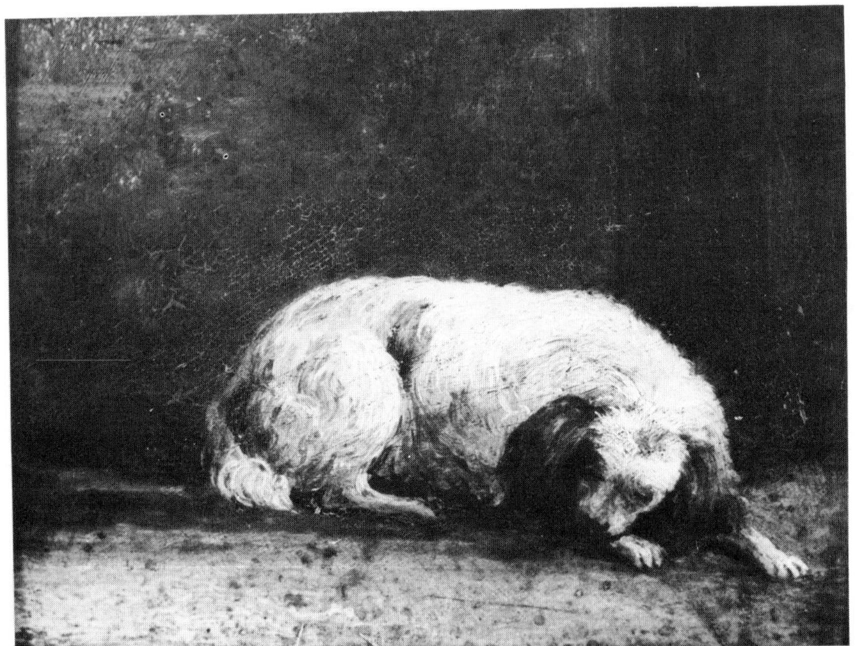

James Stark *'His dog Trim'* *Oil* $6\frac{1}{2} \times 8$ *in.*

A study handed down in the family

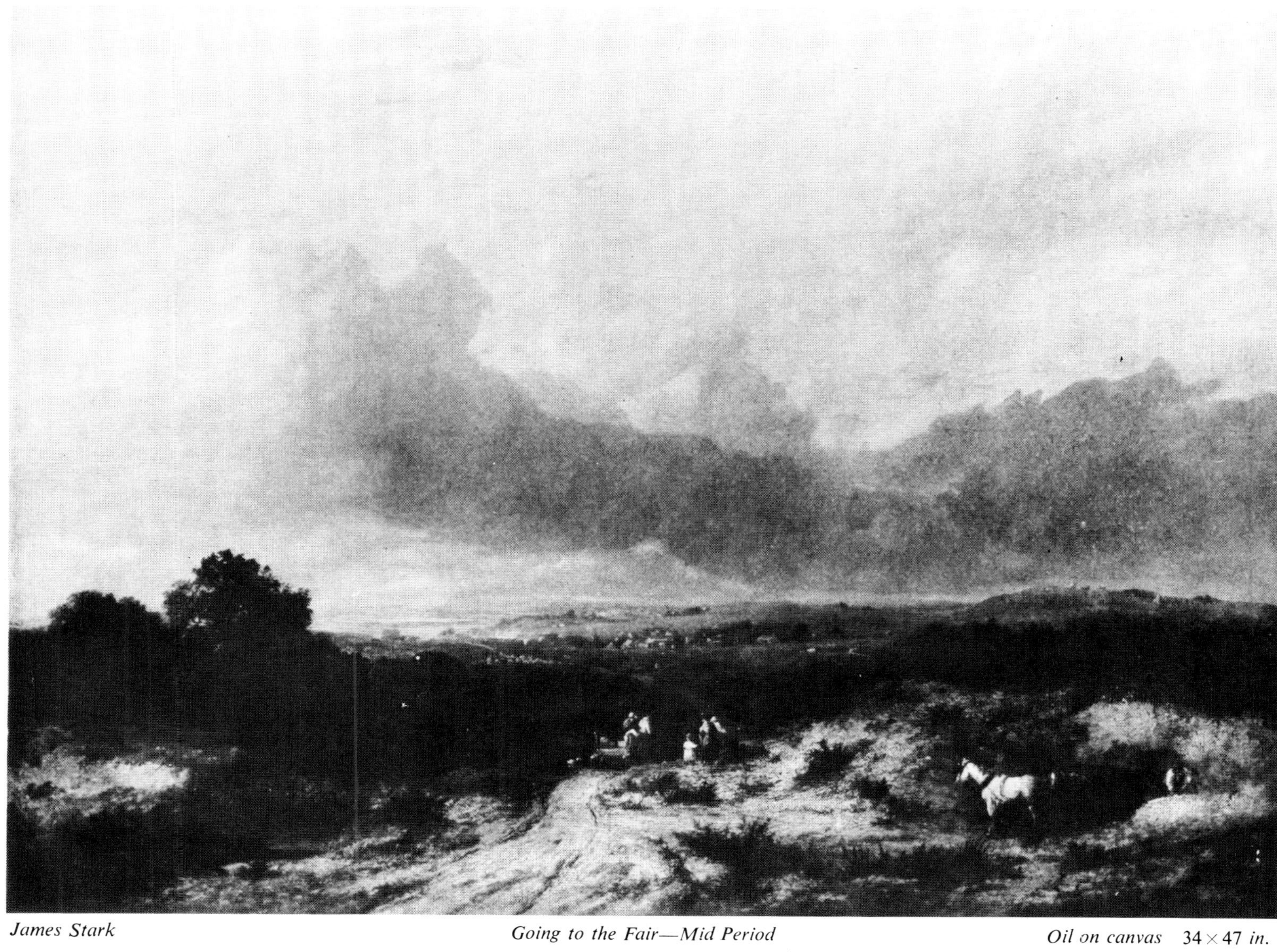

James Stark — *Going to the Fair—Mid Period* — *Oil on canvas* 34 × 47 *in.*

ARTHUR JAMES STARK

(1831-1902)

1831 Arthur James Stark was born on 6th October, 1831, the only son of James Stark, his mother being Elizabeth Young Dinmore. He was taught in the early days exclusively by his father, with whom he maintained always a very close relationship.

1839 At the age of eight years, in 1839, his father moved to Windsor. Here tuition took place for many years with the young Arthur assisting his father in the studio, occasionally
1849 painting in the animals and figures in his father's works. In 1849 it was decided that to further Arthur's career he should attend the Royal Academy School. A page from his notebook is illustrated on page 81. This involved the family moving to London, when they took up residence at 35 Norfolk Street.

His first painting, exhibited at the age of 17 years at the Royal Academy, was well received and hung in line between works by Sir Edwin Landseer and Sir Francis Grant. Whilst in London Arthur Stark executed many studies in the stables of Messrs. Chaplin & Horne, the carriers. Later, he rented for three years a studio at Tattersall's, where he perfected his horse paintings. It must have been about this time that he worked in the studio of Edmund Bristow, who is known to have been kindly disposed towards him.

1859 In 1859, James Stark, his father, became too ill to paint. They were living in lodgings at the time in Norfolk Street, Strand. Such was their poverty that they were living hand to mouth. Every picture painted by A.J. was disposed of immediately, to keep things going. When at last James became ill it was his son who cherished and nursed him to the end.

1874 Arthur James Stark, by 1874, had become widely known and was offered the post of animal painter to Queen Victoria. Due to his belief that it would hamper his development, he declined the offer. An interesting photograph preserved by the family exists, which was taken about this time. It shows our artist in the uniform of the W. Middlesex Volunteers.

On 24th November, 1878, at Ascot, our artist married Rose Isabella, youngest daughter of Thomas Fassett Kent, Counsel to the Chairman of Committees in the House of Lords. A daughter was born in 1879, and a son, James Arthur Stark, in 1887, both of whom survived him.

There is only a fragment of a letter of his preserved. This was written to his wife from Wales and contains a sketch of Snowdon. It is as follows:

> This is about the highest sketch ever taken in the Kingdom for you, being a veritable representation of the top of Snowden, taken at an elevation of above 3000 ft. . . . He then refers to characters he has met in the town. . . . they all pitch it into me right and left and worse than that *ask my opinion* though they say "Artists are the worst judges of paintings"! They are always at deadly feud respecting the originality of some old humbugging black-looking Poussin or other and if you drop a hint that there may be a mistake about it 'tis a much deeper offence than if you had said all the females of the family were ——. And the devil a one of them would give sixpence for the best modern picture going.

A. J. Stark evidently had much the same view as John Constable in thinking that many of the Old Masters were over-rated, to the detriment of artists striving for true effects.

Besides painting in Norfolk, a county with which he was associated all his life, he painted in many parts, including the Thames Valley, Hastings, Dartmoor, Knaresborough, Knole, Leith Hill, Epping Forest, Walthamstow, Wales and Shropshire.

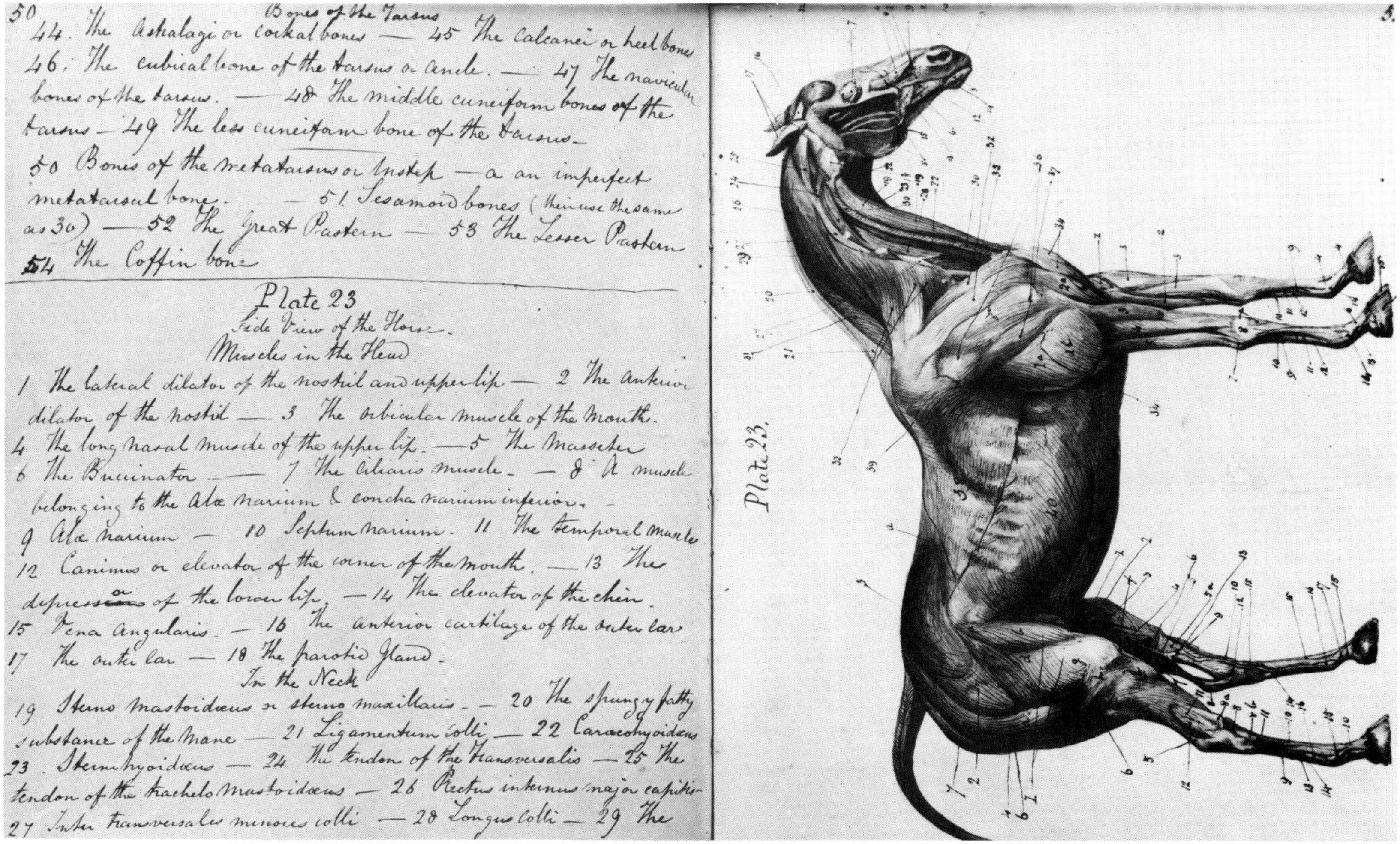

50 Bones of the Tarsus

44. The Astralagi or cockal bones — 45 The Calcanei or heel bones
46. The cubical bone of the tarsus or ancle. — 47 The navicular bones of the tarsus. — 48 The middle cuneiform bones of the tarsus — 49 The less cuneiform bone of the tarsus.

50 Bones of the metatarsus or Instep — a an imperfect metatarsal bone. — 51 Sesamoid bones (their use the same as 30) — 52 The Great Pastern — 53 The Lesser Pastern
54 The Coffin bone

Plate 23
Side View of the Horse.
Muscles in the Head

1 The lateral dilator of the nostril and upper lip — 2 The anterior dilator of the nostril — 3 The orbicular muscle of the Mouth.
4 The long nasal muscle of the upper lip. — 5 The Masseter
6 The Buccinator — 7 The Ciliaris muscle. — 8 A muscle belonging to the Alæ narium & concha narium inferior.
9 Alæ narium — 10 Septum narium. 11 The temporal muscle
12 Caninus or elevator of the corner of the mouth. — 13 The depressor of the lower lip. — 14 The elevator of the chin.
15 Vena angularis. — 16 The anterior cartilage of the outer ear
17 The outer ear — 18 The parotid gland.

In the Neck

19 Sterno mastoideus or sterno maxillaris. — 20 The spungy fatty substance of the mane — 21 Ligamentum colli — 22 Caracohyoideus
23. Sternohyoideus — 24 The tendon of the Transversalis — 25 The tendon of the trachelo mastoideus — 26 Rectus internus major capitis
27 Inter transversales minores colli — 28 Longus colli — 29 The

Plate 23.

Arthur James Stark — Page from his R.A. notebook. — Executed at the age of 16 years

Arthur James Stark exhibited thirty-six pictures at the Royal Academy, thirty-three at the British Institute of Painters in water-colours and fifty-seven at other Galleries. His works are to be seen in the British Museum, the Victoria and Albert Museum, Norwich Castle Museum and the City of Exeter.

He was a popular man who loved to attend sales in London; presumably he delighted in seeing the works of the Norwich School Painters, about whom he had many anecdotes to tell. He is said to have been a cultured man of high principle, simple and genial in his manner, though we have seen from his letter that he was a man of
1902 strong opinion. Up to the last few days before he died on 29th October, 1902, at South Nutfield, Surrey, he worked at his painting.

Portraits of him are as follows:

In miniature by H. H. Love, 1837, and in water-colour by his wife, 1883.

He is also recorded in a pencil drawing by William Collins.

Exhibitions of his works were held at the Dudley Galleries, Piccadilly, London, in 1907 and 1911.

THE PAINTINGS

Arthur James Stark, despite his study at the Royal Academy, was a loyal student of his father, James Stark, His early oils are so close to his father's in colour and handling that to the uninitiated they could be mistaken for the father's work. We find the main difference in the skies. Arthur Stark's are more sketchy in handling, though one finds the careful touches in the trees that one associates with the Norwich School. His early water-colours are very beautiful and full of Crome-like touches in the foliage.

His early days were spent in his father's studio, often adding the figures and animals. His son, J. A. Stark, made the observation that his father was almost alone in the line of Norwich School Painters to specialise in animals. In a foreword to a London Exhibition of the works of A. J. Stark at the Dudley Galleries in 1907, his son states:

> Art to him was a natural religion, its practice an ennobling worship. The passionate love of it was so deep in him, a feeling at once so real and vital, and yet so tender and intimate, that he never spoke of it. The sympathetic knew it at once, but only from quite involuntary signs; he betrayed it as a lover betrays his secret.

His mid-period oils are often quite large, interesting in composition and carefully painted, bearing little of the early Norwich School influence. In the finished work the animals are excellent and well support the wisdom of those involved in the invitation extended to him to become the Queen's Animal Painter. Respecting his oil sketches, he was strongly influenced by Constable. He executed many delightful sketches from Nature, often swept in with the minimum brush strokes, leaving the panel showing through. On occasion he could paint studies of ferns and growing corn with the greatest detail. These were later used as a basis for his foregrounds in his more important paintings. His colouring in his distance often has touches of mauve: his foregrounds having watery-green reeds or grasses with touches of indigo, sprinkled with reds, pinks and yellows. Ochres are often the main constituent of his foregrounds. He sometimes sketches on paper, using oils. By and large, his handling, especially in his later works, gives rise to a certain roughness of texture. As a water-colourist A. J. Stark was a master. Whilst his early work is careful and very detailed, his mid-period shows more freedom and movement. During his later period he was particularly pre-occupied with movement; this resulted in the development of a lyrical and free style of painting.

For many years Arthur James Stark's work was dwarfed by that of his father, but as he has become more known his merits have become firmly recognised.

A. J. Stark usually signed his finished pictures but seldom his studies and water-colours.

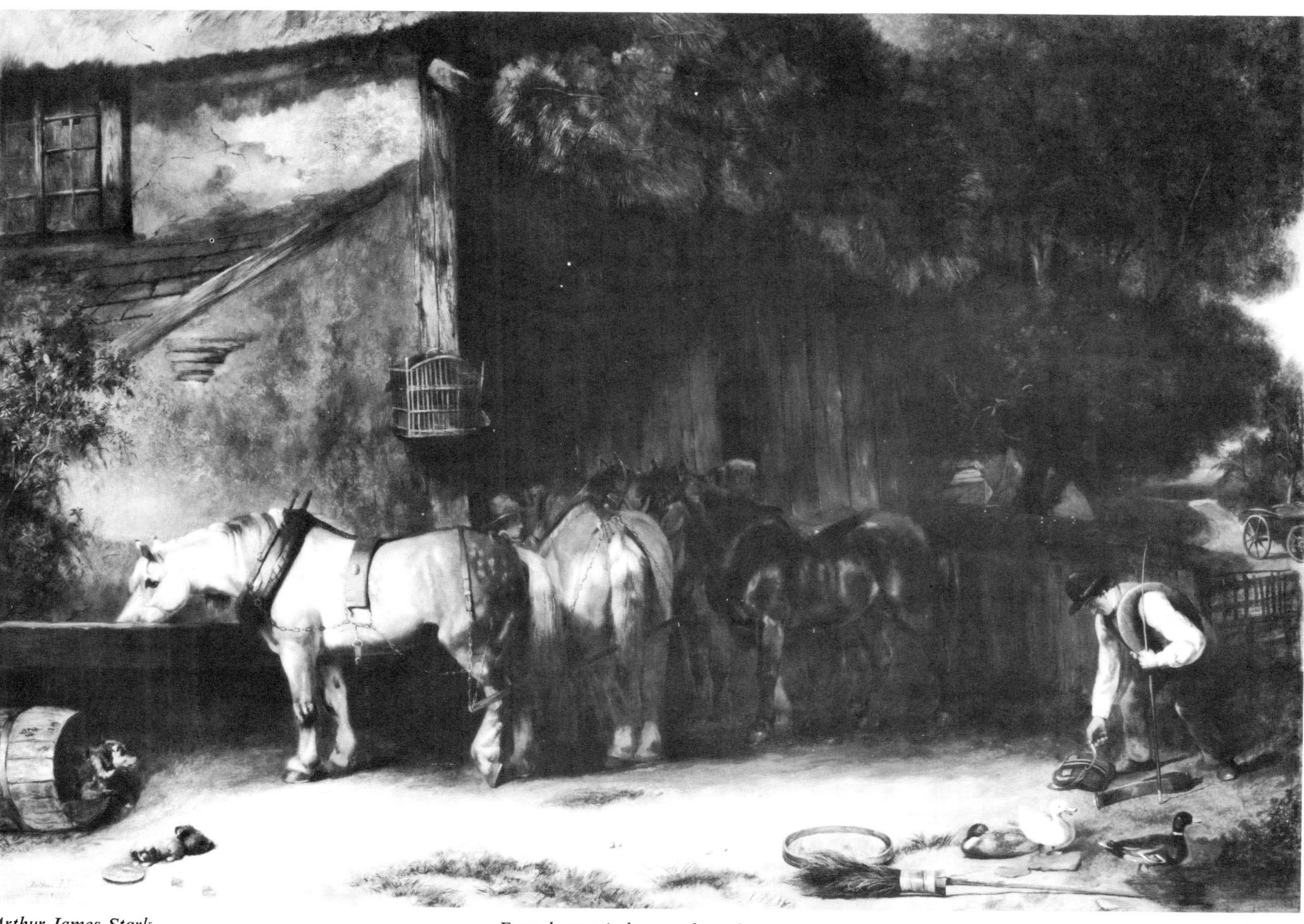

Arthur James Stark *Farm horses in harness by a farm* $26 \times 35\frac{1}{2}$ *in.*

EXHIBITS

ROYAL ACADEMY

Year	*No.*	*Subject*
1848	226	A water mill.
1849	529	An alehouse door.
1850	147	Forest scene.
1850	1259	Betts-y-Coed Bridge.
1851	347	Fetching the mallard.
	747	A study from Nature.
1852	1262	A rest from sport.
1853	126	An interior of a stable.
1852	204	Cattle and landscape.
	1260	A corner in the farmyard.
1855	303	The startled heron.
	1074	A summer afternoon.
1857	65	At rest.
	214	A quiet nook.
1858	954	Work done.
1859	157	Left in charge.
	443	On the Lighthouse Hills at Cromer, Norfolk.
1860	62	On the Teme, near Ludlow, Shropshire.
	581	Evening.
1861	481	A shady pool.
1862	323	Amateurs.
1863	709	A hunter, property of the Duke of Rutland.
1865	402	In Moor Park, Rickmansworth.
	534	Waiting at the Ferry.
1866	120	The Moor Park.
1867	401	The pasture.
1868	156	Under the beeches.
1869	213	Feeding time.
1871	334	The homestead.
1872	133	In the shade.
	175	Down in the meadows.
1873	97	The anglers nook.
1874	1390	Timber carting.
1875	1161	A farmyard.
1877	587	Dartmoor Drift. This is the name given to the unusual collection or driving of the ponies on Dartmoor. They are thus got together for the purpose of obtaining fees for pasturage and for the sorting out of trespassers. During the drift they are occasionally halted to give owners dwelling near a particular spot an opportunity of claiming the animals belonging to them. This picture is now in the Exeter Art Gallery.
1883	102	Whitening to the harvest.

BRITISH INSTITUTE

Year	*No.*	*Subject*	£	s.	d.
1848	343	Eton College. 16×21 in.		—	
1850	194	Landscape with cattle. 11×15 in.		—	
1851	458	Dead game. 17×20 in.		—	
1852	500	Repose. 25×32 in.		—	
1853	564	Cart mares and foals.	15	0	0
1854	356	At home.	10	0	0
1854	361	A meadow scene.	15	0	0
1855	41	A farm yard.	17	0	0
1855	313	Watching a bite.	10	0	0
1856	178	Noon.	25	0	0
1857	104	An interior of a stable.	12	0	0
	372	An unexpected visitor.	18	0	0

Year	No.	Subject	£	s.	d.
1858	153	On the moors.	20	0	0
	351	Harvest time.	80	0	0
1859	172	Scene in Scotland.		—	
1860	480	A quiet spot.	25	0	0
	573	On the hills—morning.	50	0	0
1861	168	The close of the day, Ben Mac Due.	60	0	0
	314	A Welsh homestead, Curig ap Conway.	25	0	0
	326	Cattle on the banks of the Yare.	15	0	0
1862	121	Run down.	8	0	0
	266	Waiting for the ——.	20	0	0
	332	Evening.	12	0	0
1863	355	Starting a wild duck.	10	0	0
	444	A farm yard.	40	0	0
1864	87	Harvest time.	15	0	0
	131	Hard fare.	18	0	0
	310	Evening.	15	0	0
1865	73	The noontide meal.	10	0	0
1866	574	A quiet pool.	20	0	0
1867	271	Horses in a straw yard.	8	0	0
	326	A farm yard.	45	0	0
	547	The path through the cornfield.	20	0	0

FIRST EXHIBITION OF THE NORFOLK AND NORWICH ASSOCIATION FOR THE PROMOTION OF THE FINE ARTS, 1848

No.	Subject
40	Cottage at Eaton.
57	Portrait of a carriage horse.
127	Eton College.
231	River scene.
306	Water mill.

SECOND EXHIBITION OF THE NORFOLK AND NORWICH ASSOCIATION FOR THE PROMOTION OF THE FINE ARTS, 1849

No.	Subject
52	An alehouse door.
414	In Clewer Meadow.

THIRD EXHIBITION OF THE NORFOLK AND NORWICH ASSOCIATION FOR THE PROMOTION OF THE FINE ARTS, 1852

No.	Subject
20	"Jockey" (the property of J. B. and H. Morgan, Esqs.)
26	Cart mares and foal.
27	"Copper Cap" (the property of J. B. and H. Morgan, Esqs.)
82	Landscape with cattle.
108	A study from Nature.

FOURTH EXHIBITION OF THE NORFOLK AND NORWICH ASSOCIATION FOR THE PROMOTION OF THE FINE ARTS, 1853

OIL-PAINTINGS

No.	Subject
113	Cart mares and foals.

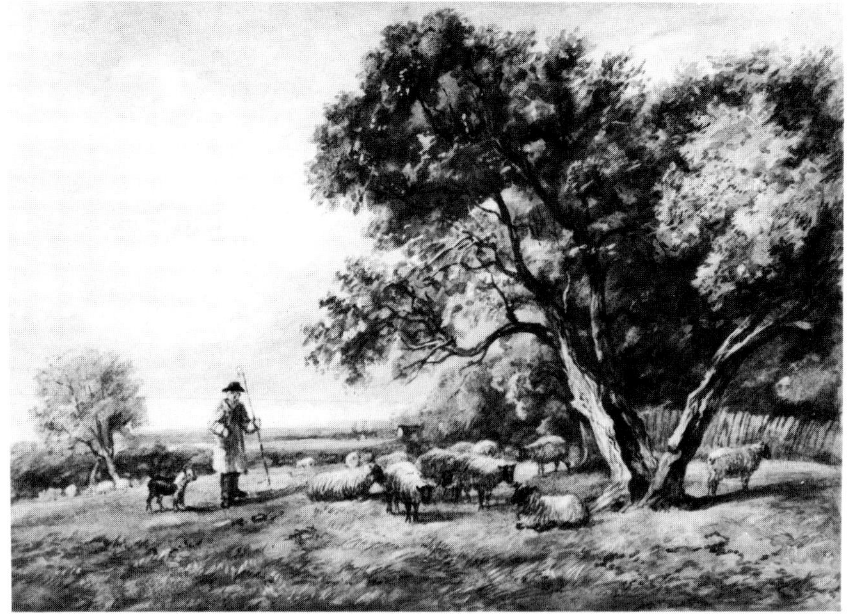

Arthur James Stark
Water-colour
app. 8×12 *in.*

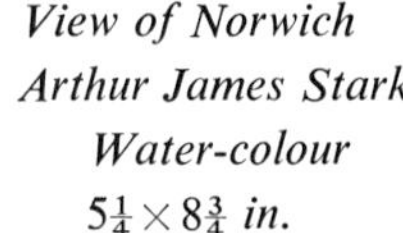

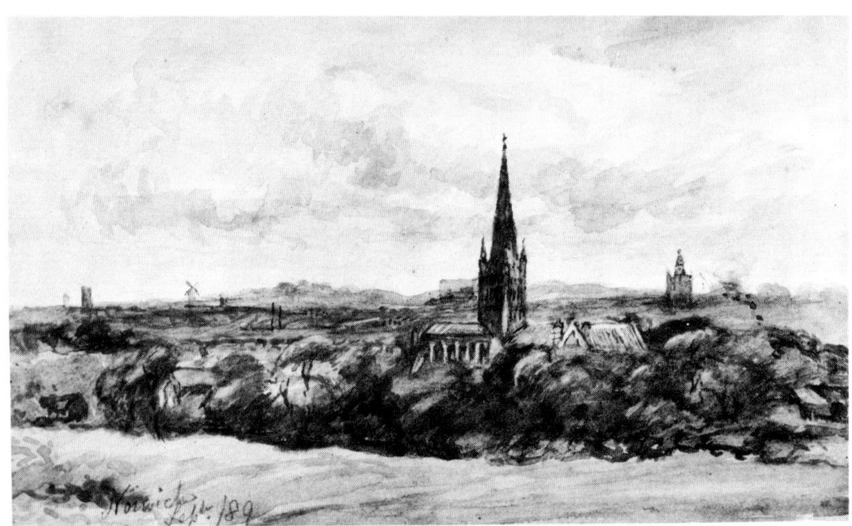

View of Norwich
Arthur James Stark
Water-colour
$5\frac{1}{4} \times 8\frac{3}{4}$ *in.*

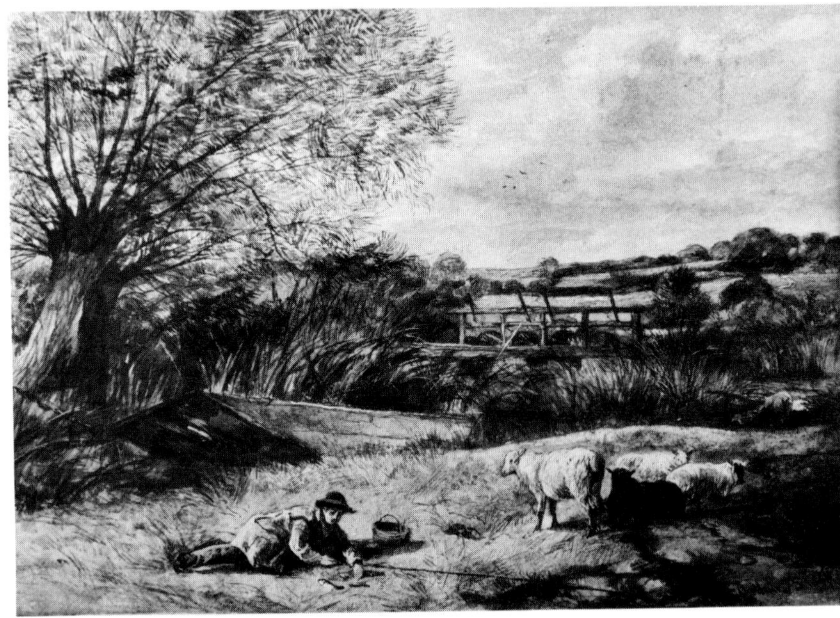

Arthur James Stark
Water-colour
5×7 *in.*

EXHIBITION OF THE NORFOLK AND NORWICH ASSOCIATION FOR THE PROMOTION OF THE FINE ARTS, 1855

No.	*Subject*	£	s.	d.
25	On the marshes—morning.	15	0	0
68	Watching a bite.	8	0	0

EXHIBITION OF THE NORFOLK AND NORWICH FINE ARTS' ASSOCIATION; AND OF THE PHOTOGRAPHIC SOCIETY, 1856

No.	*Subject*	£	s.	d.
137	Afternoon—summer time.	18	0	0
250	Summer time.	8	0	0

NORWICH FINE ART ASSOCIATION—EXHIBITION OF WORKS OF ART BY MODERN ARTISTS, 1868

No.	*Subject*	£	s.	d.
231	Passing the lock.	15	0	0
234	An English homestead.	12	0	0
264	On the Yare.	10	0	0
316	Hethersett Church.	10	0	0

NORWICH FINE ART ASSOCIATION—SECOND EXHIBITION OF WORKS OF ART BY MODERN ARTISTS, 1869

No.	*Subject*	£	s.	d.
13	Horses in the straw yard.	6	0	0
37	The haunt of the moorhen.	12	0	0
62	The forest farm.	50	0	0
187	The deer park.	15	0	0

EAST ANGLIAN ART UNION AND CITY OF NORWICH FINE ART ASSOCIATION EXHIBITION OF WORKS OF ART BY MODERN ARTISTS, 1870

OIL-PAINTINGS

No.	*Subject*	£	s.	d.
20	The Old Oak Farm, Shropshire.	20	0	0
33	Milling time.	25	0	0
167	A Berkshire homestead.	18	0	0

WATER-COLOUR

236	A lock on the Thames.	10	0	0

EXHIBITION OF WORKS OF ART BY MODERN ARTISTS, 1871

OIL-PAINTINGS

No.	*Subject*	£	s.	d.
173	A straw yard.	8	0	0
177	Removing timber.	50	0	0
206	"By the rushy-fringed brook where grow the willow and the osier dark."	15	0	0

WATER-COLOUR

241	Chiddingfold Church.	5	0	0

BRITISH MEDICAL ASSOCIATION—LOAN COLLECTION OF THE WORKS OF NORFOLK AND SUFFOLK ARTISTS, 1874

OIL-PAINTINGS

No.	*Subject*	*Lent by*
217	Windsor Park.	Mr. H. Cattermoul.
226	Carting timber.	Mr. A. J. Stark.
235	Old barn and cattle.	Mrs. Ship.
239	The close of day.	Mr. J. A. Back.

EXHIBITION OF PICTURES BY LIVING ARTISTS AT THE VICTORIA HALL GALLERY, NORWICH, 1878

No.	*Subject*	£	s.	d.
59	On the marshes.	30	0	0
103	Criccieth, North Wales.	10	0	0
124	The scattered flock.	35	0	0

NORWICH ART LOAN EXHIBITION IN AID OF THE FUND FOR THE RESTORATION OF THE CHURCH OF SAINT PETER MANCROFT, 1878

OIL-PAINTINGS

No.	*Subject*	*Lent by*
2	Sonning-on-Thames.	The Artist.
263	View of Eton College.	J. Alfred Back, Esq.
266	A favourite horse.	J. A. Back, Esq.

NORWICH ART LOAN EXHIBITION, 1885

OIL-PAINTINGS

No.	*Subject*	*Lent by*
2	A Welsh landscape.	The Artist.
6	Eventide.	The Artist.
12	Early morning.	The Artist.

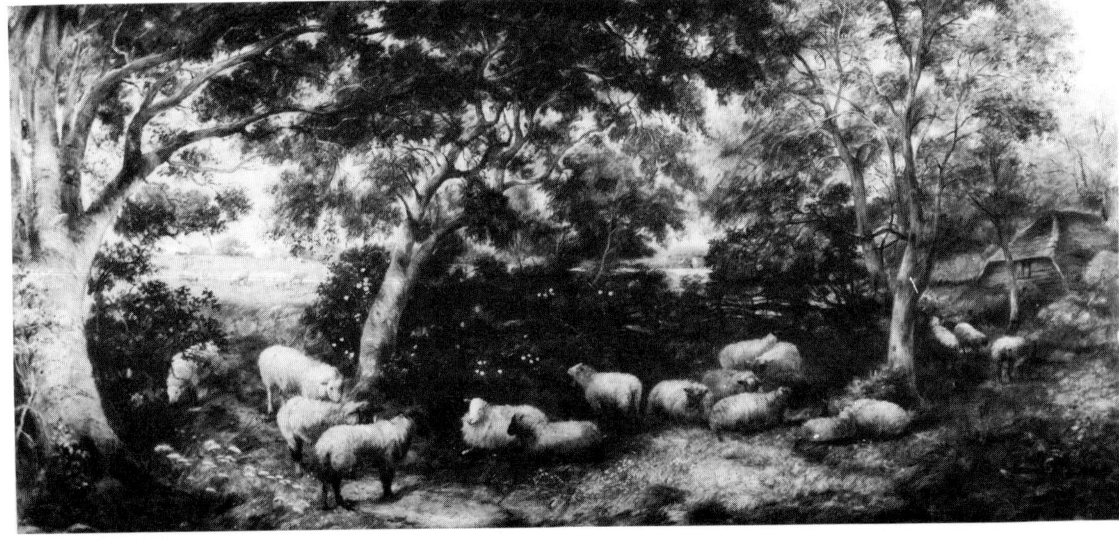

Arthur James Stark, 1893 *Oil on canvas* 26 × 54 *in.*

SEVENTH EXHIBITION OF THE NORWICH ART CIRCLE, SEPTEMBER, 1887

No.	Subject	£	s.	d.
12	A mid-day rest.	7	0	0
21	On the Bure near Wroxham.	10	0	0
73	Counting the flock.	25	0	0

EIGHTH EXHIBITION OF THE NORWICH ART CIRCLE, JANUARY, 1888

No.	Subject
9	A Sussex pasture.
15	Study for a picture.

TENTH EXHIBITION OF THE NORWICH ART CIRCLE, SEPTEMBER, 1888

OIL-PAINTINGS

No.	Subject	£	s.	d.
80	In the barley field.	10	0	0
88	"Winter lingers in the lap of Spring."	15	0	0
102	Noonday quiet.	35	0	0

ELEVENTH EXHIBITION OF THE NORWICH ART CIRCLE, JANUARY, 1889

No.	Subject	£	s.	d.
36	Evening.	4	0	0

THIRTEENTH EXHIBITION OF THE NORWICH ART CIRCLE, SEPTEMBER, 1889

No.	Subject	£	s.	d.
75	A grey day.	8	0	0
76	The brook.	30	0	0
79	A Surrey distance.	10	0	0

FOURTEENTH EXHIBITION OF THE NORWICH ART CIRCLE, JANUARY, 1890

No.	Subject	£	s.	d.
3	The hay waggon.	3	0	0

FIFTEENTH EXHIBITION OF THE NORWICH ART CIRCLE, SEPTEMBER, 1890

OIL-PAINTINGS

No.	Subject	£	s.	d.
67	The hayfield.	10	0	0
80	Early spring.	12	0	0
89	Whitening to the harvest.	20	0	0

SIXTEENTH EXHIBITION OF THE NORWICH ART CIRCLE, JANUARY, 1891

No.	Subject	£	s.	d.
1	On Dartmoor.	5	0	0

EIGHTEENTH EXHIBITION OF THE NORWICH ART CIRCLE, OCTOBER, 1891

WATER-COLOUR

No.	Subject	£	s.	d.
51	Cow shed at Nutfield.	10	0	0

TWENTIETH EXHIBITION OF THE NORWICH ART CIRCLE, OCTOBER, 1892

OIL-PAINTINGS

No.	*Subject*	£	s.	d.
50	"By quiet fields."	20	0	0
66	"Every day was Giles a shepherd."	35	0	0

TWENTY-SECOND EXHIBITION OF THE NORWICH ART CIRCLE, OCTOBER, 1893

OIL-PAINTINGS

No.	*Subject*	£	s.	d.
66	Ploughing.	7	0	0
68	Summer evening.	25	0	0
69	Five o'clock tea.	10	0	0

VICTORIA COLKETT (Mrs. HINE)

EXHIBITS AT BRITISH INSTITUTION

Year	*No.*	*Subject*
1859	196	Interior of King's College Chapel.
1860	566	Queen's Gateway, Trinity College.
1862	488	Clare College and Bridge, from King's College Grounds.
1863	195	St. John's College, Cambridge.
	511	Brecknock Castle.
1864	149	Pevensey Castle.
1865	528	Clare Hall and Bridge on the Cam.
1866	388	Norwich Cathedral from the Bishop's Palace Garden.
	607	Clare Bridge and Avenue, Cambridge.

Victoria Colkett was a pupil of S. D. Colkett and specialised in architectural subjects and road scenes. The author has seen several of her water-colours.

SAMUEL DAVID COLKETT

(PUPIL OF JAMES STARK)

(1800-1863)

1800 Samuel David Colkett was born about 1800, presumably in Norwich. He was the son of a druggist who kept a shop at 70 St. Stephen's Street, Norwich. His mother, Mrs. Mary Colkett, probably kept the shop on after his father's death. It was in this shop that Colkett probably worked during his youth. His first exhibit with the Norwich
1818 Society was in 1818, entered by Master S. Colkett.

1820 Later, about 1820 he became a pupil of James Stark. Several paintings exist which, though signed by Colkett, bear the handling of Stark. Presumably such paintings date to this period. Colkett's name features frequently in the Norwich Exhibitions between 1822 and 1833. Concurrently he was exhibiting in London at the Royal Academy, the British Institution, and Suffolk Street Galleries.

1828 In 1828, in company with several Norwich Painters, Colkett moved to London, where he successfully painted for several years.

1834 It would seem that he was married to a lady named Hamatal by the year 1834, for the birth of a son is recorded in this year, followed by the birth of a daughter, Emily Louisa, in 1836.

1836 By 1836 he had returned to his native city and established himself as a drawing master and picture dealer and restorer at Prince's Street, Tombland. By this time Colkett had achieved a reputation as a landscape painter and was painting some of his best pictures—most of them Norfolk scenes. For example, in 1839 he sent to the British Institution a view of Postwick Grove, measuring 27 by 44 in., quite a sizeable work for this artist.

1840 Colkett was still living in Tombland in 1840, where his daughter, Octavia, was born on 24th May of that year, his profession being described as drawing master.

Just as John Sell Cotman had a sale of his works when he left Norwich in 1834, Samuel David Colkett did likewise some ten years later, when he moved to Great Yarmouth. Here he established himself as formerly. The reason for his removal is not known, but it would appear that he was of a peregrinating disposition, for we find that in 1854 he made a further move to Cambridge, where he settled with his family at 54 Trumpington Street.

One may add that Colkett seldom executed sea pictures, but whilst in Yarmouth he produced several beach scenes.

After living in Cambridge for some years our artist developed a severe illness which
1863 proved fatal. He died on 24th June, 1863, leaving a daughter, Victoria Colkett, who painted in the manner of her father. She married Mr. Harry Hine, a very fine water-colourist (also a landscape painter) in 1874.

During his last years Samuel Colkett enjoyed many friendships with his new-found community, despite being afflicted with deafness. On his passing he was reported as having a transparent and genial character, always ready to instruct others.

THE PAINTINGS

Colkett is interesting because he not only painted pleasing and often fine landscapes but carried on the painting traditions of Old Crome, via James Stark. There is, of course, a lessening in the tempo of interpretation; nonetheless, the Crome idiom is faithfully carried on.

Perhaps Colkett's greatest attribute is his sense of colour, which is often quite on a par with that of any of the Norwich School. Not only is his colour good but he uses local colour with great skill—in fact, the use of local colour is a Colkett hallmark. One finds the strong blue and red touches on the figures in the foreground anchor the eye momentarily; it then progresses to further colour harmonies in the middle-distance and finally rests on the bluey distance.

The building up of his banks and grasses in the foreground of his pictures is also one of his methods. One looks for the numerous effective touches to indicate grass. This method is also used by the Cotmans. The same observation applies to his trees—they are built up.

In his early works, Colkett produced the old gnarled trees and the delightfully painted banks of the Norfolk lanes. We see plenty of impasto and rich earth colours. Prior to developing his careful point-by-point style, he did for a time paint, using a considerable amount of paint and teasing it into the forms he desired.

The skies often carry more breadth than the rest of his pictures. On his clouds he often draws his palette knife over his brush stroke.

The paintings of Samuel David Colkett will go down to posterity, not only for their charming appeal, but as being typical examples of the work of the late Norwich School.

Collett does occasionally sign in a bold primitive style.

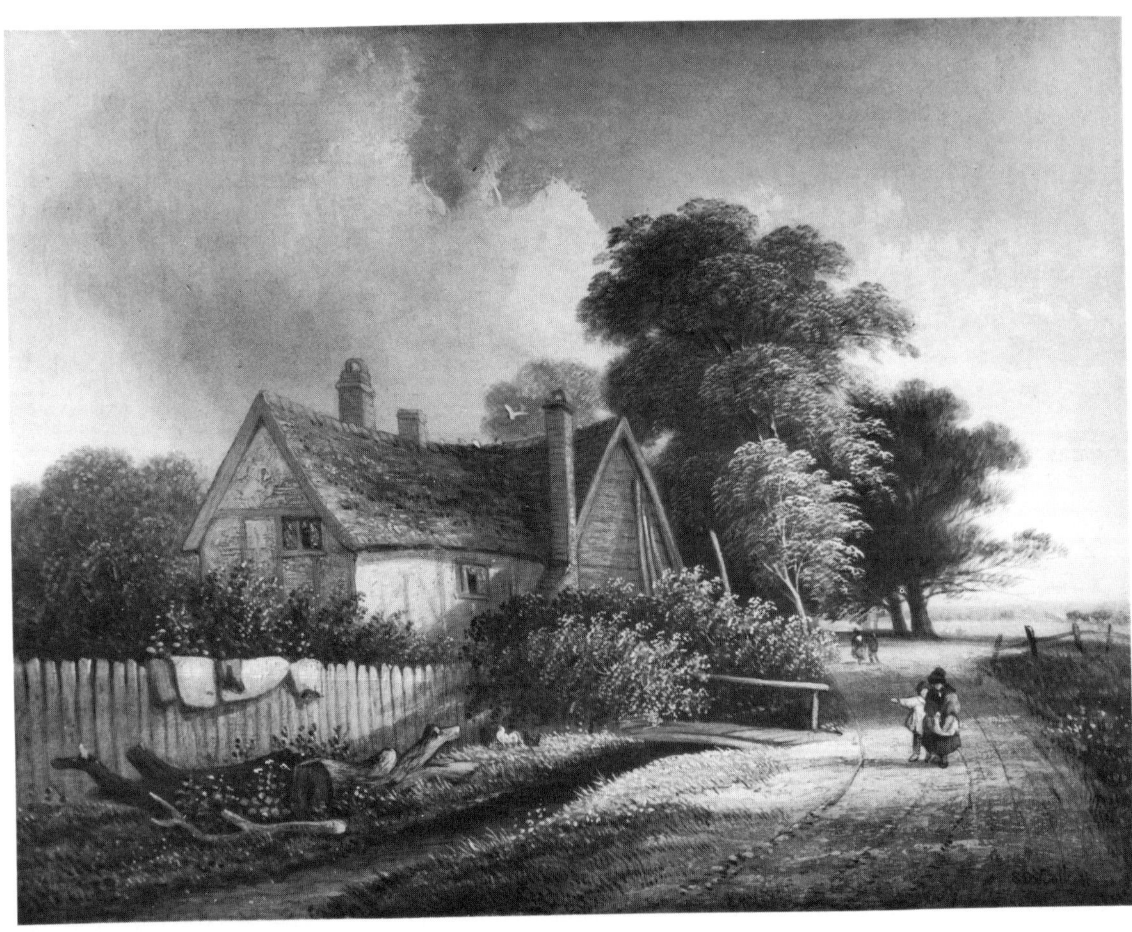

Samuel David Colkett, 1857 *Oil on canvas*

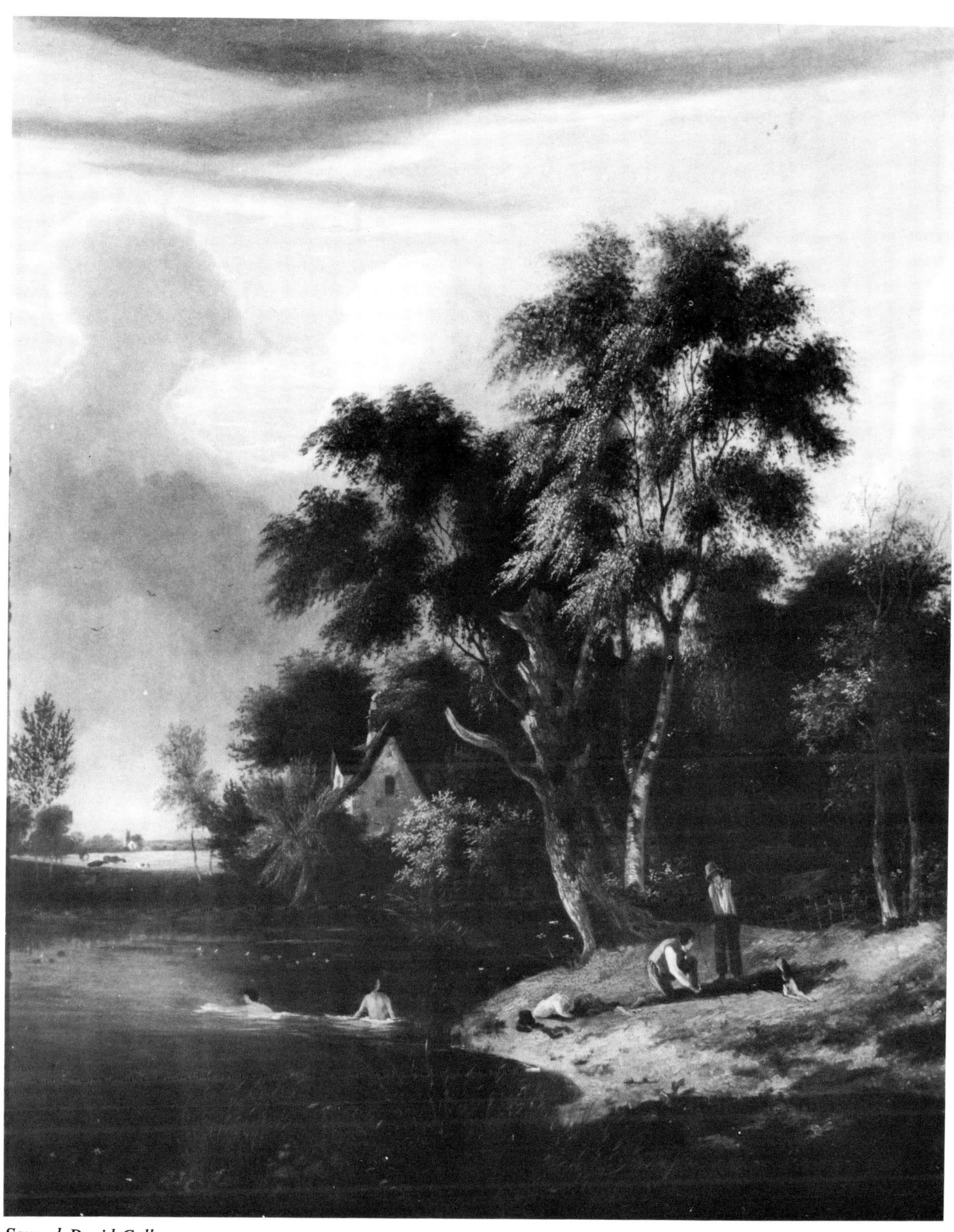

Samuel David Colkett
Probably inspired by J. Crome's Poringland Oak

Oil on Panel $29\frac{1}{2} \times 24\frac{1}{2}$ *in.*
About 1829

EXHIBITS AT THE BRITISH INSTITUTION

Year	*No.*	*Subject*
1825	133	Cattle passing a brook. 32×40 in.
1826	287	Scene near Framlingham, Norfolk. 27×30 in.
1827	219	Lane scene on the banks of the Orwell. 28×39 in.
	464	Scene at Trowse. 29×26 in.
1828	331	Wood scene with cattle. 23×29 in.
	346	Lane scene with cattle. 29×38 in.
1829	386	Sheep passing a brook. 31×38 in.
	441	View on a river. 30×38 in.
	492	Cottage scene in Norfolk. 21×25 in.
1832	351	Scene near Norwich. 23×27 in.
1839	390	Postwick Grove near Norwich. 27×44 in.
1842	252	River scene, Norwich. 25×31 in.
1846	71	Scene at Trowse, Norfolk. 24×30 in.
1847	78	Scene at Shepreth, Cambs. 15×20 in.
	412	Scene at Trowse. 15×20 in.
1848	457	The village inn door. 26×33 in.
1849	476	A water mill. 21×21 in.
1850	60	Landscape with cattle. 31×28 in.
1854	206	Cottage scene, Shepreth.
	433	Scene at Coton, Cambs.
1855	72	Scene on the Cam.
1856	504	At Bannington, Cambs.
1857	159	Lane scene, Norfolk.
	565	On the Dee.
1858	273	Lane scene, Clothall, Baldock.
1859	30	The homestead.
	182	Landscape and figures, Norfolk.
1860	144	Carrow on the Yare.
1861	472	Livemede, Suffolk.
1862	392	Study of oaks, Queen's Grove, Cambridge.

EXHIBITS AT ROYAL ACADEMY

Year	*No.*	*Subject*
1830	108	Landscape.
1831	527	Scene at Shepreth, Cambridgeshire.
1860	144	Carrow on the Yare.
1861	472	Livemede, Suffolk.
1862	393	Study of oaks, Queen's College Grove, Cambridge.

Graves also records that Colkett exhibited thirty-three works at Suffolk Street.

EXHIBITION OF NORWICH SCHOOL PICTURES

Norwich Castle Museum and Art Galleries, October, 1927

OIL-PAINTINGS

No.	*Subject*
10	Landscape. $25\frac{1}{2} \times 33\frac{1}{2}$ in.
11	River scene near Norwich. Panel, 8 in. diameter.
12	River scene near Norwich. Panel, 8 in. diameter.
13	Mill on Breydon, November, 1852. $7\frac{1}{2} \times 10\frac{1}{2}$ in.
14	Landscape with figures. $11\frac{1}{2} \times 15\frac{1}{2}$ in.
15	Landscape. $16\frac{3}{4} \times 12\frac{1}{4}$ in.
16	Landscape. 13×20 in.

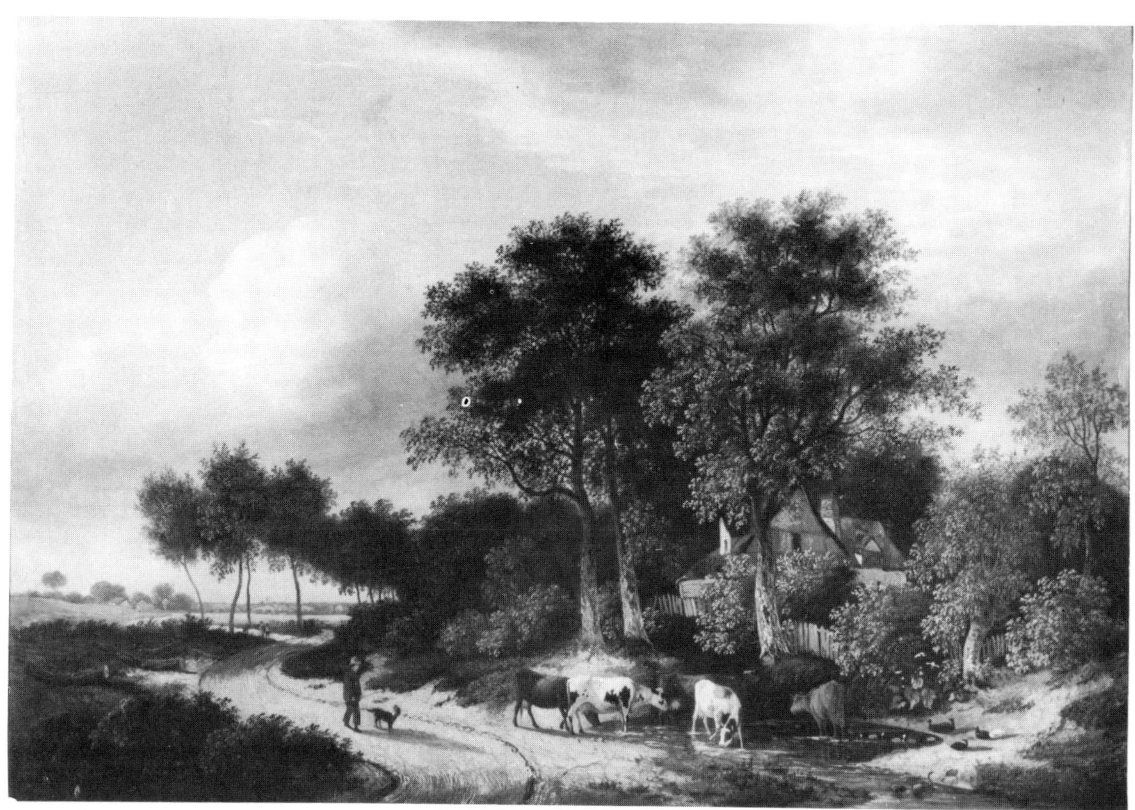

Samuel David Colkett—early period *Oil approx.* 20 × 30 *in.*

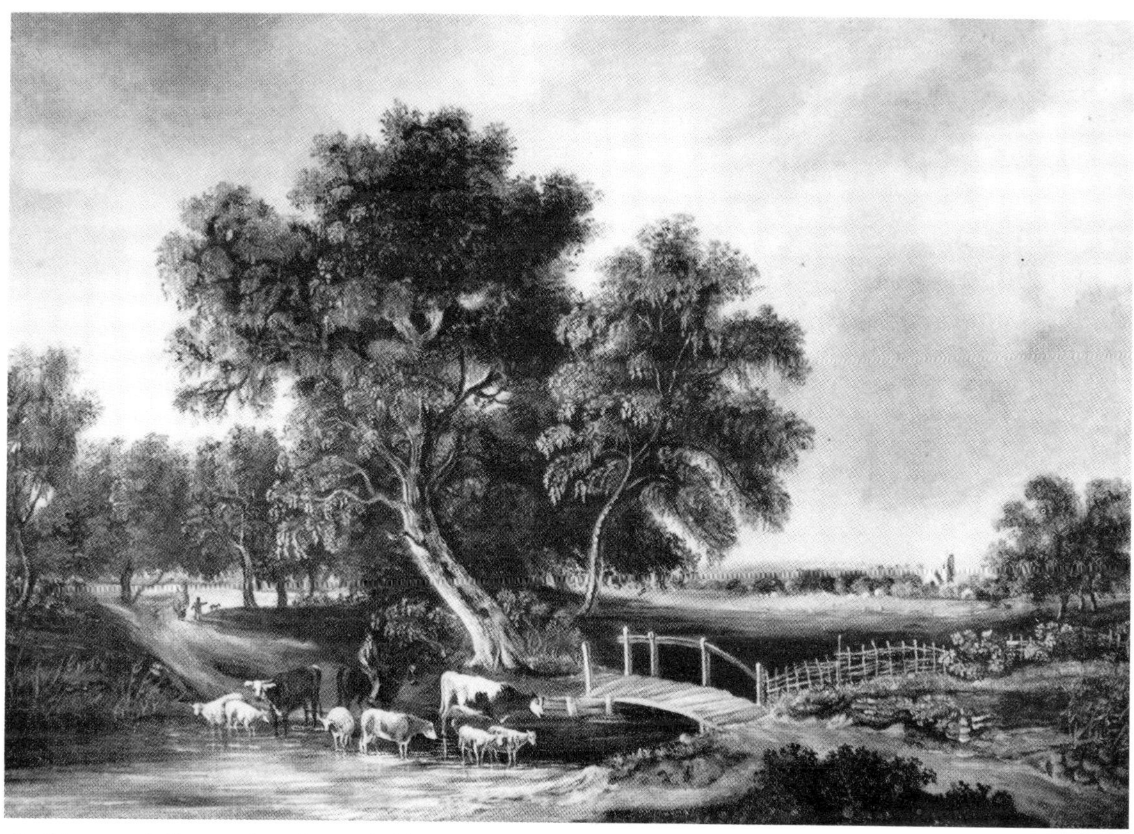

B. Silvers. A Yarmouth artist, probably a pupil of Samuel David Colkett *Oil on panel* 14 × 20 *in.*

ALFRED PRIEST

(PUPIL OF JAMES STARK)

(1810-1850)

1810 Alfred Priest was born on 12th December, 1810, the son of a Norwich chemist. His
father, wishing him to follow in his business, attended to his education, which was
described as the best available. However, he became restless and went to sea, seeking
fame and fortune. Alas, at sea he found neither, and returned to become apprenticed
to a surgeon at Downham Market. Still not finding his calling, he became interested in
Art and was placed for two years with Henry Ninham. Later he became a pupil of
1833 James Stark when he attended his studio in Chelsea. By the year 1833 his work was of
a sufficiently high standard to be accepted for the Academy.

Two years later, in 1835, he married and went to live at Pembroke Square, Kensington. Here he lived for the remainder of his London life, sending numerous exhibits to the Royal Academy, the British Institute, and Suffolk Street Galleries.

Besides being a painter he did a considerable number of etchings, many of which can be seen in the British Museum and the Colman Library, Norwich.

Priest, whilst being an intemperate man, was very good-natured with children, and
wrote poems for them, including *The Hare* and *Three Leverets*. This poetic side of his
life may well have developed had it not been for his ill-health, which caused him to
1848 leave London for Norwich in 1848. Possibly he suffered, like Joseph Stannard, with
tuberculosis, for the last years were spent at the seaside in an endeavour to recover.
Such recovery did not take place, and it is recorded that Alfred Priest died in his fortieth
1850 year, and was buried in Cringleford Churchyard, Norwich, in 1850.

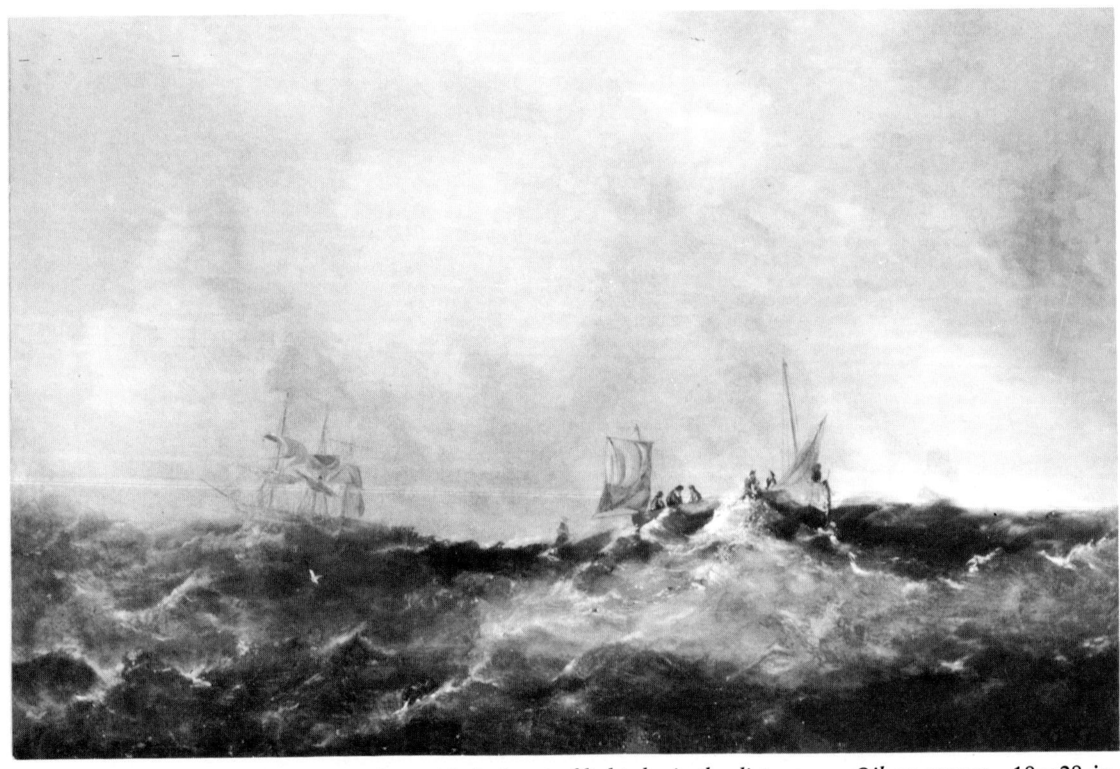

Alfred Priest *A typical Priest seapiece with the burst of light sky in the distance* *Oil on canvas* 18 × 28 *in.*

Alfred Priest was a painter who could paint either with a strong East Anglian touch, or use a very fluent smooth brushwork. By and large it is the smoother works which were painted towards the end of his relatively short life. Such an example is the *Iffley Mill* in the Castle Museum, Norwich, which was exhibited at the Society of British Artists in 1844.

His early works, under the influence of Ninham, are painted with much impasto and are generally Norwich scenes. They have a primitive quality, especially in the drawing of the figures.

From Stark, Alfred Priest learnt something of Crome's concepts respecting breadth, for we see in his sea pieces beautifully free brushwork representing both sea and sky. The ships and figures being placed with great delicacy, but in the main it is the feeling of the wind raising the sea, the roving rain clouds and the distant approach of a storm that pre-occupied Priest.

He engaged the use of Naples yellow in his skies and emerald green in his seas, sometimes glazed over with vandyke brown. Because he did not always sign his works, many have been attributed to other painters. His landscapes, painted a few years before his death, are delicate works involving the use of an interesting combination of greens, siennas and vandyke brown. In his distances he often placed animals with a characteristic touch of the brush.

EXHIBITS AT ROYAL ACADEMY

Year	*No.*	*Subject*
1833	410	Dredger on Breydon, near Yarmouth, Norfolk.
1836	192	A sea view.
1837	56	Landscape—painted on the spot.
1838	536	Scene in Gunton Park (Lord Suffield's).
1839	2	Scene at Taverham, Norfolk.
	298	At Reading, Berkshire.
1840	559	Scene in Lord Suffield's Park, Costessy, Norfolk.
	1058	Portrait of a lady.
1841	576	Sketch near Castor Castle, Norfolk.
	720	Sketch at Reading.
	843	Scene at Fulham.
1842	1103	Near Matlock Bath, Derbyshire.
1843	474	An old pollard.
	487	Scene at the back of Maple Denham Watermill, Berkshire.
1844	318	Bridge at Godstowe, near Oxford.
1845	390	Skinner's Weir, near Oxford.
	906	The ford.

SOCIETY OF BRITISH ARTISTS

Priest exhibited forty-nine paintings, the most interesting of which are as follows:

Year	*Subject*
1833	Sea view—distant vessel in distress.
1834	Storm at sea.
1835	Escaping from the wreck.
1836	Wild duck—a study from Nature.
	Coming from the wreck.
	Water mill at Reading.
1840	Gipsies at Costessy Common, at back of Lord Stafford's park.
	Tent of sails on Yarmouth Beach, for sailors driven ashore during the gales, November, 1839.
	An old poacher.
1844	Iffley Mill, near Oxford.
1845	The weir, Oxford.

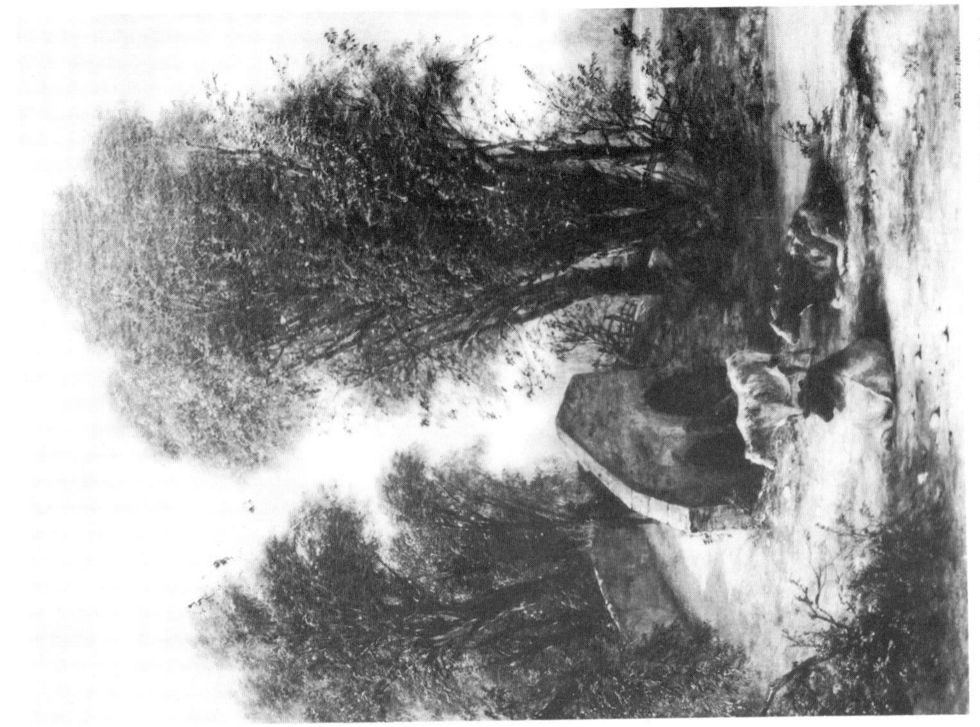

Alfred Priest *Godstone Bridge, Oxford* *Oil* $29\frac{1}{2} \times 21\frac{1}{2}$ *in.*

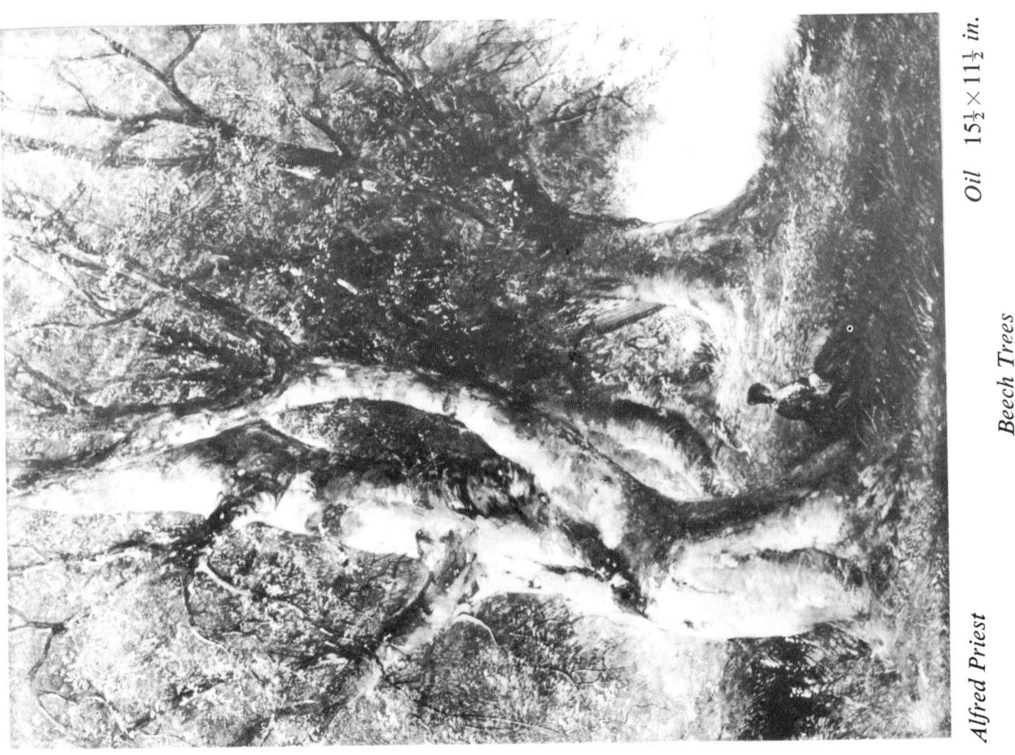

Alfred Priest *Beech Trees* *Oil* $15\frac{1}{2} \times 11\frac{1}{2}$ *in.*

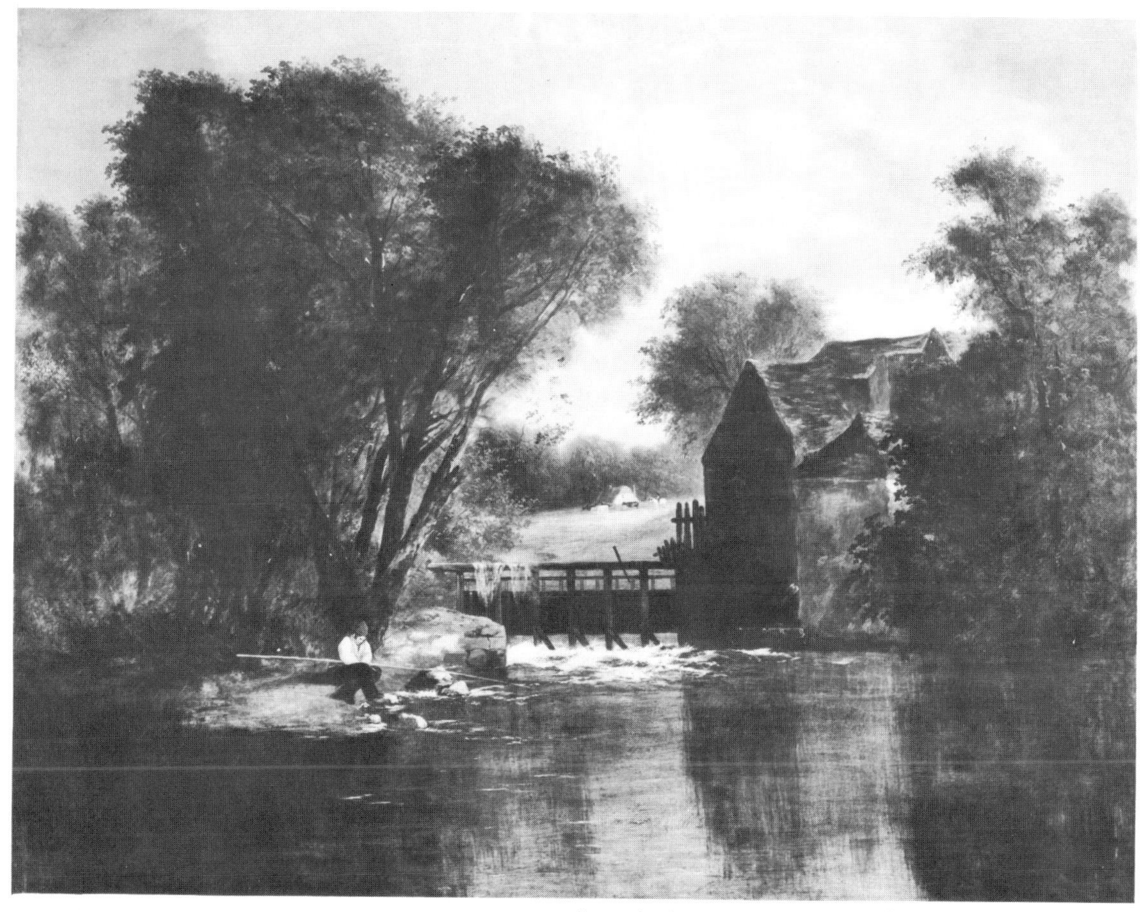

Alfred Priest *Iffley Mill, Oxford* *Oil on canvas* $27\frac{1}{2} \times 35$ *in.*

EXHIBITS AT BRITISH INSTITUTE

Year	*No.*	*Subject*
1834	384	Sea view. 18×22 in.
	506	Landscape. 21×25 in.
	513	Sea view. 28×34 in.
1835	141	Near Norwich. 18×22 in.
1836	72	Beach scene. 15×19 in.
	142	A river scene. 44×56 in.
	274	Yarmouth Beach. 16×20 in.
	367	View near Caversham Hills, Reading. 56×67 in.
1837	297	Shed at Bundle, Norfolk. 15×56 in.
1838	62	Scene at Lakenham. 44×56 in.
1840	145	Marine view. 44×56 in.
	232	The ford, Heigham, Norwich. 36×44 in.
	314	At Whitlingham, Norfolk. 33×41 in.
	335	A sketch from Nature. 18×14 in.
1841	197	On the trout stream, Pangbourne. 28×48 in.
1842	134	Scene on the road to Derbyshire.
1843	151	Avenue of pollards. 44×41 in.
1844	274	In Derbyshire. 48×41 in.
1845	75	Near Reading. 54×67 in.
1846	358	Scene in the drive, Lord Stafford's park, Costessey. 45×38 in.
	461	Scene in the drive, Lord Stafford's park, Costessey. 48×40 in.
1847	347	On the Wye, looking towards Goodrich Castle. 48×40 in.

EXHIBITION OF NORWICH SCHOOL PICTURES

Norwich Castle Museum and Art Galleries, October, 1927

OIL PAINTINGS

No.	*Subject*
79	View of Norwich (signed "A. Priest 1849"). 26½×40 in.
80	River scene, Costessy, Norfolk. 21¼×29¼ in.
81	Road by the churchyard (signed "A. Priest 1834"). 27½×35½ in.
82	Coast scene with vessel (signed "A. Priest 1849"). 13½×23½ in.
83	The hulk. 25½×35½ in.
84	Mending nets. 33½×55 in.

WATER-COLOURS

236	River scene (signed). 6¼×10¼ in.

GEORGE VINCENT

(1796-1832)

1796 George Vincent was born on 27th June, 1796, in the parish of St. John-at-Timberhill, his father being James Vincent, a cloth manufacturer. Perhaps it was the cloth manufacturing that indirectly was the cause of George Vincent becoming a pupil of John Crome, for undoubtedly James Vincent would have known the Starks, who were dyers. When James, some two years older than George Vincent, made excellent progress under Crome, it was hoped that our artist would do likewise. So, after receiving his education at Norwich Grammar School, George Vincent became a pupil of John Crome.

1816 After the Napoleonic war, in 1816 Vincent, in company with John Berney Crome and Mr. Steel, the surgeon (who married Crome's daughter) made a visit to Paris. Vincent was reported as being very seasick on the journey. There is in Norwich Museum a *View of Rouen* which probably resulted from this journey. It was perhaps on his return that he toured Essex, resulting in paintings of Ingatestone and Little Baddow. As both Vincent and Stark exhibited views of Windsor in 1816 it is likely they made the visit together. They were very close friends, as can be seen by the fact that they occupied
1817 adjoining premises when Vincent first went to London in 1817. This was in Newman Street. In this year they were both admitted as students in the School attached to the British Institution, Pall Mall. Unfortunately, in 1819 Stark was obliged to return to Norwich, due to ill-health.

1819 Presumably it was Stark's departure that caused Vincent to also leave London for a tour of Scotland in 1819. There are in the British Museum and Norwich Museum, drawings which record this visit. The large painting *View of Edinburgh from Calton Hill* exhibited, *Fishing Boats on the Firth of Clyde—Morning*, *Fishing Boats on the Banks of the Forth*, *View of St. Bernard's Well*, were all painted as a result of his Scottish visit. At this time Vincent was perhaps at the height of his powers.

When Crome died in 1821 the *Norwich Mercury* reported that Mr. Sharp and Mr. Vincent came from town to attend the funeral. With the passing of Crome, who must have been much more than a friend, Vincent must have returned to London in a sad
1822 frame of mind. However, by 1822 he married the daughter of Dr. Cugnoni and purchased a good house in Camden Town. A. J. Stark told L. G. Bolingbroke in 1882:

> Vincent married a lady who at the time of their marriage was believed to be wealthy. On the strength of his wife's supposed prosperity Vincent took a larger house than he could properly keep up in Camden Town and had therefore to paint his pictures very quickly to keep going.

It is difficult to imagine George Vincent getting himself into this scrape, but such was his artistic temperament he undoubtedly missed the stability of Crome's advice. Intemperance also played its part, this being a great cause of pain to his father, who is reported to have been very troubled.

By 1824 he had left Camden Town for a smaller and more central studio. In July 1824 he wrote the following letter to Mr. Davey, Junior:

> 28 Upper Thornhaugh Street,
> Bedford Square.
>
> To Mr. Davey Jun., Foundry Bridge Road, Thorpe. July 27th 1824.
>
> Dear Sir,
>
> As two years have passed since I had the pleasure of communicating with any of my friends, it may not be surprising if on the present occasion I should feel some difficulty in attempting to express my gratitude for your kind letter. Had not illness troubled me, I would have answered you before, but, under present circumstances, my feelings will not

allow me to excuse my pencil or pen. I regret Mr. Stark's letter to Burnet did not come to my hand sooner. That gentleman sent it to Mr. Wadmore, who gave it me the day previous to my calling upon you in the East. I had determined to give up the following week to the exhibition of old Masters, and I need not say that your company would have increased the gratification since which I have been under the necessity of deferring it until within a short period when I had the pleasure of seeing Mr. Cotman at the British Gallery. who gave me a very gratifying account of your neighbour, Mr. Stark, who, I am happy to find, enjoys a better state of health than formerly. I am very sorry the latter gentleman should be unacquainted with my address. It accounts for his not answering a letter of mine sent two years past within two months. I felt it severely at the time, and thought that, by some unknown cause, I had forfeited his friendship, and was, in some measure, led to suppose so from a statement. not at all flatering to my feelings, being circulated in town; but, upon reading his last letter and reflecting upon the subject, I could not for one moment believe an expression from him could prejudice me in the eyes of the world. I know not of any act of mine toward him, deserving censure.

Your naming my father, and his expressing feelings of concern about me, created a sensation I was not prepared for, as having understood from those I have no reason to suspect, that his feeling toward me is the very contrary to that which you named. Could anything within my power, add one moment's comfort to his declining days, it would be my utmost study to accomplish it: but so much infamy has been unjustly levelled at me, by those whose duty it was to protect, that I am not astonished a man, like my father, should express himself with severity upon my past folly, and I believe from the sufferings my mind experiences and has done for the last two years, that my stay in this world will not be for a very long duration.

I had nearly given up the hope of ever selling a picture in Norwich, but, your friend expressing a wish to possess one, I will, with your leave, take the liberty of sending, in a short time, one I have in hand. Should he not approve it, no harm is done. I am told it will make a very fair picture, but of this I am not to judge. . . . Give my best respects to Mr. Stark, and say I shall send him a few impresions of my etchings in a short time.

I remain, Your obedient Servant,

GEORGE VINCENT.

It would appear from the letter that Vincent had been etching quite recently, these etchings being very rare. The picture mentioned in the letter was sent to Mr. Davey with the accompanying letter:

To Mr. Davey Junior, Foundry Bridge Rd., Thorpe.

Dear Sir,

I feel some reluctance in troubling you with the enclosed picture, as it is not of a class to do me any good. Under such circumstances, may I beg of you to let James Stark see it before your friend, and, should he approve of its being sent for inspection, let it go: but should he consider it, as I do, a very inferior production, do not let it be seen. . . . I shall wish your friend to take it at his own price. Should he decline doing so, let J. Stark name some price, and however, trifling, it will be satisfactory to me.

The small sketch of "Pevensey Bay" I beg you to accept, and I hope to send you something better as my health returns. Have you those early productions of mine, painted about fourteen years past? They must be getting valuable. I would have sent my etchings, but I have not been in a state to use aqua fortis. In a few days I shall send down a roll of them. When you favour me with a line, give me some account of the Exhibition.

I remain, your obedient Servant,

GEORGE VINCENT.

In the following letter he refers to his beloved Whitlingham:

2 Upper Thornhaugh St.,
Bedford Square.
August 28th 1824.

To Mr. Davey Junior.

Dear Sir,

Your letter of yesterday gave me great pleasure in finding that you and Mr. Stark approved of my picture. I am apt to think it a little flattery, to give me a stimulus to do better; but

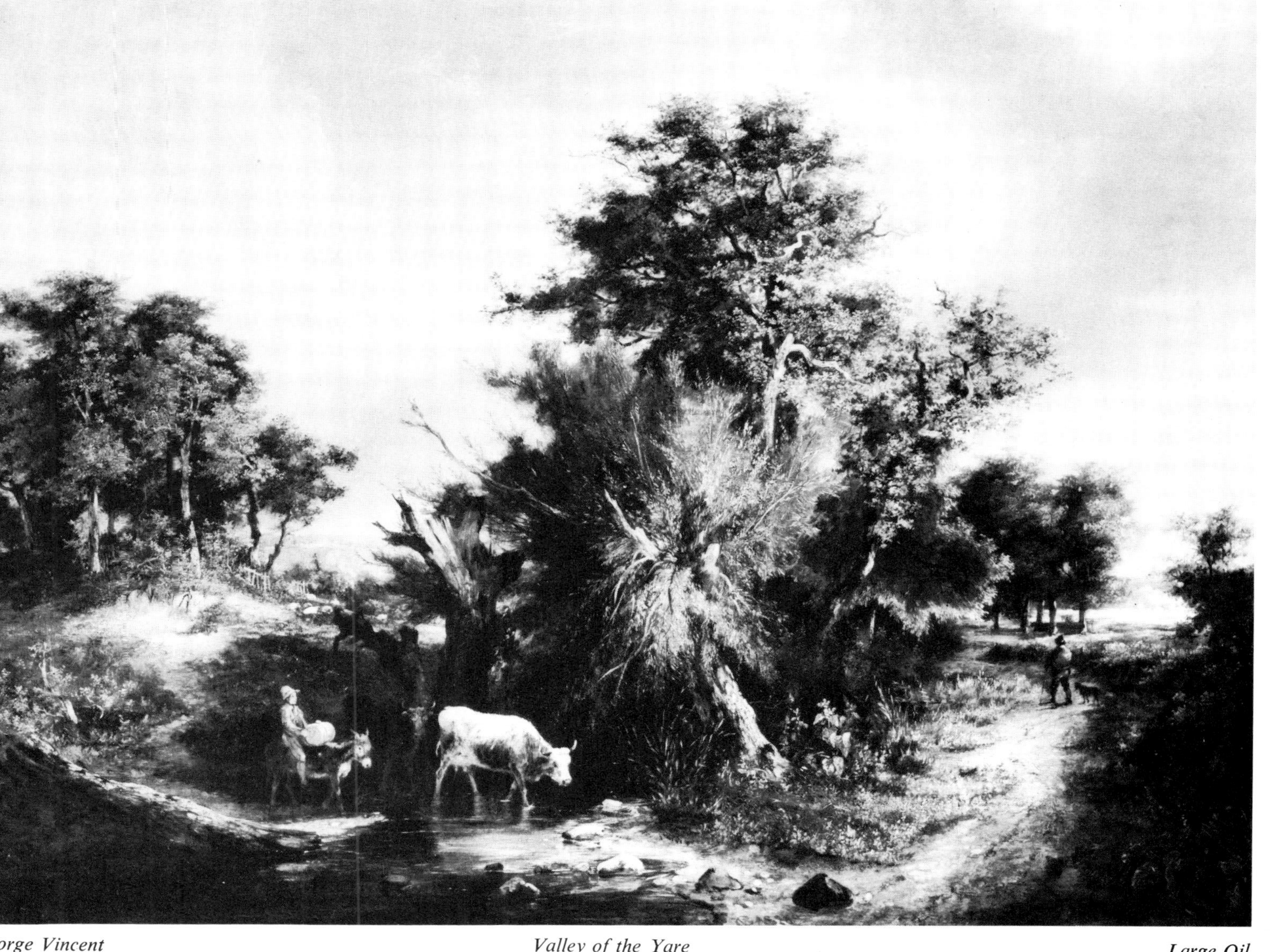

George Vincent — *Valley of the Yare* — *Large Oil*

such things the womenkind say are very agreeable, and so I thank you. I know nothing so likely to stimulate me as the smell of my old canvas I painted some years past, now in your possession. It would bring back to my mind a chain of ideas I love to dwell upon, for it was painted at the most happy period of my life. . . . Send it by all means, and as to the price, I shall consider myself well paid by receiving the ten pounds you so kindly offer. I had entertained a hope that Mr. Stark would have fixed a price for my large picture, knowing the Norwich market better than I do; but delicacy forbids him. . . . Burnet says, "Too much delicacy hurts a man", and by the following you will suppose I think so too. I beg to offer my picture at £40, but if that should be considered too much, something less will be received with as much satisfaction. My reason for sending so large a picture, was on account of your friend expressing a desire to possess one of mine, exhibited in Norwich ten years past, of the same dimensions. Should it be too much, pray light St. Clement's copper-fire with it, as I have not the least desire to see it again.

I am, thank God, very much better this week, and, should it last (to use Mr. Stark's expression) I shall ship up the French Fleet at the Battle of Trafalgar, in a short time. You must know the Directors of the British Gallery have offered two good sums of money to the Artists, to paint sketches of the battles of the Nile and Trafalgar. The Norfolk hero gained those battles, and shall it be said the Norfolk Artists would not contend for the prize now offered? You see I am not wanting in vanity or presumption. In a few days I shall go to Portsmouth to make drawings of the "Victory" and other ships engaged in those actions, and, in all probability, I shall visit a Norfolk hero living at Gatton, near Norwich, for a full account of the actions. Of this, say nothing, as I shall take a run through Norwich without stopping for a dumpling and gravy, and yet I know not a greater gratification than a day at my beloved Whitlingham. Could I but spend a few days in that delightful spot it would make me, for the time, one of the happiest fellows in the country, and I must say with my favourite, Goldsmith, "here to return and die at home at last", is my most sincere wish, and I hope a cottage will one day spring up and call me its master.

From your obedient Servant,

George Vincent.

The letter finished with a postscript:

P.S. I am sorry my letter should have troubled you yesterday. They passed each other on the road, very politely I make no doubt.

[The Directors of the British Institute offered premiums of £200 and £100 for the best and second-best sketch of the Battles of the Nile and Trafalgar, with a view of ordering two pictures to be painted of those subjects, which pictures they proposed to offer to the Governors of Greenwich Hospital, to be placed in the painted hall of that hospital, lately appropriated to a Picture Gallery. The sketches to be sent to the Gallery in the month of January, 1825. The result was that for the sketch of the Battle of the Nile, G. Arnald, A.R.A., received the £200 premium and a commission for a £500 picture from it. Now in the Maritime Museum at Greenwich. Vincent sent nothing.]

Vincent is not known to have sent a painting to be judged. From the letter it appears that Vincent had a literary turn of mind, for he refers to his favourite—"Goldsmith". His hope that "a cottage will one day spring up and call me its master", illustrates his romanticism which probably excluded any business instincts. Thus it was probably nothing to do with his wife's supposed wealth that caused Vincent to overspend on his house. A further letter again refers to the Battle of the Nile picture. Did he ever complete it?

26 Upper Thornhaugh Street.
Oct. 17th 1824.

To Mr. Davey Junior.

Dear Sir,

I have this day forwarded to March's office the picture you sent me to finish. The alteration I hope you will approve, and, should you or Mr. Stark suggest anything by way of improvement, I shall be most happy to do it when we meet. To me it has been—and

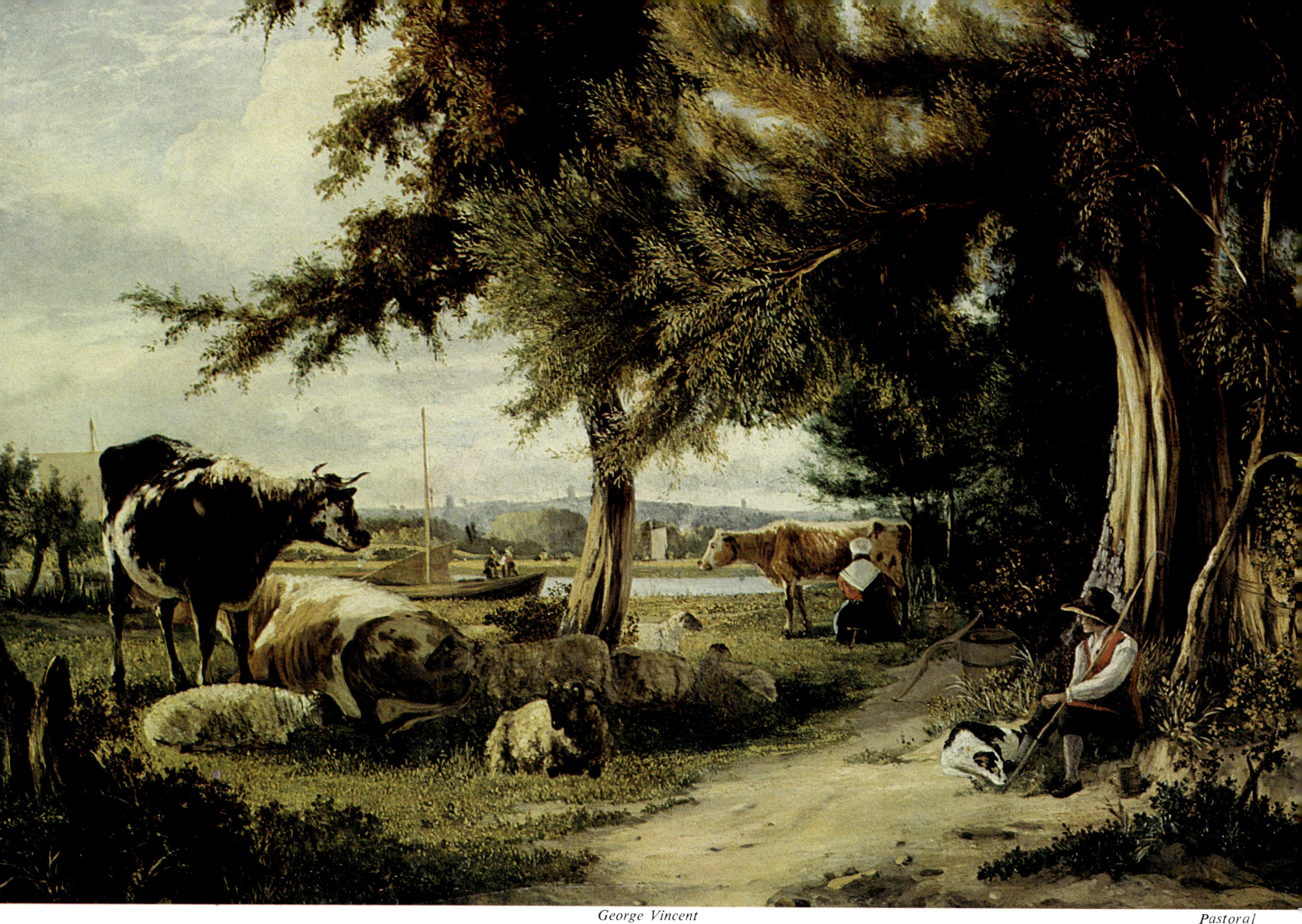

George Vincent *Pastoral*

likewise to my better half—a great source of pleasure to wander over the scenes of former days. Many circumstances have been brought to my recollection, many anecdotes told of my wanderings and very few without the name of your neighbour coupled with them. A Sunday at Bramerton not excepted. I could not resist placing in the picture a few objects omitted when making my sketch . . . The Huntman's House; Baswick's do., each and all are in my recollections and I believe it would not be difficult for me to find every object blindfold.

I am happy to say my picture of the Nile will do in point of composition, that is to say, it will make a picture. How far I shall succeed with Trafalgar, in that point, I cannot say. The former is at the time "L'Orient" blew up, and tars from the various ships are picking up the poor devils blown out of her. It is a midnight scene, and will give me an opportunity of trying my skill in Rembrandt effects.

From the above letter Vincent refers to his "better half", so he was happily married, despite all his difficulties.

The reason for Vincent's journey was ostensibly to interview the Trafalgar hero at Catton. After his return he sent the following letter to Mr. Davey:

Your great-coat I return, with many thanks; without it I should have been well sprinkled; as it was, it left me damp and chilly. I found things on my return a little out of order, which I trust a short time will rectify, but I fear it will prevent my taking the pallet in hand this week. The enclosed print will please you, I make no doubt. . . . I should have sent two by Willie, but the little disorder prevented me finding them. I must beg to express my high sense of gratitude to you and Mrs. Davey, for the kind united attention I received during my stay at Thorpe, and trust the time will soon arrive when I shall see you in Town with the same gratification. Hoping the happy trio are all quite well.

I remain, Your obedient Servant,

GEO. VINCENT.

The next letter explains the last one; he was now situated in the Third Gallery of the Fleet Prison, where persons owing money were placed. Vincent's position seems to have deteriorated.

Dec. 27. 1824.

To Mr. Davey Junior.

Dear Sir,

On the Thursday after my arrival in Town, I sent, by the Bagnet Coach, your great-coat with many thanks for its services. I have now been favoured with a line since to acknowledge its delivery, and this has more than once given me some concern. I enclosed likewise, a small parcel to J.S. and the print of "Celydon and Amelia".

I am sorry to state my situation at this time is very far from pleasant. Every hope must be given up with regard to my battle pictures being finished in time. I am at this moment, and have been for three weeks, a "prisoner in the Fleet", with many obligations to a relative for providing me with such a situation. Your kindness a few months since gave me an opportunity of paying the wretch £30, since which he had the modesty to request my large picture and four others for his debt! This undue advantage I resisted, not only as regards others to whom I stand indebted, but from his account being infamous to a degree, and the laws of my country will defend me, I am happy to say, from such overcharge.

My father-in-law came forward very handsomely and offered £50 to settle the business, and the old gentleman considered that sum too much by £3. I have not a doubt of the thing being settled very soon, but never will I acknowledge the amount of the debt.

I shall experience very great inconvenience from being shut up in this miserable place. I can paint small pictures here, but not any of size, but this is not the only evil. Being excluded from the world I shall find it no small difficulty to dispose of my works when painted, and, should I reserve them for the Exhibition, in all probability the money may not be forthcoming until after the close. Having two small pictures finished, intended for the British Gallery, the one 36×25, a View in Glen Sherrah, near Inverary, and the second 17×14 "Boats making for Home at the approaching Storm". If there are any of

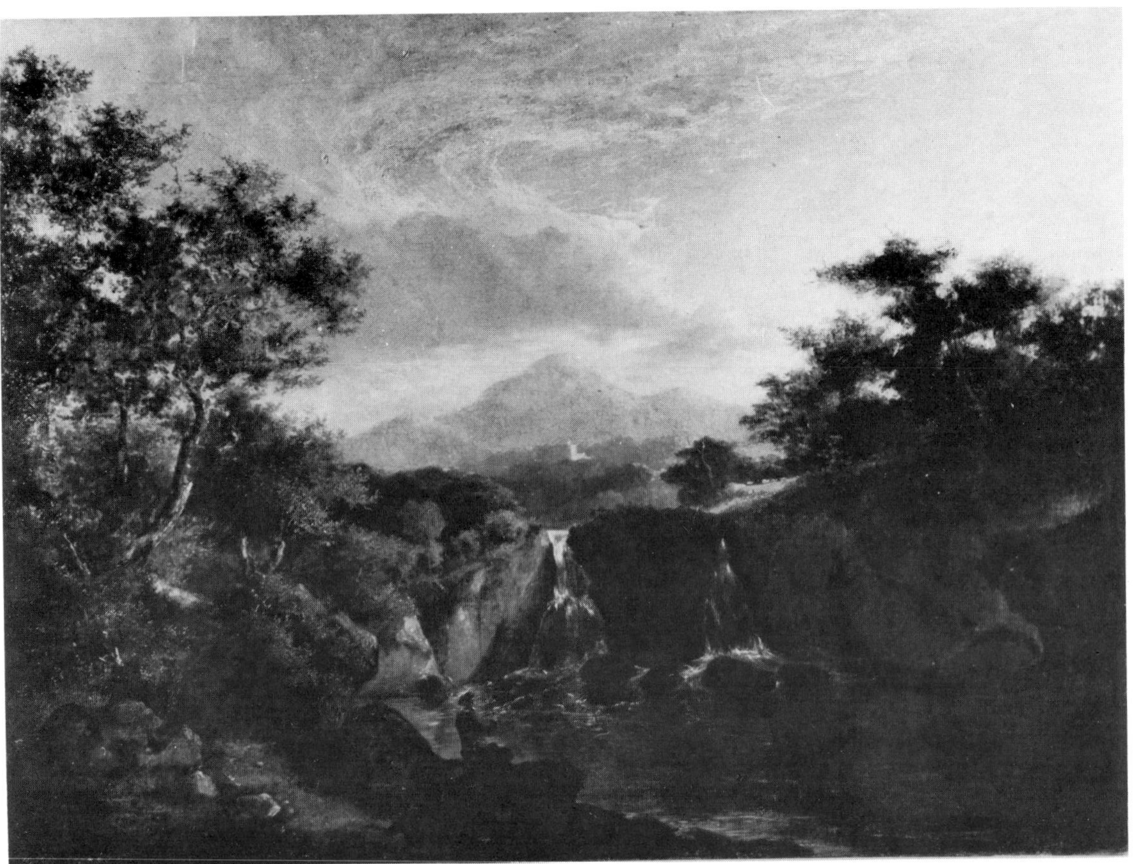

George Vincent *View in the Highlands* *Oil on canvas* 18 × 24 *in.*

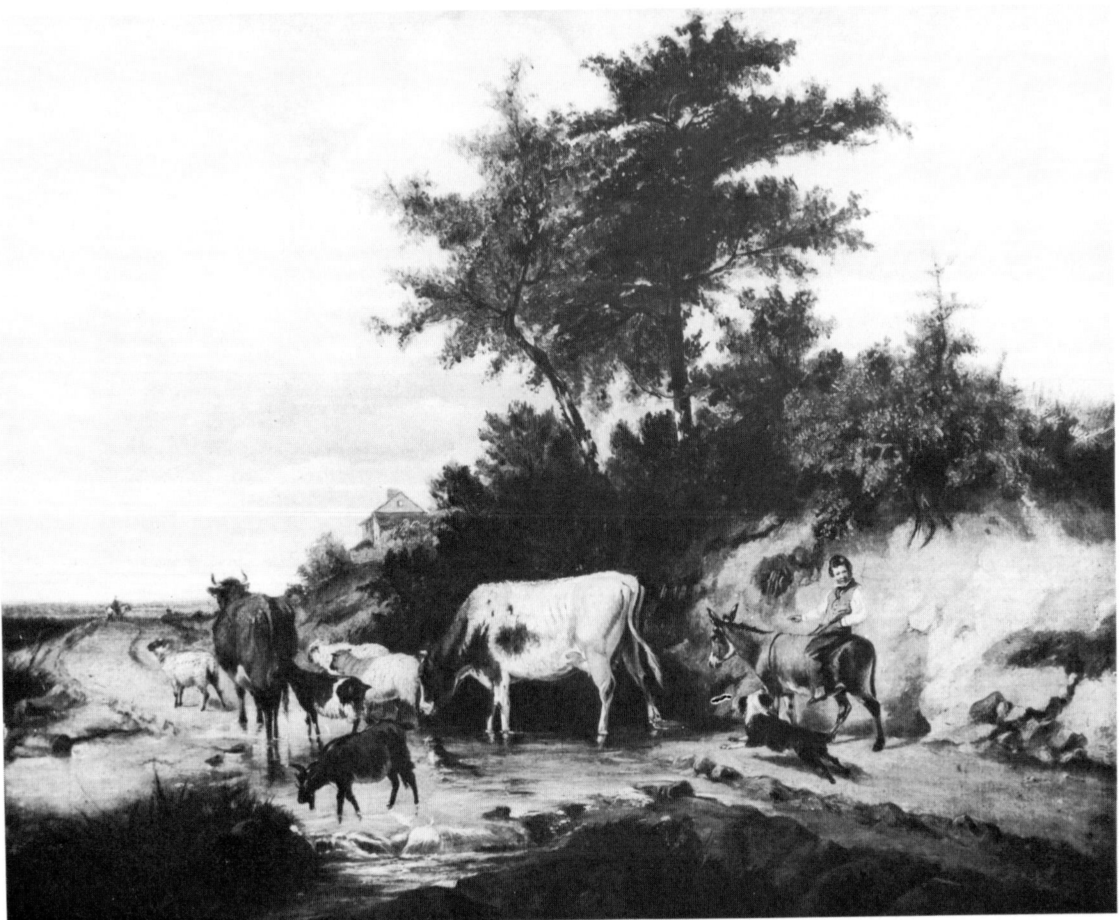

George Vincent *Crossing the Brook* *Oil on canvas* $17\frac{1}{2} \times 21\frac{1}{2}$ *in.*

your friends who would like to have them at a very low price I need not say how much it would benefit me upon the present occasion. For No. 1 I would be glad to take £15., for No. 2 £8, being half the price I should ask for them at the Gallery. As it will be necessary to name it to J.S. beg of him not to notice my residenta to a soul; and, above all, do not name it to my father, as it would make the poor old man very miserable. Pray favour me with a line and direct as usual, as I should be sorry the people at the Post Office at Norwich should see any address to me here. . . . Hoping you and Mrs. Davey and the happy trio are quite well.

I remain, Your Obedient Serv.,

GEORGE VINCENT.

No. 8 The Third Gallery, The Fleet,

Dec. 27, 1824.

Very early in 1825 Vincent visited Norwich, accompanied by a keeper. Presumably with a view to either selling his work or obtaining money in order to pay his debts. Evidently he saw James Stark, who expressed himself with some severity. Possibly he also left the paintings which were later exhibited in the Norwich Society. How he must have longed for a purchase. On his return he wrote to Mr. W. Davey again:

Fleet Prison.
12th Jan. 1825.

Dear Sir,

I beg to acknowledge receipt of your charitable letter of the 31st ultimo, with my sincere thanks for the enclosed five pounds. I should have answered yours before had not my picture retained "tacky" so long as to prevent my closing the case until today.

I am sorry that you should suppose for one moment, that I could look upon you with the slightest expectation of your becoming a purchaser of those two pictures I named in my last letter . . . but knowing of two persons in Norwich wishing to possess speciments of my pencil, I took the liberty, under present circumstances to make application to you. The gentlemen I allude to are Mr. Geo. Stacey and Mr. William Rackham. Should they, or any of your friends, like to have the pair at £20 . . . J.S. would not approve the price, therefore, do not name it to him. I hope that gentleman will not think it's my wish to undersell him in his native place. I shall not write him until I receive his pictures from Rutley's, which I doubt not to do at the beginning of next term. Previous to my coming to this place, my utmost exertions were used to send those things to Norwich, and J.S., knowing the man I have to deal with, should not express himself with severity until conscious of my neglect.

I shall be careful of its being the last thing he has to complain of. Hoping you and Mrs. Davey are quite well,

Yours &c.

1827 It was not until 13th February, 1827, that George Vincent was able to obtain his discharge from the Fleet Prison; he had been there since the beginning of December, 1824, well over two years. Had he not been able to paint during this time the punishment would have been greater still.

Various people now helped our artist, including James Wadmore, who gave him a commission for 100 guineas, resulting in *Greenwich Hospital from the River*, $47 \times 67\frac{1}{2}$ in.

It is likely that Vincent, so pleased to be released, set out for a second Scottish tour. The large Scottish view in the Fitzwilliam at Cambridge, I believe, dates to this time.
1830 The author has in his possession a water-colour *View in the Highlands*, dated 1830, possibly indicating a third visit.

Little is known about Vincent's final years. Probably he still had debts and, like George Morland, was ever being sought out. In 1832 the Society of British Artists exhibited some of his pictures at their Winter Exhibition and referred to him as G. Vincent (deceased).

It is possible that this description was true, but it is more likely that Vincent was living
quietly in the country, away from his creditors. In the Reeve Manuscript in the British
1833 Museum are references to George Vincent inheriting part of his father's estate in 1833
and that he was last seen at his father's funeral. Reeve also stated that he lived two or
three years after his father. As these reports came from the family in Norwich, a date
of 1836 for Vincent's passing seems more likely than the date of 1831 most often quoted.

One might ask what did Vincent do with himself after 1831 when he last exhibited? Did he paint under an assumed name, or take to drink and spend his inheritance, or did his mind give way? We shall probably never know but, on the other hand, research has been known to solve such problems.

An interesting statement by a Mrs. McFall (born Pinney) is preserved in the Norwich Castle Museum, dated April, 1965.

> Vincent's sister married a man called Towler; their daughter married a man called Hardesty. Their daughter, Mary Hardesty, married Richard Pinney and had a son named Harry Pinney.

Such is the story that has come to light so far respecting one of John Crome's most worthy pupils. *

THE PAINTINGS

George Vincent's fine paintings are a further example of the enthusiasm for Art instilled into all the pupils of John Crome. There is in Vincent's work an integrity of purpose—possibly at times his quality varies, but he never reduces himself to formula painting. His place in the Norwich School hierarchy is alongside James Stark.

The early works are very Crome-like, particularly in subject. The handling is tight, but we have grown to love it. The colouring is always in harmony and one can flick over the foreground and mid-distances to the pleasant touches of light on the distant buildings or animals. Vincent was an exponent of the use of local colour.

By the early 1820s he was fully developed in his art and could dash off a painting in a short time, giving it great zest and life. David Hodgson, in his *Reverie*, says George Vincent was a dashing painter and equal in his glorious depiction of ether to any other artist. The open meadow, the broad river, the wide expanse of heath and common were alike suited to his creative pencil, and Dickes notes his purple clouds with golden fringes and ability to create atmosphere.

Vincent can paint either a very broad sketchy picture, or he can take the utmost pains in order to present every detail. It was the latter type which he produced in the main, though in many of his productions are passages exhibiting the utmost freedom of handling.

His palette is very varied. It can be blue sky and subtle greens, in his early period, to the golden sky and grey blues of his mid-period, to the ochre, sienna tones of his later works.

The compositions he loved were views from the water looking towards the coast with shipping carrying the eye. Even his open sea views usually have shipping well placed to carry the eye. Crossing the brook was a favourite subject, where he paints in the figures and animals with pleasant effect, the water being used to carry the beautiful reflections. He is, perhaps, the only Norwich School painter to use the central mass, the eye being given the choice of looking to the right or left. The famous Tinker pictures at Ipswich and Norwich are of this structure.

As Vincent died at an early age, his works are comparatively rare.

He sometimes signs with a monogram followed by the date—sometimes in red but usually black. Many of his works are not signed.

*Recently discovered newspaper report gives Vincent's death as 1832.

George Vincent

A Fish Auction

Oil on canvas $25 \times 36\frac{1}{2}$ in.

EXHIBITS AT THE BRITISH INSTITUTION

Year	*No.*	*Subject*
1815	206	Near Norwich. 32×41 in.
1817	182	Landscape—evening. 25×22 in.
	146	Landscape. 25×22 in.
1818	99	A cottage scene. 37×32 in.
	103	Landscape. 25×33 in.
	217	Landscape with ruins and cattle. 66×57 in.
	246	At Whitlingham. 42×50 in.
1819	71	On the River Yare—afternoon. 68×84 in.
	206	Cottage scene. 44×52 in.
	234	On the River Wensum. 51×60 in.
1820	41	View of Edinburgh from the Calton Hill—evening. 66×90 in.
	102	Landscape and cattle. 60×78 in.
	148	Landscape and cattle. 36×30 in.
	270	View of Greenwich from Blackwall. 66×84 in.
1821	36	A Dutch Fair on Yarmouth Beach. 64×75 in.
	95	Yarmouth Beach. 45×57 in.
	148	Fishing boats on the banks of the Forth. 42×36 in.
1822	117	The Vale of Morpheal. 38×45 in.
1823	92	A view of St. Bernard's Well—evening. 48×60 in.
	208	Moonlight. 20×26 in.
	286	Poultry from Nature. 23×26 in.
1824	61	A distant view of Pevensey Bay, the landing place of King William the Conqueror. 75×111 in.
	150	View on the Thames near Gravesend. 34×41 in.
	164	Landscape. 20×24 in.
	222	Road scene. 30×26 in.
1825	74	A view near Norwich. 19×23 in.
1826	30	A grove scene. 31×36 in.
	162	A grove scene. 31×28 in.
	364	View on the River Yare. 36×42 in.
	366	The salmon fishery. 42×51 in.
1827	53	Landscape and cattle. 42×52 in.
	159	Landscape. 38×42 in.
1829	249	Landscape and cattle. 25×30 in.
	479	Fishing boats. 19×23 in.
	481	The ferry boat. 19×23 in.
	507	Landscape with cattle. 28×35 in.
1830	149	View on the coast of Sussex. 26×31 in.
	349	View in the Highlands. 42×50 in.
1831	217	Haymaking scene. 28×34 in.
	421	Lane scene near Norwich. 44×39 in.
	467	The travelling tinker. 44×39 in.

EXHIBITS AT ROYAL ACADEMY

Year	*Subject*
1814	Scene near Norwich.
1818	Forest scene—evening.
1819	Sheep crossing the brook—morning.
1821	Landscape and cattle.
1822	Grove scene.
	View at Whitlingham near Norwich.
	View of Ban An, from the island on Loch Katrine (*vide* Scott's *The Lady of the Lake*).
1823	Cottage scene.
	View of Yarmouth Quay.

EXHIBITS AT THE SOCIETY OF PAINTERS IN OIL AND WATER-COLOURS

Year	*Subject*
1818	A landscape.
	A view near Norwich.
	A view on the River Yare.
	A road scene.
1820	London from the Surrey side of Waterloo Bridge.

EXHIBITS AT THE SOCIETY OF BRITISH ARTISTS

Year	*Subject*
1824	St. Benet's Abbey and Mill, Norfolk.
	Grove scene—autumn evening.
	Cottage scene, Baddow, Essex.
1825	Shipping.
	Cottage scene.
	Landscape.
1829	Ruins of an abbey.
	A marine view.
	A river scene.
1830	Scene in Norfolk.
	Travelling tinker.
	Landscape and cattle.

EXHIBITION OF NORWICH SCHOOL PICTURES

Norwich Castle Museum and Art Galleries, October, 1927

OIL-PAINTINGS

No.	*Subject*
120	Yarmouth Quay. 30×40 in.
121	Ship building at Greenwich. 12×16 in.
122	A woodman's cottage (painted in 1827). $20 \times 15\frac{3}{4}$ in.
123	A gipsy encampment. $10 \times 12\frac{1}{2}$ in.
124	The travelling tinker. $39\frac{1}{2} \times 49\frac{1}{2}$ in.
125	Sea piece. $19\frac{1}{4} \times 26\frac{1}{2}$ in.
126	Landscape with mule, pedlar and figures. $16\frac{1}{2} \times 23$ in.
127	The travelling pedlar. $34\frac{1}{4} \times 43\frac{1}{2}$ in.
128	Fish auction at Yarmouth. 40×50 in.
129	Landscape (signed and dated 1829—exhibited British Institution 1829). $29\frac{1}{2} \times 24\frac{1}{2}$ in.

WATER-COLOURS

287	Sandlings Ferry (signed and dated 1822). $5\frac{1}{4} \times 8$ in.
288	Pencil drawing. $8\frac{3}{4} \times 6\frac{1}{4}$ in.

VINCENT'S CONTRIBUTION TO THE NORWICH EXHIBITIONS

Year	*Subject*
1811	Drawing and a painting in oils.
1812	Cottage and Landscape (both after Crome).
1813	Bishopgate Bridge.
	View of the city, near Heigham.
	Still life.
	Views in Heigham (2).

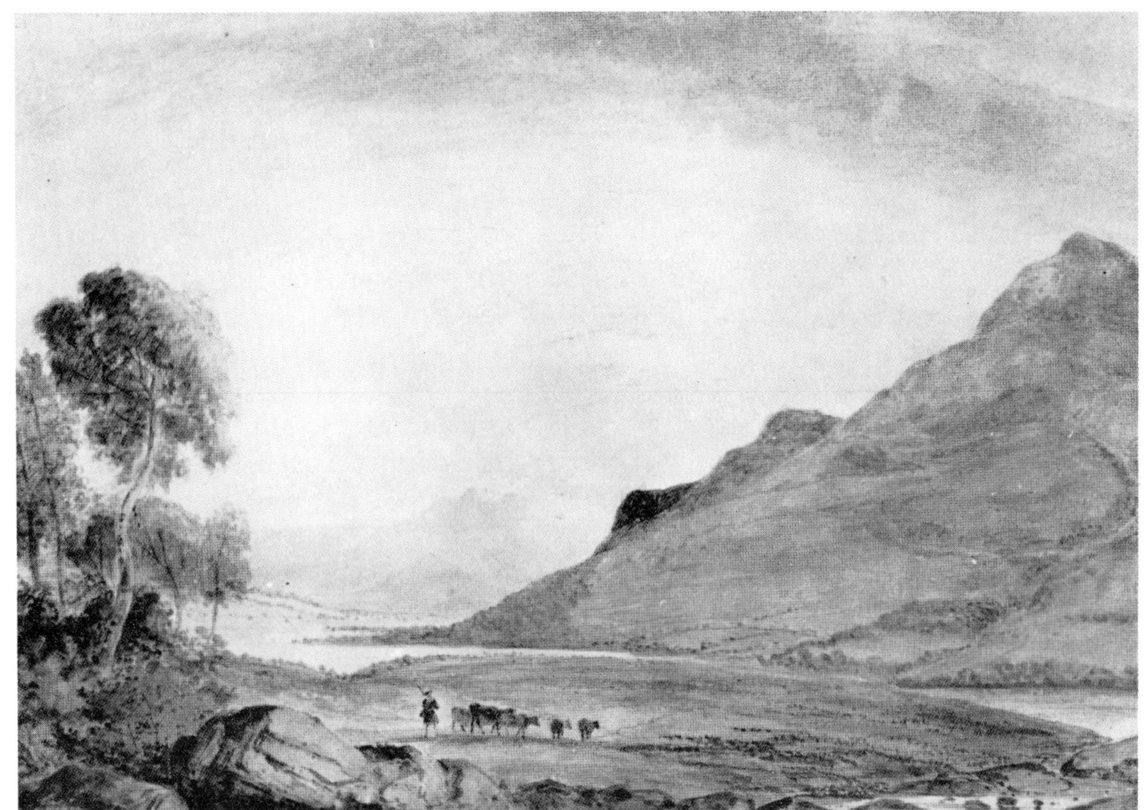

George Vincent, 1831 *View in the Highlands* *Water-colour*

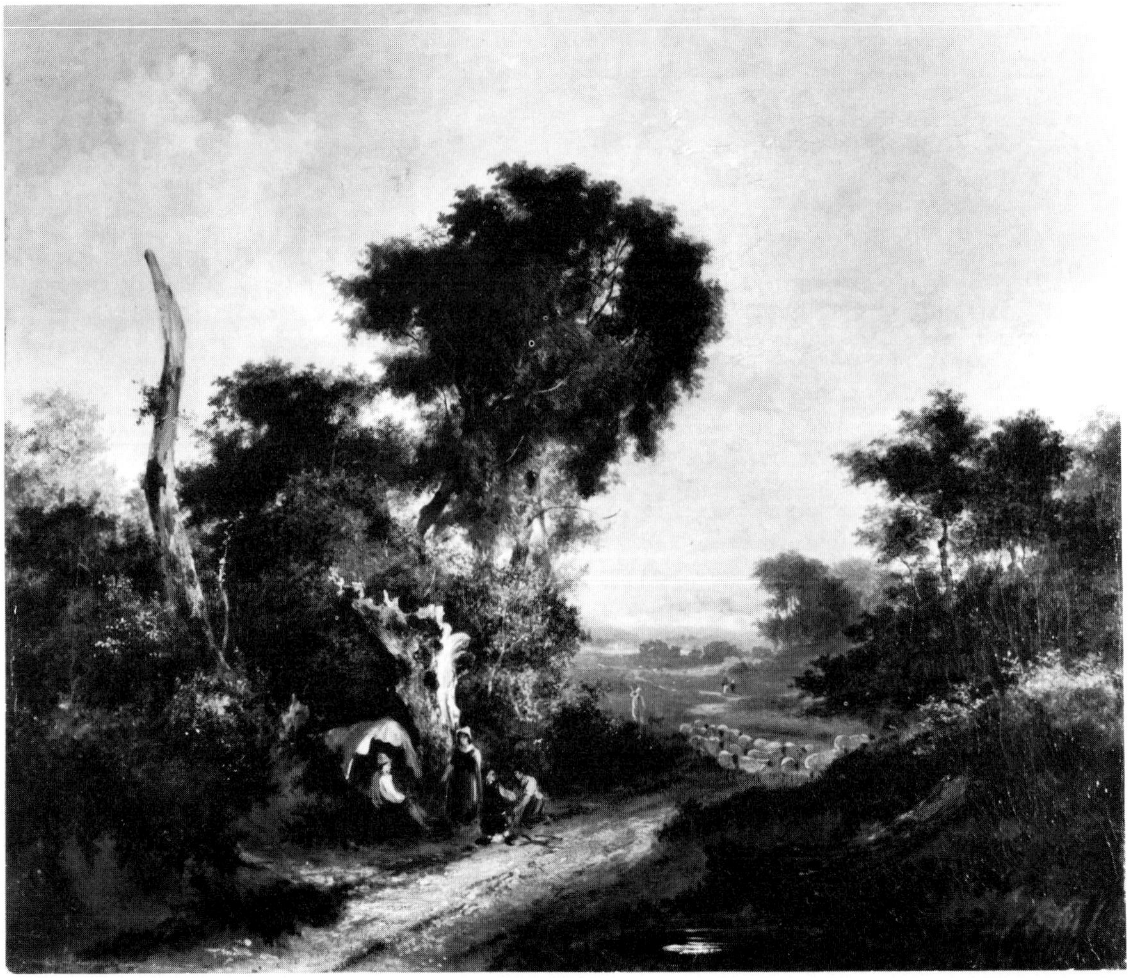

George Vincent, 1831 (one of his last recorded paintings) *Oil on canvas*

1813 Cottage at Hellesdon.
Sketch from Nature—Trowse.
1814 View in Postwick Grove.
View at Trowse Newton.
View of Norwich.
View on St. Augustine's Road.
Landscape—evening.
View near Fye Bridge.
View on St. Martin's River (2).
View of Carrow from the Foundry Bridge.
View on Mousehold Heath and five sketches, etc.
1815 Landscape and cattle—storm approaching.
View at Heigham (2).
A cow.
View at Thorpe (2).
View on the Norwich River.
Postwick Grove.
1816 Landscape and cattle—evening.
Road scene going to Whitlingham.
View near Norwich.
House on St. Martin's River.
Landscape near Little Baddow, Essex.
View at Windsor.
View near Ingatestone, Essex.
View from Bishopsgate Bridge.
Shelford Bridge—morning.
View at Little Baddow, Essex.
Forest scene.
Thorpe.
View in Suffolk.
Old houses at Heigham.
Ruins at Surlingham.
1817 View on the Yare—afternoon.
River scene.
Brighton Beach.
View from Whitlingham.
Scene near Whitlingham.
1818 Forest scene—evening.
Cottage scene.
View at Thorpe.
Landscape and cattle (2).
Lakenham Bridge.
View on the Yare.
1820 Sheep crossing a brook.
Landscape and cattle.
1821 Landscape and cattle.
Dutch Fair, Yarmouth Beach.
Bridge at Bracklin.
Hawthorn Den, on the North Esk (formerly the residence of Drummond, the poet and historian).
Yarmouth Beach.
Fishing boats on the Firth of Clyde—morning.
Coast scene, Isle of Wight.
1822 Grove scene.
View of Ben An, from the island of Loch Katrine.
Road scene (2).
View on the Yare.
1823 River scene.
Cottage scene.

Year	Subject
1825	Landscape.
	Entrance to Loch Katrine.
	Highlanders spearing salmon.
	Moonlight.
1828	Sea piece.
	Sketch—sunset.
	Farmyard.
	Norfolk scenery.
	Scene on the Yare.
	Scene at Trowse.
1831	A landscape.

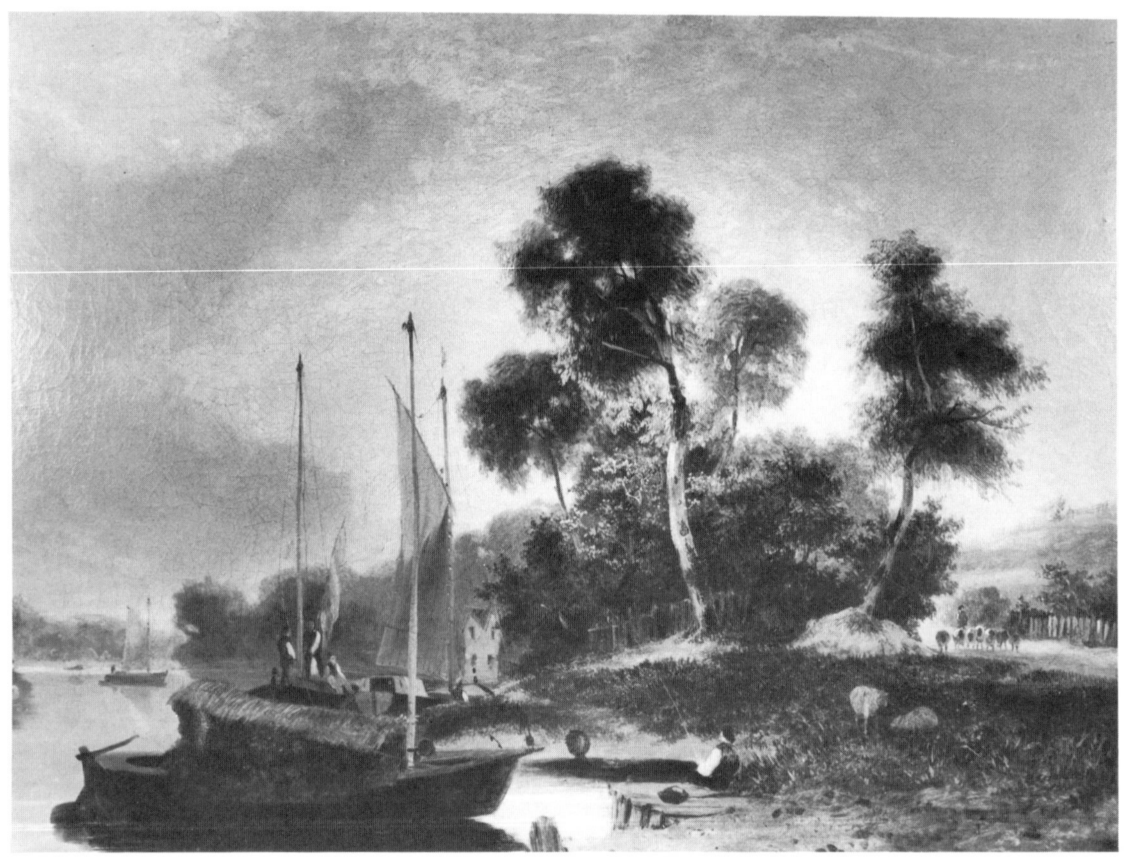

George Vincent *View on the Yare, near Norwich* *Oil on canvas* 15 × 21 *in.*
A larger version of this painting is in the Norwich Art Gallery

ROBERT LADBROOKE

(1769-1842)

1769 The circumstances of Robert Ladbrooke's upbringing are rather vague; he is said to have been related to a Sir Robert Ladbrooke who was Lord Mayor of London in 1748. We do know that he became apprenticed to a Mr. White, an artist, painter and engraver. Whilst an apprentice, he became friendly with John Crome and they took on a small room in which they painted. Crome painted landscapes, Ladbrooke portraits. Alas, our artist had little patronage.

1793 As we have already seen, J. Crome and R. Ladbrooke married sisters. Robert Ladbrooke married Mary Berney on the 3rd October, 1793. It was presumably on his marriage that he purchased a house at Scoles Green (named after William Scoles, who lived in the fifteenth century). It was this house to which Joseph Stannard repaired for his lessons. Regrettably, the house was demolished a few years ago.

Ladbrooke persevered in his art, both as a teacher and observer of Nature. His exhibits at the Norwich Society included many Welsh subjects, based on his visit with Crome
1804 in the year 1804.

An ability to recognise a Master painting enabled Ladbrooke to successfully buy and sell paintings. Indeed, at a later date he actually had a shop from which he did his dealing and frame-making.

1807 In 1807 Robert Ladbrooke had the misfortune to lose his first wife. The family left consisted of four boys and one daughter:

Robert, who did not paint;
Henry, born April, 1800, died November, 1864, Landscape painter;
John Berney, born 31st October, 1803, died July, 1869, Landscape painter;
Frederick, died October, 1865, painter of genre and Landscape.

1809 By 1809 Robert Ladbrooke was nominated president of the Norwich Society, Robert Dixon being his deputy. To the Exhibition that year he sent several paintings executed in Suffolk.

1816 So the years of painting and exhibiting continued unabated until 1816, when Ladbrooke had a disagreement with Crome and others. The result was the secession with Robert Ladbrooke, John Thirtle, Joseph Stannard, and many others withdrawing from the original Society and exhibiting on their own in a hall on Theatre Plain, Norwich.

In 1818 John Berney Ladbrooke and his brother, Henry, both exhibited with their father, but the new Exhibition gradually lost ground, most of the exhibitors returning to the original group.

1821 This very disturbing time was broken by Robert's determination to publish a series of views of Norfolk churches. Between 1821 and 1822, with the help of John Berney Ladbrooke, he lithographed in five volumes some 700 Norfolk churches. The quality of the work reflects the magnitude of the task.

1824 By 1824 J. B. Crome had become president of the Norwich Society and intimated that the Society would be pleased to have back the former exhibitors. Robert Ladbrooke, to show that there was no ill-feeling, forwarded two works.

1825 In 1825 Robert Ladbrooke lost his second wife at the age of 58 years. The effect was to make him rather a recluse, though he visited friends from time to time. A letter preserved in the British Museum relates to a visit to a friend of his by the name of Rising.

T. M. Rising, Esq.

Dear Sir,

I have sent you the sketch of the work on the Beach, and a small one of the Village of Horsey, you'll receive them safe. They are the humble efforts I made during my pleasant visit made at your house. If they give you any amusement I shall feel happy in being the means of any gratification. Be so kind a friend and pray remember me to that good and generous lady Mrs. Rising. Tell her I shall never forget her sincere attentions.

I hope the frames will please as I think my son has done them with some —— and they seem to suit the pictures—you will please return the case—pray remember me to Mr. K. Rising and family, and believe me

I remain your humble servant,

R. LADBROOKE.

Robert Ladbrooke lived on for many years in his house at Scoles Green. It must have been a great joy to him in his last years to observe the success of his three sons, John Berney, Henry and Frederick.

1838 It appears that towards the end of his life Robert Ladbrooke owned the Shakespeare Tavern, and in 1838 purchased a property in Ber Street, for which he paid £205 cash. He is said to have left a considerable amount of real estate.

1842 It was on 11th October, 1842, that Robert Ladbrooke passed away. He was buried in St. Stephen's Churchyard.

THE PAINTINGS

The main characteristic of Robert Ladbrooke's work is a certain heaviness—one might say gauntness. Whilst this produces a certain atmosphere in his work, he does sacrifice the elements in a painting which make it an entity. The dark palette is often in evidence, and the lights gentle and mellow. The most effective paintings by Robert Ladbrooke are his evening sunsets. These are usually painted with considerable verve and excellent tone. In the Castle Museum at Norwich is the *Foundry Bridge*, *Mundesley Beach*, *Yarmouth Beach*, and the small landscape panel with delicate mauve tones. *Foundry Bridge* is quite an important work. In the sky are purple tones and at the sky line touches of light. The colours tend towards heaviness, with the shadows being thinly painted. Some of his early work is very eighteenth century in character. One sees the rounder Wilson cloud, and the Wynant type figures. These early works tend to be of a lighter palette than his later work.

It would seem that he introduced black into many of his colours and had a partiality for the earth colours. Generally, he paints with considerable paint, as indeed do most of the Norwich School. He uses plenty of impasto touches, leaving some passages thinly painted.

Ladbrooke, in common with his contemporary John Crome, possibly held that an overpainted figure would detract from the picture as a whole.

At the end of the nineteenth century, and possibly later, I believe many of Henry Ladbrooke's works were sold as being the work of Robert Ladbrooke. As previously stated, Robert Ladbrooke had a good eye for a picture, his insistence on Henry Ladbrooke becoming a painter being fully justified.

He introduced a classical French influence into Norwich School painting, particularly in the treatment of skies and foliage. His work particularly influenced his sons.

One of the mysteries of the Norwich School is the whereabouts of Robert Ladbrooke's pictures, if, indeed, they do exist in number. Despite his numerous exhibits and relatively long life few of his works are to be seen.

EXHIBITS AT THE NORWICH EXHIBITIONS

Year	*Subject*
1804	A sea piece (body colour).
	Distant view of Trowse from Thorpe Grove.
	View of the fellmongers.
	View of the cathedral, Norwich, from Thorpe Grove.
	View of Norwich Cathedral, taken from Sandlings Ferry.
	View in the Vale of Llangollen, Wales.
	Conway Castle, Wales.
	Vale of Llanrwst, Wales.
	Study from Nature, North Wales.
	General view of Chepstow Castle.
	North end of Tintern Abbey.
	View from Lowestoft, Suffolk.
	Norwich Castle.
1806	View in the park at Westwick—seat of J. B. Petre, Esq.
	View in Westwick Park.
	Wood scene.
	Portrait of Lord Nelson (after the large one in St. Andrew's Hall, for the engraver).
	Lord Nelson in time of action.
	A shed at Thorpe.
	Sketch on Thorpe Meadow.
	View at Bramerton.
	Scene in Brooke, near Norwich.
	View at Brundall, Norfolk.
	The remains of Walsingham Abbey.
	View of Carrow Abbey.
	View taken near the seat of P. M. Martineau, Esq., Trowse.
	View near Worsted.
	View of Mundesley.
	View of Yarmouth Jetty.
	Sketch of Yarmouth Beach from the Old Pier Head.
	Sea piece—a swell.
	View from the Haven's Mouth from the Old Pier at Gorleston.
	Llanrwst Bridge.
	View of the Vale of Llanrwst.
	Goodrich Castle (two views).
	Conway Castle.
	View near Conway.
	Inn at Tintern.
	Interior of Tintern Abbey.
1807	Binham Abbey.
	Walsingham Abbey.
	Norwich from Trowse (a sketch).
	Composition.
	Sketch in oils.
	S.W. view of Westwick House—seat of J. B. Petre.
	Helsing Hall—seat of the Rev. R. Brown (two pictures).
	A study from Nature.
	Woodman—from Nature.
	View in Wales.
	Tintern Abbey.
	Richard and Kate.
	Evening.
	Cells at Tintern Abbey.
1808	An overshot mill, Llangollen, North Wales.
	Sea storm.
	Sea beach.
	Cottage at Sheringham.

Year	*Subject*
1808	Caister Castle.
	Ruins at Walsingham.
	View of Earlham Bridge.
	View at Brundall.
	View of the castle and cathedral from the Golden Ball Lane.
	Evening scene from Carrow Abbey.
	Distant view of the cathedral.
	Twilight.
	Two landscape compositions.
	Giles.
	Sketch on the Thorpe River.
	Three sketches from Nature.
1809	The recruits departure.
	Domestic happiness.
	Fishermen saving the wreck of a ship.
	Girl knitting at cottage door.
	Ships stranded on the beach near Cromer.
	Finding the anchor.
	Trowse Mill (sketch in oils).
	View of the city from Thorpe Meadow.
	View of a farmhouse in Suffolk.
	View of Norwich from Carrow Abbey.
	View of the Market Place.
	View on the Ipswich River.
	View on the Kind Street River.
	Five studies from Nature.
1810	A cottage with a girl fetching water, in North Wales.
	A waterfall in North Wales.
	An overshot mill in North Wales.
	Romantic tree in Lord Rosebery's park.
	Sketch of cottage near Aylsham.
	Sketch of an old shed.
	Cottage by the Old Riverside at Heigham.
	Scene near the telegraph on Mousehold.
	Wood scene near Crostwick White Horse.
	Repairing a wherry, with part of Carrow Abbey.
	View of the cottages near the New Bridge.
	View from St. Benedict's Road.
	View from St. Giles' Road.
	Sketch on Caston Heath.
	View on Mousehold Heath.
	Mackerel market on the beach at Yarmouth.
	Sailor boy just escaping shipwreck.
	Jeffries left on the Island of Sombiero.
	The fowl stealer.
	A composition.
	A view in Italy (a pencil sketch).
1811	Landscape and figures.
	Road scene with gipsies.
	A landscape composition.
	A scene on the grounds of R. Marsham, Esq.
	Wood scene at R. Marsham's, Esq.
	Scene on the road to R. Marsham's, Esq.
	A distant view of the cathedral.
	Portrait of a cow.
	Sketch of the Foundry Bridge.
	Cottages with clouds dispersing after rain.
	Caister Castle.
	View on the Aylsham Road.

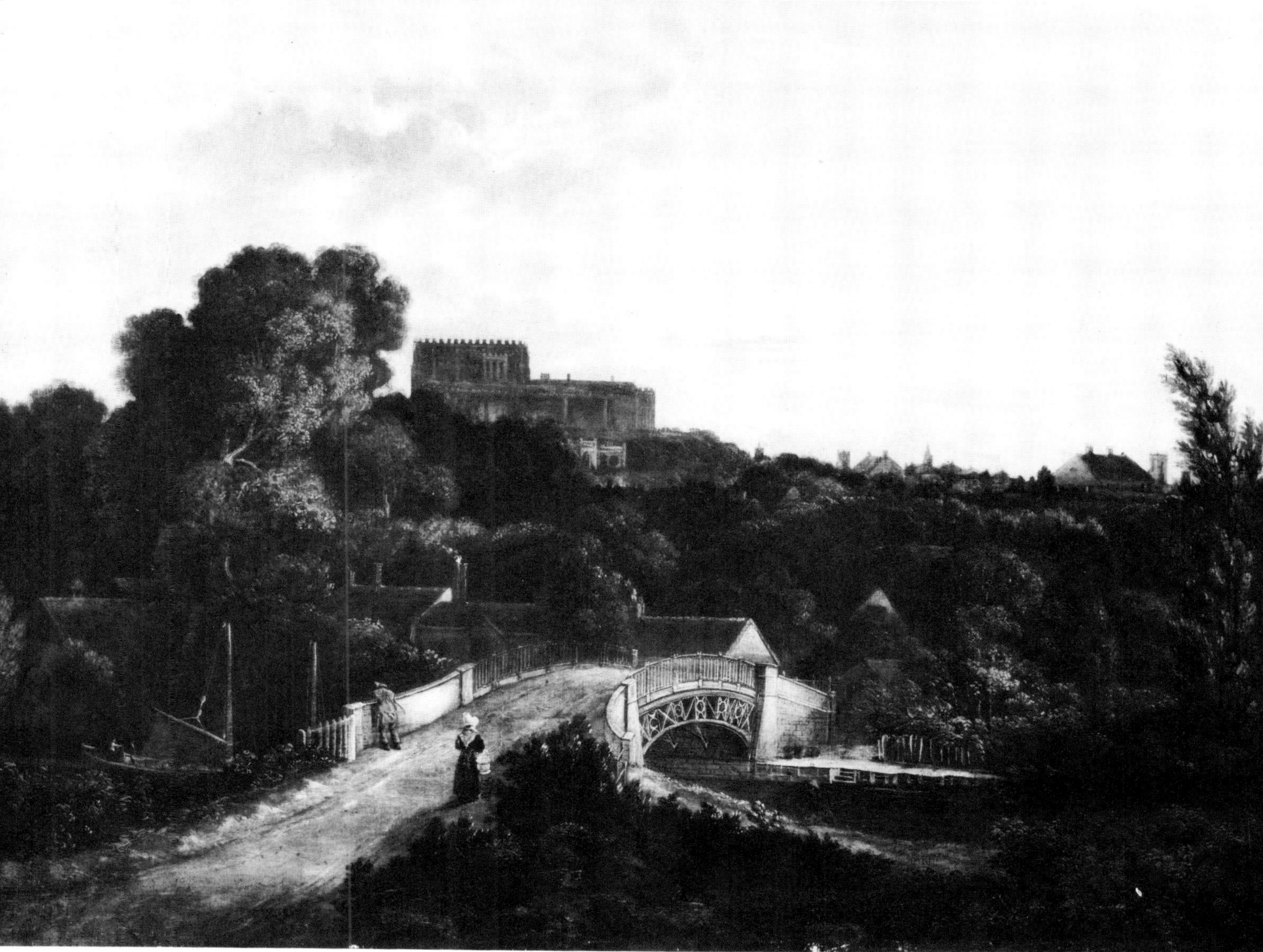

Robert Ladbrooke — *Foundry Bridge, c. 1815* — *Oil on canvas* $26\frac{1}{4} \times 38\frac{3}{4}$ *in.*

A very Gaspar-like composition

Year	*Subject*
1811	View of the castle.
	View of Trowse from Thorpe Meadow.
	A sketch on Mousehold Heath.
	Ruins of a castle.
	Hearing the lesson.
	Whitingham White House.
	A barn in the inn yard at Aylsham.
	A cottage near Sir R. Durrant's.
	A view of Thorpe.
	Sketch of the public gardens at Thorpe.
	View on Felbrigg Heath.
	Gooseberries.
	Grapes.
1812	A scene near Gorston Woodrow.
	Landscape and cattle (2).
	A scene on the Lodden Road.
	Trowse Hill, looking from the bridge.
	An interior with figures.
	View on the Thorpe Road (2).
	Gardener's cottage.
	View from Richmond Hill Gardens, near Bracondale.
	View from Mr. Ladbrooke's House.
	Wheat setters.
	The bark peelers—a study from Nature.
	Farmyard, with Giles feeding pigs.
	A view near Tivoli.
	A view near Buxton.
	Landscape composition in style of Wilson.
1813	A scene in North Wales.
	Landscape—midday.
	A view of Caister Castle.
	Landscape—sunset.
1814	Landscape composition.
	Landscape—morning.
	Landscape and castle.
	Landscape—evening.
1815	Foundry Bridge with the castle in the distance—evening.
	View of a part of the city, looking towards Bracondale—morning.

THEATRE PLAIN EXHIBITION

Year	*Subject*
1816	Merry-making, with a view of Norwich from Richmond Hill Gardens.
	View of Sandlings Ferry from Bishops Bridge.
	A misty morning, with cattle on the banks of a river.
	Figures and ruins.
	A view of the River Clitumnus, Italy.
	A calm, with fishermen on the beach.
	Sea beach with fishermen.
	Landscape and cattle.
	Conversation.
	Landscape in the style of Gainsborough.
	View on the River Dee—morning.
	A study of Nature.
	Portrait of a gentleman.
	Portrait of a young artist (may be the portrait of J. Stannard when a boy). $16 \times 12\frac{3}{4}$ in.
1817	Landscape and figures (2).

Year	Subject
1817	Corps de Garde halting at a cottage.
	Dutch fishing boats.
	Brace of partridges.
	A view on the Norwich River with figures bathing.
	A portrait of G. Harvey, Esq., M.P.
	A pheasant.
	A landscape in the style of Poussin.
	The marriage of St. Catherine.
	A cottage near Scottow.
	Ruins near Lincoln.
1818	Landscape and cattle—sunset.
	An ancient bridge at Verona.
	Landscape and figures.
	Ploughing.
	View near Ber Street, Norwich.
	A dead hare.
	A landscape composition—windy effect.
	A landscape composition—heat effect.
	The gamesters.
	Landscape—morning—after rain.
	A view on the coast of Holland.
	Landscape and ruins.
	Spring.
	Landscape and cattle.
	Autumn.
	A view of Tivoli.
1824	Landscape and cattle—a composition.
1825	A grove scene—Stratton.
1828	A landscape.
1829	A road scene.
1830	Westwick House.
	View of Langley Hall.
	A study from Nature.
1831	A landscape.
1832	A squall at sea.
1833	A sketch on the beach.
	The skirts of a wood.
	Sketch from Nature—after rain.

EXHIBITS AT THE ROYAL ACADEMY

Year	Subject
1804	A distant view of Trowse, taken from Thorpe Grove, near Norwich.
1808	Recruiting sergeant disputing with a villager.
1811	A view on Mousehold Heath.
1812	A landscape.
1815	A landscape.

EXHIBITS AT THE BRITISH INSTITUTION

Year	Subject
1811	A view on Heigham River, Norwich. 33 × 42 in.
1812	A scene on the road to Aylsham. 26 × 27 in.
	A road scene with gipsies. 28 × 24 in.
1813	A distant view of Norwich Cathedral. 28 × 36 in.

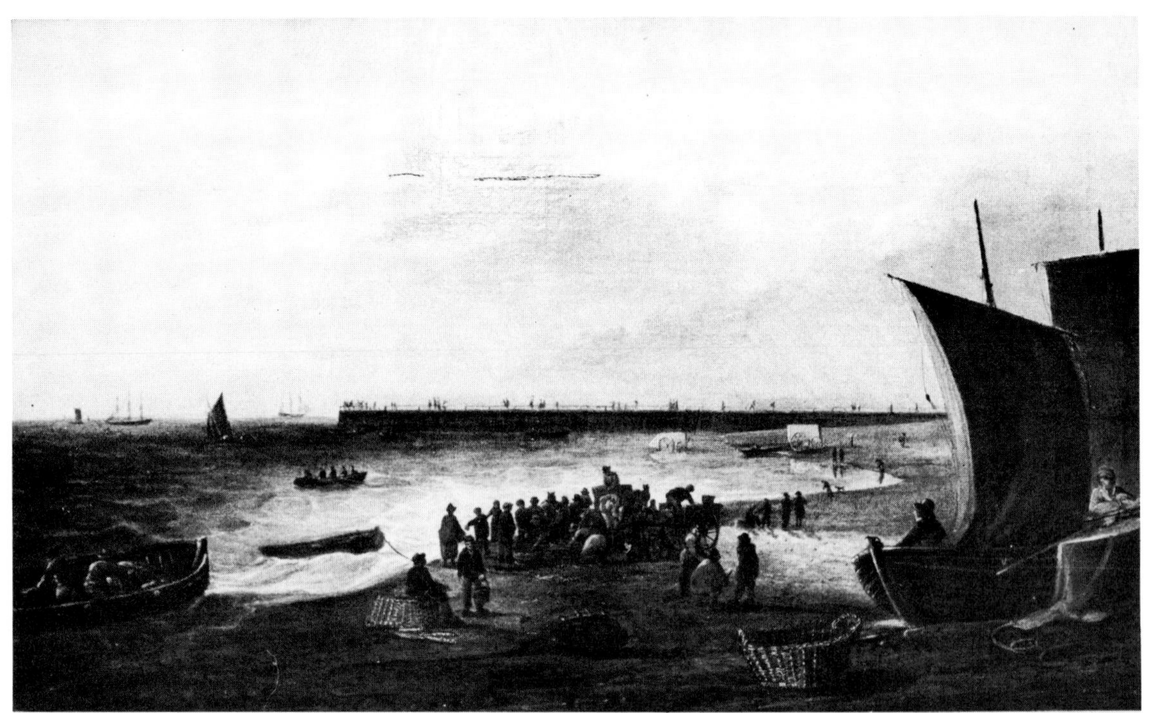

Robert Ladbrooke *Yarmouth Jetty* *Oil*

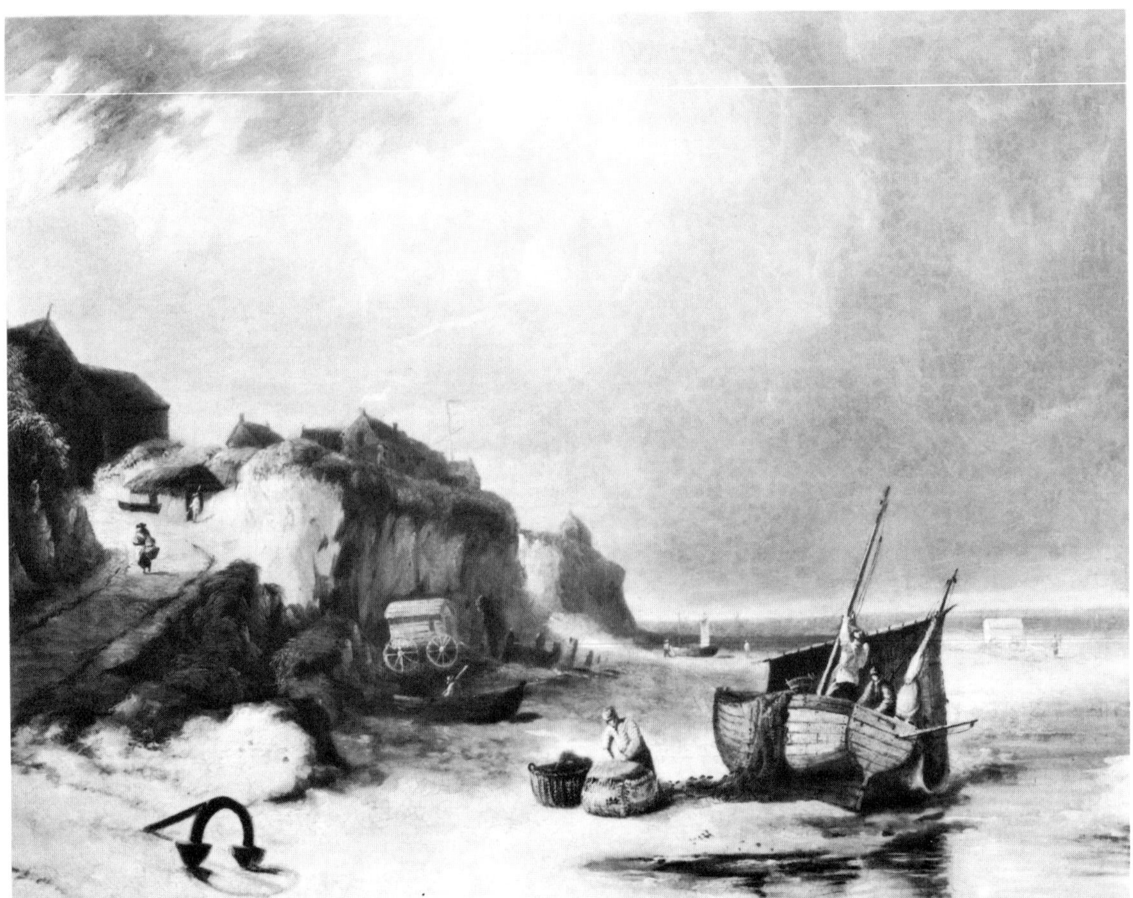

Robert Ladbrooke *Beach Scene, Mundesley* *Oil* $19\frac{1}{4} \times 24$ *in.*

No.	Subject
1819	A landscape composition. 45 × 60 in.
	A view of the Foundry Bridge, Norwich. 51 × 61 in.
1820	A landscape composition. 36 × 40 in.
1822	A landscape—cottage on Scottow Common, Norfolk. 18 × 22 in.
	Two others.

EXHIBITION OF NORWICH SCHOOL PICTURES

Norwich Castle Museum and Art Galleries, October, 1927

OIL-PAINTINGS

No.	Subject
57	Waltham Abbey. 16 × 23 in.
58	Foundry Bridge, with the castle in the distance—evening (1815). 28¾ × 38½ in.
59	Landscape. 28 × 36 in.
60	Old oaks in Buxton Park. 24¾ × 29¾ in.
61	Entrance to Yarmouth Harbour. 23½ × 37½ in.

WATER-COLOURS, DRAWINGS, ETC.

No.	Subject
191	River scene. 6 × 8½ in.
192	River scene. 8 × 13½ in.
193	River scene (sepia). 11½ × 16¾ in.

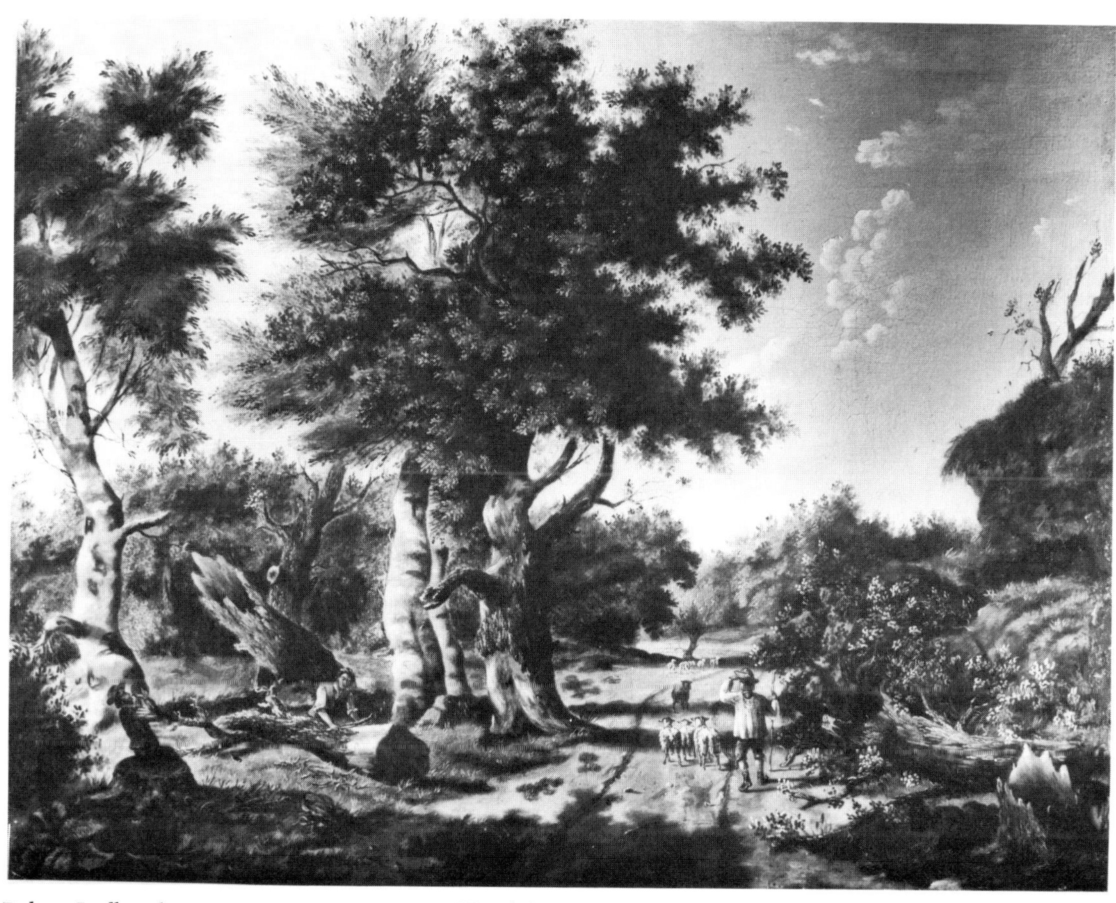

Robert Ladbrooke *Wood Scene* *Oil on canvas* 28 × 36*in.*
Possibly exhibited at the Norwich Society c.1806

HENRY LADBROOKE

(1800-1869)

1800 Henry Ladbrooke was born in April, 1800, the son of Robert Ladbrooke, landscape
painter. Little is known of his early life apart from the fact that Charles Hodgson was
one of his school masters. Leaving school he wished to enter the Church, but his father
prevailed upon him to become a painter. He was placed with his uncle, John Crome, for
a short time. Possibly he also worked with his father. By the age of fifteen he was
sufficiently accomplished to exhibit at the Norwich Society. Here he exhibited a mixed
1830 group of paintings, surprisingly few landscapes being among them. However, about 1830
he turned his full attention to landscapes. Besides his painting, he established an
extensive teaching practice, teaching at Stalham, Dilham, North Walsham, Cromer,
Holt, Dereham, Weasenham, Castle Acre, Walsingham, King's Lynn and Bury St.
Edmunds. His tolerant and pleasant manner is said to have endeared him to his pupils.

1840 About 1840 he toured Yorkshire and the North of England. As a result of this tour he
painted the *View of Bolton Abbey* now in the Castle Museum, Norwich. A further view
near Knaresborough also resulted from this trip. Possibly later visits to Yorkshire took
place, for we find a *View of the Footbridge, Houghton-in-the-Dale*, exhibited in Norwich
1848 in 1848, followed by *View on the Swale, Yorkshire*, in 1856. It is quite possible that the
1856 works of Henry Ladbrooke were at this time eagerly sought after, for an *Overshot Mill*,
exhibited towards the end of his life, was catalogued at £78 15s., a considerable sum in
those days.

It was about 1850-60 that he wrote his famous *Dottings*. These were simply notes written in an exercise book, and not published until long after his death. He explained the relationship between Joseph Stannard and John Crome and elucidated on the differences which caused the break-up of the first Norwich Society.

Towards the end of his life he is recorded as living at King's Lynn, from which town
1868 he dispatched *Moonlight on the Ouse* to the Norwich Exhibition of 1868.

It was possibly to be with his daughter in old age that he returned to Norwich, and
1869 passed away on 18th November, 1869, being buried in Norwich Cemetery.

THE PAINTINGS

Starting with small paintings, largely genre, Henry Ladbrooke graduated by the time he was thirty years of age to quite large landscapes, very carefully executed; in fact, Henry Ladbrooke is the most detailed painter in the whole of the East Anglian School. His tree work is characterised by many touches on the bole and the pencilling of innumerable leaves, contributing a most verdant type of foliage imaginable. With his foliage he is generous to a fault, simply delighting in their rendering, the foliage often being taken to the top of the picture. His distances are usually interesting, and one finds the eye carried quite comfortably from object to object. He loves an old thatched cottage nestling amongst his beautifully painted trees, with perhaps some cottagers approaching. Incidentally, his figures are very similar to those of his father. He loves to depict grasses, perhaps falling slightly over the edge of a bank. His skies are well composed often containing a touch of pink, the brushwork being sure. Due to his extensive teaching practice he had only limited time for painting. This, together with the great care lavished on his works, resulted in his output being relatively small.

EXHIBITS AT NORWICH

Year	Subject
1818	A group of flowers (at Theatre Plain).
	The interesting story (at Sir B. Wrench's Court).
1821	A group of flowers
	Domestic employment
	The pancake.
1823	Landscape.
	Buzzard and prey
	Still life.
1824	Virgin, child and St. Elizabeth.
	Flowers.
1829	North Walsham Cross and market place.
	Group of flowers from Nature.
1830	Lane scene, Knapton.
	Scene in Sheringham Park.
1831	Three landscapes.
1833	Weybourne, Norfolk.

EXHIBITION OF NORWICH SCHOOL PICTURES

Norwich Castle Museum and Art Galleries, October, 1927

OIL PAINTINGS

No.	Subject
48	The old sea bank, Lynn—moonlight. $19\frac{1}{2} \times 30\frac{1}{2}$ in.
49	Scene near Walsingham. $39\frac{1}{2} \times 29\frac{1}{2}$ in.
50	Gipsy boy. $23\frac{1}{2} \times 10\frac{1}{2}$ in.
189	Haddon Hall (pencil sketch). $12\frac{1}{4} \times 19\frac{1}{4}$ in.

AT THE BRITISH INSTITUTION

Year	Subject
1834	North Walsham, Norfolk. 24×30 in.
1835	View in Norfolk. 27×35 in.
1836	Beeston, Norfolk. 27×34 in.

FOURTEENTH EXHIBITION OF THE NORFOLK AND NORWICH SOCIETY OF ARTISTS, 1818

No.	Subject
4	Group of flowers.
52	The interesting story.

SEVENTEENTH EXHIBITION OF THE NORWICH SOCIETY OF ARTISTS, 1821

No.	Subject
8	A group of flowers.
75	The pancake.
79	Domestic employment.

NINETEENTH EXHIBITION OF THE NORWICH SOCIETY OF ARTISTES, 1823

No.	Subject
25	Landscape.
60	Buzzard and prey from Nature.
85	Still life.

TWENTIETH EXHIBITION OF THE NORWICH SOCIETY OF ARTISTS, 1824

No.	Subject
19	Virgin, child, and Elizabeth.
28	Flowers.

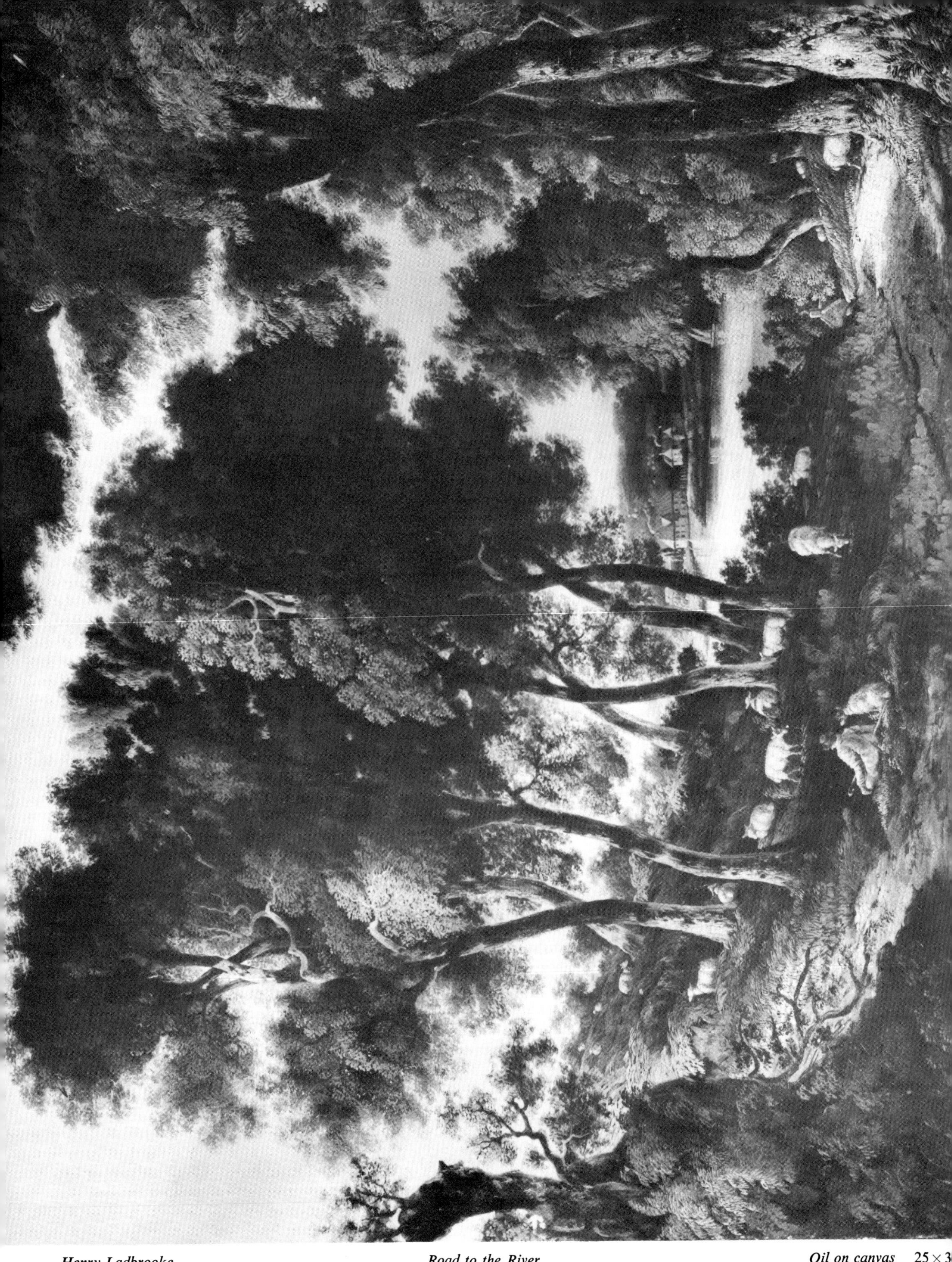

Henry Ladbrooke *Road to the River* *Oil on canvas* 25×3

TWENTY-SECOND EXHIBITION OF THE WORKS OF THE NORFOLK AND SUFFOLK INSTITUTION FOR THE PROMOTION OF THE FINE ARTS, 1828

No.	*Subject*
120	Dutch fishing boats—fresh breeze.

TWENTY-THIRD EXHIBITION OF THE WORKS OF THE NORFOLK AND SUFFOLK INSTITUTION FOR THE PROMOTION OF THE FINE ARTS, 1829

No.	*Subject*
74	North Walsham Cross and market-place.
124	Road scene, Stanninghall.

TWENTY-FOURTH EXHIBITION OF THE WORKS OF THE NORFOLK AND SUFFOLK INSTITUTION FOR THE PROMOTION OF THE FINE ARTS, 1830

No.	*Subject*
114	Lane scene, Knapton.
157	Scene in Sherringham Park, looking over Waybourne.

TWENTY-FIFTH EXHIBITION OF THE WORKS OF THE NORFOLK AND SUFFOLK INSTITUTION FOR THE PROMOTION OF THE FINE ARTS, 1831

No.	*Subject*
65	Landscape.
71	Landscape.
182	Landscape.

TWENTY-SEVENTH EXHIBITION OF THE WORKS OF THE NORFOLK AND SUFFOLK INSTITUTION FOR THE PROMOTION OF THE FINE ARTS, 1833

No.	*Subject*
142	Weybourne, Norfolk.

THE FIRST EXHIBITION OF THE NORFOLK AND NORWICH ART UNION, 1839

No.	*Subject*
84	Scene at Knaresborough, from Nature—the spot of the murder committed by Eugene Aram.
173	View from Beeston, Norfolk.

THE FIRST EXHIBITION OF THE NORFOLK AND NORWICH ASSOCIATION FOR THE PROMOTION OF THE FINE ARTS, 1848

No.	*Subject*
177	Scene in Thursford Park, Norfolk.
338	Lime Kiln, Hillington, Norfolk.
254	Lime Kiln, Congham, Norfolk.
273	Foot bridge, Houghton-in-the-Dale.

SECOND EXHIBITION OF THE NORFOLK AND NORWICH ASSOCIATION FOR THE PROMOTION OF THE FINE ARTS

In connexion with The Government School of Design, 1849

No.	*Subject*
61	Pentney Abbey, from Bilney Heath. (£69 in pencil in margin.)
243	Entrance to Riffley Wood. (3— in ink in margin.)
397	Group of trees, Thursford.
409	View on the river Ouse, near Lynn. (6g in ink in margin.)

THIRD EXHIBITION OF THE NORFOLK AND NORWICH ASSOCIATION FOR THE PROMOTION OF THE FINE ARTS, 1852

No.	*Subject*
6	Cromer, Norfolk.

FOURTH EXHIBITION OF THE NORFOLK AND NORWICH ASSOCIATION FOR THE PROMOTION OF THE FINE ARTS, 1853

No.	*Subject*
44	Footbridge over the Nar, Westacre.
48	Sketch on the Witham, Lincoln.

EXHIBITION OF THE NORFOLK AND NORWICH ASSOCIATION FOR THE PROMOTION OF THE FINE ARTS, 1855

No.	*Subject*	£	s.	d.
18	Hardingham, Norfolk.	5	5	0
94	Burnham Thorpe, Norfolk, near the spot where Nelson was born.	14	14	0
117	Gaywood, Norfolk.	5	5	0

EXHIBITION OF THE NORFOLK AND NORWICH FINE ARTS ASSOCIATION AND OF THE PHOTOGRAPGIC SOCIETY, 1856

No.	*Subject*	£	s.	d.
37	On the Swale, Yorkshire.	26	5	0

NORFOLK AND NORWICH FINE ARTS ASSOCIATION EXHIBITION OF THE WORKS OF MODERN ARTISTS, 1860

No.	*Subject*	£	s.	d.
9	Blacksmith's Shop.	12	12	0
31	Fincale Abbey.	15	15	0
113	Pallaw Wood, Durham.	26	5	0
127	The Norfolk Homestead.	21	0	0
143	Heath scene.	21	0	0
154	The Riverside Inn.	12	12	0
176a	Lane scene.	4	4	0

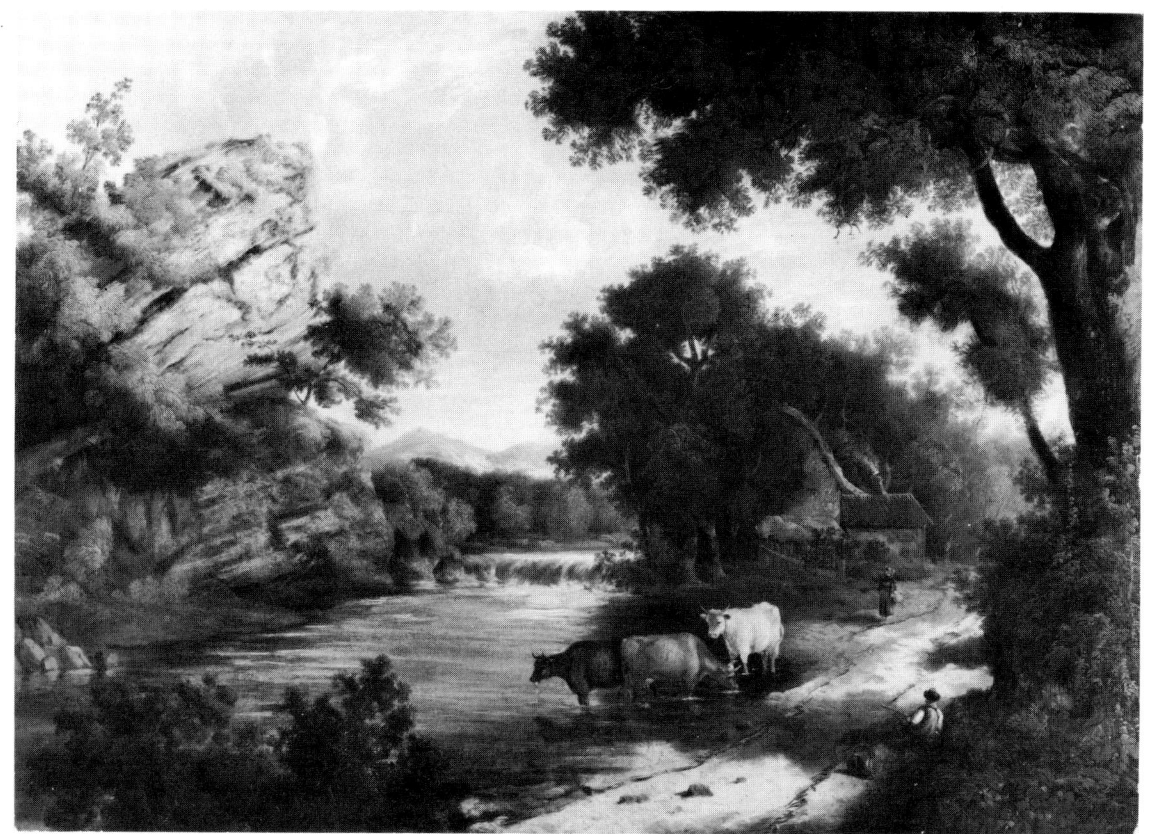

Henry Ladbrooke *View near Knaresborough, Yorkshire* *Oil*

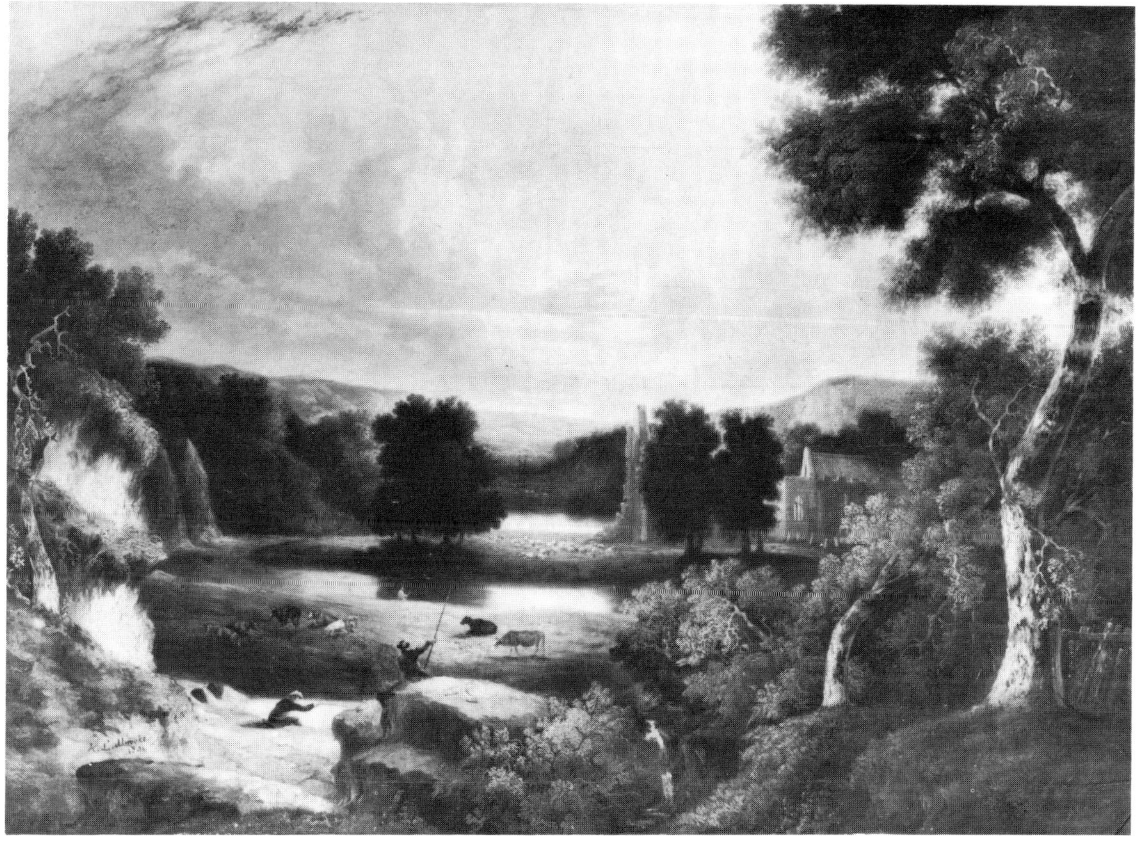

Henry Ladbrooke *Bolton Abbey* *Oil* 35 × 50 *in.*

NORWICH FINE ART ASSOCIATION—EXHIBITION OF WORKS OF ART BY MODERN ARTISTS, 1868

No.	*Subject*	£ s. d.
14	The Ford, near Durham.	36 15 0
44	Moonlight on the Ouse.	15 15 0
63	Overshot Mill.	78 15 0
110	Near Honingham, Norfolk.	50 0 0

NORWICH FINE ART ASSOCIATION SECOND EXHIBITION OF WORKS OF ART BY MODERN ARTISTS, 1869

No.	*Subject*	£ s. d.
58	Scene on the Fal, near Falmouth, from a sketch by the Rev. J. A. Ladbrooke	31 10 0
125	Foot bridge, at Westacre, on the estate of Anthony Hamond, Esq.	15 15 0
149	Wood scene.	26 5 0
175	Near Falmouth—from a sketch by the Rev. J. A. Ladbrooke, B.A.	52 10 0

NORWICH ART LOAN EXHIBITION

in aid of the Fund for the Restoration of the Church of Saint Peter Mancroft, 1878

OIL PAINTINGS

No.	*Subject*	*Lent by*
47	View at Lynn.	Mr. H. M. Vyall.
70	View in Lynn.	Mr. H. M. Vyall.
109	The village smithy.	Thomas Wells, Esq.
126	Landscape with water.	J. C. Chittock, Esq.
409	On the banks of the Coquet.	John Yule, Esq.

SWAFFHAM FINE ART EXHIBITION, 1882

No.	*Subject*	£ s. d.	*Lent by*
55	Redmount, Lynn.	25 0 0	Mr. R. Nurse.

FINE ART EXHIBITION

in aid of the new Norfolk and Norwich Hospital, 1883

No.	*Subject*	*Lent by*
34	Landscape.	Mr. J. C. Chittock.
37	Overshot Mill.	Mr. J. C. Chittock.

NORWICH ART LOAN EXHIBITION

in aid of the fund for the Restoration of St. Peter Mancroft Church, and for the completion of the Churchyard Improvements, 1885

No.	*Subject*	*Lent by*
28	View at Perran-Well near Devoran, Cornwall.	Miss Ladbrooke.
39	Lane scene at Middleton.	W. T. Bensly, Esq., LL.D.
49	The village forge.	T. Wells, Esq.

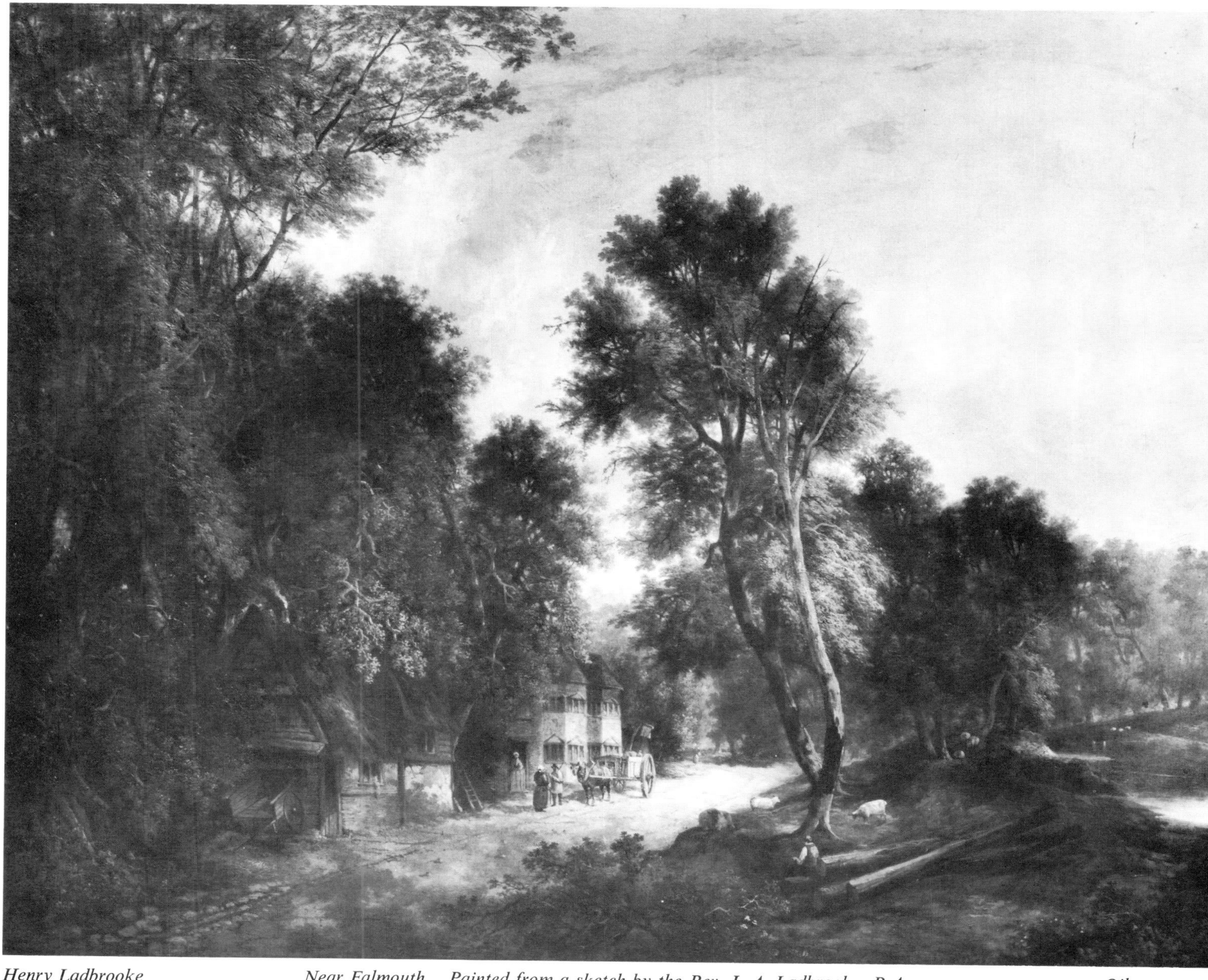

Henry Ladbrooke *Near Falmouth. Painted from a sketch by the Rev. J. A. Ladbrooke, B.A.* *Oil on canvas*

JOHN BERNEY LADBROOKE

(1803-1879)

1803 John Berney Ladbrooke was born the third son of Robert Ladbrooke on 31st October, 1803. Presumably, he was born at 5 Surrey Street, Norwich, where the family were known to be living in 1802. Rather suddenly, John lost his mother in 1807 when he was but four years old.

Little is known of his education—possibly he attended the Grammar School, for his
letters indicate a fair literary understanding. Leaving school, his father placed him with
1818 John Crome. This would be about the year 1818. It is said he studied a year with
Crome, at the end of which he exhibited seven pictures in the Norwich Society Exhibition
of 1818. The illustration (page 146) shows a view at Colney, Norfolk. John Crome
also painted this same view: it is quite possible they visited the spot together.

Having attained a certain proficiency, our painter set up as a landscape painter and drawing master. His father, having developed considerable teaching connections, gave certain of them up in favour of his sons, Henry and John. It will be remembered that Robert Ladbrooke about this time embarked on the considerable task of depicting the seven hundred churches of Norfolk.

1821- John Berney also assisted in this project between the years 1821 and 1832. Undoubtedly
1832 the extensive travelling involved resulted in many opportunities for observing Nature.
Also he commenced work on *Select Views of Norfolk and its Environs*. However, only
two parts were issued, each containing four plates.

1840 In the 1840s, probably in company with his brother Henry, he toured the North of
England and Scotland. The citizens of Norwich had the pleasure of seeing his obser-
1848- vations at the Exhibitions of 1848 and 1849, when he exhibited, amongst others:
1849

Year	*No.*	*Subject*
1848	73	Overshot Mill, Yorkshire.
1848	116	Water course near foot of Snowdon.
1848	163	View on the River Neuse, Lanarkshire.
1849	160	Head of Loch Lomond, Scotland.

John Berney Ladbrooke remained very loyal to his native Norfolk. Whilst he toured England extensively, he never moved his abode to London, as was the wont of most artists. However, he did exhibit there. At the Royal Academy three pictures:

Year	*Subject*
1821	A view near Ipswich.
1822	A view near Crostwick Common, Norfolk.
1843	Heath scene near North Walsham, Norfolk.

and to the British Institution the following:

Year	*Subject*	£	s.	d.
1823	View on Crostwick Common. 34×40 in.			
	Landscape composition. 34×30 in.			
1824	A view near Fellbridge Park, Norfolk. 32×36 in.			
1825	A heath scene. 43×52 in.			
1853	Road scene at Houghton, Norfolk.	21	0	0
1854	Overshot Mill at Ambleside.	31	10	0
1856	Recollections of a road scene in Norfolk.	21	0	0
1859	Easdale Stream, Grasmere, Cumberland.	20	0	0

Besides the above, J. B. Ladbrooke exhibited fifty paintings at the Norwich Society during his lifetime.

1857 Seeking a place for retirement John Berney bought himself a plot of land on Mousehold Heath overlooking the City of Norwich. Here, in 1857, he built his house and called it Ketts Castle Villa. Over the gate entrance he erected an arch and placed his monogram with the date; a similar monogram was built into one of the rear walls. Inside the house his monogram appeared on the fireplace and cast in stained glass windows. The central feature of the house is a tower of modest proportions, which provides an excellent view of the venerable city. Adjacent to the villa is a house said to have been owned by Robert Ladbrooke.

1865 About 1865 a Daguerreotype was taken of J. B. Ladbrooke showing him in his garden, surrounded by his young pupils. In the background there appears a huge structure, not unlike the Crystal Palace. Possibly this was his glasshouse.

Looking at the plate of our artist we see a man of great authority, a broad, scholarly forehead and the appearance of a man capable of concentration. Right up to his passing,
1879 on 10th July, 1879, he continued to paint his beloved Norfolk.

THE PAINTINGS

John Berney Ladbrooke's early works reflect the great influence of John Crome. The pictures have a silvery green appearance, strong cloud lights and many touches of light on tree trunks and strongly impastoed banks, the handling of the trees being carefully executed with strong, small, impasto touches. The skies are pale blue with mauve clouds, the lights being depicted in Naples yellow. The clouds are broadly brushed in.

In the mid-period one sees the use of sienna and ochre, the trees being beautifully detailed. The lanes are often peopled by mounted travellers. At this time he delighted in showing donkeys.

During the 1840s and 50s (the view in the Lake District illustrated belongs to this period) he attained his greatest performance, having great freedom of brushwork and beauty of colour. Certain of the works of this period were executed with detail and exquisite tone. I remember the late Major Boswell showing me a very detailed woodland scene with the light striking down through the foliage in a most effective manner. At all times John Berney Ladbrooke maintained a high standard, even in his late works, when his foliage becomes spotted, he scores successes.

In his last few years certain of his works became darker and one finds the trees painted with silver boles and dark green touches in great detail, the shadows being painted thinly.

His early works are seldom signed. The mid-period works when signed have either a monogram or a broadly lettered signature. The later works are sometimes signed in red.

J. B. Ladbrooke is a significant Master of the Norwich School.

PICTURES EXHIBITED AT THE ROYAL ACADEMY

Year	*Subject*
1821	A view near Ipswich.
1822	A view near Crostwick Common, Norfolk.
1843	Heath scene near North Walsham, Norfolk.

CONTRIBUTIONS TO THE BRITISH INSTITUTION

Year	*Subject*
1823	View on Crostwick Common. 34×40 in.
	Landscape composition. 34×30 in.
1824	A view near Fellbridge Park, Norfolk. 32×36 in.
1825	A heath scene. 43×52 in.
1850	Lane at Shambourne, Norfolk. 24×24 in.
1853	Road scene at Houghton, Norfolk.
1854	Overshot Mill at Ambleside.

No.	Subject
1856	Recollections of a road scene in Norfolk.
1857	Stock Ghyll Forge, Ambleside.
1859	Easdale Stream, Grasmere, Cumberland.

John Berney Ladbrooke exhibited three at the Royal Academy, ten at the British Institution, and thirty-five at the Sussex Street Galleries.

EXHIBITION OF NORWICH SCHOOL PICTURES

Norwich Castle Museum and Art Galleries October, 1927

OIL PAINTINGS

No.	Subject	No.	Subject
51	Landscape. $11\frac{1}{4}\times9\frac{1}{4}$ in.	54	The great oak. $23\frac{1}{2}\times35\frac{1}{2}$ in.
52	Norwich Back River. 13×12 in.	55	Landscape with figures and cattle. $19\frac{1}{4}\times29\frac{1}{4}$ in.
53	Grove scene (signed). $24\frac{1}{2}\times21\frac{1}{2}$ in.	56	Landscape with water mill, etc. $19\frac{1}{4}\times29\frac{1}{4}$ in.

WATER-COLOURS, DRAWINGS, ETC.

No.	Subject
190	Tintern Abbey. $9\frac{3}{4}\times14\frac{1}{2}$ in.

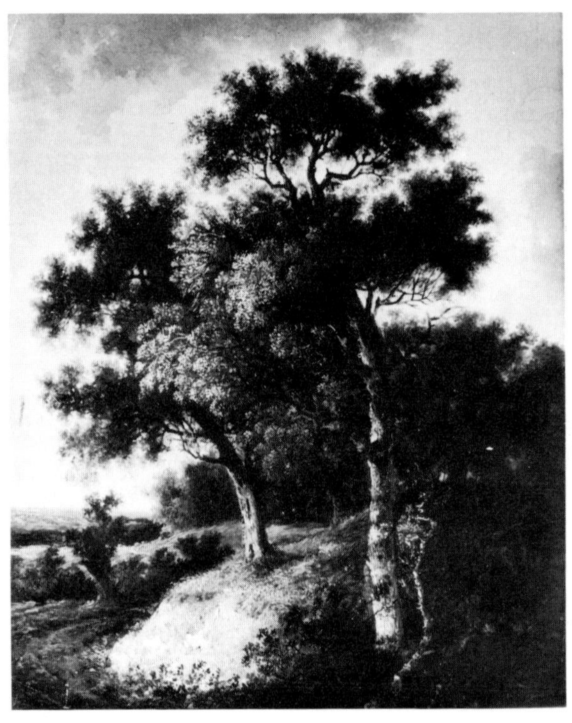

John Berney Ladbrooke Early work Oil on canvas
View at Colney, Norfolk

THIRTEENTH EXHIBITION OF THE NORFOLK AND NORWICH SOCIETY OF ARTISTS, 1817

No.	Subject	No.	Subject
5	Pea and nasturtium.		
11	Fishermen, after Morland.	30	Smugglers, after Morland.

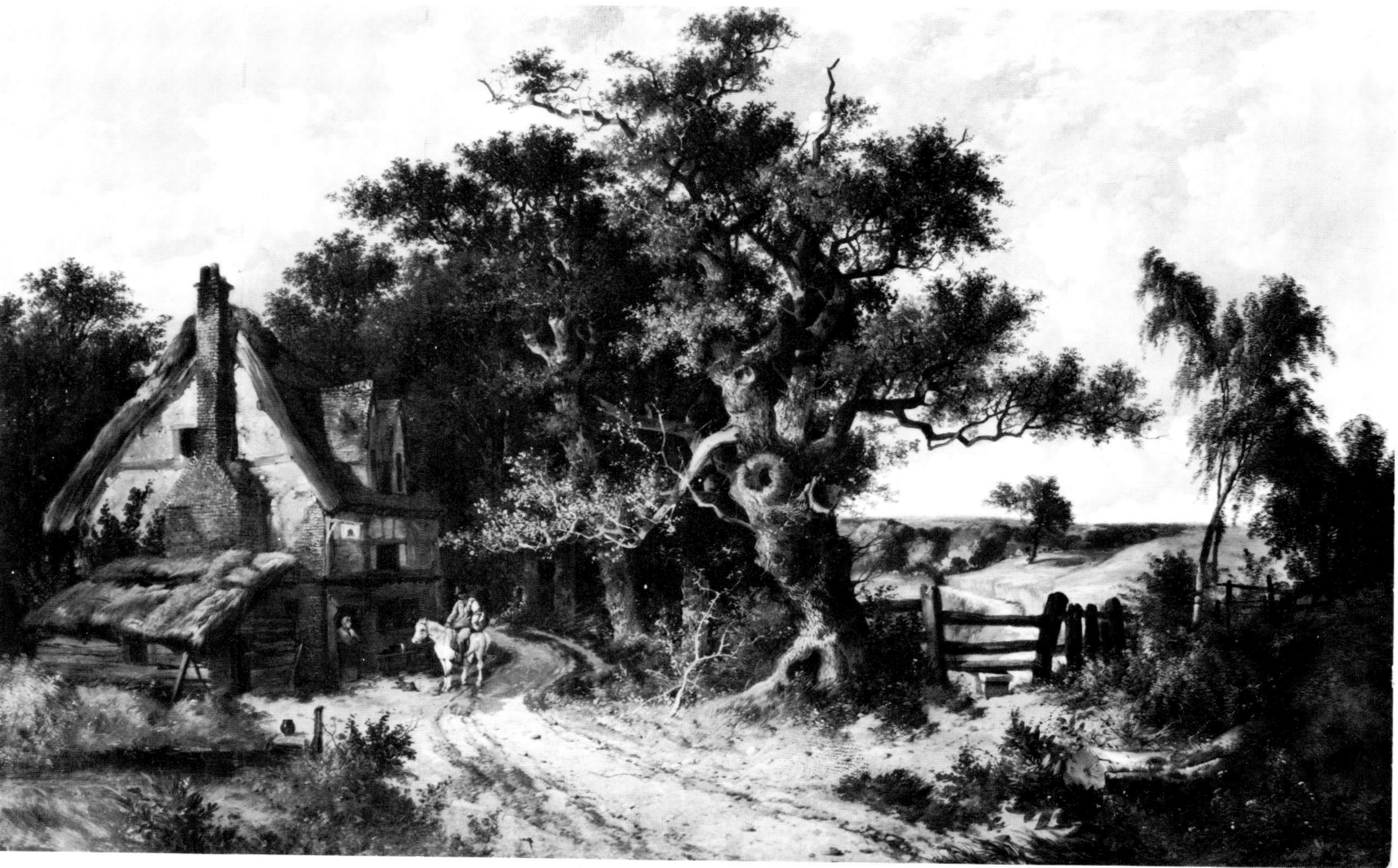

John Berney Ladbrooke — *The Bell Inn* — *Middle Period Oil on canvas* 24 × 36 *in.*

Note the sensitive painting on the old chimney stack

FOURTEENTH EXHIBITION OF THE NORFOLK AND NORWICH SOCIETY OF ARTISTS, 1818

No.	Subject
24	Ducks.
35	Landscape, with a mill.
41	The angry goose.
100	A landscape.
63	Pencil sketch.
75	Pencil sketch.
81	Pencil sketch.

SEVENTEENTH EXHIBITION OF THE NORWICH SOCIETY OF ARTISTS, 1821

No.	Subject
34	View of Tivoli.

NINETEENTH EXHIBITION OF THE NORWICH SOCIETY OF ARTISTS, 1823

No.	Subject
40	Sketch at Bentley, Suffolk.
73	View of the City of Norwich from the back of the barracks.

TWENTIETH EXHIBITION OF THE NORWICH SOCIETY OF ARTISTS, 1824

No.	Subject
8	Grove scene near Ipswich.
21	View at Bramerton.
27	Heath scene.
32	Bacchus and Ariadne.

TWENTY-FIRST EXHIBITION OF THE NORWICH SOCIETY OF ARTISTS, 1825

No.	Subject
11	Landscape and figures.
21	Landscape composition.
28	Beach scene—smugglers landing cargo.
99	Lane scene, with boys hunting a rabbit.

TWENTY-SECOND EXHIBITION OF THE WORKS OF THE NORFOLK AND SUFFOLK INSTITUTION FOR THE PROMOTION OF THE FINE ARTS, 1828

No.	Subject
23	Landscape composition—Italian scenery.
33	Landscape and cattle.
44	Landscape and cattle.
45	Sheep wash.
46	Landscape composition.
64	Sketch at Whitlingham. (Under J. B. Ladbrooke in list of exhibitors.)
98	Landscape and cattle.
99	Village ale-house.
108	Landscape and cattle.
115	Landscape, with boys hunting rabbits.
120	Dutch fishing boats—fresh breeze.
126	Heath scene—storm retiring.
229	Convolvulus Major.

TWENTY-THIRD EXHIBITION OF THE WORKS OF THE NORFOLK AND SUFFOLK INSTITUTION FOR THE PROMOTION OF THE FINE ARTS, 1829

No.	*Subject*
19	View of the River Yare from Carrow Abbey—morning.
119	View of Thorpe from the Whitlingham meadows.
173	Group of flowers, from Nature.

TWENTY-FOURTH EXHIBITION OF THE WORKS OF THE NORFOLK AND SUFFOLK INSTITUTION FOR THE PROMOTION OF THE FINE ARTS, 1830

No.	*Subject*
158	Composition.

TWENTY-FIFTH EXHIBITION OF THE WORKS OF THE NORFOLK AND SUFFOLK INSTITUTION FOR THE PROMOTION OF THE FINE ARTS, 1831

No.	*Subject*
2	Wreck, with distant view of the Black Castle, county of Wicklow, Ireland.
78	Landscape and cattle.
79	Landscape and cattle.
80	Lane scene.
129	Landscape—composition.

TWENTY-SIXTH EXHIBITION OF THE WORKS OF THE NORFOLK AND SUFFOLK INSTITUTION FOR THE PROMOTION OF THE FINE ARTS, 1832

No.	*Subject*
111	Landscape.
113	Landscape with cattle.
119	Road scene.
165	Grove scene.

TWENTY-SEVENTH EXHIBITION OF THE WORKS OF THE NORFOLK AND SUFFOLK INSTITUTION FOR THE PROMOTION OF THE FINE ARTS, 1833

No.	*Subject*
96	Storm retiring.
178	Cottage scene.
183	Return to port.

THE FIRST EXHIBITION OF THE NORFOLK AND NORWICH ART UNION, 1839

No.	*Subject*
119	Scene at Oulton.

NORWICH POLYTECHNIC EXHIBITION, 1840

No.	*Subject*
125	Heath scene—storm retiring.
137	Cattle.

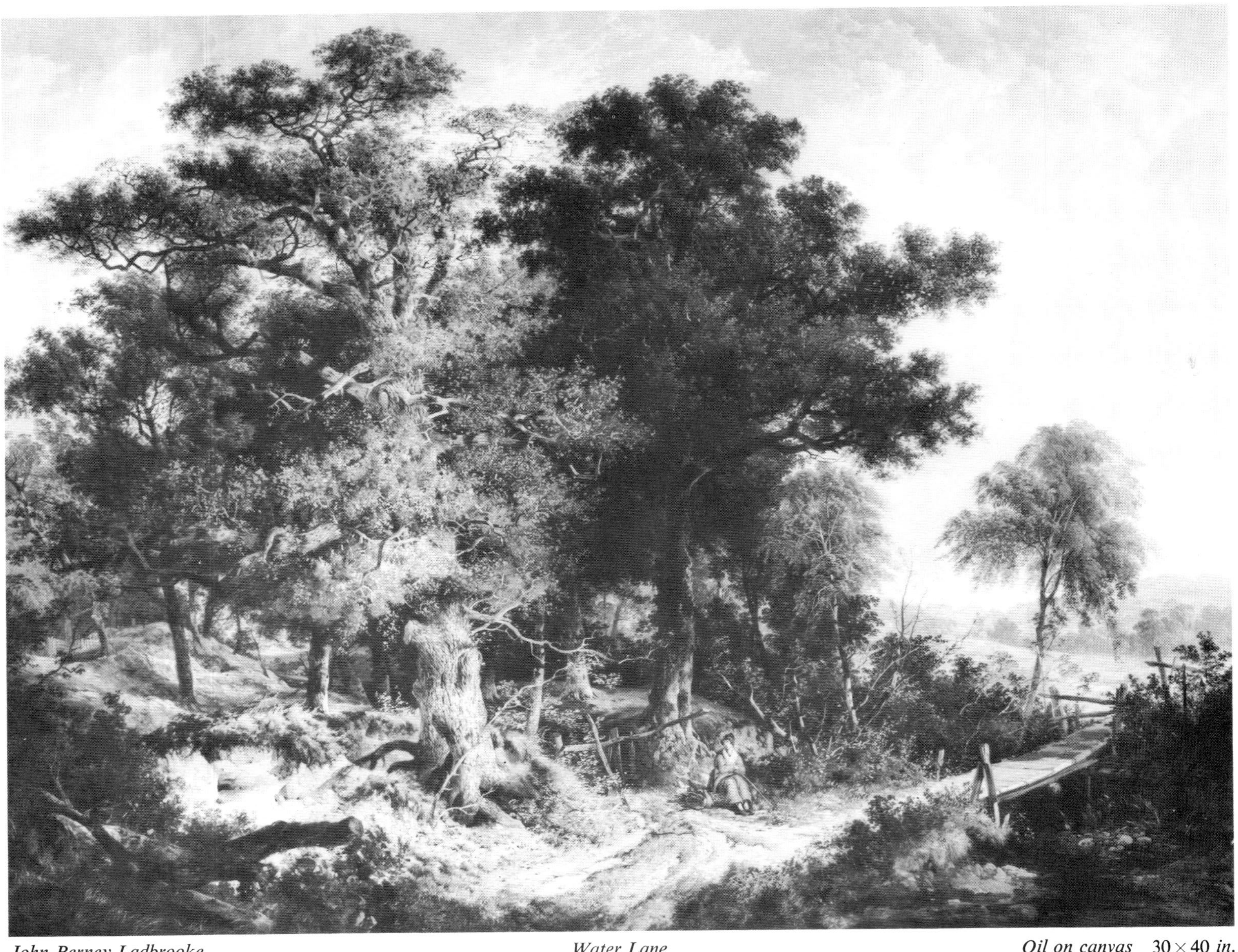

John Berney Ladbrooke — *Water Lane* — *Oil on canvas* 30 × 40 *in.*

Note how the great mass of trees in the centre are contrasted by the elegant tree to the right

THE FIRST EXHIBITION OF THE EAST OF ENGLAND ART UNION, 1842

No. *Subject*

35 Landscape and cattle.
46 The oak.

"A song for the oak, the grave old oak,
That hath rul'd in the green wood long;
Here's health and renown to his broad green crown,
With his fifty arms so strong."
(*Song*)

49 Landscape composition.
66 Heath scene, near Walsham.
93 Wood scene.
130 Landscape and cattle.

FIRST EXHIBITION OF THE NORFOLK AND NORWICH ASSOCIATION FOR THE PROMOTION OF THE FINE ARTS, 1848

No. *Subject*

46 Old sluice-gate, Heigham.
49 View on the Skid, near Bolton Abbey.
56 An avenue—composition.
73 Overshot Mill in Yorkshire.
87 Entrance of a forest.
116 Water-course near the foot of Snowdon.
163 View on the River Mouse, Lanarkshire.
166 Inverarnan, head of Loch Lomond, with the Douglas Hill in the background.
228 Waterfall at Llanberie.
263 View at Dilham, Norfolk.
286 Welsh cottage, with Snowdon in the distance.
385 View near Norwich.
386 Blacksmith's shop—moonlight.

SECOND EXHIBITION OF THE NORFOLK AND NORWICH ASSOCIATION FOR THE PROMOTION OF THE FINE ARTS, 1849

No. *Subject*

2 Beach scene, with shrimp girl.
18 Distant view of Snowdon, on the road from Beddgelert to Carnarvon.
30 Scene between North Walsham and Worstead.
78 Avenue at Whitlingham, leading to the old church.
127 Still life.
158 The homestead. (20g in ink in margin.)
164 Scene from a lane near Drayton, Norfolk.
204 Four views—Spring, Summer, Autumn, Winter.
297 Landscape—composition.
303 Landscape—composition.
310 Lane scene at Shernbourne, Norfolk.
407 Scene at Hadleigh, Suffolk.

THIRD EXHIBITION OF THE NORFOLK AND NORWICH ASSOCIATION FOR THE PROMOTION OF THE FINE ARTS, 1852

No. *Subject*

35 Lane scene leading to Wroxham Broad.
79 View on Thorpe Road—storm retiring.
89 Landscape—composition.

FOURTH EXHIBITION OF THE NORFOLK AND NORWICH ASSOCIATION FOR THE PROMOTION OF THE FINE ARTS, 1853

No.	*Subject*
5	O'Sullivan's Waterfall at the foot of the Toomies Mountain, Lower Lake of Killarney.
8	Stock Ghyll Force, Ambleside, Westmoreland.
100	Fruit piece.
122	Lower part of Stock Ghyll Force, Westmoreland.
127	Scene at Glengariff, Ireland.
140	A peep through the Gap of Dunloe.

EXHIBITION OF THE NORFOLK AND NORWICH ASSOCIATION FOR THE PROMOTION OF THE FINE ARTS, 1855

No.	*Subject*	£	s.	d.
12	The oak. (Same rhyme as 1842, No. 46.)	20	0	0
104	Millbeckforce, Cumberland.	10	0	0
111	Green lane leading to the farm.	10	0	0
172	A peep at Ullswater.	15	0	0
189	Autumn lane scene, near the railway station, Brundall.	8	8	0

EXHIBITION OF THE NORFOLK AND NORWICH FINE ARTS' ASSOCIATION AND OF THE PHOTOGRAPHIC SOCIETY, 1856

No.	*Subject*	£	s.	d.
18	Landscape—sunset. "Now the sun is in the west, Sinking slow behind the trees; And the cuckoo, welcome guest, Gently woos the evening breeze." (*Old Song*)	15	15	0
82	Mill Beck, Bowness.	8	8	0
138	On the River Yare.	4	4	0
143	Road scene—autumn.	21	0	0
268	Overshot Mill, near Beddgellert, N. Wales.	10	10	0

NORFOLK AND NORWICH FINE ARTS ASSOCIATION—EXHIBITION OF THE WORKS OF MODERN ARTISTS, 1860

No.	*Subject*	£	s.	d.
46	View of Norwich, from the artist's garden, Mousehold.	40	0	0
59	Easdale Stream, Grasmere.	12	12	0
63	View at Witlingham.	15	15	0

NORWICH FINE ART ASSOCIATION OF WORKS OF ART BY MODERN ARTISTS, 1868

No.	*Subject*	£	s.	d.
16	Old sluice-gate—early morning.	20	0	0
31	Landscape.	15	15	0
115	Landscape composition.	15	15	0

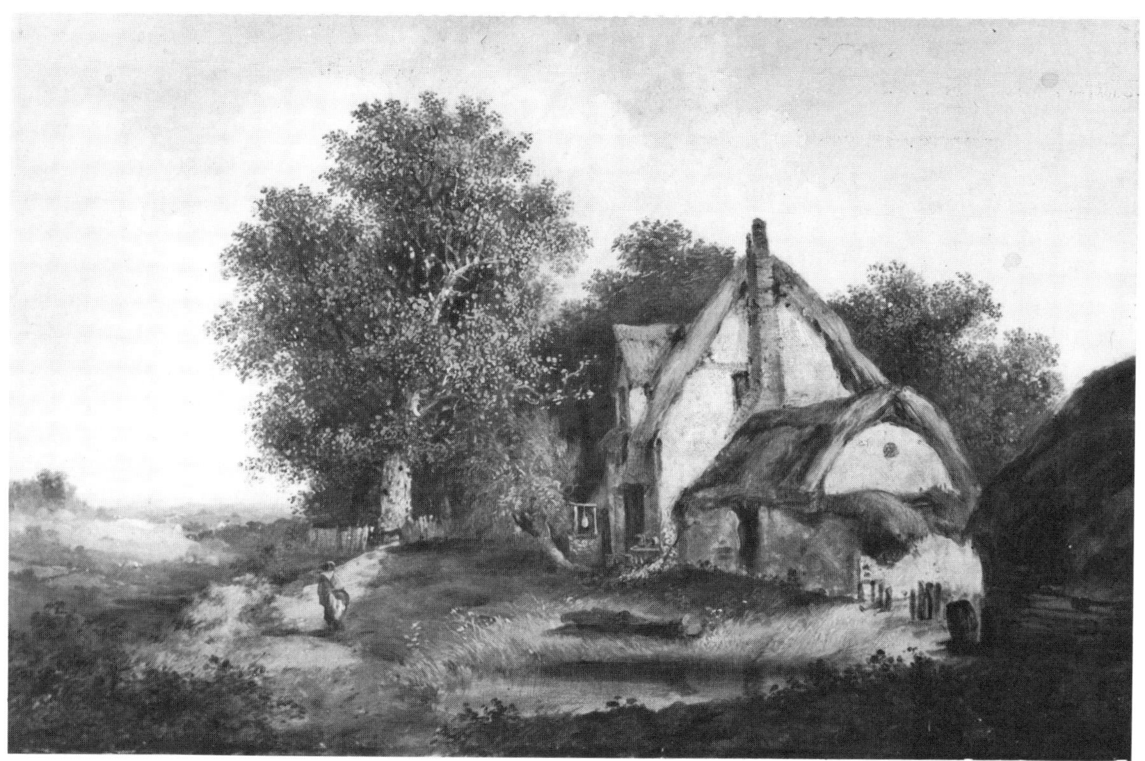

John Berney Ladbrooke *Late work Oil on canvas* 14 × 20 *in.*

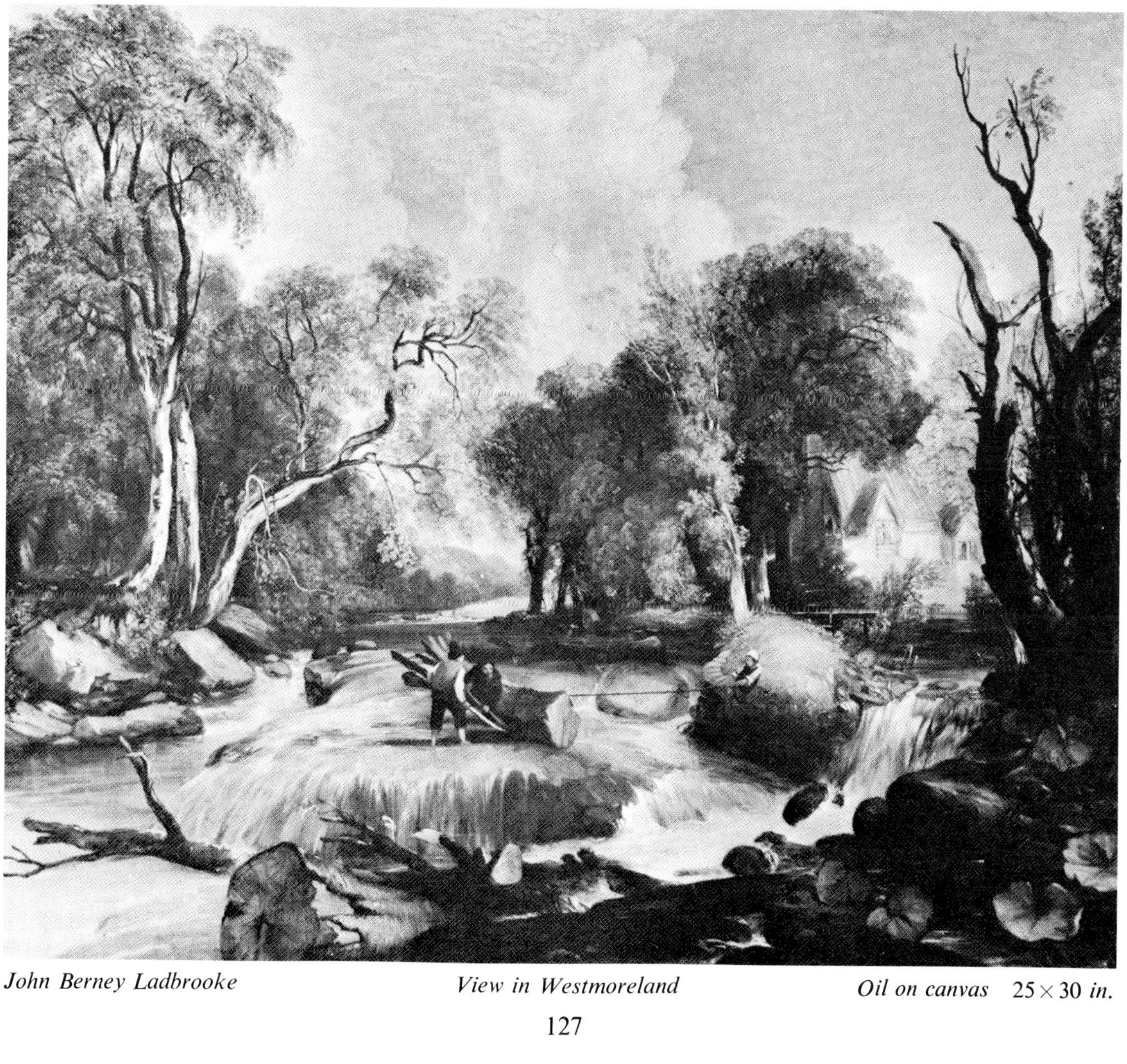

John Berney Ladbrooke *View in Westmoreland* *Oil on canvas* 25 × 30 *in.*

NORWICH FINE ART ASSOCIATION SECOND EXHIBITION OF WORKS OF ART BY MODERN ARTISTS, 1869

No.	Subject	£	s.	d.
56	Close of a stormy day, Hole, North Devon.	20	0	0
65	Road scene, formerly at Kirby, near Norwich.	40	0	0
126	View on the Rhine.	15	0	0
138	Lane scene, Norfolk.	25	0	0

EXHIBITION OF WORKS OF ART BY MODERN ARTISTS—EAST ANGLIAN ART UNION AND CITY OF NORWICH FINE ART ASSOCIATION, 1870

No.	Subject	£	s.	d.
12	Road scene with wheelwrights' shops.	40	0	0
15	Wood's End Reach—sunset.	10	0	0
89	Rustic scene.	30	0	0
148	Near Guildford, Surrey.	35	0	0
157	The frozen pool.	6	0	0
214	Ben Lomond—twilight (watercolour).	6	0	0
223	Glengarrif, Ireland (watercolour).	6	0	0

EXHIBITION OF WORKS OF ART BY MODERN ARTISTS—NORFOLK AND NORWICH FINE ART ASSOCIATION AND ART UNION, 1871

OIL PAINTINGS

No.	Subject	£	s.	d.
18	Foggy morning—early spring.	12	12	0
38	Cottage swing.	50	0	0
85	View of the city from the artist's garden—summer evening.	30	0	0
198	The foot bridge.	6	0	0
308	Glen Nives, sketched during a cruise in Sir Robert Harvey's yacht, *Clytie* (water-colour).	20	0	0
328	Upper Lake of Killarney (water-colour).	15	15	0

BRITISH MEDICAL ASSOCIATION LOAN COLLECTION

Norfolk and Sussex artists, 1874

No.	Subject	Lent by
223	Landscape.	Mr. W. Boswell.

NORWICH ART LOAN EXHIBITION

in aid of the Fund for the Restoration of the Church of Saint Peter Mancroft, 1878

No.	Subject	Lent by
359	Forest scenery.	Joseph Stanley, jun., Esq.

SWAFFHAM FINE ART EXHIBITION, 1882

No.	Subject	Lent by
21	An English cottage.	Mr. W. C. Southwell.
22	Road scene.	Mr. W. C. Southwell.

FINE ART EXHIBITION

in aid of the new Norfolk and Norwich Hospital, 1883

No.	*Subject*	*Lent by*
31	Landscape.	Dr. Eade.

NORWICH ART LOAN EXHIBITION

in aid of the Fund for the Restoration of St. Peter Mancroft Church, 1885

No.	*Subject*	*Lent by*
55	Intwood Church, near Norwich. (For sale, £31 10s.)	Mr. H. Lemmon.
86	Earlham bridge.	Mrs. Rix.
87	Landscape.	Rev. Dr. Perowne, Master of Corpus Christi College, Cambridge.
271	View of Norwich.	Mr. F. T. Knights.

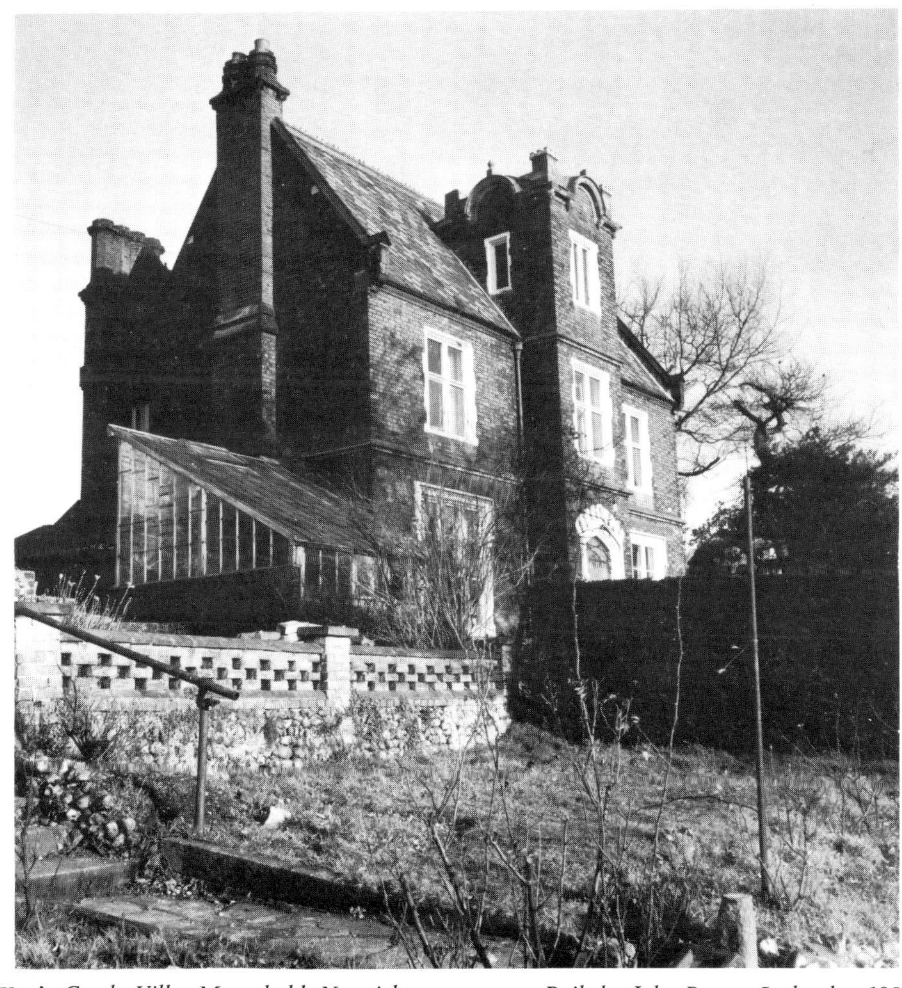

Kett's Castle Villa, Mousehold, Norwich *Built by John Berney Ladrooke, 1857*

(By kind permission of the owner)

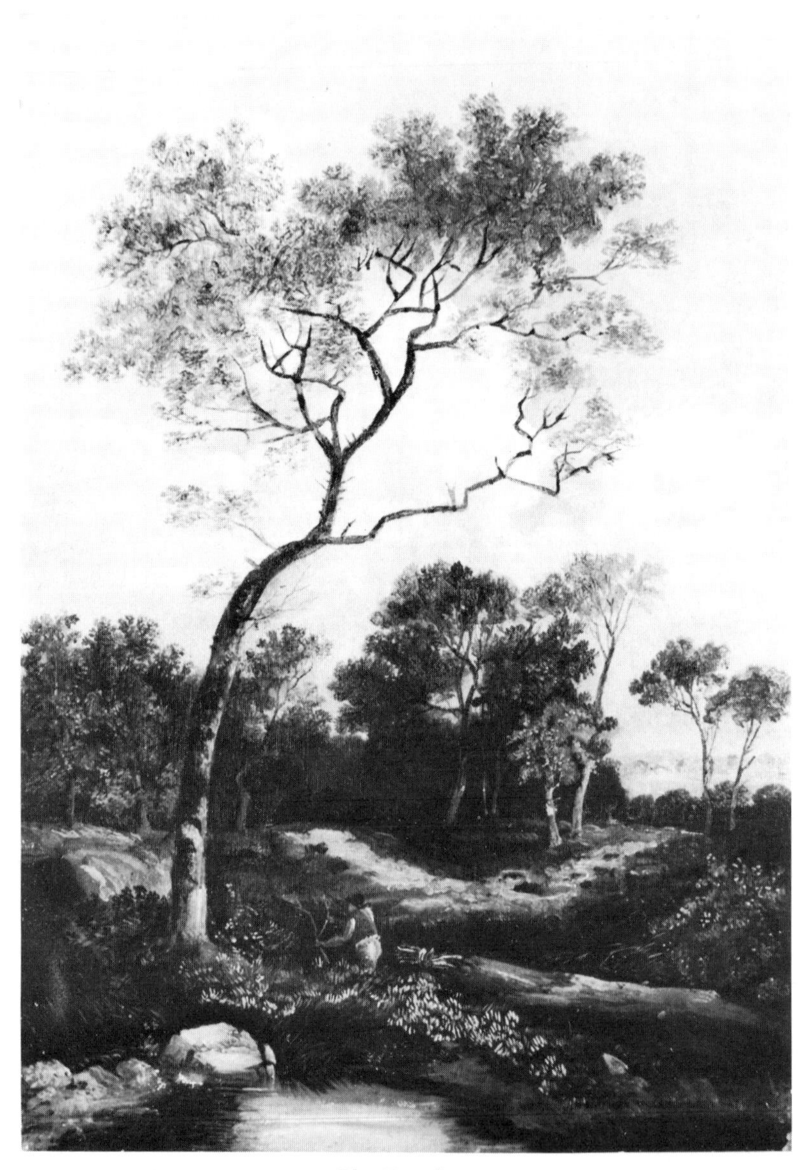

The Woodman

John Berney Ladbrooke *Mid period Oil on canvas approx.* 15×9 *in.*

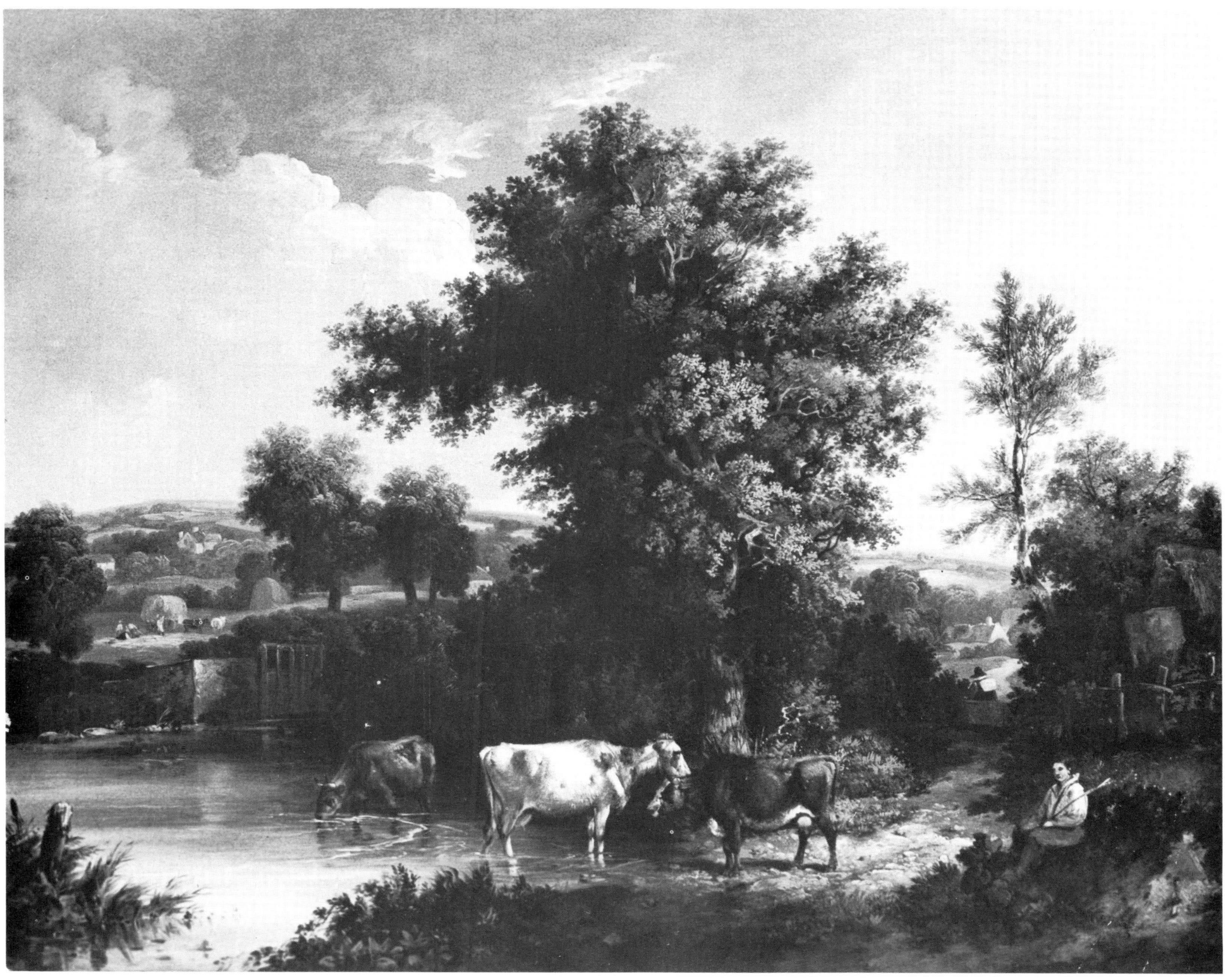

John Berney Ladbrooke *The Watering Place* *Mid period* *Canvas* *25 × 30 in.*

Cattle in landscape have always rendered important effects. Such artists as Claude, Gainsborough, Constable, and many of the Norwich School painters delighted to depict them

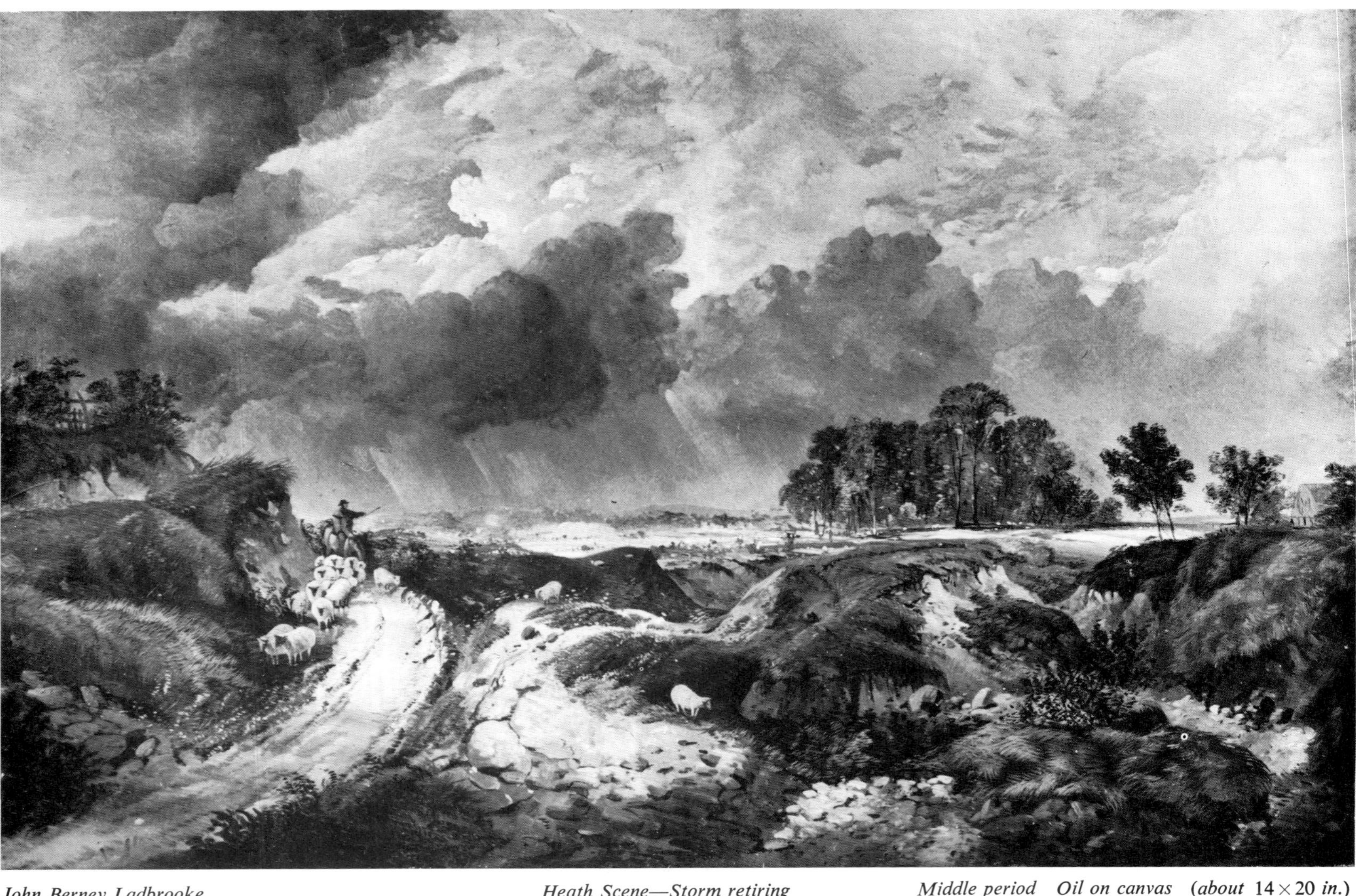

John Berney Ladbrooke *Heath Scene—Storm retiring* *Middle period* *Oil on canvas* *(about 14×20 in.)*

FREDERICK LADBROOKE

(1812-1865)

Frederick Ladbrooke was Robert Ladbrooke's youngest son and was born in 1812. Little is known of his life, apart from the fact that he moved to Bury St. Edmund's, Suffolk, where he established himself as a portrait painter. It is said that when photography was first practised he was employed as an adviser. Tradition has it that on one occasion he painted a portrait of a deceased person from a description of a relative. Not surprisingly, the relative was not convinced of the likeness, but he recognised the waistcoat!

From the illustration of a shoemaker it would seem that he was a competent portrait painter. This painting is signed on the reverse. It is one of the few paintings by Frederick Ladbrooke recorded. Miss Esther Ladbrooke, a daughter of Henry Ladbrooke, said that Frederick Ladbrooke sometimes placed figures in her father's pictures.

The *Suffolk Post* reported his death at Bury in the year 1865.

TWENTY-FIRST EXHIBITION OF THE WORKS OF THE NORWICH SOCIETY OF ARTISTS, 1825

No.	*Subject*
176	Sketch in oils.

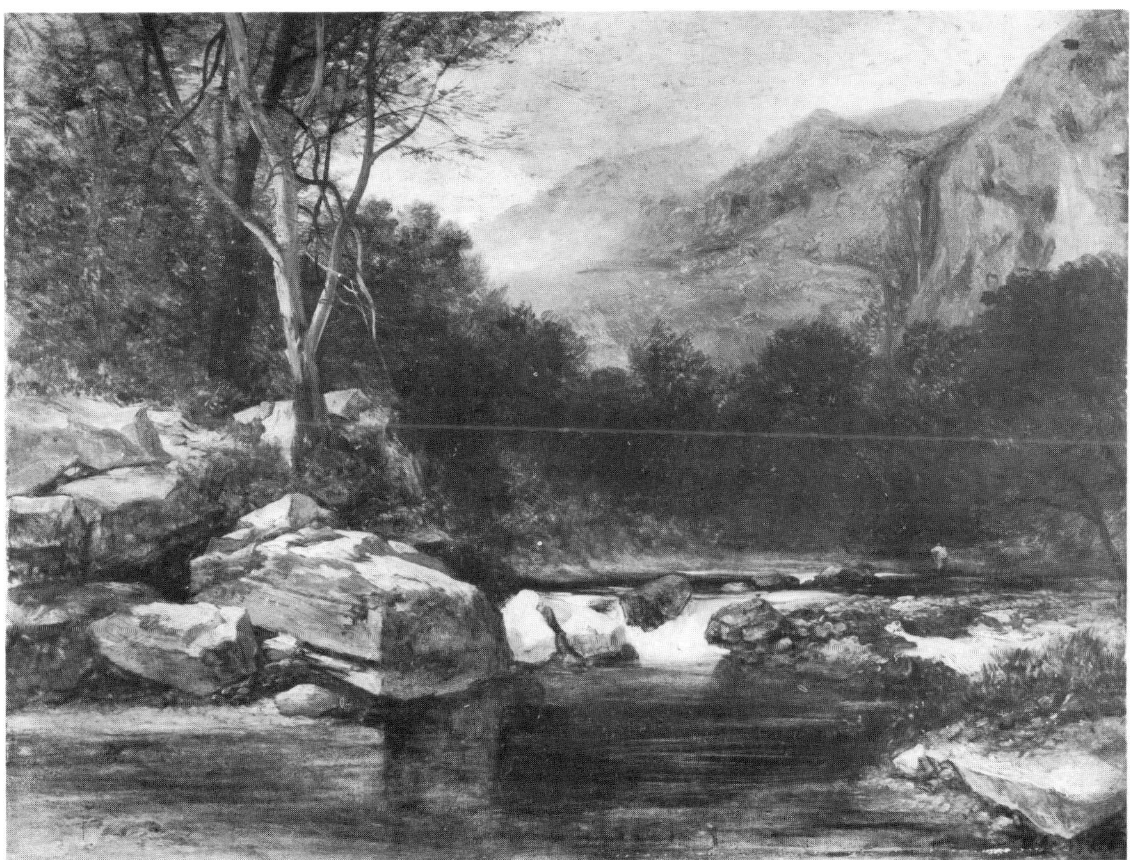

Frederick Ladbrooke *Oil on canvas*

EXHIBITION OF THE NORFOLK AND NORWICH FINE ARTS ASSOCIATION AND OF THE PHOTOGRAPHIC SOCIETY, 1856

No.	*Subject*	£	s.	d.
13	View on the Lark.	7	7	0
28	Errand boy.	7	7	0
39	View on the Stour.	7	7	0
127	The smithy.	10	10	0

NORFOLK AND NORWICH FINE ARTS ASSOCIATION—EXHIBITION OF THE WORKS OF MODERN ARTISTS, 1860

No.	*Subject*	£	s.	d.
159	The errand boy.	5	5	0
160	The errand boy.	5	5	0

EXHIBITION OF NORWICH SCHOOL PICTURES

Norwich Castle Museum and Art Galleries, October, 1927

OIL-PAINTINGS

No.	*Subject*
47	Boy and dog (signed F.L.). $19 \times 15\frac{3}{4}$ in.

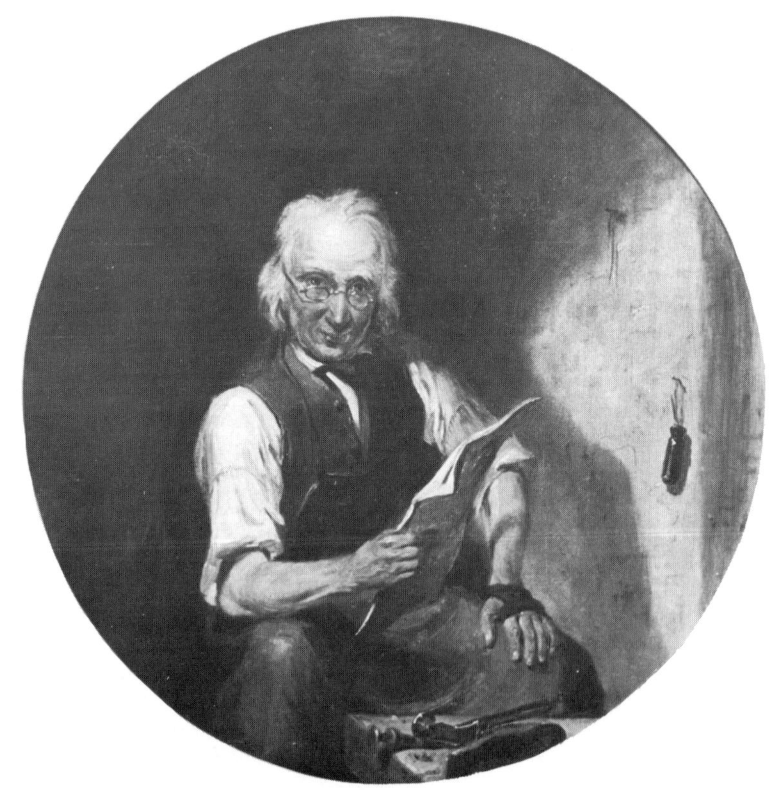

Frederick Ladbrooke *Oil*

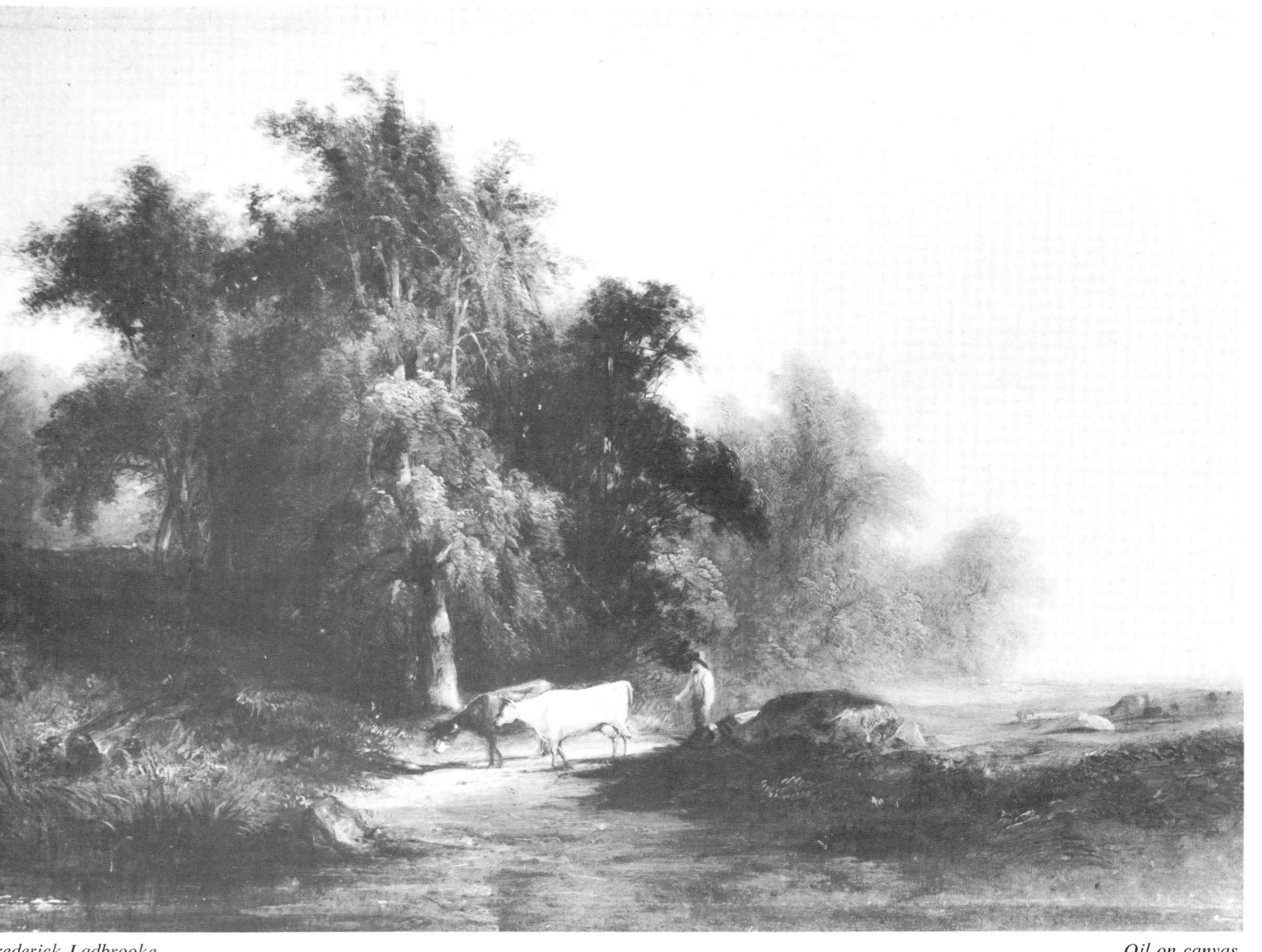

Frederick Ladbrooke   *Oil on canvas*

JAMES SILLETT

(1764-1840)

1764 The Silletts came from Eye, a small Suffolk town to the east of the Ipswich-Norwich
Road. However, by the time James Sillett was born (in 1764) the family was living in
Norwich. Here James Sillett attended school and was later apprenticed to an heraldic
painter. Being ambitious, he managed to obtain his release from the apprenticeship, and
1781 left Norwich for London where he lived at 12 Mansfield Place, 50 Georges Fields. He
1790 attended the Royal Academy School from 1781 to 1790.

In London he assisted Capon, a Norwich artist, as a scene painter at the Italian Opera
1801 House and Drury Lane. However, he did not forget his native county, for in 1801 he
married Ann Banyard from East Dereham, through whom he acquired some property.
1804 The family, in order to be near their relatives, moved to King's Lynn in 1804, where he
developed a teaching practice. During this period he executed a series of views of Lynn
which were published in Richard's *History of Lynn.*

1806 By 1806 he had acquainted himself with the Norwich Society, for in that year he
exhibited twelve pictures. Possibly it was his success at the Norwich Society Exhibitions
1810 that induced him to settle in Norwich in 1810. Such was his standing in the Society
that in 1814 he was elected vice-president, and president the following year.

It has formerly been accepted that the secession of the Ladbrooke faction in 1816 to
form the twelve Exhibitions of the Norfolk and Norwich Society of Artists, was at the
instigation of Robert Ladbrooke. Ladbrooke perhaps was not the prime mover, for in
an advertisement in the *Norwich Mercury* in 1812, Sillett states that "There is more
beauty in the delineation of flowers from the garden and human figure rather than pig
stys and cart sheds. . . ." This is obviously a dig at Crome. It is rather interesting to note
that Crome has come down to posterity as being the most gentle and popular of men.
It now becomes apparent that H. Ladbrooke, J. Stannard and James Sillett had their
1819 differences. Alas, by 1819 all was forgiven, and we find Sillett again exhibiting with the
old Society until it faded out of existence in 1833.

1828 In 1828 Sillett decided to visit Holland, painting views of Rotterdam and Leyden. Also
at this time he published fifty-nine views of churches, etc., in Norwich.

In his later years he lived at King Street, Norwich, where he gave advice to younger
artists and enjoyed talking Art. From his self-portrait we note the alert look and dimple
in his chin. He was said to be a man of great integrity. He loved his art and said,
towards the end of his life, that "Existence would no longer be desirable when deprived
1840 of the use of my pencil". He died on 6th May, 1840.

Emma Sillett, his daughter, also painted—birds, insects, fruit pieces, shells, etc., and carried on the family tradition.

THE PAINTINGS

Sillett is rather different in style to most of his contemporary Norwich School friends. This is largely attributed to his early tuition at the Royal Academy School. This instilled within him the greatest veneration for the eighteenth century painters and their traditions. Though Sillett does possess the East Anglian touch in his works, there is usually an underlying eighteenth century classical influence.

His early landscapes have a primitiveness about them which is their hallmark. Combined with this characteristic is a delightful ability to handle paint. One looks for the crisp touches on the dresses, animals and clouds. He is a great master of tone: in particular, his moonlights have beautiful dark blues, a colouring quite inimical to Sillett. Often he works on copper, and one imagines these to be early works. The foliage is a combination of siennas, light greens to warm ochres, all intermingled to give good effect. His foliage can have strong touches, rather akin to the elder Crome but much more mannered.

His figures are placed well and often shown looking into the picture. The distances, which are considerably detailed, are very thinly painted, often no more than the minimum amount of paint being used.

With his view of the Winfarthing Oak (a favourite subject) painted in 1817, he still treats his trees in an eighteenth century manner, using a predominance of yellowy green on the bole, the sky carrying gentle pink tones. However, his skies are not always painted smoothly—he can use impasto in a characteristic gnarled fashion.

It is, however, the figures which usually indicate Sillett's hand, for they have a primitive quality in which the influence of Crome is discernible, or possibly, in this respect, Sillett influenced Crome, being the elder. The figures in Crome's *Boulevard de Italian* are such an example.

From the exhibits at the Royal Academy we can deduce that Sillett spent quite a lot of time on Still Life. His flower pieces are of good colour, carefully drawn and well composed. He seems to show signs of having studied Ast and Bollongier, for one finds the flowers often large in relation to the size of the picture. Often his flowers are placed in a landscape setting. Black is often admitted into his blues, particularly skies and backgrounds. The flowers often abound with insects. Again, Sillett's classical training is made manifest in his use of classical urns and medallions. Despite Sillett's numerous exhibits of Still Life, it is his landscapes that one sees more often. Perhaps many of his Still Life paintings have yet to be recognised, for Sillett, in common with many of the Norwich painters, seldom signed. The illustrated *Winfarthing Oak* is signed "J.S. 1817".

Possibly Sillett exhibited few Landscapes knowing that Crome, Ladbrooke and several others were specialising in this form of painting.

ROYAL ACADEMY EXHIBITS

Year	*No.*	*Subject*
1796	55	Brace of Teal.
1798	21	Flowers.
	43	Group of birds.
	300	Flowers.
1802	261	Brace of partridges.
	330	An Auricula from Nature.
	464	Flowers.
	330	Primroses.
	333	Honeysuckles.
	337	Grapes.
	338	Grapes.
1804	260	Peruvian Jay.
	574	Fruit.
1807	409	Leach of tench.
	411	Dead game.
	589	Passiflora Alata: winged passion flower.
	545	The red grouse or moorcock.
	562	Study of grapes and foliage.
	562	Study of grapes and foliage.
1809	430	Flower piece.
1810	417	Dead game.
1811	22	Dead game.
	764	Composition of fruit.
1812	691	Basket of fruit.
	692	Fruit.
	695	Fruit.
1813	367	Hawk and prey.
1814	329	Hen chickens alarmed by hawk.
	650	Grapes and foliage.
	654	Grapes and foliage.
1815	125	The Galco Ossipagus or sea eagle
1816	397	An Auricula.
	485	Snake, thistle and insects.
1817	614	Fruit and flowers.
1818	158	Fish.
	618	Fruit.
1819	317	Fish from Nature.
1820	221	Dead game.
	548	Study of flowers from Nature.
1821	631	Fruit and flowers.
1823	55	Hawk and prey.
1824	488	A flower piece.
1827	1127	Interior of St. Andrew's Hall, Norwich,

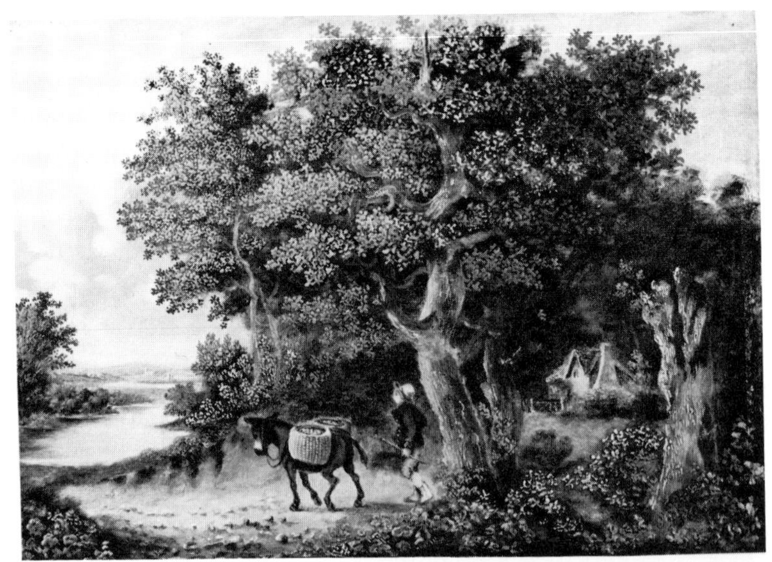

James Sillett
The Tinker
Oil on panel $5\frac{1}{2} \times 7$ *in.*

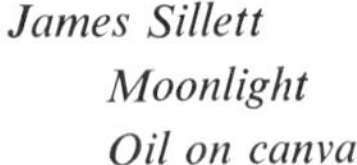

James Sillett
Moonlight
Oil on canvas

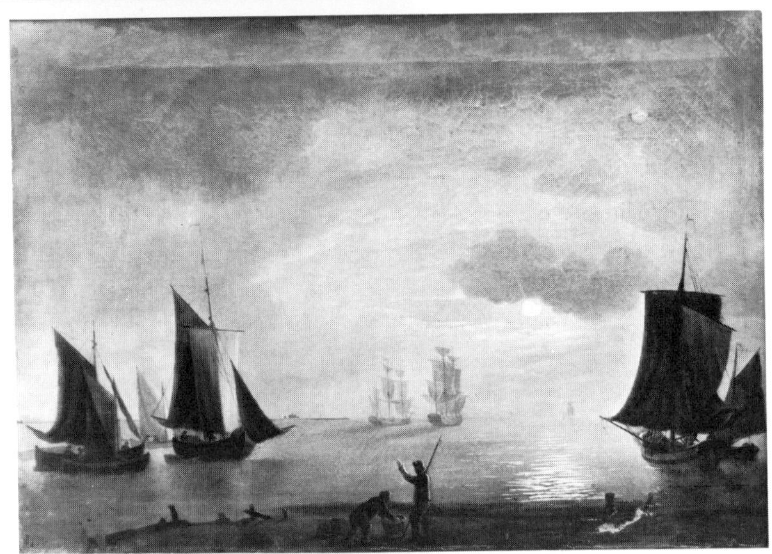

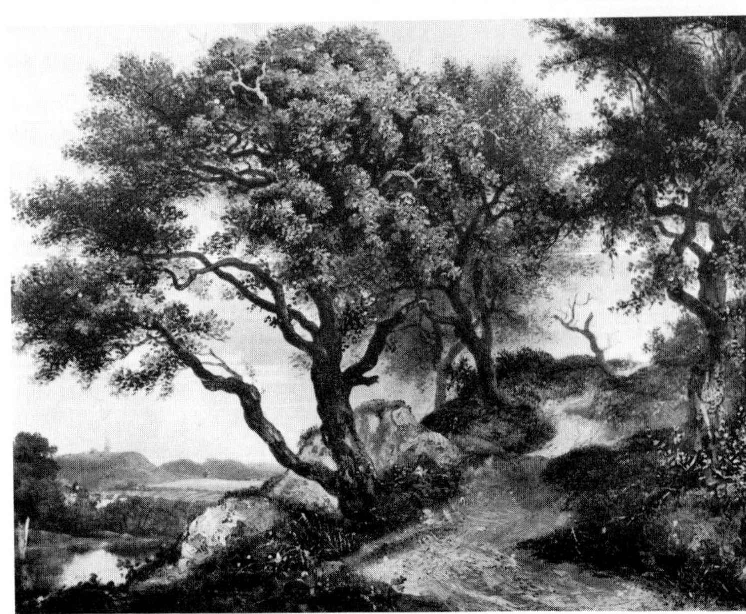

James Sillett
View near Norwich
Oil on copper, about 7×9 *in.*

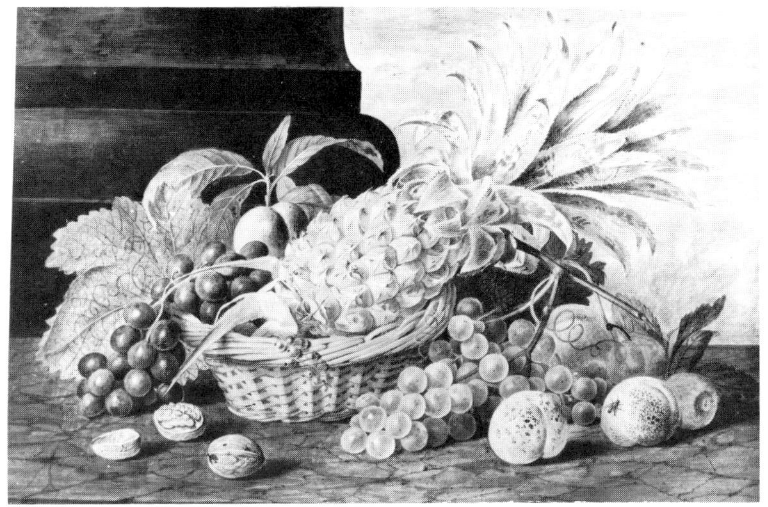

James Sillett *Water-colour* 14 × 20 *in.*

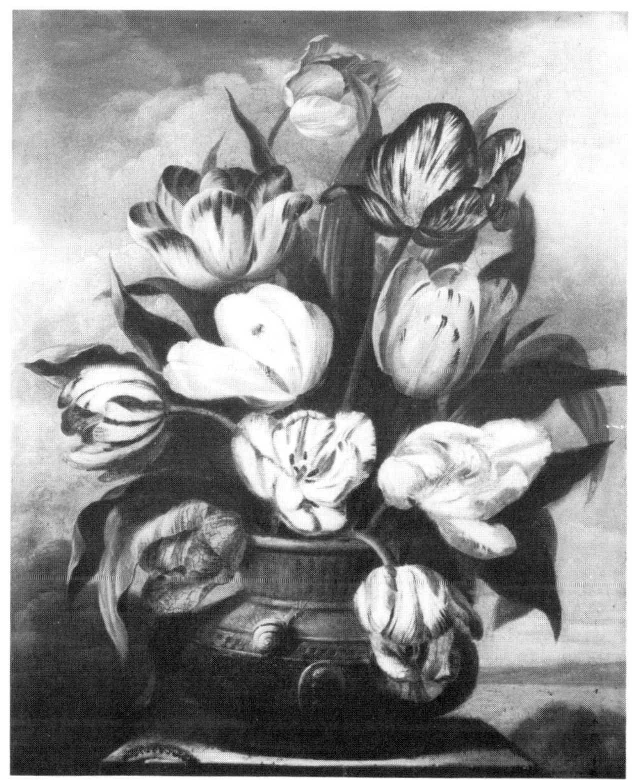

James Sillett *Oil on panel* 21 × 17 *in.*

EXHIBITION OF NORWICH SCHOOL PICTURES

Norwich Castle Museum and Art Galleries, October, 1927

OIL PAINTINGS

No.	*Subject*
88	Norwich Cathedral. $16\frac{1}{2} \times 12\frac{1}{4}$ in.

WATER-COLOURS

No.	*Subject*
238	The Old Oak at Winfarthing, Norfolk. $8\frac{1}{2} \times 12$ in.
239	Norwich Castle (given by the artist to Joseph Rudd in 1818). $12 \times 16\frac{1}{2}$ in.
240	Chestnut blooms and butterfly. 15×12 in.
241	Dead bird. 8×11 in.
242	Dead bird. 8×11 in.

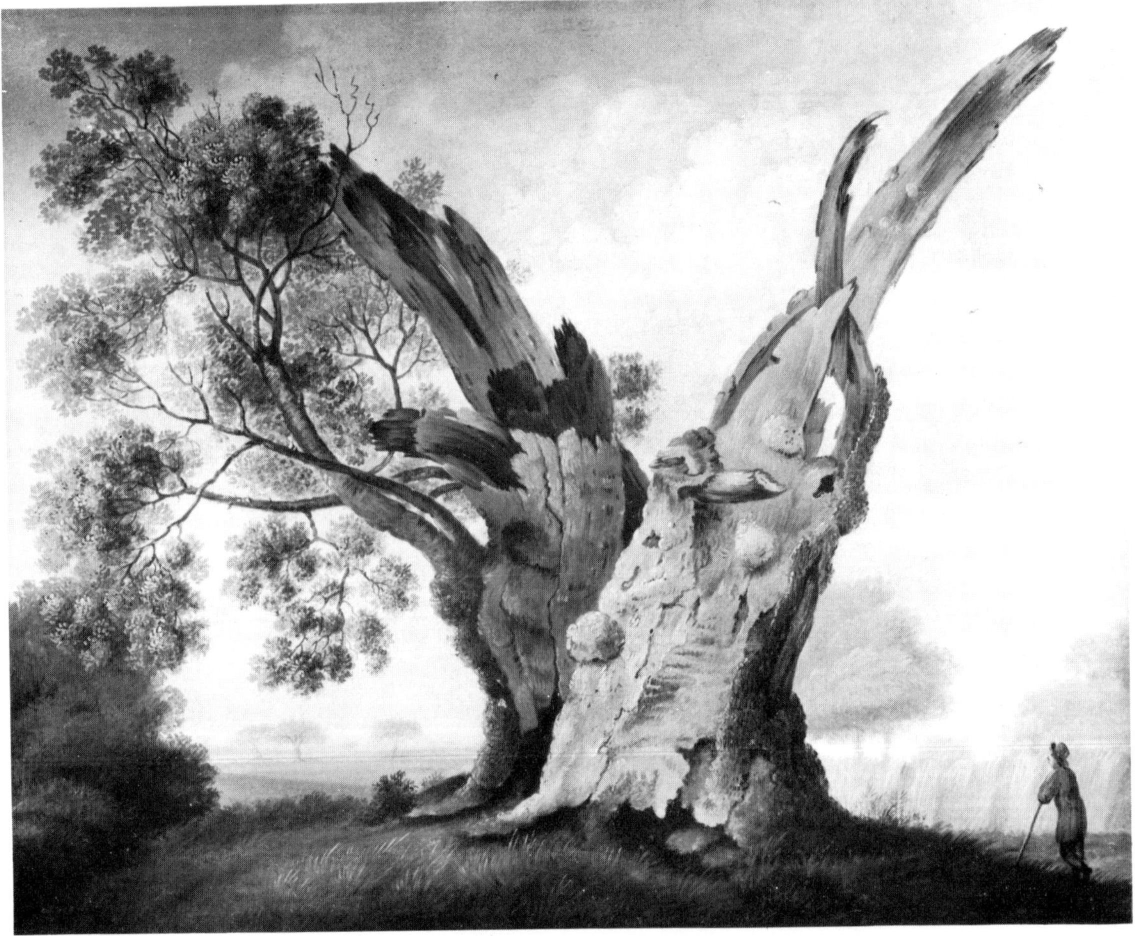

James Sillett *The Winfarthing Oak, 1817* *Oil on canvas* 20×24 *in.*

WILLIAM JOY

(1803-1867)

1803 William Joy was the son of Mr. Joy of Southtown, Yarmouth, who, for many years, was guard on the Ipswich Mail Coach. At the age of fourteen he was befriended by Captain Manby, a school friend of Nelson, an interesting character who spent a large sum of money establishing life-saving stations. As a patron of the Arts he commissioned many of the marine artists of the day. Manby had a fine room in the Royal Hospital, Yarmouth and it was from here that he allowed and encouraged William Joy and his brother to draw and paint. By copying the paintings of Pocock, Powell and Francia in Captain Manby's collection, the brothers gradually mastered the art of marine painting. Other patrons of William Joy were Mr. Croker, of the Admiralty, Mr. Freeling, of the Post Office, Mr. F. Turner, and the Rev. J. Homfray, M.A.

Later the Joys moved to Portsmouth where they did Government work, together with their marine painting. From Portsmouth they moved to Chichester, then to London,
1867 William Joy presumably passing away there in the year 1867.

JOHN CANTILOE JOY

(1806-1866)

1806 John Cantiloe Joy was born some three years after his brother, in 1806. John and William enjoyed a close relationship throughout their lives not only sharing the same profession but in many cases sharing the same commissions. It is useful to record at
1822 this point that John painted largely water-colours. In 1822, when King George IV passed Great Ormesby, Yarmouth, on his return from Edinburgh, a splendid subject for a painting was presented to the young brothers. This work is now in the Victoria and Albert Museum.

1866 John Joy died a year before his elder brother—in the year 1866. He signed quite a number of his drawings.

THE PAINTINGS

William and John Joy are painters of remarkably high merit. William, perhaps, can be identified more often than John for one occasionally sees a work signed "W. Joy" in very simple lettering. His work is very accurate indeed and will bear comparison with any of the Dutch seventeenth century Masters, the detail on the riggings, figures and boats being beautifully executed. He loves drama in a picture, and one seldom finds a William Joy without some distant rain clouds or whip in the sea. The palette tends towards grey-blue, black being admitted in many of his colours with fine effect. His works are comparatively rare.

His light often breaks through openings in the clouds and strikes down on to delightfully drawn sails giving before the wind. The ships themselves are substantial structures giving the feeling that they will withstand the lash of the storm. William Joy's seas have movement and depth and he loves depicting the foam breaking over a wave, or bursting over the bows. Without doubt many of his works rank with Brooking and Joseph Stannard in quality.

John Joy also participated in marine oil paintings but it is the gentle coastal colours in delicate sepia for which he is known. In certain of his water-colours he tends to use warm washes, giving his pictures an overall warm ochre tone.

There are several major works by the Joys in the Norwich Castle Museum, one of which has recently been cleaned, revealing a really fine painting. Birmingham Museum has also a fine example.

It would seem, according to the recorded exhibits, that the brothers mostly shared their pictures. These were signed simply "Joy", or left unsigned: there are many in the latter category.

According to the list of exhibits William Joy painted a number of landscapes: these have yet to be identified.

FIFTEENTH EXHIBITION OF THE NORWICH SOCIETY OF ARTISTS, 1819

No.	*Subject*
15	Sea storm.
26	Storm.
33	Sea piece.
43	The bathers.
51	A calm.

NINETEENTH EXHIBITION OF THE NORWICH SOCIETY OF ARTISTS, 1823

No.	*Subject*	*Lent by*
8	Lowestoft Life-boat.	

TWENTIETH EXHIBITION OF THE NORWICH SOCIETY OF ARTISTS, 1824

No.	*Subject*
5	Morning, a calm.
35	A scene on Yarmouth beach, on 3rd March, 1824.
45	A calm.

TWENTY-FIRST EXHIBITION OF THE NORWICH SOCIETY OF ARTISTS, 1825

No.	*Subject*
22	A gale.
49	A landscape.
172	A calm.

FIRST EXHIBITION OF THE NORFOLK AND NORWICH ART UNION, 1839

No.	*Subject*
21	Launching a beach boat and preparing to render assistance to ships in distress off the land.
152	Wood scene.
213	View from Harting Hill, Sussex.
215	Wreck, near the Haven's Mouth, Yarmouth.
239	Wreck.
251	Sea view.
303	Wreck.
330	Marine view.
332	The rescue of survivors from the wreck of the Killarney steamer.
334	Wreck of the Killarney steamer.
345	Marine view.

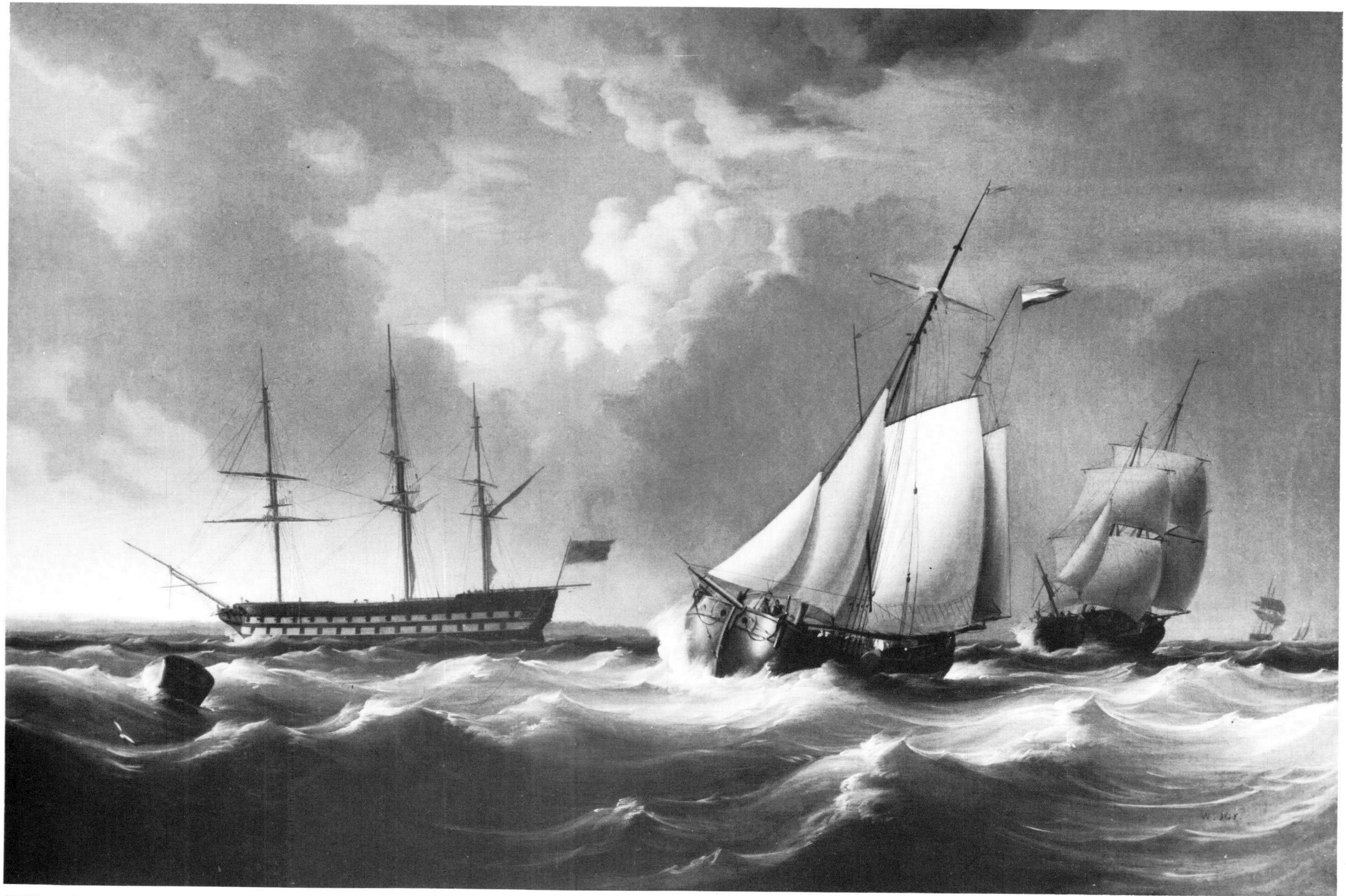

William Joy

Dutch Bomb Boat off the English Coast

Oil on canvas 20 × 30 *in.*

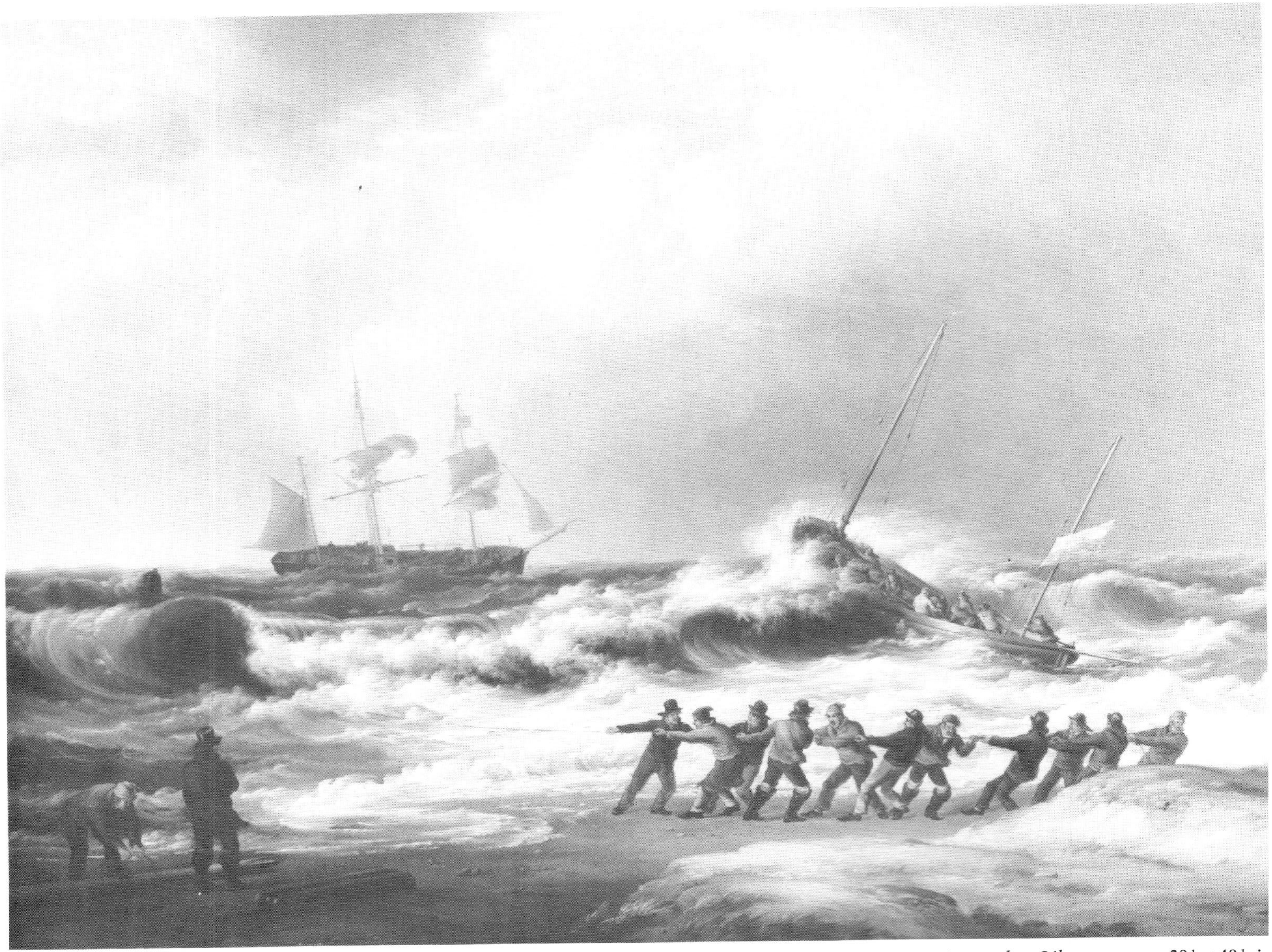

William Joy *Lifeboat going to a Vessel in Distress* *A major work* *Oil on canvas* 39¼ × 49¼ *in*

SECOND EXHIBITION OF THE NORFOLK AND NORWICH ASSOCIATION FOR THE PROMOTION OF THE FINE ARTS, 1849

No.	*Subject*
206	Marine view.
438	A sea view.
496	A sea view.

NORWICH POLYTECHNIC EXHIBITION, 1840

No.	*Subject*	*Lent by*
145	Explanatory representation of the means to give unimmergibility to all ship's boats, in a simple manner, and at small expense.	Captain Manby.

(There is the heading "Engraver" for the following entries, but drawings may be included.)

No.	*Subject*	*Lent by*
154	Going on the back of a whale to harpoon it.	Captain Manby.
156	Harpooning the whale.	Captain Manby.
209	Saving of two crews at Yarmouth.	Captain Manby.
213	Scene on Yarmouth beach.	Miss Blakely.
223	Waterlogged vessel assisted.	Captain Manby.
231	Saving a crew near Yarmouth Pier.	Captain Manby.
236	Landscape taken on the spot.	Captain Manby.
238	Vessels in a gale.	Mr. R. Scott.
246	Saving some of the crew and passengers that were wrecked in the Killarney steamer on the coast of Ireland, from the rock on which they had remained for 48 hours under most intense suffering, but were at length brought up to the height of 300 feet in a cot, on the arrival of the life-saving apparatus from Kinsale.	Captain Manby.
258	Marine view.	Mr. R. Scott.
260	Marine view.	Mr. R. Scott.
266	Going on the back of a whale to harpoon it.	Captain Manby.
267	Attacking a whale to lance it.	Captain Manby.
281	Saving of the crew of the *Jeffries*, at the distance of at least 200 yards from the shore, and on which occasion, a boat's crew, consisting of seven persons, attempted to go off against the most earnest remonstrance, being requested to wait until a line was thrown on board for them to haul themselves off by it, but disregarding the advice, and stating they could do without the tendered assistance, they made the attempt, the boat upset, and five of them paid the forfeiture of their lives, the other two were most miraculously saved.	Captain Manby.
294	Marine view.	Mr. R. Scott.

NORFOLK AND NORWICH FINE ARTS ASSOCIATION

Exhibition of the Works of Deceased Local Artists, 1860

OIL PAINTING

No.	*Subject*	*Lent by*
39	A calm.	Mr. R. B. Scott.

WATER-COLOURS

No.	*Subject*	*Lent by*
286	Sea piece.	Mr. Rossi.
296	George IV in Yarmouth roads.	Mr. Rossi.

NORWICH AND EASTERN COUNTIES WORKING CLASSES INDUSTRIAL EXHIBITION, 1867

No.	*Subject*	*Lent by*
814	Sea view—a calm.	F. E. Watson, Esq., Mayor of Norwich.

BRITISH MEDICAL ASSOCIATION LOAN COLLECTION

Norfolk and Suffolk Artists, 1874

OIL PAINTING

No.	*Subject*	*Lent by*
51	A calm.	Mr. F. E. Watson.

NORWICH ART LOAN EXHIBITION

in aid of the Fund for the Restoration of St. Peter Mancroft Church, 1885

No.	*Subject*	*Lent by*
41	Fishing boats.	F. E. Watson, Esq.
357	Fishing boats in a squall.	Mrs. Thomas Clabburn

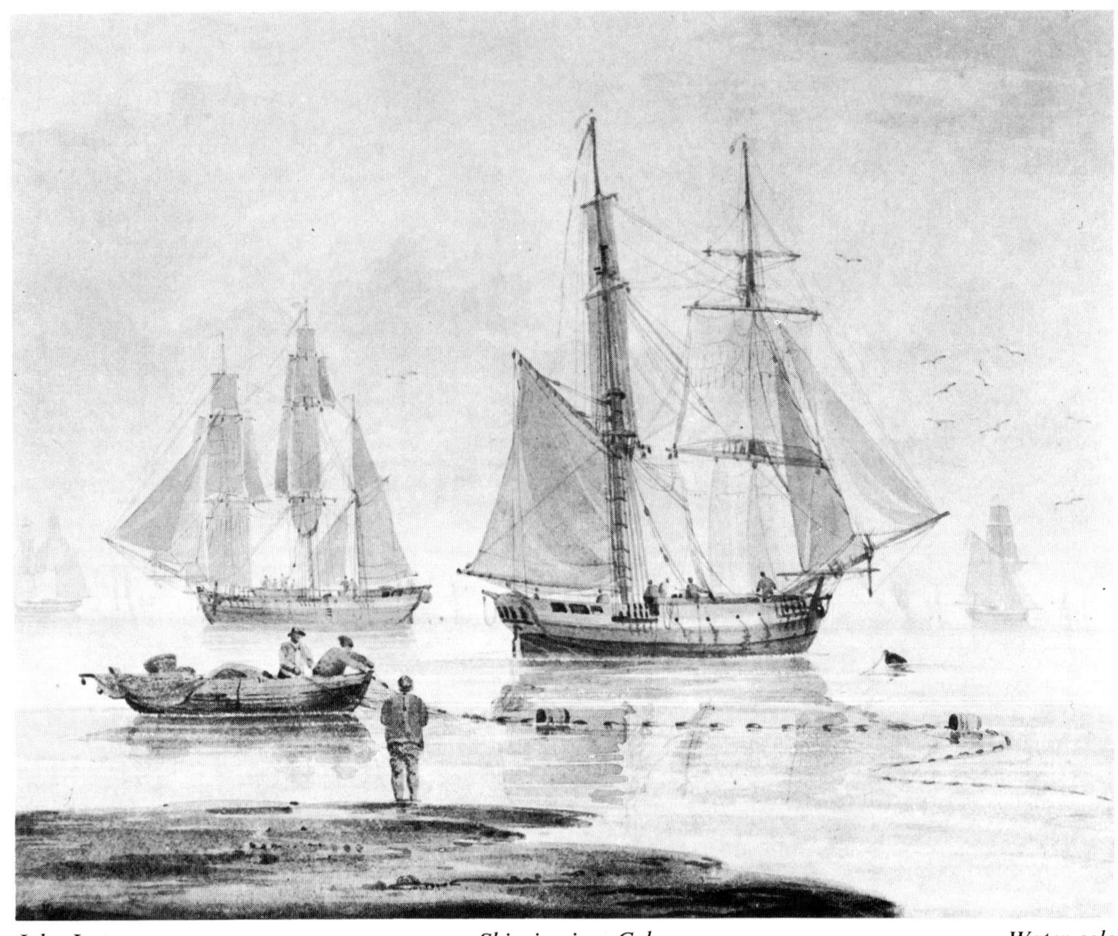

John Joy — *Shipping in a Calm* — *Water-colour*

(*One of the few signed examples*)

ART LOAN EXHIBITION

in aid of the Funds of St. George's Club for Working Girls, 1902

No.	*Subject*
265	Seascape.

EXHIBITED AT THE ROYAL ACADEMY

Year	*No.*	*Subject*
1824	325	A gale of wind breaking up.
1832	1067	Forcing a boat from a flat beach in a heavy gale by the plan brought into use by Captain Manby for affording assistance at a distance from land with facility and certainty.

EXHIBITED AT THE BRITISH INSTITUTE

Year	*No.*	*Subject*
1823	75	A view on the beach, Yarmouth. 35×46 in.
1845	382	H.M. Ship *Victory* and other ships coming to anchor. 47×63 in.

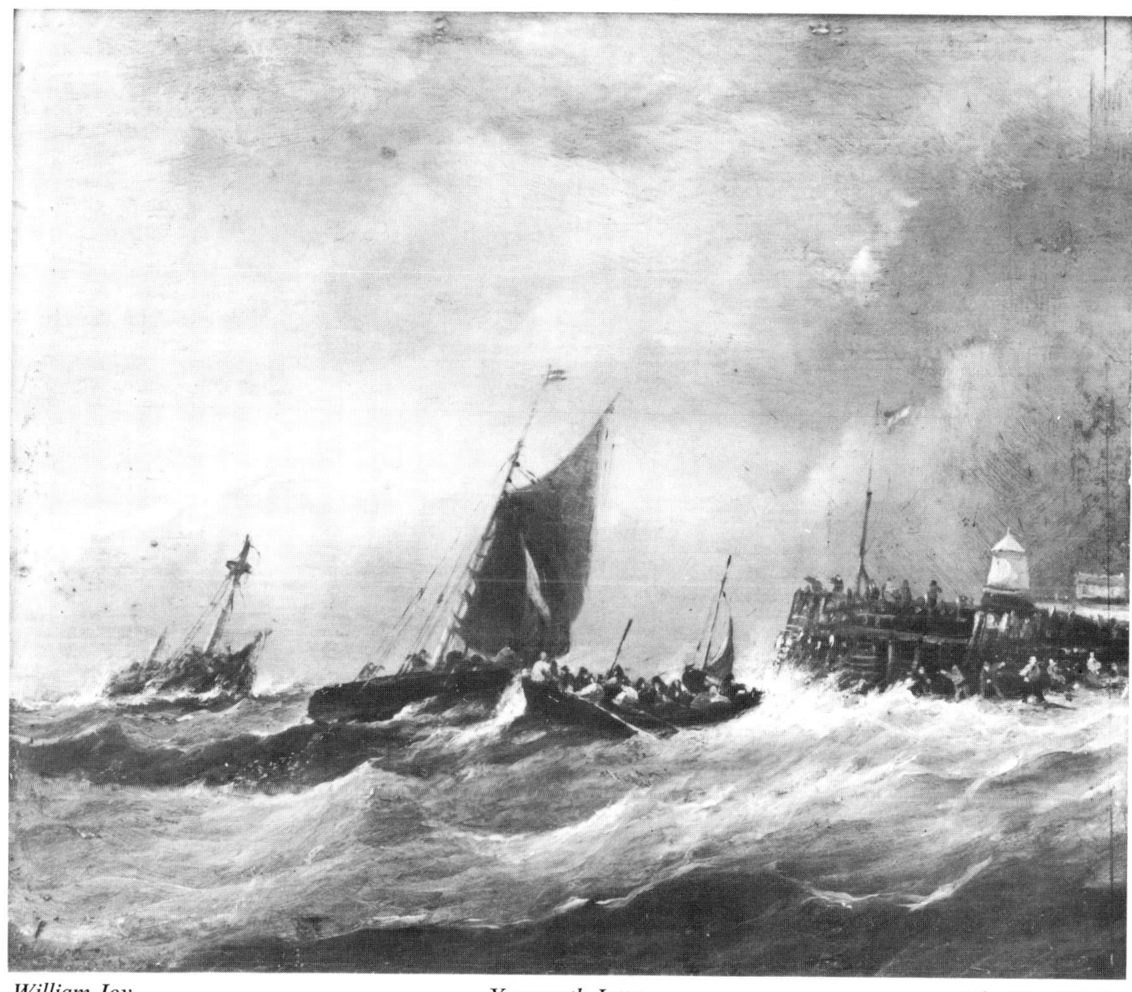

William Joy — *Yarmouth Jetty* — *Oil* 10×12⅛ *in.*

An unusually sketchy work

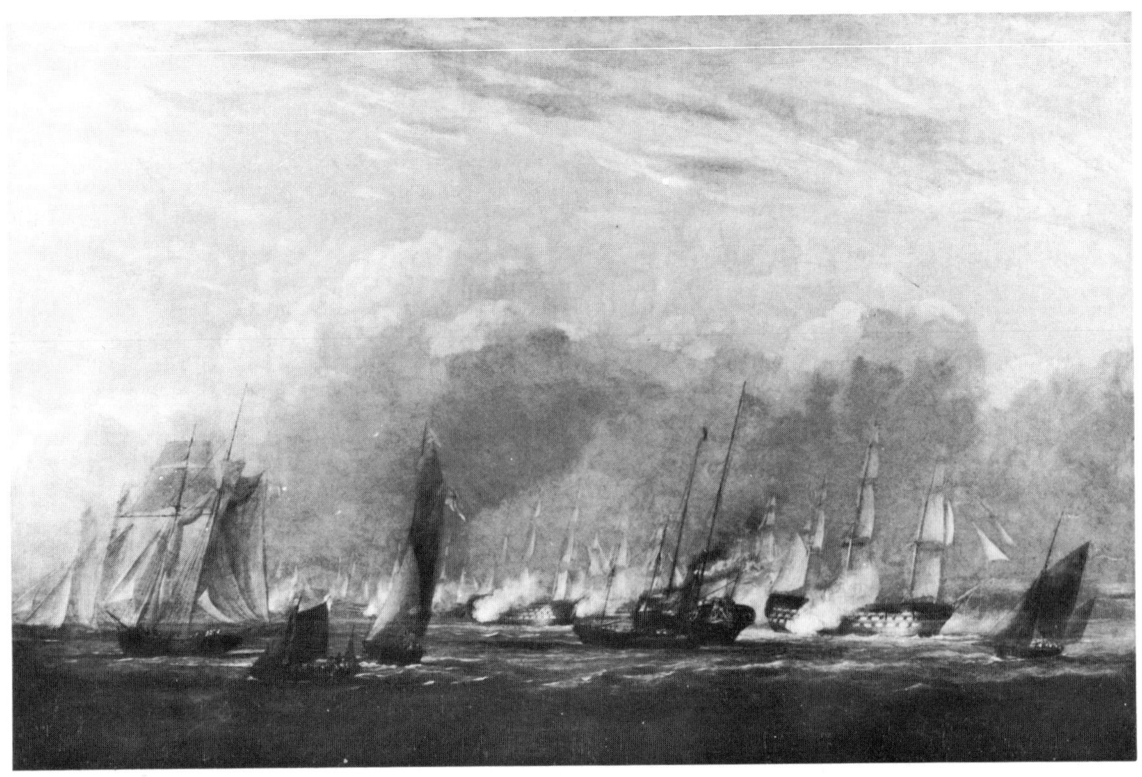

William Joy *A Review* *Oil on canvas approx.* 20×30 *in.*

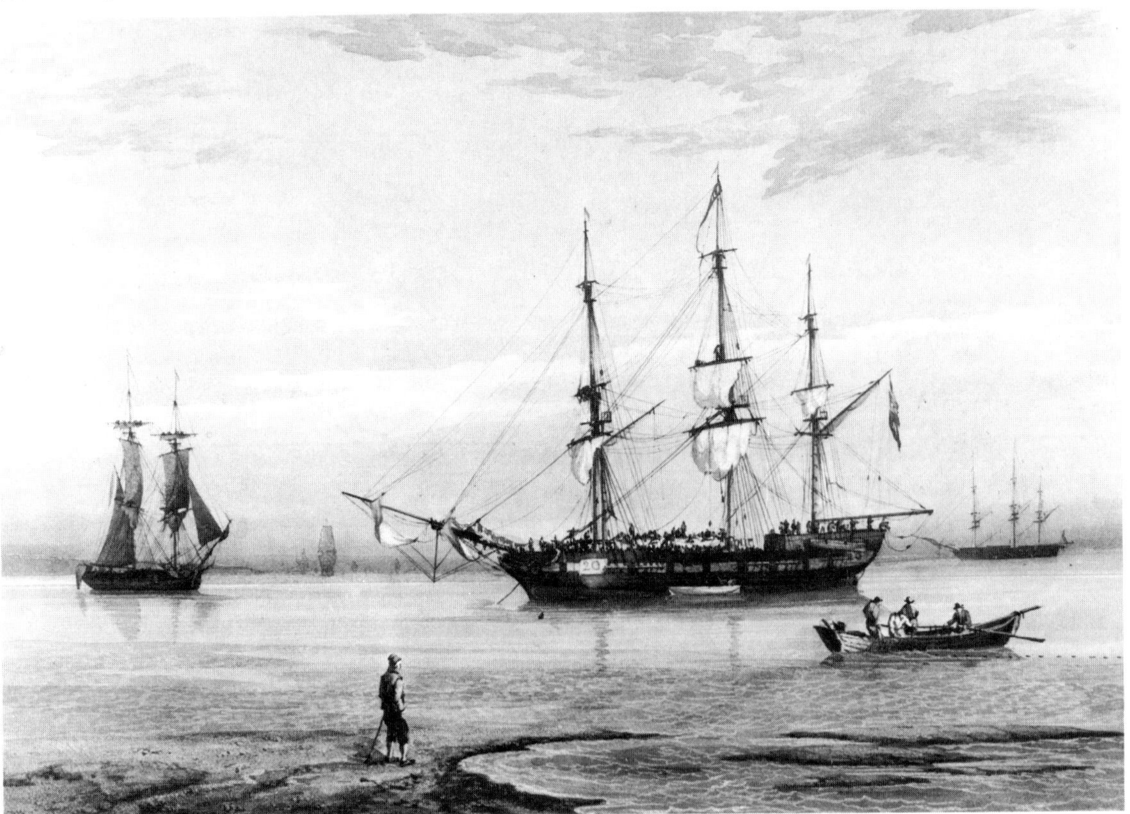

William Joy *Shipping in a Calm* *Water-colour* $10\frac{7}{8} \times 15\frac{3}{4}$ *in.*

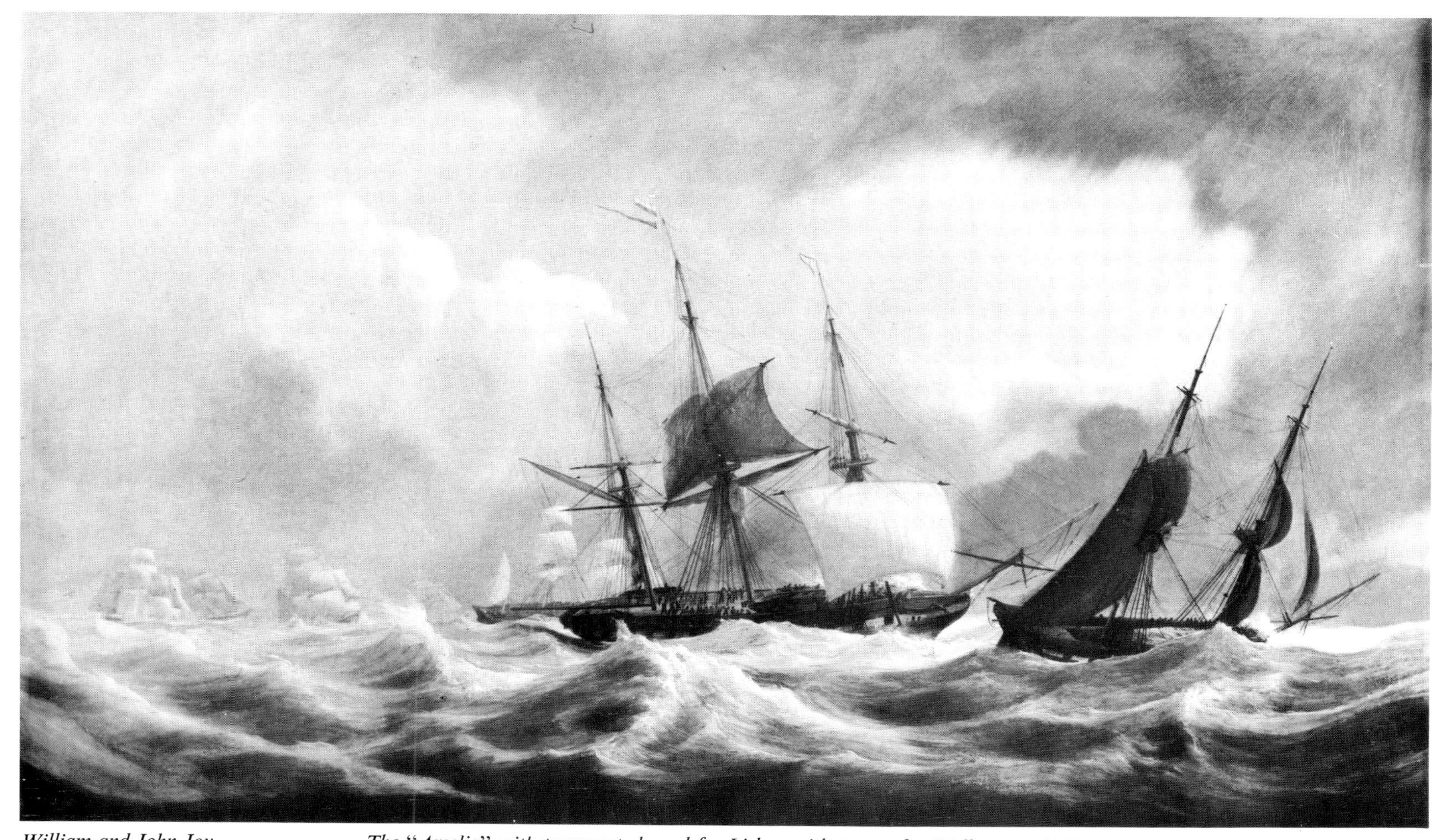

William and John Joy — *The "Amelia" with transports bound for Lisbon with troops for Wellington, 1810* — *Oil on canvas* 18 × 30 *in.*

The "Amelia" is in mourning for Princess Amelia

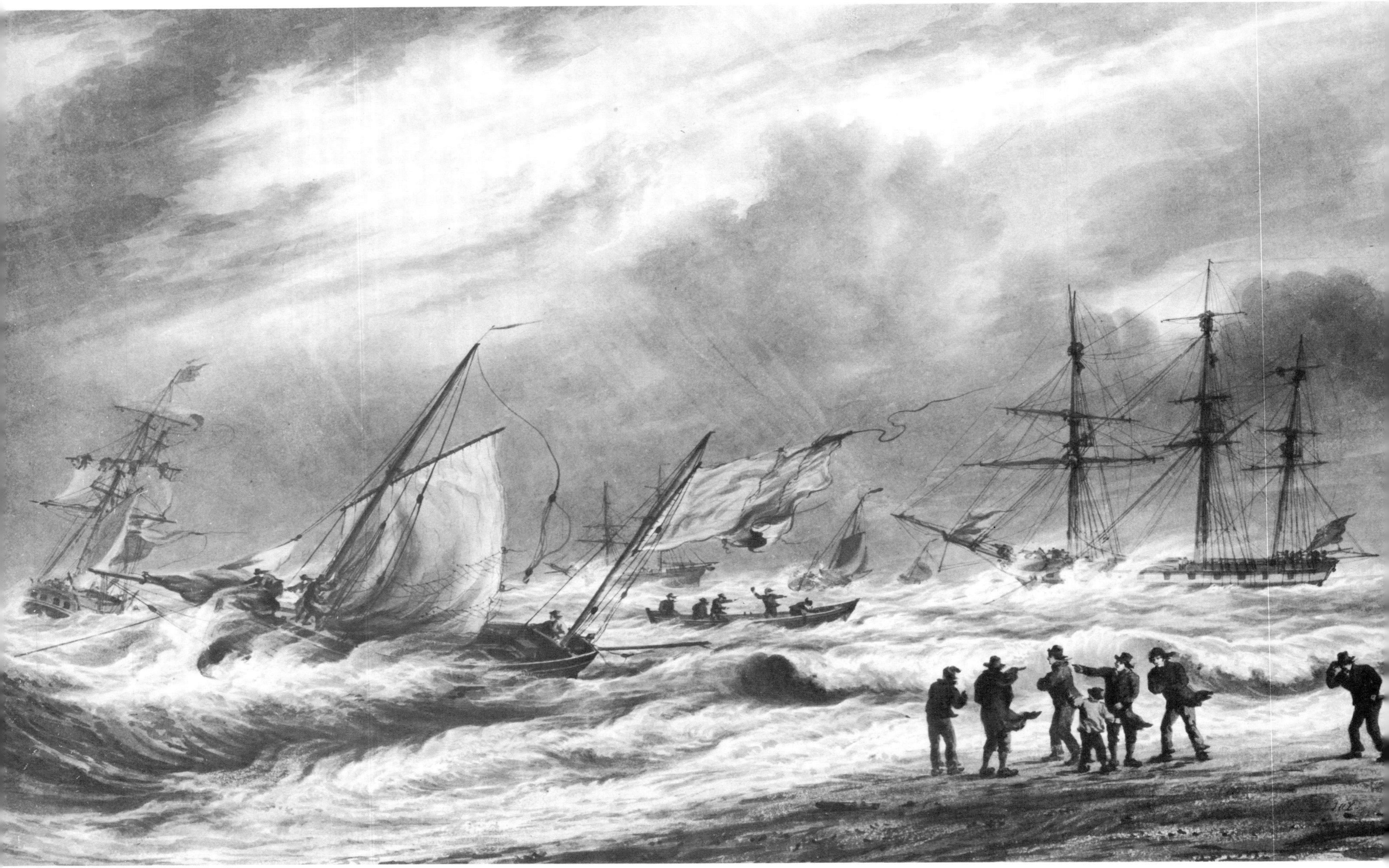

William Joy, 1828 *Note the men in the rigging* *Sepia*

JOHN NINHAM

(1754-1817)

1754 John Ninham was born in 1754 and is said to be of Huguenot descent. He carried on the business of heraldic painter and engraver at 11 Chapel Field, Norwich, specialising in the painting of panels for coaches, the coach-makers actually sending the panels to him.

He was also an engraver, his work including several views of Norwich, also a *Battle of the Nile* is recorded. Recorded in the Fitch Collection at Norwich were a series of indian ink drawings depicting the eleven Gates of Norwich.

1817 When John Ninham died in 1817 he left behind a widow and eight children. An advertisement at the time was inserted by T. and H. Ninham, stating that they were carrying on the business.

John Ninham is said to have had little advantage of education, but had an insatiable thirst for knowledge, much of which he passed on to his son, Henry. The illustrated Beach Scene, in Norwich Museum, is an interesting oil. It shows John Ninham as a truly eighteenth century artist, having his own characteristic style. The figures with their free treatment are a little reminiscent of Anderson and Pococke.

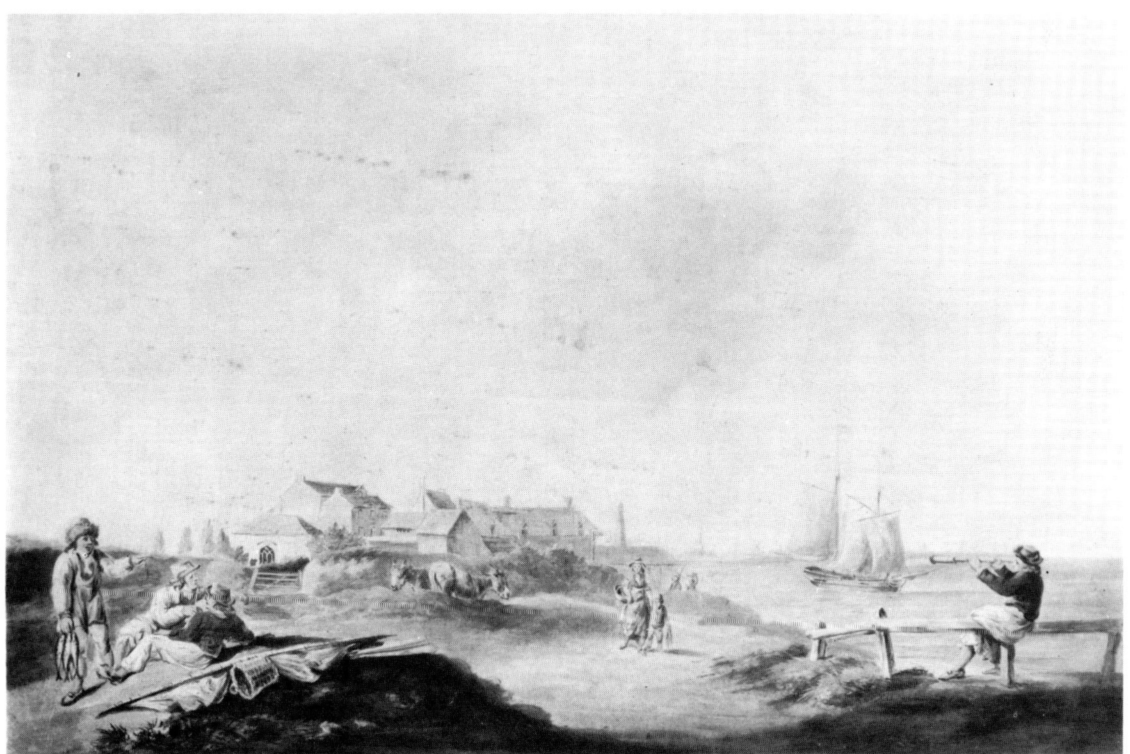

John Ninham *Beach Scene* *Oil* $13 \times 19\frac{1}{2}$ *in.*

TWENTY-FIFTH EXHIBITION OF THE WORKS OF THE NORFOLK AND SUFFOLK INSTITUTION FOR THE PROMOTION OF THE FINE ARTS, 1831

No.	*Subject*
160	Doorway to the music-house.
162	Old gate-way.

NORFOLK AND NORWICH FINE ARTS ASSOCIATION

Exhibition of the Works of Deceased Local Artists, 1860

No.	*Subject*	*Lent by*
188	A view in King Street, Norwich.	Mr. Wodderspoon.
279	View of Norwich (in water-colour room).	Mr. Mills.

HENRY NINHAM

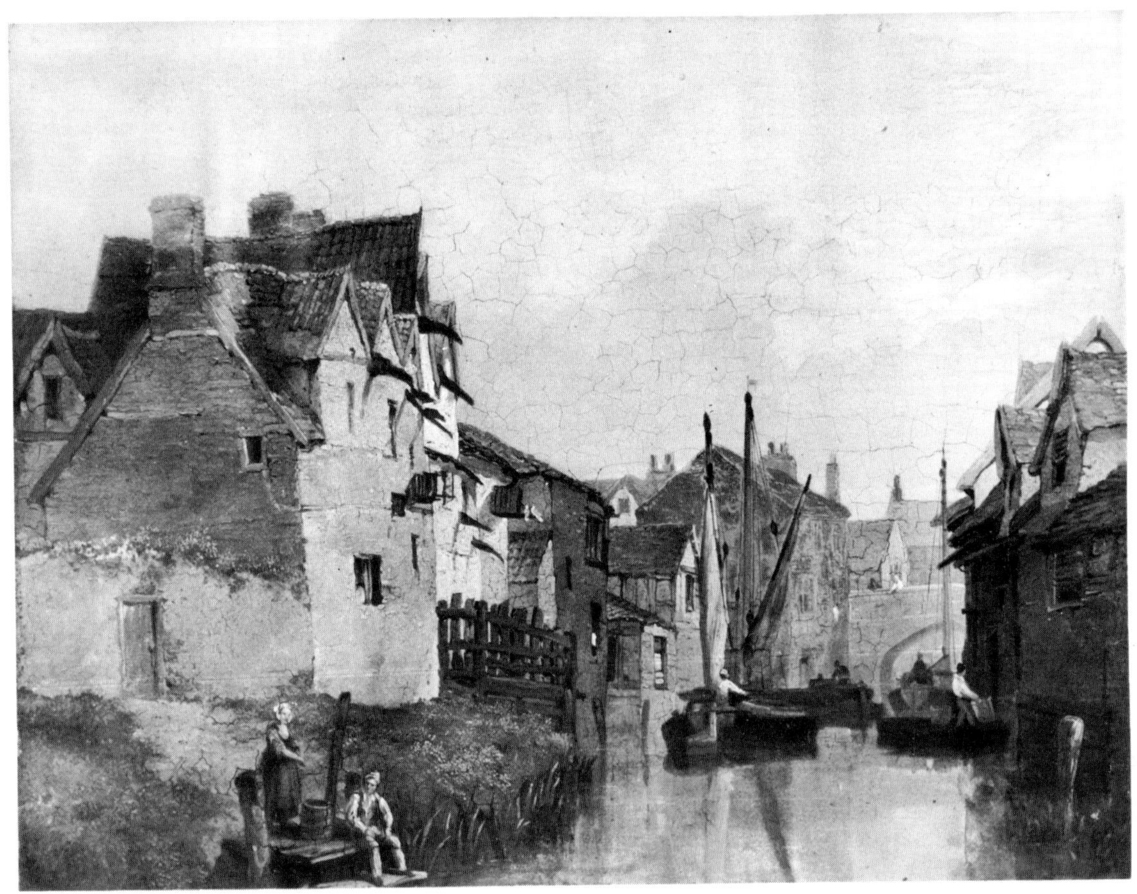

Henry Ninham *On the Wensum, Norwich* *Oil*

HENRY NINHAM

(1793-1874)

Henry Ninham, the son of John Ninham, was born on 15th October, 1793. As we have seen, he was one of eight children and as soon as he was old enough entered the family business. In the main it was as an heraldic painter and engraver that provided his means of livelihood. His engravings after Kirkpatrick of the views of the Gates of Norwich, and his engravings of numerous Norwich churches and views are his main contribution. However, he executed numerous drawings and water-colours, together with several oils. His contributions to the Norwich Society were not numerous, and in the main dealt with architectural subjects.

Henry Ninham was thought of quite highly by John Sell Cotman, who refers to him as "a very clever painter". One always looks for quality of drawing in the work of Henry Ninham. He has limited breadth and concept of handling, but directs a very skilled hand on suitably composed subjects. The study of the Norwich River Scene, bequeathed to the Norwich Castle Museum by Canon Parr, reveals a pleasing painter with a delicate sense of colour and controlled touch.

Henry Ninham was said to be a man of middle height, very heavy and stout, of genial, even jocular, disposition, and kind-hearted to a fault. It was through his friendship with the Rev. E. T. Daniel that he was introduced to J. M. W. Turner.

Ninham was married and had children, his wife, Frances, dying in 1845. Henry Ninham lived on to the age of 81, when he passed away at Chapel Field in 1874. He was buried in Norwich Cemetery.

EXHIBITS AT THE NORWICH SOCIETY'S ROOMS

Year	*Subject*
1816	A Dutch boor.
1817	The New Hall, Yarmouth.
1818	View of Flixton Hall, Suffolk.
	View of the North Aisle of Norwich Cathedral.
	The Choir of Norwich Cathedral.
1819	View of the North Aisle of Norwich Cathedral.
1820	Interior of Ely Cathedral.
1824	Interior of the Catholic Chapel of Costessey.
	South Porch of St. Michael-at-Plea Church.
	North Porch of St. Peter's, Mancroft.
1830	The Jesus Chapel, Norwich Cathedral.
	View at Cromer.
	A street scene.
	Street scene, St. Lawrence, Norwich.
1831	Street scene, near Whitefriars' bridge.
	Sir Benjamin Wrench's Court.

TWELFTH EXHIBITION OF THE NORWICH SOCIETY OF ARTISTS, 1816

No.	*Subject*
88	Dutch boor.

THIRTEENTH EXHIBITION OF THE NORWICH SOCIETY OF ARTISTS, 1817

No.	*Subject*
163	New Hall, Yarmouth.

FOURTEENTH EXHIBITION OF THE NORWICH SOCIETY OF ARTISTS, 1818

No.	*Subject*
141	View of Flixton Hall, Suffolk.
143	View from the North Aisle of Norwich Cathedral.

FIFTEENTH EXHIBITION OF THE NORWICH SOCIETY OF ARTISTS, 1819

No.	*Subject*
73	North Aisle of Norwich Cathedral.
152	Choir of Norwich Cathedral—looking east.

SIXTEENTH EXHIBITION OF THE NORWICH SOCIETY OF ARTISTS, 1820

No.	*Subject*
137	Interior of Ely Cathedral.

TWENTIETH EXHIBITION OF THE NORWICH SOCIETY OF ARTISTS, 1824

No.	*Subject*
3	Interior of the Catholic Chapel at Costessey.
102	South Porch of St. Michael's at Plea Church, Norwich.
174	North Porch of St. Peter's Mancroft Church, Norwich.

TWENTY-FOURTH EXHIBITION OF THE WORKS OF THE NORFOLK AND SUFFOLK INSTITUTION FOR THE PROMOTION OF THE FINE ARTS, 1830

No.	*Subject*
10	Jesus' Chapel, Norwich Cathedral.
58	View at Cromer.
75	A street scene.
76	Street scene, St. Lawrence.

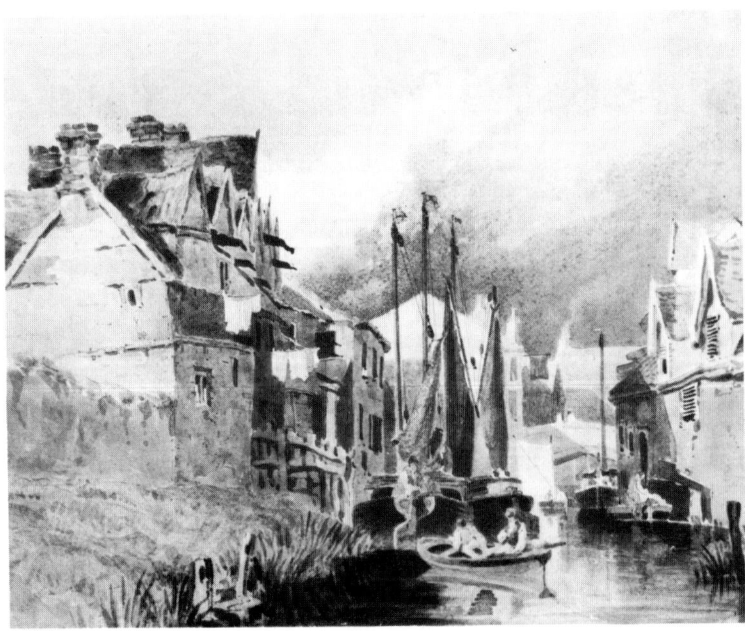

Henry Ninham *Whitefriars, Norwich* *Water-colour* 8 × 10 *in.*

TWENTY-FIFTH EXHIBITION OF THE WORKS OF THE NORFOLK AND SUFFOLK INSTITUTION FOR THE PROMOTION OF THE FINE ARTS, 1831

No.	*Subject*
6	Street scene near White Friars' Bridge.
38	Sir Benjamin Wrench's Court.

FIRST EXHIBITION OF THE NORFOLK AND NORWICH ART UNION, 1839

WATER-COLOURS

No.	*Subject*
235	Etching of part of an ancient religious house in St. John's, Maddermarket.
236	Gateway, London street.
237	Porch of the Free-school.
243	Weavers' lane.
244	Old post-office yard.
245	The kitchen in the Palace, Norwich.
246	On St. Martin's at Palace Plain.
247	Near St. Benedict's Gates.
248	Doorway in King Street.
249	Gateway Charing Cross.
	These drawings of Mr. Ninham's are intended for a series of etchings, now publishing, entitled *Picturesque Illustrations of Norwich*, accompanied by a descriptive and historical index illustrative of the plates.
255	Remains of Castleacre Priory, west front.
307	Sir Benjamin Wrench's Court, as it stood in 1810.

NORWICH AND EASTERN COUNTIES WORKING CLASSES INDUSTRIAL EXHIBITION, 1867

No.	*Subject*	*Lent by*
831	Three water-colour drawings of old post office court.	Mr. James Reeve, Curator, Norwich Museum.

BRITISH MEDICAL ASSOCIATION LOAN COLLECTION
Norfolk and Suffolk Artists, 1874

OIL PAINTINGS BY LIVING ARTISTS

No.	*Subject*	*Lent by*
212	Saint Benedict's, Norwich.	Mr. H. S. Patteson.
213	Pig Lane, Norwich.	Mr. H. S. Patteson.

WATER-COLOURS, BY LIVING ARTISTS

178	Elm Hill, Norwich.	Mr. John King.
184	Saint Lawrence, Norwich.	Mr. H. Vyall.
194	The Church Style Inn, Norwich.	Mr. John King.
206	Norwich Castle.	Mr. John King.

ART LOAN EXHIBITION
in aid of the funds of St. George's Club for Working Girls, 1902

No.	*Subject*
218	View of Norwich Cathedral from the Cow Tower.
221	Pottergate Street.
	(There are two No. 221, the other St. Peter Hungate Church by John Sell Cotman.)
226	King Street, Norwich.
230	Whitlingham, looking towards Norwich.
231	Old houses, Pottergate Street, Norwich.

EXHIBITION OF NORWICH SCHOOL PICTURES

Norwich Castle Museum and Art Galleries, October, 1927

OIL PAINTINGS

No.	*Subject*
71	The River Wensum, Norwich. $9\frac{3}{4} \times 7\frac{3}{4}$ in.
72	St. Stephen's Back Street, Norwich. $6\frac{1}{2} \times 8\frac{1}{2}$ in.
73	Houses in King Street, Norwich. 11×14 in.
74	View of Bethel Street, Norwich. 16×29 in.

WATER-COLOURS, DRAWINGS ETC.

228	Courtyard, Strangers' Hall, Norwich. $13\frac{1}{2} \times 11\frac{1}{4}$ in.
229	The Norwich Mercury Office in London Street (sepia). $10\frac{3}{4} \times 8\frac{1}{4}$ in.
230	River scene. $9\frac{3}{4} \times 11\frac{3}{4}$ in.
231	Old Post Office Court, Norwich (1). $6\frac{1}{2} \times 5$ in.
232	Old Post Office Court, Norwich (2). $6\frac{1}{2} \times 5$ in.
233	Scene in Norwich (1). $7 \times 5\frac{1}{2}$ in.
234	Scene in Norwich (2). 8×5 in.

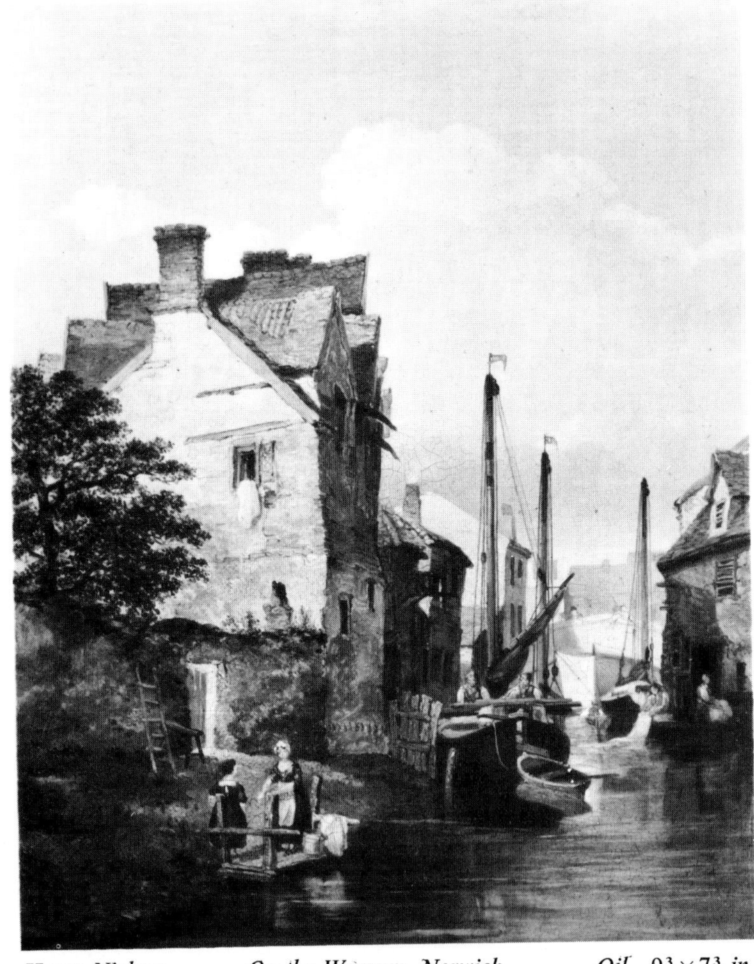

Henry Ninham *On the Wensum, Norwich* *Oil* $9\frac{3}{4} \times 7\frac{3}{4}$ *in.*

CHARLES HODGSON

(*c*. 1770-1856)

c. 1770 The exact date of birth of Charles Hodgson is not known, but we know his son, David Hodgson, was born in 1798. It is known that Charles Hodgson was an established teacher at 47 Wymer Street, Norwich, in 1802. It would therefore appear reasonable to presume that he was not born much later than 1770.

His principal teaching subject was mathematics. It was in this subject that he was appointed at the Norwich Grammar School.

In 1802 he had his first work accepted by the Royal Academy. This was followed by three other works between 1802 and 1824. In 1824 he also sent to the British Institution. Being a friend of John Crome and Robert Ladbrooke it was only natural that he banded
1805 together with them in the formation of the Norwich Society, in 1805. It will be seen from his list of exhibits that from the first he was interested principally in the painting of views containing buildings.

After Crome and Ladbrooke returned from their tour of Wales presumably Charles
1806 Hodgson kindled up the desire to see for himself. It was in the year 1806 that he gathered up his painting material and along with his very young son David he took off for distant Wales. This visit to Wales included a very significant visit to Chester, significant, because young David was so impressed by the beauty of the city he returned to it time and again to paint its alluring views. His activity in 1808 is best illustrated by the following advertisement which appeared in a Norwich paper:

> Academy, St. Andrews 24 Dec. 1808
> Mr. Chas. Hodgson
> Most respectfully informs his friends and the Public that his Academy will be open on 15 January for admission of young Ladies and young Gentlemen.
> The course of study adopted in the School leads from an enquiry into the construction of the English Language, Writing, Arithmetic.

Being a quiet, respectable and well-liked man by his fellow citizens, it is not surprising to find that in 1813 he was selected president of the Norwich Society. With the secession in 1816 Charles Hodgson remained with the Crome faction, sending to the Exhibition that year *Interior of St. Stephen's Church, Norwich*. He continued sending to the Norwich
1825 Society until 1825, when he was appointed Architectural Draughtsman to the Duke of Sussex.

Charles Hodgson died at Liverpool on 27th November, 1856.

THE PAINTINGS

David Hodgson, his son, stated in the 1860 Norwich Fine Art Society Catalogue, that his father's works were few. The author once possessed a signed water-colour by Charles Hodgson (illustrated). It was executed in cool, delicate colours, somewhat reminiscent of John Sell Cotman. It is just possible that Cotman took lessons from Charles Hodgson.

EXHIBITION OF THE NORWICH SOCIETY OF ARTISTS, 1805

No.	*Subject*
40	A landscape—body colours.
43	A landscape—body colours.
45	Moonlight—body colours.
52	Landscape—body colours.
95	Interior of the chancel of Norwich Cathedral.
107	Sketch of a Saxon screen in Norwich Cathedral.
116	View in Switzerland, after Chiparte.
121	View in Switzerland.
126	View in the cloister of Norwich Cathedral.
140	Ruins discovered in the Lower Close, Norwich.
146	View in Switzerland.
161	Fall on the River Arve.
175	One of the aisles leading from the South transcept of Norwich Cathedral.
178	View in Switzerland.

SECOND EXHIBITION OF THE NORWICH SOCIETY OF ARTISTS, 1806

No.	*Subject*
3	Eagle-tower, Carnarvon Castle, North Wales.
4	Court of Conway Castle, North Wales.
5	View in Norwich Cathedral.
6	View of Bishop Goldwell's monument, and part of Norwich Cathedral.
7	Jesus' Chapel, Norwich Cathedral.
44	Pont-y-Pair, near Llanwrst, North Wales.
95	Chester Cathedral, Cheshire.
104	Carnarvon Castle, North Wales.
115	Duke Humphrey's tomb, St. Alban's Abbey, Herts.
116	Landscape.
119	Landscape.
126	Landscape.
153	Saxon screen, Norwich Cathedral.

THIRD EXHIBITION OF THE NORWICH SOCIETY OF ARTISTS, 1807

No.	*Subject*
35	Design for a Gothic chancel.
41	Figures—a sketch.
69	Roman urn.
87	Sepulchral chapel at Tewksbury.

FOURTH EXHIBITION OF THE NORWICH SOCIETY OF ARTISTS, 1808

No.	*Subject*
65	Interior of a church—composition.
101	Spanish christening.
111	View in Staindrop Church, the tomb of R. Neville, Earl of Westmoreland, and his two wives.
249	Bishop Stanbury's Chapel, Hereford Cathedral.

SIXTH EXHIBITION OF THE NORWICH SOCIETY OF ARTISTS, 1810

No.	*Subject*
136	Interior of St. Peter's Mancroft Church, Norwich.

TENTH EXHIBITION OF THE NORWICH SOCIETY OF ARTISTS, 1814

No.	*Subject*
141	Interior of Norwich Cathedral.

ELEVENTH EXHIBITION OF THE NORWICH SOCIETY OF ARTISTS, 1815

No.	*Subject*
95	Interior of St. Peter's Mancroft Church, Norwich.

TWELFTH EXHIBITION OF THE NORWICH SOCIETY OF ARTISTS, 1816

No.	*Subject*
106	Interior of St. Stephen's Church, Norwich.

THIRTEENTH EXHIBITION OF THE NORWICH SOCIETY OF ARTISTS, 1817

No.	*Subject*
52	North entrance to the Choir, Norwich Cathedral.

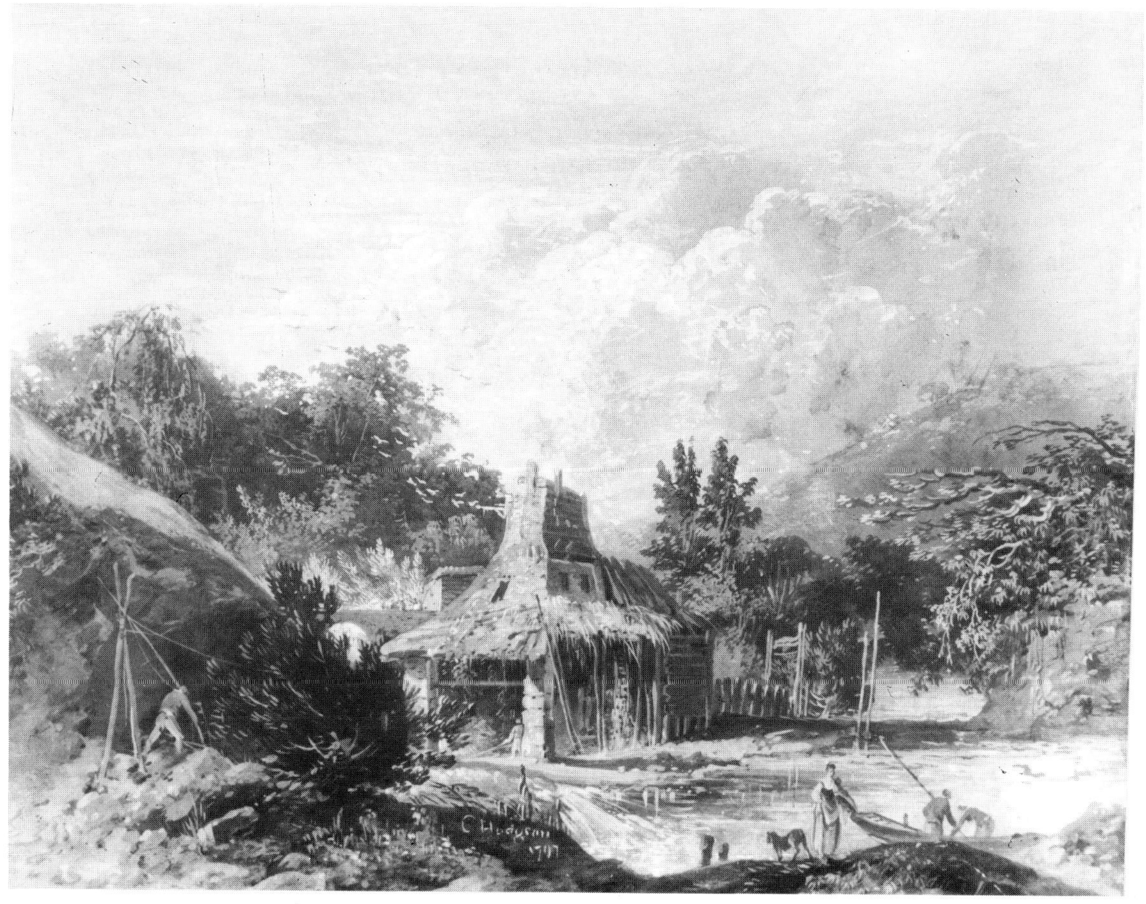

Charles Hodgson *Gouaché* $11\frac{1}{2} \times 15\frac{1}{2}$ *in.*

FIFTEENTH EXHIBITION OF THE NORWICH SOCIETY OF ARTISTS, 1819

No.	*Subject*
176	An interior, in which is introduced the monuments of the Paston family—Paston, Norfolk.

SIXTEENTH EXHIBITION OF THE NORWICH SOCIETY OF ARTISTS, 1820

No.	*Subject*
113	View of Norwich.

SEVENTEENTH EXHIBITION OF THE NORWICH SOCIETY OF ARTISTS, 1821

No.	*Subject*
51	Scene near Braintree, Essex—evening.

EIGHTEENTH EXHIBITION OF THE NORWICH SOCIETY OF ARTISTS, 1822

No.	*Subject*
83	Scene in Norwich Market.

NINETEENTH EXHIBITION OF THE NORWICH SOCIETY OF ARTISTS, 1823

No.	*Subject*
88	Street scene, Norwich.

TWENTIETH EXHIBITION OF THE NORWICH SOCIETY OF ARTISTS, 1824

No.	*Subject*
84	South transept of Rouen Cathedral.

TWENTY-FIRST EXHIBITION OF THE NORWICH SOCIETY OF ARTISTS, 1825

No.	*Subject*
46	Norwich Market.
77	Interior of the Choir, Norwich Cathedral.

In 1809, 1811, 1812, 1813 (President), 1818, 1828-32, C. Hodgson is mentioned in the list of members of the Norwich Society of Artists, but he did not exhibit in those years.

NORWICH POLYTECHNIC EXHIBITION, 1840

No.	*Subject*	*Lent by*
117	Henry VII's Chapel.	Mr. Robert Scott, jun.

NORFOLK AND NORWICH FINE ARTS ASSOCIATION

Exhibition of the Works of Deceased Local Artists, 1860

No.	*Subject*	*Lent by*
144	St. Stephen's Church.	Mr. Norgate.
151	Interior of Norwich Cathedral.	Mr. A. G. Stannard.

BRITISH MEDICAL ASSOCIATION LOAN COLLECTION

Norfolk and Suffolk Artists, 1874

No.	*Subject*	*Lent by*
24	Interior of Norwich Cathedral.	Mrs. Hodgson.

FINE ART EXHIBITION

in aid of the new Norfolk and Norwich Hospital, 1883

No.	*Subject*	*Lent by*
80	Landscape.	Mr B. E. Fletcher.

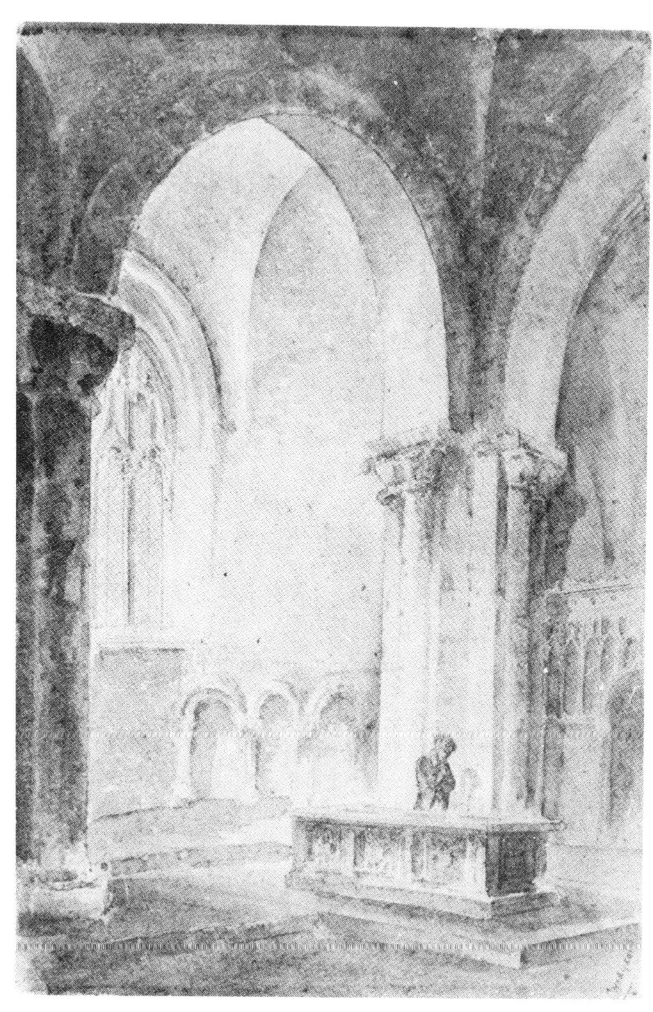

Jesus Chapel, Norwich Cathedral

Charles Hodgson *Pencil and water-colour* 9×6 *in.*

His work is rare

DAVID HODGSON

(1798-1864)

1798 David Hodgson, the son of Charles Hodgson, was born in Norwich in 1798. It will be remembered that he visited Wales with his father when he was but seven years old, in
1805 1805. It is quite possible that the Hodgsons had relatives in Liverpool, and the prime object of David's visit was to see them.

As in the case of many of the successful Norwich School painters, David was educated at the Grammar School, possibly being taught drawing by John Crome and mathematics by his father.

Such was the enthusiasm of the early Norwich painters that they often persuaded their children into taking up the profession. Charles Hodgson was no exception, for we find his son, David, exhibiting at an early age. From his fifteenth year he was a regular exhibitor; one painting at the Royal Academy, twenty-seven at the British Institution, eleven at Suffolk Street and, of course, the Norwich Society. Also at Manchester, Liverpool and Newcastle—in all, upwards of 200 pictures. His output is said not to have been great as he was an assiduous teacher. However, he was a considerable exhibitor.

1825 In 1825, with his father, he was honoured by H.R.H. the Duke of Sussex, who appointed him his painter of Domestic Architecture. About this time he was appointed drawing master at the Grammar School. Here he taught several later members of the Norwich School.

Due to his conscientious ways and gifts he had little difficulty in earning a comfortable living. From his studio in Tombland flowed many delightful views of the old City of Norwich, many of which still grace the walls of the descendants of those worthy citizens who purchased paintings from him.

1856 By 1856 he is recorded as moving from Tombland to Grey Friars, Priory Lane, King Street. He was now a well-established teacher and much loved by his pupils. One of them said of him:

> Dear Old David Hodgson! A kind and genial soul as ever lived—he taught me drawing, and I have been out sketching with the old man more than once!

1858 In 1858 he was at Ely, where he greatly admired the cathedral. The visit resulted in several fine paintings of Ely, the *View of the Octagon* (illustrated) being exhibited at the British Institution in the same year.

1861 The last London exhibit was in 1861, *Bishopgate Bridge, Norwich*, at the British Institution.

By his later days photography was coming into fashion. The illustrated plate taken by another Norwich artist, A. G. Stannard, shows our artist to be a rather care worn
1864 character. This photograph must have been taken shortly before he passed away in 1864 at Norwich.

THE PAINTINGS

The interesting aspect of David Hodgson's painting is his loyalty to one style. The *Fishmarket, Norwich*, in the Castle Museum, dating to about 1822, shows little difference in technique to the *View of the Octagon, Ely*, painted about 1858. Whilst the paint application is liberal, amounts remain similar, the palette becomes lower as time goes by. The most sparkling colour seems to date to about 1830s. In his skies he often has two blues, a light blue and touches of strong dark blue. He has an admirable eye for balancing his cloud forms with his buildings. Respecting the buildings, he developed a sensitive feeling which enabled him to indicate great age and dignity: his choice of colour in the depiction of stone is particularly subtle.

The drawing of the interiors of churches and cathedrals is never an easy task, but Hodgson seems to take it all in his stride, providing the most convincing architecture. The paintings are usually well peopled, with their black, white, blue and red costumes. Whilst the drawing is somewhat over broad, the figures are naturally grouped at their respective occupations.

His landscape—*Woodland Scene with Boys Fishing*—was probably painted shortly after John Crome painted *The Porlingland Oak*, for the composition owes much to Crome's picture. Here the trees are finished with considerable detail, especially the foreground tree. As the trees recede, the detail skilfully diminishes, the distance being made up of broad touches of slight pink, light blue, light green to slight prussian. The trunks are very Crome-like and have a gnarled texture, the foreground growth being intermingled with runners. In the sky, the clouds have numerous touches of light pink and naples, indicative of striking light.

David Hodgson's drawings and water-colours are often of high quality. The drawings in pencil are incisive and have John Crome's staccato touches—they can be confused with Crome, perhaps the latter has a softer touch. The water-colours are made up of clean washes, many carrying Stark-like green tones. He often inscribes the subject and signs.

NOTE: David Hodgson in his early years was referred to as David Hodgson, Junior. Possibly his father Charles was known as David.

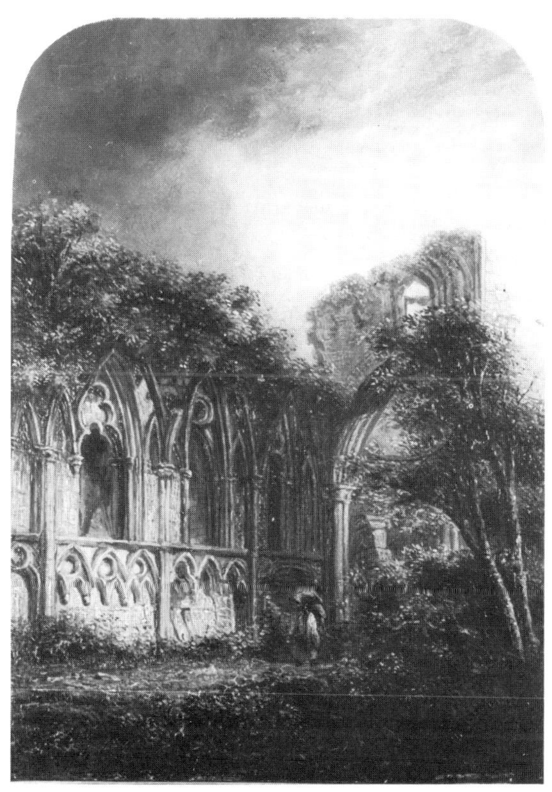

David Hodgson St. Mary's, York Oil on panel

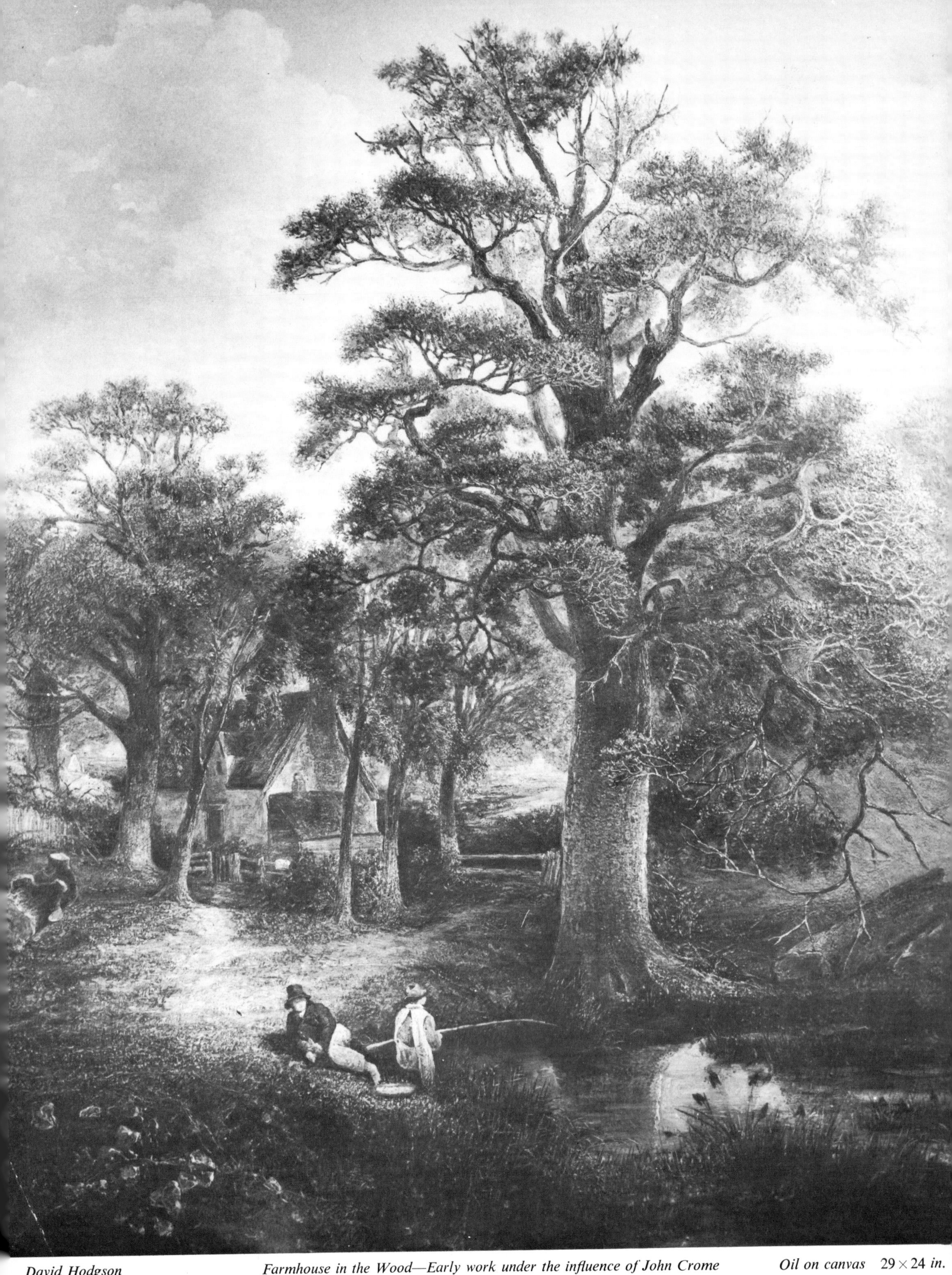

David Hodgson *Farmhouse in the Wood—Early work under the influence of John Crome* *Oil on canvas* 29 × 24 *in.*

NINTH EXHIBITION OF THE NORWICH SOCIETY OF ARTISTS, 1813

No.	*Subject*
112	Salisbury Cathedral.
122	Distant view of Dublin.

TENTH EXHIBITION OF THE NORWICH SOCIETY OF ARTISTS, 1814

No.	*Subject*
120	A cemetery—composition.
156	Norwich Castle.

ELEVENTH EXHIBITION OF THE NORWICH SOCIETY OF ARTISTS, 1815

No.	*Subject*
44	Head.
157	The gate-house, Tombland.

TWELFTH EXHIBITION OF THE NORWICH SOCIETY OF ARTISTS, 1816

No.	*Subject*
50	Sketch in oil, from the Cloister, Norwich Cathedral.
52	Flowers from Nature.
103	Transverse view from the North Aisle of the Nave, Norwich Cathedral.

THIRTEENTH EXHIBITION OF THE NORWICH SOCIETY OF ARTISTS, 1817

No.	*Subject*
77	South Aisle of the Nave of Norwich Cathedral.
85	Interior of a hall, St. John's Maddermarket, Norwich.
174	Pencil sketch.

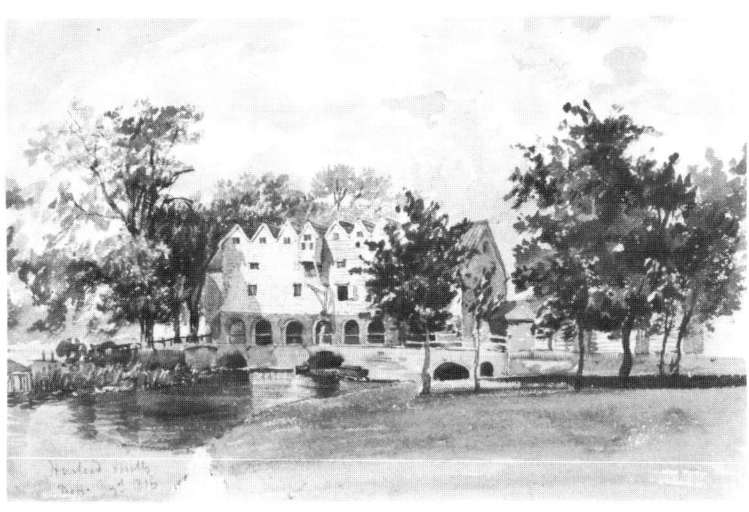

Horstead Mills, 1816

David Hodgson *Water-colour* $7\frac{3}{8} \times 11\frac{7}{8}$ *in.*

FOURTEENTH EXHIBITION OF THE NORWICH SOCIETY OF ARTISTS, 1818

No.	*Subject*
62	Interior of a church.
91	Interior of the Choir, Norwich Cathedral—looking west (unfinished).
120	View of Conway Castle, Carnarvonshire—from a sketch in 1805.
125	Great Hall, Conway Castle—from an original sketch in 1805.
135	Carnarvon Castle, North Wales—from a sketch in 1805.

FIFTEENTH EXHIBITION OF THE NORWICH SOCIETY OF ARTISTS, 1819

No. *Subject*

64 Design from Scott's Lay of the Last Minstrel.

"I would you had been there to see
How the light broke forth so gloriously,
Streamed upward to the chancel roof,
And through the galleries far aloof!

And issuing from the tomb,
Shewed the Monk's cowl, and visage pale,
Danced on the dark-browed Warrior's mail,
And kissed his waving plume,"

(Vide *Scott's Lay of the Last Minstrel, Canto II*)

76 Design for finishing the tower of St. Peter's Mancroft, Norwich.
117 A design for an ornamental building, adapted to park scenery.
203 Sketch of the tower of St. Peter's Mancroft, Norwich.

SIXTEENTH EXHIBITION OF THE NORWICH SOCIETY OF ARTISTS, 1820

No.	*Subject*
66	Archway under the steeple of St. John's Maddermarket, Norwich.
90	Interior of St. Stephen's Church, Norwich.
96	Transverse view of Hellesdon Church.
114	Sketch in sepia.
116	Two prison scenes—sketches for pictures.
119	The Queen's Gate, Carnarvon Castle—evening.
128	Waterfall in North Wales.
130	Perspective view of the residence of P. M. Martineau, Esq.
134	Two sketches—designs for pictures.
139	View of Greenwich.
156	View at Brighton.

SEVENTEENTH EXHIBITION OF THE NORWICH SOCIETY OF ARTISTS, 1821

No.	*Subject*
23	Landscape.
57	The Chancel, shewing the monuments of Lord and Lady Paston, Paston Church, Norfolk.
67	Scene in St. Martin's at Oak.
88	Group of trees in Tuck's Wood, Lakenham.
109	A triumphal arch, to celebrate the Coronation of King George IV.

EIGHTEENTH EXHIBITION OF THE NORWICH SOCIETY OF ARTISTS, 1822

No.	*Subject*
58	The Norwich Fish Market.
64	Woodland scenery.
94	Landscape.
128	A storm retreating.

NINETEENTH EXHIBITION OF THE NORWICH SOCIETY OF ARTISTS, 1823

No.	*Subject*
71	Scene at Coltishall.
79	Scene in the interior of Norwich Cathedral.
105	Interior of St. Stephen's Church, Norwich.
143	Scene—St. Martin's at Oak.
150	Scene from Nature.
190	The South Porch of Chester Cathedral—sepia drawing.
196	West central entrance of Norwich Cathedral.
198	Ruin in the Bishop's Garden, Norwich—sepia drawing.

TWENTIETH EXHIBITION OF THE NORWICH SOCIETY OF ARTISTS, 1824

No.	*Subject*
39	Guild-Hall Porch, Norwich.
59	Distant view from Bracondale.
65	Landscape.

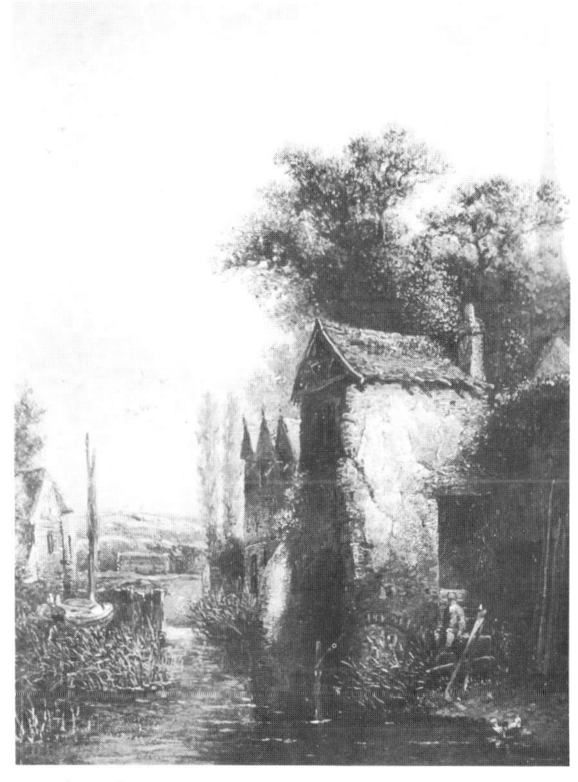

David Hodgson *From Whitefriars Bridge, Norwich*

A similar view is published in Dickes' 'Norwich School Painters', page 205

Exhibited in Hodgson's centenary at the Castle, Norwich

TWENTY-FIRST EXHIBITION OF THE NORWICH SOCIETY OF ARTISTS, 1825

No.	*Subject*
54	Scene, composed near Norwich.
60	Distant view, from Bracondale.
64	Distant view, from Acle.
79	Scene, near Stratton Strawless.
81	Street scene, Norwich—afternoon.
87	Landscape.
160	South Entrance, Chester Cathedral.

TWENTY-SECOND EXHIBITION OF THE NORFOLK AND SUFFOLK INSTITUTION FOR THE PROMOTION OF THE FINE ARTS, 1828

No.	*Subject*
53	The Bishop's Great Gate, St. Martin's at Palace, Norwich.
79	Haymarket, Norwich.
80	Norwich Fish Market.
96	All Saints' Church, Norwich.
101	Scene on Tombland, with a view of the Erpingham Gate.
102	St. James' Street, Norwich.
103	Scene in Norwich Market Place.
106	View of a part of Norwich Market.

TWENTY-THIRD EXHIBITION OF THE NORFOLK AND SUFFOLK INSTITUTION FOR THE PROMOTION OF THE FINE ARTS, 1829

No.	*Subject*
8	Bishop-gate Bridge, Norwich, painted to illustrate the *Architectural Antiquities of Cities* now publishing by John Britton, Esq., F.S.A.
43	St. James's Street, Norwich.
48	Guildhall Porch, Norwich.
91	Street scene, with a view of the Town Hall, King's Lynn, Norfolk.
175	Study from Kimberley Park.
182	Study of ash trees.
183	Study of ash trees.

TWENTY-FOURTH EXHIBITION OF THE WORKS OF THE NORFOLK AND SUFFOLK INSTITUTION FOR THE PROMOTION OF THE FINE ARTS, 1830

No.	*Subject*
19	Sir Benjamin Wrench's Court, taken down in 1826.
36	Lamb Row, Chester.
52	Old Post-office Court, Norwich, taken down in 1826.
79	Landscape.
94	Interior of part of Norwich Cathedral.
117	Bishopgate Bridge.
145	Old Ferry House.
164	Landscape.
165	Landscape.
192	A study in Kimberley Park.

TWENTY-FIFTH EXHIBITION OF THE WORKS OF THE NORFOLK AND SUFFOLK INSTITUTION FOR THE PROMOTION OF THE FINE ARTS, 1831

No.	*Subject*
39	Interior of St. Mary's Chapel, Chester.
54	Old buildings in Chester, taken down in 1829.
58	Cottages at Chester.
63	Erpingham Gate-house, Norwich.
66	Draining mill.
94	Lower Bridge Street, Chester.
126	Town Hall, Chester.
—	Landscape and cattle.

TWENTY-SIXTH EXHIBITION OF THE NORFOLK AND SUFFOLK INSTITUTION FOR THE PROMOTION OF THE FINE ARTS, 1832

No.	*Subject*
44	Mausoleum, Wroxham, erected to the memory of S. T. Southwell, Esq.
93	Bishop's Gate, Norwich, painted for the *Picturesque Antiquities of Cities* by J. Britton, Esq.
110	St. Margaret's Church, Lynn—West Front.
118	Scene from the New Mills—morning.

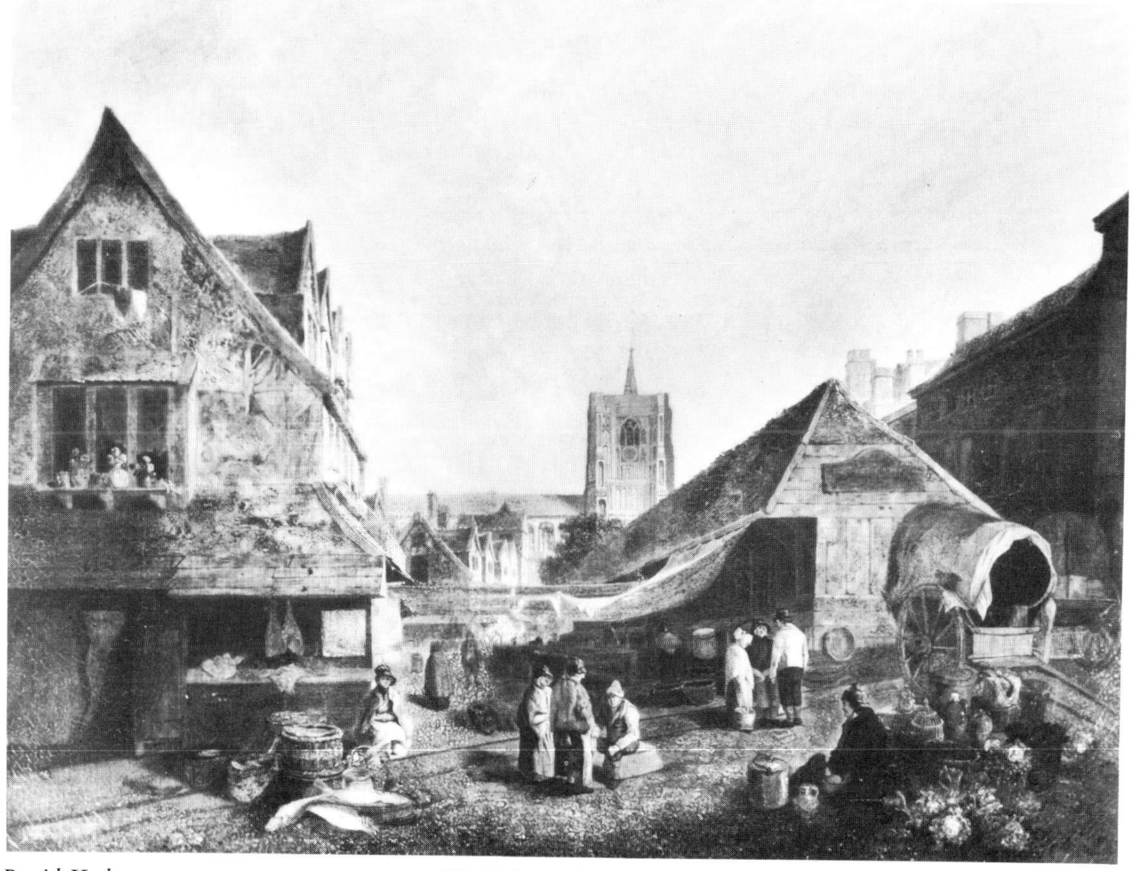

David Hodgson *Old Fish Market, Norwich* *Oil* $26\frac{3}{4} \times 34\frac{1}{2}$ *in.*

TWENTY-SEVENTH EXHIBITION OF THE WORKS OF THE NORFOLK AND SUFFOLK INSTITUTION FOR THE PROMOTION OF THE FINE ARTS, 1833

No.	*Subject*
9	In the Cloister, Chester Cathedral.
10	The Keep, Castle Rising.
11	In the Cloister, Chester Cathedral.
55	Interior of the Cloister of Chester Cathedral.
56	Old houses in Bristol.
70	The Crypt, Norwich Cathedral.
83	St. Michael's Porch, Chester, shewing the interior of one of the Rows.
92	Interior of Godmanham Church, Yorkshire.
93	The mendicant. "O grant relief and Heav'n will bless your store."
102	Interior of St. Mary's Chapel, Chester.
148	Trees at Cringleford.

WORKS OF ANCIENT AND MODERN MASTERS, 1828

No.	*Subject*
89	Principal entrance to the Bishop's Palace, Norwich.

SECOND EXHIBITION OF THE WORKS OF ANCIENT MASTERS, 1830

No.	*Subject*
2	Interior of a church.
42	Landscape.
47	Landscape.

FIRST EXHIBITION OF THE NORFOLK AND NORWICH ART UNION, 1839

No.	*Subject*
1	Part of the remains of Castleacre Priory.
45	View at Lakenham.
55	In Kimberley Park.
60	Market scene, Norwich.
64	Street scene, Chester.
67	Entrance to a wood.
77	Near Whitlingham.
115	Town-hall, Lynn.
130	St. Bennet's Abbey.
175	Scene at Reedham.
191	Gateway of the Abbey of St. Bennet's, at Holme.
194	Street scene, Chester.
217	View in Kimberley Park.

NORWICH POLYTECHNIC EXHIBITION, 1840

No.	*Subject*	*Lent by*
114	View in the Precincts, Norwich.	The Artist.
129	Meadow scene, Trowse.	The Artist.

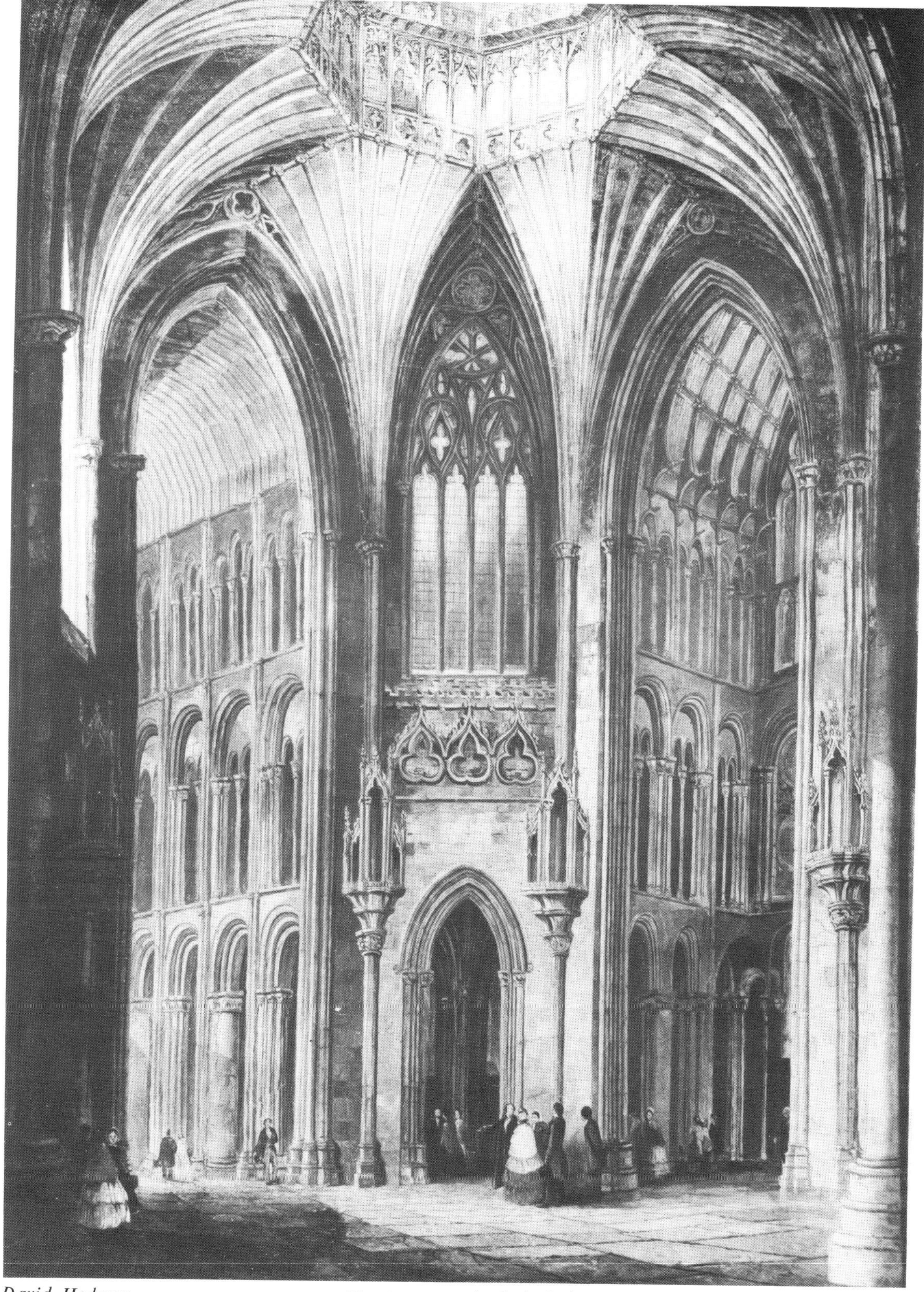

David Hodgson — *The Octagon, Ely Cathedral* — *Oil on canvas* 33 × 24 in.
Exhibited at the British Institute, 1858
NOTE—*The Octagon was built in the 13th century and is supported by a timber superstructure behind the stone façade*

FIRST EXHIBITION OF THE EAST OF ENGLAND ART UNION, 1842

No.	*Subject*
32	Lane scene, Whitlingham.
37	A study of trees from Nature, near Whitlingham.
39	Entrance to a wood, near Norwich.
45	Composition in Kimberley Woods.
48	Trees painted from Nature in Trowse Wood.
92	Meadow scene, Trowse, near Norwich.
100	In Trowse Wood—afternoon.

FIRST EXHIBITION OF THE NORFOLK AND NORWICH ASSOCIATION FOR THE PROMOTION OF THE FINE ARTS, 1848

No.	*Subject*
18	At Witton, Norfolk.
23	At Whitlingham, Norfolk.
161	St. Peter's Mancroft Church.

SECOND EXHIBITION OF THE NORFOLK AND NORWICH ASSOCIATION FOR THE PROMOTION OF THE FINE ARTS, 1849

No.	*Subject*
7	Kimberley Park, Norfolk.
22	Lane at Eaton.
28	View from the Hospital Meadow, Norwich.
64	Interior, attached to the Roman Catholic Chapel, Saint John Maddermarket, Norwich.
68	The Kitchen of the Palace of the Right Rev. Lord Bishop of Norwich.
115	Street scene, Chester.
236	The Nave of Norwich Cathedral, looking east.
240	Meadow scene, Heigham.
255	Interior of a monastic building, St. Martin at Palace, Norwich.
375	Norwich Castle previous to its restoration.

THIRD EXHIBITION OF THE NORFOLK AND NORWICH ASSOCIATION FOR THE PROMOTION OF THE FINE ARTS, 1852

No.	*Subject*
57	Garden House, Heigham, Norfolk.
84	On the Wensum, Norwich.
86	Sandling's Ferry House, Norwich.
121	The Crypt under the Grammar School, Norwich.

FOURTH EXHIBITION OF THE NORFOLK AND NORWICH ASSOCIATION FOR THE PROMOTION OF THE FINE ARTS, 1853

No.	*Subject*
3	In the Cloister, Chester Cathedral.
6	The Town Hall, Lynn.
30	St. Michael's Porch, Chester.
135	Landscape and building.

EXHIBITION OF THE NORFOLK AND NORWICH ASSOCIATION FOR THE PROMOTION OF THE FINE ARTS, 1855

No.	*Subject*	£	s.	d.
60	Bishop's Palace Gateway, Norwich.	12	12	0
63	St. Mary's Abbey, York.	5	15	6
95	Great Hall, Conway Castle, N. Wales.	5	15	6
180	Lower Bridge Street, Chester.	26	5	0

EXHIBITION OF THE NORFOLK AND NORWICH FINE ARTS' ASSOCIATION AND OF THE PHOTOGRAPHIC SOCIETY, 1856

No.	*Subject*	£	s.	d.
3	Town Hall, Chester.	10	10	0
31	Lamb Row, Chester.	6	6	0
156	Village church near Ely.	6	6	0
162	Framingham Church, Norfolk.	5	5	0
289	Interior in St. Simon's, Norwich.	5	5	0

NORFOLK AND NORWICH FINE ARTS ASSOCIATION

Exhibition of the Works of Modern Artists, 1860

No.	*Subject*	£	s.	d.
10	Bishopgate Bridge.	16	10	0
21	Bishop Hall's Palace, Heigham, Norwich.	6	6	0
30	Octagon Tower, Ely Cathedral.	30	0	0
35	Ruins at Castle Priory.	5	0	0
37	St. Mary's Chapel, Chester; Burnham Priory, Norfolk; North Aisle, Norwich Cathedral; Heydon Church, Norfolk.	15	15	0
43	Sir Benjamin Wrench's Court, Old Post Office, St. John's Maddermarket, in St. Martin's at Palace.	15	15	0
51	View of Norwich.		—	
52	Demolition of the Old Fish Market, Norwich.	18	0	0
61	Bishopgate Bridge, South.	16	10	0
70	Bowthorpe, near Norwich.	6	6	0
75	White Friars' Bridge.		—	
96	Elizabethan house, St. Martin's at Oak, Norwich.	10	10	0
102	Monks' Entrance, Ely Cathedral.	6	6	0
110	Street scene, Cossey, Norfolk.	12	12	0
120	Prior's Entrance, Ely Cathedral.	6	6	0
123	Landscape at Caister, Norwich.	4	0	0
131	Cottages at Witlingham.	5	0	0

NORWICH AND EASTERN COUNTIES WORKING CLASSES INDUSTRIAL EXHIBITION, 1867

No.	*Subject*	*Lent by*
918	Portion of Ely Cathedral.	A Friend.

BRITISH MEDICAL ASSOCIATION LOAN COLLECTION

Norfolk and Suffolk Artists, 1874

No.	*Subject*	*Lent by*
9	Nave of Norwich Cathedral.	Mrs. Hodgson.
13	The Old Fishmarket, Norwich.	Mr. Robert Geldart.
20	At Witton, near Norwich.	Mrs. Hodgson.
25	Becket's Chapel.	Mr. Robert Geldart.
30	Bishop Bridge.	Mrs. Hodgson.
35	Bishop's Palace Gateway, Norwich.	Mrs. Hodgson.

NORWICH ART LOAN EXHIBITION

in aid of the Fund for the Restoration of the Church of Saint Peter Mancroft, 1878

No.	*Subject*	*Lent by*
89	The Old Fishmarket, Norwich.	Mr. J. H. Ladyman.
90	Norman Chancel Archway.	Henry F. Butcher, Esq.
124	Newstead Abbey.	Mr. E. M. Edwards, Junr.
129	Guildhall, Norwich.	Miss Bignold.
148	The Bishop's Palace Gate, Norwich.	Miss Bignold.
161	On the Back River.	Mrs. Norgate.
168	The south end of the Old Fishmarket, Norwich.	Mr. George Wilson.
178	All Saints' Hill, Norwich.	William Dixon, Esq.
181	The south end of the Old Fish Market, Norwich.	Wm. Dixon, Esq.
329	The Spiral Column, Norwich Cathedral.	Philip Back, Esq.

FINE ART EXHIBITION

in aid of the new Norfolk and Norwich Hospital, 1883

WATER-COLOUR

No.	*Subject*	*Lent by*
28	Bishop Bridge.	Mr. I. B. Coaks.

NORWICH ART LOAN EXHIBITION

in aid of the Fund for the Restoration of St. Peter Mancroft Church, 1885

No.	*Subject*	*Lent by*
61	Old Fishmarket, with St. Peter's Church in distance (painted in 1858).	John N. Waite, Esq.
62	Chapel of St. Thomas à Becket, formerly underneath part of the Convent of the Black Friars, St. Andrew's, Norwich.	Robert Geldart, Esq.
67	Cowgate Street as it was, with the tower of St. Martin at Palace and cathedral spire in the distance.	Mr. W. W. Stanley.
78	Town Hall, King's Lynn.	S. Harvard, Esq.
99	King Street Gates.	J. J. Colman, Esq., M.P.
112	Interior of a church near Ely.	W. T. Bensly, Esq., LL.D.

A LOAN COLLECTION OF PICTURES AND WATER-COLOUR DRAWINGS

exhibited at the Agricultural Hall Gallery, Norwich, during the Grand Oriental Bazaar, 1894

No.	*Subject*	*Lent by*
39	King Street Gates.	J. J. Colman, Esq., M.P.
49	Chester.	Samuel Hoare, Esq., M.P.
52	Bishop Bridge.	Samuel Hoare, Esq., M.P.

ART LOAN EXHIBITION

in aid of the Funds of St. George's Club for Working Girls, 1902

No.	*Subject*
156	The Old Fishmarket, Norwich.
169	Old Guildhall, Norwich.

LOAN COLLECTION OF DRAWINGS

in the New Picture Gallery in the Norwich Castle Museum, 1903

No.	*Subject*	*Lent by*
96	Fuller's Hall, Norwich—the house in which Alderman Fuller served his Mayoralty. 8 × 9 in.	Mr. James Reeve.

EXHIBITED AT THE BRITISH INSTITUTION

Year	*Subject*
1822	Wood scene. 31 × 35 in.
1824	The interior of St. Stephen's Church, Norwich. 29 × 27 in.
1825	Landscape composition. 30 × 24 in.
1826	A scene near Norwich. 43 × 53 in.
1827	Scene in Norwich Market Place. 17 × 16 in.
1828	The Erpingham Gate House, Norwich. 43 × 38 in.
	St. James' Street, Norwich. 15 × 17 in.
	Guildhall Porch, Norwich. 15 × 17 in.
1829	Tombland, Norwich. 37 × 43 in.
	Tombland, Norwich. 25 × 32 in.
1838	Lower Bridge Street, Chester. 27 × 32 in.
	In Watergate Street, Chester. 27 × 32 in.
1852	The Choir of Norwich Cathedral, looking east. 48 × 39 in.
1853	The Bishop's Palace Gate.
1854	The Town Hall, Lynn, Norfolk.
1856	Lamb Row, Chester.
	Ship Tavern, Lynn, Norfolk.
1857	Becket's Chapel, Norwich.
1858	The Octagon, Ely Cathedral.
1861	Bishopgate Bridge, Norwich.

EXHIBITION OF NORWICH SCHOOL PICTURES

Norwich Castle Museum and Art Galleries, October, 1927

OIL PAINTINGS

No.	*Subject*
41	Tombland, Norwich, 1827. 12½ × 18½ in.
42	Fish Market, Norwich. 30½ × 20½ in.
43	Framingham, near Norwich—church interior. 8½ × 11½ in.
44	Norwich Guildhall. 24½ × 29¾ in.
45	Norwich Guildhall, 1863. 11½ × 13½ in.
46	Norwich Fish Market, 1859. 19½ × 23½ in.

HENRY BRIGHT

(1810-1873)

1810 Henry Bright, unlike most of the Norwich School painters, was born in the neighbouring county of Suffolk, at Saxmundham, on 5th June, 1810. His father was a jeweller and clockmaker who commanded much respect in the town. It is known that the family at one time attended the Congregational Chapel at Rendham, a nearby village.

Little is known of his early education, but he was probably educated privately. In
1825-30 his teens his father apprenticed him to a chemist at Woodbridge. This would be about 1825-30. It is interesting to note that a drawing by John Berney Crome of the Deben, near Woodbridge, in the collection of Mr. Denis Thomas, was executed
1828 about 1828. So it is quite possible the young chemist was befriended at this time by John Berney Crome, who is recorded as having given lessons to our painter. It is hardly surprising that his next move was to Norwich, the mecca of East Anglian artists at that time. Here he continued his work as a chemist's assistant with Paul Squire, who was also a collector of Norwich School paintings. Having attained proficiency in chemistry, he later became a dispenser at the Norfolk and Norwich Hospital. Concurrently with this work, he studied painting and drawing under John Berney Crome and John Sell Cotman. Two other associates at this time were Thomas Lound and John Middleton. The former purchased some of his work and the latter is said to have been taught water-colour drawing by him.

1835 According to a letter in the British Museum, Henry Bright was married on 10th May, 1835, to Eliza Brightly.

1836 Newly married and full of good prospects he moved to London in 1836 and established himself at 12 Spring Terrace, Paddington, where he lived for ten years. A year later, in 1837, he first exhibited at the British Institution and in this year visited North and South Wales. The year 1843 saw his first exhibit at the Royal Academy. This was later followed by forty-nine oil and thirty-three water-colour exhibits in London.

1843 In 1843, whilst living at Paddington, he wrote to his friend, Thomas Lound, inviting him to join him in a visit to some of the London galleries. It is possible Lound was living in London at this time, for Bright upbraids him for not coming sooner.

1844 In 1844, at the Royal Academy, he exhibited a picture entitled *Entrance to an Old Prussian Town*. This was purchased by H.M. Queen Victoria.

1848 Unfortunately, in 1848 he lost his wife, who died at the age of 31 years. This probably resulted in him moving his residence to Grove Cottage, Ealing, where he continued to paint and teach. It is said that his income about this time was £2,000 per year—a truly remarkable sum for those days.

Henry Bright was not only admired by the great Turner and Ruskin, but sold several of his works to admiring fellow-painters such as Clarkson Stanfield. With his fame spreading, his pupils became more distinguished. Thus the Grand Duchess Marie of Russia became a pupil. It is said that one day, when sketching with her near Broderick Castle, they were stranded by a swollen stream. It says much for the strength and chivalry of Henry Bright when we learn that he carried her on his back through the roaring waters.

In the 1840s he made several trips to the Continent, visiting Holland, Germany and
1847 France. In 1847 he exhibited at the Royal Academy *Ruined Castle on the Banks of the Rhine: Sunset Effect*. Possibly the picture illustrated on page 221.

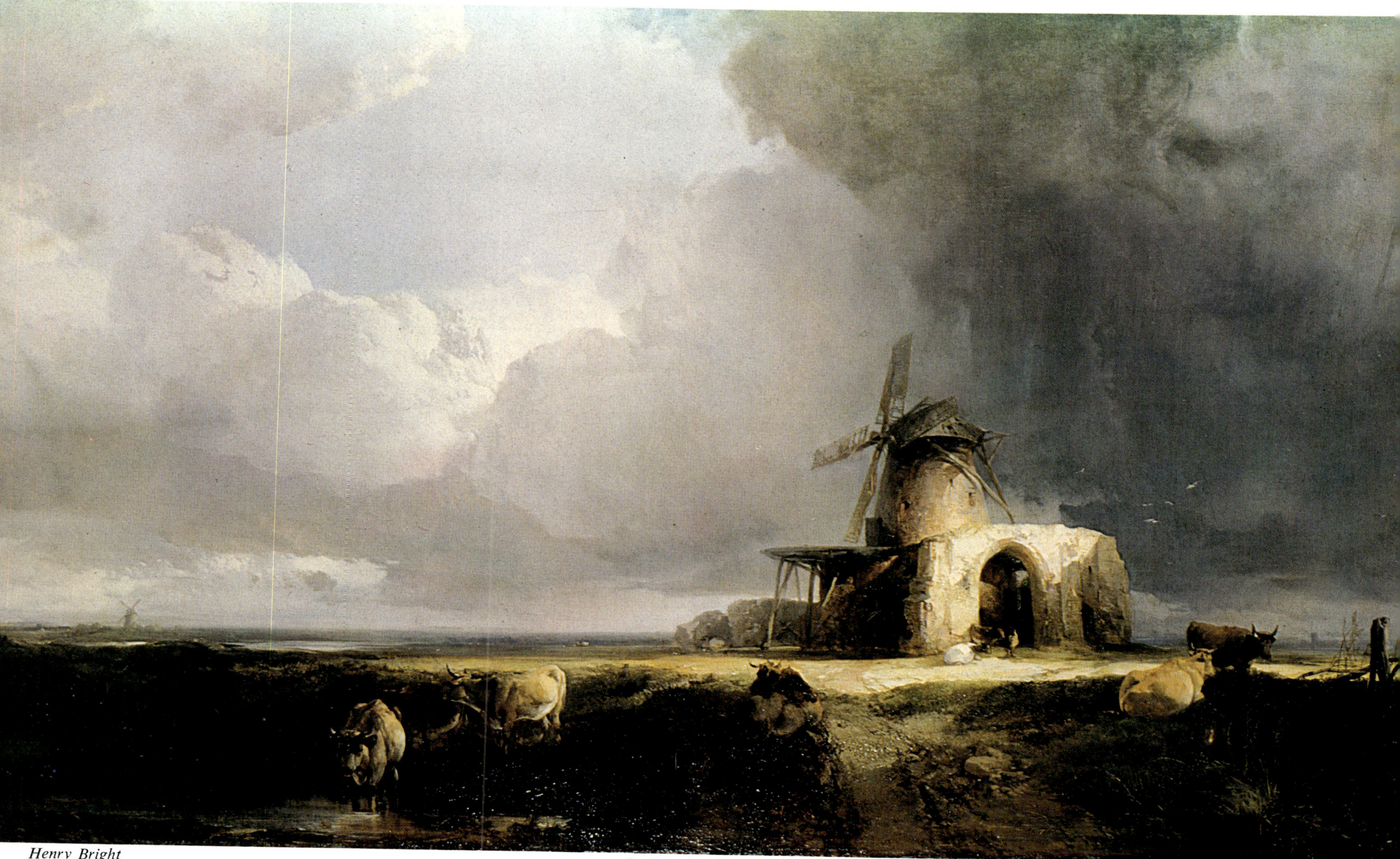

Henry Bright

St. Benet's Abbey

1869 The year 1869 saw Bright giving up his cottage at Ealing and moving into Vine Cottage,
The Oval, Kensington: at this time he used the Windham Club, St. James's, as his
address. In his last years he moved from London to Norwich, and finally to Ipswich,
1873 where he passed away at his residence, 22 Lesser Road, on 21st September, 1873.

THE PAINTINGS

Painting and drawing seemed to Henry Bright second nature. His fluency and delicacy of touch are almost unrivalled. He had a great flair for crystallising a subject and accenting salient points in such a way that the viewer is carried into the picture, the eye compulsively following the beautiful flowing lines. It is perhaps as a draughtsman that Bright shows his mastery, though he had the most sensitive feeling for colour which, on occasion, gives rise to great atmosphere in his works. The distant rain cloud or glancing sun rays are depicted with an ease which makes their effect convincing. The use of a palette knife in the sky gives a crisp touch to the impasto cloud—sometimes the cloud by means of the knife is splintered, to give a delicious spattering of light. Added to this masterful handling, Bright sometimes introduces his "electric" blue pigment.

In his early works one sees the pigment very sparingly used with abundant use of vandyke brown and naples yellow. The drawing is always convincing, even early on. The mid-period yields a great show of confidence and dexterity of handling of paint, with the plump figures producing an excuse for the use of earthy reds and glistening white, often carrying an enamel-like texture. To this period belong the large canvases—views across the marshes with the windmills being silhouetted against the sinking sun; great river scenes with the setting sun casting its delicious mantle. They all have much grandeur. It is difficult to find a Henry Bright painting or drawing without great merit: he is perhaps the most consistent East Anglian artist. Even in his very late period one can only say they lack the strong light we associate with his earlier works.

Our painter usually signed his works, though many unsigned works are recorded. The signature on his pastels is often so carried into the composition that it can be missed by the uninitiated. This very freely written signature is sometimes found on his oils, though clearly lettered signatures are to be seen. He often signs dark on dark.

In passing, it is my experience that he painted very few water-colours (illustrated is one dated 1836), a fair number of oils, and drew many pastels, for which he attained a great reputation. His sketches in pencil are fairly numerous—I do not recall seeing pen-and-ink drawings, though he undoubtedly executed some.

There are at least two other Henry Brights, one a painter of birds, the other a landscape painter, but quite pedestrian.

Our Henry Bright's works are to be seen in number at Norwich and Ipswich museums. Other galleries exhibiting his works are Glasgow, Leicester, Victoria and Albert, Montreal, Nottingham, Salford, and Sheffield.

EXHIBITS AT THE BRITISH INSTITUTION

Year	*Subject*
1837	Heath scene. 15×21 in.
1838	Waterfall near Dolgelly, North Wales, called the Black Cataract. 25×21 in.
	Old cottages near Pevensey, Sussex. 20×25 in.
	Winter. 18×22 in.
1839	Coast scene. 16×23 in.
1840	Scene in the woodlands of Suffolk. 19×26 in.
	Ruin of a mill on the heath, Sizewell-on-Sea, Suffolk. 30×41 in.

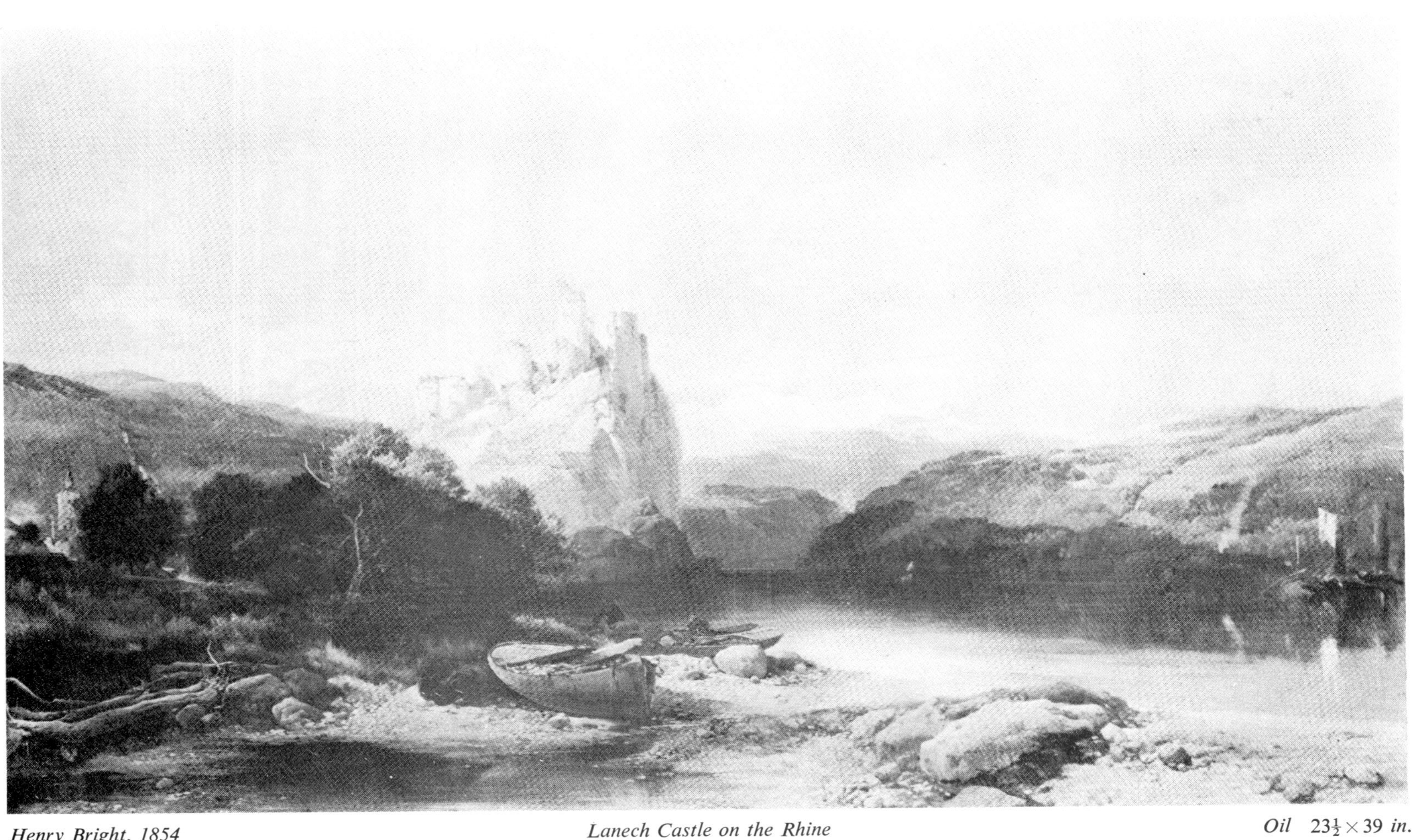

Henry Bright, 1854 *Lanech Castle on the Rhine* *Oil* $23\frac{1}{2} \times 39$ *in.*

Year	Subject
1841	Evening. 11 × 15 in.
	Ruin of an old mill on the marshes near Loddon.
1842	A coast scene. 13 × 18 in.
	Landscape and cattle. 13 × 18 in.
1844	A Dutch village—twilight—moonrise. 26 × 35 in.
	A landscape, Cornwall—autumnal morning. 26 × 35 in.
	On the River Lydd. 15 × 20 in.
	Rocky coast, Polperro. 17 × 23 in.
	Bilston Tor, Dartmouth. 17 × 23 in.
	On the River Bure—moonlight. 16 × 20 in.
	Near Newport, Isle of Wight. 19 × 30 in.
1845	A Cornish mountain scene. 44 × 68 in.
1846	Scene on the Yorkshire Moors—early morning. 38 × 49 in.
	The Vale of the Wharfe, Bolton. 28 × 40 in.
	Near Pulham St. Mary the Virgin, Norfolk. 22 × 29 in.
	A Welsh mountain stream. 22 × 29 in.
1847	Evening. 19 × 24 in.
	Welsh mountain scene—autumnal cloudy weather. 54 × 78 in.
	An old water mill at Iffley, Oxon. 37 × 58 in.
1848	A "bit" from a sketch near Bolton. 19 × 24 in.

EXHIBITED AT THE ROYAL ACADEMY

Year	Subject
1843	Water-colour sketch of the Rhine.
1845	On the River Yare, Norfolk—morning (purchased by Charles Stanfield).
1846	Scene in Holland—afternoon effect.
1847	A ruined castle on the banks of the Rhine—sunset effect.
	Remains of St. Benet's Abbey on the Bure—thunderstorm clearing off.
1848	An overlook on the southern coast of England.
1849	Old mill at Stiffkey, near Wells, Norfolk—once the seat of Sir Nicholas Bacon.
1850	A mountain stream, Borrowdale, Cumberland.
	On the River Yare, Norfolk.
1869	The ray after the storm.
1871	The battle of the frogs and mice—Homer.

EXHIBITED AT THE NEW SOCIETY OF PAINTERS IN WATER-COLOURS

Year	Subject
1839	Scene near St. Donat's Castle, South Wales.
	Winter.
	Two coast scenes.
	Evening.
1840	Scene on the banks of the Rhine near Meder Wesel.
	Lane scene, Trowse, Norwich.
	Scene on the Rhine—evening.
	On the river near Leyden, Holland—moonrise.
	On the River Ore, Suffolk.
	Conway Castle.
	Winter scene near Leyden, Holland—Dutch people returning from market in a sledge.
	Scene on the French coast—hazy morning.
	Landscape, Holland—early morning.
	Unloading a wreck on the sands near Orford Lights, coast of Suffolk.
	Dutch boats on the river near Rotterdam.
	In Shrubland Park, Suffolk.
	On the coast of France—sunrise.

Year	Subject
	Rocky shore, Pembrokeshire, South Wales.
	On the Suffolk coast—sunset.
1841	Ruins of an old mill on the marshes near Loddon, Norfolk—early morning.
	Old mill near Clovelly, North Devon.
	Sketch of a Devonshire cottage.
	Waterfall, Devonshire.
1843	River Lynn, Devon (two pictures).
	Scene in North Devon.
	On the Thames.
	River scene—sunrise.
	Moonrise.
1844	Entrance to an old Prussian town—evening effect, winter (purchased by H.M. Queen Victoria).
	Scene on the border of Dartmoor, Devon.

EXHIBITION OF THE NORFOLK AND NORWICH FINE ARTS' ASSOCIATION AND OF THE PHOTOGRAPH SOCIETY, 1856

No.	Subject	Lent by
256	River scene:	Mr. Rossi.

NORFOLK AND NORWICH FINE ARTS' ASSOCIATION

Exhibition of the Works of Modern Artists, 1860

No.	Subject
68	Evening.
77	Landscape.
98	Morning.
177	The water mill.

NORWICH AND EASTERN COUNTIES WORKING CLASSES INDUSTRIAL EXHIBITION, 1867

OIL-PAINTINGS

No.	Subject	Lent by
758	Marsh mills—sunset.	Wm. Dixon, Esq.
774	Crayon drawing.	J. B. Morgan, Esq.
801	View in the Isle of Arran.	Mr. Theodore Rossi.

NORWICH FINE ART ASSOCIATION

Second Exhibition of Works of Art by Modern Artists, 1869

No.	Subject
181	St. Bennet's Abbey.
184	River scene near Norwich.

NORWICH AND EASTERN COUNTIES INDUSTRIAL AND FINE ARTS EXHIBITION. NORFOLK AND NORWICH FINE ART ASSOCIATION AND ART UNION

Exhibition of Works of Art by Modern Artists, 1871

WATER-COLOUR

No.	Subject	£	s.	d.
318	Phalz Castle on the Rhine—moonlight.	50	0	0

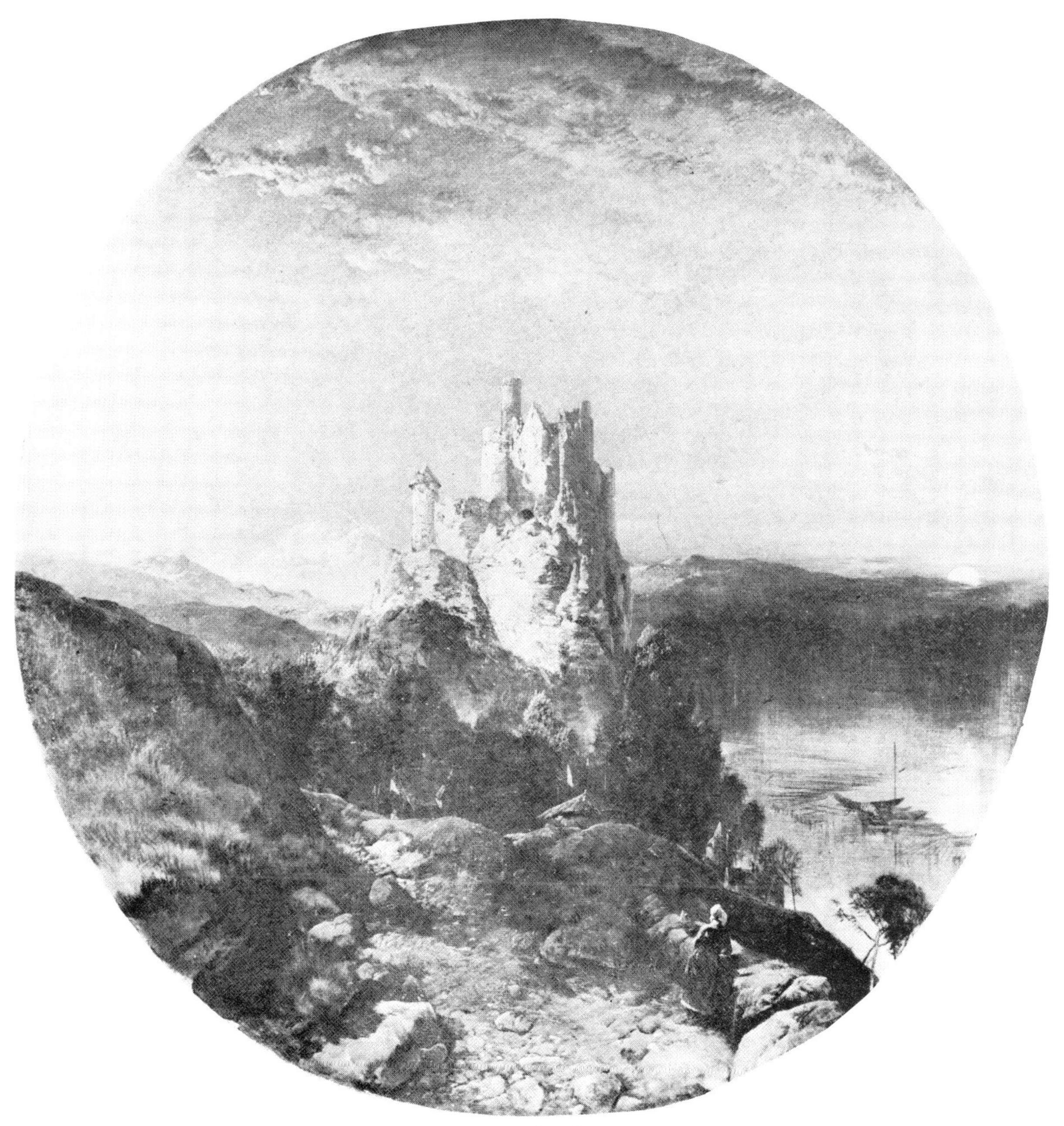

View on the Rhine

Henry Bright *Oil on canvas tondo approx.* 36 *in.*

BRITISH MEDICAL ASSOCIATION LOAN COLLECTION

Works of Norfolk and Suffolk Artists, 1874

OIL-PAINTINGS

No.	Subject	Lent by
1	Barges—sunset.	Mr. G. Holmes.
75	Marsh mills—sunset.	Mr. G. Holmes.

WATER-COLOURS

No.	Subject	Lent by
85	The shrimpers.	Mr. James Reeve.
92	Study from Nature.	Mrs. J. Middleton.
97	On the Rhine.	Mr. James Reeve.
111	Sepia sketch.	Mr. G. H. Christie.
158	Hemsby, near Yarmouth—evening effect.	Mr. James Reeve.

NORWICH ART LOAN EXHIBITION

in aid of the Fund for the Restoration of the Church of Saint Peter Mancroft, 1878

No.	Subject	Lent by
131	Landscape with windmill.	T. Brightwell, Esq.
153	A sketch.	Clare Sewell Read, Esq., M. P.
166	Lake Leman.	Mr. T. Moore.
448	The rising storm (crayon).	J. C. Barnham.
517	View on the Rhine (water-colour).	E. Farrer.
543	Sketch.	J. H. Browne.
552	An old barn.	J. B. Morgan.
560	A sketch.	J. H. Browne.
567	Sketch in Cumberland (water-colour).	E. Farrer.

SWAFFHAM FINE ART EXHIBITION, 1882

No.	Subject	£	s.	d.	Lent by
98	Moonlight scene, North Wales.	14	14	0	Mr. C. T. Thompson.
184	Crayon drawing.	10	0	0	E. Farrer, Esq.
185	Crayon drawing.	10	0	0	E. Farrer, Esq.

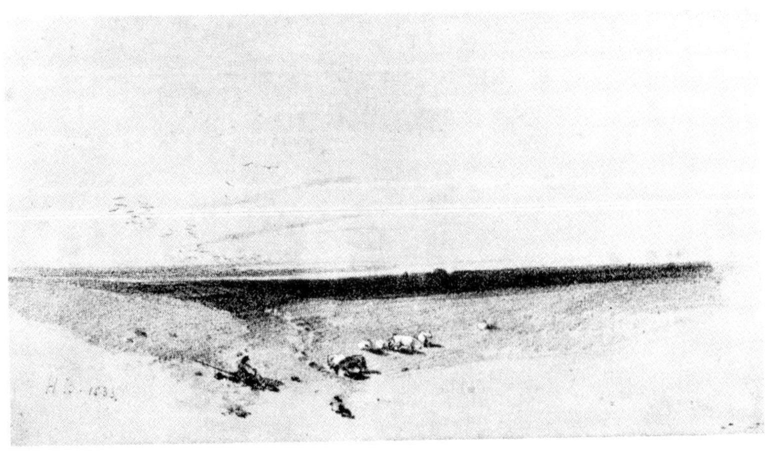

Henry Bright, 1833 *Pastel*

FINE ART EXHIBITION

in aid of the new Norfolk and Norwich Hospital, 1883

No.	*Subject*	*Lent by*
23	Sherringham Mill.	Mr. Cadge.
11	Landscape.	Mr. J. J. Colman, M.P.
29	Old windmill.	Mr. J. J. Colman, M.P.
3	Norwich, from Trowse (water-colour).	Mr. George H. Christie.

ART LOAN EXHIBITION

in aid of the Fund for the Restoration of St. Peter Mancroft Church, 1885

No.	*Subject*	£ s. d.	*Lent by*
51	Snowdon.	—	Clare Sewell Read, Esq., M.P.
63	Sherringham Mill.	—	William Cadge, Esq.
73	A sketch.	—	Clare Sewell Read, Esq., M.P.
75	Landscape—evening.	—	J. J. Colman, Esq., M.P.
674	Evening.	12 12 0	Messrs. Hogarth and Sons.

ART LOAN EXHIBITION

in aid of the funds of St. George's Club for Working Girls, 1902

No.	*Subject*
128	Landscape.
128	View on a mere.
158	Sheringham Heath.
162	Churchyard.

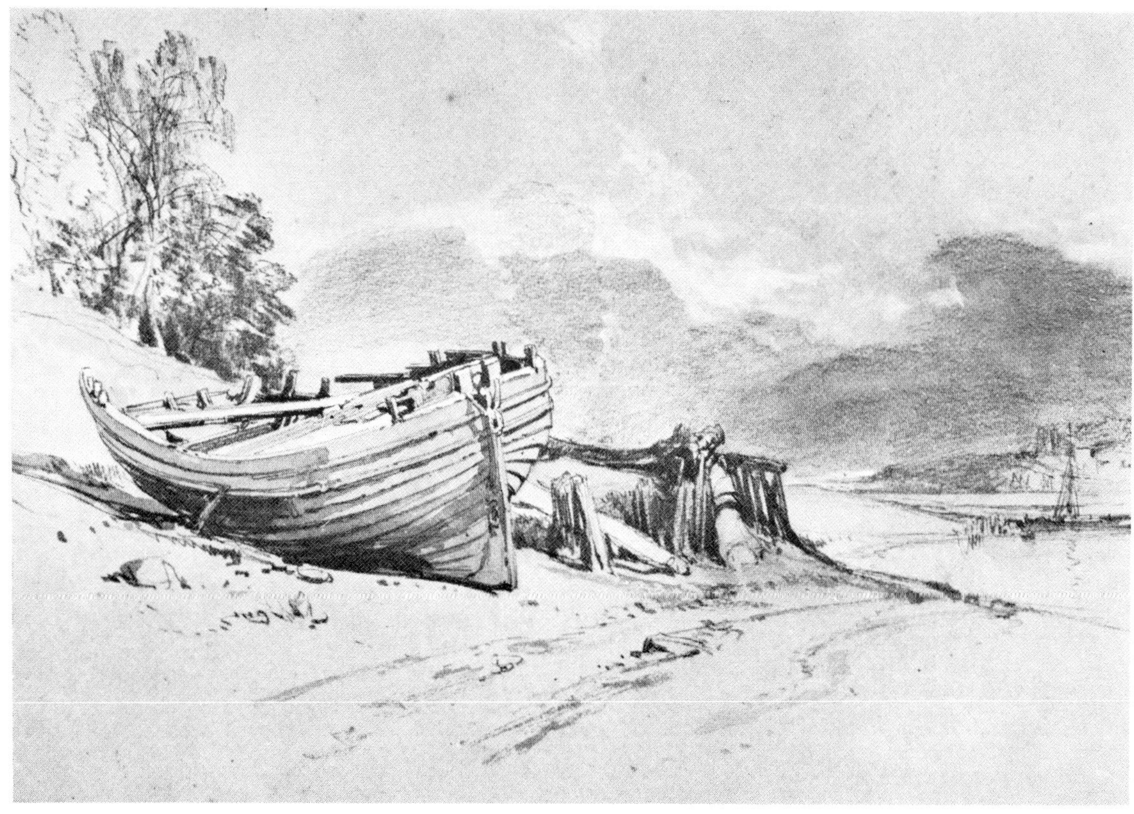

Henry Bright *Pastel*

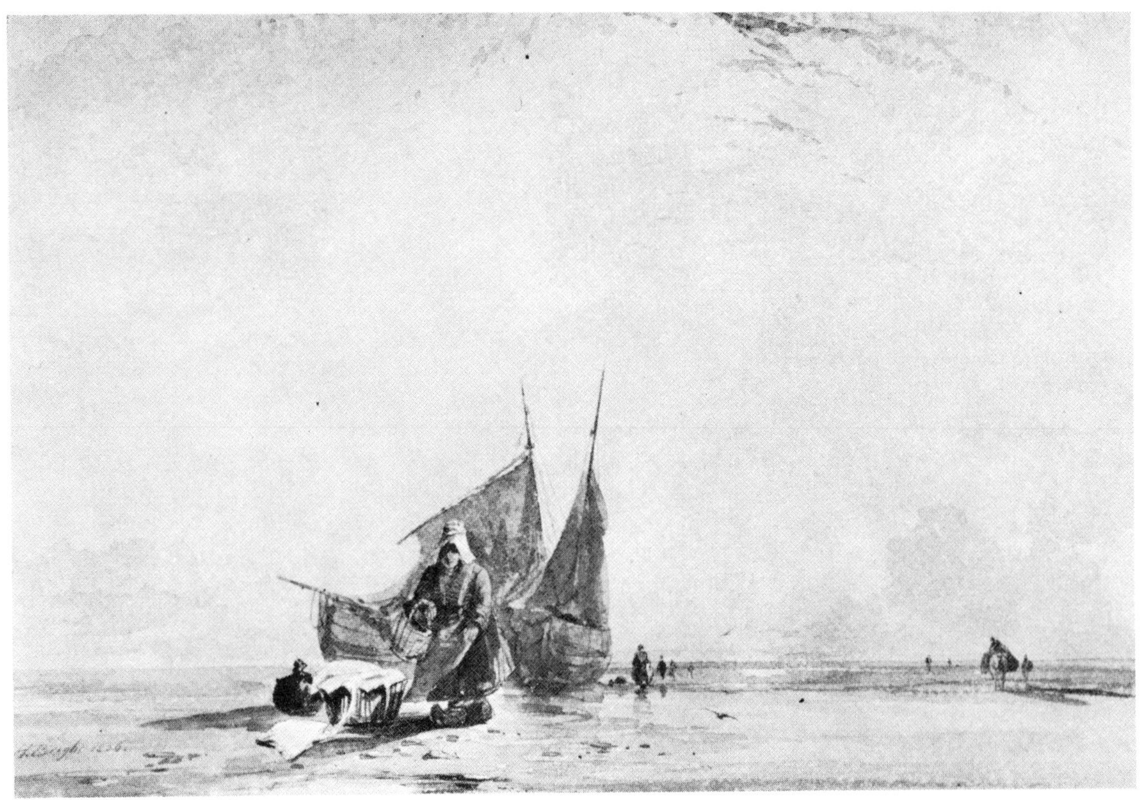

Henry Bright *Beach Scene, 1836* *Water-colour*

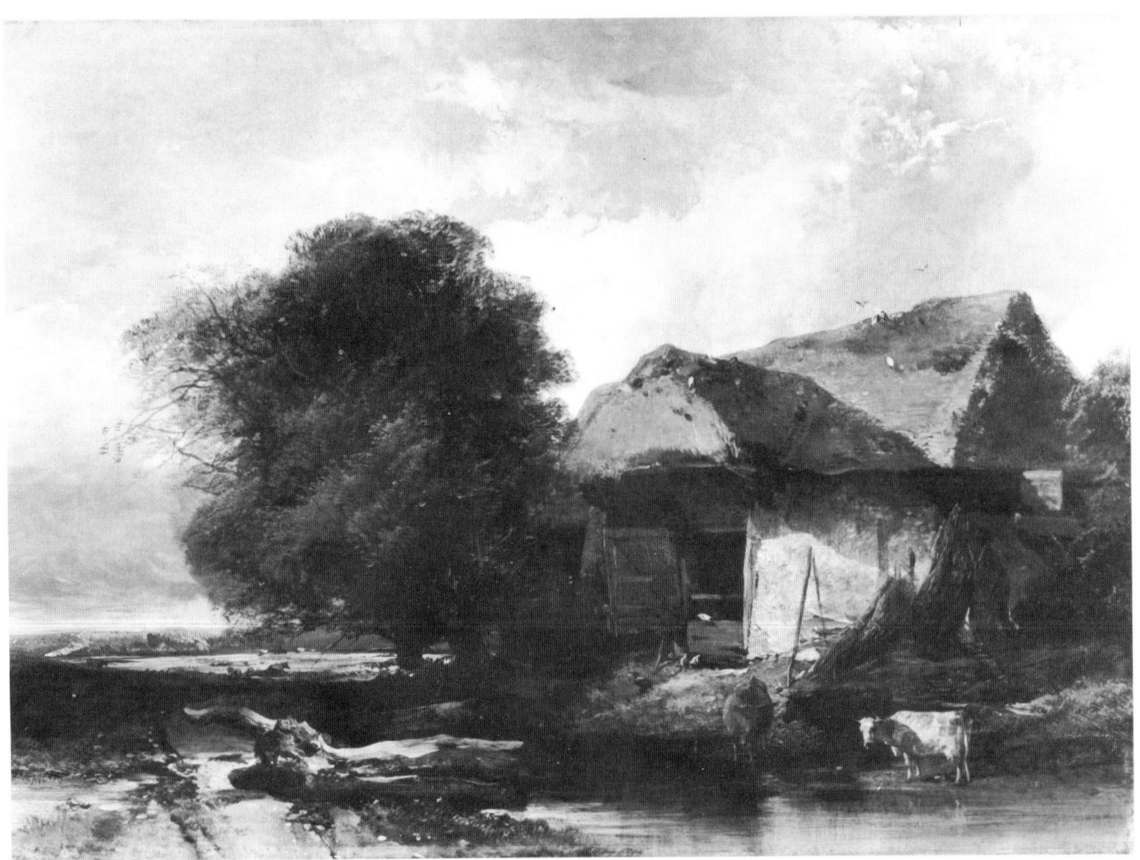

Henry Bright *Old Barn, Suffolk* *Oil* $14\frac{1}{2} \times 20\frac{1}{2}$ *in.*

LOAN COLLECTION OF DRAWINGS IN THE NEW PICTURE GALLERY IN THE NORWICH CASTLE MUSEUM, 1903

No.	*Subject*	*Lent by*
98	North West Tower, Great Yarmouth. Shed in front of tower in centre, river in foreground. $10\frac{1}{4} \times 6\frac{3}{4}$ in.	Mr. James Reeve.
99	On the Rhine (pastel drawing). Castle and hills in middle distance, snow-capped mountains in distance. River with boats and logs of timber in foreground. $9\frac{1}{2} \times 13$ in.	Mr. James Reeve.

EXHIBITION OF NORWICH SCHOOL PICTURES

Norwich Castle Museum and Art Galleries, October, 1927

OIL-PAINTINGS

No.	*Subject*
1	North Beach, Gt. Yarmouth. $15\frac{1}{2} \times 30\frac{1}{2}$ in.
2	A Welsh mountain scene with water, sheep and cottage in foreground. 12×19 in.
3	A Welsh scene. $11\frac{3}{4} \times 15\frac{1}{4}$ in.
4	Norfolk Broads with boats. $9 \times 12\frac{1}{2}$ in.
5	Shore scene. $8\frac{1}{2} \times 13\frac{1}{2}$ in.
6	Horstead Mill. 11×17 in.
7	Windmill. $6\frac{3}{4} \times 5\frac{1}{4}$ in.

WATER-COLOURS, DRAWINGS, ETC.

130	Seashore scene (pastel). $9\frac{1}{4} \times 12\frac{3}{4}$ in.
131	The City of Norwich from Trowse. $14\frac{1}{2} \times 27\frac{3}{4}$ in.
132	Tunbridge Wells. $8\frac{1}{4} \times 13\frac{3}{4}$ in.
133	The gipsy encampment. $7 \times 13\frac{3}{4}$ in.
134	Landscape. $13\frac{1}{4} \times 10\frac{1}{4}$ in.
135	Mt. Blanc from Lausanne (crayon). $14 \times 20\frac{1}{4}$ in.
136	Orford Beach—a storm (crayon in colours). $11 \times 17\frac{1}{2}$ in.

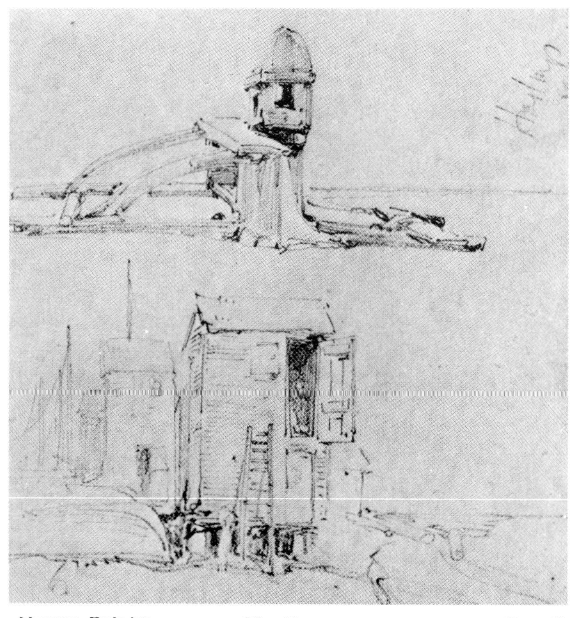

Henry Bright *Hastings* *Pencil*

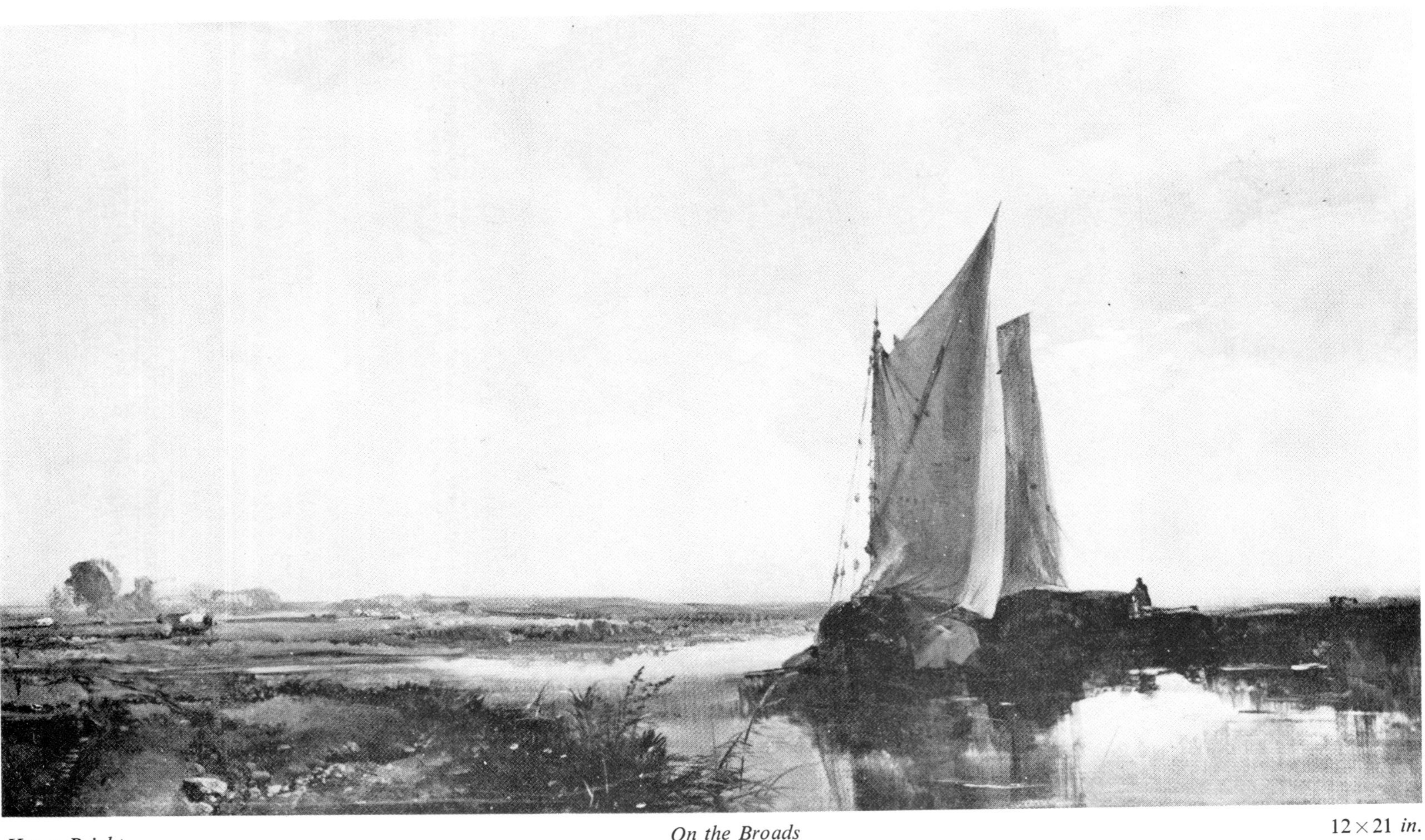

Henry Bright *On the Broads* 12 × 21 *in.*

OBADIAH SHORT

(1803-1886)

1803 Obadiah Short was born in 1803 in the parish of St. Augustine, Norwich. His father, who was an officer in the Army of Sir John Moore, lost his life at Corunna in 1809. His mother was actually with his father at the time and is thought to have died in Lisbon Hospital. Obadiah was thus left in very poor circumstances to be brought up by his grandmother. It is therefore not surprising to find that he received no formal education, but by his wit and powers of observation he was able to make his way in
1816 the world. At an early age he started work as a weaver—thus he continued from 1816 to 1829, when he replaced his loom for a painter's easel. His interest in art is said to have been stimulated by seeing a man named Harbord copying a work by Crome.

1832 In 1832 Short walked from Norwich to Holkham with a letter of introduction from Dr. Dalrymple to the Earl of Leicester. The Earl treated the artist with great kindness and gave him the freedom of his home. It is not known how long he stayed to study the paintings, but he returned to Norwich on foot.

Mr. Sparshall, the wine merchant, friend of Crome, lent Short two pictures by James Stark to copy. After much hard work in copying, Short launched himself as a landscape painter. He was at this time commissioned by Dr. Dalrymple to draw birds and pathological subjects in the Norwich Museum.

1834 In 1834 he accepted a position as a designer with Willetts of Norwich. This post he retained for about fifty years. In his time off he continued to develop his landscape painting.

Short is said to have been a kindly man without ambition. He asked very little for his work and actually refused to take extra money when patrons offered it. He was, all his life, a devout and humble Christian and regularly attended the Church of England services.

1886 It was in his 84th year he passed away—to be precise, on 15th July, 1886.

Several years ago the writer met a descendant of the artist, living at Felixstowe, who owned a large water-colour of Mousehold Heath, a subject painted many times by Obadiah Short.

THE PAINTINGS

Obadiah Short was not one of the great men of the Norwich School but he could paint a very charming picture. At times he raised himself almost into the Ladbrooke class. One picture of his I examined, which was signed and dated 1839, showed such beautiful handling on the trees that it could well have been the work of J. B. Ladbrooke had not the palette been different.

Short's trees tend to be brown in colour and the paint in his later works may be described as rather heavily placed. James Reeve noted that his later work came under the influence of Alfred Priest.

Many of his works are to be seen in the Norwich Castle Art Gallery.

TWENTY-SIXTH EXHIBITION OF THE WORKS OF THE NORFOLK AND SUFFOLK INSTITUTION FOR THE PROMOTION OF THE FINE ARTS, 1832

No.	*Subject*
17	Cottages at Thorpe.
30	Beach scene, Yarmouth.

TWENTY-SEVENTH EXHIBITION OF THE WORKS OF THE NORFOLK AND SUFFOLK INSTITUTION FOR THE PROMOTION OF THE FINE ARTS, 1833

No.	*Subject*
223	Beach scene at Corton.
224	Scene at Trowse.

EXHIBITION OF THE NORFOLK AND NORWICH ASSOCIATION FOR THE PROMOTION OF THE FINE ARTS, 1855

No.	*Subject*
4	Lane scene.
30	Lane scene.

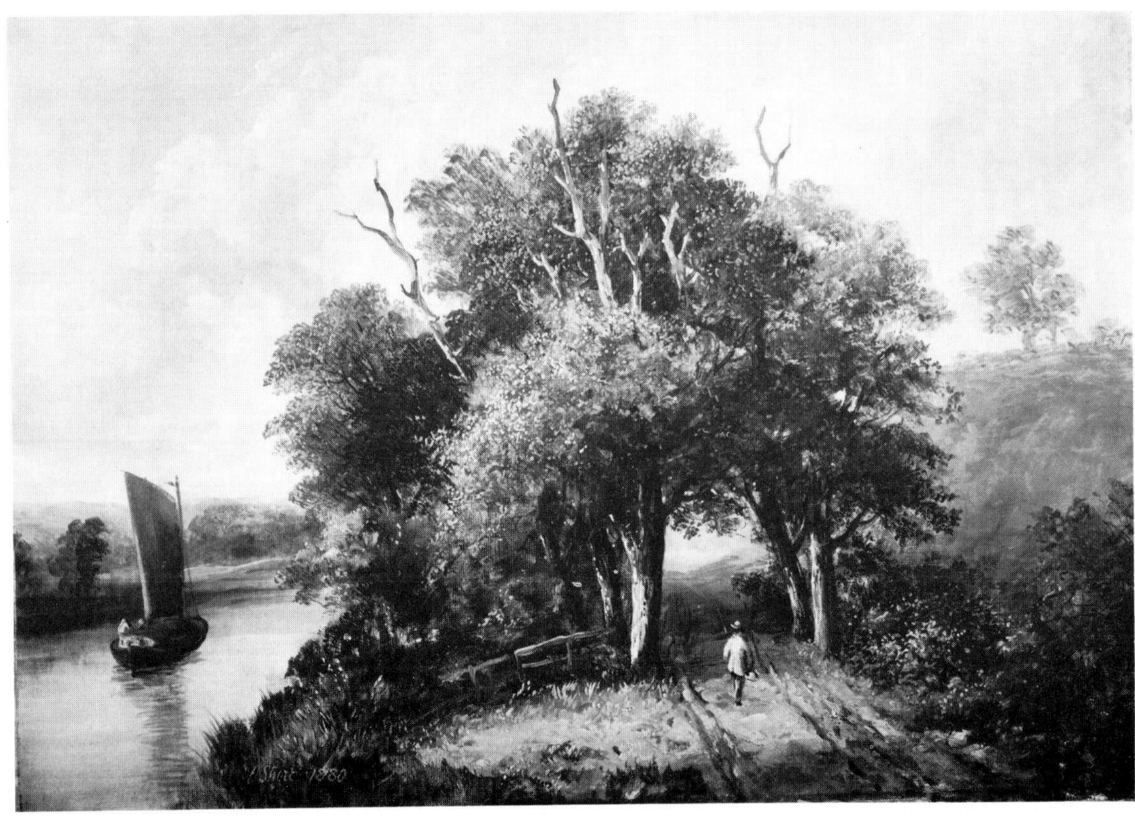

Obadiah Short *Late work Oil on canvas* $8\frac{1}{2} \times 12\frac{1}{4}$ *in.*

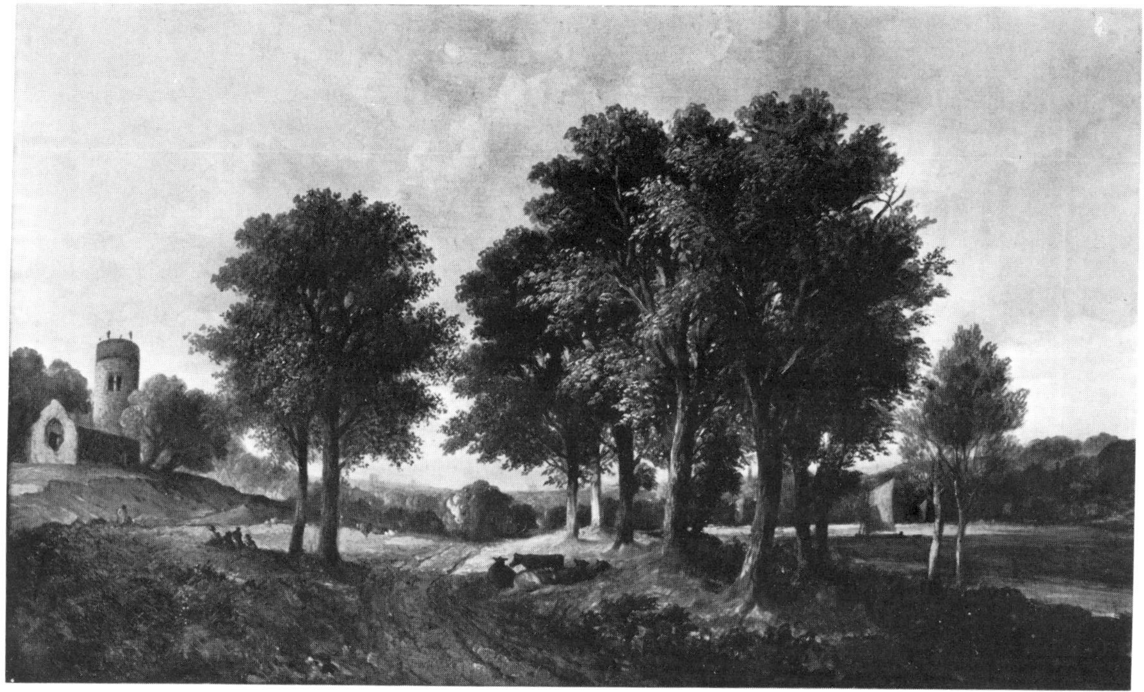

Obadiah Short *Middle Period* *Oil on canvas* $18\frac{1}{4} \times 30$ *in.*

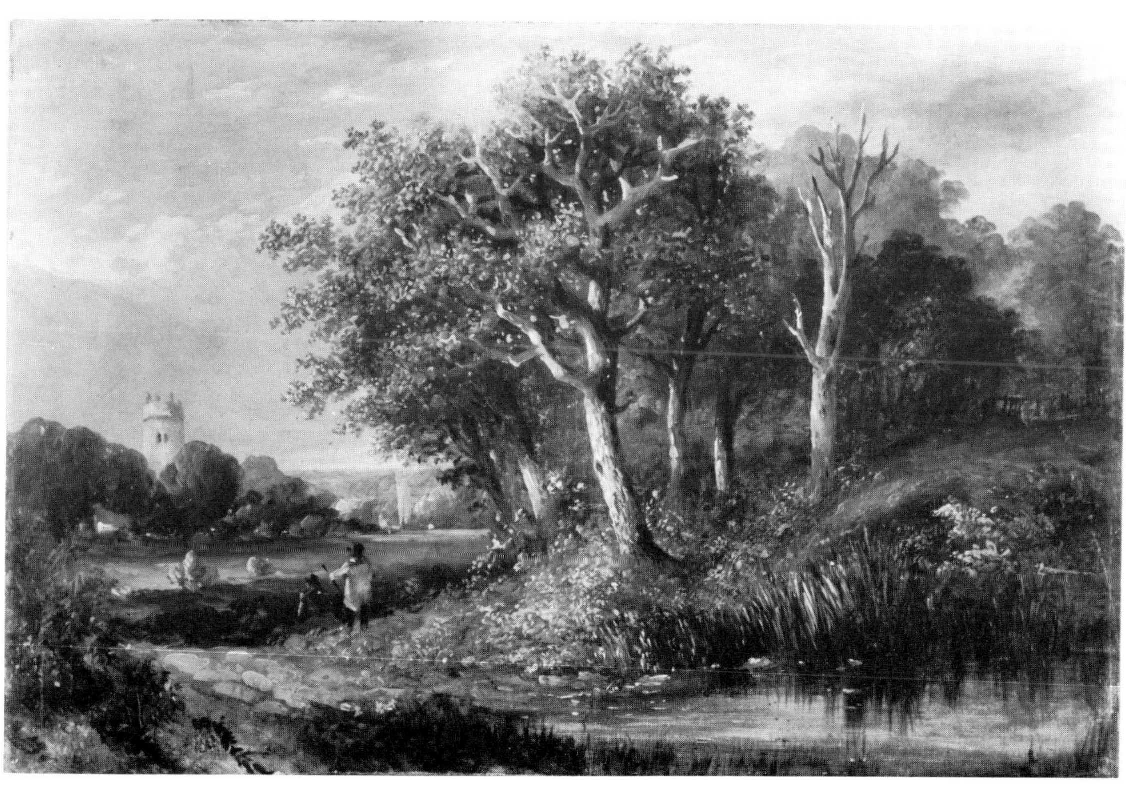

Obadiah Short *Fairly early example* *Oil on canvas* 10×16 *in.*

EXHIBITION OF THE NORFOLK AND NORWICH FINE ARTS' ASSOCIATION AND OF THE PHOTOGRAPHIC SOCIETY, 1856

No.	*Subject*
113	Norwich from Crown Point.
145	Coast scene, Lowestoft.

BRITISH MEDICAL ASSOCIATION LOAN COLLECTION

Works of Norfolk and Suffolk Artists, 1874

WATER-COLOURS

No.	*Subject*	*Lent by*
190	Old houses, Saint Lawrence, Norwich.	Mr. O. Short.
205	Fuller's Hole, Saint Martin's, Norwich.	Mr. O. Short.

OIL-PAINTING

232	Landscape.	Mr. O. Short.

EXHIBITION OF PICTURES BY LIVING ARTISTS

Victoria Hall Gallery, Norwich, 1878

No.	*Subject*
108	Landscape.
130	Landscape with sheep.

EXHIBITION OF NORWICH SCHOOL PICTURES

Norwich Museum and Art Galleries, October, 1927

OIL-PAINTINGS

No.	*Subject*
85	Whitlingham lane. $19\frac{1}{2} \times 29\frac{1}{2}$ in.
86	Study of trees. 8×11 in.
87	Lane scene with cottages. $8\frac{1}{2} \times 11\frac{1}{2}$ in.

WATER-COLOURS

237	Landscape at Costessey, Norfolk. $8\frac{1}{2} \times 17$ in.

MARIA MARGITSON

(1832-1896)

Miss Maria Margitson was the niece of John Berney Ladbrooke. It is known that she taught at the residence of her uncle in Bridge Street, St. Andrew's, Norwich. This information is confirmed by an advertisement which appeared on 27th July, 1850. In the Fine Art Exhibition of 1883 a painting by Miss Margitson and Ladbrooke is recorded. Presumably this is J. B. Ladbrooke—possibly being a landscape background. She is said to have studied with Eloise Harriet Stannard, the fruit and flower painter.

Unfortunately, details of her life are scarce but we do know that she passed away in Norwich in 1896 at the age of 64 years.

THE PAINTINGS

Miss Margitson painted flowers and still life, probably specialising in the latter. Her works are of very high quality and well composed. The paintings are few and only one exhibit at the British Institution is recorded. She exhibited in Norwich in 1855, 1869, 1871, 1878, and 1883. At her best she can rival most still-life painters of the nineteenth century.

EXHIBIT AT THE BRITISH INSTITUTION

Year	*No.*	*Subject*
1857	113	Autumn fruit.

EXHIBITION OF THE NORFOLK AND NORWICH ASSOCIATION FOR THE PROMOTION OF THE FINE ARTS, 1855

No.	*Subject*	£	s.	d.
71	Fruit and flowers.	8	8	0

EXHIBITION OF THE NORFOLK AND NORWICH FINE ARTS' ASSOCIATION AND OF THE PHOTOGRAPHIC SOCIETY, 1856

No.	*Subject*	£	s.	d
79	Fruit and flowers.	15	0	0
94	The produce of the Abbey garden.	21	0	0
160	Autumn fruit.	8	8	0
269	Basket of flowers.	4	4	0

NORFOLK AND NORWICH FINE ARTS' ASSOCIATION

Exhibition of the Works of Modern Artists, 1860

No.	*Subject*	£	s.	d.
86	Fruit.	15	15	0
185	Fruit.	10	10	0

NORWICH FINE ART ASSOCIATION

Second Exhibition of Works of Art by Modern Artists, 1869

No.	*Subject*	£	s.	d.
77	Fruit.	8	0	0
88	Study of grapes.	8	0	0
127	Fruit.	10	0	0

EAST ANGLIAN ART UNION AND CITY OF NORWICH FINE ART ASSOCIATION

Exhibition of Works of Art by Modern Artists, 1870

No.	*Subject*	£	s.	d.
23	Fruit.	15	0	0
31	Fruit.	12	0	0

NORWICH AND EASTERN COUNTIES INDUSTRIAL AND FINE ARTS EXHIBITION, 1871

OIL-PAINTINGS

No.	*Subject*	£	s.	d.
63	Fruit.	8	0	0
69	Fruit.	8	8	0
184	Fruit.		—	

NORWICH ART LOAN EXHIBITION

in aid of the Fund for the Restoration of the Church of Saint Peter Mancroft, 1878

No.	*Subject*	*Lent by*
252	Fruit.	The Artist.
254	Fruit.	The Artist.

EXHIBITION OF PICTURES BY LIVING ARTISTS

Victoria Hall Gallery, Norwich, 1878

No.	*Subject*	£	s.	d.
6	Fruit.	15	0	0
132	Fruit.	15	0	0

FINE ART EXHIBITION

in aid of the new Norfolk and Norwich Hospital, 1883

No.	*Subject*	*Lent by*
22	Fruit (Miss Margitson and Ladbrooke).	Mr. J. Gunn.

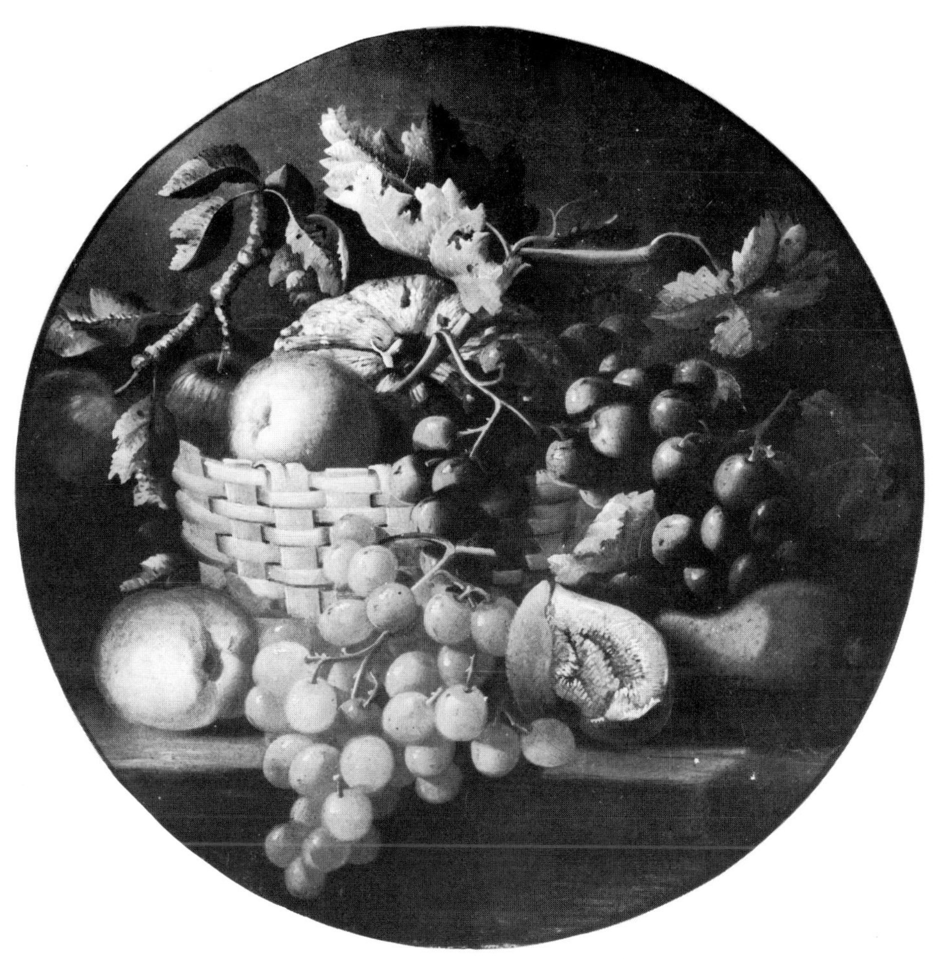

Maria Margitson, 1860 *Niece of J. B. Ladbrooke*
Oil on canvas 14 *in. dia.*

JOSEPH PAUL

(1804-1887)

Joseph Paul was born in Norwich about the year 1804, his father probably being a Robert Paul, who is recorded as a portrait painter. Many of Robert Paul's works were exhibited at the Norwich Society.

There is no record of Joseph Paul actually taking lessons from any members of the School, but he imbibed the brushwork and palette of John Crome. Many of his skies are reminiscent of George Vincent. It is more than likely he had associations with the latter. Paul is alleged to have entered into conflict with the authorities and fled to London about the year 1830.

We know that Paul made his way to London and executed copies of Canaletto, Rembrandt and other Masters. Presumably the purpose of doing copies was to prevent recognition. Later, however, he became more bold and reverted to his Norwich School paintings.

It is on record by a Mr. Hinds of Yarmouth, who knew Paul late in life, that he was given to heavy drinking and was something of a character. It is alleged he had some reputation as a singer.

Paul resided in later years at 53 St. William Street, St. Pancras. He died at the age of 83 years in 1887, having been married five times.

THE PAINTINGS

It is only of late years that Joseph Paul has been recognised. Years ago his works sold under the names of Constable, Stark, Crome, Cotman, or any name that the vendor liked to associate with the painting. Because Paul attained the reputation for doing pastiches of the "Greats", he was never given credit for his own style. Even when he is painting a Constable pastiche of Salisbury Cathedral the initiated at once recognise Paul, for he just cannot restrain his exuberant and free style of painting. For all his pastiches, Paul knew something of the elements of painting.

Beneath his trees and foregrounds, one finds warm, red grounds and beneath his skies, white and sometimes faint pink. On these colours he built his pictures. Whilst it is true his pictures lack observation, they are often quite beautiful in effect. Crome's teaching is present respecting the figures in the landscape. There are no figures so exquisitely executed that they steal the picture. Paul's pictures are as Crome taught "a whole effect". Without doubt most of Paul's works are studio compositions. They contain usually a church, windmill, rain, figures, trees, distant fields and a well-rutted road. Despite the formula, Paul usually presents a painting which is not only interesting but stimulating. Such was his success that many people have been induced to part with quite large sums of money in the belief that his work was that of a greater painter.

Paul's early works often depict the city of his birth, but these pictures are fairly rare and are, from a collector's point of view, his most valuable. Then we have his Norwich School landscapes. Finally his pastiches.

For many years Joseph Paul was regarded as a copyist, but his own landscapes have a vigorous charm which will merit him a place in the Norwich School.

It is rare indeed to find a Paul which has not been lined: such a work would possibly be by his son, John Paul.

EXHIBITION OF NORWICH SCHOOL PICTURES

Norwich Castle Museum and Art Galleries, October, 1927

OIL-PAINTINGS

No.	*Subject*
75	Landscape (sold as an "Old Crome" for £300). $29\frac{1}{2} \times 24\frac{1}{4}$ in.
76	Landscape with cottage. $10\frac{1}{4} \times 13\frac{1}{2}$ in.
77	Cottage and mill. $6\frac{3}{4} \times 9\frac{3}{4}$ in.

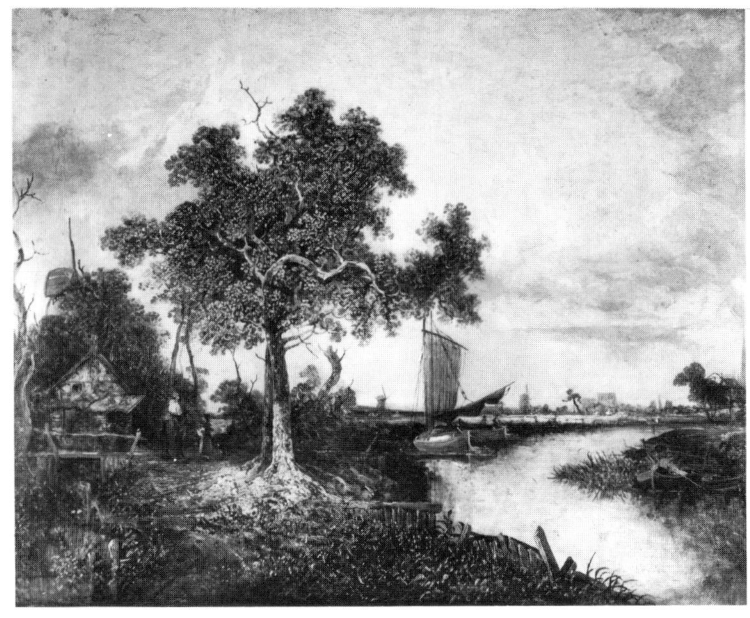

Joseph Paul *View of Norwich* *Oil on canvas* 28 × 36 *in.*

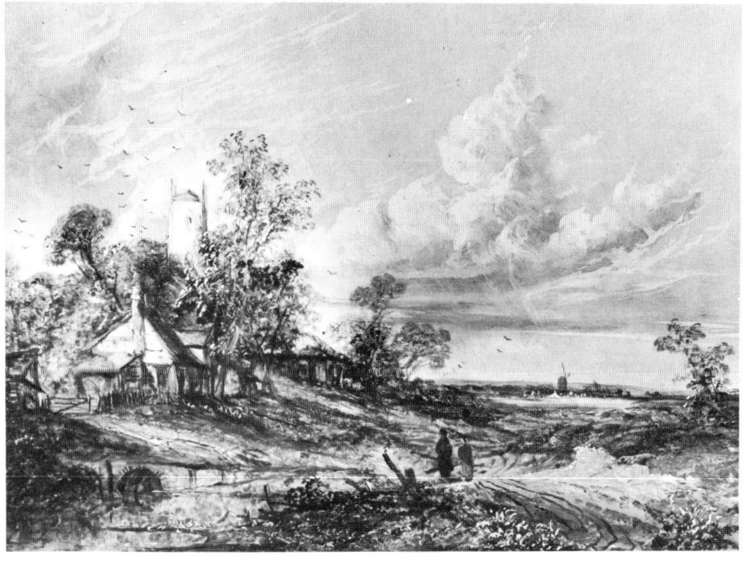

Joseph Paul *Oil on canvas*
One of a pair

JOHN PAUL

John Paul was one of Joseph Paul's sons. He was known to have painted views of London, often on paper. These are sometimes signed "J. Paul". Joseph Paul, his father, also painted similar views, but seldom signed.

John Paul also painted horses, two such paintings are illustrated. His work shows considerably more refinement than that of his father, the drawing being more exact and the colour more subdued. One can see the Norwich School influence in the sky of the hunting picture, which is inscribed on the reverse "J. Paul, London". The paint is thinly applied with delicate touches.

The horse portrait illustrated is dated 1874.

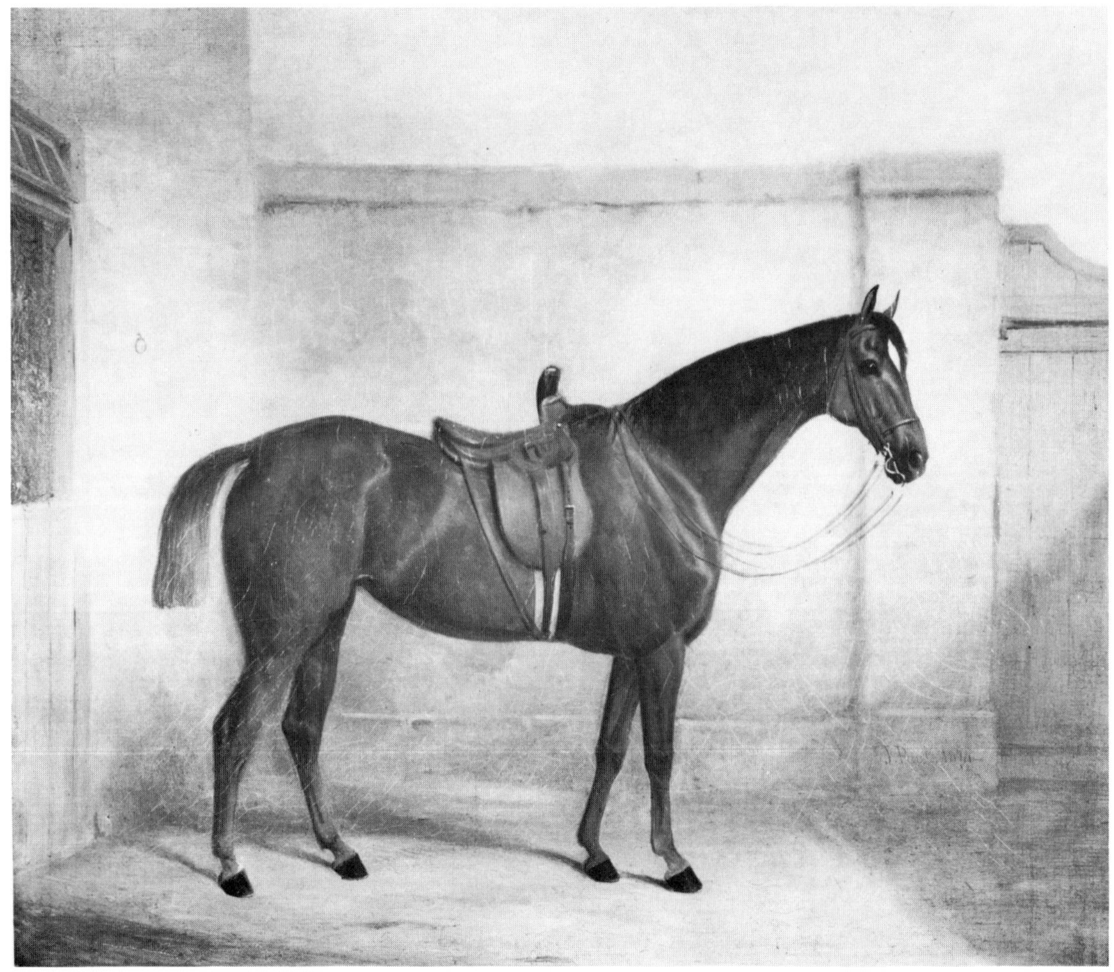

John Paul, 1874 *Oil on canvas*

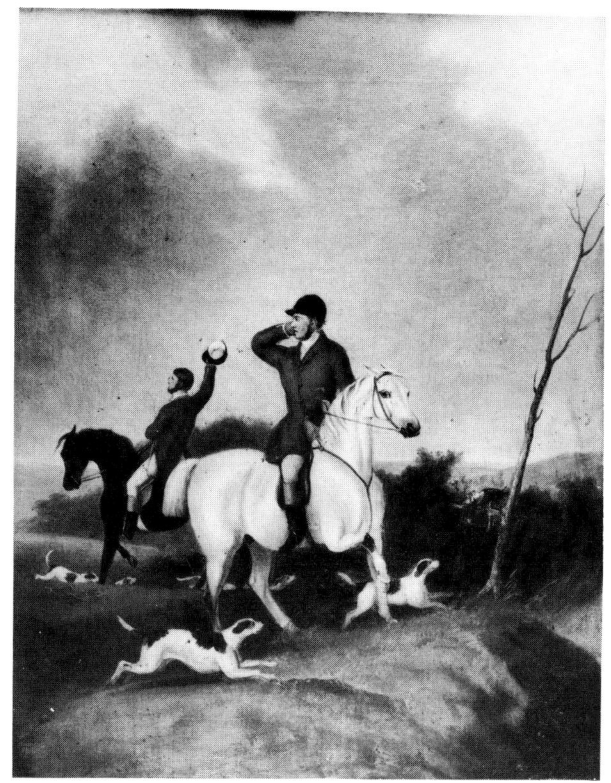

John Paul *Landscape with Huntsmen* *Oil on canvas*

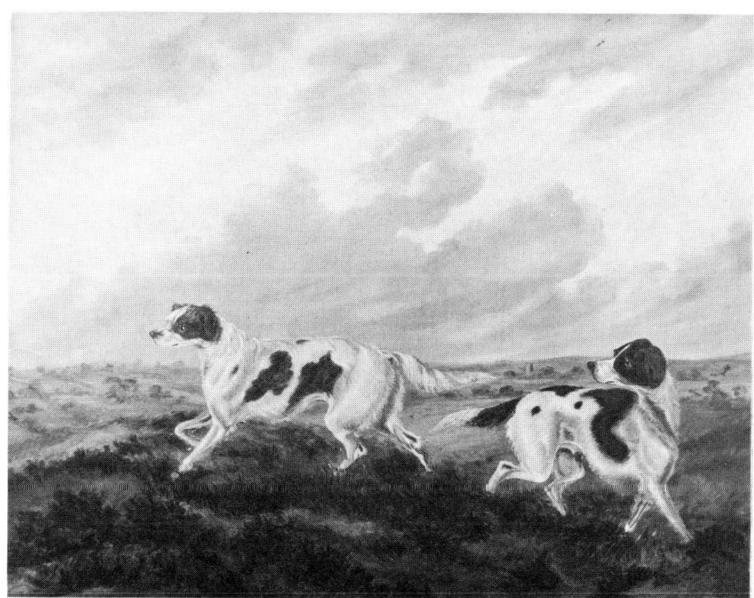

Edwin Cooper *Oil* 49 × 64 *cms.*

EDWIN COOPER

(1785-1833)

1785 Edwin Cooper was born on 1st January, 1785, in the parish of Saint James, Bury St. Edmund's, Suffolk. His father was Daniel Cooper, a miniature painter and Drawing Master to Bury School. Presumably Edwin Cooper attended his father's school. It is known that he was capable of producing a very good drawing at the tender age of eight years. Tradition has it that he became acquainted with John Crome from an early age, and is said to have painted inn signs with him at Yarmouth.

We know that he married, but details are lacking; evidently his wife was named
1806 Anne. By 1806, when he was twenty-one years of age, he was a fully professional painter for we find him exhibiting with the newly-formed Norwich Society. In this year he exhibited four paintings, all of them portraits of horses.

It would appear that such was his ability that even at this early age he was entrusted with many commissions.

1810 By 1810 he was exhibiting horses and cattle at the Norwich Society, many of them being commissions. Undoubtedly his reputation in Norfolk was growing.

When the disruption of the Norwich Society occurred, Cooper was evidently tactful enough to exhibit with both factions; keeping his most important exhibits for the Crome faction, thus underlying his relationship with John Crome.

The exact date of Cooper's removal to Beccles is not known, but it was probably about 1810. This would place him closer to his point of exhibition and put him in close touch with his Norwich patrons.

It is said that Cooper at one time had a studio at Newmarket. This was probably
1824 about 1824, for in that year he is recorded as painting several race-horses.

It has been said that Cooper was a pupil of Marshall. As Marshall had few, if any, associations with Norwich it is more likely that he shared a studio with Marshall when he worked at Newmarket.

1825 In 1825 he executed several commissions for Sir Jacob Astley, three of which were exhibited at the Norwich Society in 1825. A portrait of Mr. J. Hewitt, huntsman to Sir Jacob, later found its way into the Hutchinson collection. This is the only recorded portrait by Edwin Cooper, though undoubtedly he executed several. It would appear that the exhibitors at the Norwich Society were rather scrupulous in keeping to their subjects, *e.g.* Crome and his School painted landscapes, Sillett still life, Clover portraits, and Edwin Cooper animals. We know, of course, that Sillett painted landscapes but seldom exhibited them.

Possibly the extensive travelling under arduous conditions, and coming into contact with numerous patrons resulted in Cooper forming a great alliance with the bottle. It was said of him late in life that he never undertook a picture before drinking a bottle of port. If such was the case it is hardly surprising to find our painter departing
1833 this life at the early age of forty-eight, in the year 1833. The *Suffolk Chronicle* of 12th January, 1833, reported the sad news.

Thus passed the earliest Norwich School painter of animals.

The works of Edwin Cooper have typical East Anglian strength of touch. He endeavours at all times to render his animals with a sensitive exactitude. Whilst many of his works are commissions, one feels that Cooper always cared; he never descended to the level of the mannerist horse painters.

Painting usually on a cross-grained canvas, he often, in his early works, uses slight reds on his buildings and skies, reserving the browns and blacks for his animals. Often his animals have small touches of white impasto, whether to pick out a bridle, body markings, or facial features. He can at times attack the canvas with wonderful bravuro such as we see in the *Grey Mare with Foal* (illustrated). The figures introduced in his pictures are competent, but he has much more feeling when dealing with animals; possibly the accent on his animals is intentional.

Whilst he uses a reasonable paint thickness, the rather course cross-grained canvas is apt to show through, particularly in the foregrounds and skies. One tends to look for this in his work; however, it would be very unlikely that he always worked on such canvas.

His dogs show the influence of certain of the Dutch seventeenth-century painters: one can imagine him having studied Hondius fairly closely.

A drawing of the artist in the Norwich Museum shows Cooper in his hunting apparel with his dog. As this drawing compares with others by him, it is presumably a self-portrait, carrying the inscription "died 9th January 1833 at 1 o'clock morning".

A further drawing illustrated is that of a four-year-old horse. The inscriptions indicate the mottled parts and high-lights. The lines are quite firm without being hard.

Cooper's water-colours are gentle in colour, rather eighteenth century in feel, the general colouring often being ochre.

Cooper usually signs "Edw Cooper Pinxt" with date or simply "E. Cooper Pinxt", occasionally in red, but usually black.

Though Edwin Cooper enjoyed associations all his life with the Norwich School, by virtue of his residence at Beccles in Suffolk, he is also eligible for inclusion in the Suffolk School.

EXHIBITS AT THE NORWICH SOCIETY

Year	*No.*	*Subject*	*Owner*
1806	66	Portrait of a hunter.	Capt. Heath.
	69	Portrait of a charger.	Capt. Heath.
	71	Portrait of a pointer.	—
	249	Portrait of an Arabian and charger.	Lord Paget.
1810	196	Portrait of a horse.	—
	197	Portrait of a horse.	—
	198	Portrait of Mr. Hussey's grey hunter.	—
	199	Portrait of a horse.	—
	200	Portrait of Mr. Hussey's roan horse and Gryier, a famous hound belonging to the Berkeley Hunt.	—
	201	Horse racing.	—
	202	Cattle.	—
	203	Bull.	—
	204	Hunters.	—
1812	18	Horses.	J. Sayers, Esq.
1816	41	Sketches of race horses.	—
	81	Study of horse.	—
	259	Four original drawings of the fox chase: Going out.	—

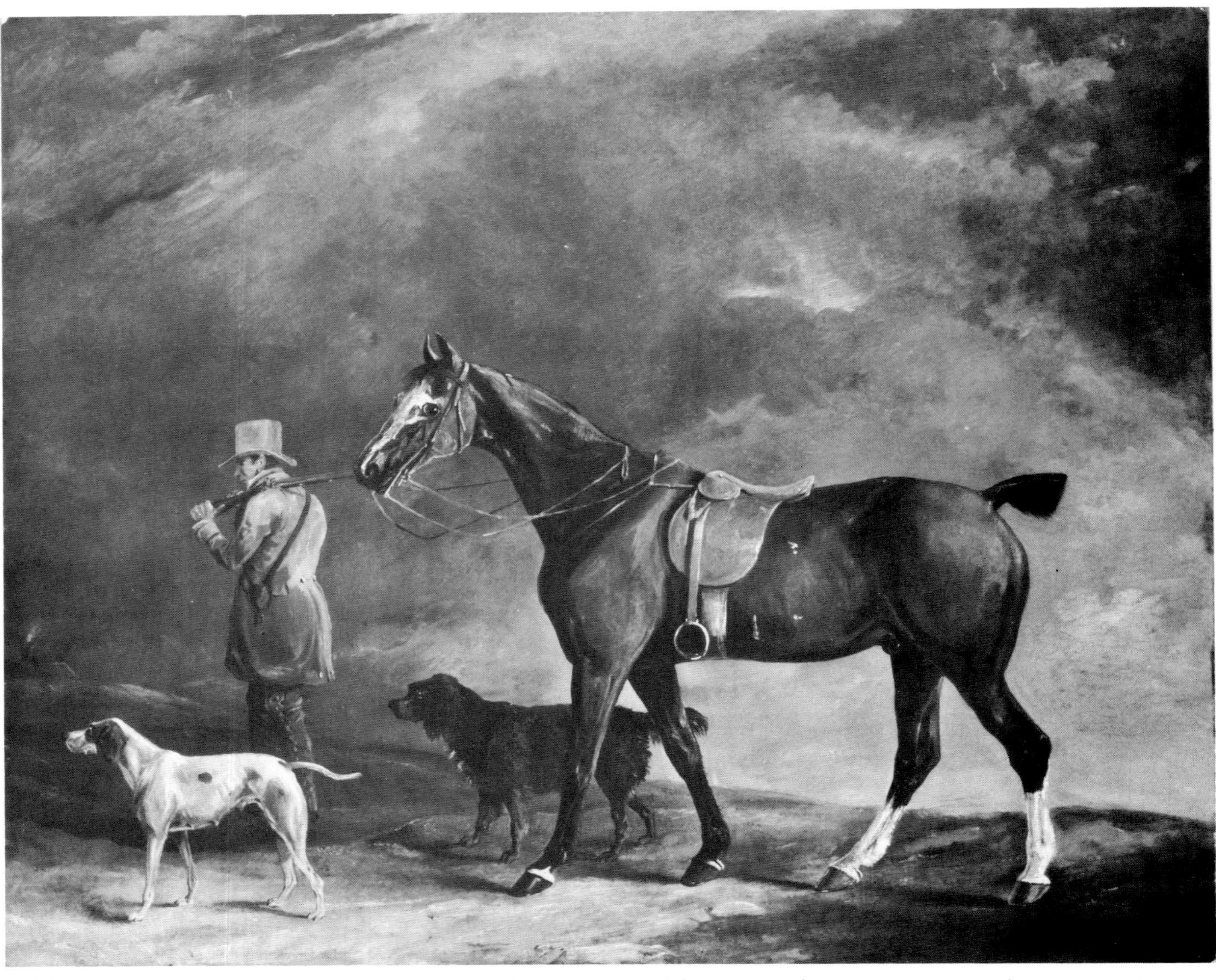

Edwin Cooper — *Sportsman with his gun, horse and dogs in a Landscape* — *Oil on canvas* 25 × 30 *in.*

Year	No.	Subject	Owner
1816	260	Breaking cover.	—
	241	The chase.	—
	262	The death.	—
1817		*Breakaway Society*	
	22	Portrait of horse.	—
	47	Sketches of horses.	—
	71	Sketches of horses.	—
	72	Sketches of horses.	—
	136	Portrait of mare and foal.	—
	17	Portrait of a terrier.	Wm. Samuels.
	24	Hunting subject.	—
	25	Portrait of a shooting pony and pointers.	Thomas Farr.
	32	Portrait of a hackney, greyhound and terrier pup.	Mr. Mapes.
	36	Lively.	N. Micklethwaite, Esq.
	38	Brood mares—the black one the portrait of Wousley by Mentor, the dam of Smolensko.	—
	42	Boy and ass.	—
	64	A fox.	—
	78	Portrait of a hunter.	Rev. R. Gooch.
	86	Portrait of a horse.	—
	182	Boy and ass.	—
	183	Hunting piece.	—
	184	Hunting piece.	—

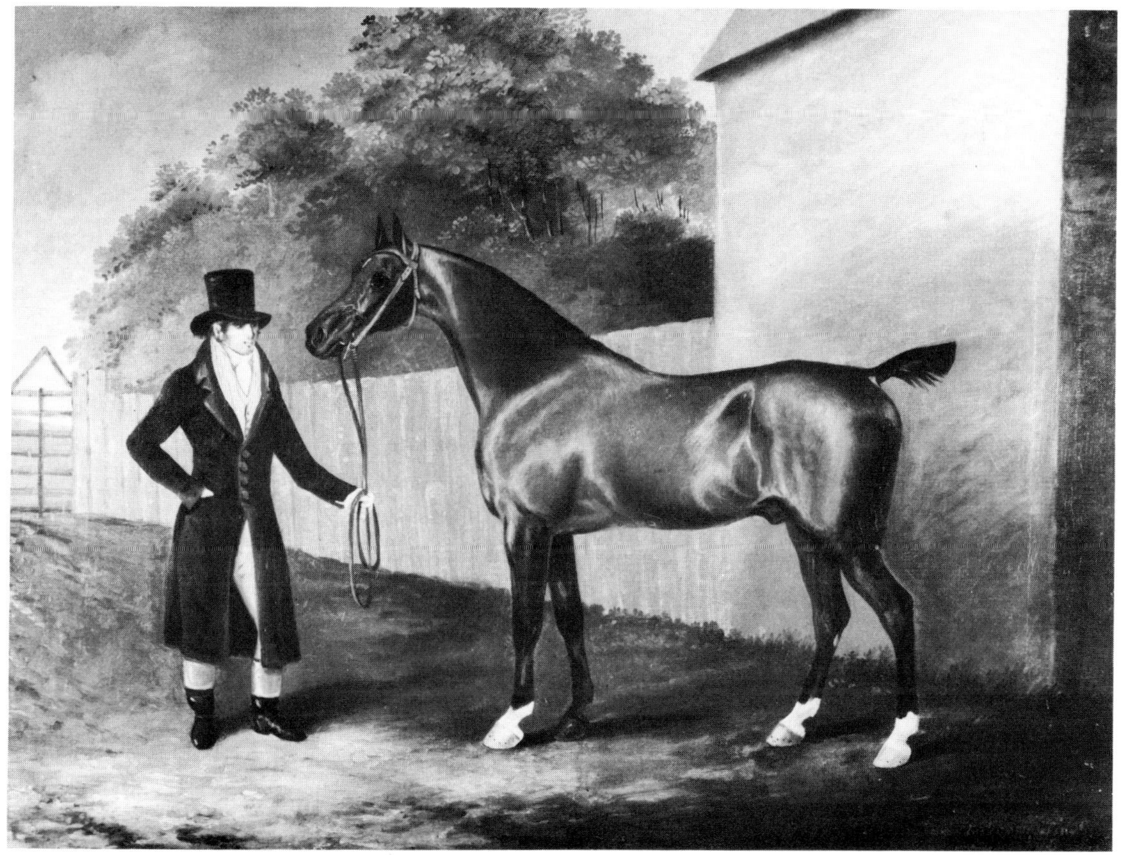

Edwin Cooper, 1806 *Oil on canvas* 18 × 24 *in.*

Year	*No.*	*Subject*	*Owner*
1817	185	Hunting piece.	—
	186	Hunting piece.	—
1818		*Breakaway Society*	
	38	A tiger.	—
	15	Portrait of a mare.	Mr. Eastaugh.
	70	Portrait of a horse and dog.	Mr. Harsent.
	100	Portrait of a cow and running calf.	Mr. Harsent.
1819	29	Portrait of a hunter and pony.	T. Saul.
	41	Portrait of a hunter.	F. Alexander.
	180	A pointer.	—
1820	32	Brood mare.	Mr. James Shaw.
	35	Lilliput, a favourite hunter.	J. Freshfield.
1821	208	Bullock, fattened by Mr. T. Brown Thrigby.	—
1822	68	Portrait of Tosser, a favourite old hunter, and hounds.	E. Jenney.
	82	Portrait of a hunter and hounds.	E. Jenney.
1823	49	A hunter.	A Gentleman.
1824	17	Phenomenon Fireaway.	S. and D. Sewell.
	24	Marshland Shales.	J. J. R. Hawes.
	60	Fetch it, Neptune.	—
	215	The fox.	—
1825	1	Portrait of a hunter.	Sir J. H. Ashley, Bart.
	5	Portrait of a hackney.	Sir J. H. Ashley, Bart.
	15	Portrait of hunter and hounds.	Sir J. H. Ashley, Bart.
	139	Portrait of a hunter.	—
1828	52	Portrait of Intruder by Smolensko, a stud horse.	Mr. Hindes.
	110	Portrait of a terrier.	W. W. Cergat.
	111	Fox hounds in chase—fox beats.	—
	112	Fox hounds—bitch and puppies.	—
	113	Horses at harrow surprised by hunters.	—
	116	Portrait of a horse.	A Gentleman.
	195	Mare, foal and greyhounds at play.	—
1829	7	A hunter.	—
	18	Portrait of bullocks.	R. H. Gurney.
	22	Portrait of hunter.	—
	23	Horses alarmed by thunder—sketch.	—
	45	Portrait of a favourite pony and dogs.	W. Carpenter.
1829	75	Portrait of a favourite.	—
	76	Spot and Hector.	J. Carr.

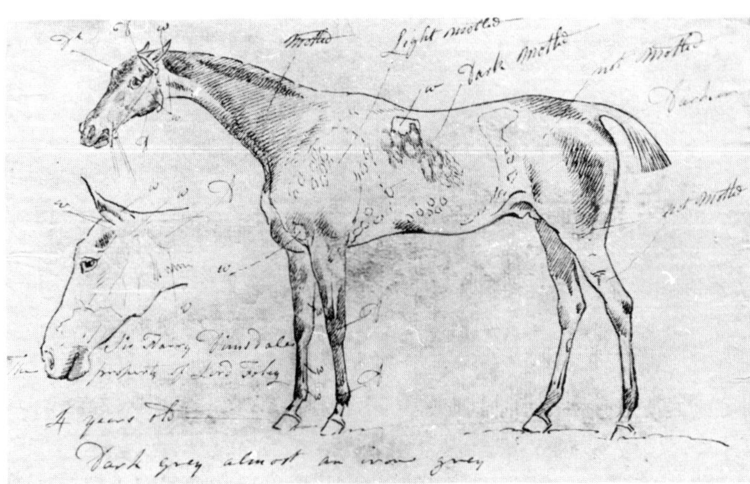

Edwin Cooper *Pencil* $4\frac{1}{4} \times 6\frac{7}{8}$ *in.*

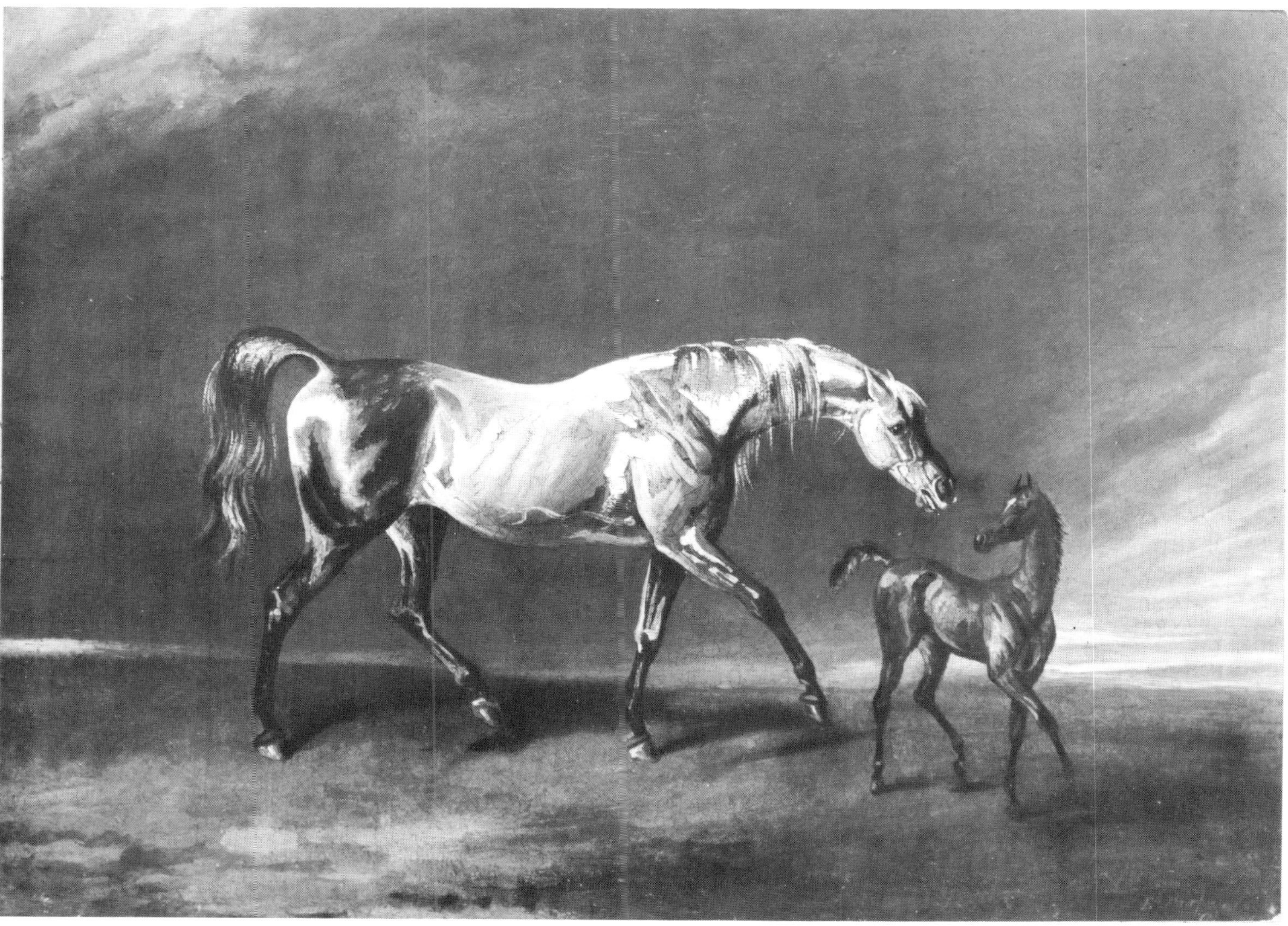

Edwin Cooper *Grey Mare with Foal in a Landscape* *Canvas* 18 × 24 *in.*

Year	*No.*	*Subject*	*Owner*
1830	86	Favourite terrier pups.	Rev. R. Gooch.
	101	Portrait of Tristram.	Alfred Parsons.
	116	Portrait of trotting pony.	—
	148	Portrait of a horse.	G. Legge.
	162	Old favourites.	—
	186	Buck shooting.	—
	188	The charger.	—
	189	Deer.	—
	191	A tiger couchant.	—
1831	102	It's nearly up with him.	—
	133	Portrait of Michael Beasley on his favourite hunter, with portraits of his leading hounds and mare ridden by the whipper-in.	—
1832	56	Portrait of hunter.	R. H. Gurney.
	65	Frightened horses.	—
	140	Portraits of horses.	R. Thornton.
	166	Going to cover—Ward, Esq., on a favourite mare.	—

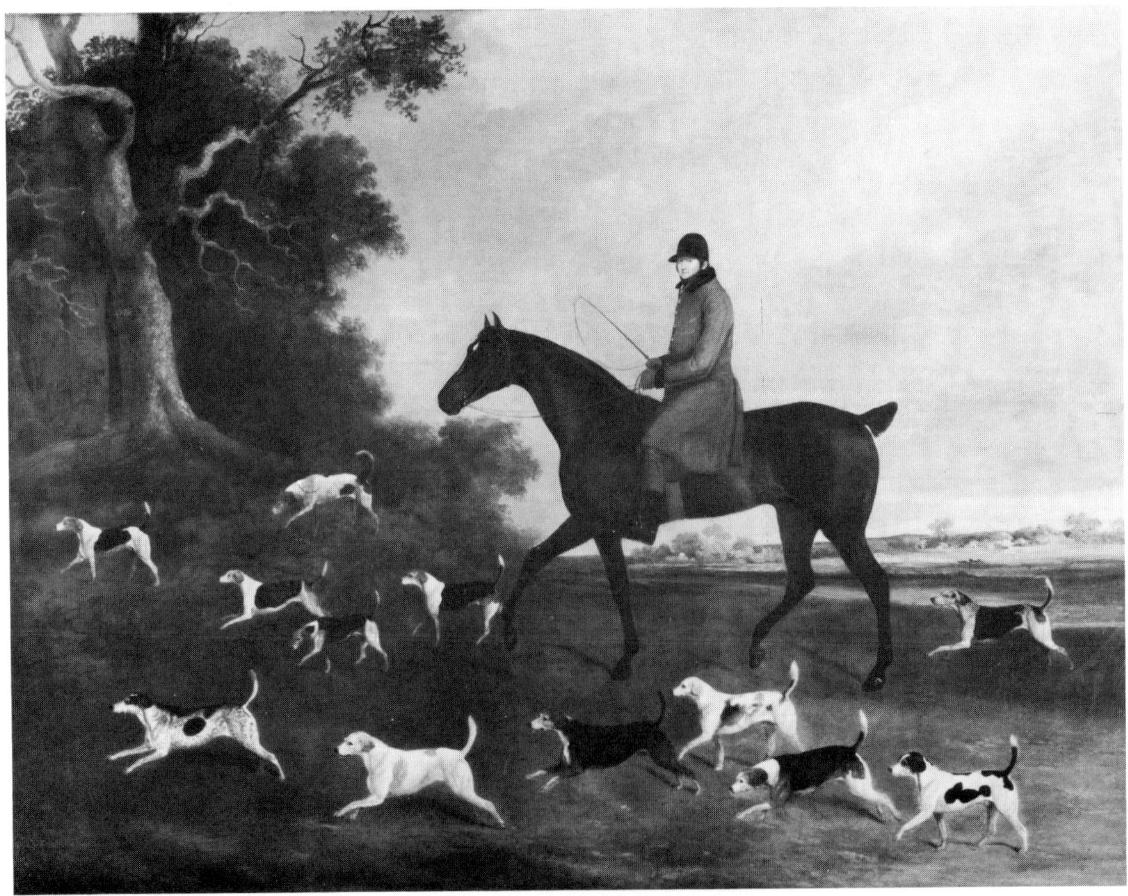

Edwin Cooper *Edward Lombe on Sparkle, with Hounds* *Oil* 41 × 54½ *in.*

HENRY WALTON

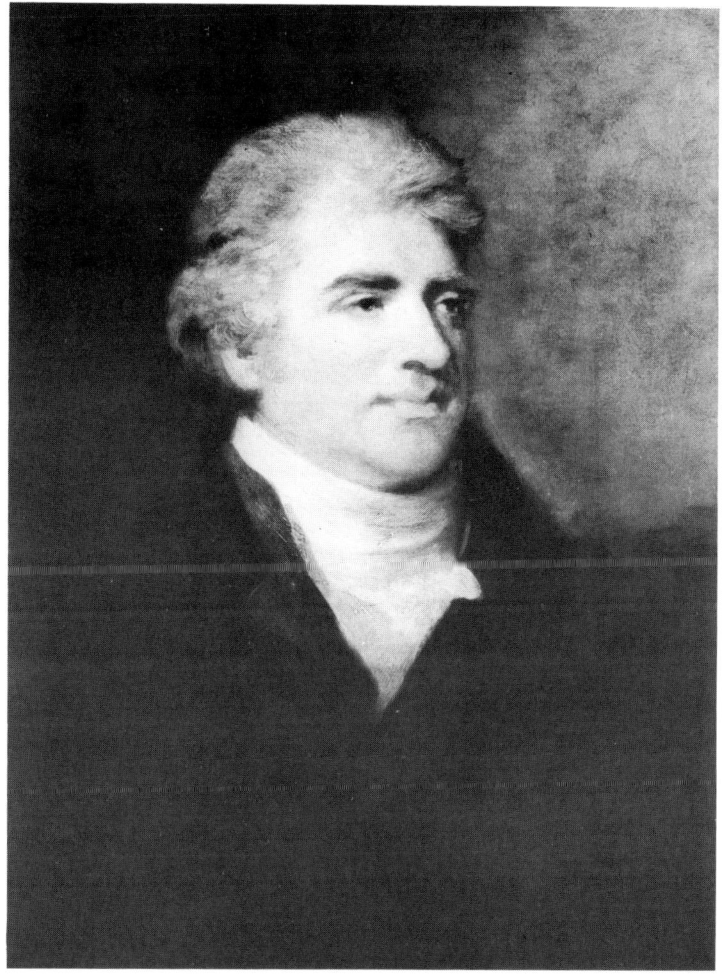

Entienne Dumont

Painted by Henry Walton *Oil on canvas* 30 × 25 *in.*

HENRY WALTON

Norfolk School

(1746-1813)

1746 Henry Walton was born in 1746, probably in Dickleburgh, being baptised on 5th June, 1747, in the neighbouring church of Tivetshall St. Mary. His father, Samuel Walton, was a farmer, and as churchwarden was appointed Overseer of the poor.

1770 Of his early education and activities we know little, but in the year 1770 he applied to be a student at the Maiden Lane Academy established by the Incorporated Society of Artists. According to William Mason, a person who appeared in a painting entitled *Actual Scene at Harrow School*, Walton was a pupil of Zoffany; this fact being borne out by his adopted technique.

1771 In 1771 Walton exhibited at the Incorporated Society (the forerunner of the Royal
1772 Academy) and was followed by his election as a director in 1772. His exhibited paintings were portraits for a number of years, but in 1776 a genre painting called *Plucking the Turkey* was exhibited. It is said that his genre painting was painted under the influence of the French eighteenth-century painters; certainly Walton's work bears some resemblance to that of Jean Baptiste Simeon Chardin.

1777 From 1777 to 1779 Walton sent his exhibits to the Royal Academy, where he unsuccessfully put forward his name for Associateship of the Academy. Undoubtedly, Walton's genre pieces were fine and almost unrivalled; that he was unsuccessful in his application probably caused him to forsake London for his native Norfolk. He returned with his wife, Elizabeth Rust (a miniature painter), to a farm he had bought at Burgate, a few miles from his birthplace. Here he set up in practice and became probably the leading East Anglian portrait painter.

1780 In the 1780s he painted some of his finest portraits, including Sir Edmund Bacon and the Buxton family group.

Besides being an artist it is known that Walton was also engaged in art dealing. It is known that he advised Lord Fitzwilliam respecting certain of the purchases for his Collection (now at the Fitzwilliam, Cambridge): also the Collection of Sir Thomas Beauchamp at Langley Hall, Norfolk, was formed on his advice.

It was somewhat unfortunate that Walton had such great contemporaries; had he appeared at any other period his work would have been given more recognition and he would probably have responded accordingly.

Being a regular visitor to the London sales enabled him to purchase some fine paintings. One such picture Farington mentions in his diary. It would appear that Walton purchased a Titian for £250, cleaned it, and offered it to Sir Thomas Lawrence for £2,500. The Academician turned it down because the price was unreasonably high!

1813 It was probably a picture that caused Walton to visit London in May, 1813, for it was on 19th May of that year that he suddenly died on returning from a party.

His friend, Dawson Turner (also Crome's patron), exhibited after his death a notice of the painter (Outlines in Lithography from a small collection of Pictures, Yarmouth, pages 7, 21-22), in which he said:

> There was in him a singular *bonhomie*, united to much shrewdness, with a vivacity sure to please, and a knowledge of Art, a fund of anecdotes connected with it equally sure to interest and instruct.

THE PAINTINGS

Whilst Henry Walton is essentially an eighteenth-century painter, he probably made a certain contribution in the development of the portrait sketch. He seems to have two methods: his sketchy portraits, which involves Zoffany's palette and handling, plus an original use of strong lights. It is possible that John Constable saw Walton's portraits for the strong impasto touches of light and the thinly painted shadows are to be seen in Constable's portraits. Walton's fame, however, rests not on his sketchy work, but rather on his more highly finished pieces. Such pictures as *Sir Robert and Lady Buxton and their daughter Anne*, in the Norwich Castle Museum, illustrate this. Here we have Walton depicting a typical titled family of the late eighteenth century in what would appear to be an authentic homely setting.

In this picture Walton brings out a feeling of serenity and composure, not an easy feat, and certainly requiring gifts possessed only by the few. One might say his sitters often look relaxed.

Certain of his portraits are painted on a very thinly painted burnt umber ground. The facial recesses, such as under the eyebrows and ear-holes, are simply the umber ground untreated.

The genre paintings, such as the *Girl with Turkey*, have about them a romantic stillness reminiscent of Vermeer.

Having just seen an exhibition of paintings by J. H. Mortimer it would seem that at one period Walton was strongly influenced by this painter, though in the main his extra strength of brushwork is a means of identification.

EXHIBITS AT THE ROYAL ACADEMY

Year	*No.*	*Subject*	*Owner*
1777	360	A market girl.	—
1778	322	A girl buying a ballad.	—
1779	338	A scene in *The Spanish Bosher*—Act 1, Scene 1.	—
	339	A group of figures with a fruit barrow.	E. Cooper.
1803	267	Portrait of a grey Arabian mare.	Duke of York.
1831	1019	Horses frightened.	—

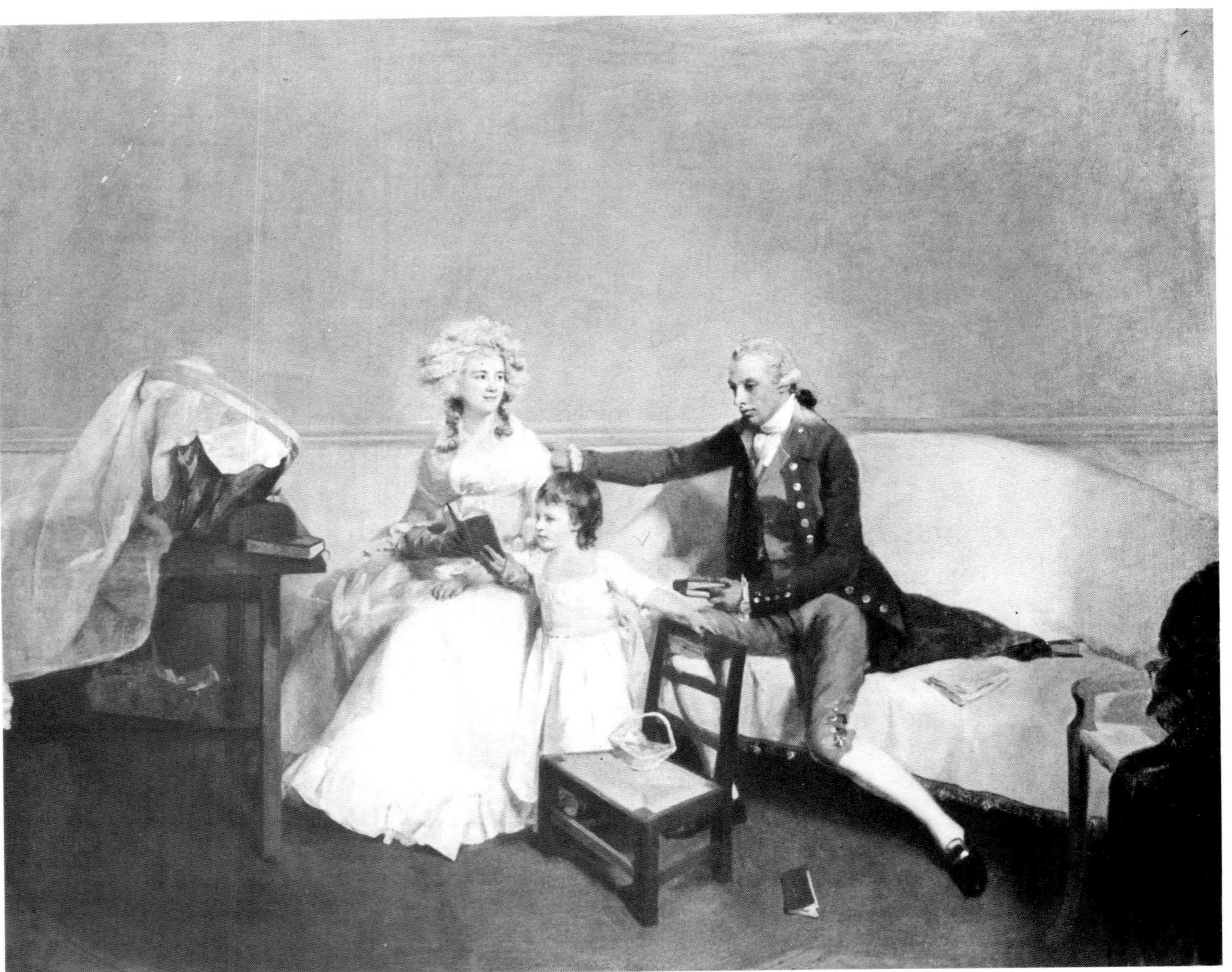

Henry Walton — *The Buxton Family* — *Oil on canvas* $29 \times 36\frac{1}{2}$ *in.*

JOHN SELL COTMAN

(1782-1842)

1782 John Sell Cotman was born in the Parish of St. Mary Coslany in Norwich on 16th May
1782. He appears to have come from merchant stock, for his father, after spending some
1793 time as a hairdresser, became a haberdasher, mercer and dealer in foreign lace. In 1793
he attended the Grammar School in the Cathedral Close—probably his presence near
the Cathedral gave him his interest in the drawings of buildings, which seems to occupy
so much of his time in later years.

Long before leaving the Grammar School Cotman showed his proficiency as an Artist—even at the age of twelve years his landscape studies are quite advanced. It was probably through Opie that he made London contacts and came under the notice of the famous Doctor Monro, who encouraged so many great artists. Apart from studying in the Monro circle it is difficult to find more concerning his art education.

1799 As a youth he lived in London and in 1799 visited Wales and Surrey on sketching tours.
1803 This was followed in 1803 by his trip to Yorkshire, resulting in many of his famous
subjects. During the first few years of the century he resided in London, periodically
venturing off on his tours. This continued until 1806, when he decided to return to his
native city. Here he took a house in Lucketts Court, Wymer Street, and opened a
School of Drawing and Design. Cotman at this time described himself as a portrait
painter. (John Crome is included among his sitters.)

1805 This year Cotman visited Lincolnshire, arriving back with such drawings as *Croyland Abbey* and studies of *Drainage Mills*.

1809 In 1809 Cotman married Ann Miles, who came from Felbrigg near Cromer. This probably accounts for several drawings of Cromer that Cotman produced at this time.

Having successfully established his teaching, he founded his "Circulating Drawings", the idea being for people to hire these works with a view to copying them under supervision. The quarterly subscription being one guinea.

1810 1810 heralded his first son, Miles Edmund Cotman, and in this year he was left £100 by Mrs. Cholmeley. Francis Cholmeley wrote him telling him of his mother's passing. ". . . her friendship for you extended beyond the grave and she left you a bequest of one hundred pounds."

1811 Etchings* seem to have occupied a lot of our artist's time during this period and in 1811 was published by Messrs. Boydell "Etchings of John Sell Cotman". They were largely architectural. These were followed by many other publications dealing with Norfolk and Normandy, France.

1812 In April 1812 Cotman moved to Southtown, Yarmouth, where he lived until December
1823. On 13th July, 1812, Ann Cotman was born, followed by John Joseph Cotman on
1814 29th May, 1814.

1817 The year 1817 saw our painter touring Normandy. He must have had sympathetic feelings for the country, for he visited Normandy again in 1819 and yet again in 1820.

---

*Under the influence of Dawson Turner, Cotman, in 1814, produced more etchings depicting the Grand Festival at Great Yarmouth. These were followed in 1817 by *Specimens of Norman and Gothic Architecture in the County of Norfolk* and *Specimens of the Castellated and Ecclesiastical Remains in the County of Norfolk*.

In 1818 appeared a series of etchings illustrative of the Architectural Antiquities of Norfolk, 60 plates.

Apart from the Yarmouth etchings the other subjects were republished in 1838 by H. G. Bohn, who bought the plates. A volume which has come to light recently is *Specimens of Norman and Gothic Architecture in the County of Norfolk*, 50 plates, by J. S. Cotman, 1816, 1817 and 1818; printed by C. Sloane of Yarmouth.

1823 In 1823 he sent 19 drawings, largely the result of his Normandy tour, to the Norwich Society. In the same year he changed his abode, moving to St. Martin-at-the-Palace, Harwich.

1825 In 1825, through the good offices of Lady Palgrave, Cotman was offered Associate Membership of The Water Colour Society, without having to submit a work. This came at an opportune moment, for the Norwich Corporation decided to demolish Sir Benjamin Wrench's Court where the Norwich Society Exhibitions had been held. This resulted in the cessation of Norwich Exhibitions for several years.

It is rather interesting to note that in the 1820s there is a great affinity between the work of Samuel Prout and that of Cotman. I think the honours go to Cotman, who first painted Continental Architecture in 1817, whilst Prout's first visit was in 1819. However, as Ruskin has observed, Prout's feeling and depiction of buildings is unsurpassed in water-colour.

Cotman had little success in selling his work; had it not been for his teaching he would have been in dire straits indeed. He insisted in adopting his own style in drawing and painting, which was not readily accepted. Dawson Turner, his friend, prevailed upon him to adapt his work to public taste. In the 1820s Cotman did make endeavours in this direction.

1833 With the termination of the Norwich Society Exhibitions in 1833 Cotman began to look towards London. Fortunately, on the recommendation of J. M. W. Turner, Cotman was appointed Drawing Master at King's College, London, and life became full of
1834 optimism, despite a rather unsuccessful sale of his works in Norwich in 1834.

1836 In 1836 Cotman arranged for his son, Miles Edmund, to take over his teaching duties at King's College. He then took up his palette and painted in his natural style with great freedom of line and colour. Again the critics rose up and Cotman's spirits fell.

1841 However, in 1841 he took to drawing with black and white chalk. The effect was electric, and works of this period represent the culmination of his powers. In the New Year of
1842 1842 he was back in London, feeling unwell. His health gradually declined until on 28th July he departed this world.

THE PAINTINGS

Cotman, in his day, was not understood. His work was well in advance of his times. It was only when the Impressionists, fifty years later, began to use bright colours, that his work became acceptable. Though much of Cotman's work is in bright colour, he did have the greatest feeling for tonal values, as we see in much of his early work and occasionally later. Most of the East Anglian Painters based their art on an intense study of nature. Cotman did not paint nature but used nature to inspire him in his art. This lack of study of nature resulted in our artist forming a style. However, his originality was such that he could by no means be classed as a mannerist.

His work in oil is more extensive than formerly considered. Going through his early Norwich Society Exhibits one comes across numerous oil sketches. In 1834, in the Norwich Sale, are recorded forty-seven paintings in oil. After the Artist's death, Christies, in 1843, sold a further sixty-seven oil paintings. Thus over 130 oils are recorded, without those disposed of other than in sales.

Cotman is undoubtedly a major East Anglian Artist, and at his best a superb draughtsman. One has only to study his *View of Dieppe*—there are few painters who could have achieved such effects with such apparent ease. More than anything he was original and his style formed the successful basis upon which later painters, such as Henry Bright, Miles Edmund Cotman and John Joseph Cotman, were founded.

Cotman's technique with oil-painting was in the main very uncharacteristic of the remainder of the Norwich School, such was his individuality. *The Waterfall* in the Norwich Museum, an early work, suggests classical influence but the coarse gritty handling is very much Cotman's. *The Banks of the Yare* at Leeds is not so happy a composition and in it we see Cotman using Crome's formula for balancing masses. By the 1820s we see our artist endeavouring to produce paintings more to the public taste. Cotman's mastery was such that he was able to model his figures with a turn of the brush—a strong characteristic of a J. S. Cotman oil from the 1820s onwards. A further characteristic was the placing of local colours in the mid-distance.

Undoubtedly many J. S. Cotman oils were left in an unfinished state. It is quite possible that many of them were worked over by others.

Later he reverted to his own style, and pictures like the *Baggage Wagon* and the *Drop Gate* probably influenced William Muller with their broad and bold conception. It is at the end of Cotman's life that he produced his finest pictures and amongst these is *Postwick Grove* or *Scene on the Bure*, formerly in the collection of the late Viscount Mackintosh of Halifax.

With his oil painting J. S. Cotman tends to be very varied and experimental in his approach. One can only conclude that the medium was not always suited to his excitable temperament as water-colour.

Alec Cotman has made the observation that the work of J. S. Cotman is usually associated with a "blocking in" technique.

EXHIBITS AT ROYAL ACADEMY—DRAWINGS

Year	*No.*	*Subject*
1800	334	A watermill near Dorking.
	342	A cottage near Guildford churchyard.
	343	Back of an inn near Guildford.
	424	Leatherhead Church, Surrey.
	550	Harlech Castle, Wales.
	596	Cottage—Dorking, Surrey.
1801	311	Brecknock.
	410	Llantony Abbey.
1802	420	Carnarvon Castle.
	430	A grindstone, near Harlech, North Wales.
1803	381	Morning.
	446	Buildwas Abbey.
	576	Banwell, Somersetshire.
1804	375	Near Barmouth, North Wales
	409	Newburgh Park, Yorkshire—the seat of T W. Belasyse, Esq.
	418	Newburgh Park, Yorkshire.
	461	East window of Howden Church.
	498	Rivaulx Abbey, Yorkshire.
	465	Fountain Abbey, Yorkshire.
	928	Gormire, Yorkshire.
1805	325	A study of trees.
	448	A draining mill.
	509	Croyland Abbey, Lincolnshire.
	626	Gateway of Croyland Abbey.
1806	341	In Castle Eden Dean, Durham.
	460	Horses drinking.
	461	Durham Cathedral.

Year	No.	Subject
1806	494	Distant view of Greta Bridge, Yorkshire.
	524	On the River Greta, Yorkshire.
	540	Barnard Castle, from Towler Hill.

THE ASSOCIATED PAINTERS IN WATER-COLOURS

Year	No.	Subject
1810	5	A mill on Mousehold Heath, near Norwich.
	17	A Blakeney fishing boat.
	36	Fishing boat—morning.
	81	Richmond Castle, Yorkshire.
	83	Landscape—composition.
	140	Landscape—composition.
	156	A cottage door.
	195	A study of trees.
	201	Durham Cathedral.
	225	A sketch.

THE NORWICH SOCIETY OF ARTISTS AT NORWICH

Year	No.	Subject
1807	9	Ancient Bath—composition.
	18	Durham Cathedral.
	45	Croyland Abbey.
	47	Durham.
	48	Window between St. Andrew's Hall and the Dutch Church.
	67	Distant view of Cader Idris, North Wales.
	94	A portrait.
	99	Portrait.
	103	Portrait of a lady.
	104	Portrait.
	105	Sketch after Vandyke.
	106	Portrait.
	112	Watermill, Surrey.
	124	Norwich Castle—a sketch.
	129	Harlech Castle, North Wales.
	130	A coloured sketch of the market-place, Norwich, taken from Mr. Cooper's.
1807	133	View of Norwich from Whitlingham Church.
	139	Dutch boat driving before wind, and vessels in the offing.
	140	St. Botolph's Priory, Colchester.
	154	Portrait of a lady
1808	1	Portrait.
	2	Portrait.
	3	Portrait.
	4	Portrait.
	5	Portrait of a lady.
	6	Beggar boy.
	7	Boy at marbles.
	8	Portrait of Mr. Freeman.
	9	Portrait of a lady.
	15	Dealers waiting the coming in of the herring boats, Yarmouth.
	21	Sketch in oils.
	22	Sketch in oils.
	27	Sketch from Nature in oils.
	29	Sketch from Nature.

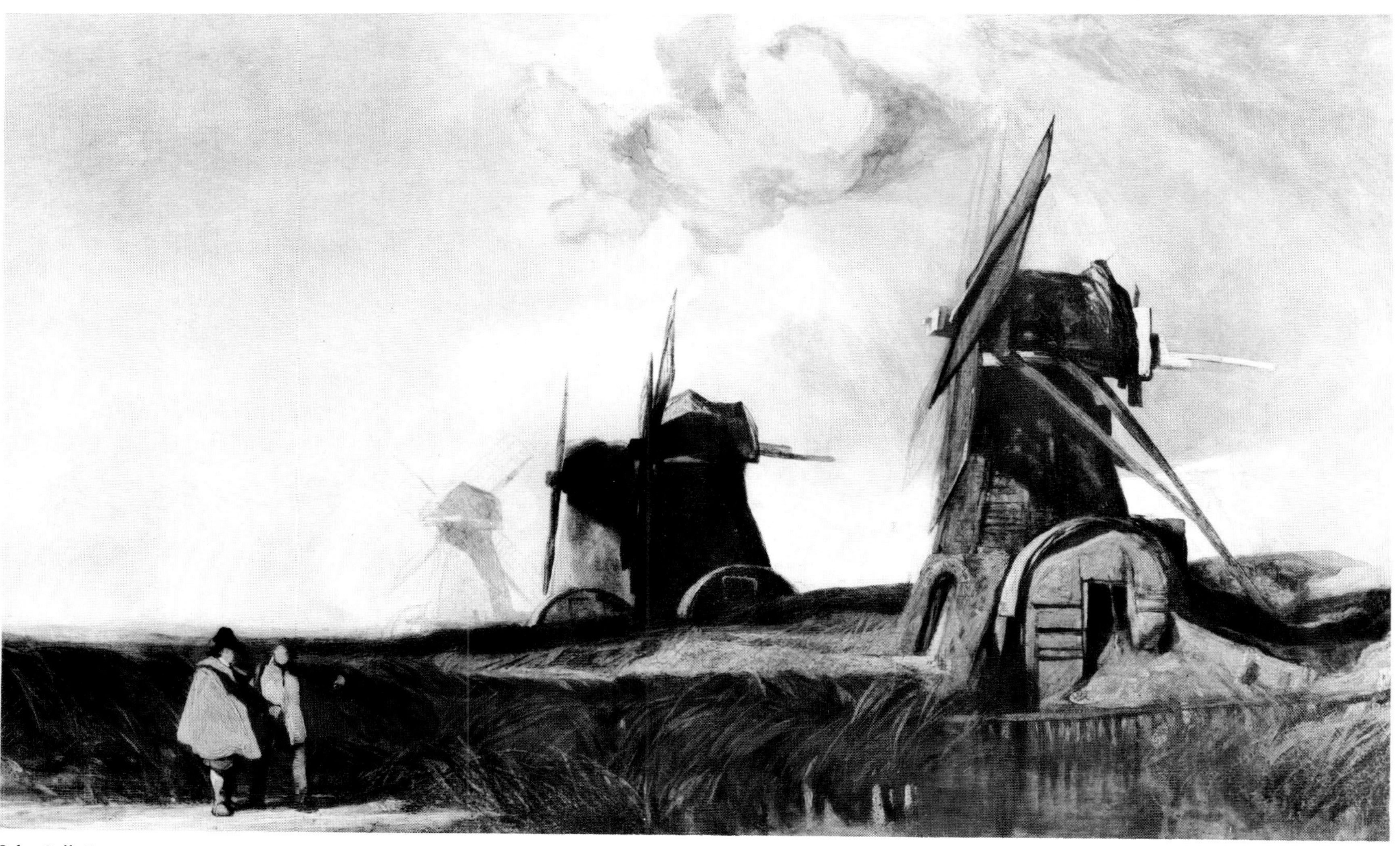

John Sell Cotman — *The Windmills* — *Oil on canvas* 23 × 36 *in.*

Year	*No.*	*Subject*
1808	30	Sketch from Nature.
	33	Sketches from Nature.
	34	Sketches from Nature.
	46	Sketch in oils.
	47	Claude (from Lewis's Monk)
	52	Huntress
	75	Horses drinking—a sketch for a large picture.
	84	A study
	88	Portrait ("For, I had heard of battles, and I long'd to follow to the field some warlike Lord"—Douglas).
	95	Woodcutter and landscape composition—two drawings.
	104	Study of a rock, Greta River.
	107	Coal shaft—coloured sketch.
	108	Mare and foal—sketch in bistre.
	109	The charioteer—a composition.
	119	Cottage.
	124	Two historical designs.
	128	Byland Abbey—coloured sketch.
	137	Dutch boats—two sketches in chalk.
	140	Sketch in oils.
	143	On the Greta River, Yorkshire—sketch from Nature.
	157	Study in oils—still life.
	158	Thunder storm, composed for a large picture.
	161	Norwich craft.
	162	Cromer Beach.
	164	The shepherd.
	165	Dutch hoys, Yarmouth River.
	173	Portrait.
	176	My dog.
	184	Hell Caldron, Rokeby Park.
	186	Snowdon, North Wales.
	188	Twickenham, mid-day.
	189	Portrait.
	191	Packet boats working to windward, Beaumaris Bay.
	193	The *Mars*, riding at anchor off Cromer.
	196	Ferry House, Bristol.
	199	Llynn Ogwen, North Wales.
	203	Portrait.
	204	Landscape composition.
	211	View of Breydon—twilight.
	214	Sketch.
	215	Portrait.
	217	Portrait.
	219	Lane near Thorpe.
	220	Old Merton Hall, Cheshire.
	221	Waterfall—composition.
	222	Barrow, etc.
	224	Banditti.
	220	Cromer fisherman.
	234	Sketch in oils.
	245	Portrait.
	246	Old house at Bristol.
	250	The action of the *Windsor Castle* packet, sketched for a large picture.
	252	Dutch fishing boats—a calm.
1809	6	Carrow Abbey.
	7	St. Mary's Abbey, York.
	9	A portrait.
	10	St. Mary's Abbey, York.
	11	The Dutch Fair, Yarmouth (unfinished).

Year	*No.*	*Subject*
1809	13	Bridge at Knaresborough, Yorkshire
	22	Boats at Cromer Beach.
	25	An old house on Orford Hill, Norwich.
	27	Smelt fishing—evening (unfinished).
	28	From Catterick Bridge (unfinished).
	33	An old house, Fye Bridge, Norwich.
	80	Portrait.
	82	Hampstead Heath.
	85	North side of Hampstead Heath.
	87	Portrait.
	136	Ferry House, York.
	140	Dutch shipping.
	144	Portrait.
	149	The old shepherd of Elmerton.
	159	The Sheep Walk, near Alnwick Castle, Northumberland.
	160	Landscape, with cows·
	161	Gleaner.
	162	Richmond Castle, Yorkshire.
	163	The Ouse Bridge, York.
	150	A Welch peasant.
	153	Rivaulx Abbey, Yorkshire.
	159	A chamber in Wenlock Prison, in Shropshire.
	164	A skirmish between Lord Paget's Regiment of Hussars and the French, wherein the latter were totally routed (the sketch for his large picture)
	168	Boats on the shore at Blakeney.
	169	Fish swills, rudder, tec.
	172	Old houses, Elm Hill.
	173	Bone-house, Heigham.
	174	East end of Weldon Church, Yorkshire.
	177	Part of Warwick Castle.
	181	View on Mousehold Heath.
	191	Scene near Norwich.
	206	Near Llanrwst, North Wales.
	208	Norwich market-place (a plate of this drawing is now in the hands of the engraver).
1810	4	Wells Harbour.
	25	Swedish fishing boats.
	43	Kirby Bedon Tower.
	54	Mousehold Heath.
	55	View of Jungfrau-Horn, a glacier in the Canton of Bern, Switzerland.
	57	Croyland Abbey, Lincolnshire.
	59	Harlech Castle, North Wales.
	60	Mousehold Heath.
	62	Draining mill, Lincolnshire.
	67	Composition.
	69	Scene near Cromer.
	88	Portrait of a horse, the property of Dennis Howard, Esq.
	93	Fishermen, with a distant view of Creke Castle, Durham.
	106	End of a barn at Diss.
	115	Penmanmaur, North Wales.
	121	Durham Castle and Cathedral.
	124	Harvest field—a pastoral.
	134	Dolbaddern Castle.
	138	North end of Battersea Bridge.
	140	View of Snowdon, from the Lake of Llanberris, North Wales.
	161	Harlech Castle, North Wales.
	172	Fastolf's Tower, Caistor Castle.
	175	Kett's Castle.
1811	51	West front of Binham Abbey, in Norfolk, for Cotman's *Antiquities of Norfolk*.
	52	A doorway on the south side of Brayesworth Church, Suffolk.

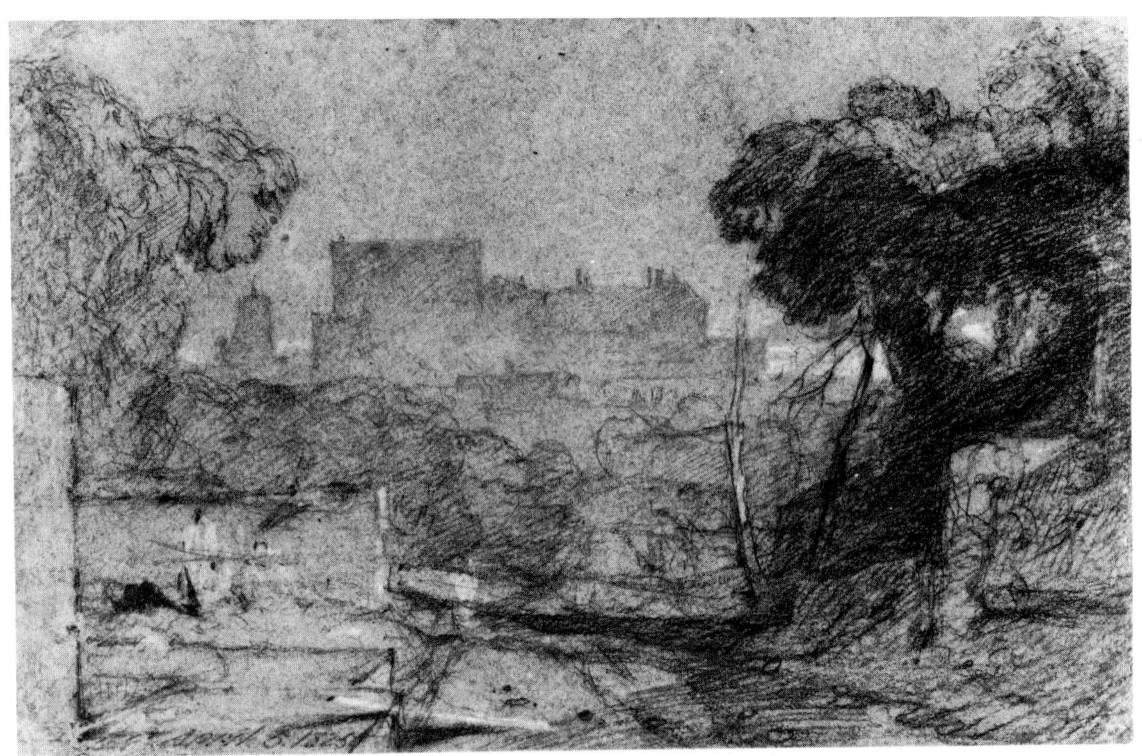

John Sell Cotman *View of Norwich Castle* *Chalk drawing*

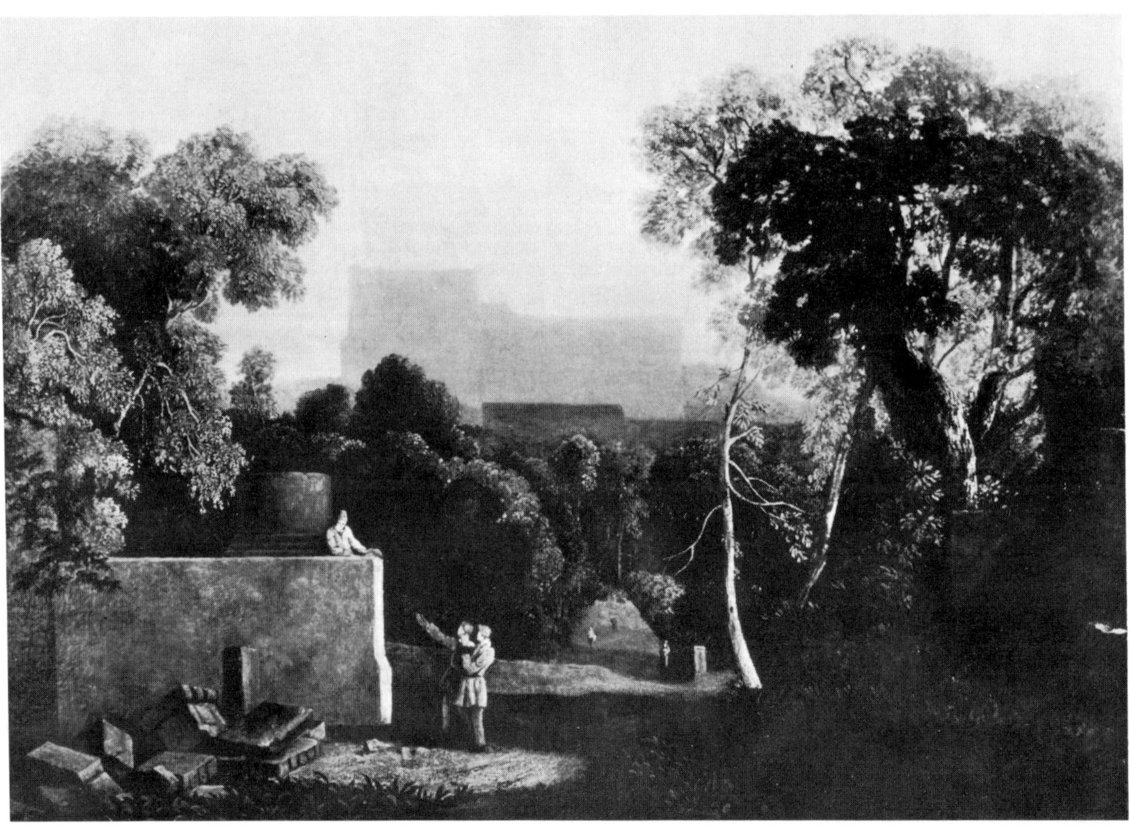

John Sell Cotman *View of Norwich Castle (with artist's licence)* *Oil on canvas*

Whilst additions to this painting may have been made in the nineteenth century the main structure is Cotman.

Year	*No.*	*Subject*
1811	53	Part of Easeby Abbey, Yorkshire.
	54	A curious doorway on the north side of Brayesworth Church, Suffolk
	55	Rivaulx Abbey, Yorkshire.
	56	St. Mary's Abbey, Yorkshire.
	57	The Old Cottage House, Conway, North Wales.
	58	West front of Byland Abbey, Yorkshire.
	59	The east end of Howden Collegiate Church, Yorkshire.
	60	A doorway to the Manor House, Yorkshire.
	61	The frontispiece to J S. Cotman's *Etchings.*
	62	A garden house on the River Yare.
	63	West end of Brayesworth Church, Suffolk.
	64	West front of Croyland Abbey, Lincolnshire.
	65	West front of Kirkstall Abbey, Yorkshire.
	66	Part of the refectory of Rivaulx Abbey, Yorkshire.
	67	A Saxo-Norman doorway, Kirkham Priory, Yorkshire.
	68	The reverse view of the same.
	69	An entrance to the refectory of Rivaulx Abbey, Yorkshire.
	70	North Creak Abbey, Norfolk.
	71	Part of the refectory of Fountain Abbey, Yorkshire.
	72	Trees, Duncomb Park, Yorkshire.
	73	A window in St. Stephen's Chapel, St. Andrew's Hall.
	74	A sketch for Cotman's *Antiquities of Norfolk.*
	78	The prospectus to J. S. Cotman's *Architectural Antiquities of Norfolk.*
	79	A doorway, Valle Crucis Abbey, North Wales.
	80	The dedication.
	81	The west front of St. Botolph's Priory, Colchester, Essex.
	82	A draining mill, Lincolnshire—a pencil sketch.
	124	A screen—south transept of Norwich Cathedral.
	129	A shrine, Norwich Cathedral—a sketch for Cotman's *Architectural Antiquities of Norfolk.*
	133	Part of Walsingham Abbey, Norfolk—a sketch for Cotman's *Antiquities of Norfolk.*
	151	Part of the south transept of Norwich Cathedral—a sketch for Cotman's *Antiquities.*
	198	Part of Basham Hall.
1812	59	Part of Bromholme Priory.
	60	St. Lawrence's Pump, Norwich.
	61	Vicarage House, Methwold.
	62	A doorway of Little Snoring Church.
	63	South Gate, Yarmouth.
	64	Arches under the tower of Castle Rising Church.
	65	Tower of West Dereham Church.
	66	Chapel on the Mount, Lynn.
	67	A doorway of Holme Church.
	68	Interior of the Priory, Yarmouth.
	69	West front of the chapel, Houghton in the Dale.
	70	Font in Walsingham Church.
	71	Gateway of Walsingham Abbey.
	72	Middleton Tower.
	73	Tower on the walls, Yarmouth.
	74	Part of Walsingham Abbey.
	75	Interior of South Runcton Church.
	76	Doorway of Wimbotsham Church.
	83	West front of Binham Priory.
1815	16	South porch of St. Nicholas' Chapel and the west end of St. Margaret's Church, Lynn, Norfolk, forming part of the eighth number of the *Antiquities of Norfolk* to be published in August.
	198	Ancient brasses.
1818	132	Holkham Hall.
1820	213	West front of the Abbey Church at Caen, in Normandy.
	214	Cathedral Church of Notre Dame, Rouen—south transept, from La Place de la Calende.

Year	*No.*	*Subject*
1821	129	West front of the cathedral at Rouen.
	131	West front of the Church of St. Peter, at Lisieux.
1823	33	William, Duke of Normandy, at the head of his followers, previous to the Battle of Hastings—a sketch.
	113	Draining mill, near Downham, Norfolk—a pencil drawing.
	124	Fountaine de la Crosse, Rouen.
	126	House in the Place de la Pucelle, at Rouen.
	127	Castle of Mortaine, Normandy.
	146	Chateau of Containe-le-Henri, the residence of the Viscount De Canissy.
	147	Domfront, Normandy—view from the town.
	153	Entrance into the town of Falaise, the birthplace of William the Conqueror.
	154	Mount St. Michael, Normandy, on the approach from Pontorson, under the appearance of the mirage.
	155	Rouen, looking up the Seine, between the Island de la Mocque and the Quay Royal; the Fauxbourg d'Eauplet and Mount St. Catherine in the distance.
	156	Dutch boats.
	157	Screen to a chapel on the north side of the Church of St. Lawrence, at Eu, Normandy.
	161	Pont de L'Arch, on the Seine, with a distant view of the ruined Abbey of Deus Amants.
	162	Domfront, Normandy—view of the town, etc.
	163	Dieppe—from the heights to the east of the port, looking down upon the harbour, castle, churches of St. Jacques, St. Eemi, and along the coast towards St. Vallery.
	164	Castle of Alencon, Normandy, said by Bloemfield to have been the model from which the Castle of Caistor, near Yarmouth, was built by the Duc D'Alencon, as the price of his ransom to Sir John Fastolf.
	168	An old house, France—pencil drawing.
	171	Arches on the west side of the Abbey Church of St. George's de Bocherville.
	201	E. W. C. Hay, Esq.
1824	9	A landscape cmpoosition.
	15	Trees at Kimberley—clearing up after a storm at mid-day.
	18	View from Yarmouth Bridge, looking towards Breydon, just after sunset. Painted for J. Bridgman, Esq.
	41	Dutch boats off Yarmouth—prizes during the war.
	48	An old house at St. Alban's.
	63	Swimming a feather—a scene at Reedham. Painted for Mr. J. Eager.
	64	A Cromer fishing boat on the shore in Wells Harbour. Painted for Mr. Eager.
	72	Old houses and figures.
	74	Snowdon, with the Lake of Llanberris, from Dolbaddern Castle, North Wales.
	75	Dieppe, from the heights to the east of the port, looking down upon the harbour, castle, churches of St. Jacques and St. Remi, and along the coast to St. Vallery. Painted for J. Brightwen, Esq.
	76	Trees at Bramerton.
	77	Study of trees, Ashted Park, Surrey.
	78	Study of trees, at Rokeby, Yorkshire.
	81	Ruins in Bedfordshire.
	82	Study of trees.
	85	East end of Fountain's Abbey, Yorkshire.
	88	Frame containing doorway of Arminghall Hall—and north doorway of Hales Church, Norfolk.
	89	Frame containing tower of Kirby Bedon Church, and ruins at Llantissilio, North Wales.
	90	Arches under the tower of Fountain's Abbey, Yorkshire.
	92	View of the Jungfrauhorn, Pic de la Vierge, situated in the Valley of Lauterbrunnen, in the Canton of Berne.
	93	St. Mary's Abbey, York.
	94	Abbatial house of the Abbey of St. Ouen, at Rouen, taken down in 1817. Painted for the Rev. C. P. Burney, D.D.
	95	Mount St. Michael, on the side of Pontorson, showing the phenomenon of the mirage. Painted for J. Brightwen, Esq.
	97	Frame, containing remains of an old tower and doorway of Shingham Church, Norfolk.

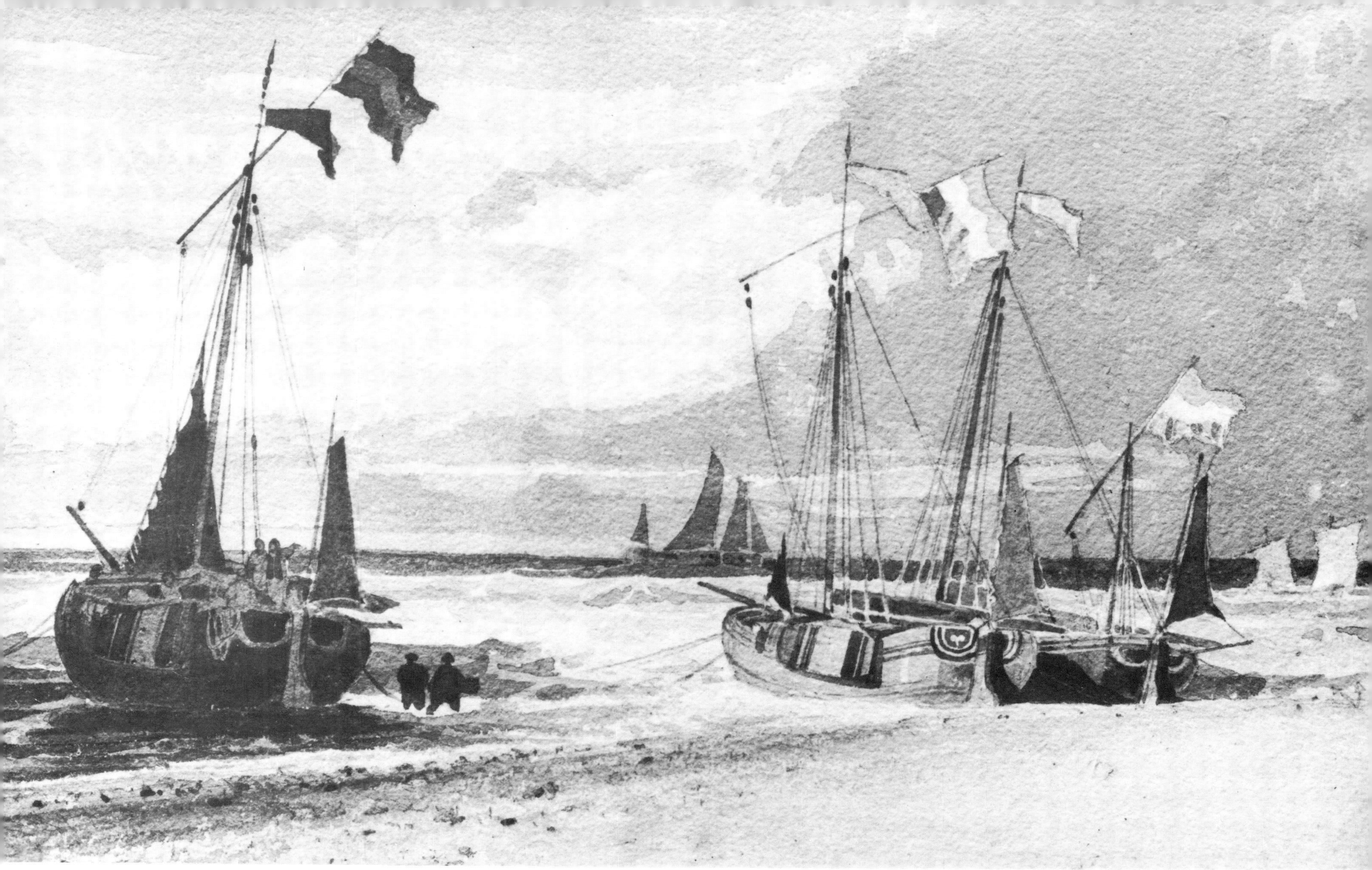

John Sell Cotman — *Dutch Fishing Boats* — *Water-colour* $8 \times 12\frac{3}{4}$ *in.*

Year	No.	Subject
1824	98	Just in from a walk, or "Studies Resumed"—a portrait.
	100	Frame, containing two views of the ruins of the Abbey of Fontenaye le Marmion, France.
	101	Peasant girl.
	104	Trees at Shickleton, Yorkshire.
	108	Trees at Catton—a study in chalk.
	124	D. B. Murphy, Esq.—a pencil drawing.
	144	Welsh cottager's child.
	146	Trees in Duncombe Park, Yorkshire.
	152	Trees on the Seine at Pont de L'Arche.
	154	Collegiate house at Conway.
	155	Frame, containing sketches of horses.
	160	Cottage at Hanworth.
	161	A landscape composition.
	164	Study of trees, at Reedham.
	171	A landscape, with the Fable of the Judgment of Midas, and a view of Whitby, Yorkshire—part of a series of designs intended to illustrate a work now publishing on landscape composition.
	172	Millbank on the Thames, and Kilgarren Castle, Pembrokeshire—part of a series, etc.
	179	St. Benet's Abbey, Gate and Mill.
	183	Castle of Mortain, France.
	189	Study of trees, at Caistor next Yarmouth.
	191	Rouen from Mount St. Catherine.
	194	Trees at Blofield—study in chalk.
	198	Distant view of Mount St. Michael and Tomblane, from the terrace of the Cathedral of Avranches, part of which was standing in 1817.
	199	Boats on the River Sarthe, below Alencon.
	200	Castle of Arques, France—a sketch.
	204	Castle of Cruelly, France.
	208	The Abbey, Fontenaye de la Marmion, France.
	216	Frame, containing two sea views.
1825	111	Landscape.
	112	Boats.
	113	Landscape.
	117	Landscape.
	132	A study.
	135	Boats on the shore at Cromer.

THE OLD WATER-COLOUR SOCIETY

Year	No.	Subject
1825	104	Dieppe from the heights to the east of the port, looking down upon the harbour, churches of St. Jacques and St. Remi, and along the coast towards St. Vallery.
	105	Abbatial house of St. Ouen, at Rouen, taken down in 1817.
	109	Mount St. Michael, on the side of Pontorson, Normandy, showing the phenomenon of the mirage.
1826	91	Landscape—composition.
	93	View on the Scheldt.
	185	Landscape, near Pont Audemer.
	192	Porch of the church of Louviers.
	199	Town of Alencon.
	215	Abbey church of St. Stephen, at Caen.
	242	Boats on the beach, at Cromer.
1828	203	Cliffs on the north-east side of Point Lorenzo, Madeira.
	260	A street scene at Andely's, Normandy.
1829	35	Fishing boat off Cromer.
	162	Danish merchant ship off Yarmouth, unloading timber.

Year	No.	Subject
1829	248	Fountains in the fish market at Basle (from a sketch by W. H. Harriott, Esq.).
1830	3	Fishing smack in a gale.
	81	Man-of-war tender off Yarmouth.
	237	Abbey gate of St. Martin at Aumale.
	354	City scene—composition.
1831	47	Crosby Hall.
	102	Hotel de Ville, Ulm.
	105	Abbatial house of the Abbey of St. Ouen, Rouen.
	380	Fishing boats off Yarmouth.
1832	58	Sir Simon Spruggins, Knt., the tall fellow of the family of that ilk (*vide* Lady Morley's *Spruggins Family*).
	106	Dutch galliot in a breeze.
	150	Entrance to Gunton Park, Norfolk.
1833	21	Barge on the Medway.
	36	Landscape—composition.
	45	Landscape—composition, with the story of Bathsheba.
	83	The interior of Spruggins Hall, Manor of Dulfuddle, Bedfordshire, leading to the picture gallery; Arms of Spruggins, Gull, Whittingham, Bagnigge, Kiltwaddle and Sucklethumbkins, over the doorway (*vide Spruggins Gallery*).
	96	Sea view.
	222	King John and Prince Henry at Swineshead Abbey, attended by the Earls of Salisbury, Oxford, Pembroke, Essex and Warrenne; after their defeat and loss at crossing the Lynn Wash.
	249	A painter's study.
	304	Italian peasant at a fountain in the valley of Coriati.
1834	237	No title.
	144	A landscape.
1836	49	The drawing lesson.
	127	Sea view.
	161	Figures on the sands at Blakeney.
	187	Italian boys with a lady of Loretto.
	194	Velaquez designing his celebrated picture of the Crucifixion.
	247	A dutch canal.
	255	A sketch.
1838	223	Russian merchant ship on a lee shore.
1839	152	A lady of Alencon.
	162	Corridor in the castle at Falaise.
	250	Interior of the Abbey, Jumieges.
	310	Vessels off Yarmouth

THE NORFOLK AND SUFFOLK INSTITUTION, NORWICH

No.		Subject
1828	43	Landscape.
	62	Landscape.
	68	Landscape.
	72	Landscape.
	151	Composition.
	154	West front of the Abbey Church of St. Stephen at Caen.
	155	The investigation.
	163	The High Street at Alencon, in France.
	164	Street scene at Andely's, France.
	166	An old house in Rouen.
	167	Chateau Navarre, the late property of Beauharnais.
	172	Street at Evreux.
	177	A galliot in a gale, off Yarmouth.

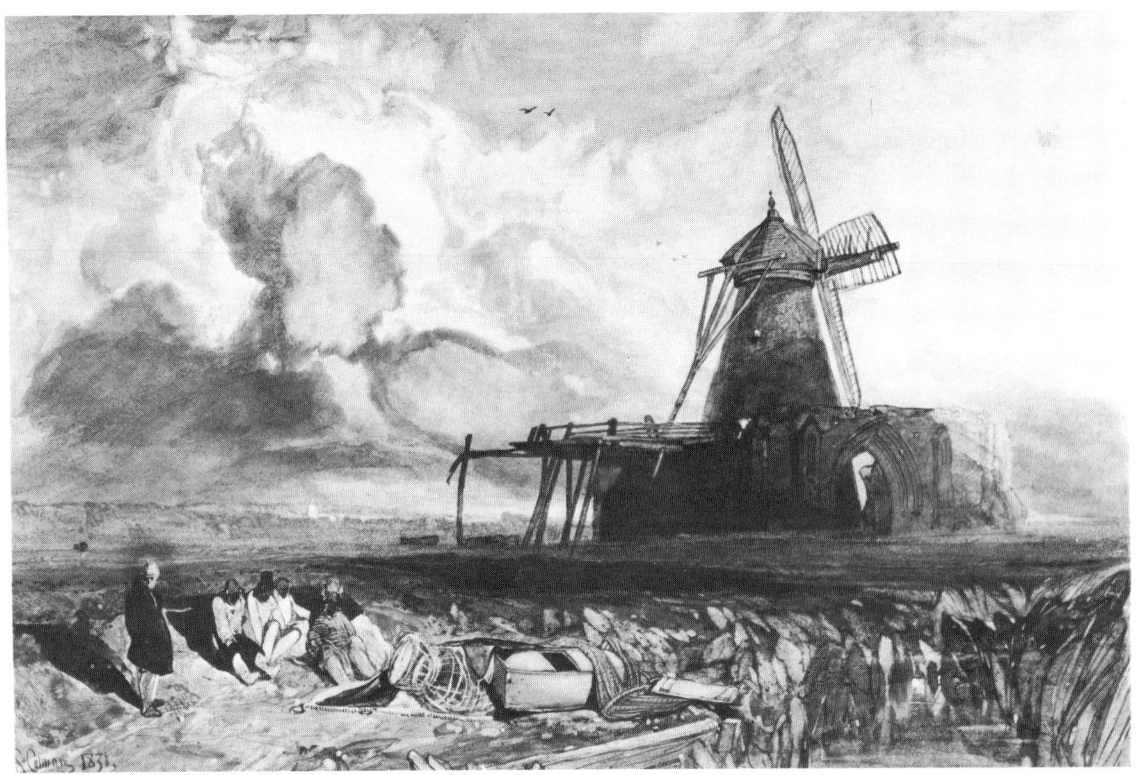

John Sell Cotman *St. Benet's Abbey, 1831* *Water-colour* $12\frac{3}{8} \times 18\frac{1}{2}$ *in.*

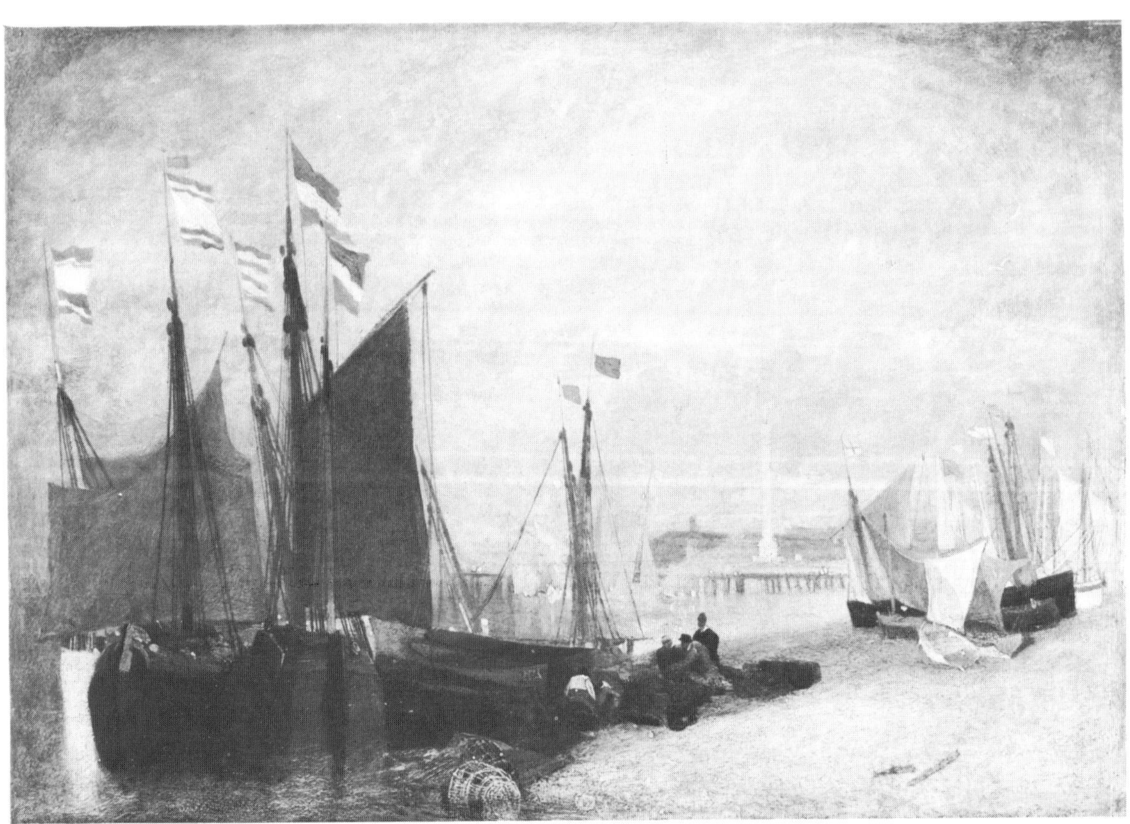

John Sell Cotman *Dutch Boats off Yarmouth* *Oil on panel* $17 \times 24\frac{1}{2}$ *in.*

EXHIBITION OF THE WORKS OF ANCIENT AND MODERN MASTERS
in the Gallery of the Norfolk and Suffolk Institution

Year	*No.*	*Subject*
1828	109	A mill.

TWENTY-THIRD NORFOLK AND SUFFOLK INSTITUTION EXHIBITION

Year	*No.*	*Subject*
1829	125	View near Barmouth, North Wales.
	132	Abbatial house of the Royal Abbey of St. Ouen, Rouen.
	133	A city.
	134	A bishop, etc.
	135	Hotel de Ville, Brussels.
	142	A cardinal, etc.
	147	City, harbour, and the Colossus of Rhodes—composition.
	148	Schaffhausen, Switzerland.
	150	Departure of Ulysses from the Island of Calypso.
	159	Mount St. Michael, Normandy, with the appearance of the mirage.
	198	A Spanish General describing a plan to his Aide de Camp.
	199	Sea beach.

SECOND EXHIBITION OF THE WORKS OF ANCIENT MASTERS

Year	*No.*	*Subject*
1829	84	Le Presentiment, or the departure of Pierre, first Duc de Bourbon, Earl of Clermont, and March, etc., for the Battle of Poietiers, in which he was killed.
	87	" Dost thou call me fool, boy ? "—Shakespeare.
	88	William the Conqueror presenting the Deeds of the Castle and Town of Tamworth to Robert de Marmion—sketch.
	89	Green mantle.
1830	13	Dutch boats in a gale off Dunkirk.
	14	The Old Manor House, St. Mary Wiggenhall, Norfolk.
	20	Scene near Bristol.
	23	Landscape composition.
	28	Sketch of works at Lowestoft, as now proceeding.
	30	Sheriff Hutton Castle, Yorkshire—sunset.
	32	Sevre, Etruscan, and other vases.
	35	Mount St. Michael, France, under the effect of the mirage at sunset.
	40	Crosby Hall, London.
	41	Hotel de Ville at Ulm.
	44	A gentleman of the 15th century.
	47	A Scotch mist in the Highlands, from the drovers.
	49	Alder Carr Reach.
	59	Middleton Tower, near Lynn.

Mr. Cotman, Vice-President

1831	43	Sir Simon Spruggins, Knt., the tall fellow of the family of that ilk (*vide* Lady Morley's *Spruggins Family*).
	190	A Norman stable—a sketch.

J. S. Cotman, Vice-President

TWENTY-SIXTH NORFOLK AND SUFFOLK INSTITUTION EXHIBITION

1832	24	Introduction of Mary Queen of Scots to her prison chamber in Fortheringay Castle.
	39	A study of armour, etc.

J. S. Cotman, President

TWENTY-SEVENTH NORFOLK AND SUFFOLK INSTITUTION EXHIBITION

Year	*No.*	*Subject*
1833	29	On the ramparts at Cologne.
	35	King John and Prince Henry at Swinstead Abbey, attended by the Earls of Salisbury, Oxford, Warwick, Pembroke and Essex.
	36	Landscape composition.
	41	A castle on the French coast.
	42	The Duke of York and the Earl of Sandwich hoisting signals and standing off Solebay, prior to the action with Admiral de Ruyter in 1672.
	44	Mont Blanc.
	45	Interior of Manor House.
	47	Landscape composition.
	61	Banditti attacked.
	69	A wood scene at Irstead.
	77	Italian peasant at a fountain, in the valley of Corriati.

THE BURY ST. EDMUND'S INSTITUTION

at the Gallery in the Great Market Place, Bury

J. S. Cotman, Norwich

Year	*No.*	*Subject*
1828	132	The investigation.
	136	A street scene at Andely's, in France.

EXHIBITS AT BRITISH INSTITUTION

Year	*No.*	*Subject*
1810	82	Dutch fishing boats. 27 × 35 in.
	289	Dutch fishing boats. 27 × 35 in.
	293	Dutch fishing boats laying in the river, Yarmouth. 17 × 24 in.
	306	Old Morton Hall, Cheshire. 35 × 40 in. J. S. Cotman, Yarmouth.
1823	8	Dutch prizes off Yarmouth. 20 × 24 in.
	253	Wood scene in the marshes near Yarmouth. 38 × 48 in.

FRAMED WORKS IN OIL

sold September 1834 at Norwich

Subject

View of Norwich Castle from Foundry Bridge (unfinished).
Landscape.
Ditto (the mishap)—companion to the above.
Landscape and Palace of the Prince Beauharnois.
Sea view, with fishing boat off Yarmouth.
Yarmouth Beach with figures.
Merton Hall, in Chester, with figures.
Horse in stable.
Old house at Yarmouth.
Landscape (salmon spearing).
Ditto (ditto).
Sea view (Dutch galliots).
Landscape (unfinished).
Sea view (Dutch boats).
Sea view (fishing boats).
Wherries on Breydon.
Wheelbarrow, basket, etc.—a sketch.

OIL SKETCHES (unfinished)

sold at Christies 18th May 1843

Subject	*No. of Sketches*
Sketches of landscapes.	4
A pair of upright woody scenes; and two others.	4
A bandit; and a castle. A cottage.	3
A sea piece; and a woody river scene.	2
Scarborough Castle.	1
A woody landscape, with a waterfall—very richly coloured.	1
A Savoyard boy with dancing dogs. Dutch vessels in a river—small, brilliantly coloured.	2
A willow tree near a stile.	1
The mouth of Gorleston Harbour, with vessels in Yarmouth Roads.	1
A woody scene, with sheep in a meadow, near a brook.	1
Carnival figures at Rome.	1
A white horse in a stable.	1
A lane scene at Gunton Park, with figures near a gate.	1
A priest in his robes before the altar in a church.	1
Dutch vessels on a river—calm; a capital picture.	1
A valley, with a waterfall and deer.	1
A romantic landscape, with a waggon escorted by horsemen (unfinished).	1
View in a Swiss town—a sketch.	1
A Dutch galliot and a hay barge—a pair.	2
A horse and figures (unfinished).	1
A Dutch and English river scene.	2
A rocky valley.	1
Carnival figures in Rome.	1
A landscape, with a fishing boat in a stream.	1
Eel baskets in a river—small.	1
A woody scene in Gunton Park.	1
Fishing boats in a breeze off Yarmouth.	1
Four windmills near a stream, with rushes—coloured with admirable effect.	1
A Dutch brig at anchor, off the coast.	1
Fishermen on the shore, near Yarmouth.	1

MILES EDMUND COTMAN

(1810-1858)

1810 Miles Edmund Cotman was born in Southtown, Yarmouth, on 5th February, 1810. He was named after his grandfather on his mother's side, a farmer from Felbrigg.

At the age of thirteen years he contributed his first exhibit to the Norwich Society. It is said that his early work was so like his father's that they could only be distinguished by the inscriptions. At a later date, when he assisted with the teaching practice, he relates that a certain Mrs. Chapman, the mistress of a school, assured him that she had a pupil who will not learn of a Cotman either father or son. Such an affront to a man as sensitive as Miles Edmund probably caused him to reflect on the sagacity of maintaining the Cotman style such as perpetrated by his father, John Sell Cotman. Indeed, such considerations probably resulted in Miles Edmund devising a method which extracted the fluency from his father and traditional standards from his own observations. So in 1836, when Miles Edmund was appointed to assist in the teaching of Art at King's College, alongside his father, it is quite possible that his talents were more acceptable than those of his father. Thus we find that some years later Miles Edmund assumed the entire responsibility for the teaching there.

That Miles Edmund and John Sell Cotman shared pictures there can be no doubt, for
1838 Cotman senior refers in his letters of 1838 to their joint efforts—neither specialising in any particular aspects.

Besides teaching, Miles Edmund Cotman painted industriously. He was fortunate in so much that he found several patrons, including an amateur artist, James Bulwer, a clergyman. Numerous water-colours by Miles Edmund found their way into the Bulwer Collection. Bulwer, besides befriending Miles Edmund on occasion, accompanied John Sell Cotman on his expeditions.

From our artist's list of exhibits we can see that he not only painted in water-colour but executed almost as many works in oil, many of the works being ambitious not only in subject but also in size.

It appears that Miles Edmund married and had three children. A pupil giving her recollections of him describes him as gentle and easy-going but suggests rather ominously that there may be more in his character than appears on the surface. Despite these speculations there is little doubt that Miles Edmund was a man of quiet temperament, integrity, and genius, though several writers have overlooked his splendid artistic qualities, so intoxicated were they by his father's work.

1846 In 1846 Miles Edmund etched eleven subjects which were published under the title "Eleven Original Etchings" by Charles Muskett, Old Haymarket, Norwich. Also he lithographed twelve works executed by his father in chalk, these impressive drawings and others are now in the British Museum.

1852 In 1852 Cotman, after many years of teaching and painting in London, began to find life a strain: probably for this reason he wisely retraced his steps to Norwich. One may add that after the death of John Sell in 1842 Miles Edmund had supported his mother and family; during this time they resided at 42 Hunter Street, Brunswick Square.

On returning to Norwich Miles Edmund lived with his brother, J. J. Cotman, at
1855 Thorpe until 1855, when they moved to The Smee, Great Plumstead, a suburb of Norwich.

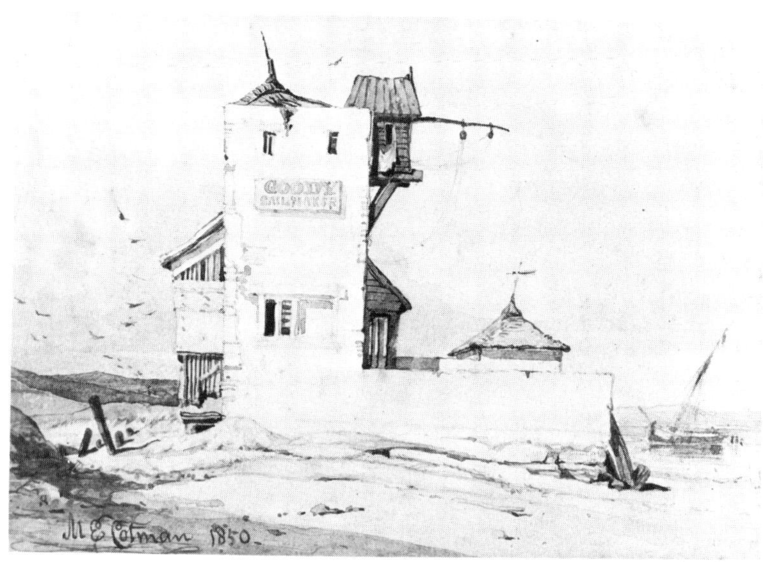

Miles Edmund Cotman, 1850 *Sepia Drawing*

We do not know how M.E. reacted to the unpredictable J.J., but he probably immersed himself in his work and sought the quietude of the countryside. It was during a sketching tour that he fell and fractured an ankle, which resulted in him being taken to the Norfolk and Norwich Hospital and being treated by his surgeon, Mr. Cadge. It must have come as a great surprise to the citizens of Norwich when it was announced that he had passed away on 23rd January, 1858.

Miles Edmund Cotman was a kindly man and much respected by all his students. Though he suffered with depression most of his life, he battled incessantly against it, producing fine pictures and supporting his family. I am sure it would be most revealing if at some future time an exhibition of his works can be held.

THE PAINTINGS

The early works are very like John Sell and have in some cases probably been given to that master. However, M.E. did break away with his own style. There is about Miles Edmund Cotman's water-colours more detailed observation than his father's. One sees the added detail and extra toning touches which make for greater realism. His palette is balanced, in that he contrasts very often his cool greens with certain burnt sienna or venetian reds. Often his drawings are clearly signed "M. E. Cotman", followed by the date, although in the 1927 Exhibition about half the water-colour exhibits were unsigned. None of the six oils was signed

His work in oil is quite different from that of his father, being more clearly drawn and containing an abundance of detail, combined with a good delineation of subject. Miles Edmund often achieves a splendid breadth especially

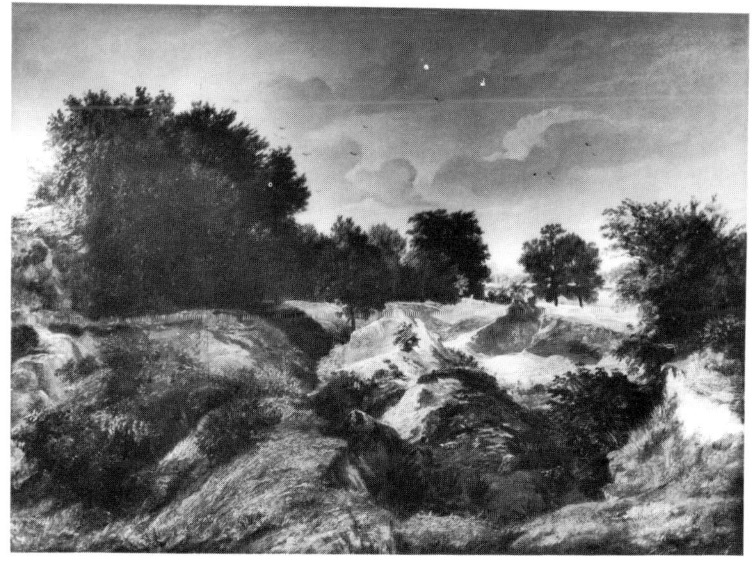

Sand Hills near Norwich
Miles Edmund Cotman *Oil on canvas* 18 × 24½ *in.*

in his skies. Perhaps in certain of his pictures the paint probably appears a little devoid of medium but in others it is just as beautiful, having a very luminous quality. The *Boats on the Medway* in the Norwich Castle Museum is a splendid example of his use of siennas and umbers. His study of ships details, rigging and sails, and their relationship to weather conditions seems to leave little to be desired.

In his skies his brushwork is often very free. One notices his bluey greys sensitively brushed over a soft beige ground. His high lights being placed in with a firm brush with paint containing Naples yellow and warm white. Whilst his cattle sometimes appear rather masculine and a trifle gaunt, his figures are sometimes rather small.

Finally, in his skies he loves to place his high lights behind his darker clouds and often designs his clouds at an angle to the subject.

EXHIBITS AT BRITISH INSTITUTION

Year	*No.*	*Subject*	£ s. d.
		42 Hunter Street, Brunswick Square	
1840	146	Indiaman ashore. 40×51 in.	
		3 Henrietta Street, Brunswick Square	
1845	107	Sea view. 21×26 in.	
	237	Boats on the Medway—a calm. 31×29 in.	
	456	Scene at Whitlingham, Norfolk. 22×26 in.	
		9 Hollis Place, Haverstock Hill	
1852	362	Vessels leaving port. 21×27 in.	
1854	191	Boats on the Medway—calm.	15 15 0
	536	Yarmouth fishing boats.	12 12 0
		The Smee, Great Plumstead, Norfolk	
1856	81	On the banks of the river at Whitlingham.	10 10 0
		Sea view (companion picture to "On the banks of the river at Whitlingham").	

EXHIBITS AT THE ROYAL ACADEMY

Year	*No.*	*Subject*
1840	452	Sea view.
1841	440	Boats becalmed.
	583	A lee shore.
		9 Holles Place, Haverstock Hill
1851	771	Near the coast—a recollection.

EXHIBITS AT THE WATER-COLOUR SOCIETY OF BRITISH ARTISTS

Year	*Subject*
1835	Hay barges on the Thames.
	Taking out stores for a fishing boat off Great Yarmouth.
	A boat waiting for passengers off Cromer.

Year	*Subject*
1836	Sea view (oil painting).
	Yarmouth fishing boat (lugger) off Lowestoft.
1838	A Dutch galliott passing through a fleet of shrimpers off Great Yarmouth (oil painting).
	Beach scene, Great Yarmouth.
1839	The mouth of the Yare (water-colour).
1840	Sea view (oil painting).
	Vessels on the bar at the mouth of the Yare (oil painting).
	Dutch fishing boats off Yarmouth (water-colour).
	Eel catcher on Breydon Water (water-colour).
1841	Scene at Gunton, Norfolk (oil painting).
	A lugger in a gale (oil painting).
	Scene at Bramerton, Norfolk (oil painting).
	Boats in a calm (oil painting).
	Yarmouth Beach after a gale (water-colour).
	The *News of Peace* arriving in Yarmouth during a gale, December 27th, 1814 (water-colour).
1842	Sea view—a fresh breeze.

EXHIBITION OF NORWICH SCHOOL PICTURES

Norwich Castle Museum and Art Galleries, October 1927

OIL PAINTINGS

No.	*Subject*
19	Yarmouth Beach and Jetty. 14 × 44 in.
20	Landscape. 29 × 46¾ in.
21	Shipping scene. 4¾ × 8 in.
22	Woodland and water. 7 × 11¼ in.
23	Wreck on Yarmouth Beach. 22½ × 35 in.
24	Seascape. 13½ × 20¼ in.

WATER-COLOURS, DRAWINGS, ETC.

147	Thorpe Valley on the River Yare (signed) (sepia). 5¼ × 9¾ in.
148	Landscape—classical composition. 11 × 16½ in.
149	The *Dreadnought* and *Grampus* as hospital ships in the Thames (signed and dated 1830). 17 × 22½ in.
150	Seascape—evening (signed and dated 1833). 14 × 18 in.
151	Seascape (signed and dated 1831). 11¾ × 14½ in.
152	Portrait of Alfred Priest (charcoal). 12½ × 9½ in.
153	Waterfall (signed and dated 1836) (monochrome). 9 × 13 in.
154	Mountain scene (monochrome). 9¼ × 13 in.
155	Castle and tree (monochrome). 9 × 13 in.
156	Fishing boats. 6½ × 9¾ in.

NINETEENTH EXHIBITION OF THE NORWICH SOCIETY OF ARTISTS, 1823

No.	*Subject*
165	Pencil drawing.
167	Summer-house on River Waveney (pencil drawing).

TWENTIETH EXHIBITION OF THE NORWICH SOCIETY OF ARTISTS, 1824

No.	*Subject*
192	View on the River Sarthe at Alencon.

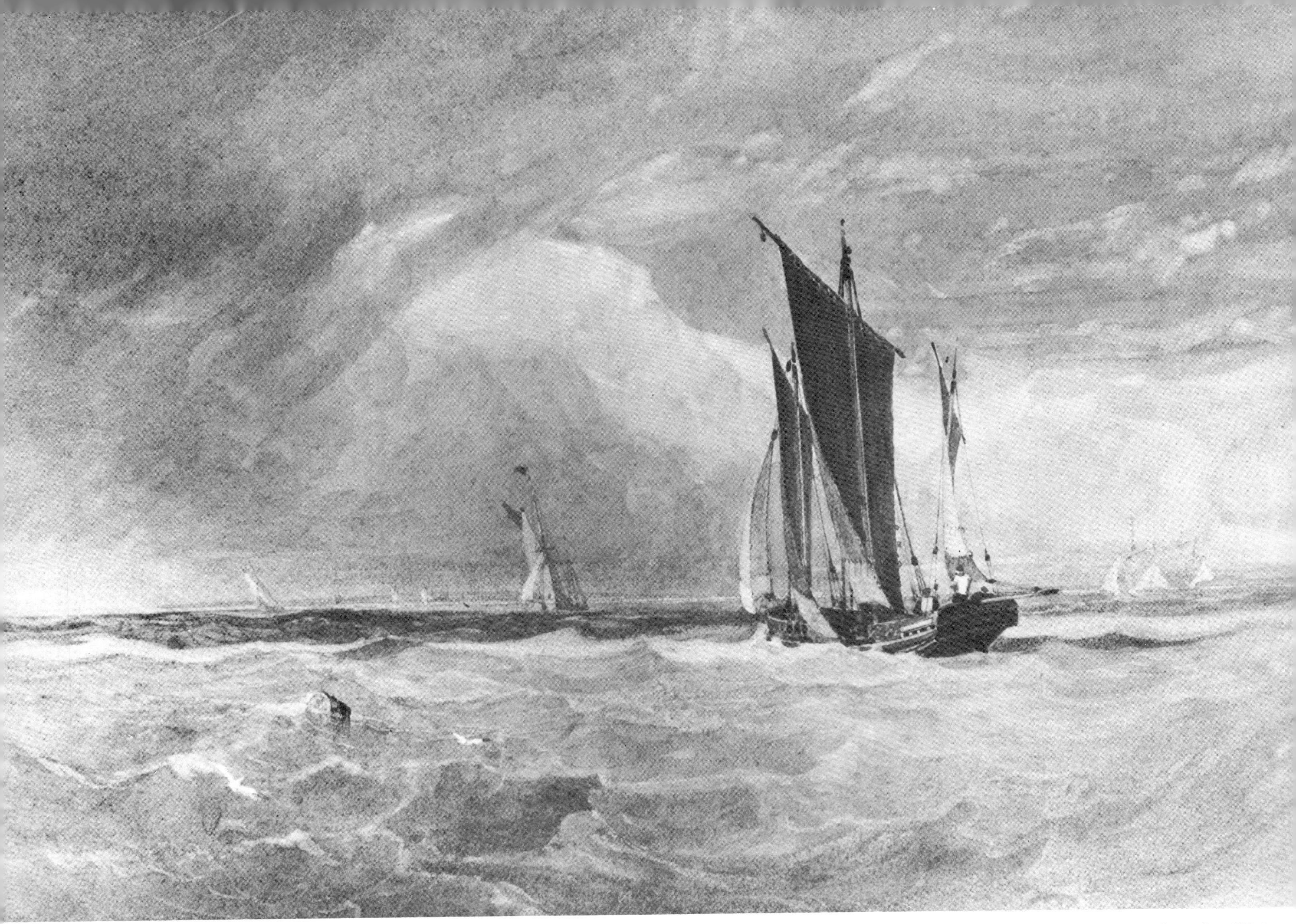

Miles Edmund Cotman *Marine View* *Water-colour* $8\frac{7}{8} \times 12\frac{1}{2}$ *in.*

TWENTY-FIRST EXHIBITION OF THE NORWICH SOCIETY OF ARTISTS, 1825

No.	*Subject*
119	An arquebusier of the reign of Elizabeth.
128	A bandoleer of the reign of Elizabeth.
131	Boats.
136	A bandoleer of the reign of Elizabeth.
142	A bandoleer of the reign of Elizabeth.

TWENTY-SECOND EXHIBITION OF THE NORFOLK AND SUFFOLK INSTITUTION FOR THE PROMOTION OF THE FINE ARTS, 1828

No.	*Subject*
143	A Yarmouth coble.
147	Fishing boats in calm.
150	Anchors, etc.
156	Humber keel in the Thames.
157	Wood barges.
159	Barges at Yarmouth.
165	A Thames sailing barge.

TWENTY-THIRD EXHIBITION OF THE NORFOLK AND SUFFOLK INSTITUTION FOR THE PROMOTION OF THE FINE ARTS, 1829

No.	*Subject*
126	Fishing boats, Carrow.
128	Dutch fishing boats on the beach at Yarmouth.
131	Bacharact on the Rhine.
138	Scene in Gunton Park.
139	Norwich wherries.
140	View from the bridge over the Sambre at Namur.
141	Fishing boats in a gale.
144	A galliott.
146	Cromer fishing boats.
151	Thuilleries, from the Quay, Orsay.
152	Fountain of the Stone Cross at Rouen.
154	Dutch passage boats on the Meuse.
155	Scene at Hackney.
160	Dog, from plaster.
181	Bruges.
191	Fishing boat.
192	Two views of Cromer.
195	Scene in Petersham Wood.
197	Scene at Peckham.
201	Thorpe Reach.

TWENTY-FOURTH EXHIBITION OF THE NORFOLK AND SUFFOLK INSTITUTION FOR THE PROMOTION OF THE FINE ARTS, 1830

No.	*Subject*
21	Hotel de Ville and fountain at Weisbaden.
24	Humber keel.
26	The Grand Square of the Jesuits, the Panfilu Palace to the right, etc.
33	Fishing boat, off Yarmouth.

No.	Subject
37	Dutch galliott.
38	Street scene and fountain at Weisbaden.
42	Man-of-war tender, off Portsmouth.
54	Entrance to the Great Canal at Venice.
56	A river scene.

TWENTY-FIFTH EXHIBITION OF THE NORFOLK AND SUFFOLK INSTITUTION FOR THE PROMOTION OF THE FINE ARTS, 1831

No.	Subject
8	Fishing boat in a squall (in the collection of J. S. Cotman).

TWENTY-SIXTH EXHIBITION OF THE NORFOLK AND SUFFOLK INSTITUTION FOR THE PROMOTION OF THE FINE ARTS, 1832

No.	Subject
9	Boats in the Medway—sunset.
22	Study of tapestry.
23	Sea view.
32	Study of armour and tapestry.
38	Boats on the Medway.
46	Hay boats on the Thames.
50	A seventy-four in a gale.
52	Convoy dispersed.

TWENTY-SEVENTH EXHIBITION OF THE NORFOLK AND SUFFOLK INSTITUTION FOR THE PROMOTION OF THE FINE ARTS, 1833

No.	Subject
7	Sketch—Norwich Cathedral.
8	Sketch—Norwich Cathedral.
16	Scene on the Thames—morning.
17	Sketch—Norwich Cathedral.
27	Sketch—Norwich Cathedral.
62	The *Dreadnought* and *Grampus* hospital ships on the Thames.
78	Sketch—Attleburgh Church.

FIRST EXHIBITION OF THE NORFOLK AND NORWICH ART UNION, 1839

No.	Subject
34	Sea view.
106	Wreck.
135	Sketch on Breydon Water, near Yarmouth.
230	Sea view.
241	Deptford dockyard.
261	Interior of a shed.
333	Sea view—evening.
346	Sea view—mouth of the Thames.

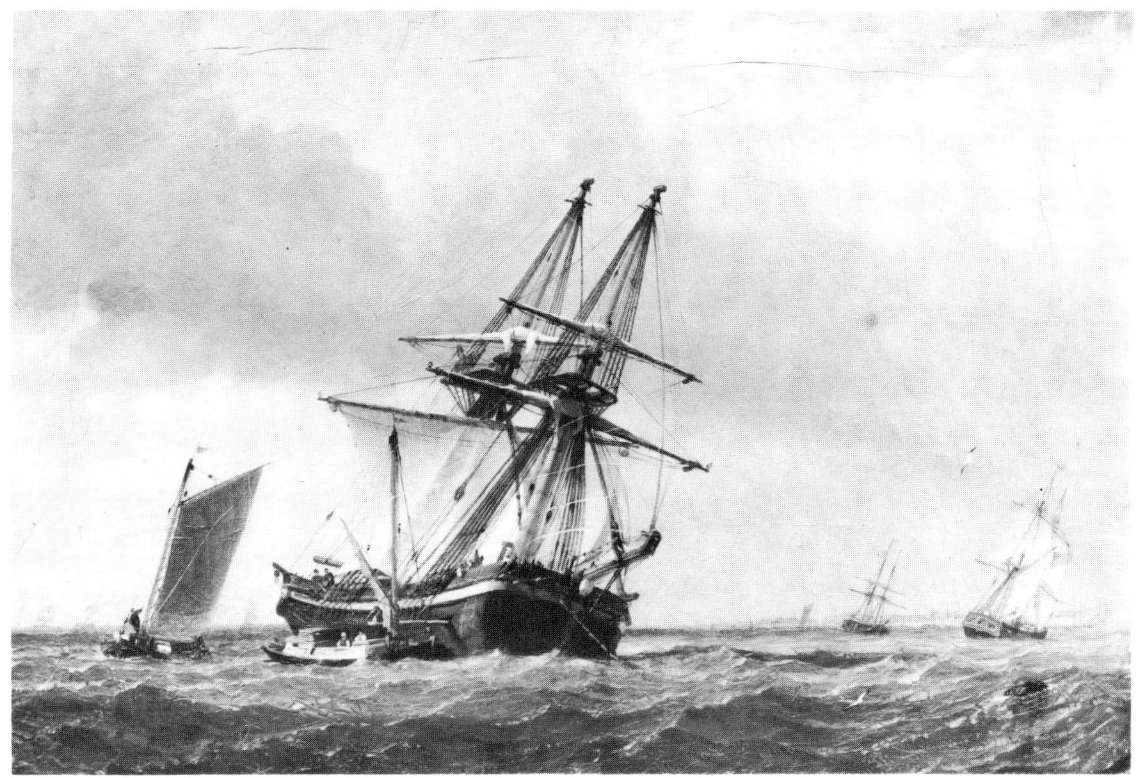

Miles Edmund Cotman *Sea Piece—Unloading Timber* *Oil* $12\frac{3}{4} \times 19$ *in.*

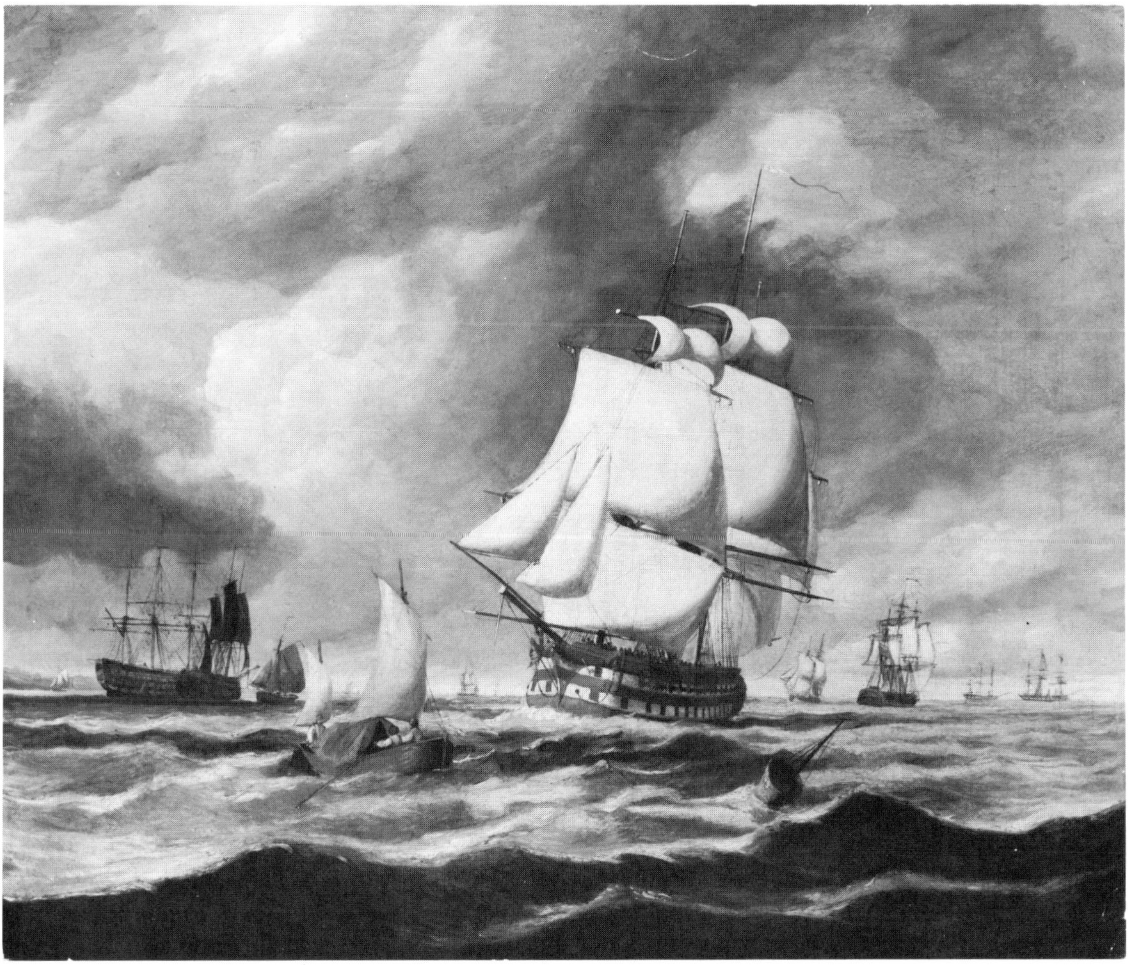

Miles Edmund Cotman *Oil on canvas* 25×30 *in.*

FIRST EXHIBITION OF THE EAST OF ENGLAND ART UNION, 1842

No.	*Subject*
22	South-east corner of the reindeer paddock, Gunton Park, Norfolk.
24	Scene at Whitlingham, Norfolk.
110	Off the Dutch coast.
123	Hanworth Common, Norfolk.

FOURTH EXHIBITION OF THE NORFOLK AND NORWICH ASSOCIATION FOR THE PROMOTION OF THE FINE ARTS, 1853

No.	*Subject*
21	Boats on the Medway—a calm.
29	Yarmouth fishing boats off the coast.

EXHIBITION OF THE NORFOLK AND NORWICH ASSOCIATION FOR THE PROMOTION OF THE FINE ARTS, 1855

No.	*Subject*	£	s.	d.
28	North Beach, Yarmouth.	26	5	0
47	On the Yare.	7	0	0
77	Sea view.	7	7	0
190	Sea view.	7	7	0
196	Boats on Medway—calm.	12	12	0
317	Outhouse at Hanworth.	8	8	0

EXHIBITION OF THE NORFOLK AND NORWICH FINE ARTS' ASSOCIATION AND OF THE PHOTOGRAPHIC SOCIETY, 1856

No.	*Subject*
263	Coast scene.
287	Dutch galliott running into port.

NORFOLK AND NORWICH FINE ARTS ASSOCIATION
Exhibition of the works of Deceased Local Artists, 1860

No.	*Subject*	*Lent by*
82	Rustic bridge.	Mr. Norgate.
304	Woody landscape.	Mr. C. Steward, Yarmouth.

NORWICH AND EASTERN COUNTIES WORKING CLASSES INDUSTRIAL EXHIBITION, 1867

No.	*Subject*	*Lent by*
769	Dover Pier.	Ben. Wilkinson, Newmarket Road.
819	Back of the Mills.	Mr. Boswell, Exchange Street, Norwich.
820	Sea view.	Mr. Boswell, Exchange Street, Norwich.
881	Drawing.	Mr. James King.

BRITISH MEDICAL ASSOCIATION LOAN COLLECTION
of the Works of Norfolk and Suffolk Artists, 1874

No.	*Subject*	*Lent by*
28	Lane to Whitlingham.	Mr. W. Boswell.
60	Off the Dutch coast.	Mr. G. H. Christie.
76	Yarmouth Beach and Jetty.	Mr. John King.
	WATER-COLOURS	
87	Near the coast.	Mrs. Kye.
93	Marine subject, after Stanfield.	Mrs. Kye.
107	River bank with trees.	Mr. T. J. Mott.
115	On the Waveney.	Mr. John King
162	Greenwich Reach, looking towards Blackwall.	Mr. James Reeve.

NORWICH ART LOAN EXHIBITION
in aid of the Fund for the restoration of the Church of St. Peter Mancroft, 1878

No.	*Subject*	*Lent by*
111	Dutch boats.	R. W. Burleigh, Esq.
160	Yarmouth Jetty and Beach.	Mr. John King.
445	Sea piece.	Thomas Edwards, Esq.
457	Sea view.	Thomas Edwards, Esq.
476	A sea piece.	G. H. Christie, Esq.
494	Sea piece.	Dowager Lady Buxton.

FINE ART EXHIBITION
in aid of the new Norfolk and Norwich Hospital, 1883

No.	*Subject*	*Lent by*
6	On the Medway.	Mr. J. J. Colman, M.P.
45	Gorleston.	Mr. J. J. Colman, M.P.
47	Beach scene.	Mr. J. J. Colman, M.P.

NORWICH ART LOAN EXHIBITION
in aid of the Fund for the restoration of St. Peter Mancroft Church, 1885

No.	*Subject*	*Lent by*
32	On the Medway.	J. J. Colman, Esq.

LOAN COLLECTION OF PICTURES AND WATER-COLOUR DRAWINGS
exhibited at the Agricultural Hall Gallery during the Grand Oriental Bazaar, 1894

No.	*Subject*	*Lent by*
33	Unloading timber at Yarmouth.	I. B. Coaks, Esq.

CATALOGUE OF THE LOAN COLLECTION OF DRAWINGS
in the New Picture Gallery in the Norwich Castle Museum, 1903

No.	*Subject*	*Lent by*
44	Barges. Hay barge in centre, small boat and two figures on right. $6\frac{1}{2} \times 9\frac{1}{4}$ in.	Mr. Russell J. Colman.
46	River scene. Bramerton Hills on right, river in foreground, wherry on left. $7\frac{1}{2} \times 11\frac{1}{2}$ in.	Mr. Russell J. Colman.
48	Marine view. Sailing vessels on right and in distance, buoy and sea birds on left. 9×13 in.	Mr. Russell J. Colman.

SOCIETY OF BRITISH ARTISTS

Year	*No.*	*Subject*
1835	636	Hay barge—Thames (water-colour).
	673	Taking out stores for a fishing boat off Great Yarmouth (water-colour).
	694	A boat waiting for passengers off Cromer.
1836	228	Sea view (oil painting).
	467	Yarmouth fishing boat (lugger) off Yarmouth (oil painting).
1838	239	A Dutch galliott passing through the fleet of shrimpers off Great Yarmouth (oil painting).
	329	Beach scene, Great Yarmouth (oil painting).
1839	523	The mouth of the Yare.
1840	156	Sea view (oil painting).
	352	Vessels on the bar at the mouth of the Yare (oil painting).
	546	Dutch fishing boats off Yarmouth (water-colour).
	644	Eel catcher on Breydon Water (water-colour).
1841	74	Scene at Gunton, Norfolk (oil painting).
	147	Lugger in a gale (oil painting).
	191	Scene at Bramerton, Norfolk (oil painting).
	479	Boats—calm (oil painting).
	627	Yarmouth Beach after a gale (water-colour).
	637	The *News of Peace* arriving at Great Yarmouth during a gale, December 27, 1814 (water-colour).
1842	89	Sea view—fresh breeze (oil painting).

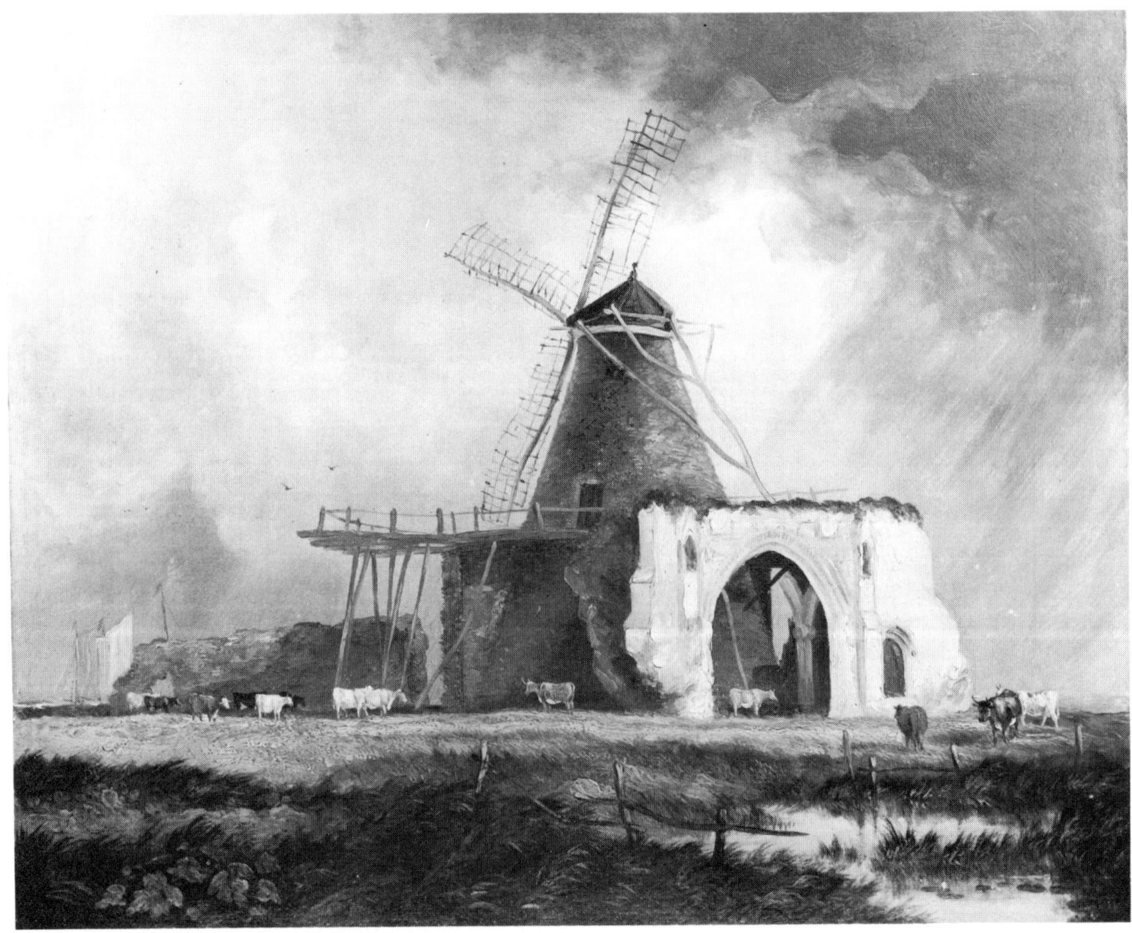

Miles Edmund Cotman *St. Benet's Abbey, near Norwich* *Oil on canvas* 16×20 *in.*

JOHN JOSEPH COTMAN

(1814-1878)

1814 John Joseph Cotman, the second son of John Sell Cotman, was born on the 29th May, 1814.

1824 In 1824 the family moved to St. Martin's at Palace Plain, Norwich. John Joseph was sent to school where he found the lessons short. Of his lessons he later recorded, "I determined to evade them, and did so, I fear, at my cost".

In his early teens he was placed with his uncle, Edmund Cotman, a haberdasher, but abandoned the business to take up sketching. Presumably his father, being an artist himself, could offer small resistance. About this time he became friendly with a well-to-do youth named Joseph Geldart who had given up a solicitor's office to travel in search of the colouring used by the old Venetian painters.

1835 Besides painting, our artist also taught, and we learn that in 1835 he took over Miles Edmund's teaching duties in Norwich, whilst his brother released his father from some of his duties at King's College, London.

An entry in his diary for 1838 tells us his sad position:

> Thursday Dec. 20th 1838. Rose late. Nothing done before breakfast not even shaved. Sad shame. Must mend. Delightful ride to Thorpe—gave a lesson to Mrs Clive—very nice agreeable woman, Lady of the Poor Law Commissioner. Afterwards rode till two—Dined too late to answer father's letter . . . containing kind handsome unexpected Christmas box. Write tomorrow morning before breakfast to send with Turkey on Saturday. . . . Good account from Joseph Geldart at Florence. I am almost afraid to say that I count on his return. I have since his time gone back far! far!

This entry rather suggests that Geldart had befriended him and tried to help over the difficulties.

From an early age he had been rather excitable and subject to moods, which resulted in a decline in the number of pupils. However, after he moved to Thorpe his fortunes changed and his teaching practice grew. It was probably on the strength of his newly found income he decided to marry a certain Miss Helen Cooper*, daughter of a silversmith. There were six children by the marriage, one of whom later became Dr. Cotman†, who formed a collection of pictures.

1858 In 1858 he was living at Plumstead. Evidently living with him was Miles Edmund Cotman.

1861
1862 We do know that many Cotman drawings found their way to the pawnbroker and sales from such drawings were held 16th May 1861 and 26th November and 27th November 1862. This same year our artist's sister Ann (herself an artist) died leaving John Joseph the sum of £400. He was then living in Albert Terrace, Unthank Road, Norwich, but later took lodgings at New Catton. Still his health was troublesome, but his drawings sold quite readily. Despite this brief success it was said that he stayed indoors for long periods. Finally he developed cancer of the tongue and attended Norwich Hospital where he was operated upon by Sir James Paget.

---

*Evidently the marriage took place after 4th September, 1841, for in the British Museum is a letter bearing that date, from J. S. Cotman to J. J. Cotman, reprimanding John Joseph for becoming engaged to Miss Cooper.

†Dr. Cotman was born in 1848. He was the second son.

1878 Prior to entering hospital he sent this note to James Reeve, the Curator of the Museum:

Feb. 21 1878
Thursday Morning

To James Reeve.

Dear Sir,

If you have a few minutes to spare I should be pleased to see you as I am going to the hospital this evening—and know not when I may leave it, if ever alive.

Yours faithfully,
J. J. COTMAN.
[In pencil]

The operation was a success but shortly afterwards the patient became excitable and left his bed, resulting in a relapse. He passed away on 15th March, 1878.

His obituary stated that he was talented but eccentric. The latter characteristic is confirmed by the following story:

> It appeared that J.J. had been advanced money by a certain gentleman against a picture. One day he saw the gentleman concerned and bolted into an inner room and locked the door. After much calling for him a note appeared under the door with the criptic message, "I am out!"

THE PAINTINGS

It is undoubtedly as a water-colour painter that J. J. Cotman will go down to posterity. These are delightfully freely handled works, spontaneous, emotional and strikingly coloured. One looks for the blues often appearing in the shadows and foliage, in fact in any appropriate place the artist can place it. To contrast the blue, delicate yellows often appear, which combined with much red give the drawing a very rich appearance. The line drawing can also be quite remarkable. Just as his father, J. S. Cotman, loved to model a figure with the turn of his, brush, J. J. Cotman would sometimes place in his landscape an animal produced simply by a single stroke of his pencil.

His oils have not the spontaneity of his drawings, but they have a powerful richness. Again the reds and blues predominate. Presumably to satisfy his palette he indulged often in evening scenes, featuring a low sun. These oils are perhaps some of the most romantic works found in the Norwich School.

EXHIBITS AT THE BRITISH INSTITUTION

Year	*No.*	*Subject*
1852	54	Wood scene, Norfolk—a study from Nature. 22×30 in.
	323	View from the Whitlingham Mills, near Norwich. 32×48 in.
	446	View from Bramerton Common, Norfolk. 15×25 in.
1853	330	Sketch on the banks of the river at Whitlingham.
	349	View by the river, near Thorpe Church.
1855	236	A sketch from the river at Thorpe, Norwich.
	335	Landscape with timber wain.
1856	297	An English cottage home.

EXHIBITS AT THE ROYAL ACADEMY

Year	*No.*	*Subject*
1853	198	A landscape.

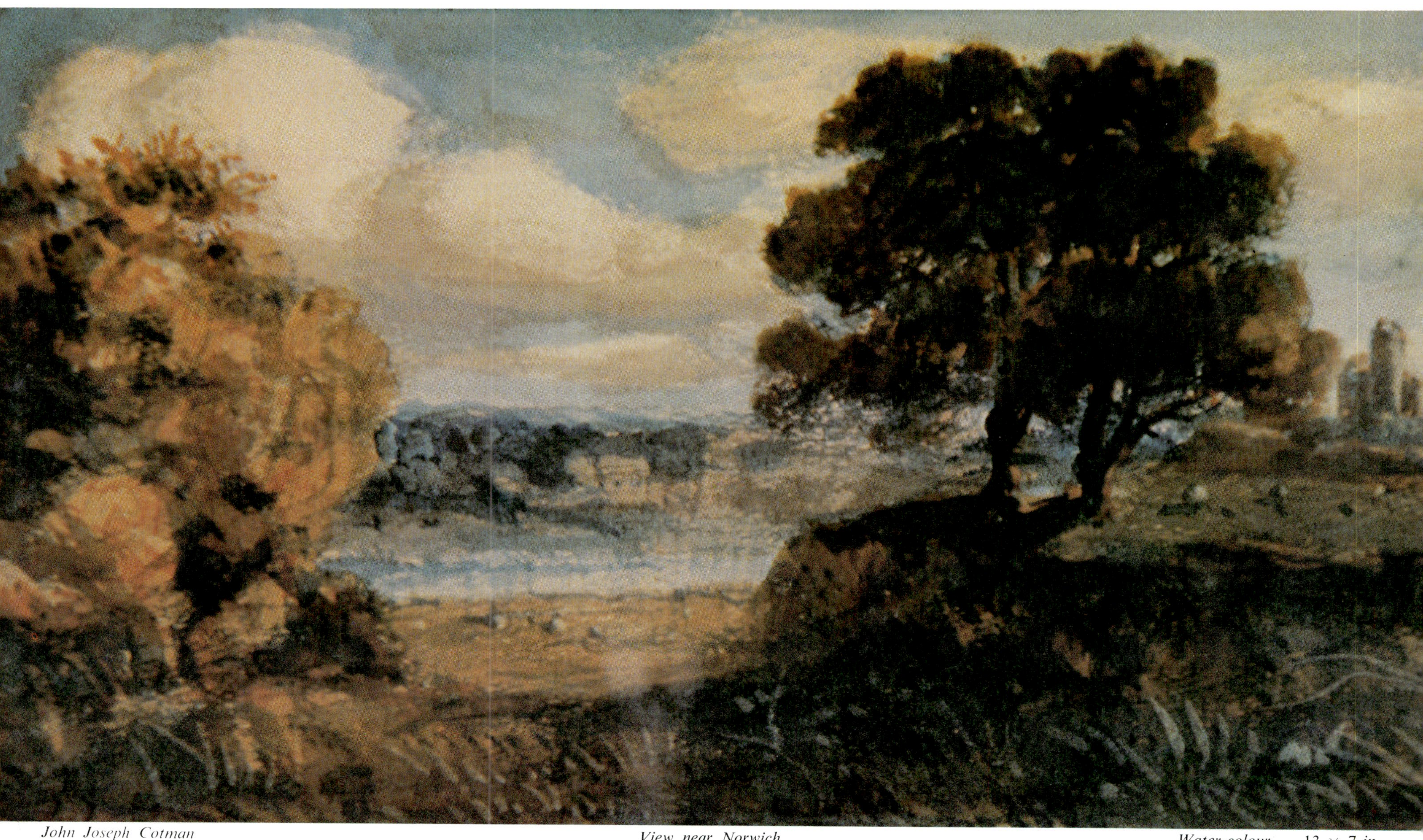

John Joseph Cotman — *View near Norwich* — *Water-colour* — 13 × 7 *in.*

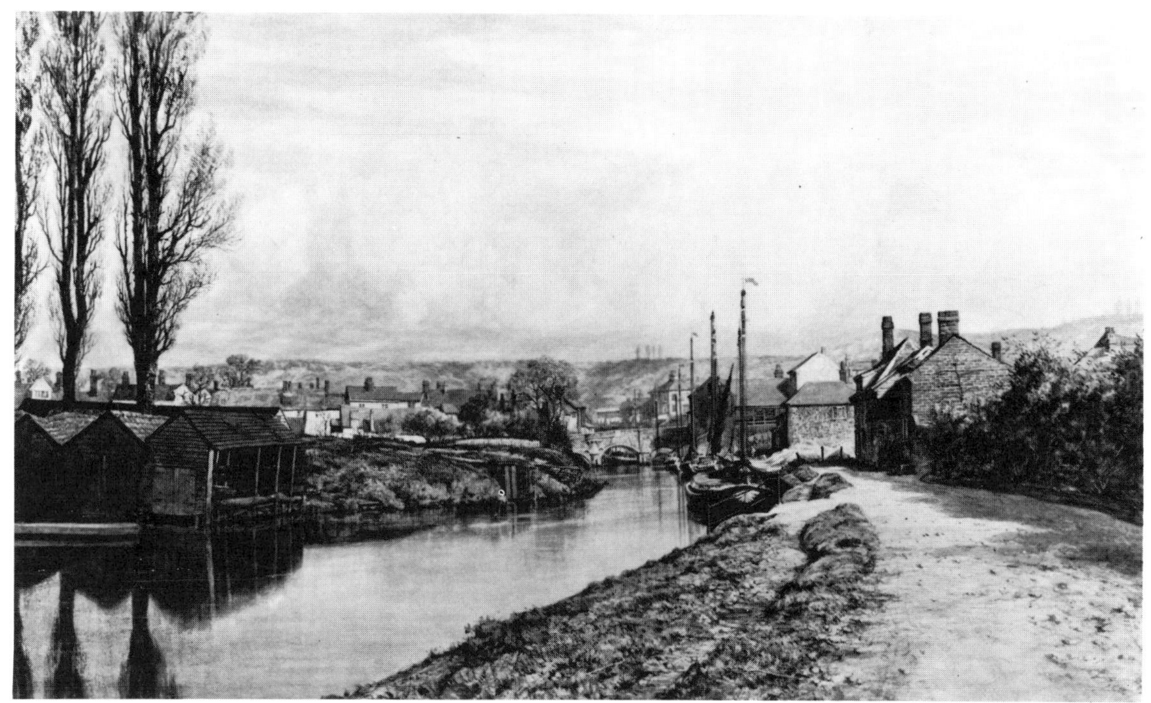

John Joseph Cotman *Bishop Bridge, Norwich, 1875* *Water-colour* $15\frac{1}{2} \times 27$ in.

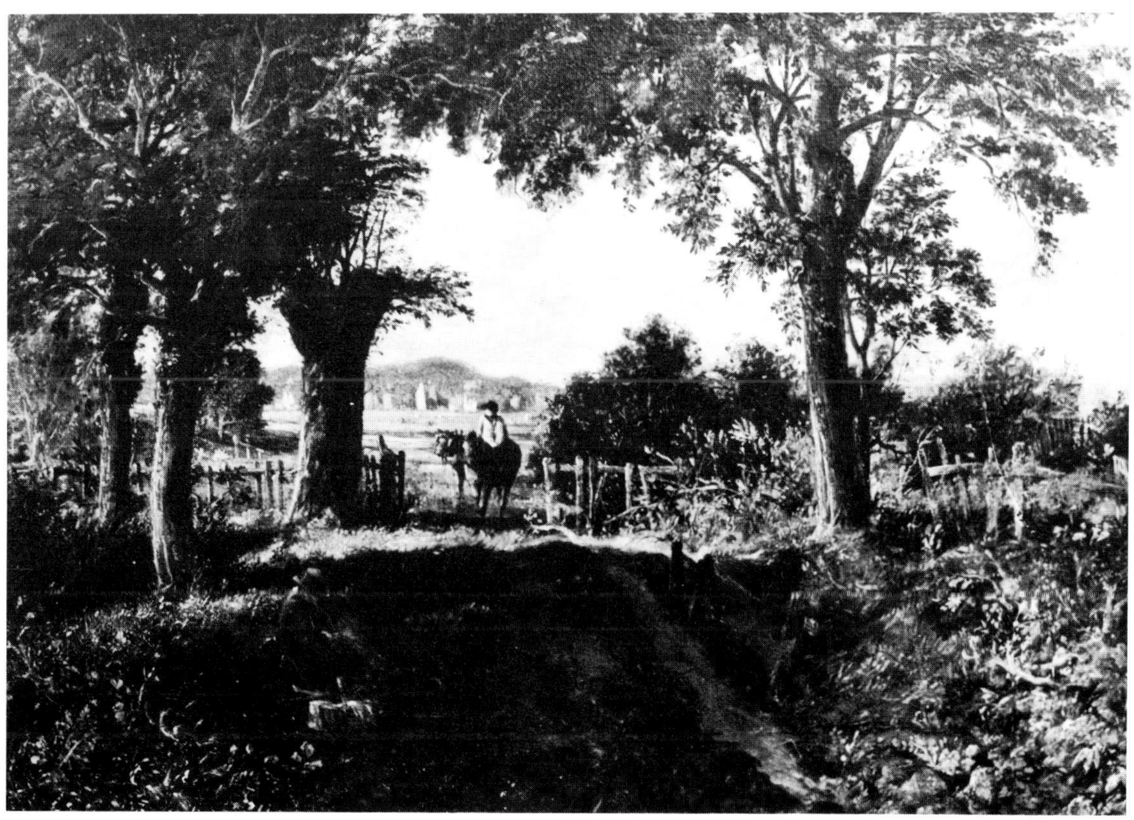

John Joseph Cotman *Lane near Carrow* *Oil* $15\frac{1}{4} \times 22\frac{1}{4}$ in.

TWENTY-FIFTH EXHIBITION OF THE NORFOLK AND SUFFOLK INSTITUTION FOR THE PROMOTION OF THE FINE ARTS, 1831

No.	*Subject*
46	Sketch.

TWENTY-SIXTH EXHIBITION OF THE NORFOLK AND SUFFOLK INSTITUTION FOR THE PROMOTION OF THE FINE ARTS, 1832

No.	*Subject*
34	View on the mouth of the Thames.

TWENTY-SEVENTH EXHIBITION OF THE NORFOLK AND SUFFOLK INSTITUTION FOR THE PROMOTION OF THE FINE ARTS, 1833

No.	*Subject*
20	Sketch—Whitlingham.
53	Two studies.

FIRST EXHIBITION OF THE NORFOLK AND NORWICH ART UNION, 1839

No.	*Subject*
69	Sketch of a shell.
210	Sketch of a bacchante.
279	Watercress Gatherer.
280	Pencil drawing—an old woman gathering sticks.
281	Pencil drawing.
284	Study, from the antique.
285	Monumental drawing.
299	Study from the antique.
317	Study from Nature, in chalk.
319	Study from the antique.
322	Study from Nature.

FIRST EXHIBITION OF THE EAST OF ENGLAND ART UNION, 1842

No.	*Subject*
198	Study of a young man's head.
199	Sketch of a child's head.
200	Study of a child's head.

SECOND EXHIBITION OF THE NORFOLK AND NORWICH ASSOCIATION FOR THE PROMOTION OF THE FINE ARTS, 1849

No.	*Subject*
47	A view at Thorpe, near Norwich.

THIRD EXHIBITION OF THE NORFOLK AND NORWICH ASSOCIATION FOR THE PROMOTION OF THE FINE ARTS, 1852

No.	*Subject*
92	View by the river, near Thorpe Church.
96	View from the Whitlingham Hills, Norfolk.
98	Sketch on the bank of the River Whitlingham.
126	Landscape with figures, Whitlingham.
132	Study from Nature.

FOURTH EXHIBITION OF THE NORFOLK AND NORWICH ASSOCIATION FOR THE PROMOTION OF THE FINE ARTS, 1853

No.	*Subject*
18	Vale of Todmorden, Lancashire.
130	Mill at Maple Durham, near Reading.

EXHIBITION OF THE NORFOLK AND NORWICH ASSOCIATION FOR THE PROMOTION OF THE FINE ARTS, 1855

No.	*Subject*	£	s.	d.
52	The angler's resort.	5	5	0
108	On the Colne, North Bridge, Colchester, Essex.	3	3	0
131	Road scene.			
207	An English cottage home.	21	0	0
213	View at Thorpe.			

EXHIBITION OF THE NORFOLK AND NORWICH FINE ARTS' ASSOCIATION; AND OF THE PHOTOGRAPHIC SOCIETY, 1856

No.	*Subject*	£	s.	d.
177	Sketch at Brundall, Norfolk.	10	10	0
230	Boats becalmed. (Contributed by Mr. Rossi.)			

NORWICH FINE ART ASSOCIATION—SECOND EXHIBITION OF WORKS OF ART BY MODERN ARTISTS, 1869

No.	*Subject*	£	s.	d.
237	Norwich Castle.	21	10	0
262	Norwich, from Whitlingham Lane.	26	5	0

EXHIBITION OF WORKS OF ART BY MODERN ARTISTS, 1870—EAST ANGLIAN ART UNION AND CITY OF NORWICH FINE ART ASSOCIATION

No.	*Subject*	£	s.	d.
193	Group of curiosities.	9	9	0
199	Landscape. (Lent by a member of the committee.)			
249	Chepstow.	5	5	0
258	Earlham, near Norwich.	5	5	0

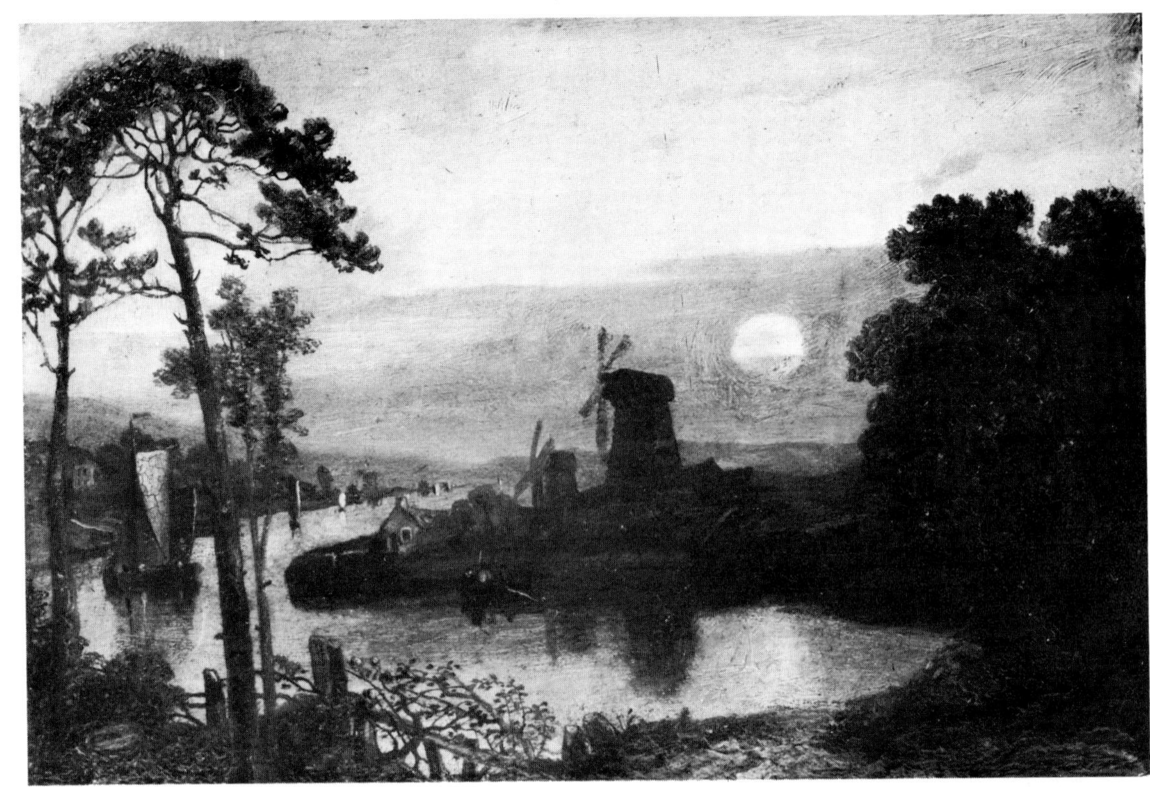

John Joseph Cotman

View near Norwich

Oil on board

8×12 in.

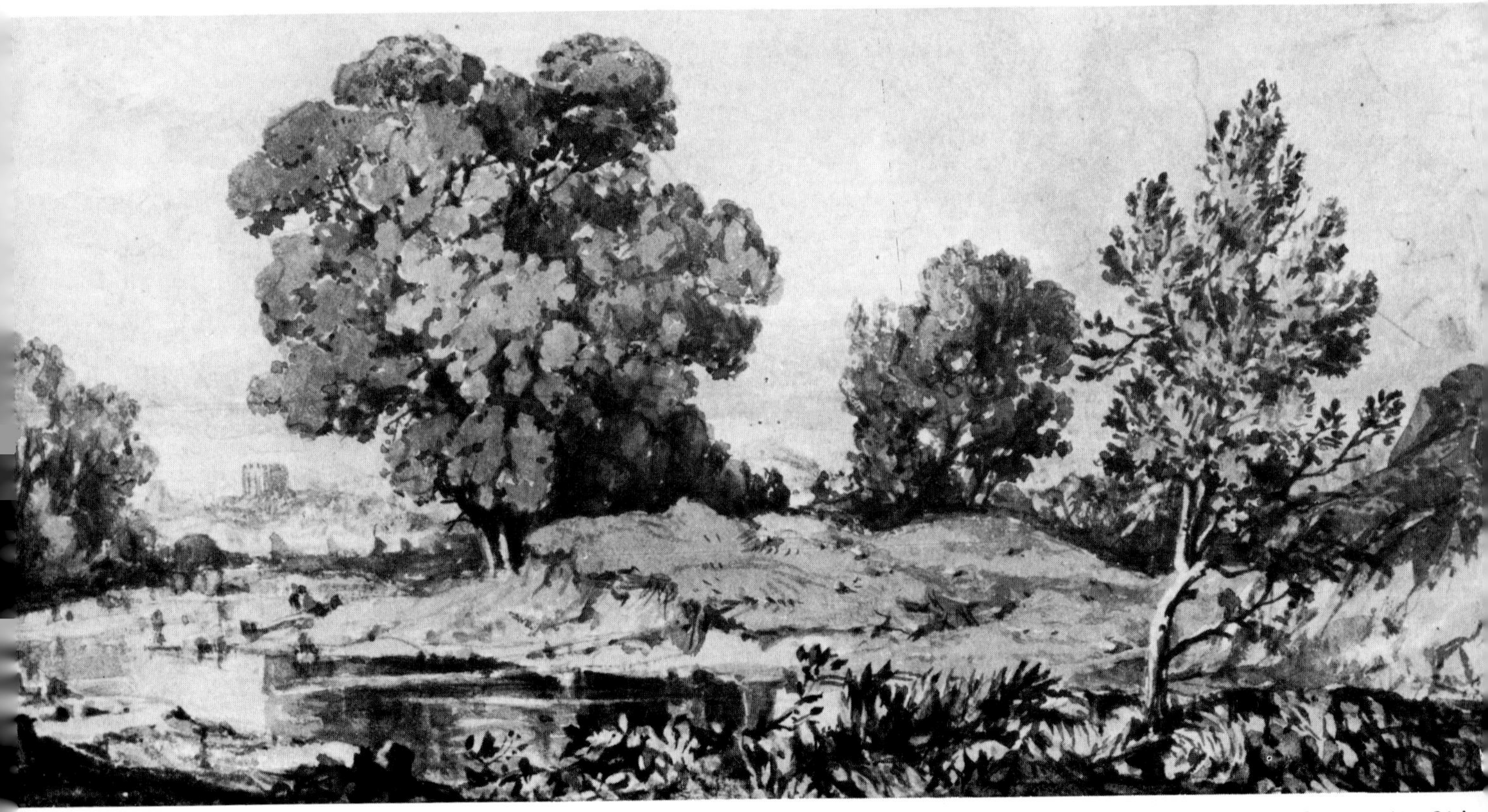

John Joseph Cotman, 1866 *View of Norwich* *Water-colour* $4\frac{3}{8} \times 8\frac{3}{8}$ in.

BRITISH MEDICAL ASSOCIATION LOAN COLLECTION
of the Works of Norfolk and Suffolk Artists, 1874

WATER-COLOURS

No.	*Subject*	*Lent by*
172	Whitlingham.	Mr. John King.
191	Bishop Bridge.	Mr. Henry Stevenson.
199	After sunset.	Mr. R. P. Burcham.

NORWICH ART LOAN EXHIBITION
In aid of the fund for the restoration of the Church of Saint Peter Mancroft, 1878

No.	*Subject*	*Lent by*
452	Gibraltar, Heigham.	Mr. E. M. Edwards.
481	Mousehold Heath.	Mr. James Reeve.
485	Carrow Gardens.	Mr. James Reeve.

FINE ART EXHIBITION
In aid of the new Norfolk and Norwich Hospital, 1883

No.	*Subject*	*Lent by*
33	"Righteousness and Peace have kissed one another" (copy of Rubens).	Mr. John Gunn.
107	Thorpe from Whitlingham.	Mr. H. G. Barwell.
21	Lane near Whitlingham.	Dr. Eade.
25	Cornfield.	Dr. Eade.
58	Whitlingham Lane.	Mr. H. G. Barwell.

NORWICH ART LOAN EXHIBITION
In aid of the fund for the restoration of St. Peter Mancroft Church, 1885

No.	*Subject*	*Lent by*
310	Vale of Thorpe.	E. M. Edwards, Esq.
312	Foundry Bridge—south.	J. Farrar Ranson, Esq.
315	Landscape.	W. T. Bensly, Esq., LL.D.
317	Near St. Martin's Gates, Norwich.	J. J. Colman, Esq., M.P.
325	Foundry Bridge—north.	J. Farrar Ranson, Esq.
337	Landscape.	F. T. Keith, Esq.
447	Caister Castle.	Rev. Dr. Raven.
448	Thorpe, Norwich. (For sale, £12 12s.)	Messrs. J. Hogarth & Sons.
455	Old Whitlingham Road. (For sale, £15 15s.)	Messrs. J. Hogarth & Sons.
460	Trowse. (For sale, £12 12s.)	Messrs. J. Hogarth & Sons.

ART LOAN EXHIBITION
In aid of the funds of St. George's Club for Working Girls, 1902

No.	*Subject*	*Lent by*
236	Old Carrow Gardens.	James Reeve, Esq.
240	Old Foundry Bridge.	Miss Wells.

CATALOGUE OF THE LOAN COLLECTION OF DRAWINGS

In the New Picture Gallery in the Norwich Castle Museum, 1903

No.	Subject	Lent by
50	Landscape composition. Building on right, two figures in mid-distance, trees beyond and on left. $7 \times 9\frac{3}{4}$ in.	Mr. James Reeve.
54	Landscape. Cottage and trees on right, bridge in foreground, cattle in roadway on left. 9×12 in.	Mr. James Reeve.

EXHIBITION OF NORWICH SCHOOL PICTURES

Norwich Castle Museum and Art Galleries, October, 1927

OIL PAINTINGS

No.	Subject
17	Landscape with figures, Whitlingham, Norwich. $18\frac{1}{4} \times 29$ in.
18	Station Road, Brundall. 17×24 in.

WATER-COLOURS, DRAWINGS, ETC.

No.	Subject
137	Landscape. $15 \times 21\frac{1}{2}$ in.
138	Thorpe Village (signed and dated 1874). $10\frac{3}{4} \times 17$ in.
139	Seascape (signed J. J. Cotman 1859). 13×26 in.
140	Scene on the Broads, 1874. $9\frac{1}{4} \times 14\frac{3}{4}$ in.
141	Landscape. $9\frac{1}{2} \times 13\frac{1}{4}$ in.
142	River scene. $8\frac{1}{2} \times 11\frac{1}{2}$ in.
143	Ten small water-colour drawings done by the artist for the late Benjamin Samuel.
144	Five small water-colour drawings done by the artist for the late Benjamin Samuel.
145	Study of trees—predominating colours red and orange. Done by the artist for the late Benjamin Samuel. $29 \times 21\frac{1}{2}$ in.
146	Bishop's Bridge, Norwich. $14\frac{3}{4} \times 26\frac{3}{4}$ in.

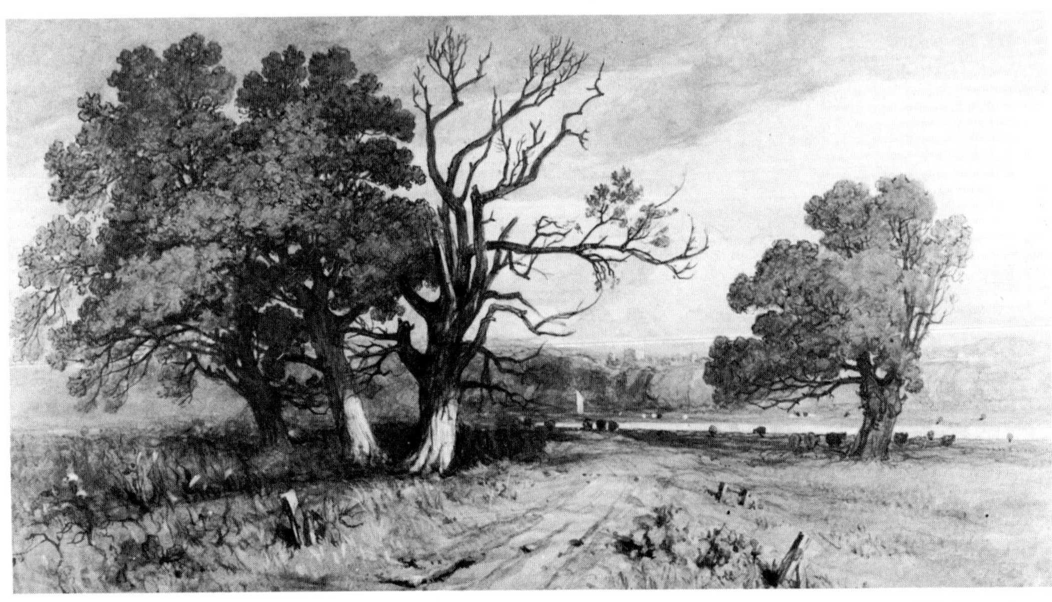

John Joseph Cotman *View near Norwich* *Water-colour*

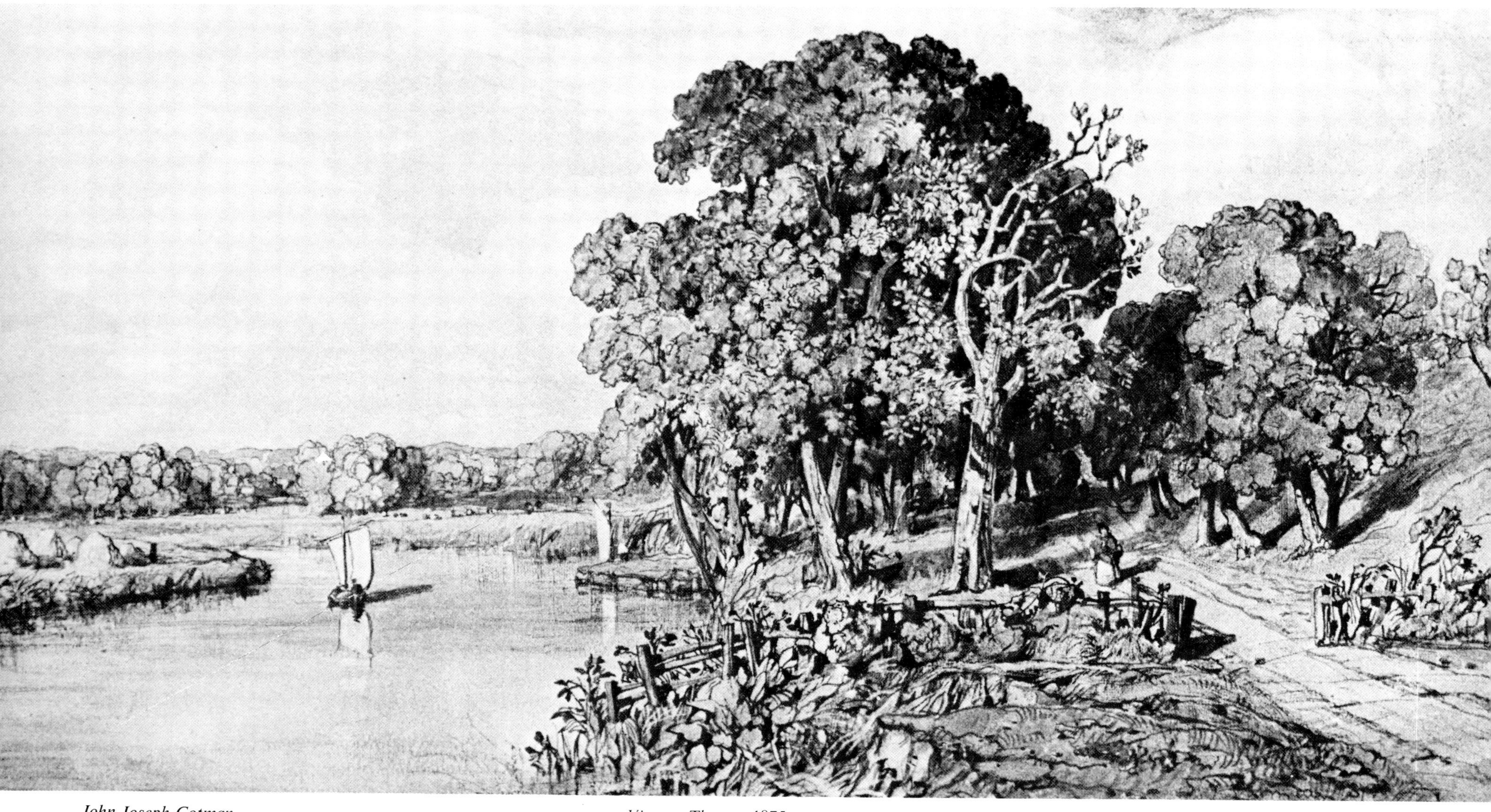

John Joseph Cotman — *View at Thorpe, 1875* — *Water-colour* — 12 × 23 *in.*

THOMAS LOUND

(1802-1861)

1802 Our artist was born in the year 1802 about the time Old Crome was cogitating on the formation of the Norwich Society. He was born into a family of brewers and all his life retained business interests.

Early in life he took lessons from John Sell Cotman, but later he became more more influenced by J. Crome, J. Stannard and Thirtle.

We know that he married, for there is a record of two of his daughters, Matilda Lound who married a Thirkettle, and Harriet Lound who married a Barham. Lound's sons-in-law, like himself, collected paintings. Lound purchased about seventy-five water-colours by Thirtle, in fact most of the Norwich School artists were represented in his folios. There is a record in the catalogue of his pictures sold after his death of works by Joseph Stannard and John Sell Cotman and John Crome. What a wonderful time collectors had in those days; from the Lound catalogue we read: Lot 75—Two hundred studies, principally in crayon, by Old Crome, Stannard, Lound and others, mounted and bound. This lot was purchased for four guineas! Lot 252—Pair Yarmouth River Scenes (on marble stands) by J. Stannard—were sold for the remarkable sum of 42s.!

Such was Lound's enthusiasm for art that he had few other than art books in his library when he died. Amongst his books were J. S. Cotman's *Architectural Antiquities of Normandy* and Constable's *English Landscape*.

Thomas Lound lived most of his life in King Street, Norwich, where he entertained his fellow artists and friends. A further interest was sailing, for he owned a yacht named *The Kathleen*. It is said that the cabin was adorned with seven river and sea views.

By the year 1850 he must have toured Yorkshire and possibly Wales, for in the Norwich Exhibitions of the 1850s we find views of Harlech Castle, Caerphilly, Byland Abbey, Yorkshire, Chepstow Castle, Bolton Abbey and Richmond, Yorkshire.

Between 1845 and 1857 he contributed no less than twenty-nine water-colours to the Royal Academy and British Institution.

1860 In 1860 he contributed six water-colours to the Norfolk and Norwich Fine Arts Associ-
1861 ation. This was to be his last exhibits for the following 18th January, 1861, he passed away, much missed by the people of Norwich.

It would seem that Lound had a very pleasant personality, which enabled him to mix freely with some of the finest water-colour painters of the age, including not only the Norwich School, but David Cox and Peter de Wint.

THE PAINTINGS

Lound was essentially a water-colour painter but from the list of work left in his studio at his death it is apparent that he did paint a number in oils.

His water-colours are painted with clean washes and with a spontaneous touch. His style is not particularly original, but he certainly transcribed Nature with loving and effective touches. As for his oils, they are often painted under the influence of John Sell Cotman—his oils show greater Cotman influence than his water-colours. His oils can sometimes be confused with those of Henry Bright, as they were contemporaries, and both probably subjected to the same influences. Many of his charcoal drawings are very like Joseph Stannard, but on closer examination prove not to be so incisive.

It would appear that he seldom signed his works. None of the exhibits in the 1927 Exhibition was signed.

SALE ON WEDNESDAY, 6TH MARCH, 1861
at the Exhibition Room in the Bazaar, St. Andrew's, Norwich

PAINTINGS BY THE LATE THOMAS LOUND

LOOSE SKETCHES

Lot	*Subject*
1	Thirty studies, sketches, etc.
2	Forty ditto.
3	Ditto.
4	Ditto.
5	Fifty ditto.
6	Seventy ditto.
7	Twelve sepia drawings.
17	Twelve sepia sketches.
18	Ditto.
19	Ditto.
20	Ditto.
21	Portfolio for above.

ENGRAVINGS, ETCHINGS, ETC.

52	Chalk studies.
53	Twenty-seven drawings in sepia, principally scenes on the Norfolk coast.

WATER-COLOUR SKETCHES
(unframed)

91	Yarmouth Beach.
92	St. Benet's Abbey.
93	Carrow.
94	The old fishmarket.
95	Four sketches, on boards.

WATER-COLOUR DRAWINGS

130	Nine drawings.
131	Ditto.
132	Ten ditto.
133	Ditto.
134	Six drawings.
135	Ditto.
136	Ditto.
137	Ditto.
138	Four ditto.
139	Portfolio.
140	Four drawings.
141	Ditto.
142	Ditto.
143	Ditto.
144	Ditto.
145	Ditto.
146	Two ditto.

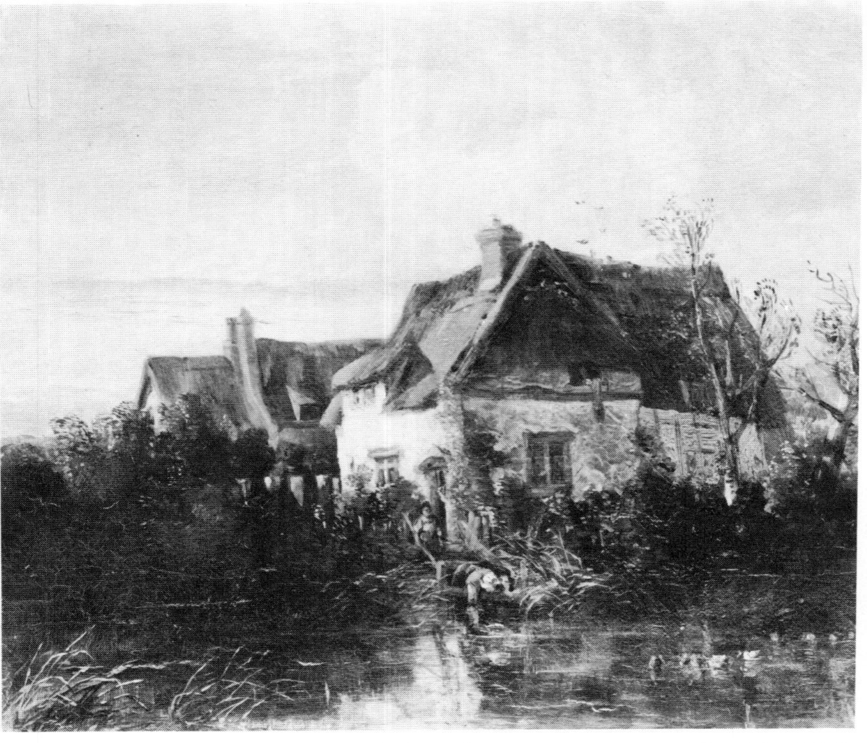

Thomas Lound *At Lakenham* *Oil* $12\frac{1}{2} \times 14\frac{1}{4}$ *in.*

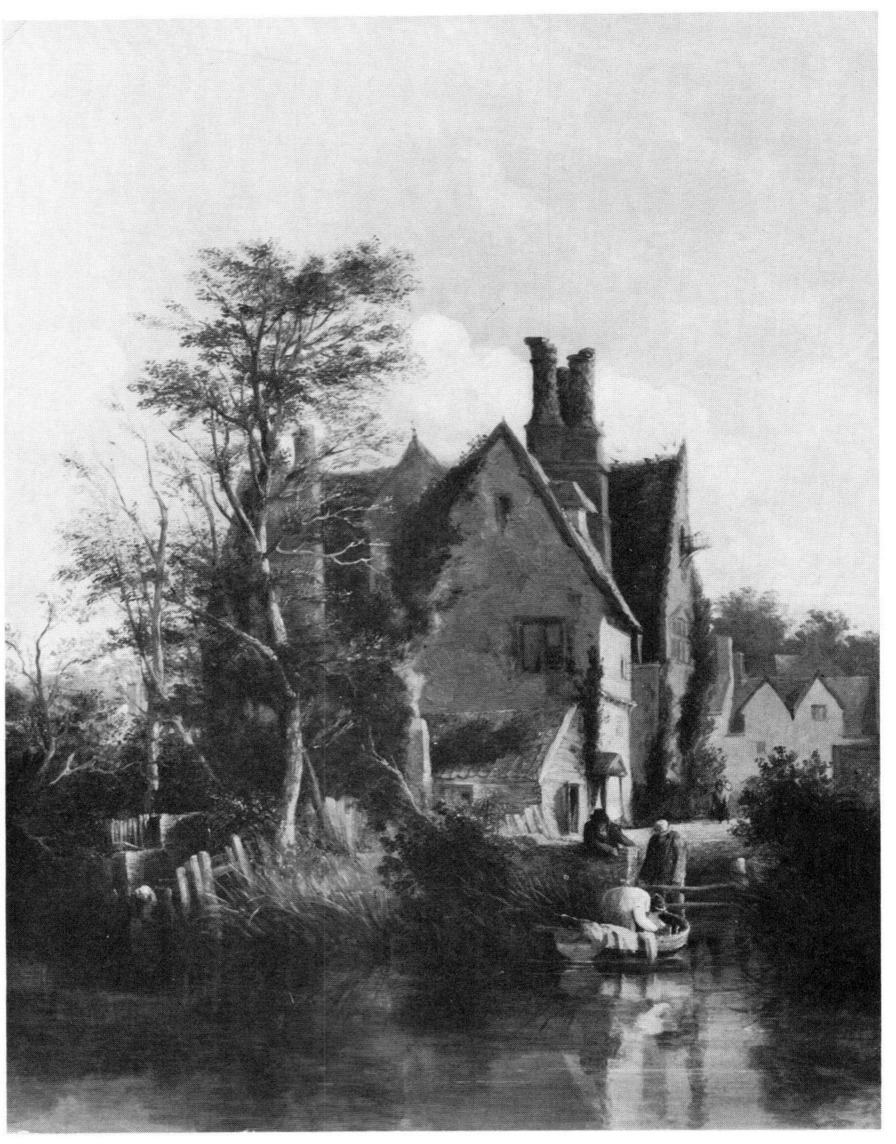

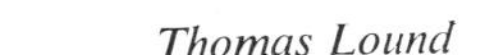

Thomas Lound *St. Martin's River and Gate* *Oil on panel* $19 \times 15\frac{1}{2}$ *in.*

No	*Subject*
147	Portfolio.
148	Four drawings.
149	Ditto.
150	Ditto.
151	Ditto.
152	Ditto.
153	Portfolio.
153A	Five drawings.
153B	Ditto.
153C	Ditto.
153D	Ditto.
153E	Portfolio.
154	Two drawings—the East and South-East Towers, Great Yarmouth.
155	Two drawings—Honingham Fields and Norwich from Trowse.
156	Ditto—Ely from the river and Caistor Castle.
157	Ditto—Horsford Heath and Mundesley Beach.
158	Ditto—Old cottage at Cawton and Mundesley Beach.
159	Ditto—Reedham and Norwich from Crown Point.
160	Ditto—Caistor and Bramerton.
161	Ditto—Caistor and Mundesley.
162	Ditto—Yarmouth from Caistor and Ely, south-west.
163	Ditto—Croyland Abbey and Beeston.
164	Ditto—Coldham Hall and Norwich from the north-east.
165	Ditto—Norwich from the Thorpe Meadows and Norfolk coast.
166	Ditto—Caistor Castle and Yarmouth.
167	Ditto—Caistor Castle, south-east, and houses at Heigham.
168	Wymondham Priory.
169	Trowse Bridge.
170	Old Houses, St. Martin's at Palace.
171	Churchyard, Tombland.
172	Part of Norwich market.
173	Old houses, Colchester.
174	Old houses, Ipswich.
175	Castle Rising Castle.
176	The same subject.
177	Bolton Abbey.
178	Conway.
179	The Wye at Chepstow.
180	Tintern Abbey.
181	Caerphilly Castle.
182	Tintern Abbey.
183	Sheriff Hutton Castle.
184	Caerphilly Castle, south-east.
185	Chepstow Castle.
186	Hasboro' Beach.
187	Valle Crucis Abbey.
188	Cockermouth Castle.
189	Barden Tower.
190	Harlech Castle.
191	Valle Crucis Abbey.
192	Wenloch Priory.
193	Kidwelly Castle.
194	Wenloch Abbey.
195	Brougham Castle.
196	Cockermouth Castle.
197	Conway.
198	Byland Abbey.
199	Furness Abbey.
200	Pair of heath scenes.

WATER-COLOUR DRAWINGS
(framed)

Lot	*Subject*	
202	Sea shore.	
204	Pair river scenes.	In oils. Four lots painted by Mr. Lound for the cabin of the *Kathleen*.
205	Ditto sea views.	
206	Ditto river scenes.	
207	Beach scene (circular).	
208	Harlech Castle.	
210	Unfinished sketch.	
211	Fast Castle.	
212	Caistor Castle.	
213	Beach scene.	
214	Pembrokeshire coast.	
215	Cardigan Bay, with Harlech Castle.	
216	Conisborough.	
217	Warkworth Castle.	
218	On the Tees.	
223	Wymondham Church.	
224	Beach scene.	
227	Bolton Abbey.	
229	Tintern Abbey.	
232	Fishing boats (Lound, after Cotman).	
233	Heath scene (Lound, after Cox).	
237	Lancaster Sand.	

PAINTINGS
(in gilt frames)

246 Beach scene, Yarmouth.
217 Cottages and timber yard.
248 Ely, with cathedral in the distance.
249 St. Benet's Abbey.
250 Fishing boats.
251 Castle Rising.
253 Welsh Mill.
254 Bramerton Hills.
255 Cottage—Thorpe.
256 Yarmouth Old Tower, North River.
257 Mundesley Beach.
258 Beach scene, Yarmouth.
260 Marsh Mill.
261 Boat house, Reedham.
262 Ely Cathedral—sunset (Bright and Lound).
263 Boat builder's yard.
266 Sketch—sunset.
267 Cottages, Heigham.
268 Street scene, St. Michael's at Coslany.

PAINTINGS BY LOUND
(unframed)

272 Yarmouth Beach (after Stannard).
273 Ditto.
274 Caistor Castle.
275 Beach scene.
276 St. Benet's Abbey.
277 Moonlight.
278 Bolton Abbey.

Lot	Subject
279	Cottages at Heigham.
280	Ditto.
281	Landscape (after Old Crome) (framed).
282	Cottages.
283	Beach scene.
284	Mousehold.
285	View of the river, King Street.
286	White Friars' Bridge.
287	The Gibraltar, Heigham.
288	River scene.
289	Landscape (after Smyth) (framed).
290	Old houses.
291	Conway Castle.
292	Pair of small beach scenes.
293	Yarmouth Beach.
294	Old houses.

ROYAL ACADEMY EXHIBITS

Year	No.	Subject
1845		Old houses on the banks of the river at Norwich.
1846	333	River scene, Whitlingham, Norfolk.
	379	Beach scene, Great Yarmouth.
	409	Sea view, Lowestoft, Suffolk.
	700	Heigham, Norfolk.
1849	199	On the River Bure, Norfolk.
	215	The beach, Great Yarmouth.
	859	Caistor Castle, Norfolk (water-colour).
1850	247	A Norfolk marsh mill.
	607	Caistor Castle, Norfolk.
	1240	Coast scene—barque on shore (water-colour).
1851	83	Old houses, Norwich.
1852	126	Summer morning, near Great Yarmouth.
	207	The fisherman's rendezvous near the jetty, Great Yarmouth.
	402	Old houses in Crown Court, Norwich.
1853	495	On the Yare, Norfolk.
1854	781	Richmond, Yorkshire, from the south-west (water-colour).
1855	473	On the Norwich River.
	1318	At Lakenham, Norfolk (water-colour).

BRITISH INSTITUTION

Year	No.	Subject
1846	353	Cromer Beach, Norfolk. 18×25 in.
1847	102	St. Benet's Abbey on the Bure, Norfolk. 11×15 in.
	399	Mundesley Beach, Norfolk. 12×15 in.
1850	468	On the beach, Great Yarmouth. 16×21 in. (A label on the back of a picture by Crome, in the Norwich Castle Museum, of this same subject (17×22 in.) says, "Copied by Lound".)
1850	356	Ely from the meadow—evening. 23×32 in.
1851	52	Coast scene. 16×21 in.
	180	A boatwright's yard. 25×20 in.
1852	253	The North-West Tower, Great Yarmouth. 23×32 in.
1854	277	Cottages near Norwich.
1857	21	At Lakenham, Norfolk.

SIXTEENTH EXHIBITION OF THE NORWICH SOCIETY OF ARTISTS, 1820

No.	*Subject*
141	St. Benet's Abbey.

SEVENTEENTH EXHIBITION OF THE NORWICH SOCIETY OF ARTISTS, 1821

No.	*Subject*
99	Croyland Abbey.

EIGHTEENTH EXHIBITION OF THE NORWICH SOCIETY OF ARTISTS, 1822

No.	*Subject*
93	West Front of Castleacre Abbey.

TWENTY-FIRST EXHIBITION OF THE NORWICH SOCIETY OF ARTISTS, 1825

No.	*Subject*
184	View of Lake Windermere.

TWENTY-THIRD EXHIBITION OF THE NORFOLK AND SUFFOLK INSTITUTION FOR THE PROMOTION OF THE FINE ARTS, 1829

No.	*Subject*
166	Shipping.

TWENTY-SIXTH EXHIBITION OF THE NORFOLK AND SUFFOLK INSTITUTION FOR THE PROMOTION OF THE FINE ARTS, 1832

No.	*Subject*
62	Scene, looking from Carrow Bridge.
69	Bishopgate Bridge.

TWENTY-SEVENTH EXHIBITION OF THE NORFOLK AND SUFFOLK INSTITUTION FOR THE PROMOTION OF THE FINE ARTS, 1833

No.	*Subject*
30	Trowse Mill.
31	Whitlingham Marl Staithe.
58	Scene at Trowse.
59	Sea View.
194	Bridge—Croyland. (Under T. Lound in list of exhibitors.)

FIRST EXHIBITION OF THE NORFOLK AND NORWICH ART UNION, 1839

No.	*Subject*
41	Yarmouth Beach.
43	River scene—Thorpe.
53	Yarmouth Jetty, early in the morning.
143	Draining mill, Limpenhoe.
172	Cromer Beach.
238	The old tower.
250	Yarmouth Beach.
308	Gateway of St. Benet's Abbey.
337	Sketch of the south doorway, Hillington Church.
342	Street scene, Beccles—a sketch.

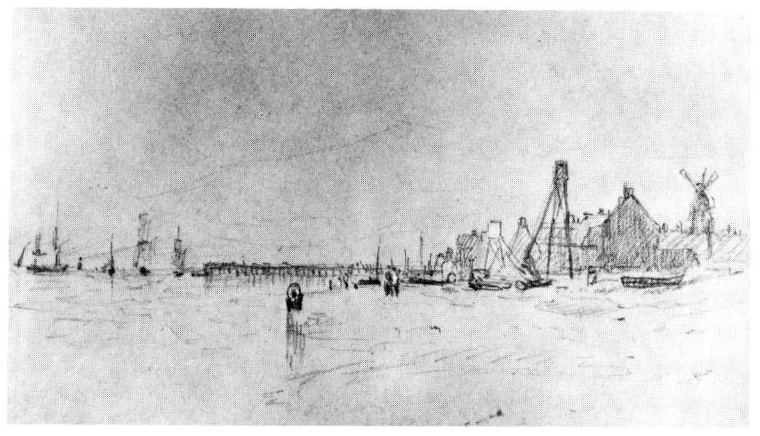

Thomas Lound *Yarmouth Jetty—Nelson's column in the distance*

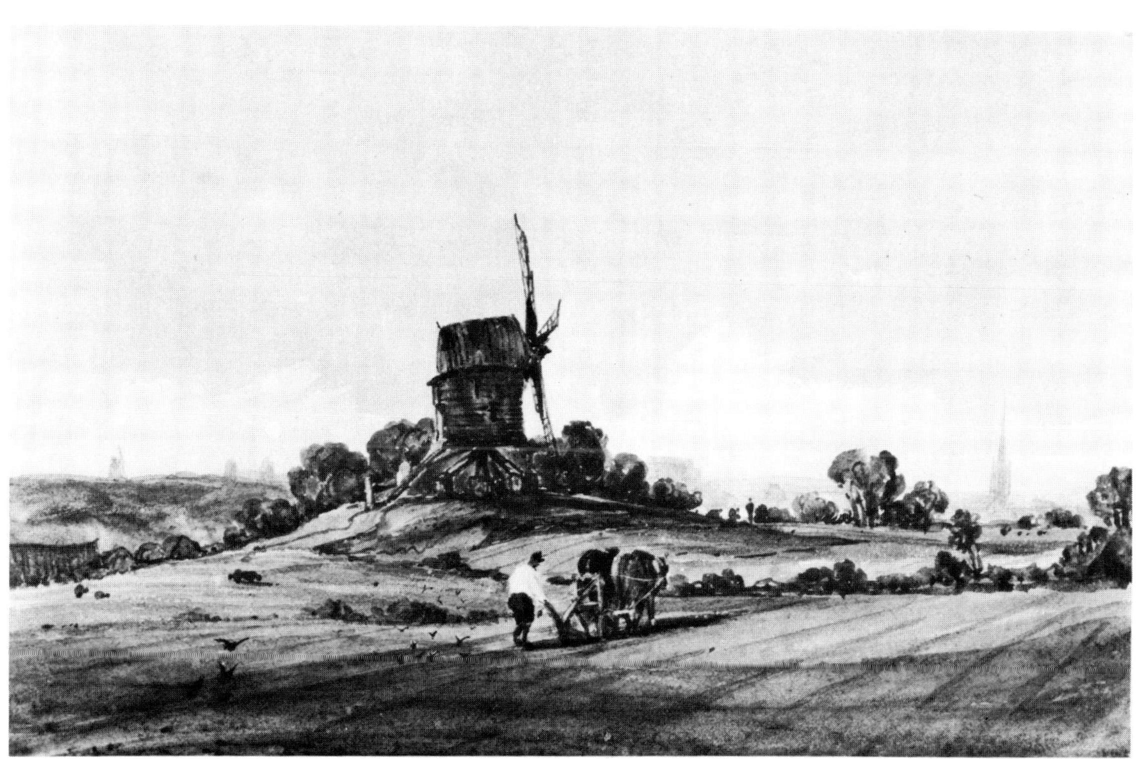

Thomas Lound *View of Norwich* *Water-colour*

FIRST EXHIBITION OF THE EAST OF ENGLAND ART UNION, 1842

No.	*Subject*
13	A brook at Merkshall.
82	Hasbro' Beach.
208	Old mill at Eye.

FIRST EXHIBITION OF THE NORFOLK AND NORWICH ASSOCIATION FOR THE PROMOTION OF THE FINE ARTS, 1848

No.	*Subject*
25	Marsh mill on the Bure, Norfolk.
38	Caistor Castle.
43	Beach scene.
84	Marsh mill at Reedham.
122	An old mill, near Wymondham.
211	Yarmouth Beach.
259	River scene.
262	St. Benet's Abbey.
267	Off Lowestoft.
268	Cromer Beach.
276	Mundesley Beach.
293	Marsh mill, near Ely.

SECOND EXHIBITION OF THE NORFOLK AND NORWICH ASSOCIATION FOR THE PROMOTION OF THE FINE ARTS, 1849

No.	*Subject*
70	St. Benet's Abbey. 10 g. (in ink in margin).
71	Yarmouth Beach. 10 g. (in ink in margin).
120	Breydon. 10 g. (in ink in margin).
209	Beach scene. 8 g. (in ink in margin).
275	On the Bure, Norfolk. 10 g. (in ink in margin).
280	River scene. 8 g. (in ink in margin).
325	Coast scene.
386	Beach scene. 5 g. (in ink in margin).

THIRD EXHIBITION OF THE NORFOLK AND NORWICH ASSOCIATION FOR THE PROMOTION OF THE FINE ARTS, 1852

No.	*Subject*
51	The beach, Great Yarmouth.
53	Summer morning, near Great Yarmouth.
60	A barque on shore.
70	The fisherman's rendezvous, Great Yarmouth.
110	A boatwright's yard.
137	Tintern Abbey on the Wye.
139	The Chequers-yard, St. Michael's Coslany.
144	Caister Castle, Great Yarmouth.
147	A Welsh cottage.
148	Caerphilly Castle from the north-west.
157	Caerphilly from the Cardiff Road.
158	Tintern Abbey from the ferry.
161	Norwich, from above Trowse.
163	Norwich, from Drayton Road.

FOURTH EXHIBITION OF THE NORFOLK AND NORWICH ASSOCIATION FOR THE PROMOTION OF THE FINE ARTS, 1853

No.	*Subject*
25	Ely, from the meadows.
53	On the Waveney.
58	Sea shore.
63	Richmond, from the south-west, Yorkshire.
67	Byland Abbey, Yorkshire.
69	Llangharne Castle, South Wales.
74	Eastby Abbey, Yorkshire.
75	Chepstow Castle, Monmouthshire.
78	Evening on the Bure.
81	Morning.
87	Heigham, Norwich.
104	On the River Yare.

EXHIBITION OF THE NORFOLK AND NORWICH ASSOCIATION FOR THE PROMOTION OF THE FINE ARTS, 1855

No.	*Subject*	£	s.	d.
9	On the Bure—evening.			
44	Bramerton Heath.	15	15	0
55	Coast scene.	13	13	0
122	Norfolk coast.	6	6	0
126	Marsh mill.	5	5	0
167	A windmill.	5	5	0
203	Beach scene, Great Yarmouth.	6	6	0
284	On the Bure, Yarmouth.	6	6	0
296	At Conway, North Wales.	6	6	0
298	Richmond, Yorkshire—south-west.	8	8	0
308	Bolton Abbey, Yorkshire—north-west.	12	12	0
313	Bolton Abbey, Yorkshire—south-east.	8	8	0
328	Richmond, Yorkshire, from the east.	8	8	0
361	A Welsh mill.	6	6	0

EXHIBITION OF THE NORFOLK AND NORWICH FINE ARTS' ASSOCIATION AND OF THE PHOTOGRAPHIC SOCIETY, 1856

No.	*Subject*	£	s.	d.
298	From Richmond Hill.	8	8	0
324	Harlech, North Wales.	12	12	0
342	Sea shore.	5	5	0
347	Harlech Castle, North Wales.	8	8	0
355	Marsh mill, near Ely.	8	8	0
364	Sketch of Buildwas Abbey, Shropshire.	6	6	0
388	Shore of Cardigan Bay, North Wales.	8	8	0
409	Castle Rising, Norfolk.	8	8	0

NORFOLK AND NORWICH FINE ARTS ASSOCIATION
Exhibition of the Works of Modern Artists, 1860

WATER-COLOURS

No.	*Subject*
188	Hunstanton Beach.
191	Cardigan Bay.

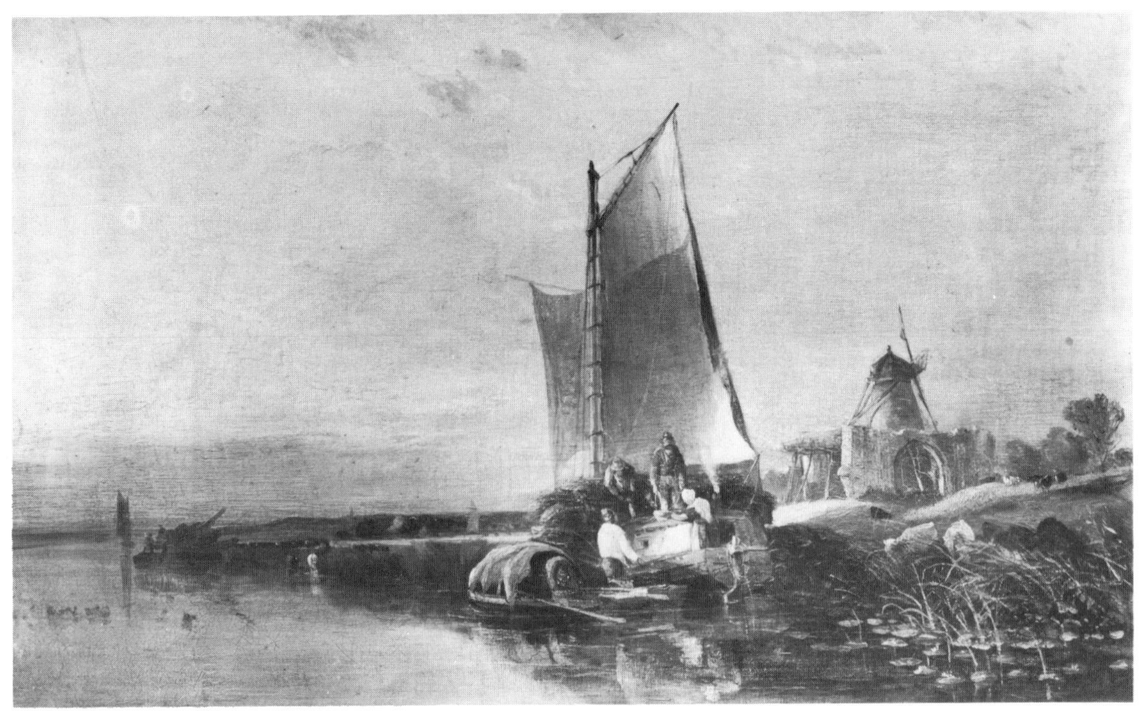

Thomas Lound *St. Benet's Abbey* *Oil* $17\frac{1}{2} \times 29\frac{5}{8}$ *in.*

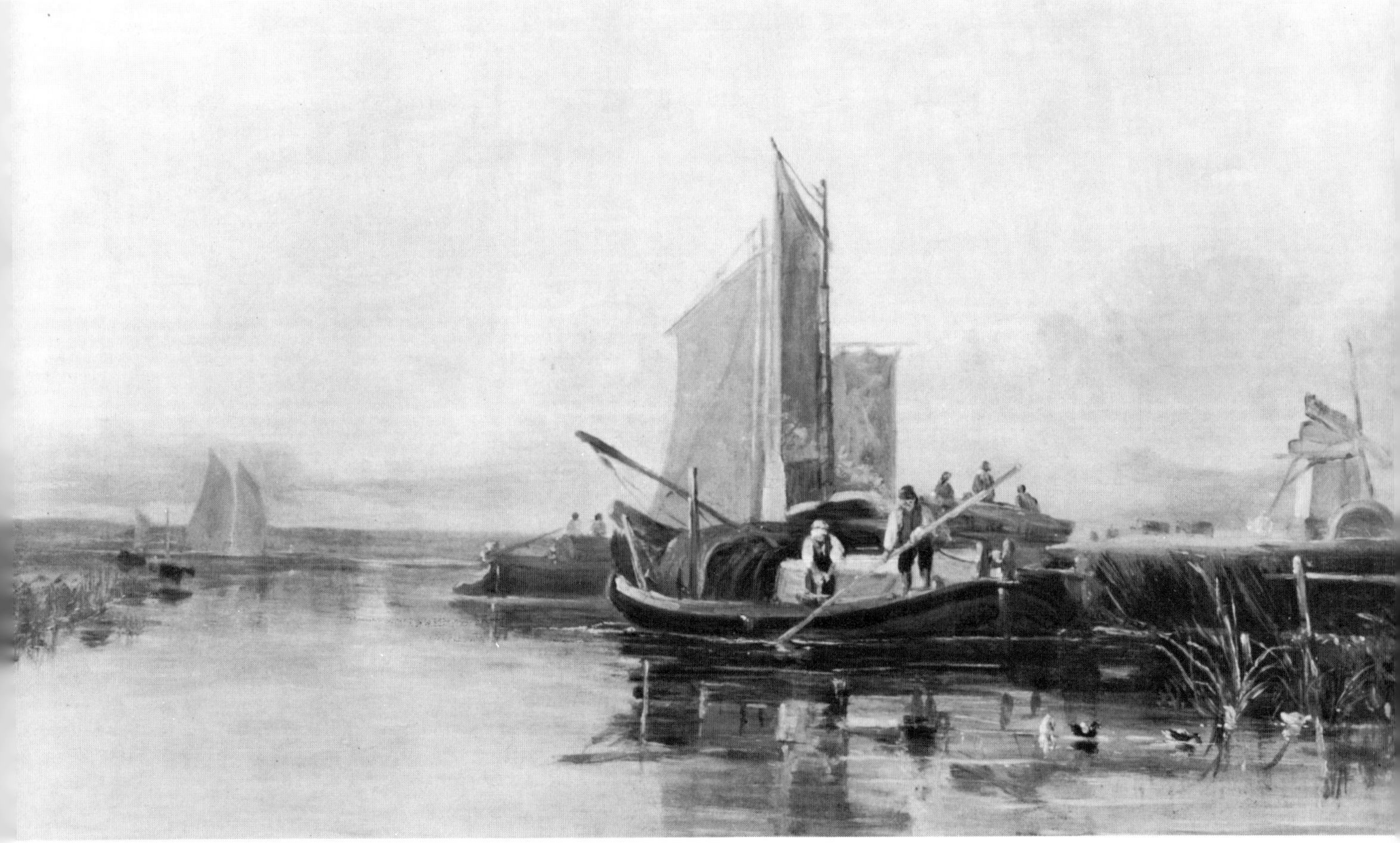

Thomas Lound *Norfolk Broads Landscape* *Oil on Canvas* 11×19

Lot	Subject
200	Conisborough, Yorkshire.
224	On the Tees, near Barnard Castle.
247	Warwick Castle.
255	Bramerton House.

NORWICH AND EASTERN COUNTIES WORKING CLASSES INDUSTRIAL EXHIBITION, 1867

No.	Subject	Lent by
771	Water-colour drawing.	P. E. Hansell, Esq., Thorpe.
786	Sea view.	Mr. John King, Princes Street.
789	Water-colour drawings by Leman, Lound, Thirtle, Cotman and Old Crome.	Mr. John King, Princes Street.
837	Mill and cattle.	Sir J. P. Boileau, Bart., Ketteringham.
866	Oil painting.	Mr. James King.
903	View of King Street Wharfs.	J. J. Colman, Esq.
927	Water-colour sketches by Thirtle, Leman, Lound, etc.	A Friend.

BRITISH MEDICAL ASSOCIATION LOAN COLLECTION
of the Works of Norfolk and Suffolk Artists, 1874

WATER-COLOURS

No.	Subject	Lent by
116	Caister Castle, Yarmouth.	Rev. W. R. Collett.
121	Beach scene—morning, taking nets on board.	Mr. T. H. Edwards.
127	Ely Cathedral.	Mr. T. H. Edwards.
134	Richmond Castle, Yorkshire.	Mr. James Reeve.
135	Sepia sketch.	Mr. John King.
140	Caerphilly Castle.	Mr. T. H. Edwards.
141	White Friars, Norwich.	Mr. P. E. Hansell.
151	Castle Rising, Norfolk.	Mr. W. R. Collett.
156	Ebb tide.	Mr. J. B. Morgan.
159	Saint Benet's Abbey.	Rev. W. R. Collett.

NORWICH ART LOAN EXHIBITION
in aid of the Fund for the Restoration of the Church of Saint Peter Mancroft, 1878

No.	Subject	Lent by
175	View on the North River.	Mr. Thomas Bingham.
274	Marsh mill, near Ely.	W. Butcher, Esq.
295	Bramerton Hills.	Clare Sewell Read, Esq., M.P.
305	Near Yarmouth Bridge.	Mr. W. Boswell.
455	Old houses on Tombland.	R. W. Burleigh, Esq.
461	Old houses, from St. George's Tombland Churchyard.	R. W. Burleigh, Esq.
475	Mundesley Beach.	J. B. Morgan, Esq.
480	Beach scene—evening.	T. H. Edwards, Esq.
484	Marsh mill, near Ely.	

SWAFFHAM FINE ART EXHIBITION, 1882

No.	Subject	Lent by
82	St. Benet's Abbey. (£5 5s.)	Mr. C. T. Thompson.

FINE ART EXHIBITION IN AID OF THE NEW NORFOLK AND NORWICH HOSPITAL, 1883

No.	*Subject*	*Lent by*
2	Marsh mill near Ely.	Mr. George Wilson.
90	Whitlingham Reach.	Mrs. Bolingbroke.
147	Mill.	Mr. Theodore Rossi.
46	Below the New Mills.	Mr. J. J. Colman, M.P.

ART LOAN EXHIBITION IN AID OF THE FUND FOR THE RESTORATION OF ST. PETER MANCROFT CHURCH, 1885

No.	*Subject*	*Lent by*
76	Watermill.	T. Wells, Esq.
77	Bramerton Hills.	Clare Sewell Read, Esq., M.P.

ART LOAN EXHIBITION IN AID OF THE FUNDS OF ST. GEORGE'S CLUB FOR WORKING GIRLS, 1902

No.	*Subject*	*Lent by*
147	Old houses, Norwich.	B. E. Fletcher, Esq.
151	North-West Tower, Yarmouth.	James Mottram, Esq.

LOAN COLLECTION OF DRAWINGS IN THE NEW PICTURE GALLERY IN THE NORWICH CASTLE MUSEUM, 1903

No.	*Subject*	*Lent by*
100	East Barsham, Norfolk. Gable end of cottage on left, trees on right and figures in roadway. 9×13 in.	Mr. James Reeve.
101	The Devil's Tower. Tower with boats and figures on right, trees and cattle on left, river in foreground. 11½×18¾ in.	Mr. Russell J. Colman.
102	Yarmouth Beach. Fishermen on shore on left, sailing vessels in distance on right. 5½×8¾ in.	Mr. James Reeve.
103	Coast scene. Cliffs, and men unloading vessel on right; sea on left. 12½×19½ in.	Mr. Russell J. Colman.
105	St. Benet's Abbey. Abbey on right, sailing barges on left distance, cattle in foreground. 13¾×20½ in.	Mr. Russell J. Colman.

EXHIBITION OF NORWICH SCHOOL PICTURES
Norwich Castle Museum and Art Galleries, October, 1927

OIL PAINTINGS

No.	*Subject*
62	At Lakenham. 12½×14¼ in.
63	River scene, Ely. 13×22 in.
64	Sunrise on the Yare, 1853. 9½×17½ in.
65	St. Benet's Abbey—river scene. 12×21 in.
66	View from Crown Point, Norwich. 10×18 in.

THOMAS LOUND

WATER-COLOURS, DRAWINGS, ETC.

No.	*Subject*
207	Beach scene (sepia). $10\frac{1}{2} \times 22$ in.
208	Two water-colour drawings (in one frame).
209	Augustine Steward's House, Tombland, Norwich. $16\frac{1}{4} \times 12\frac{1}{4}$ in.
210	Tombland Alley, Norwich. $17\frac{1}{4} \times 13\frac{1}{2}$ in.
211	Rivaulx Abbey, Yorkshire. $13\frac{1}{4} \times 20\frac{1}{4}$ in.
212	Castle Rising from the meadows. $12\frac{1}{2} \times 21\frac{1}{2}$ in.
213	At the head of Breydon Water (unfinished). $13\frac{1}{2} \times 26\frac{3}{4}$ in.
214	River scene, Norwich. $9 \times 12\frac{1}{2}$ in.
215	Castleacre, Norfolk. 12×16 in.
216	Mousehold, Norwich. $14\frac{1}{2} \times 22$ in.

JOHN THIRTLE

NORWICH EXHIBITS 1927

DRAWINGS

No.	*Subject*	*Lent by*
259	Miniature portrait of Charles Turner, Mayor of Norwich 1834, as a child. $12 \times 9\frac{1}{2}$ in.	Mrs. Alston.
260	Portrait of Mr. Hay Gurney. $16\frac{1}{4} \times 12$ in.	Mrs. Charles Barnard.
261	View from Hellesdon. $4\frac{1}{2} \times 16$ in.	Mr. F. R. Beecheno.
262	Windmill. $10\frac{1}{4} \times 15\frac{1}{2}$ in.	
263	Near Postwick. $9 \times 13\frac{1}{4}$ in.	
264	Quayside, Norwich (sepia). $6\frac{3}{4} \times 10\frac{1}{2}$ in.	Mrs. L. G. Bolingbroke.
265	Bishop's Bridge, Norwich. $13 \times 16\frac{1}{2}$ in.	Mr. G. Buxton.
266	Norwich from Mousehold. $13\frac{1}{2} \times 38\frac{1}{2}$ in.	J. Cator.
267	Bishop's Bridge, Norwich. $19\frac{1}{4} \times 26\frac{1}{4}$ in.	A. T. Chittock.
268	Dilham Staithe. $7\frac{1}{2} \times 12\frac{1}{2}$ in.	The Misses Colman.
269	St. Benet's Abbey. $7\frac{1}{4} \times 12\frac{1}{4}$ in.	H. P. Gowen.
270	Costessey Park. $19\frac{1}{2} \times 26\frac{1}{2}$ in.	
271	River scene with sailing boat. $19\frac{1}{2} \times 28\frac{1}{2}$ in.	
272	River scene. $19\frac{1}{2} \times 26\frac{1}{2}$ in.	
273	View of Norwich with Cow Tower. $6\frac{1}{4} \times 13\frac{1}{4}$ in.	C. R. Bignold.
274	Five miniature portraits.	Dr. R. J. Mills.
275	Two miniature portraits.	
276	Portrait, signed. $15 \times 11\frac{1}{2}$ in.	H. W. Parr.
277	Three children on a beach, one holding a fishing net. $8 \times 10\frac{1}{4}$ in.	A. M. Samuel.
278	Thatched cottage. $9\frac{1}{2} \times 13\frac{1}{2}$ in.	E. B. Southwell.
279	Four crayon sketches of boats.	
280	Huntsmen panel. $11\frac{1}{4} \times 14\frac{1}{4}$ in.	
281	Huntsmen panel	W. W. Rix Spelman.
282	Tombland, Norwich. $13\frac{1}{2} \times 21$ in.	
283	River scene. $9\frac{1}{4} \times 12\frac{1}{2}$ in.	
284	Cromer. $9\frac{1}{2} \times 13\frac{3}{4}$ in.	
285	Unloading the cargo. $5 \times 7\frac{1}{2}$ in.	
286	Portrait. $4\frac{1}{4}$ in. diameter	P. M. Turner.

JOHN THIRTLE

(1777-1839)

1777 John Thirtle was born in 1777 in a modest house in Elephant Yard, Magdalen Street,
Norwich, the son of John and Susannah Thirtle. His baptism is entered in the register of
St. Saviour's Parish, Norwich, as taking place on the 22nd June, 1777.

At an early age he went to live in London to learn the craft of picture-frame making.
Little is known of his life in London, but we do know that he was back in his native City
practising as a frame-maker in premises near to those of his father (a shoemaker) in
1800 Magdalen Street about 1800.

Besides making frames he had interested himself in painting and discovered within himself certain gifts respecting portraiture. We find in the early Norwich Society Exhibitions (he was a founder member) that he exhibited a considerable number of portraits, many of them miniatures.

1808 In 1808 he exhibited his only Royal Academy work—*Walter and Jane*, No. 642.
Gradually, as the years passed, he became more and more interested in the challenge of
1809 landscape painting. In 1809 he omitted to send any portraits to the Norwich Society
1811 Exhibition. By 1811 he became very friendly with John Sell Cotman, accepting in his
shop subscriptions for Cotman's first series of etchings, Thirtle's name being mentioned
on the title page. The friendship with Cotman undoubtedly led to Thirtle being introduced to Elizabeth Miles, whose sister, Ann Miles, had already married John Sell Cotman.
1812 It was on 2nd November, 1812, that Thirtle married at Felbrigg Church.

It will be remembered that in 1816 the disagreement amongst members of the Norwich Society caused the secession, in which many members, including John Thirtle, started up their own Exhibition on Theatre Plain. Thirtle actually contributed fifteen works which proved his interest in making the new Exhibition a success.

The secession must have been a time of real crisis for Thirtle, as he was primarily a picture-frame maker. The division of opinion probably affected his business. Thus he judiciously concluded in 1818 that he would probably be better off remaining a neutral agent. So in this year he refused to exhibit. His absence was lamented by the writer in the *Norwich Mercury*.

It was not until the reorganisation of the Norfolk and Suffolk Institute in 1827-28 that our artist exhibited again. Until the end of his life he continued to send exhibits to various exhibitions but he was bothered by an infection of the lungs. On medical advice he refrained from visiting the river he dearly loved, but nothing would stop him going out on Castle Hill to witness a good thunderstorm.

Despite his attempts to contain his infection it gradually affected him more and more
1839 until he passed away on 30th September, 1839, in his 63rd year. His business to which
he had devoted himself was taken over by the Boswell family, who remained in business
in Norwich until about 1960. Thirtle's wife survived her husband by many years and
died in 1882 at the age of ninety-five, a very great age for Victorian times.

THE PAINTINGS

John Thirtle at his best is a master of water-colour painting. He has a great sense of composition and attained delightful freedom of execution. One usually recognises his work by his palette, which is often dominated by sienna. The appearance of his work is often of a faded character—in company with John Crome he used a very unstable blue which in time has almost disappeared.

His other main characteristic is the broken line—whether he is depicting the stones in an old wall, or the sides of a boat, he tends to use the short line and dot technique. At times his distances tend to receive only brief treatment, often with blunt lines.

Occasionally he signs his work in plain lettering, "J. Thirtle", sometimes followed by the date. Of the twenty-eight exhibits in the Norwich School Exhibition of 1927 only one was signed.

NORWICH SOCIETY EXHIBITS

Year	*Subject*
1805	Portrait of his sister.
	Portrait of a lady.
	Venus and Cupid (after Westall).
	Cottages.
	Welsh cottages.
1806	Thorpe Hall.
	Portrait of Mr. James Thirtle.
	A mill on Mousehold Heath.
	View on the River Wensum, St. George's, Norwich.
	Mettingham Castle.
	Bishop's Bridge, Norwich.
	Portrait.
	Portrait of his mother.
	Portrait of a lady.
	Nymph bathing.
	The mushroom gatherer.
	Portrait of a lady.
	Despairing lover.
	Portrait of a lady.
	Lakenham Mills.
	The lime kiln.
	The font in Binham Abbey, Norfolk.
1807	View on the river, near the Devil's Tower.
	Bishop's Bridge.
	Fye Bridge, Norwich.
1808	View on the River Wensum, near King Street Gates.
	Part of the interior of Binham Abbey.
	Walter and Jane.
	Portrait of a lady.
	Tan yard, Thorpe, near Norwich.
1809	Cottage.
	Mill and cottage on Mousehold Heath.
	Cottages—study from Nature.
	North-west view of Fye Bridge, Norwich.
	View near Thorpe—evening.
	Interior from part of Norwich Cathedral.
	The Deveil's Tower, near King Street Gates—evening.
1810	Norwich—evening.
	View on the river, looking from Carrow Bridge—evening.
	Sketch on the river, near Heigham.
	Boat-builder's yard, Norwich.
	View on the river, near Cow Tower, Norwich.
	Cottage, Lakenham.
	Southgates, Yarmouth.

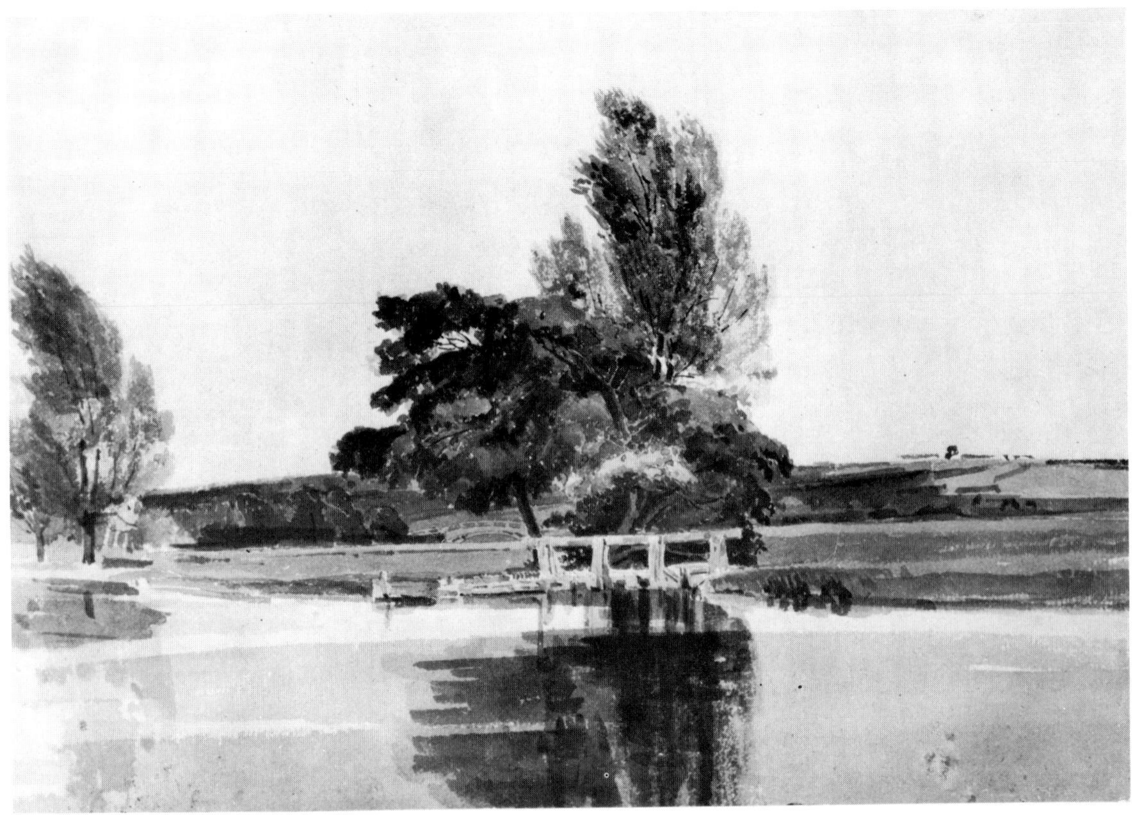

John Thirtle *Riverside Scene, near Norwich* *Water-colour* $8\frac{3}{4} \times 12\frac{3}{8}$ *in.*

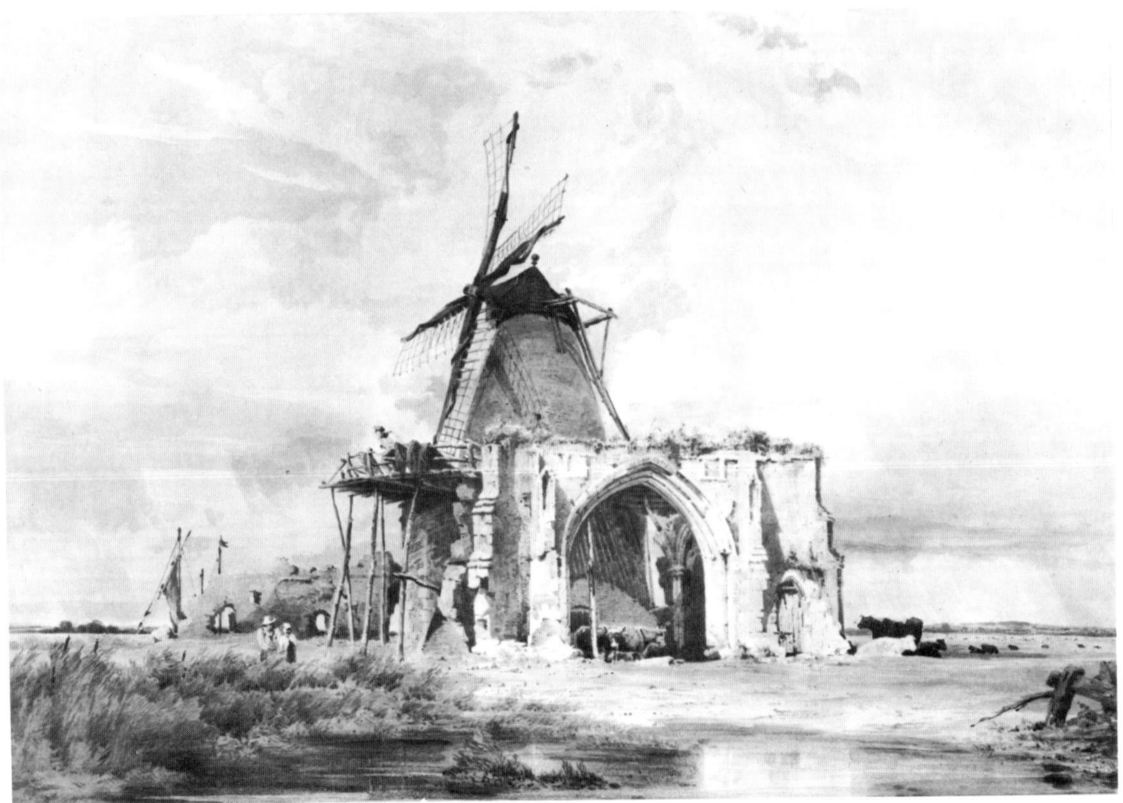

John Thirtle *St. Benet's Abbey* *Water- colour* $19\frac{1}{2} \times 28\frac{1}{2}$ *in.*

Year	*Subject*
1811	Lakenham Mills.
	View on the river, from the arch of Bishop's Bridge.
	Sketch on the River Wensum.
	Ferry Lane, Norwich.
	Draining mill, St. Benet's Abbey, on the North River.
1812	A view of the approach of the troops to the attack on Rasil Kymer.
	A view of the bombarding of Fort Shinaas.
	Mill and cottage—a composition.
	Boat-builder's yard, near the Cow Tower, Norwich.
1813	View on the river.
	Carrow Bridge—evening.
	Portrait.
1814	Horstead Mills, near Coltishall on the Bure. Representing the mill surrounded by trees in the distance. River and reeds in the foreground to the left. A girl and a dog on the tow path under a pollard to the right. $16\frac{3}{4} \times 25$ in. Now the property of T. C. Blofeld.
	A drawing.
	Catton Church—a sketch.
	Cottage at Thorpe.
	Scene at Cossey (or Costessy)—the seat of Sir G. Jerningham.
	Study of dead birds.
	Fishmarket, Norwich.
1815	Trowse Bridge, near Norwich.
	A view of Thorpe, with the steam barge working up—evening.
	A view of Fuller's Hole, Norwich—morning.
1816	Croyland Abbey and Bridge, Lincolnshire.
	A drawing—evening.
	Norwich from Hellesdon—morning.
	Sea beach—low water.
	A view on the Thames.
	A view on the Thames.
	An outlet, near Cossey (or Costessy) Mills.
	A view of Norwich from Mousehold Heath—evening.
	A cottage scene.
	Fishing boats—storm coming on.
	Fishing boats—calm.
	A landscape.
	Three portraits, one being of himself.
1817	View near the Horse Barracks, Norwich.
	Part of City Hall, Norwich, in 1809.
	Rainbow effect on the river, King Street, Norwich.
	Drawing—Welsh scenery.
	Bishopgate Bridge, Norwich—evening.
	View from Thorpe, looking towards Bracondale—evening.

NORFOLK AND SUFFOLK INSTITUTION

Year	*Subject*
1828	St. Benet's Abbey.
1829	Boat builders—Carrow.
	Scene on the river at Thorpe—evening.
	View from Thorpe to Whitlingham—evening.
1830	Dilham Staithe.
	Duke's Palace Bridge.
	Scene—Cromer.
	An east view of Norwich.
	Cromer Beach.

NORFOLK AND NORWICH FINE ARTS ASSOCIATION
Exhibition of the Works of Deceased Local Artists, 1860

WATER-COLOUR ROOM

No.	*Subject*	*Lent by*
241	Beach scene.	Mr. Fitch.
249	Outlet at Cossey.	Mr. T. Bignold.
251	Landscape and houses.	Mr. R. B. Scott.
252	Norwich River, with rainbow.	Mr. C. Turner.
257	Bishop's Bridge.	Mr. T. Bignold.
262	Landscape, with children.	Mr. R. B. Scott.
271	View of Norwich.	Mr. Ladbrooke.
276	Landscape.	Mr. H. Bolingbroke.
277	Landscape—Wales.	Mr. R. B. Scott.
278	Norwich from the river.	Mr. H. Bolingbroke.
284	Carrow Bridge.	Mrs. Thirtle.
289	St. Benet's Abbey.	Mr. J. N. Waite.
295	The Harvest Waggon.	Mr. Root.
301	Dilham Staithe.	Mrs. Thirtle.
305	View down Norwich River.	Mrs. Thirtle.
306	River scene, opposite Duke's Palace.	Mr. J. Mills.
307	View of Norwich from Mousehold.	Mrs. Thirtle.
310	Beach scene.	Miss Master.
311	Thorpe Old Hall.	Mr. T. Bignold.
314	S'udy of willows.	Mr. Boswell.

NORWICH AND EASTERN COUNTIES WORKING CLASSES INDUSTRIAL EXHIBITION
at St. Andrew's Hall, Norwich, 1867

WATER-COLOURS

No.	*Subject*	*Lent by*
764	Norwich from Mousehold—evening.	Wm. Dixon, Mount Pleasant.
770	Four water-colour drawings.	P. E. Hansell, Thorpe.
789	Water-colour drawings by Leman, Lound, Thirtle, Cotman and Old Crome.	Mr. John King, Princes Street.
897	Sketches by John Thirtle and Cotman.	Mr. T. G. Bayfield.
927	Water-colour sketches by Thirtle, Leman, Lound, etc.	A Friend.

BRITISH MEDICAL ASSOCIATION LOAN COLLECTION
of the Works of Norfolk and Suffolk Artists, 1874

WATER-COLOURS, ETC. BY DECEASED ARTISTS

No.	*Subject*	*Lent by*
82	Group of children.	Mr. Robert Cooper.
87	Near the coast.	Mrs. Kye.
90	View at Heigham.	Mrs. Kye.
98	Gorleston River.	Mr. James Reeve.
102	Portrait of a lady.	Mrs. Kye.
105	Earlham Bridge.	Rev. W. N. Ripley.
108	Dilham Staithe.	Mrs. Kye.
113	The Harvest Waggon—Trowse, looking towards Crown Point.	Mr. James Reeve.

No.	Subject	Lent by
125	Horstead Mills.	Rev. T. Blofield.
138	View at Trowse.	Mr. John King.
139	Yarmouth Beach.	Mr. John King.
157	View at Hethel, Norfolk.	Mr. John King.

NORWICH ART LOAN EXHIBITION
in aid of the Fund for the Restoration of the Church of Saint Peter Mancroft, 1878

WATER-COLOUR DRAWINGS

No.	Subject	Lent by
419	Bishop's Bridge, Norwich.	Miss Bignold.
420	On the Wensum, Norwich.	Rev. Charles Turner.
425	The Devil Tower and Carrow Bridge.	Mr. Wm. Runacres.
435	Off Yarmouth.	Miss Bignold.
450	Bishop Bridge.	R. W. Burleigh, Esq.
465	Trowse Old Bridge.	Mr. J. B. Aldis.
466	Beach scene.	Mr. John King.
468	Landscape.	Miss Parr.
470	Whitlingham Reach.	Samuel Harvard, Esq.
495	Landscape.	Mr. John King.
569	Landscape.	Miss Bignold.
576	Water-colour—river scene near Norwich.	Miss Bignold.

FINE ART EXHIBITION
in aid of the new Norfolk and Norwich Hospital, 1883

No.	Subject	Lent by
56	River at Thorpe.	Mr. H. G. Barwell.
57	Landscape.	Mr. I. B. Coaks.

ART LOAN EXHIBITION
in aid of the fund for the Restoration of St. Peter Mancroft Church, 1885

No.	Subject	Lent by
322	Whitlingham.	Samuel Harvard, Esq.
351	The Devil's Tower.	J. J. Colman, Esq., M.P.
358	Portrait of Hudson Gurney, Esq., of Keswick, date 1806.	Alfred Barnard, Esq.
361	Scene on the Yare, near Norwich.	Miss Bignold.
362	A view in Costessey Park, near Norwich.	Miss Bignold.
657	Bishop's Bridge.	Mr. W. Rupert.
666	Portrait of a child.	Mr. W. Rupert.

A LOAN COLLECTION OF PICTURES AND WATER-COLOUR DRAWINGS
exhibited at the Agricultural Hall Gallery, Norwich, during the Grand Oriental Bazaar, 1894

WATER-COLOURS

No.	Subject	Lent by
54	View over Norwich from Mousehold.	H. G. Barwell, Esq.
55	Tombland.	Samuel Hoare, Esq., M.P.
62	Thorpe.	J. J. Colman, Esq., M.P.
64	The Devil's Tower.	J. J. Colman, Esq., M.P.
68	Trowse Bridge.	Samuel Hoare, Esq., M.P.

ART LOAN EXHIBITION

in aid of the Funds of St. George's Club for Working Girls, 1902

No.	*Subject*	*Lent by*
214	Tanyard, Heigham, Norwich.	James Reeve, Esq.
219	Water Gate, Lower Close, Norwich.	James Reeve, Esq.
223	Lenwade Mills, Norfolk.	James Reeve, Esq.
237	Norwich from Back River.	
238	Whitlingham Reach with steamboat.	The Worshipful the Mayor of Norwich (Russell Colman, Esq.).
274	Bishop's Bridge.	Miss Bignold.

CATALOGUE OF THE LOAN COLLECTION OF DRAWINGS

in the New Picture Gallery in the Norwich Castle Museum, 1903

No.	*Subject*	*Lent by*
82	Tan Yard, Norwich. Old tan house, with dial, at Heigham; figures in foreground, palings on right. $6\frac{3}{4}\times10\frac{1}{2}$ in.	Mr. James Reeve.
83	Thorpe Staithe. The river, with wherries, sailing boat and billy-boys on right; wherry, with mast down, on left—evening. $9\frac{3}{4}\times13\frac{3}{8}$ in.	Mr. J. B. Aldis.
84	Lakenham Mills. Old Lakenham Post Office on right, mill in centre, and cottage on left. $7\frac{5}{8}\times9\frac{7}{8}$ in.	Mr. Russell J. Colman.
85	Thorpe Watering. Horses in foreground, trees and church on left, river, with Whitlingham in the distance on right. $12\frac{3}{4}\times18\frac{3}{4}$ in.	Mr. Russell J. Colman.
86	View of Norwich. View looking from the north-east. $9\times28\frac{1}{2}$ in.	Mr. Russell J. Colman.
87	Whitlingham Reach. View looking along the river, showing the first steamer which plied between Norwich and Yarmouth. $18\frac{1}{4}\times30\frac{1}{2}$ in.	Mr. Russell J. Colman.
88	Fye Bridge, Norwich. Old houses on left and right, bridge and wherry in left centre. This bridge was removed in 1829. $7\frac{3}{4}\times11$ in.	Mr. Russell J. Colman.
89	Lamas-Buxton, Norfolk. River in foreground, wherry and buildings on right, boat and figures on left, trees above and in distance. $10\frac{1}{2}\times15\frac{1}{2}$ in.	Mr. James Reeve.
90	Lenwade Mills, Norfolk. Mills on right, cottages on left, bridge in centre, river in right foreground. 8×13 in.	Mr. James Reeve.
91	Norwich, from Mousehold. Sunset effect, cathedral in centre, ruins of St. Leonard's Priory on left. $8\frac{3}{4}\times12\frac{3}{4}$ in.	Miss Barwell.
92	St. Benet's Abbey. Gateway in centre, sails of draining mill on left, cattle on right. $9\frac{1}{4}\times12\frac{3}{4}$ in.	Mr. Russell J. Colman.
93	Water Gate, Lower Close, Norwich. Cottage with figure right foreground, gateway in centre, high land in the distance, with a portion of St. Leonard's Priory to left. $11\frac{1}{2}\times15\frac{1}{4}$ in.	Mr. James Reeve.
94	View of Norwich. Cathedral on right, river in distance on left. $7\frac{1}{2}\times16\frac{5}{8}$ in.	Mr. James Reeve.
95	Duke's Palace, Norwich. View taken previous to erection of bridge. Stark's dye houses on right, wherries on left, river in foreground. St. Giles's Church in the distance. $10\frac{1}{2}\times18\frac{1}{2}$ in.	Mr. James Reeve.
97	Thorpe Reach. Men unloading wherry on left, meadows on right, trees in distance. $5\frac{3}{8}\times10\frac{1}{2}$ in.	Miss Barwell.

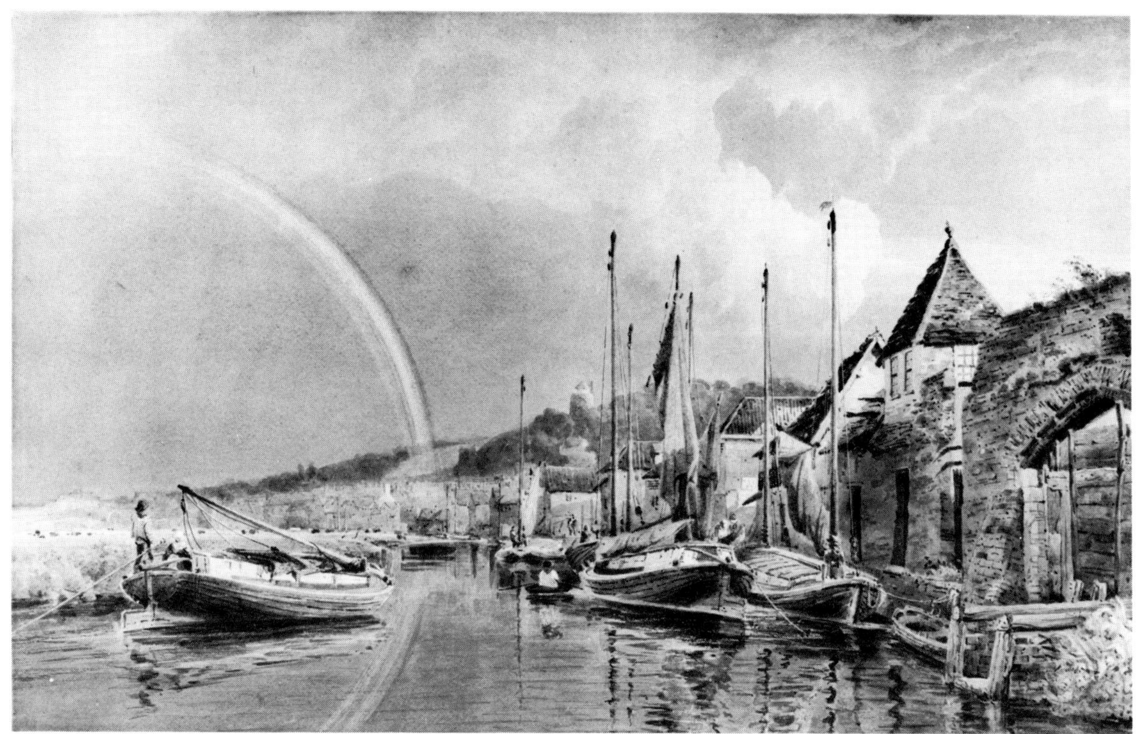

John Thirtle *River scene with rainbow (King Street, Norwich) 1817* *Water-colour* $15\frac{7}{8} \times 25\frac{1}{8}$ *in.*

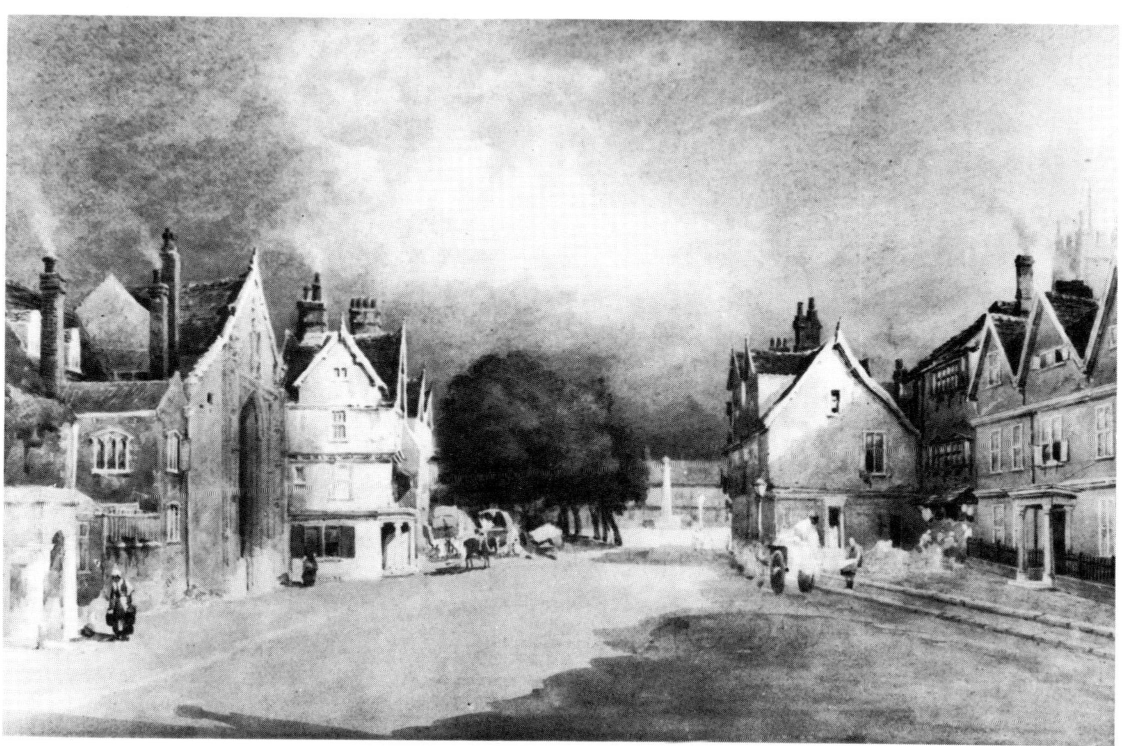

John Thirtle *Tombland, Norwich* *Water-colour* $13\frac{1}{2} \times 21\frac{1}{4}$ *in.*

JOHN MIDDLETON

(1827-1856)

1827 John Middleton was born the son of a well-to-do family on 9th January, 1827, in the
Parish of St. Stephen, Norwich. It is likely he attended the Grammar School, where he
probably became enthused with the feeling to become an artist. He was taught by
John Berney Crome, who may have been his teacher at school; later by Henry Bright and
Henry Jutsom, probably by the latter in London, for he moved to the Metropolis in
1847 1847 taking a house No. 1 The Terrace, South Kensington. It was in this year that he
commenced sending to the Royal Academy and British Institution. Despite the fact that
Middleton had independent means he struggled hard to master his art; indeed the Cantley
1848 Beck Plate (Norwich Museum) painted in 1848 is progress worthy of any professional
artist. This year he also visited the South of England resulting in the View near Tunbridge Wells exhibited at the British Institute. He also executed a water-colour
inscribed "Tunbridge Wells". He is said to have interested himself in etching about the
1852 year 1852, when he issued some small plates under the title "Nine Etchings by John
Middleton".

It must have been while staying in London that he wrote to James Reeve from the Riddler Hotel, Holborn, in which he refers to a mistake made by his servant. From this one gathers that he didn't suffer fools gladly. Incidentally he had an interesting habit of cross-writing his letters—a trait which probably accounted for the family's prosperity!

John Middleton was not an extensive traveller, perhaps his delicate state of health
proved a problem. However, he did get up to the Isle of Arran which resulted in at least
one water-colour study and an oil of the subject—the latter being sent to the British
1854 Institution in 1854.

Perhaps it was due to consumption, from which he suffered, that our artist never
1856 married. By 1856 this disease had become a great trial to him. On the 7th of October
he wrote his Will and some six days later a codicil. By 11th November, 1856, his energy
finally ran its course. His passing was much lamented by his mother and family. His
mother lived on to exhibit in Norwich certain of his works; in passing, one may observe
that she also painted flower pieces. According to the obituary John Middleton was one
of the most amiable of men. It said that as long as he could hold a pencil he turned to
his easel with the same affection.

THE PAINTINGS

John Middleton was recognised in his day as having genius. A writer of his obituary stated that he would have travelled far in the Arts had he lived a normal span. Dying as he did at the early age of twenty-nine years his production is necessarily limited. Those collectors possessing his works cherish them greatly.

We are fortunate in so much that Cantley Beck (page 113) is dated 1848, for it shows us the fluency that he had attained even at 21 years of age. Whilst one could mistake it for a work by Henry Bright, it seems to have a little more serenity and the tree forms are more individual. In the 1927 Norwich School Exhibition of the six water-colours by Middleton only one is signed and dated, and of the four oils only one is signed and dated. Until more research is done it is not at the moment possible to date his work.

The water-colours are delightfully free, often they carry a predominant green hue, also occasionally he employs texture with his brush strokes, for example on the bol of a tree. I have seen his water-colours signed and inscribed, sometimes with a J.M. and sometimes in the monogram form. Although Middleton didn't have lessons from James Stark, he was undoubtedly in touch with Stark, and would see his work in various exhibitions. I mention this because it would seem that Stark most strongly influenced his water-colour technique.

WORKS OF JOHN MIDDLETON FROM THE COLLECTION OF MRS. MIDDLETON (JOHN MIDDLETON'S MOTHER)

Sale, 13th, 14th and 15th June, 1883

The following drawings are mostly sketches for pictures:

No.	*Subject*
355	Four—Weybourne.
356	Four—Scotland, etc.
357	A pair of uprights—rocks and water.
358	Ditto—trees.
359	Two—a study in March on the Norfolk coast, for the picture in the Academy, 1852—Isle of Arran.
360	Two—Clovelly.
361	Six—Devon and Norfolk.
362	Four—landscapes.
363	Four—trees.
364	Two—Lynmouth and Clovelly.
365	Six—landscapes.
366	Three—Devon.
367	Three—Devon.
368	Two—landscapes.
369	Three—Weybourne and study of lichens.

EARLY SKETCHES

370	A series of thirteen sketches, the first of John Middleton's (when a pupil of J. B. Crome).
371	Two—Richmond and mountain scenery.
372	Four—Norfolk views.
373	Four—Costessy, Wales, etc.
374	Six landscapes.
375	Three—St. Benet's Abbey, etc.
376	Four uprights—Earlham, Whitlingham and Eaton.
377	Four ditto—Caistor Castle, Yarmouth Tower, old houses, etc.
378	Three ditto—landscapes.
379	Two—Carrow and Trowse.
380	Two—views near Norwich.
381	Two—bridges near Norwich.
382	Two—Keswick.
383	Two—old houses.
384	Two uprights—The Close, Norwich, and river scene.
385	Two ditto—Norfolk views.
386	Two ditto—ditto.

PENCIL DRAWINGS

387	Eight sketches.
388	Four ditto.
389	Twenty ditto.
390	Twenty ditto.

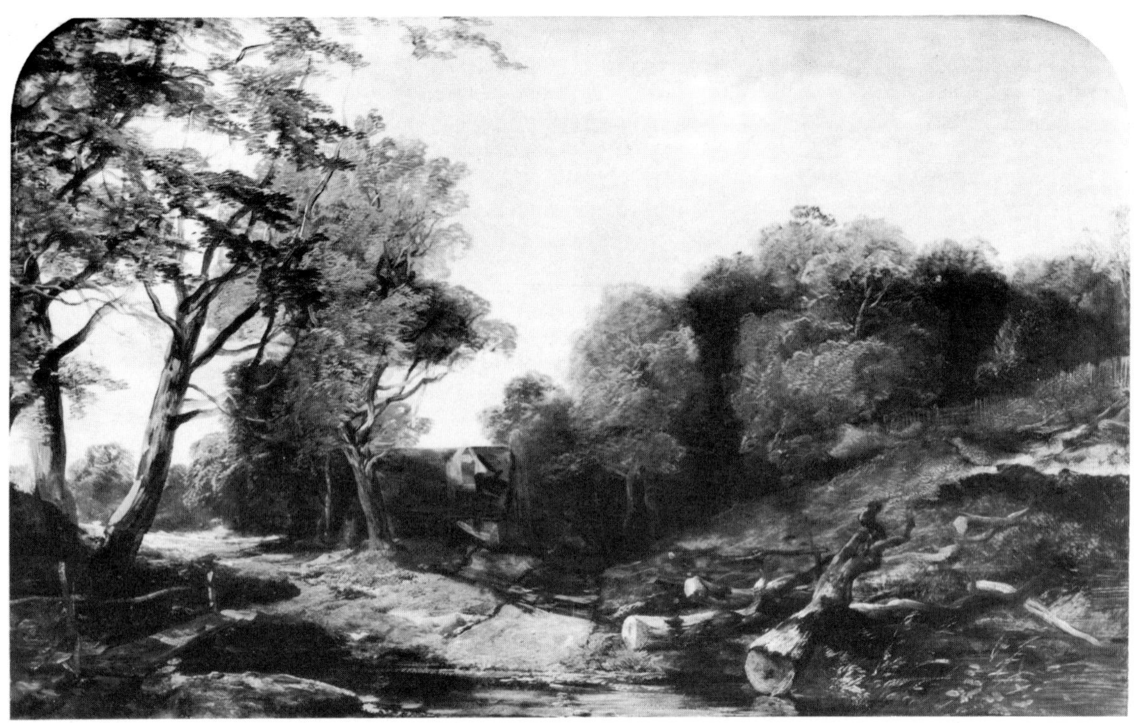

John Middleton *Road scene with felled timber in foreground* *Oil* $13\frac{1}{4} \times 21\frac{3}{4}$ *in.*

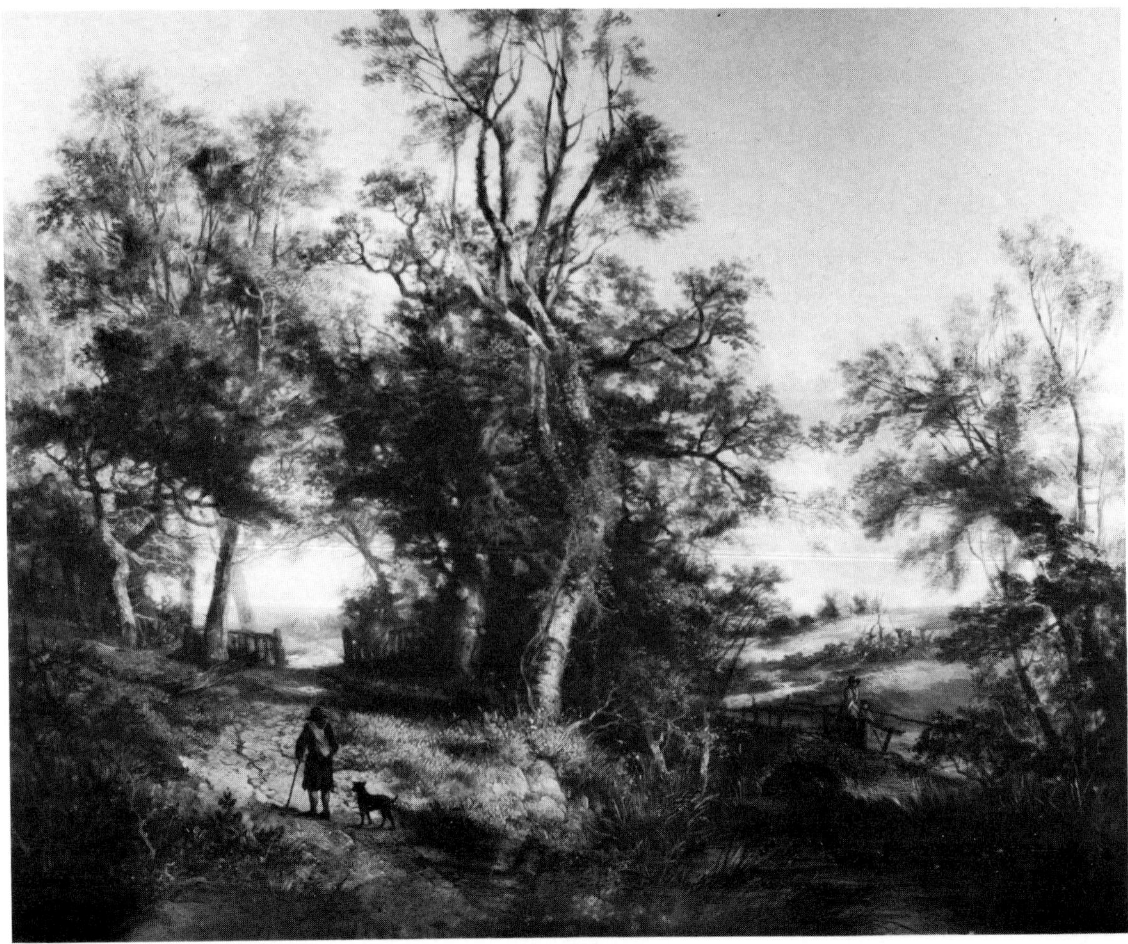

John Middleton *The Rustic Bridge* *Oil on canvas* 25 × 30 *in.*

No.	*Subject*
391	Twenty ditto.
392	Thirty-six ditto.
392A	Three sketching books, containing pencil sketches by John Middleton.
392B	Sketch book containing sketches by John Middleton, taken in the Isle of Arran.

ETCHINGS

393	A set of eighteen etchings, mounted and named, several of them duplicate subjects, showing the different states of the plates.
394	A set of nine etchings, one plate of each subject named and described with references to the pictures from which they were taken.
395	Another set.
396	Seven etchings, various.
397	Six ditto.
398	A set of nine copper plates etched by John Middleton, *viz.*: at Hellesdon, a fine day in February; felled timber at Barningham; Ivy Bridge, South Devon; Weybourne; Gunton Park, near Cromer; Hatfield; and two compositions—see etchings, lot 394.

DRAWINGS IN WATER-COLOUR
(in folios)

427	Two—departure of the Grand Duchess from Brodick, September 1853; Kent's Cavern, Torquay.
428	Two—Clovelly; and study of rocks and water.
429	One—near Ivy Bridge, South Devon.
430	Mile End Ferry, Henley.
431	The Thames, Henley.
432	In North Devon.
433	Weybourne.
434	Clovelly.
435	At Blofield.
436	Hatfield.
437	Two—Kent's Cavern, Torquay; old sheds.
438	Two—Crown Point; old sheds at Eaton.
439	Two—Stratton Stawless Park and lane scene.
440	Two—Hatfield; Lane Mill, Woolfardisworthy, N.D.
441	Two—Tunbridge Wells.
442	Two—Tunbridge Wells.
443	Two—Withyham, Kent; and North Devon.
444	Two—river scenes, North Devon.
445	One upright—farmyard.
446	Two—Devonshire.
447	A pair—the Thames, Henley.
448	One—study of rocks and trees.
449	Study of trees.
450	Hatfield.
451	Magpie Island, the Thames.
452	Walton-on Thames.
453	Hatfield.
454	Clovelly.
455	North Devon.
456	Isle of Arran. (The picture of this subject was exhibited at the Royal Academy and is now in the possession of J. Arden, Esq.)
457	Billingstone, Kent.
458	Alby, Norfolk.
459	Withyham, Kent. (Bought by Reeve.)
460	Lynmouth, North Devon.
461	Ivy Bridge, South Devon—"Sunshine and Shadow".

No.	*Subject*
462	Isle of Arran.
463	Ditto.
464	Clovelly, North Devon.
465	Hatfield.
466	Old Barn, Kent.
467	Berrinarboor, North Devon.
468	Arran.
469	Limestone quarry, Coombe Martin, North Devon.
470	Coombe Martin, North Devon.
471	Clovelly street, North Devon.
472	Weybourne, Norfolk.
473	Avenue of limes at Hatfield.
474	Ivy Bridge, South Devon.

OILS

554	Road scene, with timber. 22 × 13 in.
555	Landscape, with gipsy tent and figures. 24½ × 17½ in.
556	Woods at Weybourne. 21 × 15 in.
557	Ivy Bridge, South Devon—"Sunshine and Shadow". 30 × 20 in. (The Royal Academy, 1855.)
558	Near Ivy Bridge, South Devon. 21 × 15 in.
559	Gunton Park—a beech glade. 19 in. circular.
560	At Hatfield. 24 × 10½ in.
561	At Thorpe. 8 × 6 in.
562	Near Southwold. 9 × 7 in.
563	Landscape. 8 × 6 in.
564	Norfolk coast. 6 × 5 in.

WATER-COLOUR DRAWINGS
(framed)

566	River scene.
567	Bright day in February—Hellesdon meadows (an etched drawing).
568	Dahlias.

SKETCHES IN OIL

569	Old barn. 34 × 20 in.
570	River scene. 16 × 12 in.
571	Trees. 14 × 9 in.
572	Landscape. 42 × 24 in.
573	Ditto. 24 × 16 in.
574	Ditto. 17 × 12 in.
575	Ditto. 22 × 13 in.
576	Ditto and river. 16 × 12 in.
577	St. Benet's Abbey. 14 × 9 in.
578	Landscape. 18 × 12 in.
579	River scene. 12 × 9 in.
580	Road scene. 12 × 9 in.
581	Landscape. 15 × 12 in.
582	Ditto. 11 × 9 in.
583	Ditto. 28 × 18 in.
584	Wood scene. 19 in. circular.
585	Beeches. 19 × 16 in.
586	Road scene with trees. 24 × 15 in.
587	Two sketches.

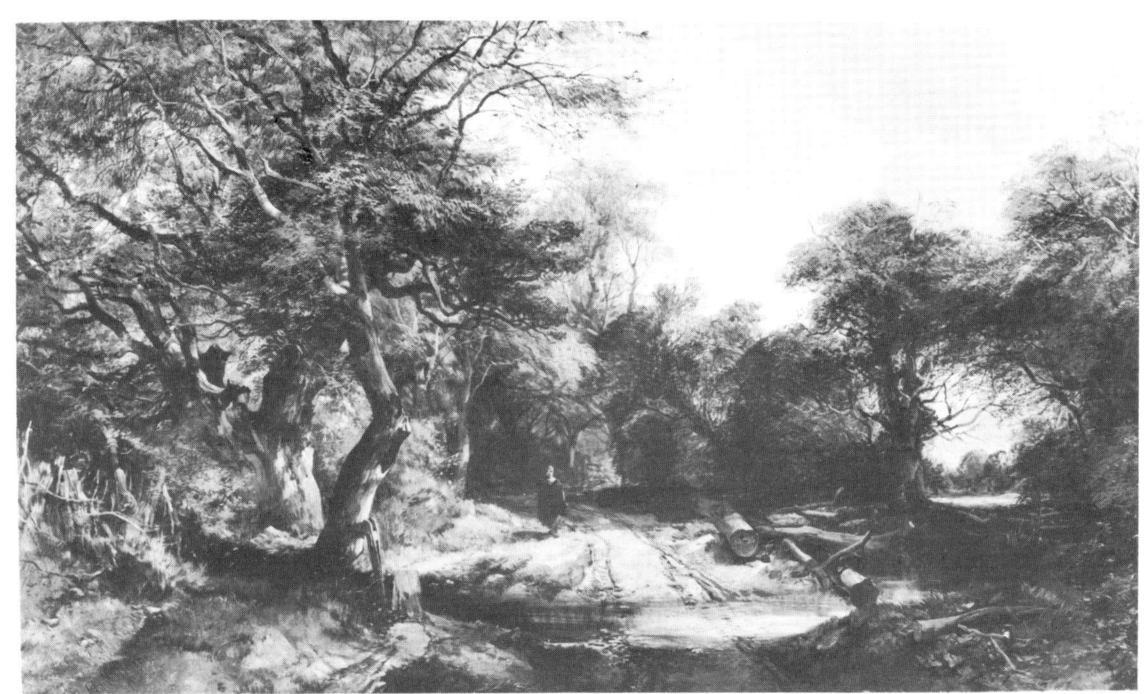

John Middleton *Cantley Beck*, 1848 *Oil* 19½ × 33¾ *in.*

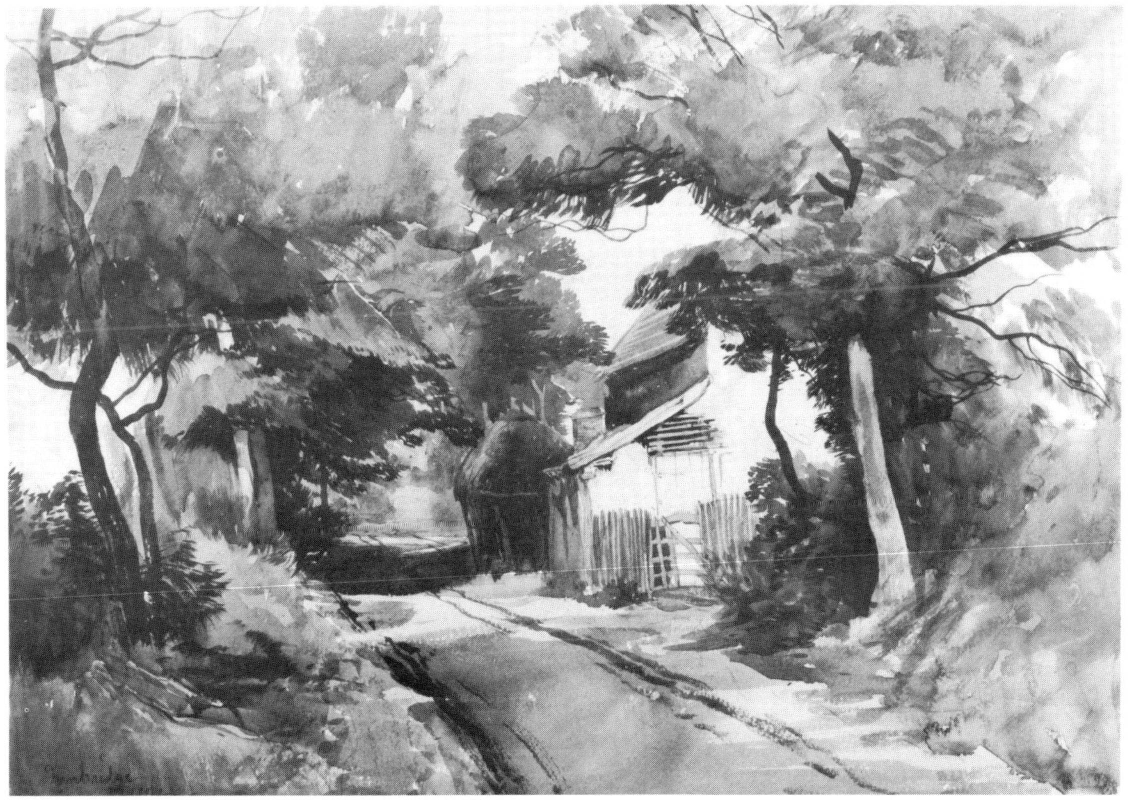

John Middleton *Tunbridge* (*Kent*) *Water-colour* 13 × 19 *in.*

EXHIBITION OF NORWICH SCHOOL PICTURES
Norwich Castle Museum and Art Galleries October 1927

OIL-PAINTINGS

No.	*Subject*
67	A fine day in February. $6\frac{3}{4}\times 11$ in.
68	Landscape. 19 in. in diameter.
69	A study in March on the Norfolk coast (signed J. Middleton 1852). $20\frac{1}{2}\times 32\frac{1}{2}$ in.
70	Landscape with pollards. $19\frac{1}{2}\times 23\frac{1}{2}$ in.

WATER-COLOURS, DRAWINGS, ETC.

222	Landscape (monochrome). $13\frac{1}{2}\times 20$ in.
223	Thatched sheds, etc. $11\frac{3}{4}\times 18\frac{1}{2}$ in.
224	Barn and cut wood (signed and dated 1847). $13\times 18\frac{3}{4}$ in.
225	Landscape. $15\frac{1}{2}\times 25\frac{1}{2}$ in.
226	Landscape. 11×17 in.
227	Lynmouth. $19\times 12\frac{1}{2}$ in.

EXHIBITS AT NORWICH
THE EXHIBITION OF THE NORFOLK AND NORWICH ASSOCIATION FOR THE PROMOTION OF THE FINE ARTS, 1848

No.	*Subject*
209	Cantley Beck, near Ketteringham.
317	The beech forest, in autumn.
370	A sketch from Nature, in Kent.
376	A sketch from Nature, in Kent.

SECOND EXHIBITION OF THE NORFOLK AND NORWICH ASSOCIATION FOR THE PROMOTION OF THE FINE ARTS, 1849

No.	*Subject*
66	A sketch from Nature.
83	The Grove at Gunton (painted on the spot).
307	The saw mills in Gunton Park, Norfolk.

THIRD EXHIBITION OF THE NORFOLK AND NORWICH ASSOCIATION FOR THE PROMOTION OF THE FINE ARTS, 1852

No.	*Subject*
124	Near Sheringham, Norfolk.
152	Sketch at Linton, North Devon.

FOURTH EXHIBITION OF THE NORFOLK AND NORWICH ASSOCIATION FOR THE PROMOTION OF THE FINE ARTS, 1853

No.	*Subject*
66	At Weybourne (a sketch in oils).

EXHIBITION OF THE NORFOLK AND NORWICH ASSOCIATION FOR THE PROMOTION OF THE FINE ARTS, 1855

No.	*Subject*
102	Sunshine and shade.

EXHIBITION OF THE NORFOLK AND NORWICH FINE ARTS' ASSOCIATION AND OF THE PHOTOGRAPHIC SOCIETY, 1856

No.	*Subject*	*Lent by*
237	Scene in Devonshire.	Mr. Rossi.

NORFOLK AND NORWICH FINE ARTS ASSOCIATION
Exhibition of the Works of Deceased Local Artists, 1860

No.	*Subject*	*Lent by*
12	Beech trees, Buckhurst Park.	Mr. Dixon.
41	Scene in Kimberley Park.	Rev. J. H. Steward.
42	Scene in Gunton Park.	Mr. J. Barwell.
84	Fishing scene.	Mr. Rossi.
85	Sketch in Isle of Arran.	Mr. Norgate.
88	Wayborne Overlook.	Mrs. Middleton.
98	Cantley Beck, near Ketteringham.	Mr. J. J. Colman.
110	Woods in autumn.	Mr. Mott.
112	The beech forest.	Mr. P. Back.
113	The rustic bridge.	Mr. P. Back.
146	Sunshine and shade.	Mrs. Middleton.
180	Weyborn Wood (painted on the spot).	Mrs. Middleton.
199	Hatfield Park (studied on the spot).	Mr. J. Barwell.
221	A fine day in February.	Rev. S. Titlow.
224	Lane scenery.	Mr. A. A. H. Beckwith.
283	Scene in Isle of Arran (water-colour) (sketch for the picture in oils).	Mr. Norgate.
308	Waterfall (water-colour).	Mr. G. Middleton.
315	Beach scene (water-colour).	Mr. G. Middleton.

NORWICH AND EASTERN COUNTIES WORKING CLASSES INDUSTRIAL EXHIBITION, 1867

No.	*Subject*	*Lent by*
852	View in Hatfield Park.	J. Barwell, Esq., Surrey Street.
853	View in Gunton Park.	J. Barwell, Esq., Surrey Street.

BRITISH MEDICAL ASSOCIATION LOAN COLLECTION
of the Works of Norfolk and Suffolk Artists, 1874

No.	*Subject*	*Lent by*
31	Weybourne, looking towards the Beeston Hills.	Mr. T. H. Edwards.
57	Gunton Park.	Mr. J. Barwell.
64	Devonshire.	Mr. F. E. Watson.
66	An oast house in Kent (figures by Boddington).	Mr. G. H. Christie.
68	Beeches.	Mr. G. H. Christie.
70	Grove scene in Gunton Park.	Mr. J. Everett.
163	"Down the stony vale I wind."	Mr. P. E. Hansell.

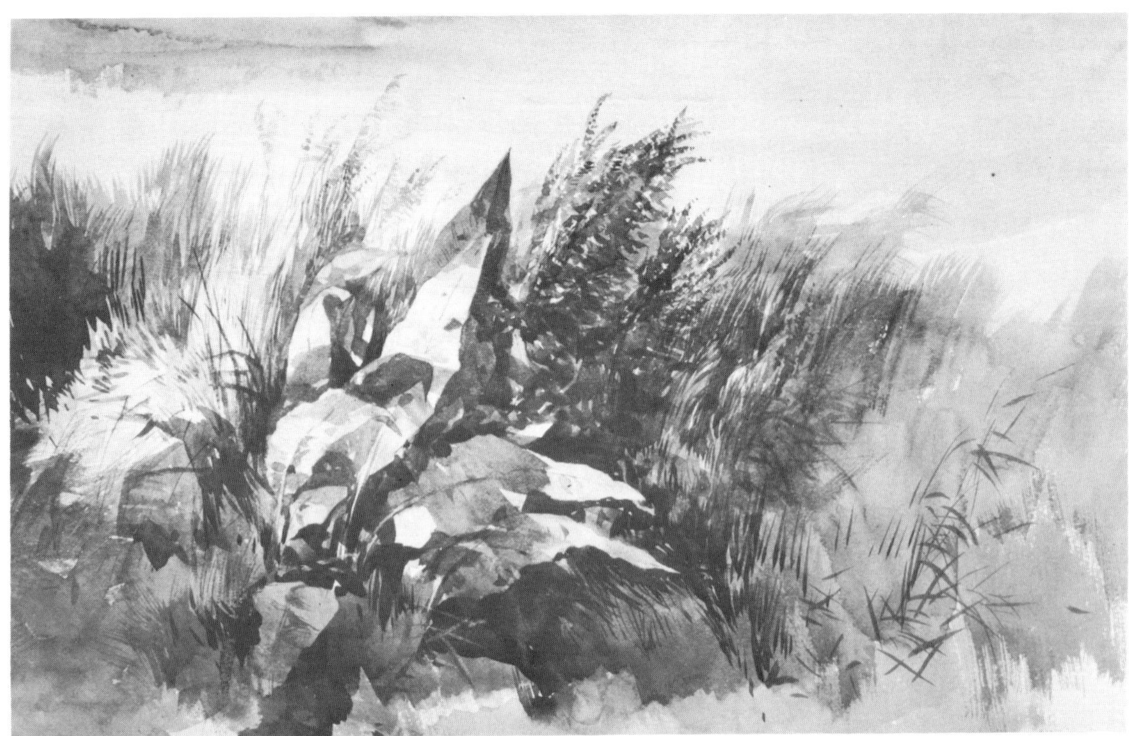

John Middleton *Dock Leaves* *Water-colour* $8\frac{3}{4} \times 13\frac{1}{2}$ *in.*

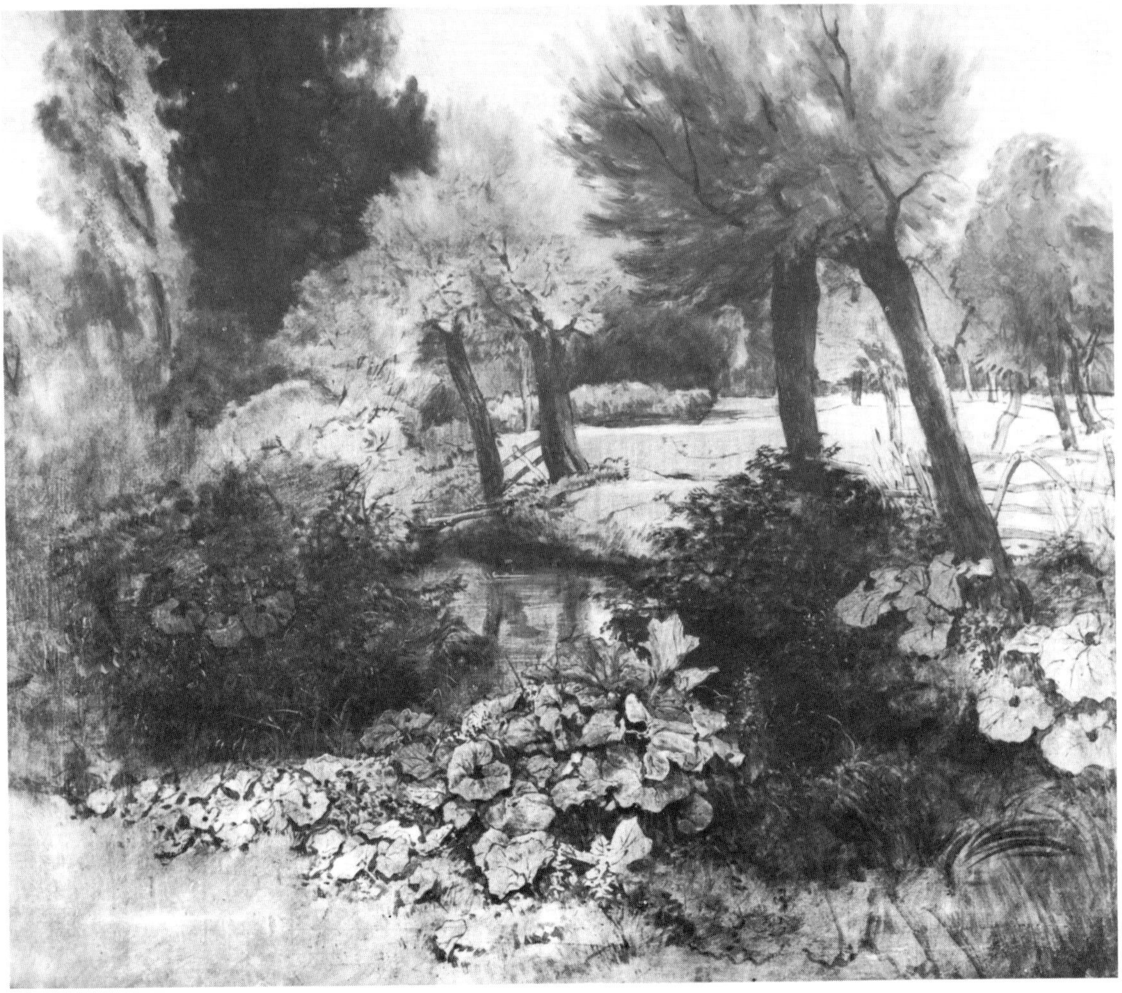

John Middleton *Landscape with Pollards* *Oil on canvas* $20\frac{1}{4} \times 24\frac{1}{4}$ *in.*

NORWICH ART LOAN EXHIBITION
in aid of the Fund for the Restoration of the Church of Saint Peter Mancroft, 1878

No.	*Subject*	*Lent by*
50	Hatfield Park.	Philip Back, Esq.
73	Hatfield Park—beech forest.	Philip Back, Esq.
118	Oast house in Kent (figures by Boddington).	G. H. Christie, Esq.
120	A beech wood.	G. H. Christie, Esq.
155	View near Tunbridge Wells.	Philip Back, Esq.
297	View of Weybourne.	Thomas Edwards, Esq.
432	View on the Llyn.	F. T. Keith, Esq.
437	River scene, Devonshire.	J. B. Morgan, Esq.
444	View near Tunbridge Wells.	Miss Bignold.

SWAFFHAM FINE ART EXHIBITION, 1882

No.	*Subject*	*Lent by*
289	Japanese lily.	Miss M. B. Marriott.

FINE ART EXHIBITION
in aid of the new Norfolk and Norwich Hospital, 1883

No.	*Subject*	*Lent by*
95	Hatfield.	Mr. H. G. Barwell.
109	Oasthouse, Kent.	Mr. George H. Christie.
121	Landscape.	Mr. George H. Christie.
129	Gunton Park.	Mr. H. G. Barwell.
20	Ivy Bridge, North Devon.	Mr. J. J. Colman, M.P.
23	Cantley Beck.	Mr. J. J. Colman, M.P.
34	March day, near Hellesdon Mills.	Mr. J. J. Colman, M.P.
40	Landscape.	Mr. J. J. Colman, M.P.

ART LOAN EXHIBITION
in aid of the Fund for the Restoration of St. Peter Mancroft Church, 1885

No.	*Subject*	*Lent by*
71	Weybourne.	Clare Sewell Read, Esq., M.P.
98	A fine day in February.	J. J. Colman, Esq., M.P.
103	Landscape.	F. E. Watson, Esq.
313	Landscape with trees.	F. T. Keith, Esq.
365	Sketch of a gateway.	Edward Preston Willins, Esq.

LOAN COLLECTION OF DRAWINGS IN THE NEW PICTURE GALLERY
in the Norwich Castle Museum, 1903

No.	*Subject*	*Lent by*
104	Near Norwich. River in foreground. Group of trees in centre.	Mr. James Reeve.

ROYAL ACADEMY EXHIBITS

Year	Subject
1847	Autumn.
	"But see the fading, many coloured wood."
	The field-barn.
1848	The beech forest—evening.
1849	Avenue of limes at Hatfield.
1850	Clearing the wood—early spring.
1851	Clovelly, on the coast of Devonshire.
	A fine day in February.
1852	The stream in June.
	A study in March on the Norfolk coast.
1853	Felled timber—early spring.
1854	A stream in Arran.
	In the Isle of Arran, looking over the Firth of the Clyde.
1855	Looking down the stream.

BRITISH INSTITUTION

Year	Subject	£	s.	d.
1847	Scene in North Wales. 25 × 32 in.	—		
1848	Scene near Tunbridge Wells, Kent. 23 × 32 in.	—		
1849	The village common. 32 × 46 in.	—		
	The roadside barn. 19 × 27 in.	—		
1850	The greenwood glade. 33 × 38 in.	—		
	The woods in autumn. 39 × 57 in.	—		
1852	A fine day in February. 13 × 17 in.	—		
	Weybourne, on the Norfolk coast. 34 × 49 in.	—		
	Summer—a study from Nature. 30 × 41 in.	—		
1853	A tributary of the Lynn.	25	0	0
	Sand hills on the Norfolk coast.	10	0	0
1854	The woods in autumn.	10	0	0
	Glensheraig, Isle of Arran.	50	0	0
1855	Sunshine and shade.	30	0	0

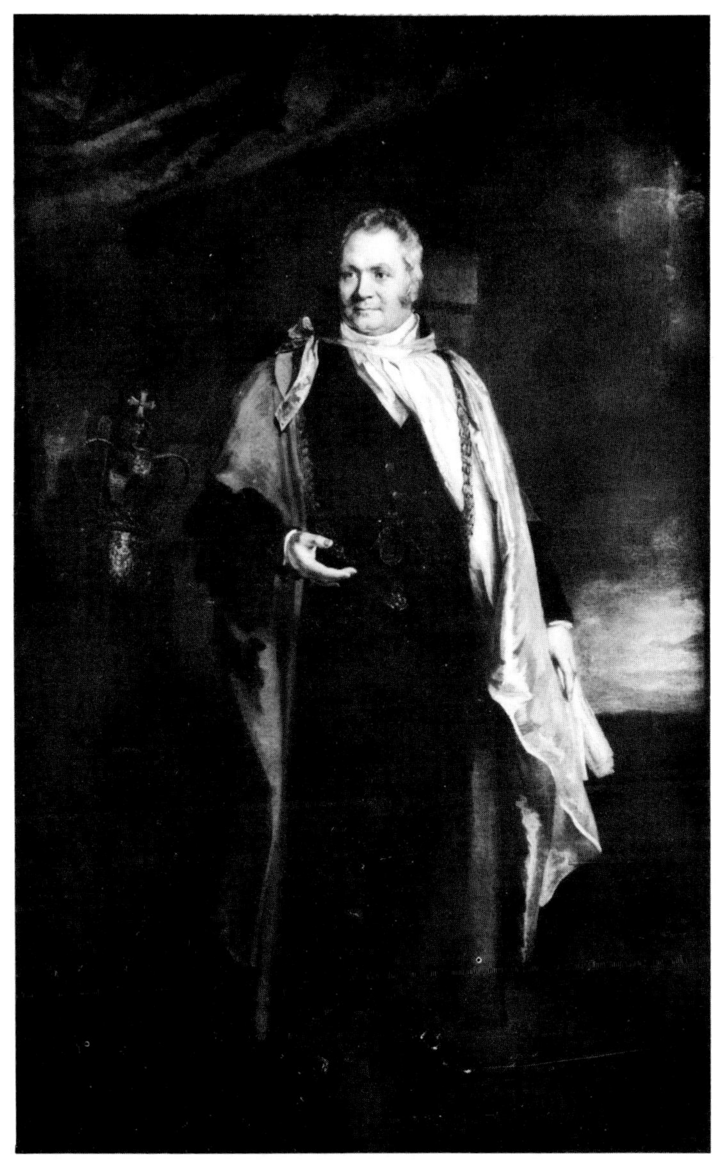

Portrait of Crisp Brown
by
Joseph Clover

JOSEPH CLOVER

(1779-1853)

1779 Joseph Clover was born in Aylsham, Norfolk, in 1779. He was the grandson of Joseph Clover 1725-1811, said to be the father of Veterinary Art.

Our Joseph Clover was interested first in engraving but whilst watching Opie painting a portrait of his uncle he resolved to become a painter. He actually studied with Opie in London over a period of four years, commencing in 1807. He actually assisted Opie in the painting of his portraits.

1809 By the year 1809 Clover was sufficiently established as a portrait painter to be commissioned to paint the Mayor of Norwich, now hanging in St. Andrew's Hall, together with several others of his civic portraits. Thus he became one of the major portrait painters in Norwich. His portraits of James Stark and George Vincent can be seen in the Sexton Room in the Assembly House, Norwich.

1816 In 1816, after the defeat of Napoleon, Joseph Clover visited Paris, probably on the recommendation of John Crome.

1828 During the years of the decline of the Norwich Society, 1828-1831, he contributed to the
1831 funds, which reflects well on his ability to earn a substantial income from his work.

1828 He seemed to spend his time between London and Norwich with the occasional tour. In 1828 he made a tour of Wales and left on record numerous water-colours, including a view of Kidwelly Castle.

Little is known of Clover's later years, but he probably lived in London most of the
1853 time. However, his death was reported there on 28th April, 1853.

THE PAINTINGS

Joseph Clover was primarily a portrait painter. He tends to use his paint quite freely and is not afraid of the use of colour. In his small lively sketches he sometimes leaves the ground paint for effect. He has a predeliction for the use of red. In his oil landscapes his approach is that of a sketcher, with a Constable-like touch he uses strong colour, sometimes painting on a warm ground. The water-colour landscapes, of which there are numerous examples in the Norwich Castle Museum, are at times painted with remarkable mastery. His use of the white of the paper for high lighting being one of his characteristics. His signature sometimes appears on the reverse of his water-colours.

NINTH EXHIBITION OF THE NORWICH SOCIETY OF ARTISTS, 1813

No.	*Subject*
55	Portrait of Mr. Thomas Mickelburgh, merchant, who has most respectably filled the chair in the Farmers' Club, Cromer, for thirty years, and for whom this portrait is painted.

ELEVENTH EXHIBITION OF THE NORWICH SOCIETY OF ARTISTS, 1815

No.	*Subject*
60	A girl sewing.
94	Return from market.

TWELFTH EXHIBITION OF THE NORFOLK AND NORWICH SOCIETY OF ARTISTS, 1816

No.	*Subject*
23	Child washing its feet at a brook.
98	Girl's head.
121	A lady presenting to a cottager an edition of the Sacred Scriptures, given by the Bible Society.
128	Portraits of the Rev. Pendlebury Houghton and his daughter.
146	A lady drawing flowers.

TWELFTH EXHIBITION OF THE NORWICH SOCIETY OF ARTISTS, 1816

No.	*Subject*
7	Portrait of the late Mr. Frewer.
34	View in Pagwell Bay, near Ramsgate—fishermen returning from shrimping.
113	Portrait of the late Mrs. Frewer.

THIRTEENTH EXHIBITION OF THE NORFOLK AND NORWICH SOCIETY OF ARTISTS, 1817

No.	*Subject*
10	Boy with a starfish.
29	Portrait of James Meredith, Esq.
89	Portrait of the Rev. C. Townley, LL.D.
98	Portrait of General Cookson.
109	Portrait of a lady.

THIRTEENTH EXHIBITION OF THE NORWICH SOCIETY OF ARTISTS, 1817

No.	*Subject*
21	Charity (unfinished). "For I was hungry and ye gave me meat; I was thirsty and ye gave me drink; I was a stranger and ye took me in."—St. Matthew, XXV, 35.
41	Portrait of a lady.
53	Portrait of Mr. Schofield.
54	Charity. "I was sick, and ye visited me."—St. Matthew, XXV, 36.

FOURTEENTH EXHIBITION OF THE NORWICH SOCIETY OF ARTISTS, 1818

No.	*Subject*
82	Portrait of J. Stark, Esq. (landscape by J. Stark).

FIFTEENTH EXHIBITION OF THE NORWICH SOCIETY OF ARTISTS, 1819

No.	*Subject*
27	Portrait of E. Rigby, M.D., F.L.S., F.H.S.
50	Portrait of Mr. Priest.
53	Portrait of B. Leman, Esq., Mayor of Norwich 1819, painted in his second Mayoralty, to be placed in the Hall of St. Andrew's, Norwich.
159	Portrait of Osborne Butcher, Esq.

SIXTEENTH EXHIBITION OF THE NORWICH SOCIETY OF ARTISTS, 1820

No.	*Subject*
30	Portrait of a gentleman.
48	Portrait of an officer.
51	Portrait of a lady.

EIGHTEENTH EXHIBITION OF THE NORWICH SOCIETY OF ARTISTS, 1822

No.	*Subject*
50	Portrait of a gentleman.
76	Portrait of C. Brown, Esq.

NINETEENTH EXHIBITION OF THE NORWICH SOCIETY OF ARTISTS, 1823

No.	*Subject*
59	Portrait of a gentleman.
69	Portrait of a lady.
104	Divided attention.

TWENTY-FIRST EXHIBITION OF THE NORWICH SOCIETY OF ARTISTS, 1825

No.	*Subject*
161	The truant discovered—scene on banks of Loch Lomond, in Highlands of Scotland.

TWENTY-SECOND EXHIBITION OF THE NORFOLK AND SUFFOLK INSTITUTION FOR THE PROMOTION OF THE FINE ARTS, 1828

No.	*Subject*
4	Portrait of Charles Augustus Tulk, Esq., late M.P. for Sudbury.
22	Portrait of the Rev. P. Candler.
32	Portrait of Mrs. Candler.
134	Portrait of Mrs. E. Smyth.

TWENTY-FOURTH EXHIBITION OF THE NORFOLK AND SUFFOLK INSTITUTION FOR THE PROMOTION OF THE FINE ARTS, 1830

No.	*Subject*
99	Portrait of the son of Onley Onley, Esq.
100	Portrait of James Gay, Esq.
110	Portrait of Omer Effendi, Private Secretary to the Pacha of Egypt.
136	Portrait of Mrs. Gay.

TWENTY-SIXTH EXHIBITION OF THE NORFOLK AND SUFFOLK INSTITUTION FOR THE PROMOTION OF THE FINE ARTS, 1832

No.	*Subject*
78	The novel.
79	The sketch book.
137	Portrait of Mrs. Blofield.
141	Portrait of G. Cubitt, Esq.

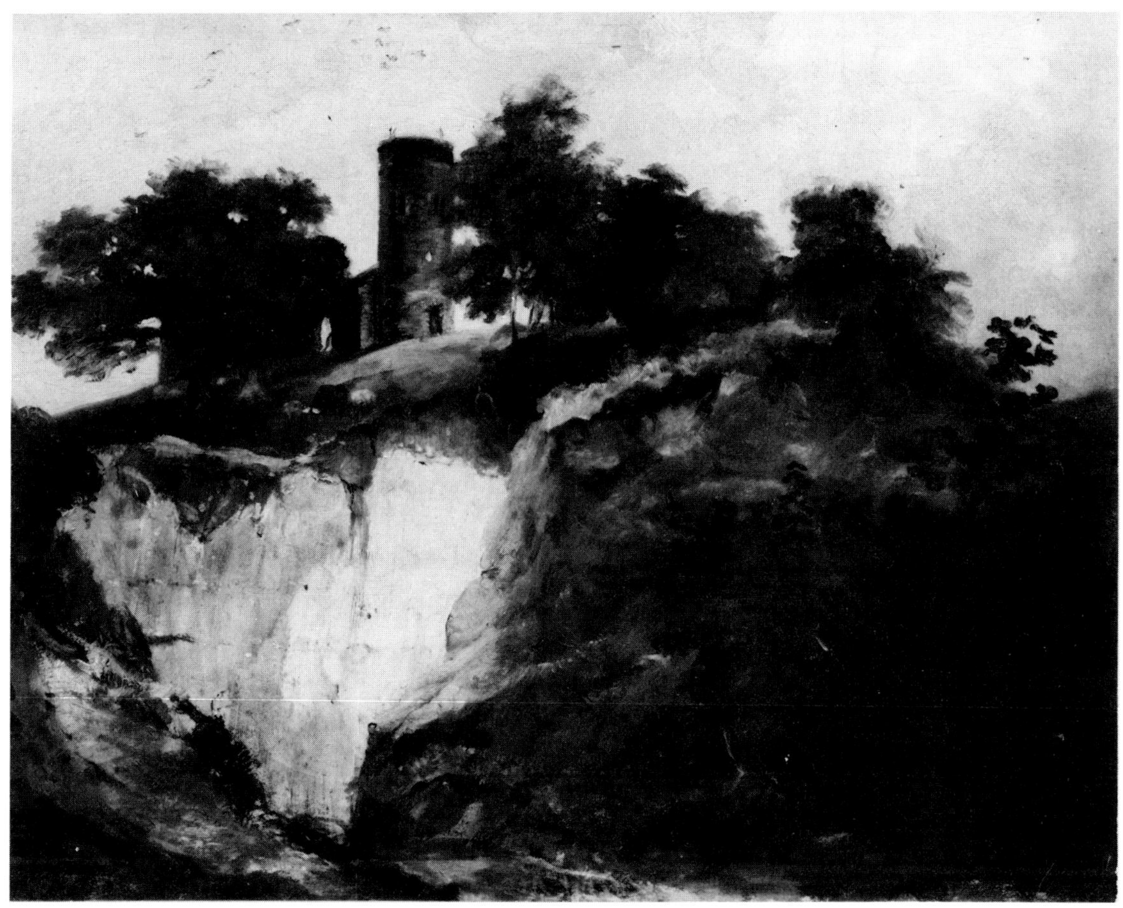

Joseph Clover *Whitlingham Church, 21st September, 1822* *On board* $10\frac{1}{2} \times 13\frac{1}{2}$ *in.*

NORWICH POLYTECHNIC EXHIBITION, 1840

No.	*Subject*	*Lent by*
232	Female on the beach.	Mrs. Thirtle.

NORFOLK AND NORWICH FINE ARTS ASSOCIATION
Exhibition of the Works of Deceased Local Artists, 1860

No.	*Subject*	*Lent by*
17	Portraits.	Mr. F. Noverre.
18	Portrait of the late James Stark.	Mrs. Bolingbroke.
45	Portrait of a dog.	Mr. J. S. Muskett.
90	Portrait.	Mr. F. Noverre.
103	Portrait of Glover, the Vetenarian.	Mr. Wells.
105	An old lady.	Mr. R. B. Scott.
114	The slipper.	Mr. G. Etheridge.
116	Portrait of the late Mrs. Cubitt.	Mr. W. J. Cubitt.
118	Divided attention.	Mr. C. Turner.
142	Crossing the brook.	Mrs. Thirtle.
178	A lady.	Mrs. Thirtle.

NORWICH AND EASTERN COUNTIES WORKING CLASSES INDUSTRIAL EXHIBITION, 1867

No.	*Subject*	*Lent by*
818	Lady Beechey on the sands at Cromer.	Mr. Boswell, Exchange Street, Norwich.

BRITISH MEDICAL ASSOCIATION LOAN COLLECTION
of the Works of Norfolk and Suffolk Artists, 1874

No.	*Subject*	*Lent by*
16	Portrait of an old lady.	Mr. H. G. Barwell.
43	Portrait of Mr. Back.	Mr. Henry Back.
244	Portrait of the Rev. Bransby Francis.	Mr. W. B. Francis.

ART LOAN EXHIBITION
in aid of the fund for the Restoration of the Church of Saint Peter Mancroft, 1878

No.	*Subject*	*Lent by*
87	Divided attention.	Rev. Charles Turner.
269	Portrait of Alderman John Browne, Norwich.	His grandson, J. H. Browne, Esq.

FINE ART EXHIBITION
in aid of the new Norfolk and Norwich Hospital, 1883

No.	*Subject*	*Lent by*
2	Portrait of Robert Priest, Chemist, with Indenture and Card of Invitation from Holkham, 1788. (Probably the father of Alfred Priest, the Norwich painter)	Mr. Thomas Priest.

ART LOAN EXHIBITION
in aid of the fund for the Restoration of St. Peter Mancroft Church, 1885

No.	*Subject*	*Lent by*
48	Portrait of Vincent (background by Vincent).	J. J. Colman, Esq., M.P.

NORWICH SCHOOL EXHIBITION, 1927

No.	*Subject*	*Lent by*
8	Portrait of Clover's great-grandmother, Mrs. Withington. $16\frac{1}{4} \times 12\frac{1}{4}$ in.	Miss A. M. Geldart.
9	Portrait of Dr. Edward Rigby. $35\frac{1}{4} \times 27\frac{1}{2}$ in.	Norfolk & Norwich Hospital.

ROBERT LEMAN

(1799-1863)

1799 Robert Leman was born in 1799 and judging by his portrait comes down to us as being a man of firm decision and integrity. Presumably both these characteristics would be necessary to fulfil his role in life as the managing clerk to the Norwich Union Fire Office.

We have glimpses of him sketching with Lound and winning a prize at the Art Union. Like Lound, he was essentially an amateur of great merit who also collected paintings.

In the British Museum is a letter to Mr. James Reeve, Curator of the Norwich Museum at the time:

> Dear Sir,
>
> I send by the bearer my servant the piece of crystalized iron as a specimen for your museum. She is accompanied by my two little nieces. I would be glad if you would show them the museum and contents.
>
> I am dear Sir,
>
> Yours truly,
>
> R. Leman.

This short letter, much to the point, illustrates how the people interested in the Norwich Castle Museum have, over the years, given their full support.

Robert Leman was one of the younger members of the Norwich Society, and in league with David Hodgson formed the Norwich Amateur Club for practise in sketching. He became Honorary Secretary of the Norfolk and
1839 Norwich Art Union in 1839.

We hear little of Leman again until the report which appeared in the *Norwich Mercury*, 21st
1863 March, 1863. "On the 18th inst., at his residence, Newmarket Road, Mr. Robert Leman, aged 64, passed away."

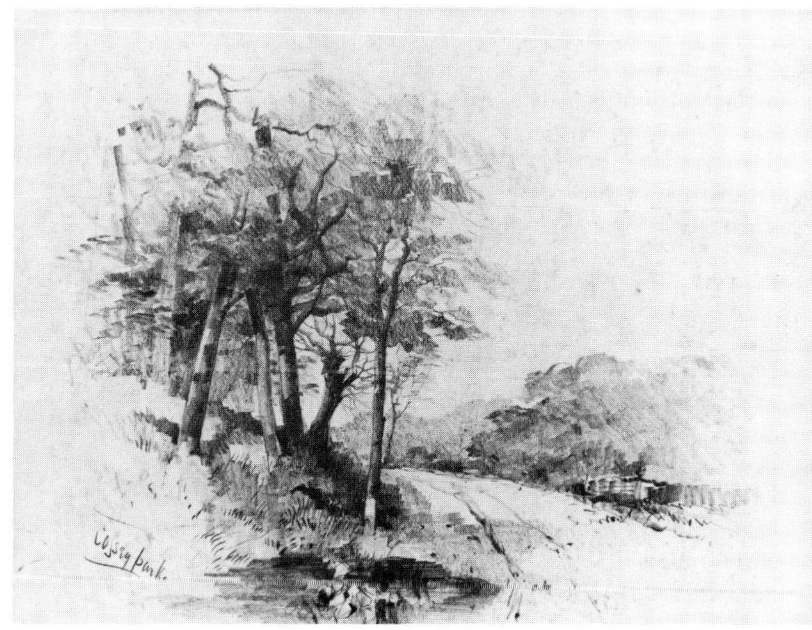

Robert Leman *Cossey Park* *Pencil* $11\frac{1}{8} \times 15\frac{1}{4}$ *in.*

THE PAINTINGS

The writer is conversant only with his pencil and water-colours. The fact that Leman was strongly influenced by Henry Bright is indisputable, and in a more minor way by John Sell Cotman. Bright's water-colours may be said to be more controlled. Perhaps Leman's most noticeable hallmark is his fondness for blues.

No.	*Subject*	*Lent by*
194	Four water-colour sketches.	Trustees of the British Museum.
195	The shepherd on the heath.	The Misses Cotman.
196	Mountain scene. $12\frac{1}{2} \times 19\frac{1}{4}$ in.	
197	On the Greta, Yorkshire. $12 \times 18\frac{1}{2}$ in.	
198	Back of Pull's Ferry, Norwich. $9\frac{1}{4} \times 12\frac{3}{4}$ in.	
199	Bromholm Bacton. $9\frac{1}{4} \times 12\frac{3}{4}$ in.	R. J. Cotman.
200	Gorleston. $9\frac{1}{4} \times 13$ in.	A. G. Howlett.
201	Landscape with figures. $12\frac{1}{4} \times 9$ in.	
202	Landscape with figures. $12\frac{1}{4} \times 9$ in.	
203	Seascape (sepia). $9\frac{1}{4} \times 13$ in.	
204	Marshland scene (sepia). $7\frac{1}{2} \times 11$ in.	
205	Landing the catch (sepia). $8\frac{3}{4} \times 12$ in.	Dr. Colvin B. M. Smith.
206	Landscape. $12 \times 9\frac{1}{4}$ in.	Mr. E. B. Southwell.

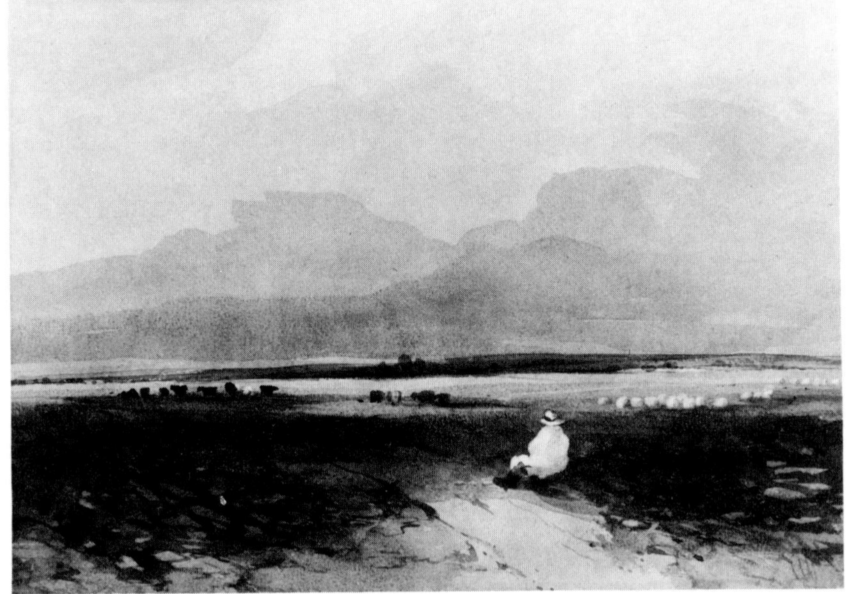

Robert Leman *Heath scene* *Water-colour* $7 \times 10\frac{1}{4}$ *in.*

ANTHONY SANDYS

(1806-1883)

1806 Anthony Sandys was born in the year 1806 possibly of Italian parentage. His family may have been of some distinction as a gold seal was found amongst his effects when he died. Little is known of his very early life apart from the fact that he is said to have worked as a dyer at Stark & Mills. It is quite possible that he met James Stark (whose father was a dyer) and became determined to make his way as an artist. The aspect of art he chose
1830 was portraiture. By 1830 we find him exhibiting a portrait at the Norfolk and Suffolk Institute.

1832 Evidently he was married by 1832 for we know that his brilliant artist son, Antonio Frederick Augustus Sandys, was born in this year.

1849 He continued to exhibit portraits until 1849 when he introduced a new branch of Art—"A
1852 Study of Wild Duck" and "A Sketch of Fruit and Flowers". Then in 1852 we find him turning to landscape painting, resulting in *A Sketch at Colney* and *A Sketch at Lakenham.* It was probably his interest in landscape that prompted him to make a tour of the Lake
1858 District in 1858. He sketched at Sorodore Grange, Lodore, Windermere and Skiddaw. Included in a group of drawings executed about this time, is a self-portrait sketched first thing in the morning!

1859 In 1859 he was living at 9 St. Giles Hill, Norwich. From here he despatched for exhibition at the British Institute No. 116, *A Quiet half-hour with the time.*

1862 By 1862 he again developed itching feet and took off for a tour of Derbyshire. He was at Peveril of the Peak on 1st September, 1862, Cave Dale later in the month, and then with a burst of effort he arrived at Ben Nevis by 10th September 1862. Following this he visited Fort William and many other places in Scotland. All his drawings are carefully signed with monogram and inscribed.

Anthony Sandys had at least two children, Antonio Frederick Augustus and Emma Sandys, both of whom became portrait painters.

Anthony was also something of a collector, for he bought several lots at J. B. Crome's sale and had in his collection works by many of the Norwich School Painters. It is recorded that he was working on the restoration of a painting attributed to Titian at the
1883 time of his death in 1883.

THE PAINTINGS

Anthony Sandys' landscape paintings, probably because of his original palette, have not received a lot of notice. He does, however, have a fine sense of composition and his drawing has a sureness about it found with the great Masters. He loves to produce the feeling of late evening with the last rays of the sun catching the side of a windmill or illuminating a nearby path. His skies are usually a warm purply red with touches of Naples Yellow. His mid-day scenes are more rare, but he has a predeliction for duck-egg blue and scattered clouds, which sometimes appear open-ended. He sometimes introduces a purple effect. A favourite motive is animals standing in water, giving warm reflections for the foreground of the picture. His works have an affinity with those of Thomas Lound, but Lound uses much more paint.

---

*Whilst Frederick Sandys was born in Norwich he is not usually associated with the Norwich School of Painters, largely due to his domicile being in London and his style of painting being related to the Pre-Raphaelite group.

A portrait of Frederick Sandys is in the National Portrait Gallery.

Sandys' drawings are very controlled, but not stiff, he has on occasion the ability to delineate with the minimum of effort. Another time he can meticulously draw every stone in a bridge—to great effect I may add. As a portraitist he probably regarded his subject seriously and produced a portrait that was more honest than appealing. Had he specialised in landscape from the beginning posterity would have been much the richer.

EXHIBITS AT BRITISH INSTITUTE

Year	*No.*	*Subject*
1859	116	A quiet half-hour with the time.

TWENTY-FOURTH EXHIBITION OF THE WORKS OF THE NORFOLK AND SUFFOLK INSTITUTION FOR THE PROMOTION OF THE FINE ARTS, 1830

No.	*Subject*
115	Portrait of an old lady.

TWENTY-FIFTH EXHIBITION OF THE WORKS OF THE NORFOLK AND SUFFOLK INSTITUTION FOR THE PROMOTION OF THE FINE ARTS, 1831

No.	*Subject*
87	Portrait of a gentleman.
99	Portrait of a lady.

TWENTY-SIXTH EXHIBITION OF THE WORKS OF THE NORFOLK AND SUFFOLK INSTITUTION FOR THE PROMOTION OF THE FINE ARTS, 1832

No.	*Subject*
161	Portrait of a lady.

TWENTY-SEVENTH EXHIBITION OF THE WORKS OF THE NORFOLK AND SUFFOLK INSTITUTION FOR THE PROMOTION OF THE FINE ARTS, 1833

No.	*Subject*
94	Portrait of a lady.

THE FIRST EXHIBITION OF THE NORFOLK AND NORWICH ART-UNION, 1839

No.	*Subject*
62	Portrait of Mr. Paraman.
102	Sketch of a lady.
114	Portrait of a gentleman.
120	Hearing the task.
134	Portrait of a boy.
170	Portrait of a lady.
278	Minerva, drawn from the cast (A. F. A. Sandys). (In pencil in the margin is written "Exhibited by his father A.S. See list of exhibitors". In the list of exhibitors 278 is listed under Anthony and under him is A. F. A. Sandys (aged 10) Norwich, and written in pencil next to this is "278—Antonio Frederic Augustus in Register St. Stephen's Ch.")

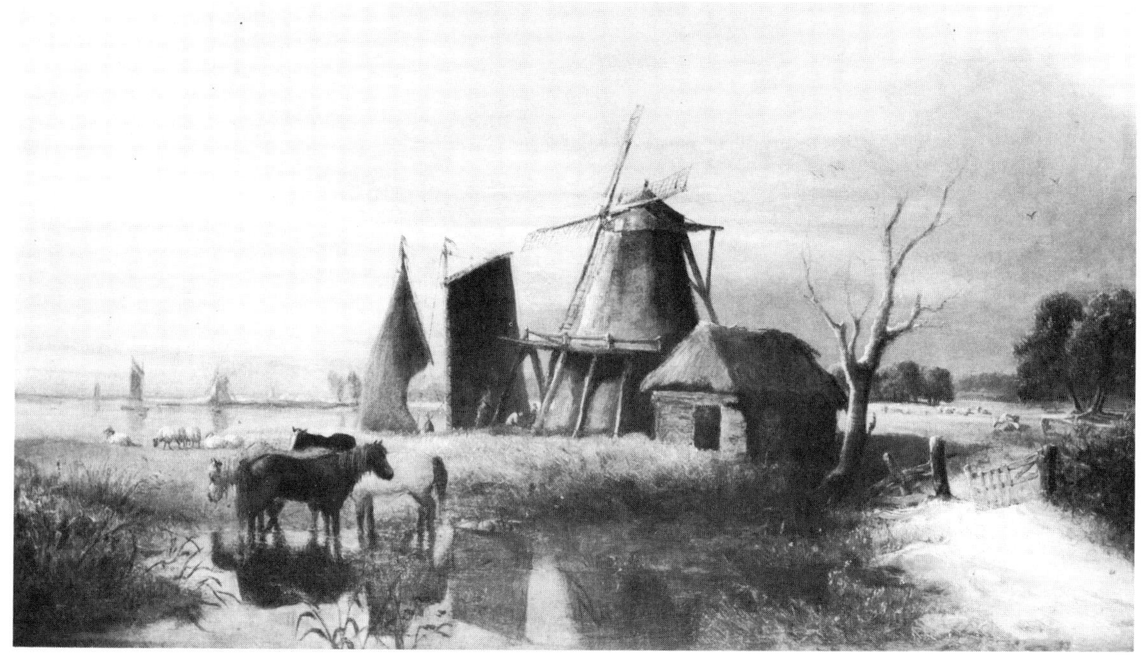

Anthony Sandys *Norfolk Windmills* *Oil on canvas* $14\frac{1}{2} \times 24\frac{1}{2}$ *in.*

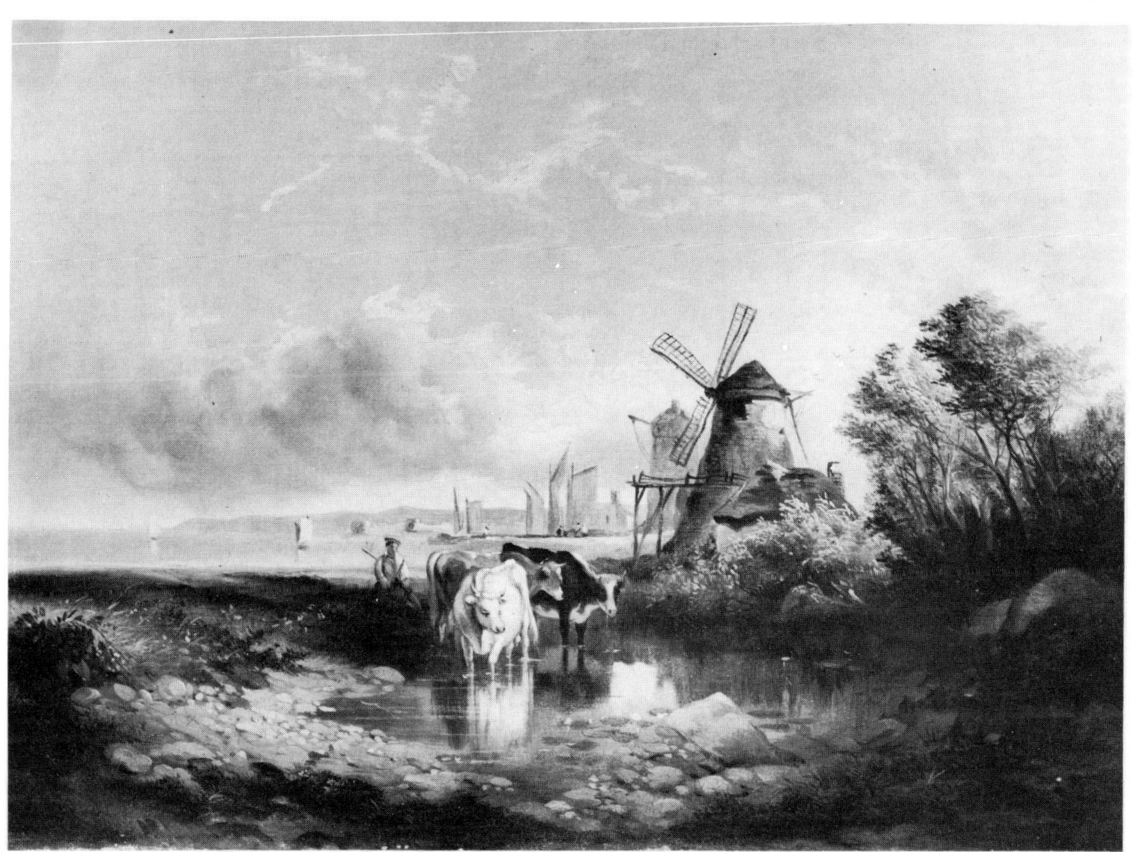

Anthony Sandys *On the Norfolk Coast* *Oil on canvas* 13×19 *in.*

NORWICH POLYTECHNIC EXHIBITION, 1840

No.	*Subject*	*Lent by*
4	Portrait.	The Artist.
5	Portrait of a lady.	The Artist.

THE FIRST EXHIBITION OF THE EAST OF ENGLAND ART UNION, 1842

No.	*Subject*
156	The disappointed.

THE FIRST EXHIBITION OF THE NORFOLK AND NORWICH ASSOCIATION FOR THE PROMOTION OF THE FINE ARTS, 1848

No.	*Subject*
30	Portrait.

SECOND EXHIBITION OF THE NORFOLK AND NORWICH ASSOCIATION FOR THE PROMOTION OF THE FINE ARTS, 1849

No.	*Subject*
6	A portrait.
59	A portrait.
169	A study of wild ducks.
250	A sketch of fruit and flowers.

THIRD EXHIBITION OF THE NORFOLK AND NORWICH ASSOCIATION FOR THE PROMOTION OF THE FINE ARTS, 1852

No.	*Subject*
34	Portrait.
113	A sketch at Colney.
122	A sketch at Lakenham.

EXHIBITION OF THE NORFOLK AND NORWICH ASSOCIATION FOR THE PROMOTION OF THE FINE ARTS, 1855

No.	*Subject*	£	s.	d.
1	A portrait.		—	
93	A lane scene near Norwich.	6	0	0
132	Study of a head.		—	

NORFOLK AND NORWICH FINE ARTS ASSOCIATION
Exhibition of the Works of Modern Artists, 1860

No.	*Subject*	£	s.	d.
79	A scene on the Norwich River.	6	0	0
80	A sketch at Trowse.	4	0	0
93	A portrait.		—	
130	Scene on the Back River.	5	0	0
182	Portrait.		—	

IDENTIFIED PICTURES AT THE SALE OF THE ARTIST'S EFFECTS
on 16th October, 1883, at Norwich

No.	*Subject*
22	Two original drawings for *Norfolk Portraits*.
53	Oil sketches. Portrait of Sandys and two others.
106	Oil painting, framed. Portrait of Inigo Jones.
107	,, ,, ,, ,, ,, A. Sandys.
110	,, ,, ,, ,, ,, C. Hall.
111	,, ,, ,, ,, ,, Austin Piper, painted in 1854.
112	,, ,, ,, ,, ,, Captain H. Roberts, painted in 1860.
113	,, ,, ,, Three heads in one picture—portraits of the artist.
114	,, ,, ,, Portrait of the artist, after Gainsborough.
127	,, ,, ,, ,, ,, a lady.
129	,, ,, ,, Two flower pieces.
130	,, ,, ,, The twin sisters.
131	,, ,, ,, Landscape, Mousehold.
131A	,, ,, ,, ,, Thorpe.
132	,, ,, ,, Portrait of Carlyle.
133	,, ,, ,, Whitlingham Lane.
134	,, ,, unframed. ,, ,,
135	,, ,, ,, Hayfield.
136	,, ,, framed. Road scene, with pollard oak.
137	,, ,, ,, Trowse Eye.
138	,, ,, unframed. Coldham Hall.
139	,, ,, ,, Meditation and small landscape.
140	,, ,, ,, Landscape with windmills.
141	,, ,, ,, Still life.
143E	,, ,, framed. Alder Car.
144	,, ,, unframed. Portrait of the artist.
146	,, ,, ,, ,, ,, ,, ,, (unfinished).
150	,, ,, ,, Italian landscape.
155	,, ,, ,, Landscape, Thorpe.

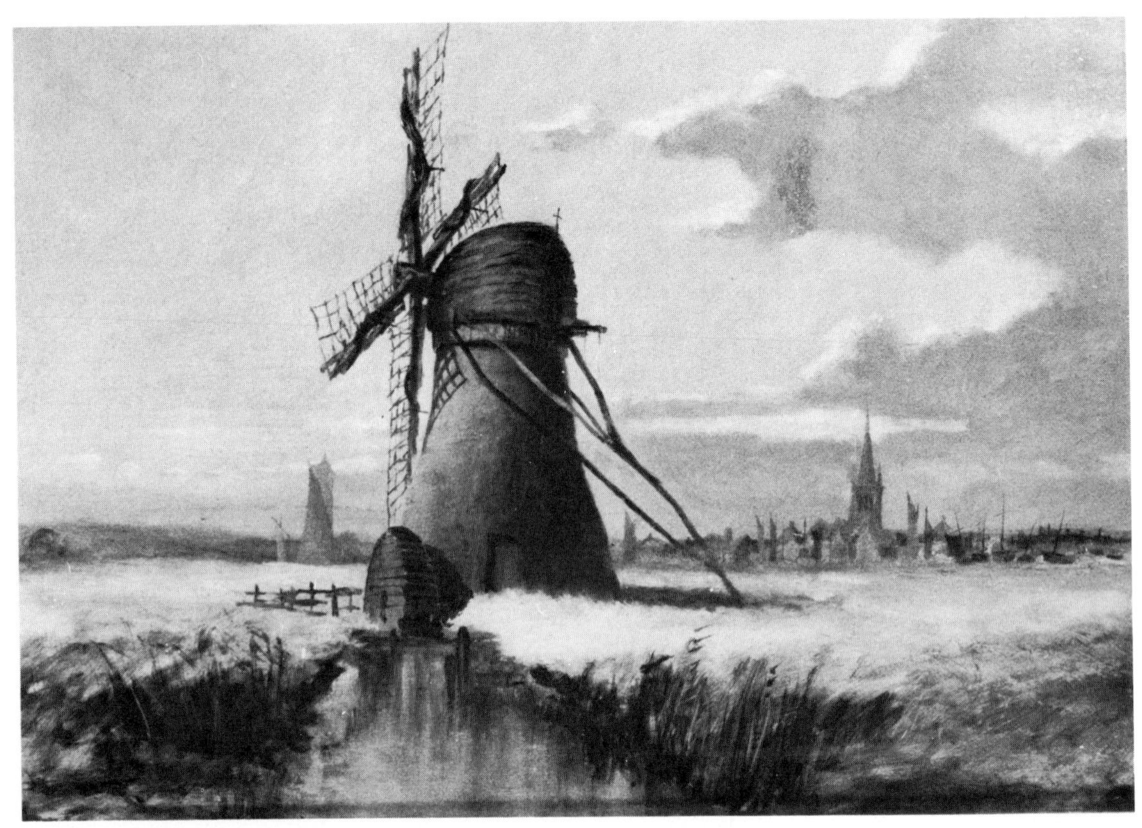

Anthony Sandys *Oil on board*
15×11 *in.*

(*Note the open-ended cloud form*)

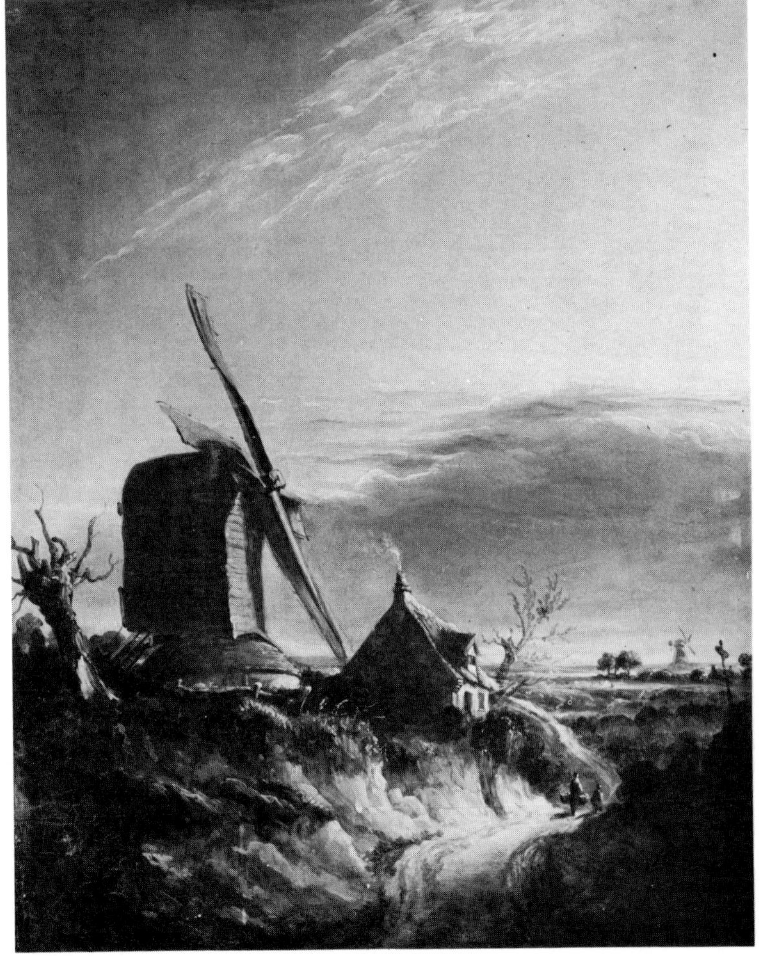

Anthony Sandys *Oil*

ROBERT DIXON

(1780-1815)

Along with Joseph Stannard, George Vincent and John Middleton, Robert Dixon
1780 died young. Born in 1780, at an early age he became interested in drawing.

After going through the course of studies at the Royal Academy School, London, he
1800 settled in Norwich as scene painter to the theatre about the year 1800.

To the first Norwich Society Exhibition in 1805 he contributed sixteen studies. He
1809 continued to support the Society until the year 1809 when he was elected Vice-President
to Robert Ladbrooke. It is not known if he had disagreements with the President, but
the year 1810 was the last year he exhibited with the Society. Possibly his activities as
drawing master and scene painter fully occupied his time.

1810- In 1810-11 he published his Norfolk Scenery, containing thirty-eight folio plates of soft
1811 ground etchings. A contemporary William Capon, who left Norwich to become one of
London's foremost theatre designers, sought out Robert Dixon and offered him a post
in the Metropolis. However, this offer was declined, possibly on health grounds, for our
artist suffered greatly with ill-health during his last years. It is said that he faced ill-
health and death with exemplary fortitude. When the certainty of death appeared he
thought not of himself, but only of his family. The people of Norwich were greatly
1815 saddened to learn of his death on 1st October, 1815. He left a widow and six children,
evidently in a state of penury, for the citizens of Norwich organised a benefit exhibition
of the artist's works in the artist's room in Sir Benjamin Wrench's Court, commencing
16th October, 1815. Tickets were obtained from Mr. Coppin, Mr. Freeman and Mr.
Thirtle.

Robert Dixon was said to have been an intelligent man with a gentlemanly disposition, which made his society much sought after; to his friends he was a feast of genius, intelligence, and good humour.

THE PAINTINGS

Robert Dixon was a water-colour painter, first painting in the style of the late 18th century painters when he came under the influence whilst in London of George Barret. Later, when he moved to Norwich, his style became much more free, the simple washes probably being developed as a result of looking at the work of his contemporaries. In technique his work at times compares closely with James Stark, but in general they are less sophisticated. Even in his later work one often sees the tree shapes so closely associated with the painters of the 18th century. His oils have something in common with James Sillett. They have a strong 18th century feel and are confidently handled with pleasing impasto. He introduces warm touches and sometimes Crome-like greens. He has a predilection for cottage scenes.

ROBERT DIXON EXHIBITS

EXHIBITION OF THE NORWICH SOCIETY OF ARTISTS, 1805

No.	*Subject*
14	Fye Bridge, Norwich, from the water.
17	View up the river from Fye Bridge, Norwich.
24	Thorpe Hall, Norfolk, from the water—a sketch.
36	Part of St. Andrew's Workhouse, Norwich—a sketch.
48	A sketch in Thorpe Hall yard.
70	Part of St. Andrew's Workhouse, since taken down.

No. *Subject*

78 Unloading a wherry.
100 Drawing from Nature.
103 Part of a tan yard, Halesworth, Suffolk.
119 Sketch at Lakenham, Norfolk.
131 Near Magdalen Gates, Norwich.
143 Mill on Mousehold, near Norwich—a sketch.
148 Cottage in Heigham, Norwich.
154 Horning Ferry.
172 Lakenham—a sketch from the farm-yard.
216 Fellmonger's yard—a sketch.

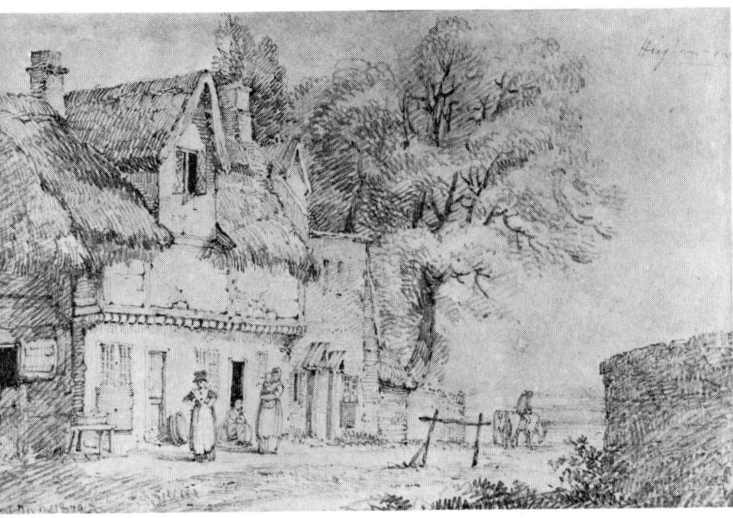

Robert Dixon 1809 *View at Heigham, Norwich* *Pencil* $9\frac{3}{4} \times 5\frac{3}{4}$ *in.*

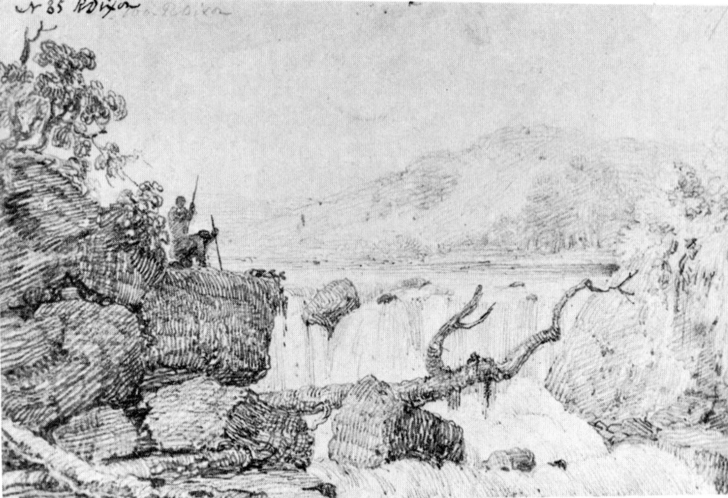

Robert Dixon *Pencil drawing* $6\frac{1}{4} \times 10$ *in*

SECOND EXHIBITION OF THE NORWICH SOCIETY OF ARTISTS, 1806

No. *Subject*

12 Head of Laocoon—a study, from plaster.
38 Owen's cottage.

" 'Mid Cambria's hills a lowly cottage stood,
Circled with mossy tufts of sombre green:
A vagrant brook flow'd wildly through the wood,
Flashing in lucid lapse the shades between;
And, clothed in mist, a distant hut was seen:
A village-spire above the copse rose white;
And oft, when summer closed the day serene,
The broad horizon glistens golden-bright,
Beskirted here and there with purple-tinted light."
(*Vide* Mrs. Robinson's *Poem of the Foster-Child.*)

50 Scene, at Halesworth, Suffolk.
54 Landscape.
64 Imitation of bronze, bas-relief.
83 Cottage and figures.
90 Cottage from Nature—evening.
123 Cupid benighted.

"Soon as he began to glow,
'Now', says he, 'let's try my bow,
Whether still the strings remain
Quite uninjured by the rain'."
(*Vide* Girdlestone's *Anacreon*, Ode III.)

No.	*Subject*
142	The Dolphin, at Heigham.
149	Coslany Bridge.
162	Fye Bridge Quay—a sketch.
164	St. Michael's Coslany Church (looking from St. George's).
173	Cupid benighted. "Then exulting leaps the boy— . . . . 'Sound I find my bow indeed, But thy heart with pain must bleed'." (*Vide* Girdlestone's *Anacreon*, Ode III.)
185	Imitation of bronze, bas-relief.
194	Cottages—a sketch.

THIRD EXHIBITION OF THE NORWICH SOCIETY OF ARTISTS, 1807

No.	*Subject*
1	Imitation of *basso relievo*—a compartment for a drawing-room.
12	The ale-house door—composition.
27	Pencil-sketch.
42	Pencil-sketch.
43	Cannock Gate, Lynn, drawn for Bell's *Antiquities of Norfolk*.
61	Compartment for a drawing-room.
62	Burlingham Church—a sketch.
79	Sketch—evening.
93	Compartment for a drawing-room.
96	Head, in chalks.
118	Grey Friar's Tower, Lynn, drawn for Bell's *Antiquities of Norfolk*.

FOURTH EXHIBITION OF THE NORWICH SOCIETY OF ARTISTS, 1808

No.	*Subject*
97	Indian-ink drawing.
125	Cottages, Filby.
138	The dispute between Hudibras and Sidrophel—sketch "At this dress Sidrophel look'd wise, And staring round with owl-like eyes, He put his face into a posture Of sapience, and began to bluster." (*Hudibras*, Part 2, Canto 3.)
148	Ralpho interceding for the Fiddler—sketch. "But Ralpho now in colder blood, His fury mildly thus withstood; Great Sir, quoth he, your mighty spirit Is raised too high; this slave doth merit To be the hangman's business, sooner Than from your hand to have the honour Of his destruction." (*Hudibras*, Part 1, Canto 2.)
152	Drawing from Nature—evening. "The God of day does to his Thetis haste, In clouds of gold, and shining purple dress'd: Each labouring husbandman his setting waits, And to his coarse but welcome home retreats." (Mountford.)
153	Drawing from Nature.
160	Drawing from Nature.
187	Cottage door—composition.

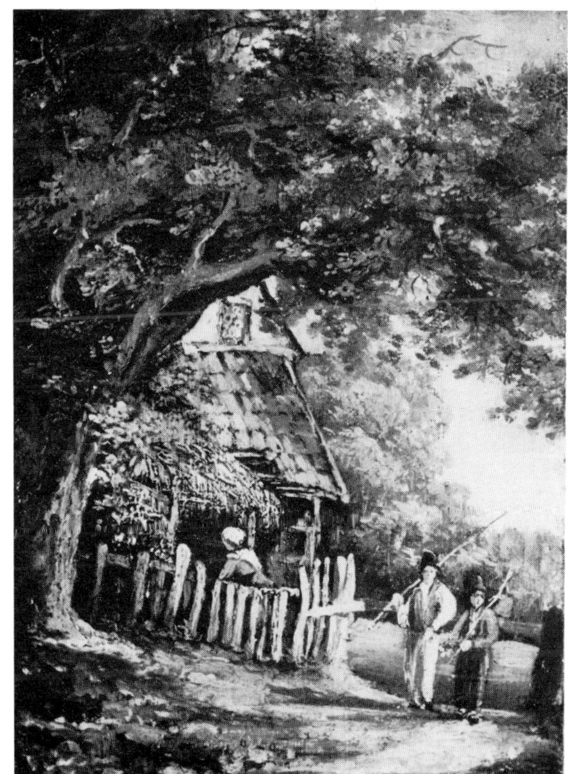

Robert Dixon *On panel* 6×4 *ins.*

FIFTH EXHIBITION OF THE NORWICH SOCIETY OF ARTISTS, 1809

No.	*Subject*
15	Flordon Black Horse.
18	View at Lakenham, Norwich.
54	Pencil sketch at Flordon.
55	Ditto at Newton.
73	Pencil sketch at Caistor.
118	Cottage scene (indian ink).
123	Pencil sketch at Filby.
137	Cottage (indian ink).
139	View on Mousehold Heath.
186	Drawing from Nature.
192	Entrance to Cromer, on the Aylsham Road.
197	Ruins of a tower on the city walls.

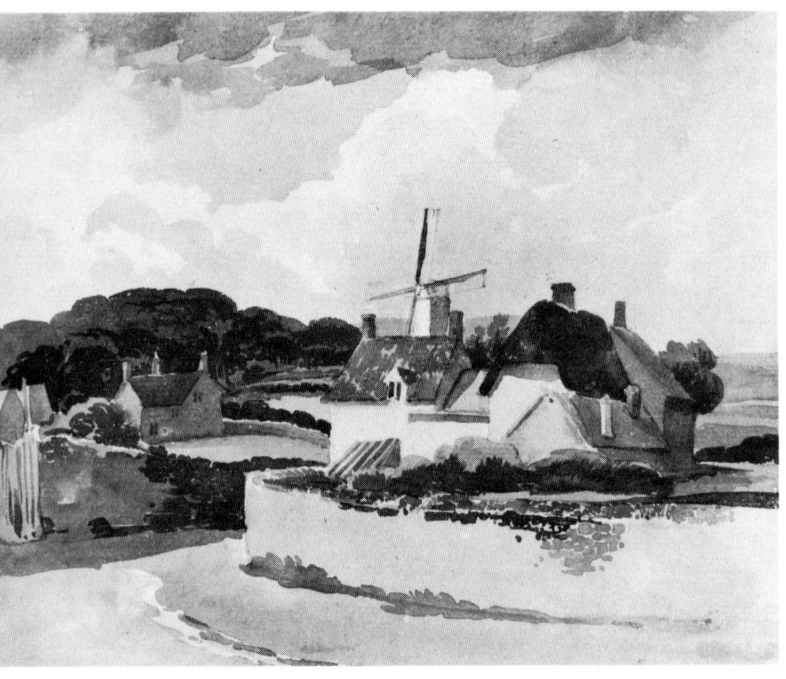

Robert Dixon *The Mill at Cromer* *Water-colour* $7 \times 9\frac{3}{4}$*in.*

SIXTH EXHIBITION OF THE NORWICH SOCIETY OF ARTISTS, 1810

No.	*Subject*
9	Deloraine opening the grave of Michael Scott.

"I would you had been there, to see
How the light broke forth so gloriously;
No earthly flame blazed e'er so bright;
It shone like heaven's own blessed light,
And, issuing from the tomb,
Shewed the Monk's cowl, and visage pale,
Danced on the dark brow'd warrior's mail,
And kissed his waving plume."

(*Vide* Scott's *Lay of the Last Minstrel*, Canto 2d.)

No.	*Subject*
50	Pencil sketch.
61	View between Overstrand and Cromer—evening.
74	Whitford Bridge, near Hockring.
83	Cottage door—composition.
109	Cromer Mill—evening.
110	Runcton Common—morning.
120	Beach scene, Cromer.
128	Pencil drawing.
130	Cottage scene.
143	Pencil sketch.
145	Beach scene, Cromer.
154	Runcton and Beeston (looking from Howard's Hill, Cromer)—evening.
158	Landscape.
162	Pencil sketch.
179	Pencil sketch—Cromer.

NORFOLK AND NORWICH FINE ARTS ASSOCIATION
Exhibition of the works of Deceased Local Artists, 1860

No.	*Subject*	*Lent by*
122	Cottage door.	Mr. Norgate.

BRITISH MEDICAL ASSOCIATION LOAN COLLECTION
of the works of Norfolk and Suffolk Artists, 1874

WATER-COLOURS

No.	*Subject*	*Lent by*
89	Cottages and figures.	Mr. W. N. H. Turner.
112	The cottage by the brook.	Mr. W. Runacres.
124	The homestead.	Miss Martineau.

NORWICH ART LOAN EXHIBITION
in aid of the Fund for the Restoration of the Church of Saint Peter Mancroft, 1878

No.	*Subject*	*Lent by*
482	An old cottage.	Mr. W. Runacres.

CATALOGUE OF THE LOAN COLLECTION OF DRAWINGS
in the New Picture Gallery in the Norwich Castle Museum, 1903

No.	*Subject*	*Lent by*
62	Near Cromer. Waves breaking on shore. $5\frac{1}{2} \times 8\frac{1}{4}$ in.	Mr. James Reeve.

1927 EXHIBITION, NORWICH

No.	*Subject*	*Lent by*
172	Cottage and figures. $11 \times 16\frac{1}{4}$ in.	
173	Pencil sketch. 6×10 in.	British Museum.
174	Farm house. $13\frac{1}{4} \times 19$ in.	Mr. R. Lee Barber.
175	Beeston Hill. $6\frac{1}{4} \times 12$ in.	
176	Cromer Mill. $7\frac{3}{4} \times 10\frac{1}{4}$ in.	
177	Near Cromer. $7\frac{1}{2} \times 12$ in.	
178	Cromer Cliffs. $5\frac{3}{4} \times 9\frac{1}{2}$ in.	Russell J. Colman.

JOSEPH STANNARD

(1797-1830)

Joseph Stannard, who may be called the first of the Stannards, was born in Norwich
1797 in the year 1797, his father being Abraham Stannard, probably a musician, and his mother prior to marriage being Mary Bell.

In all probability Joseph attended the Grammar School, for there is a mention of a Stannard attending at this period. However, from his letters it is apparent that he received a fair measure of education. At an early age he showed an aptitude for art and was sent to Robert Ladbrooke at Scholes Green, Norwich, for lessons. Such was his ability that Robert Ladbrooke quickly invited him to work in his studio.

When Joseph was sixteen years of age the most eminent man of Art in Norwich was John Crome. The family must have considered an apprenticeship with Crome to be desirable, so he was duly approached; Crome, to their consternation, asked the surprisingly high fee of £50—something like £750 in current figures. The Stannards, not being wealthy, regarded this as tantamount to his refusal to accept Joseph. On the other hand Crome's works by
1811 1811 were becoming sought after and probably he just didn't have a lot of time.

Whilst Robert Ladbrooke's teaching was regarded as somewhat pedestrian, there is little doubt that his strong emphasis on good drawing encouraged Joseph to develop his art in this respect.

The year 1816 saw the secession with Robert Ladbrooke taking his faction away from the Crome group. Naturally
1818 Joseph sided with Ladbrooke. By 1818 he had fledged his wings and was working on his own, executing certain portrait commissions and open air landscape studies.

Probably the portraiture led to an interest in the stage, for we find our painter executing "character" studies. In the 1927 Norwich School Exhibition we find such characters as Richard Roe, Old Lying Plummer, Old Peter the Huntsman, and others, including Old Blind Dan. The illustrated *Norwich Rat Catcher*, dates to this period.

Probably at the Norwich Society Joseph met Emily Coppin (about whom we shall read later). She readily understood his genius and probably realised that a

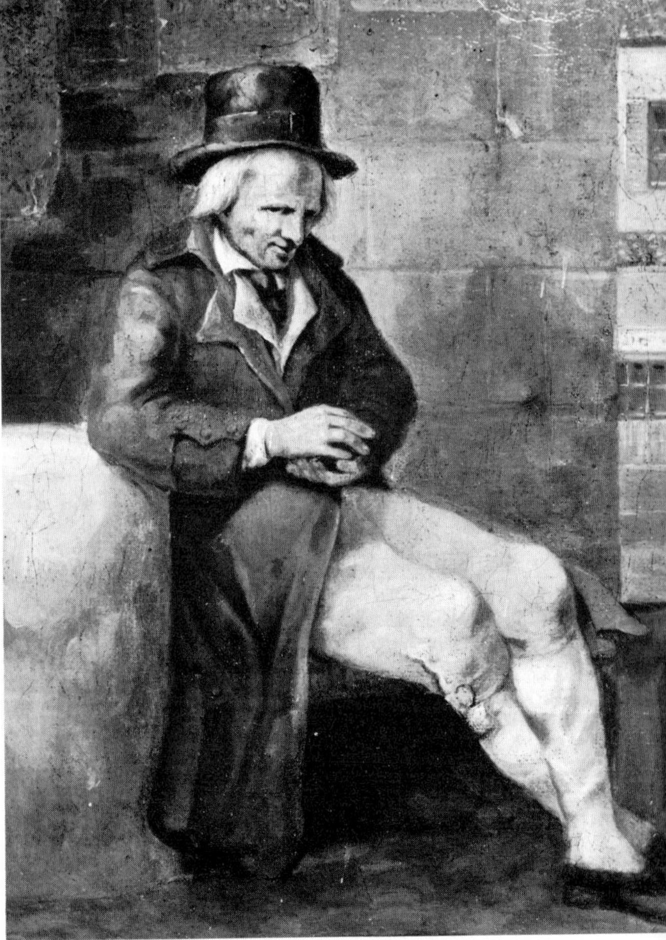

Joseph Stannard *A Norwich ratcatcher* *Oil* *About* 18×1
(*One of the "characters"*)

which not only outrivalled most of his fellow painters, but most of the painters of the 19th century.

The late Major Boswell, whose family had dealt in Norwich School paintings for generations, maintained that Joseph Stannard was the greatest genius of the School.

SEVENTH EXHIBITION OF THE NORWICH SOCIETY OF ARTISTS, 1811

No.	*Subject*
118	Sketch in Bister.

EIGHTH EXHIBITION OF THE NORWICH SOCIETY OF ARTISTS, 1812

No.	*Subject*
187	Back of the ferry.

NINTH EXHIBITION OF THE NORWICH SOCIETY OF ARTISTS, 1813

No.	*Subject*
99	Dead birds.
151	Cherries.
152	Strawberries.

TENTH EXHIBITION OF THE NORWICH SOCIETY OF ARTISTS, 1814

No.	*Subject*
12	Shell, from Nature.
107	Old building.

ELEVENTH EXHIBITION OF THE NORWICH SOCIETY OF ARTISTS, 1815

No.	*Subject*
38	Landscape, after Ladbrooke.
64	The Weighing House, Castle Ditches—evening.

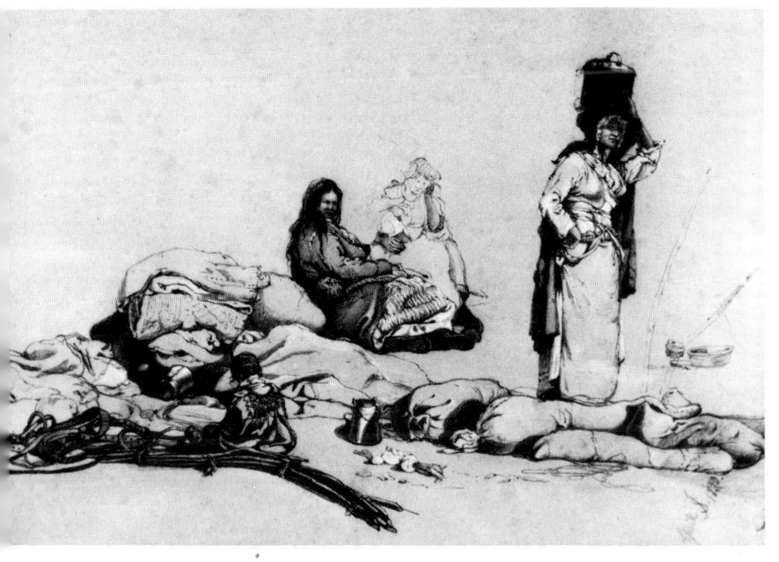

seph Stannard *The Gleaners* *Coloured crayon and chalk* $10\frac{1}{2} \times 18$ *in.*

THIRTEENTH EXHIBITION OF THE NORFOLK AND NORWICH SOCIETY OF ARTISTS, 1817

No.	*Subject*
6	Landscape.
8	Landscape.
12	A study.
16	Landscape.
18	Landscape.
104	Landscape and cattle.
107	Landscape.
113	Landscape.
116	Landscape and cattle.
121	Head of a saint.
125	Landscape composition.
129	Head of a saint.
135	Landscape on the Thorpe Road.

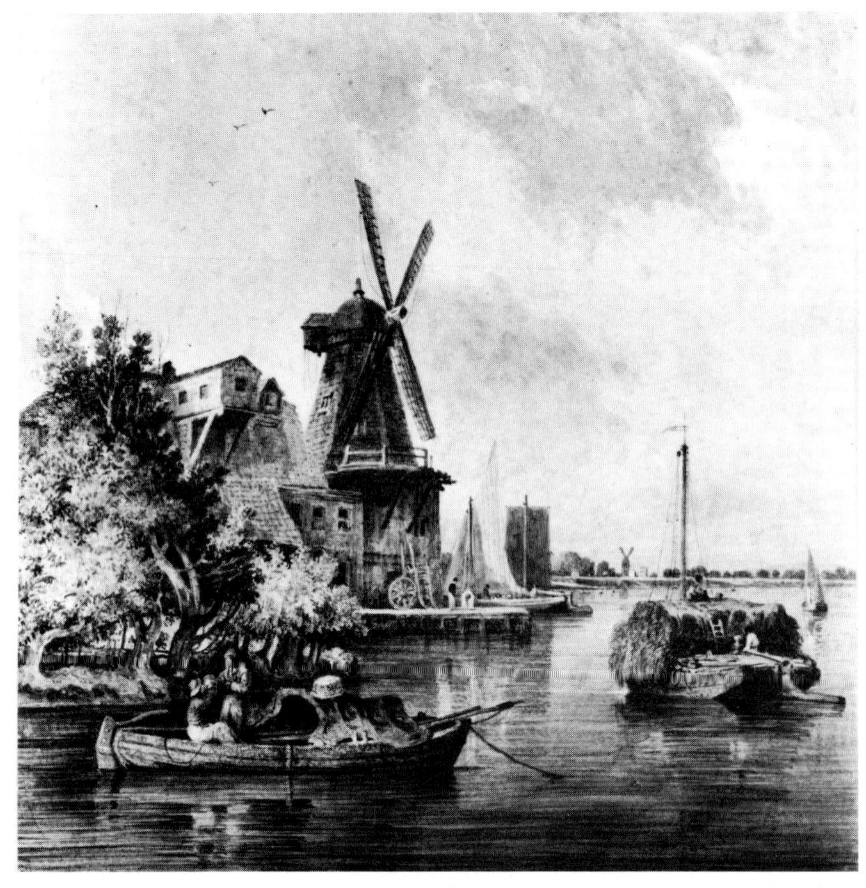

Joseph Stannard *On the Thames* *Water-colour* $8\frac{3}{4} \times 8\frac{3}{4}$ *in.*
Probably dates to his London visit

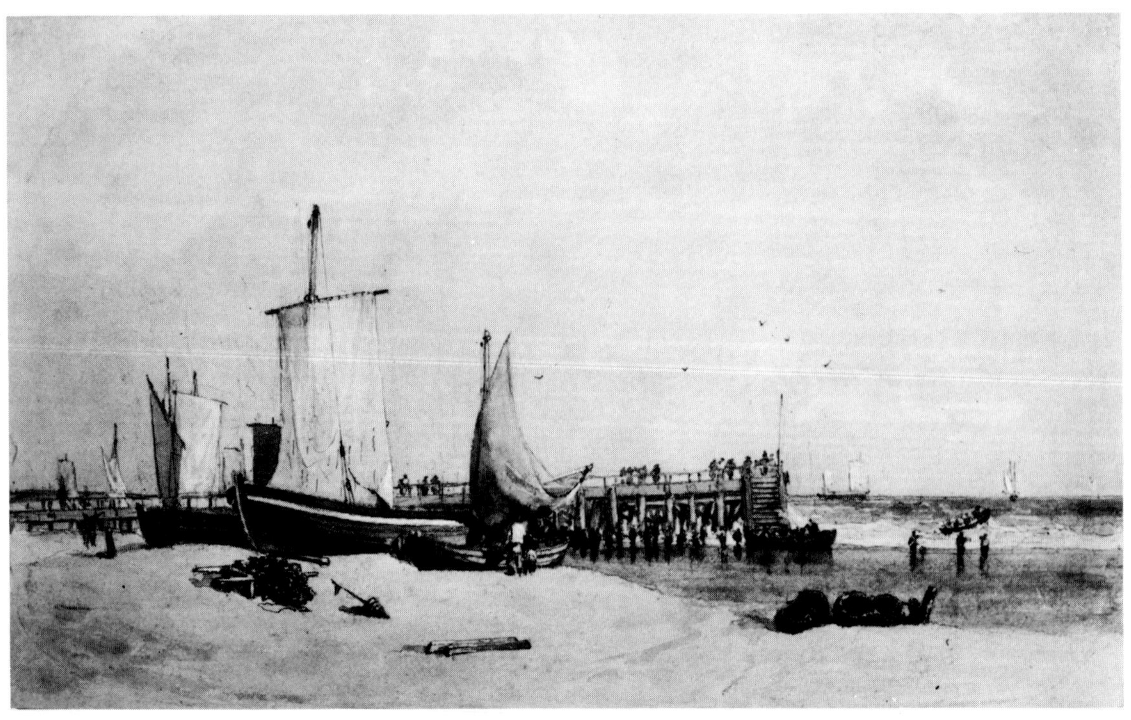

Joseph Stannard *Old Yarmouth Jetty*
(Ochre is a dominant colour in this water-colour)

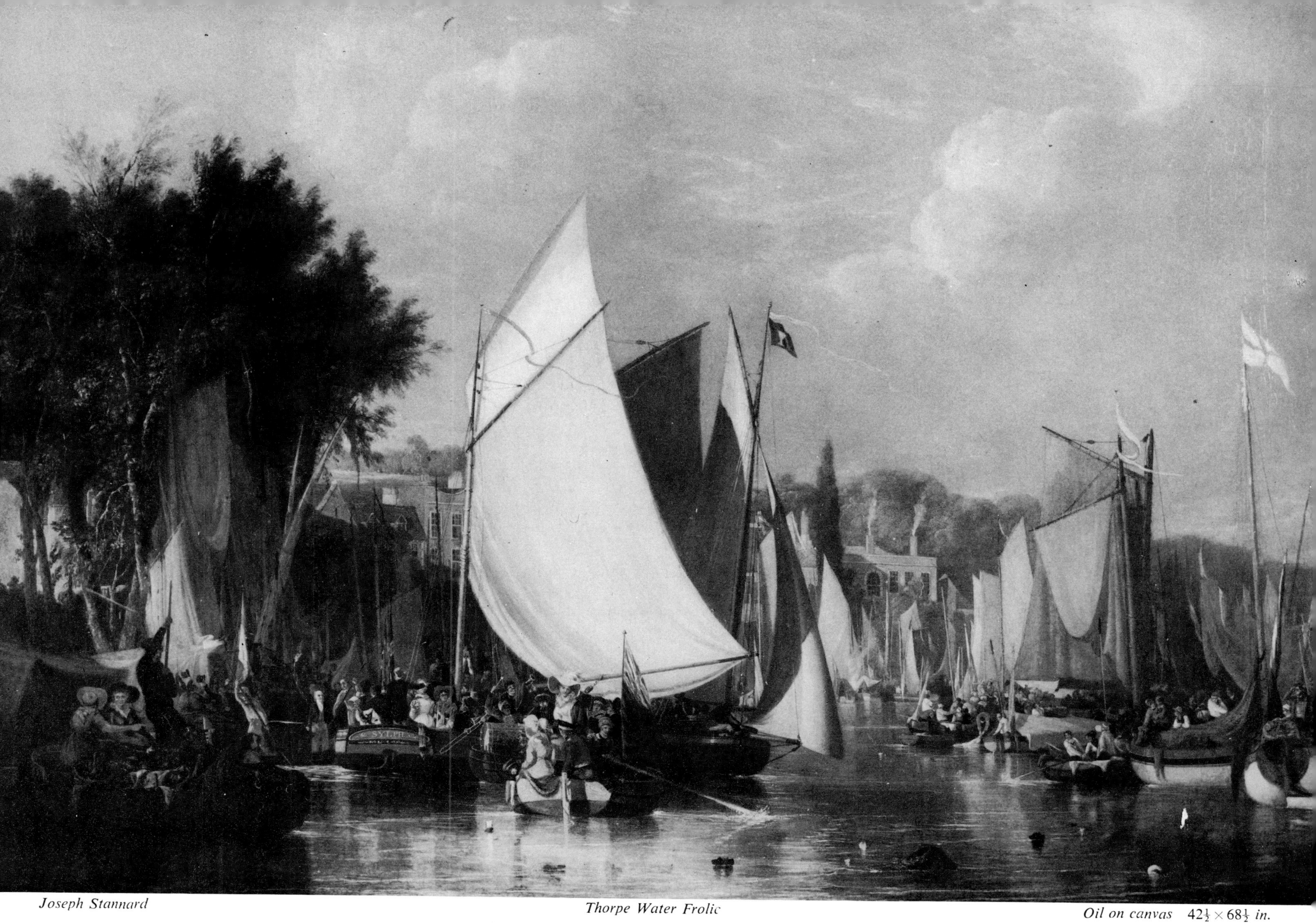

Joseph Stannard *Thorpe Water Frolic* *Oil on canvas* $42\frac{1}{2} \times 68\frac{1}{2}$ *in.*

FOURTEENTH EXHIBITION OF THE NORFOLK AND NORWICH SOCIETY OF ARTISTS, 1818

No.	*Subject*
6	Study from Nature.
10	Mackerel, from Nature.
20	Landscape composition.
26	Study, from Nature.
29	Landscape—sunset.
59	Landscape composition.
69	Landscape—evening, sun setting.
89	Landscape composition.
98	View on the river at Heigham.
116	Landscape composition.

FIFTEENTH EXHIBITION OF THE NORWICH SOCIETY OF ARTISTS, 1819

No.	*Subject*
8	Landscape.
13	Portrait of a gentleman.
23	Scene in the melodrama of *The Broken Sword.*
39	Portrait of Mrs. Hammond, Theatre Royal, Norwich.
148	Portrait of a gentleman.
160	Scene in a Norwich ale-house.

SIXTEENTH EXHIBITION OF THE NORWICH SOCIETY OF ARTISTS, 1820

No.	*Subject*
13	Scene at Thorpe, looking towards Norwich.
100	Landscape and goats.
215	Portrait of Mr. Beacham, in the character of Riber, in *The Miller and his Men.*

EIGHTEENTH EXHIBITION OF THE NORWICH SOCIETY OF ARTISTS, 1822

No.	*Subject*
3	The ferry, from a celebrated picture of Berghem's in the "Musee des Tableaux", Amsterdam.
43	Scene on the Wensum—the sun breaking out after a storm.

TWENTY-FIRST EXHIBITION OF THE NORWICH SOCIETY OF ARTISTS, 1825

No.	*Subject*
8	Breydon.
9	Thorpe Water Frolic—afternoon.
26	Beach scene.
29	Scene on Breydon—morning.
38	Misty morning.
85	Yarmouth Beach.

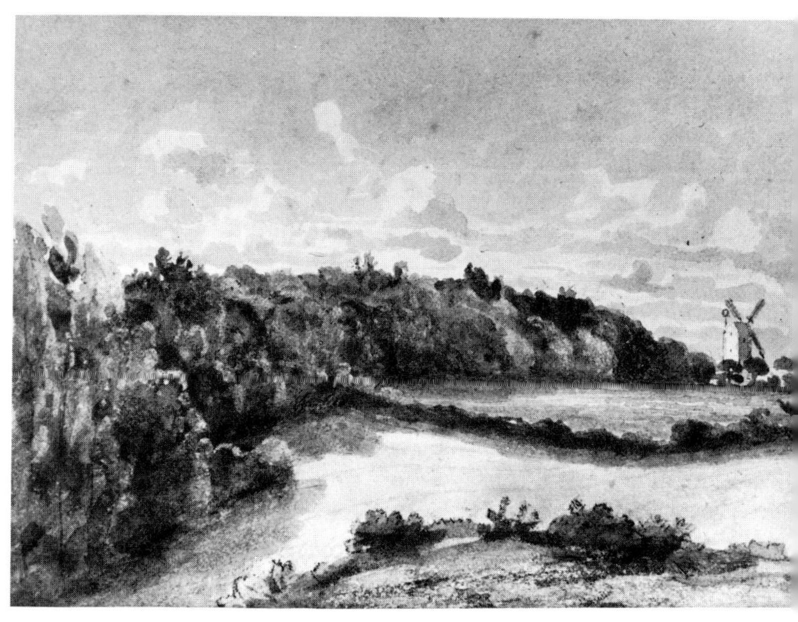

Joseph Stannard *Water-colour and chalk* *Size* $7\frac{3}{4} \times 12$ *in.*

TWENTY-THIRD EXHIBITION OF THE NORFOLK AND SUFFOLK INSTITUTION FOR THE PROMOTION OF THE FINE ARTS, 1829

No.	*Subject*
30	Fisherman going off.
40	Fishing boats going out—Hasbro' in the distance.
63	Portrait of a gentleman.
84	Fishermen, Yarmouth Beach.
85	Shrimpers, looking from Gorleston Pier towards Lowestoft—morning.
103	Fresh breeze off Lowestoft.
110	Fishing along shore—Yarmouth in the distance.
224	Painted and etched by Joseph Stannard.

TWENTY-FOURTH EXHIBITION OF THE NORFOLK AND SUFFOLK INSTITUTION FOR THE PROMOTION OF THE FINE ARTS, 1830

No.	*Subject*
142	Portrait of the Rev. W. Gordon.

NORWICH POLYTECHNIC EXHIBITION, 1840

No.	*Subject*	*Lent by*
111	Portrait of Hunting Peter.	Mr. S. Woolsey.
112	Portrait of Joe Doe.	Mr. S. Woolsey.
120	Yarmouth Jetty.	John Gordon, Esq.
134	Thorpe Regatta.	Colonel Harvey.

NORFOLK AND NORWICH FINE ARTS ASSOCIATION
Exhibition of the Works of Deceased Local Artists, 1860

No.	*Subject*	*Lent by*
15	View of Thorpe.	Mr. H. S. Patteson.
34	Sketch—Thorpe Water Frolic.	Mr. Norgate.
111	Breydon.	Mr. Norgate.
133	Whitlingham Reach.	Mr. H. Hansell.
147	Norwich characters.	Mr. R. B. Scott.
200	Yarmouth Old Jetty.	Mr. J. Gordon.
224	View of Keswick.	Rev. S. Titlow.
	WATER-COLOUR ROOM	
245	The beachman.	Mr. Boswell.

NORWICH AND EASTERN COUNTIES WORKING CLASSES INDUSTRIAL EXHIBITION, 1867

No.	*Subject*	*Lent by*
768	River scene.	Ben Wilkinson, Esq., Newmarket Road.
816	Cattle.	F. E. Watson, Esq., Mayor of Norwich.
858	View of Breydon.	J. Barwell, Esq., Surrey Street.

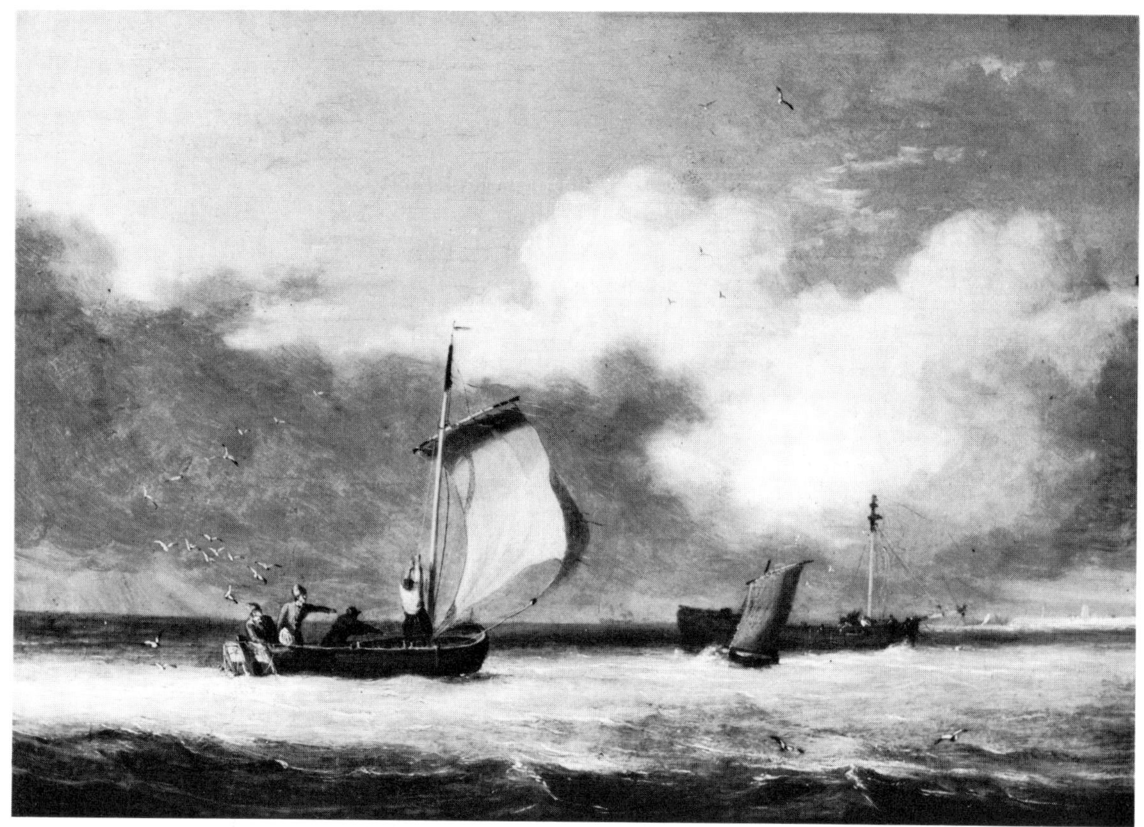

Joseph Stannard *Exhibited at Stannard Exhibition, 1934, No. 92* *Oil on panel* 13 × 9 *in.*

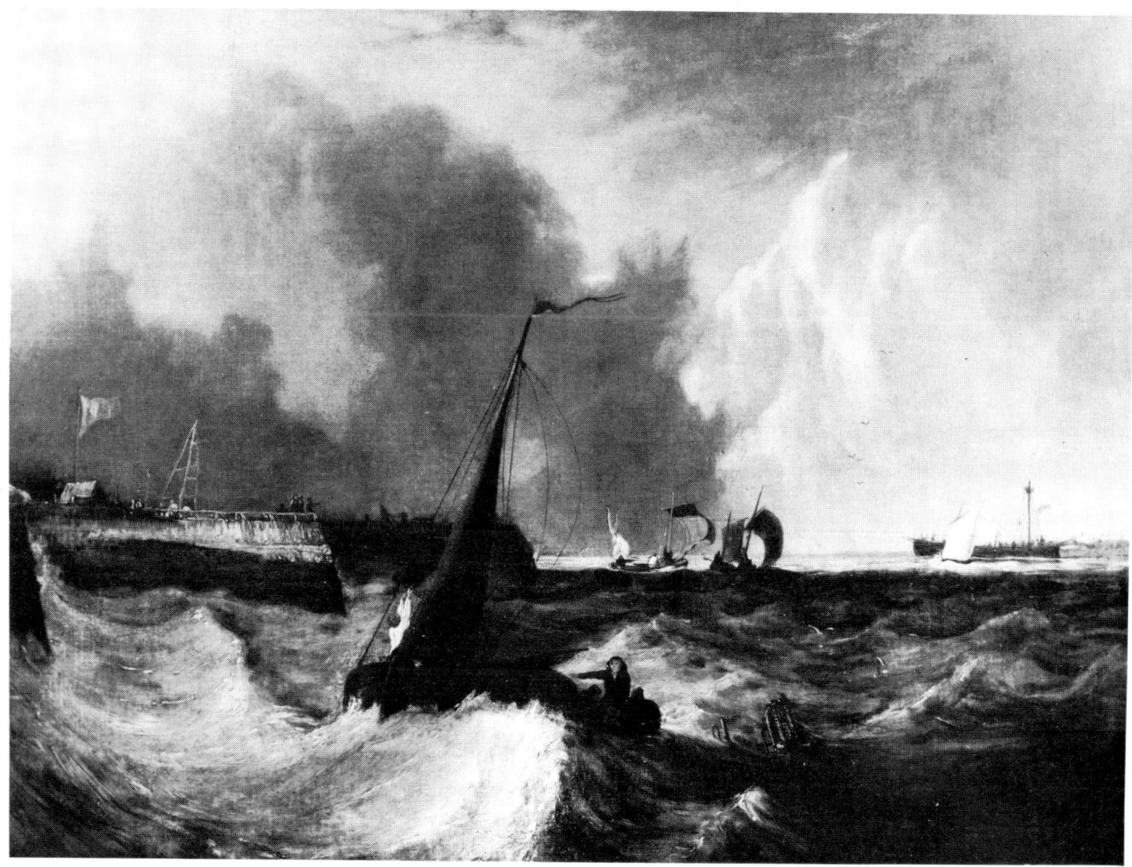

Joseph Stannard. *Gorleston Pier* *Oil on canvas* 18 × 24 *in.*

NORWICH FINE ART ASSOCIATION
Second Exhibition of Works of Art by Modern Artists, 1869

No.	*Subject*	£ s. d.
97	Sunday evening.	5 5 0
170	Sketch in a country churchyard.	10 10 0

BRITISH MEDICAL ASSOCIATION LOAN COLLECTION
of the Works of Norfolk and Suffolk Artists, 1874

No.	*Subject*	*Lent by*
14	Yarmouth Jetty.	Miss Martineau.
29	Thorpe Reach.	Mr. J. Barwell.
67	The river at Thorpe.	Mr. H. S. Patteson.
80	The gleaners.	Mr. G. H. Asker.
	WATER-COLOURS	
91	Study of boats.	Norwich Exhibition.
119	Study of a figure.	Mr. A. Master.
120	Study of a figure.	Mr. A. Master.
123	Vessels at sea.	Mr. F. Fox.

NORWICH ART LOAN EXHIBITION
in aid of the Fund for the Restoration of the Church of Saint Peter Mancroft, 1878

No.	*Subject*	*Lent by*
82	Yarmouth Beach.	Isaac B. Coaks, Esq.
88	River scene.	Rev. J. Thackray.
94	Yarmouth Roads.	I. B. Coaks, Esq.
116	The River Yare at Whitlingham.	R. W. Burleigh, Esq.
122	The River at Thorpe, looking towards Carrow.	J. J. Colman, Esq., M.P.
151	Beach scene, Great Yarmouth.	I. B. Coaks, Esq.
156	View of Old River, Thorpe.	H. Staniforth Patteson, Esq.
271	Sea piece.	George Barker, Esq.
339	Yarmouth River.	Mr. J. H. Ladyman.

FINE ART EXHIBITION
in aid of the New Norfolk and Norwich Hospital, 1883

No.	*Subject*	*Lent by*
57	View of Cromer.	Mr. John Gunn.
65	Beach.	Mr. I. B. Coaks.
74	Sea piece.	Mr. I. B. Coaks.
106	Yarmouth Jetty.	Mr. I. B. Coaks.
16	Fishing boats.	Mr. J. J. Colman, M.P.
51	Off Corton.	Mr. H. G. Barwell.

NORWICH ART LOAN EXHIBITION
in aid of the fund for the Restoration of St. Peter Mancroft Church, 1885

No.	*Subject*	*Lent by*
69	Fishing boats.	J. J. Colman, Esq., M.P.

LOAN COLLECTION OF PICTURES
exhibited at the Agricultural Hall Gallery during the Grand Oriental Bazaar, 1894

No.	*Subject*	*Lent by*
3	Thorpe Watering.	Miss Barwell.
12	River at Thorpe.	J. J. Colman, Esq., M.P.
32	Yarmouth Beach.	I. B. Coaks, Esq.
41	The Marl Staithe, Whitlingham.	George Holmes, Esq.
51	Village of Thorpe.	H. S. Patteson, Esq.
	WATER-COLOUR	
60	Off Gorleston.	H. G. Barwell, Esq.

ART LOAN EXHIBITION
in aid of the Funds of St. George's Club for Working Girls, 1902

No.	*Subject*	*Lent by*
174	Marl Staithe, Whitlingham.	George Holmes, Esq.
251 to 255	Old Norwich characters.	Charles Foster, Esq.

WORKS EXHIBITED AT THE BRITISH INSTITUTION

Year	*Subject*
1824	Breydon, looking towards Yarmouth. 20 × 26 in.
	Mundesley Cliffs, looking towards Cromer. 21 × 26 in.
	A view of Norwich. 39 × 47 in.
1825	Breydon—morning. 20 × 36 in.
	On the Norwich River. 23 × 25 in.
1826	A marine view. 17 × 21 in.
1827	Gorleston Pier — pilot's boats going off. 29 × 33 in.
1828	Fresh breezes—Lowestoft Roads. 36 × 45 in.

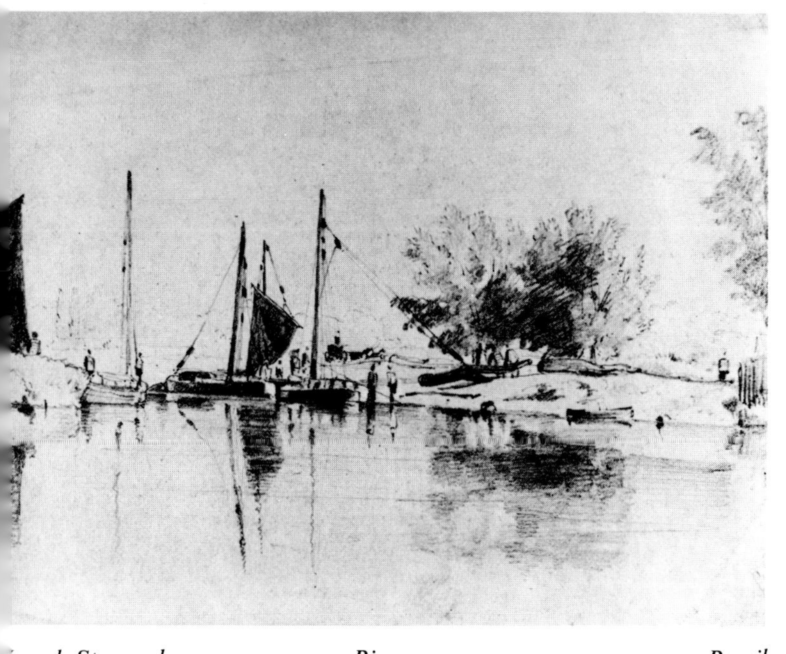

Joseph Stannard *River scene* *Pencil*

WORKS EXHIBITED AT THE SOCIETY OF BRITISH ARTISTS

Year	*Subject*
1824	Boats—morning.
	A village inn door (drawing in British Museum).
1825	Horning Ferry—morning.
	Cottage scene.

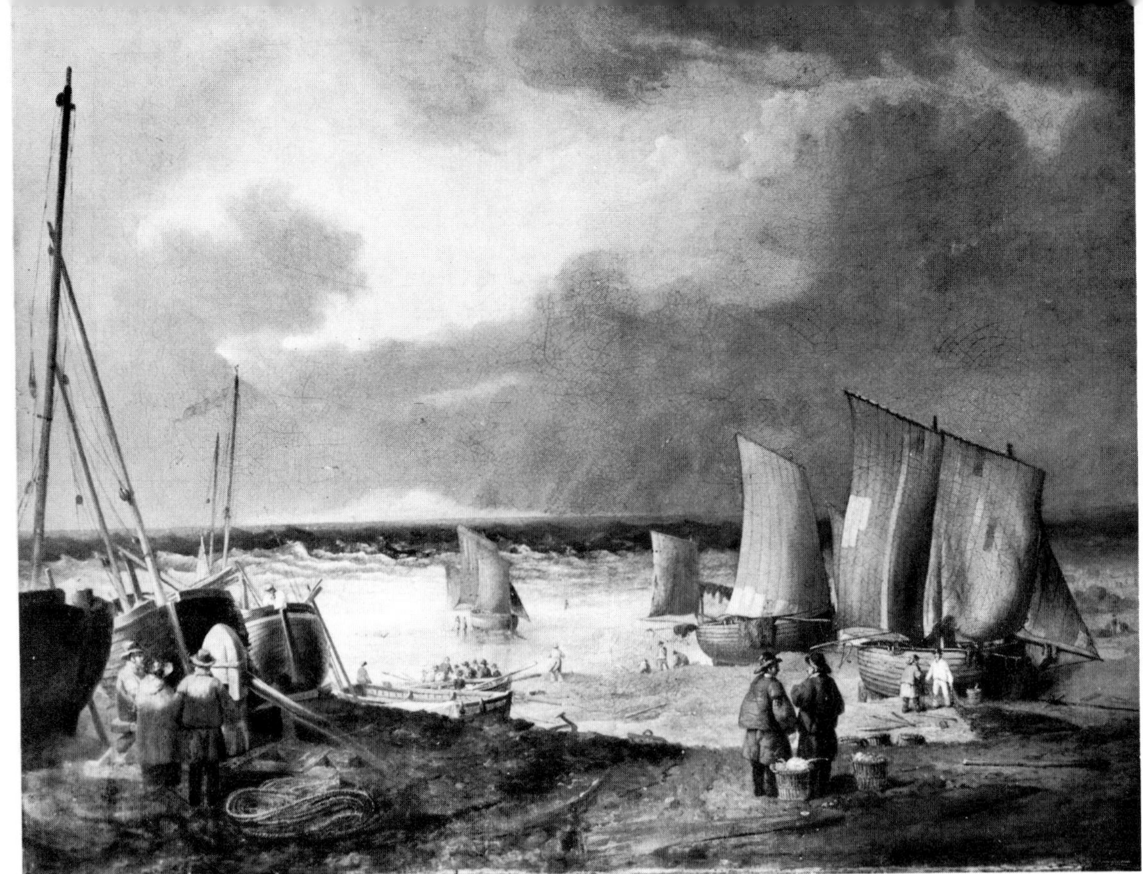

Joseph Stannard, early period *Yarmouth Beach* *Oil on canvas* 28 × 36 *in.*

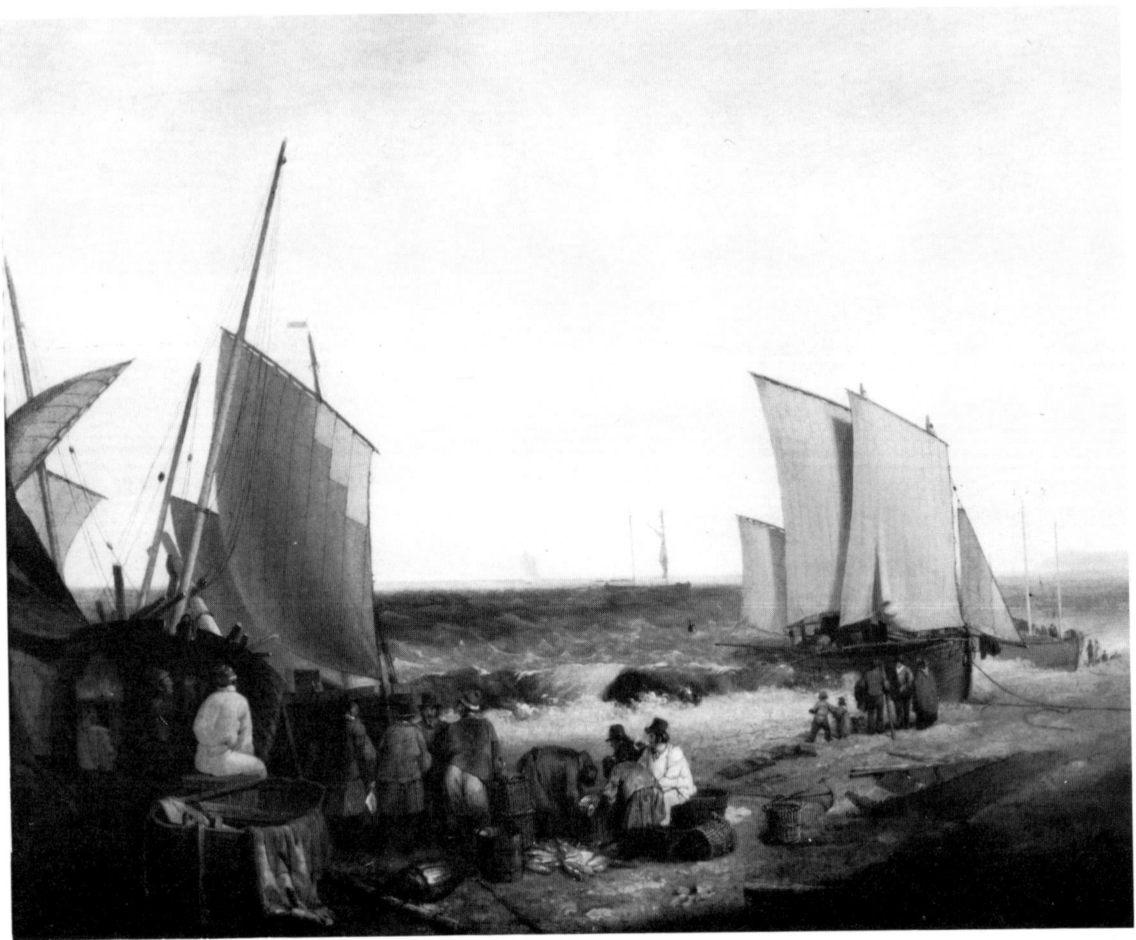

Joseph Stannard, early period *Beach Scene* *Oil* 33 × 26¼ *in.*

EXHIBITION OF NORWICH SCHOOL PICTURES
Norwich Castle Museum and Art Galleries, October, 1927

OIL-PAINTINGS

No.	*Subject*
97	Near Surlingham Ferry. $19\frac{1}{2} \times 29\frac{1}{2}$ in.
	Five sketches of old Norwich characters:
98	Richard Roe, a fighting man. $11 \times 7\frac{1}{2}$ in.
99	Old Lying Plummer (lived in St. James', Norwich). $12\frac{1}{2} \times 7\frac{3}{4}$ in.
100	Old Peter, the huntsman (lived in St. Augustine's and sold hare skins, etc.). $12 \times 7\frac{1}{2}$ in.
101	Joe Doe, the butcher's porter (sold his body for dissection after death). $13\frac{3}{4} \times 10$ in.
102	Old Wire, the coal porter (a great drunkard). Charles Grimmer (died at the age of 112). Long Blind Dan (Daniel Northern), lived in Magdalen Street. $14 \times 15\frac{1}{2}$ in.
103	River scene at Bramerton. 18×25 in.
104	Yarmouth Sands (Old Masters' Exhibition, Burlington House, 1878). $29 \times 39\frac{1}{2}$ in.
105	Sunrise on the sea shore (Old Masters' Exhibition, Burlington House, 1878). 19×27 in.
106	Loading rushes. $20 \times 31\frac{1}{2}$ in.
107	Yarmouth Beach. $4\frac{1}{2} \times 10$ in.

WATER-COLOURS

243	Shore scene (signed and dated 1838). $6 \times 18\frac{1}{2}$ in.
244	River scene (pencil). $6\frac{1}{2} \times 9\frac{1}{2}$ in.
245	Water Gate. $10\frac{1}{4} \times 9$ in.
246	Studies of figures (J.S. 1829) (chalk). $5 \times 11\frac{1}{4}$ in.
247	Coltishall Lock. $7 \times 17\frac{1}{2}$ in.

"STANNARD" EXHIBITION, 1934

No.	*Subject*	*Lent by*
56	Sketch—three figures (signed and dated 1824) (crayon). 6×6 in.	Rev. E. A. Parr.
57	Sketch from beach (crayon). $5\frac{7}{8} \times 11$ in.	Rev. E. A. Parr.
58	Seascape (monochrome). $15\frac{5}{8} \times 20\frac{1}{2}$ in.	Sir Hugh Beevor, Bart.
59	Dish of mackerel (water-colour). $11 \times 6\frac{3}{4}$ in.	Mr. W. Browne.
60	Beach and cliffs (signed and dated 1829) (pastel). $9\frac{1}{4} \times 16\frac{1}{2}$ in.	Miss Cowper Johnson.
61	A sailing barge (signed and dated 1829) (pastel). $11\frac{3}{4} \times 14\frac{5}{8}$ in.	Miss Cowper Johnson.
62	The Water Gate (water-colour). $10\frac{1}{4} \times 9$ in.	Mr. R. J. Colman.
63	Coltishall Lock (water-colour). $7 \times 17\frac{1}{2}$ in.	Mr. F. J. Thompson.
64	Seascape (pastel). $12 \times 16\frac{3}{8}$ in.	Miss Cowper Johnson.
65	The rat catcher (water-colour). $11\frac{1}{2} \times 8$ in.	Colonel S. Garerd Hill, V.D.
66	Hurdy-gurdy man (signed and dated 1830) (pastel). 10×7 in.	Mrs. Bolingbroke.
67	Etching, after picture by Alfred Stannard. $5\frac{3}{8} \times 8\frac{1}{2}$ in.	Mr. H. W. Hunt.
68	Etching (signed and dated 1827). $4 \times 6\frac{3}{8}$ in.	Mr. H. W. Hunt.
69	Boat scene (signed and dated 1825) (etching). $5\frac{3}{8} \times 8\frac{1}{2}$ in.	Mr. G. J. Burton.
69A	Study of head (water-colour). $3\frac{1}{4} \times 2\frac{1}{2}$ in.	Mr. W. Lincolne Sutton.
70	Pastry seller (water-colour). $11\frac{5}{8} \times 8\frac{1}{8}$ in.	Colonel S. Garerd Hill, V.D.
71	Hurdy-gurdy man (signed and dated 1830) (pastel). 10×7 in.	Mrs. Bolingbroke.

OILS

72	River scene. $17\frac{1}{2} \times 9\frac{1}{2}$ in.	Tolhouse Museum, Great Yarmouth.
73	River scene at Bramerton. Panel, $17\frac{3}{4} \times 25$ in.	Mr. Donald D. Day, F.R.C.S.
74	Beach scene. Panel, 11×15 in.	Mr. Henry N. Holmes.
75	Near Surlingham Ferry. $19\frac{1}{2} \times 29\frac{1}{2}$ in.	Mrs. Lincolne Sutton.
76	Old River at Thorpe. $37\frac{1}{2} \times 43\frac{1}{4}$ in.	Mr. R. J. Colman.
77	Seascape (signed and dated 1830). Panel, $12\frac{1}{2} \times 16\frac{1}{2}$ in.	Mrs. L. J. Mills.
78	Thorpe, near Norwich. $17\frac{1}{2} \times 25\frac{1}{2}$ in.	Mr. R. J. Colman.

No.	*Subject*	*Lent by*
79	Sailing boats. $4\frac{5}{8}\times8\frac{1}{2}$ in.	Mr. C. R. Oury.
80	Wherries on Yare. Panel, $8\frac{7}{8}\times16\frac{3}{4}$ in.	Mr. Percy Moore Turner.
81	Yarmouth Beach. $4\frac{1}{2}\times10$ in.	Mrs. Murray Morrison.
82	Early morning at sea. Panel, $9\times5\frac{3}{4}$ in.	Mr. Ralph H. Mottram.
83	Breydon Water, near Yarmouth. $9\frac{1}{2}\times11\frac{7}{8}$ in.	Mr. Percy Moore Turner.
84	Beach scene with boats and figures. $14\frac{5}{8}\times19\frac{1}{2}$ in.	Mr. A. E. Barham.
85	Boat house, figures, etc. (signed J.S.). Panel, $18\frac{1}{2}\times14\frac{3}{4}$ in.	Mr. W. Browne.
86	Landscape with road and figures. Panel, $6\times9\frac{1}{2}$ in.	Mr. Percy Moore Turner.
87	Cottage and landscape. $9\frac{3}{4}\times11\frac{1}{2}$ in.	Mr. Wm. Hubbard.
88	Loading rushes. $20\times31\frac{1}{2}$ in.	Mr. A. G. Howlett.
89	Landscape with cottage and bridge. Panel, $13\frac{5}{8}\times12$ in.	Mr. C. F. Bond.
90	Woody landscape with figures and sheep. Panel, $6\times9\frac{1}{4}$ in.	Mr. Percy Moore Taylor.
91	Beach scene. $9\frac{3}{4}\times11\frac{1}{2}$ in.	Mr. Edward M. Hansell.
92	Seascape (signed). $9\times12\frac{3}{4}$ in.	Mr. Bassett F. Hornor.
93	Shipping scene. $15\times18\frac{1}{4}$ in.	Sir Arthur Michael Semuel, Bart., M.P.

Joseph Stannard *Fresh breeze off Lowestoft* *Oil About 20 × 30 in.*

ALFRED STANNARD

(1806-1889)

1806 Alfred Stannard was born in the year 1806, the brother of Joseph Stannard. Being nine years younger than Joseph he became his pupil at an early age. Several works are recorded upon which both Joseph and Alfred worked.

1820 He is first recorded as exhibiting *Study of an Old Man* in 1820. He was described in the
1825 Catalogue as Master A. Stannard. This was followed by a group of exhibits in 1825.

1827 In 1827 he married a Miss Sparkes and the following year his illustrious daughter—Eloise Harriet Stannard—was born. In all he had fourteen children including Alfred George Stannard.

1830 With the loss of his brother Joseph in 1830 Alfred concentrated his efforts in his studio in Upper King Street, Norwich. From this address he despatched numerous exhibits to the British Institute and Suffolk Street Exhibitions.

Alfred Stannard also took pupils at his King Street Studio and it is said that his wife
1840 assisted with this work. In the 1840s tragedy struck the Stannard household, causing Alfred to lose three of his children and his elderly mother. Despite all these reverses
1852- our artist continued to paint fine pictures, and in 1852-3 painted one of the finest pictures
1853 of the whole of the Norwich School, *Scene at Trowse, Norfolk*. This painting depicts old Trowse Hall and its environs together with a distant glimpse of the City of Norwich. Alas, such were the difficulties facing artists at this time that he found it extremely difficult to meet his commitments.

The only known letter by Alfred Stannard concerns two pictures presumably belonging to Eloise. It is written from St. Andrew's Hall Plain, Norwich and dated 16th February, 1878.

> Dear Sir,
>
> On my daughter's return to me I mentioned your offer for the two little pictures. She is vexed that I refused (wishing you should have her *best* works in that neighbourhood). Under the circumstances if you still remain in the same mind, I am willing to accept the £22.10.0. Please telegraph in reply if its to prevent these going to London.
>
> Yours faithfully,
>
> ALFRED STANNARD.

The letter is interesting. It shows a proud man not wishing to accept less than he asked, but probably having to accept an offer under force of circumstances. The ingenious terms in which the letter is couched suggests that Alfred was a man of considerable intelligence.

As old age approached the misfortunes of former years began to take their toll on his health and he found himself unable to produce paintings of former quality. When in
1878 1878 his *Sluice Gates on the Wensum*, painted many years earlier made £330 at auction, it must have been food for thought.

Alfred wasn't a great traveller; in all his years his most distant journeys seem to have been to London and Peterborough. His *View on the Thames, Hammersmith*, was the property of James Reeve, Curator at the Norwich Museum and the *Peterborough Cathedral*, the property of a Donald Steward.

At the end of his life Alfred Stannard became something of a legend in his life-time, being known as one of the last of the Norwich School painters to have known the great John Crome.

In spite of his many hardships our artist lived until 26th January, 1889, leaving only his daughter Eloise to carry on the great Stannard tradition.

THE PAINTINGS

The early work of Alfred is strongly influenced by his brother Joseph; occasionally he signs his name on the joint works. Perhaps when Joseph died the few works which were left in the studio were completed by Alfred.

It is said that as a boy Alfred had lessons from John Crome. This influence is certainly felt in Alfred's early landscapes. In these early works one looks for concisely executed weeds, rather rounded clouds, and in his landscapes, contrasting warm brown trees with lots of foliage touches. By 1850 one looks for light blue skies and more thinly laid paint and great subtlety of colouring. The *Yarmouth Jetty* in the Castle Museum, dated 1861, has a beautiful gentle fluency and is superbly composed.

After 1860 he executed views looking into the sun which were rather daring in concept. In these works he proved his worth, for it takes a great painter to successfully paint the sun without the balance of colours going astray. The *View at Gorleston*, Plate 000, painted in 1870, is such an example—the secondary light touching the man in the boat and the side of the boat is worthy of Claude, so beautiful are the tones.

After 1870 the quality of his work is a function of his state of health. However, he painted almost until the end of his life.

His water-colours are made up of very clean washes—the only ones I have seen are in the Museum at Norwich. Alfred was commissioned by Lord Harvey to paint views on his estate. Very freely drawn crayon drawings exist, heightened with white.

Alfred Stannard signed many of his works, but others I have seen are not signed. The early signatures are often initials, other variations are A. Stannard and Alfred Stannard. The date sometimes appearing below the signature.

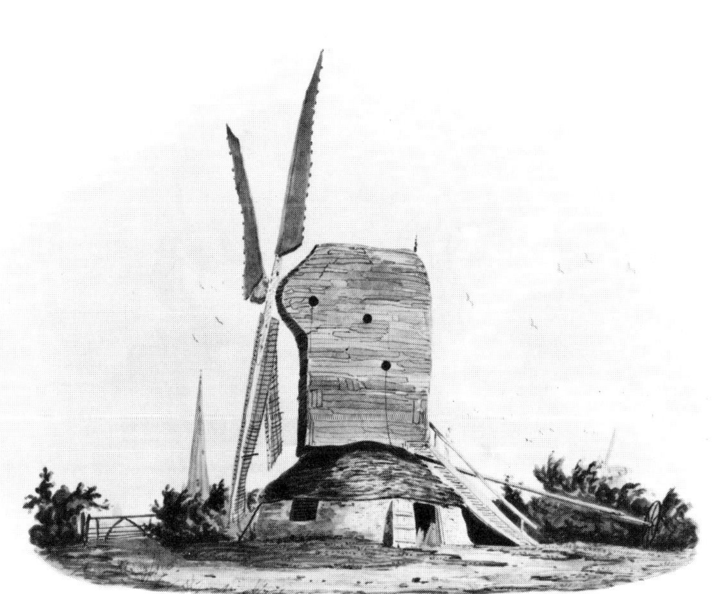

fred Stannard *The Black Mill on Mousehold Heath*
One of a series of commissioned drawings

EXHIBITION OF NORWICH SCHOOL PICTURES
Norwich Castle Museum and Art Galleries, October, 1927

OIL-PAINTINGS

No.	*Subject*
89	Penning the sheep—scene at Crown Point, Norwich. 38×49 in.
90	Keel and boats at Breydon. $24\frac{1}{4} \times 15$ in.
91	Yarmouth Harbour. $9\frac{1}{4} \times 12\frac{3}{4}$ in.
92	Seascape. $12\frac{1}{2} \times 16\frac{1}{2}$ in.
93	Sluice gate on the River Wensum. $22\frac{1}{2} \times 31\frac{1}{2}$ in.
94	Burgh Castle, near Great Yarmouth. 21×31 in.

THE BRITISH INSTITUTION

Year	*No.*	*Subject*
1826	159	A scene near Norwich. 14×18 in.
1828	152	Trowse Hill, Norwich (painted on the spot). 46×56 in. (Critics took exception to the statement "painted on the spot" remarking that a picture so highly finished could not have been produced so.)
	233	A scene at Lakenham, near Norwich. 26×31 in.
	271	Langley Staithe, Norfolk (painted on the spot). 22×26 in.
1829	504	Penning the fold. 54×64 in.
1830	219	Wood scene, near Norwich. 34×42 in.
1851	227	Scene at Whitlingham. 23×34 in.
1860	539	Yarmouth Quay, from the south.

THE SOCIETY OF BRITISH ARTISTS, SUFFOLK STREET

Year	*Subject*
1825	Cottage scene.
1827	Lane scenes—Kirby, Norfolk (2).
	A scene near Lodden, Norfolk.
1828	Sluice-gate on the River Wensum.
1829	A mill.
1830	Scene on the River Yare.
1843	Gorleston, looking towards the pier-head.

SIXTEENTH EXHIBITION OF THE NORWICH SOCIETY OF ARTISTS, 1820

No.	*Subject*
97	Study of an old man.

TWENTY-FIRST EXHIBITION OF THE NORWICH SOCIETY OF ARTISTS, 1825

No.	*Subject*
12	Road scene, at Herringfleet.
17	Cattle passing a brook—morning.
37	A scene at Trowse.
78	Lane scene, near Whitlingham.
88	Scene at Bramerton.

TWENTY-SECOND EXHIBITION OF THE NORFOLK AND SUFFOLK INSTITUTION FOR THE FINE ARTS, 1828

No.	*Subject*
41	Penning the fold. "On came the comely sheep, From feed returning to their pens and fold. And these the kine, in multitudes, succeed; One on the other rising to the eye; As watery clouds which in the heavens are seen, Driven by the South or Thracian Boreas, And, numberless, along the sky they glide."
47	Scene at Lakenham—evening.
63	Lane scene at Whitlingham.
73	Scene at Kirby Bedon.
81	Scene on Bramerton Common.
86	Sluice gate on the River Wensum.
109	Lane scene—Trowse.
132	Langley Staithe.

TWENTY-THIRD EXHIBITION OF THE NORFOLK AND SUFFOLK INSTITUTION FOR THE PROMOTION OF THE FINE ARTS, 1829

No.	*Subject*
12	Lane scene—Trowse.
13	Scene in Crown Point Wood, with wood cutters.
34	Lane scene—Trowse
38	Trowse Hall.
69	The remains of Burgh Castle looking towards Reedham, painted on the spot.
228	Etching of Keswick Sluice.

TWENTY-FIFTH EXHIBITION OF THE NORFOLK AND SUFFOLK INSTITUTION FOR THE PROMOTION OF THE FINE ARTS, 1831

No.	
67	Marsh Mill, near Hardley Cross.

TWENTY SIXTH EXHIBITION OF THE NORFOLK AND SUFFOLK INSTITUTION FOR THE PROMOTION OF THE FINE ARTS, 1832

No.	*Subject*
98	Tower on King Street Meadows.
146	Caistor Castle.
159	Caistor Castle, near Yarmouth.

FIRST EXHIBITION OF THE NORFOLK AND NORWICH ART UNION, 1839

No.	*Subject*
13	Old Tower, near Carrow Bridge.
14	Keswick Sluice Gate.
56	Road scene—Lakenham.
93	Scene in Billockby, Norfolk.
181	Sheep washing.

NORWICH POLYTECHNIC EXHIBITION, 1840

No.		*Lent by*
18	Landscape.	Mr. W. Horton.
59	Landscape.	Mr. W. Horton.
123	View of Crown Point, Trowse.	Mr. Fish, Yarmouth.

FIRST EXHIBITION OF THE EAST OF ENGLAND ART UNION, 1842

No.	*Subject*
98	Vessels in a calm off Lowestoft.
104	Scene on the Wensum—Sun breaking out after a shower.
106	Yarmouth Beach, with figures

FIRST EXHIBITION OF THE NORFOLK AND NORWICH ASSOCIATION FOR THE PROMOTION OF THE FINE ARTS, 1848

No.	*Subject*
19	Sketch of the Interpreter to Ibrahim Pacha, who visited London in 1846.
26	Vessel passing a lock.
70	Carrow Old Staithe.
112	Drainage Mill.
138	The evening train.
236	Gorleston River sunrise.
325	Caistor.

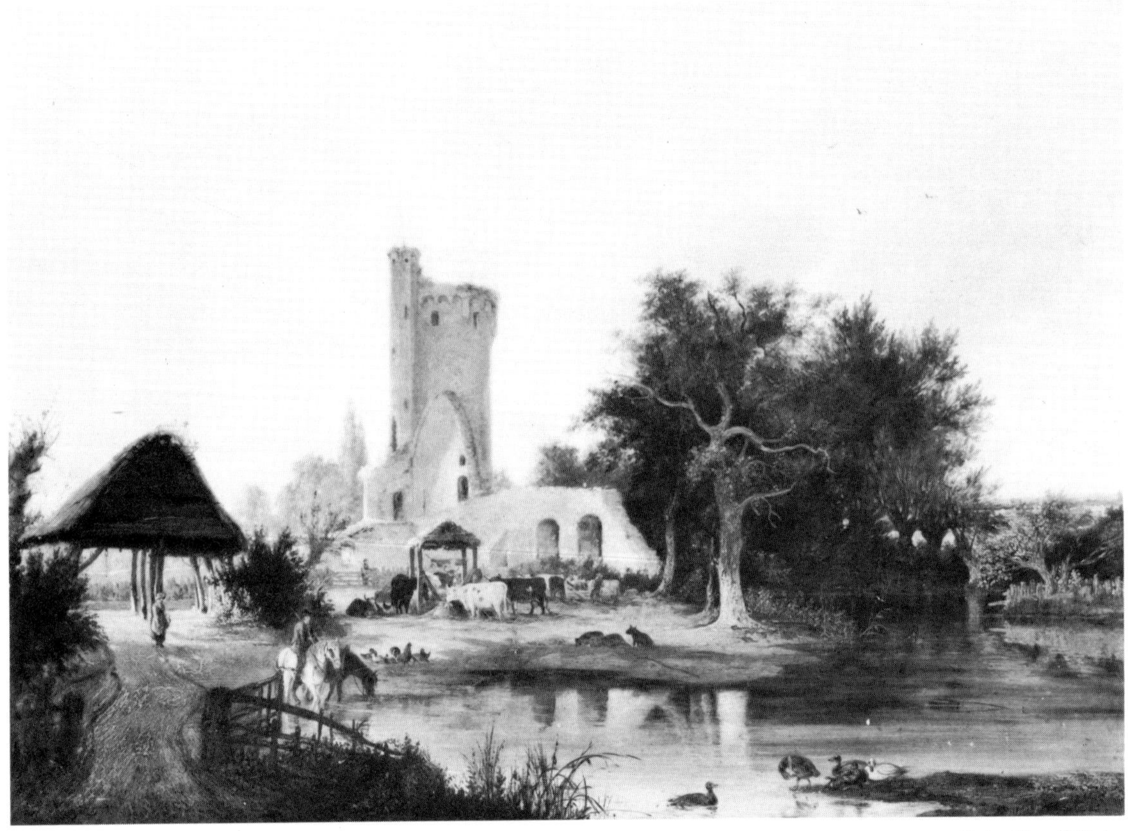

Alfred Stannard *Caistor Castle 1851* *Oil* 21 × 29½ *in.*

EXHIBITION OF THE NORFOLK AND NORWICH ASSOCIATION FOR THE PROMOTION OF THE FINE ARTS, 1849

No.	*Subject*
11	Fishing boats.
19	Seashore—morning.
53	On the River Deben.
87	Gorleston Pier Head, from the south.
93	Beach scene.
333	Pilot cutter coming in.
394	At Trowse.
398	Postwick Grove.
416	Sheep washing.

THIRD EXHIBITION OF THE NORFOLK AND NORWICH ASSOCIATION FOR THE PROMOTION OF THE FINE ARTS, 1852

No.	*Subject*
125	Scene at Trowse, Norfolk.

EXHIBITION OF THE NORFOLK AND NORWICH FINE ARTS' ASSOCIATION AND OF THE PHOTOGRAPHIC SOCIETY, 1856

No.	*Subject*	£	s.	d.
48	Sheep washing.	12	12	0
247	Caistor Castle.	8	8	0
276	River scene.	5	5	0
284	Lane scene, Trowse.	4	4	0

NORFOLK AND NORWICH FINE ARTS ASSOCIATION
Exhibition of the Works of Modern Artists, 1860

No.	*Subject*	£	s.	d.
28	Gorleston, looking towards Yarmouth.	10	0	0

BRITISH MEDICAL ASSOCIATION LOAN COLLECTION
of the Works of Norfolk and Suffolk Artists, 1874

No.	*Subject*	*Lent by*
218	Fisherman's cottage (oil painting).	Mr. Jacob Mills.

NORWICH ART LOAN EXHIBITION
In aid of the Fund for the Restoration of the Church of St. Peter Mancroft, 1878

No.	*Subject*	
75	Whitlingham Lane	Mr. W. C. Lowne.
104	View on the Norfolk Coast.	Mr. E. M. Edwards.
169	Sea piece.	Mrs. Norgate.
174	Fishing boats off Yarmouth.	Mr. W. C. Lowne.
188	Landscape.	Samuel Aldred, Esq., M.D.
259	Beach scene.	Rev. J. Thackray.
334	Cottage at Thorpe.	Rev. J. Thackray.
340	View at Upper Sherringham.	H. Staniforth Patteson, Esq.
418	Pakefield Beach, near Lowestoft.	Rev. J. Thackray.

SWAFFHAM FINE ART EXHIBITION, 1882

No.	*Subject*	*Lent by*
159	On the Thames, Hammersmith.	Mr. J. Reeve.

FINE ART EXHIBITION
In aid of the new Norfolk and Norwich Hospital, 1883

No.	*Subject*	*Lent by*
29	Whitlingham Lane.	Mr. W. C. Lowne.
7	Mouth of the Yare.	Mr. J. J. Colman, M.P.
44	Sea piece.	Mr. J. J. Colman, M.P.
9	Yarmouth Quay	Mr. W. C. Lowne.
38	Fishing boats off Yarmouth.	Mr. W. C. Lowne.

NORWICH ART LOAN EXHIBITION
In aid of the Fund for the Restoration of St. Peter Mancroft Church, 1885

No.	*Subject*	*Lent by*
15	Yarmouth Beach.	J. J. Colman, Esq., M.P.
20	Peterborough Cathedral.	Donald Steward, Esq.

LOAN COLLECTION OF PICTURES AND WATER-COLOUR DRAWINGS
Exhibited at the Agricultural Hall Gallery, Norwich, during the Grand Oriental Bazaar, 1894

OIL-PAINTINGS

No.	*Subject*	*Lent by*
29	Gorleston.	J. J. Colman, Esq., M.P.
30	Sea Piece.	J. J. Colman, Esq., M.P.

EXHIBITS AT THE "STANNARD" EXHIBITION, 1934

No.	*Subject*	*Lent by*
1	Seascape. Panel $11\frac{3}{4} \times 13\frac{3}{4}$ in.	Mr. H. C. Townsend.
22	Whitlingham. Signed and dated 1828. Panel, $14 \times 18\frac{3}{8}$ in.	Mr. C. R. Bignold.
3	Sluice gates on the River Wensum. Panel, $22\frac{1}{2} \times 31\frac{1}{2}$ in.	Mr. F. J. Nettlefold.
4	Beach with figures and boats. $13\frac{1}{2} \times 17$ in.	Mr. George Dipple.
5	Beach scene. Signed and dated 1834. Panel, $12\frac{1}{2} \times 17\frac{3}{4}$ in.	Mrs. E. J. Mills.
6	Yarmouth Beach scene with boats and figures. Signed and dated 1847. $30\frac{1}{4} \times 49\frac{1}{2}$ in.	Tolhouse Museum, Great Yarmouth.
7	Coast scene with boats. $8\frac{1}{2} \times 14$ in.	Mr. Henry N. Holmes.
8	Beach scene with hut. Signed and dated 1834. $18\frac{1}{2} \times 23\frac{1}{2}$ in.	Mr. Henry N. Holmes.
9	A view near Trowse (by Alfred Stannard and Beattie, probably Mrs. Alfred Stannard). $23 \times 41\frac{1}{2}$ in.	Mr. H. K. Henderson.
10	Yarmouth Harbour. $9\frac{1}{2} \times 12\frac{3}{4}$ in.	Mr. Frank Hill.
11	Loading Timber. $16\frac{1}{2} \times 21\frac{5}{8}$ in.	Mr. Bernard Boswell.
12	Lowestoft Beach. Signed and dated 1871. $14\frac{3}{4} \times 19\frac{1}{2}$ in.	Mr. Bernard Boswell.
13	Early morning, Pakefield Beach. $19\frac{1}{2} \times 23\frac{1}{2}$ in.	Mrs. Blofield.
14	River scene with boats and figures. Signed and dated 1873. $22\frac{1}{2} \times 29\frac{1}{2}$ in.	Mr. George Dipple.

No.	*Subject*	*Lent by*
15	Beach scene. Signed and dated 1882. $9\frac{5}{8}\times13\frac{3}{4}$ in.	Mr. L. R. Nightingale.
16	Yarmouth Beach. $12\frac{1}{2}\times18\frac{7}{8}$ in.	Mr. A. E. Barham.
17	Caistor Castle. Signed and dated 1849. $40\frac{1}{2}\times40$ in.	Mr. Crauford Jordan.
18	Landscape and cottage. $7\frac{1}{2}\times5\frac{1}{2}$ in.	Miss Turner.
19	Landscape—windmill and wherries. $5\frac{3}{4}\times9\frac{3}{4}$ in.	Mr. Edward M. Hansell
20	Woodland scene—panel, $7\frac{5}{8}\times11\frac{1}{8}$ in.	Mr. Donald D. Day, F.R.C.S.
21	Farmhouse with man and sheep. Signed and dated 1880. $10\frac{1}{2}\times14\frac{1}{4}$ in.	Miss Turner.
22	Landscape, cottage and Church. $11\frac{3}{4}\times15\frac{3}{4}$ in.	Mr. Bassett F. Horner.
23	Cottage at Trowse. $7\frac{3}{4}\times6$ in.	Mr. A. H. Gray.
24	Landscape with figures. Initials A.S. $6\frac{1}{8}\times9\frac{1}{2}$ in.	Mr. Percy Moore Turner.
25	Yare below Norwich. Signed. $8\frac{1}{2}\times11\frac{5}{8}$ in.	Mr. E. D. Tillett.
26	Seascape from beach. Signed and dated 1884. $13\frac{1}{2}\times16\frac{5}{8}$ in.	Colonel S. Garerd Hill, V.D.
27	Caistor Castle. Signed and dated 1830. Pastel, $18\frac{1}{4}\times29$ in.	Mr. R. B. Angell.
28	The Devil's Tower, Norwich. Pastel, $11\frac{1}{2}\times9$ in.	Mr. Bernard Boswell.
29	Landscape near Norwich. Millboard, 11×15 in.	Mrs. S. W. Jackson Cook.
30	Crayon sketch. Signed and dated 1830. $12\frac{1}{4}\times7\frac{5}{8}$ in.	Rev. E. A. Parr.

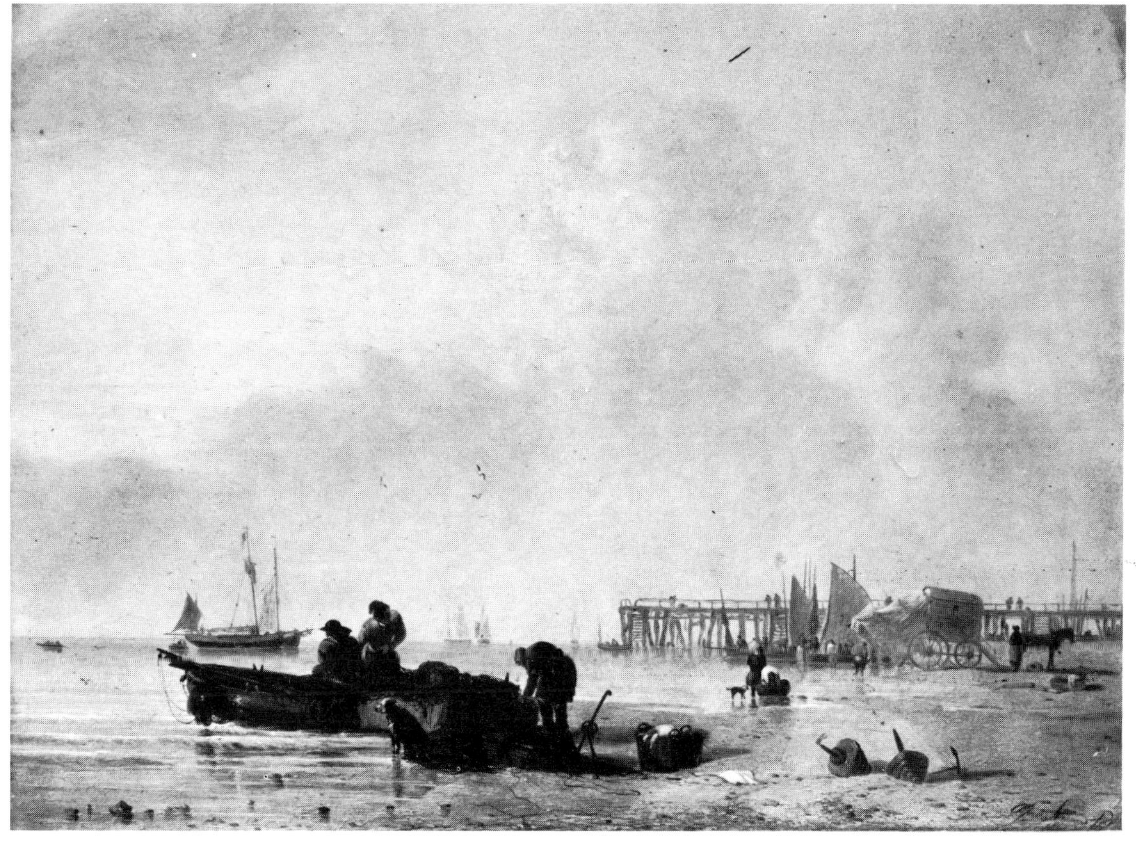

Alfred Stannard *Old Yarmouth Jetty 1861* *Oil on canvas*

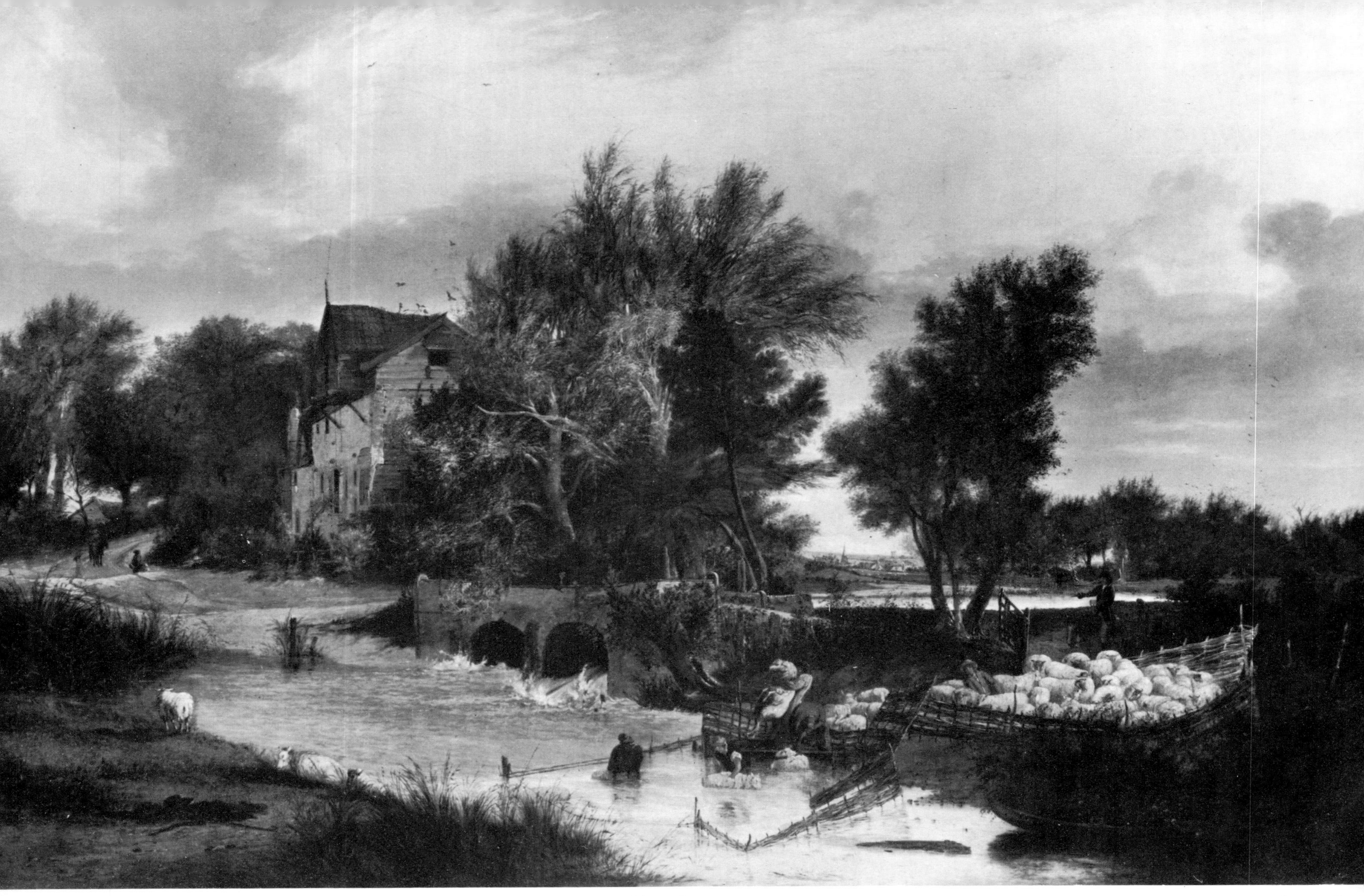

Alfred Stannard *Sheep dipping* *Large oil*

ALFRED GEORGE STANNARD

(1828-1885)

1828 Alfred George Stannard was the eldest son of Alfred Stannard and was born on 15th July, 1828. It is not to be wondered that being the son of Alfred Stannard and the brother of Eloise Harriet Stannard that he decided early in life to become an artist.

1848 At the age of twenty years he left his native city to tour Wales, returning with numerous studies from which were developed many exhibits. His tour included Snowdon, Caernarvon, Llanberis, Harlech Castle and Circaeth Castle.

After studying under his father his work attained such quality that a work was
1851 accepted by the British Institution in 1851. It is interesting to note that his first exhibit
1852 was a still life. The following year, 1852, the following notice appeared in the Norwich
Mercury:

> Married on Saturday last at St. George's Tombland, by the Rev. S. Hodgson, brother of the bride, Mr. A. G. Stannard, eldest son of Mr. A. Stannard, Artist, to Anna Maria, youngest surviving daughter of Mr. D. Hodgson and grand-daughter of the late Francis Stone, Architect.

1854 In 1854 the family moved to London to seek fame and fortune and for a year resided at
No. 25, London Street, Fitzroy Square. Perhaps the cost of living in London proved
1856 too great for we find our artist living at Castle Meadow, Norwich, in the year 1856,
dispatching to the Exhibition at the British Institution *The Roadside Barn*.

Plate *The Woodlands* was one of his Royal Academy exhibits in 1858. This delightful example was in the author's collection some twelve years ago.

1867 In 1867 A. G. Stannard exhibited several Swiss views, which rather suggests that he may have joined forces with one of the other members of the Norwich School and ventured abroad.

1878 In 1878 two collectors, Rev. S. Thackray and G. L. Coleman, loaned two of his works to a Norwich Exhibition.

It would seem that Alfred George Stannard moved to Great Yarmouth at the end of his life and died there in 1885. He left a wife and many children, several of whom emigrated to New Zealand and America.

THE PAINTINGS

Alfred George Stannard in his early work was very careful in his drawing, using bright colours as he painted the rising or setting sun. In his mid to late period one looks for a broken sky and much use of impasto. By using a coarse brush stroke he achieves considerable movement. His seas tend to be rather dramatic at times, when the atmospheric conditions permit. When calms are depicted the reflections are effected by extraordinary excellent tones. His Welsh pictures, painted about 1848, often have a characteristic warm light pervading the buildings and other objects reflecting the light. To obtain distance, shipping is often shown receding in size. In the distance, a building will often be shown, leaving one wondering at its remarkable size. Our artist executed many pastels, sometimes of considerable size. I have seen views of Sheringham and Wales in this medium.

About 1858 he was probably influenced by W. H. Crome, and painted several paintings in a green key. Plate *The Woodlands* is such a painting.

A. G. Stannard only signs occasionally, his signature appears sometimes running along a pathway into the picture.

There is about A. G. Stannard's work a great sense of idealism—the shepherd tending his flock beneath a summer sky, or a boy resting in the shadow of an oak whilst his sheep gracefully graze. As we accustom our eyes to his idiom I believe we shall grow to admire more and more this painter from one of the great Norwich painting families.

EXHIBITION OF NORWICH SCHOOL PICTURES

Norwich Castle Museum and Art Galleries, October, 1927

OIL PAINTINGS

No.	*Subject*
95	View of Gresham, near Cromer. $20\frac{1}{2} \times 26\frac{1}{2}$ in.
96	Woodland scene (in the style of Stark). $7\frac{1}{2} \times 11$ in.

ROYAL ACADEMY EXHIBITS

Year	*No.*	*Subject*
1856	414	The Village brook.
1858	386	Woodlands.
	774	A sunny afternoon.
1859	434	The woodland—spring.

BRITISH INSTITUTE

Year	*No.*	*Subject*
1851	74	Fruit from Nature. 34×38 in.
	225	Road to the Mill. 42×50 in.
	3	Chalk Hill Terrace, Thorpe Hamlet.
1856	410	The roadside barn, Castle Meadow.
1857	396	An English Village.
	524	The harvest field.
1859	385	A bit of the meadows.
	409	The hamlet—a sketch from nature.
1864	291	Cottage home.

SOCIETY OF BRITISH ARTISTS

Year	*Subject*
1854	In early spring.
1855	A gypsy's haunt.
	Evening.
1856	The Dairy Farm.
	An English road.
1857	The breakwater.

STANNARD EXHIBITION, 1934

No.	*Subject*	*Lent by*
31	Whitlingham Church and the Yare Valley. Signed and dated 1856. $35\frac{3}{4} \times 27\frac{5}{8}$ in.	Mr. Aubrey Blake.
32	Old water mill. $14\frac{5}{8} \times 17\frac{5}{8}$ in.	Mr. Alfred Boswell.
33	View of Bredon with wherries. $21 \times 29\frac{3}{8}$ in.	Mr. P. G. Back.

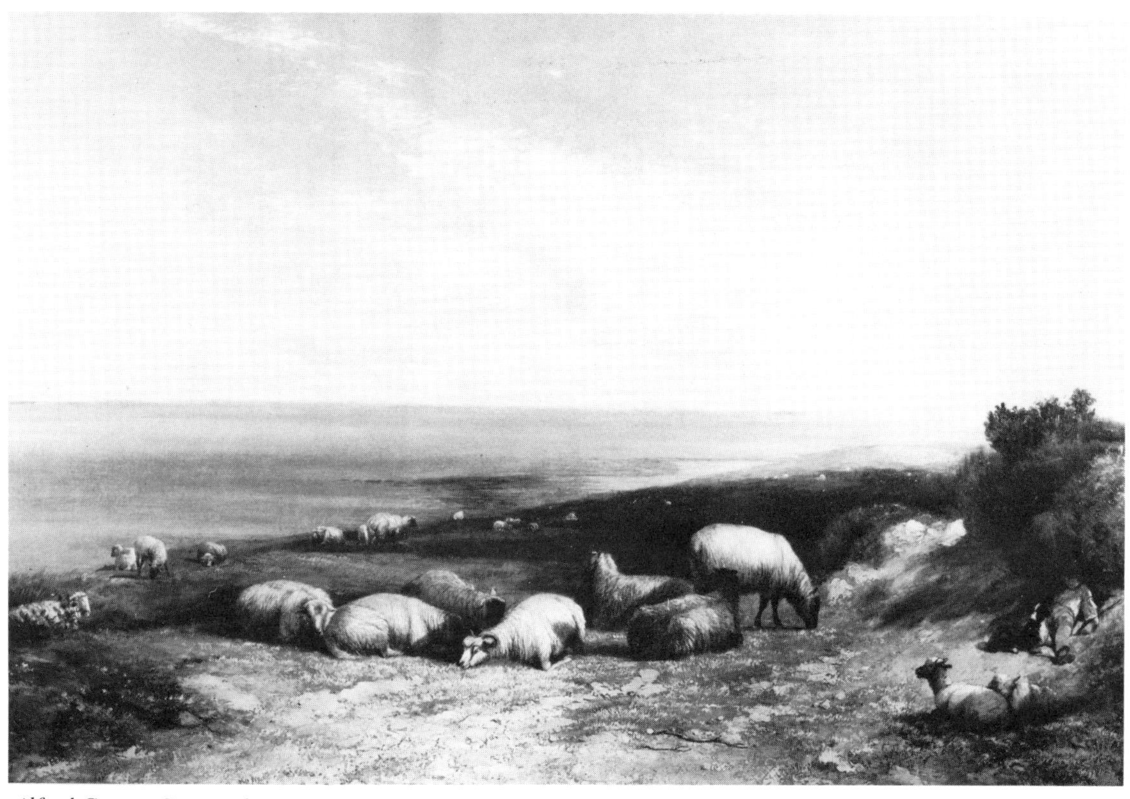

Alfred George Stannard *A Sunny Afternoon* *Oil on canvas* 24 × 36 *in.*

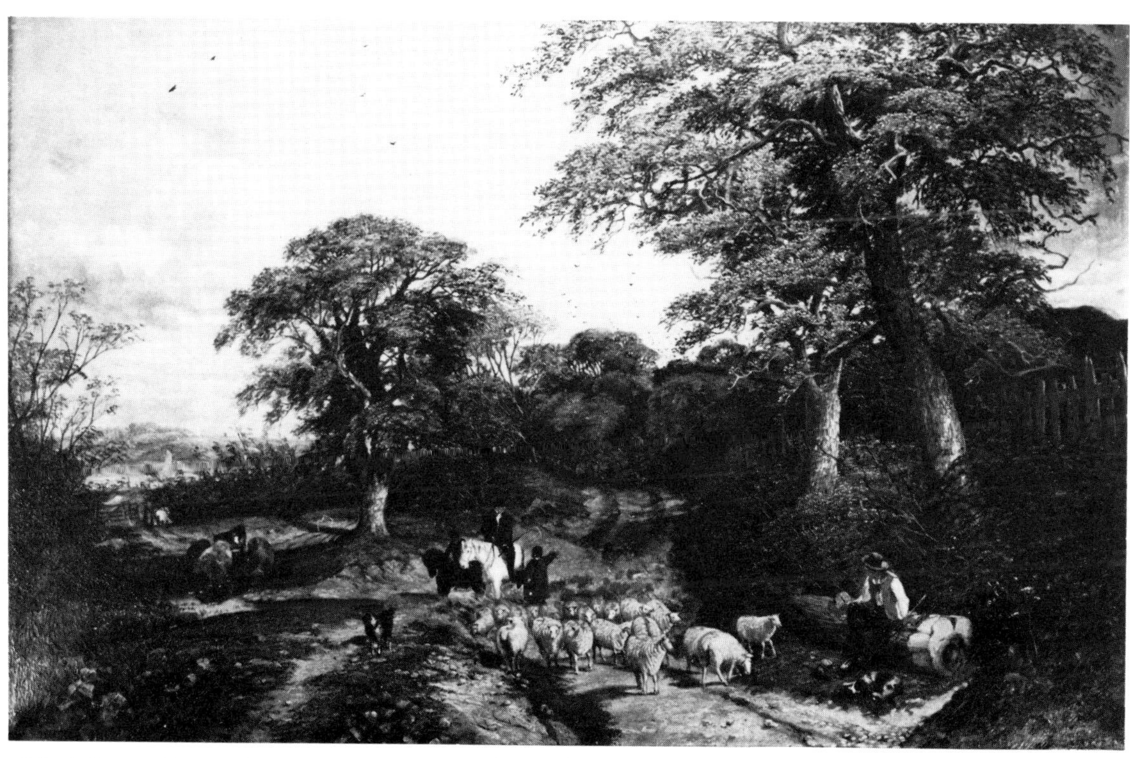

Alfred George Stannard *An English Road* *Oil on canvas* 22 × 35 *in.*

No.	*Subject*	*Lent by*
34	Yarmouth Jetty. $8\frac{1}{2} \times 11\frac{3}{8}$ in.	Mr. J. T. Havard.
35	Sea piece. $19\frac{3}{4} \times 29\frac{1}{2}$ in.	Mr. Henry E. Humphris.
36	The breakwater. Signed and dated 1883. $15\frac{7}{8} \times 13\frac{5}{8}$ in.	Mr. W. Browne.
37	River scene between Trowse and Lakenham. $25\frac{3}{8} \times 29$ in.	Mr. C. F. Bond.
38	Landscape with ruin. Signed. Pastel, $20\frac{1}{4} \times 29\frac{3}{4}$ in.	Mr. John Potter.
38A	Evening—Trowse Church. Panel, $4\frac{3}{4} \times 7\frac{1}{2}$ in.	Mr. H. Leeds.

NORWICH EXHIBITS

FIRST EXHIBITION OF THE EAST OF ENGLAND ART UNION, 1842

No.	*Subject*
2	Light air of wind.
157	Black tower, painted on the spot.
210	A study of a ruin.

FIRST EXHIBITION OF THE NORFOLK AND NORWICH ASSOCIATION FOR THE PROMOTION OF THE FINE ARTS, 1848

No.	*Subject*
36	Bala Lake.
47	A Welsh river—moonrise.
48	Snowdon, North Wales.
77	Caernarvon.
285	Lake of Llanberis, North Wales.
304	Trout stream—evening.
351	Gorleston Pier—heavy weather.
367	Campsey Ash High House, Suffolk, the seat of J. G. Sheppard, Esq.
378	Scene on the Welsh Coast.
379	A mountain torrent.
388	Scene in North Wales—sunrise.

SECOND EXHIBITION OF THE NORFOLK AND NORWICH ASSOCIATION FOR THE PROMOTION OF THE FINE ARTS, 1849

No.	*Subject*
9	Scene on the Dee—sunset.
20	Pont-y-pair.
26	Sherringham Hills, Norfolk.
45	Evening.
63	Harlech Castle.
67	Pilot boat going off.
162	River scene, with part of Flint Castle.
183	Welsh Mill scene.
222	Welsh foot bridge.
285	A quiet lake.
306	Study from nature, North Wales.
319	Peterborough.
334	Mackerel boats—a light breeze.
402	River scene.
440	Criciceth Castle.
457	Moonlight—Chester.

THIRD EXHIBITION OF THE NORFOLK AND NORWICH ASSOCIATION FOR THE PROMOTION OF THE FINE ARTS, 1852

No.	*Subject*
63	The rustic bridge.
77	Trout fishing.
105	The stepping stone.

EXHIBITION OF THE NORFOLK AND NORWICH FINE ARTS' ASSOCIATION AND OF THE PHOTOGRAPHIC SOCIETY, 1856

No.	*Subject*	£	s.	d.
9	A summer sunset.	36	15	0
19	An English road.	26	5	0
24	The cottage farm.	5	5	0
75	Summer showers.		—	
154	The wooden bridge.	5	5	0
169	A gipsy's haunt.	10	10	0
288	A roadside barn.	4	4	0

NORFOLK AND NORWICH FINE ARTS ASSOCIATION EXHIBITION OF THE WORKS OF MODERN ARTISTS, 1860

No.	*Subject*	£	s.	d.
22	The village stream.	5	0	0
23A	The sunset hour.	20	0	0
48	The cottage farm.	12	0	0
122	An overlook—sketch on the spot.	8	0	0
142	Summer time.	40	0	0
146	A bit on the meadows.	4	4	0
169	Trowse Bridge.	4	4	0
173	Handy Willie.	6	6	0

NORWICH FINE ART ASSOCIATION

Second Exhibition of Works of Art by Modern Artists, 1869

No.	*Subject*	£	s.	d.
78	Thurn, Switzerland.	15	15	0
85	Street in Bern, Switzerland.	5	5	0
91	Winter.	6	6	0
92	Spring.	6	6	0
118	Autumn.	6	6	0
119	Summer.	6	6	0
129	Bernese Alps—sunset.	8	8	0

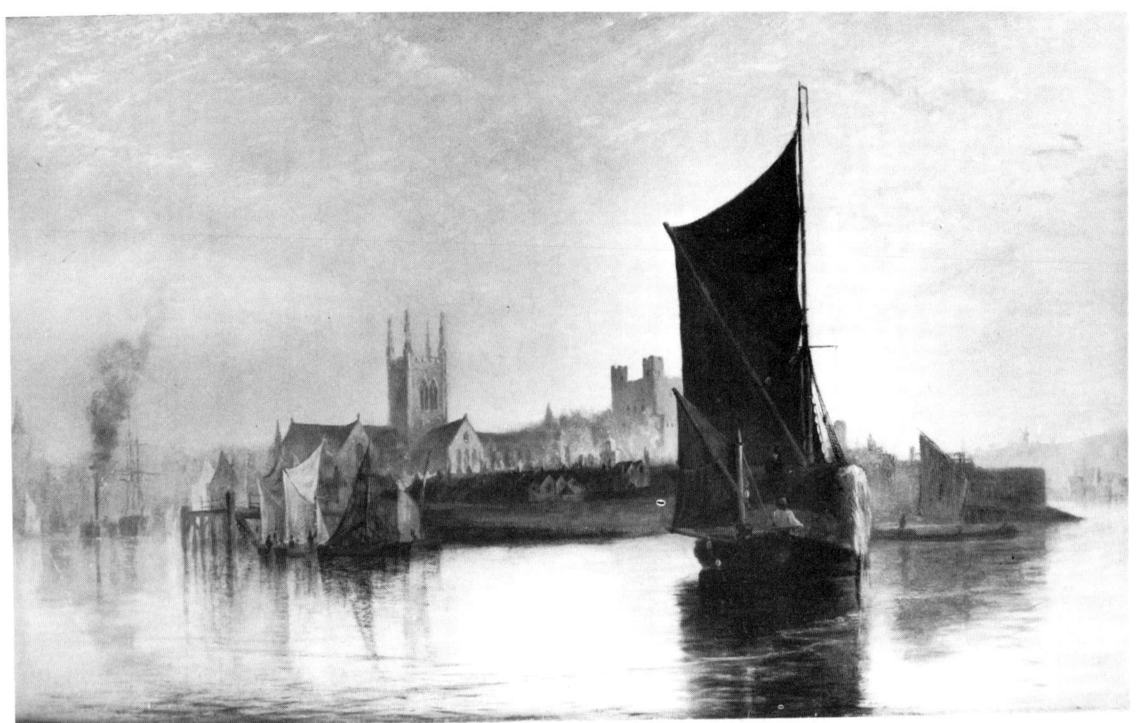

Alfred George Stannard *View of Rochester* *Oil on canvas* 18 × 30 *in.*

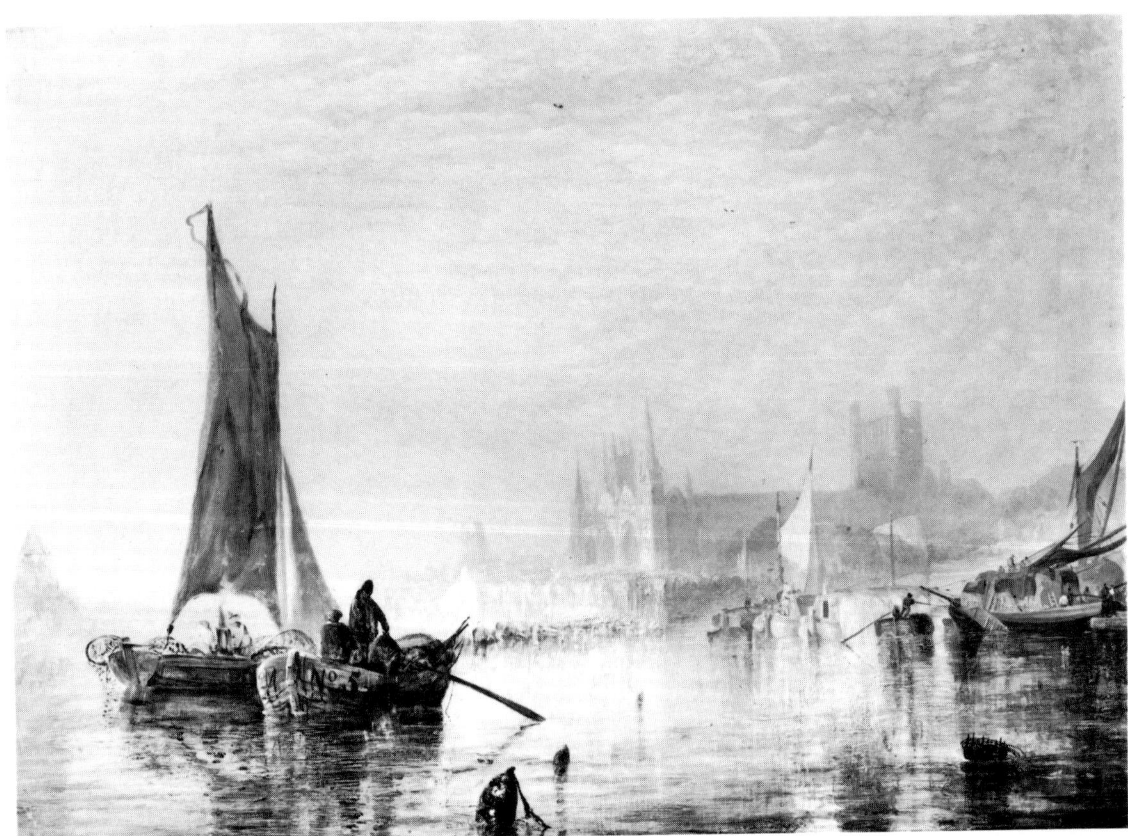

Alfred George Stannard *Ely Cathedral* *Oil* $18\frac{1}{2} \times 25\frac{1}{2}$ *in.*

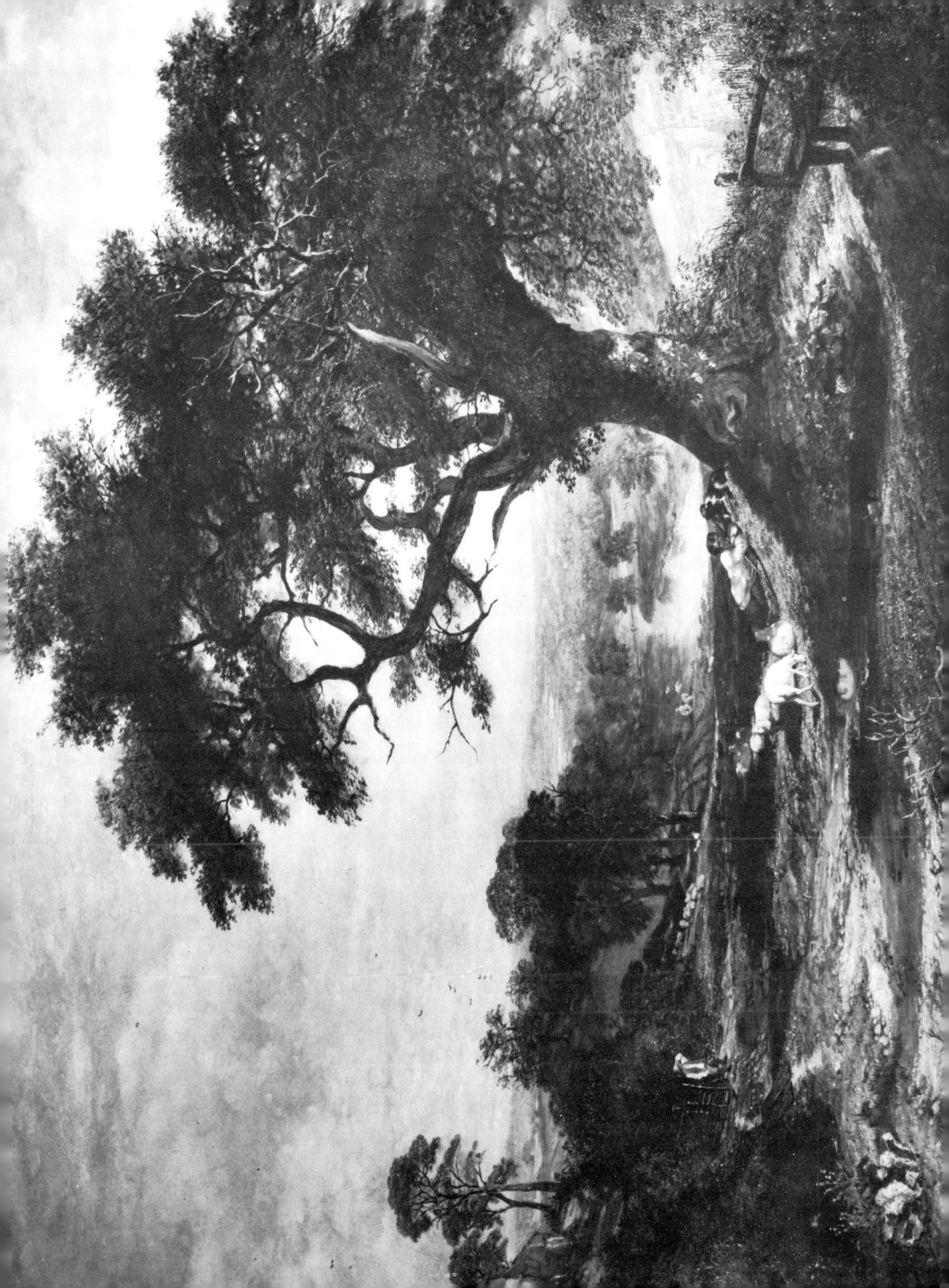

EAST ANGLIAN ART UNION AND CITY OF NORWICH FINE ART ASSOCIATION

Exhibition of Works of Art by Modern Artists, 1870

No.	*Subject*	£	s.	d.
27	River scene, Lakenham.	30	0	0
48	A winter's sunset.	10	0	0
93	The Castle of Thun, Switzerland.	6	0	0
104	Moonrise at Berne, Switzerland.	6	0	0

NORWICH ART LOAN EXHIBITION

in aid of the Fund for the Restoration of the Church of St. Peter Mancroft, 1878

No.	*Subject*	*Lent by*
117	View near Cromer.	Rev. J. Thackray.
388	An old cottage.	G. L. Coleman, Esq.

Page 327

Alfred George Stannard *The Woodlands* *Oil* 34 × 45 *in.*

Exhibited at the Royal Academy, 1858

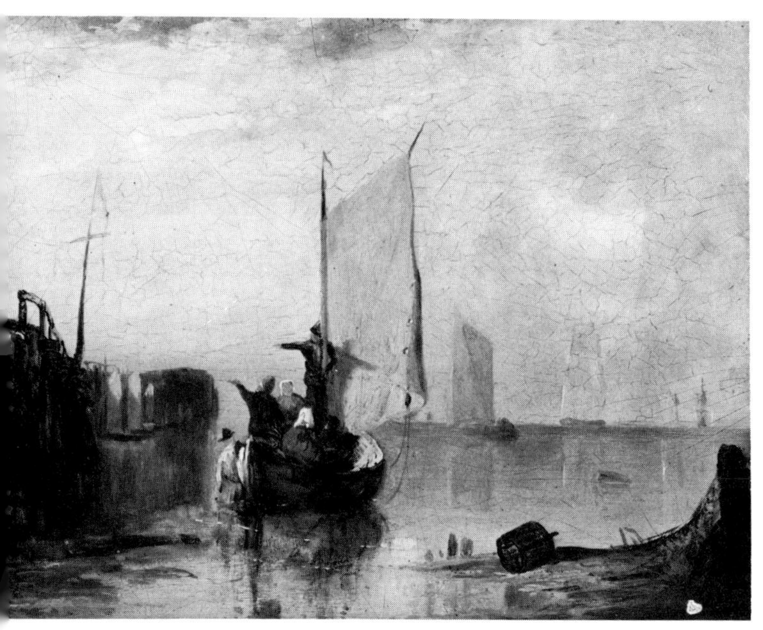

fred George Stannard *Yarmouth Jetty* *Oil on panel* $9\frac{1}{2} \times 7$ *in.*

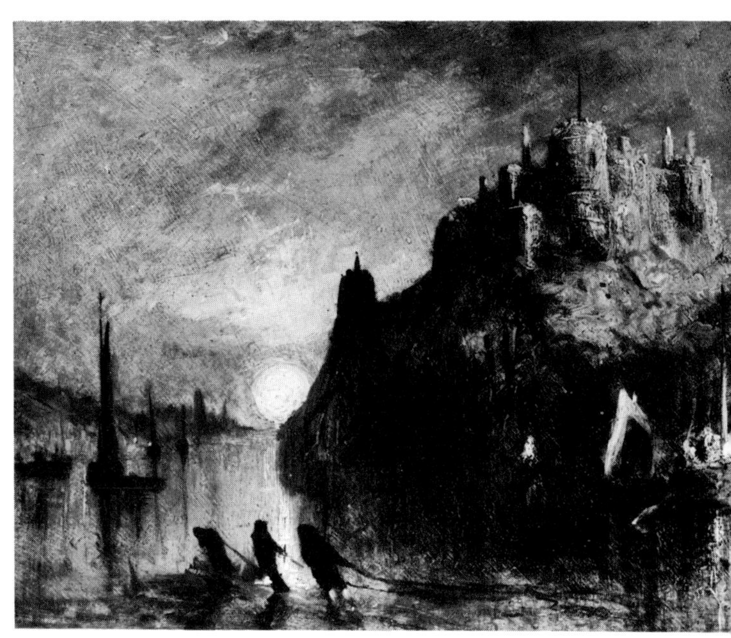

Alfred George Stannard *Harlech Castle* *Oil on panel* $9\frac{1}{2} \times 7$ *in.*

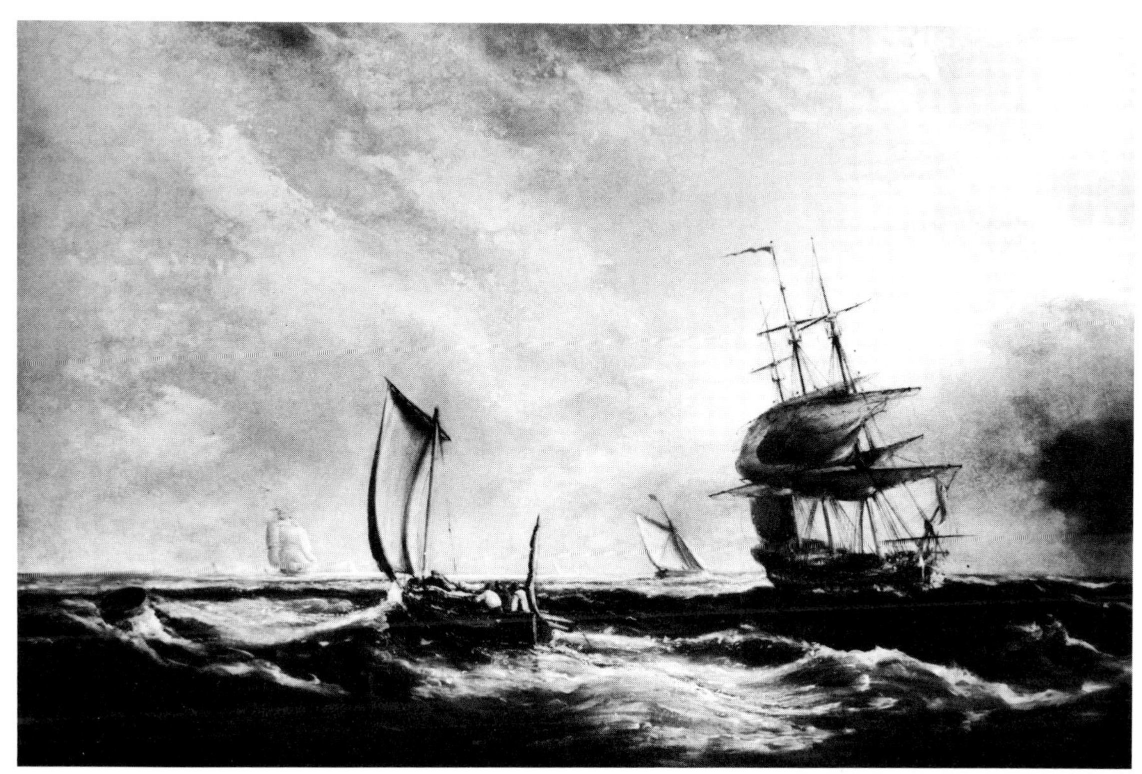

Alfred George Stannard *Oil on canvas* $19\frac{3}{4} \times 29\frac{1}{2}$ *in.*
Exhibited 1934 in "The Stannard Exhibition", No. 35

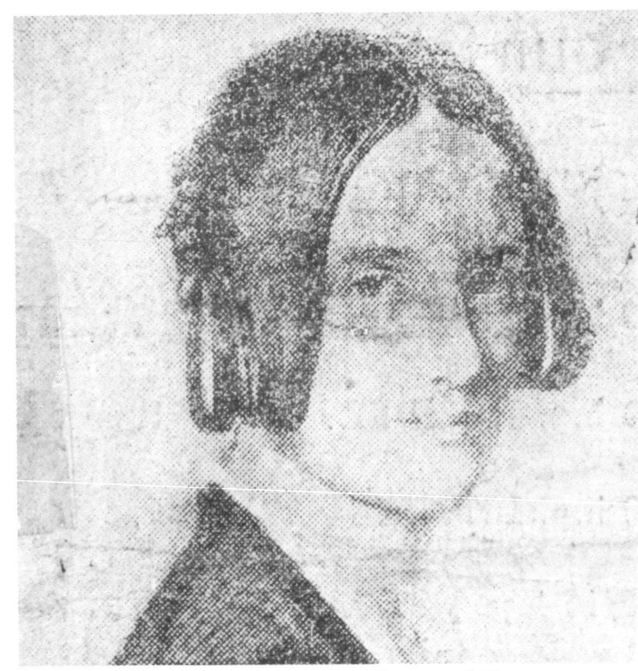

Eloise Harriet Stannard at the age of 18 years
(From an old newspaper cutting)

ELOISE HARRIET STANNARD

(1829-1915)

1829 Eloise was born in 1829, the daughter of Alfred Stannard. Alfred himself at this time being aged twenty-three years. This rather suggests that she was one of the first born of his fourteen children—alas, not all survived the rigours of Victorian hygiene. Her mother before marriage was a Miss Sparkes.

Little is known of her early education; possibly she attended her father's Art Classes and generally assisted him in the studio. As a scholar she probably attended school in company with her cousin Emily Stannard (Joseph Stannard's daughter).

1847 Our first real glimpse of her is from a photograph taken in 1847 when, as a girl of eighteen years, she appears with her hair parted down the middle in true Victorian style. Even in early life she had delicate health due to a weak heart. This resulted in her having to confine many of her activities to an indoor life. Just when her interest in still life painting developed we do not know exactly but she is said to have been quite competent by the age of eighteen years.

1852 By the year 1852 she exhibited for the first time at the British Institution. This was
1856 followed by her first exhibit at the Royal Academy in 1856. It is said that she always sold the work sent to London. There were thirty exhibits at the Royal Academy and twenty-nine at the British Institution. For many of her works she received over sixty guineas. We know from the numerous people who generously loaned her works to the Norwich Exhibitions that she sold successfully locally. Alfred Stannard often dealt with her business matters, on one occasion telling a local buyer that there were London buyers interested in his daughter's pictures should he be not forthcoming. The ring of independence made up the Stannard character. They were honest, straightforward and independent. Being proud, they set forth to the world a show of respectability.

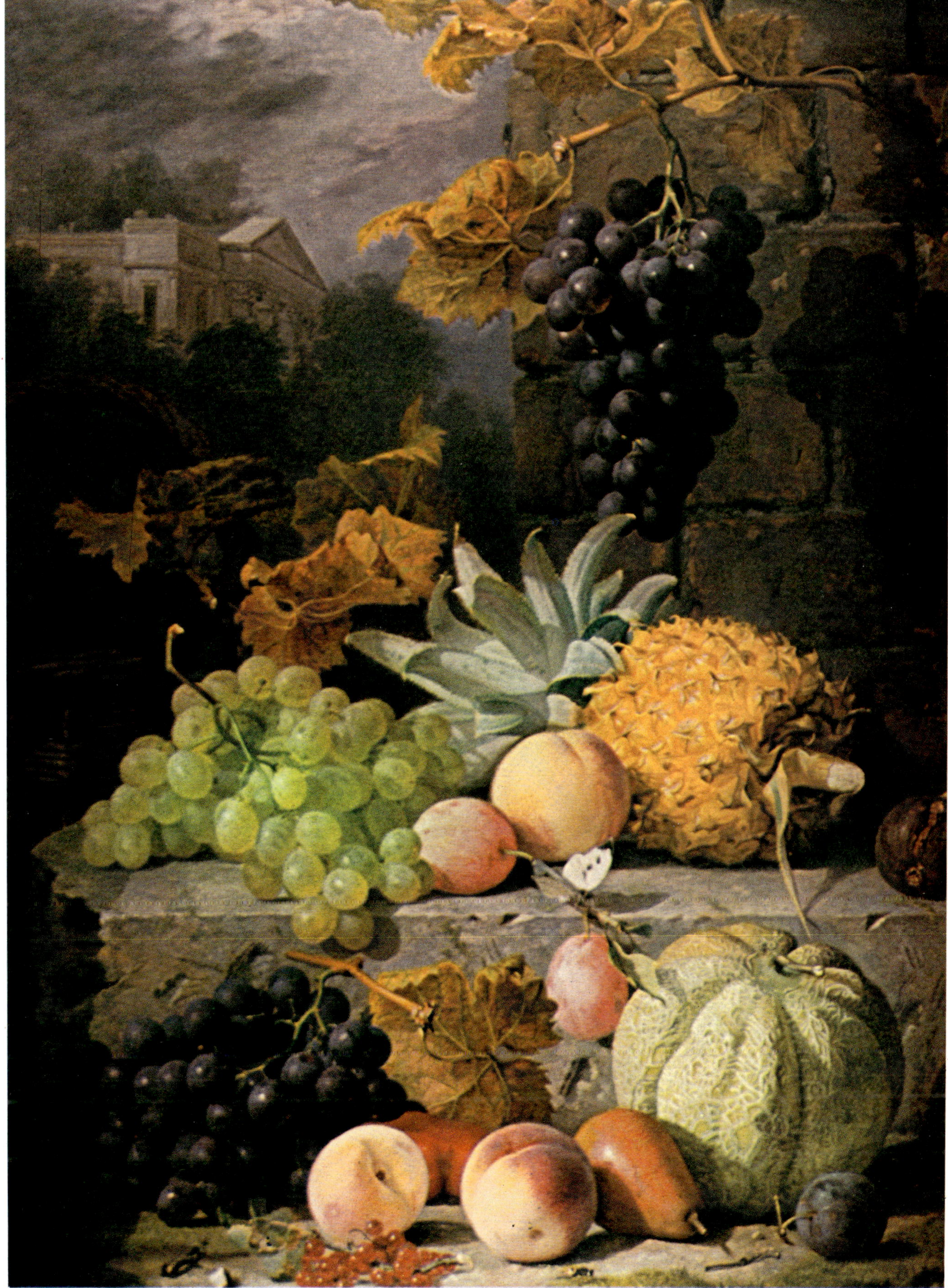

Eloise Harriet Stannard — *By the Old Garden Wall* — *Oil on canvas* 25 × 32 in.

Exhibited at the Royal Academy, 1864

1864 In 1864 our artist was living with her family in Opie Street, Norwich; by 1865 they had moved to St. Andrew's Hall Plain, in which year she despatched two exhibits to the
1865 British Institution.

Presumably it was due to her success in painting still life that she found little time for pupils, but Miss Maria Margitson, a niece of J. B. Ladbrooke, is said to have spent time in her studio.

1873 When her mother passed away in 1873, presumably being one of the eldest daughters the responsibility of the family fell upon her. This burden was unfortunate for it reduced the time she could devote to her art; thus we find that she only sent one more exhibit to London after this sad event. It was up to this time her policy to send to London her major works each year—possibly there were few collectors locally who could afford them.

Misfortune again attended her some sixteen years later when she lost her father,
1889 Alfred Stannard, in 1889. The size of the household must by this time have diminished considerably, for A. G. Stannard, her brother, had died in 1885. It must have been about this time that she moved to smaller but still generous premises at Chappel Field Road. Here she took a pleasant house partly built out of the old City wall, her studio being an upper room having an unbroken Northern light and overlooking Chappel Field Gardens.

With the departure of her family she suffered somewhat from loneliness in her later life, but always found her work a haven. It is possible that she received visits from her numerous relatives. In later life, Mr. Townsend, the picture dealer and framer, took the part her father had taken in dealing with the business aspects. When a painting was completed Mr. Townsend would send along his son to collect for framing and sale. In this way our artist was able to concentrate her attention in the creating of her pictures. As years went by she no longer attempted the larger productions of her earlier years, but painted small studies and occasionally restored paintings.

Towards the end of her life she gave an interview to a reporter. After explaining that she painted only from Nature she was asked how she occupied herself during the winter time.

"Oh", she replied, "I used to paint the gold in my paintings".

"The gold?"

"Yes, the gold objects I used to paint into my paintings for background or contrast effects. I have had lent to me several pieces from the Corporation Plate".

"The Corporation Plate?"

"Yes, I have had the Salt, the Rosewater Dish and even a ewer and tankard."

She confided to the visitor that she believed an artist should get right close to the subject and paint not one's imaginings but reality. The author had a letter from a Mr. Davidson of Norwich whose father actually supplied much of the fruit used in our artist's pictures.

Right up to the end she painted at least for an hour each day. However, she caught a severe cold which proved too much for her enfeebled strength, and she passed away at 4.30 a.m. on 2nd February, 1915—the last of the great Stannard family which had painted consistently in Norwich for over a hundred years.

THE PAINTINGS

Eloise Harriet Stannard's painting effects are so beautiful that it seems almost sacrilegious to probe beneath the surface to endeavour to discover her technique. But like all still-life painters she did have a technique.

The author has not seen any of her really early works, the earliest being a delightful carefully executed picture dating to about 1850. This was very much in the De Heem manner and pervaded throughout by a delicate blue hue. By 1864, when she painted *By the Old Garden Wall*, illustrated page 213, she had emerged with her own characteristic technique, having moved from Dutch light and shadow to real sunlight and shadow. The idea of painting a subject out of doors resulted in greater contrasts of light and extra luminosity. The blue black of grapes painted in full sunlight are under-painted with crimson lake, which is often allowed to come through their blue glaze, giving greater transparency. The masses of fruit are juxtaposed judiciously; thus two peaches are backed unobtrusively by a large tomato to great effect. Textures of fruit also receive attention, thus a foreground pear has the appearance of being a hard fruit in contrast to its neighbour, a delicious soft peach.

The placing of sienna leaves around a light passage gives great effect. The wall shadow also acts as a complement to an area of light. The backgrounds at this period are often grey blue.

About 1865 when she exhibited *In the Outhouse* at the Royal Academy, illustrated page 218, she painted some of her largest works. The introduction and use of Vandyke brown shadows seems to date from about this time.

The Plate on this page, which is dated 1890, is representative of her later period. By and large the subjects are more simple. No longer is she painting her large Academy pieces. However, her genius is just as evident, for though the subjects are smaller, they are more directly painted. The warm colours are under painted with burnt sienna and the shadows often Vandyke brown—very thinly painted. Her very late works, often dating into the twentieth century, are often broadly painted without glazes. Whilst most of her works are of fruit, many flower paintings are recorded.

Eloise Harriet Stannard usually signed her works. Her earlier works are signed in a fluent hand, the letters often being joined. Her later signature usually take the form of simple lettering. Often the "E.H.S." is quite clear, but sometimes in her written signature the "H" is like an "M".

Artists are in the interesting position of not only being able to draw inspiration from the Old Masters they admire, but can actually set out to excel them. It is more than likely that Mrs. Joseph Stannard followed the precepts of Jan Van Huysum. Whilst Eloise admired Van Huysum and drew inspiration from him, such was her individual and fluent interpretation of Nature that it may be said she rivalled her great predecessor in the creation of beautiful and natural effects.

When one considers the work of E. H. Stannard the outstanding feature is her extraordinary good taste; this, combined with her sensitive technique and genius, places her in the very top rank of British 19th-century still life painters.

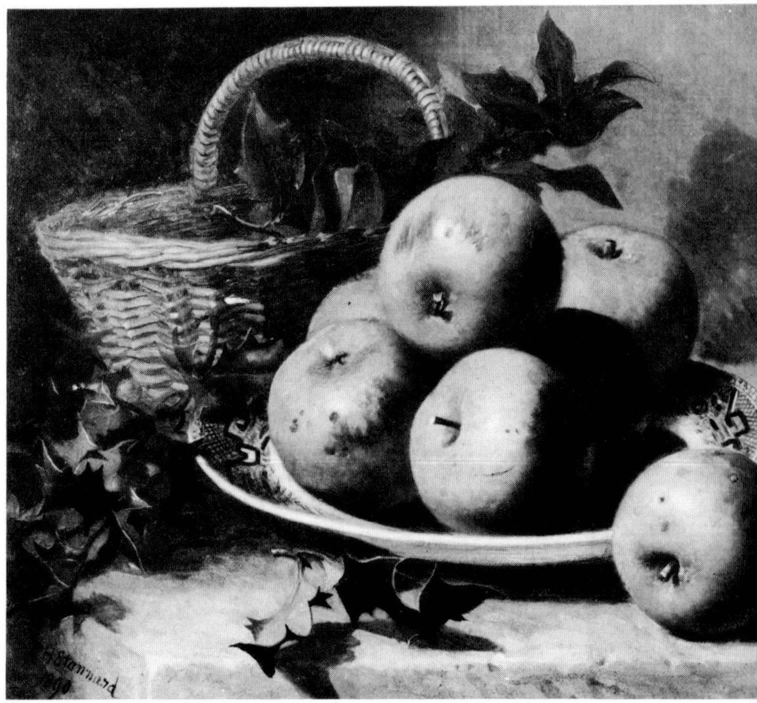

Eloise Harriet Stannard, 1890 *Oil on canvas* 12 × 1(

EXHIBITS AT ROYAL ACADEMY

Year	*No.*	*Subject*
1856	72	Autumn.
	291	Summer.
	302	Winter.
	1128	Spring.
1857	1138	Fruit.
1859	509	Fruit.
1860	157	Fruit.
	274	Fruit.
1861	477	Fruit.
	487	Fruit.
1862	281	Fruit.
	405	Melon, etc.
	418	Fruit.
1863	344	Fruit.
	373	Fruit.
1864	457	By the old garden wall (Opie Street).
1865	285	Fruit.
	329	In the outhouse.
1866	323	Fruit.
1867	554	Fruit.
1868	430	The gardener's bench.
	447	Fruit.
1869	752	Grapes and other fruit.
	892	Black grapes.
1870	6	Fruit.
1871	272	Fruit with ewer, salt, etc., belonging to the Corporation of the City of Norwich.
1872	372	Fruit.
	428	Peaches.
1873	295	Fruit.
1893	1	Russets.

EXHIBITS AT THE BRITISH INSTITUTE

Year	*No.*	*Subject*	*Price*
1852	130	Fruit from nature. 35 × 40 in.	
1853	197	Flowers from nature.	10 gns.
	358	Fruit from nature.	12 gns.
1854	167	Fruit from nature.	25 gns.
1855	35	Fruit from nature.	30 gns.
	43	Fruit from nature.	40 gns.
1856	470	Fruit from nature.	50 gns.
1857	43	Fruit from nature.	35 gns.
	301	Fruit from nature.	45 gns.
1858	39	Fruit from nature.	50 gns.
	188	Fruit from nature.	50 gns.
1859	70	Fruit from nature.	50 gns.
	129	Fruit from nature.	50 gns.
1860	99	Fruit from nature.	50 gns.
	297	Fruit from nature.	50 gns.
1861	202	Fruit from nature.	25 gns.
	542	Fruit from nature.	50 gns.
1862	415	Fruit from nature.	30 gns.
	484	Fruit from nature.	60 gns.

Year		Subject	
1863	290	Fruit from nature.	50 gns.
	321	Black grapes.	30 gns.
	391	White grapes.	30 gns.
1864	53	Fruit.	60 gns.
	208	Autumn.	50 gns.
1865	44	Fruit.	40 gns.
	232	Fruit, etc.	40 gns.
1866	144	Cottage Fruit.	50 gns.
	410	Fruit.	50 gns.
1867	396	Fruit, etc. from nature.	50 gns.

EXHIBITION OF THE NORFOLK AND NORWICH FINE ARTS ASSOCIATION AND OF THE PHOTOGRAPHIC SOCIETY, 1856

No.	Subject	£ s. d.
10	Auriculas, from nature.	10 10 0
120	Fruit, painted from nature.	31 10 0

NORFOLK AND NORWICH FINE ARTS ASSOCIATION
Exhibition of the Works of Modern Artists, 1860

No.	Subject	£ s. d.
41	Fruit, painted from nature.	—
97	Roses, a sketch from nature.	10 10 0
121	Fruit.	—

NORWICH ART LOAN EXHIBITION
in aid of the Fund for the Restoration of the Church of St. Peter Mancroft, 1878

No.	Subject	Lent by
78	Grapes.	Joseph Stanley, Jun., Esq.
101	Strawberries—"The President".	Joseph Stanley, Jun., Esq.
135	Fruit piece.	H. Staniforth Patteson, Esq.
150	Fruit.	Mr. Thomas Bingham.
285	Fruit piece.	Rev. J. Thackray.
291	Fruit piece (into which is introduced the Norwich Corporation Plate.	J. Womersley, Esq.
293	Summer fruit.	Mr. Hugh Fox.
304	Autumn fruit.	Mr. Hugh Fox.
312	The last hanging bunch.	Mr. Robert Thorns.
405	Fruit (oil painting).	J. C. Chittock, Esq.

SWAFFHAM FINE ART EXHIBITION, 1882

No.	Subject	Lent by
109	Red currants.	Mr. J. Reeve.
110	White currants.	Mr. J. Reeve.
158	Study of Strawberries.	Mr. J. Reeve.
162	Study of strawberries.	Thomas Palmer, Esq.

NORWICH ART LOAN EXHIBITION

in aid of the Fund for the Restoration of St. Peter Mancroft Church, 1885

OIL PAINTINGS

No.	*Subject*	*Lent by*
7	Fruit piece.	Alfred Kent, Esq.
8	Fruit piece.	Alfred Kent, Esq.
23	Fruit—strawberries.	S. Garerd Hill, Esq.
25	Basket of flowers.	S. Garerd Hill, Esq.
269	Flower piece.	Henry S. Patteson, Esq.
273	Fruit.	Henry S. Patteson, Esq.
273A	Fruit—raspberries.	S. Garerd Hill, Esq.
275	Fruit—grapes.	S. Garerd Hill, Esq.

STANNARD EXHIBITION, 1934

No.	*Subject*	*Lent by*
98	Winter scene. Signed and dated 1862. $10\frac{1}{2} \times 13\frac{5}{8}$ in.	Mr. Wm. Payne.
99	Dead birds and nest. $8\frac{3}{4} \times 14\frac{3}{4}$ in.	Mr. C. R. Oury.
100	Dead partridge among turnips. $13\frac{1}{2} \times 17\frac{3}{8}$ in.	Mr. Madoc Powell.
101	Melon and grapes. Signed and dated 1854. $27\frac{1}{2} \times 22\frac{1}{2}$ in.	Mr. C. R. Bignold.
102	Pineapple and grapes. $19\frac{1}{2} \times 23\frac{1}{2}$ in.	Mr. R. G. Belson.
103	Spring. Signed and dated 1866. $11\frac{5}{8}$ in. diameter.	Mrs. Spashett.
104	Spring. Signed and dated 1866. Oval, $10\frac{3}{8} \times 13\frac{1}{2}$ in.	
105	Summer. Signed and dated 1866. Oval, $10\frac{3}{4} \times 13\frac{1}{2}$ in.	Colonel S. Garerd Hill, V.D.
106	White Grapes. Diameter, $19\frac{1}{2}$ in.	Mr. C. F. Bond.
107	Pineapple and peaches. Signed and dated 1867. Diameter, $25\frac{1}{2}$ in.	Dr. L. B. Mills.
108	Winter. Signed and dated 1866. Diameter, $11\frac{5}{8}$ in.	Mrs. Spashett.
109	Autumn. Signed and dated 1866. Oval, $10\frac{1}{2} \times 13\frac{1}{2}$ in.	
110	Winter. Signed and dated 1866. Oval, $10\frac{1}{2} \times 13\frac{3}{8}$ in.	Colonel S. Garerd Hill, V.D.
111	Black and white grapes. $25 \times 20\frac{1}{2}$ in.	
112	Grapes and pineapple. $20 \times 25\frac{3}{8}$ in.	Mr. Roland F. Hornor.
113	Wild roses. Signed and dated 1890. $6\frac{3}{4} \times 9\frac{1}{2}$ in.	Mr. J. T. Havard.
114	Rabbit and turnips. Signed and dated 1878. Diameter, $17\frac{5}{8}$ in.	
115	Ducklings and meadowsweet. Signed and dated 1877. Diameter, $17\frac{3}{8}$ in.	The Exors. of Mr. Frank Hill.
116	Grapes and poppies. Signed and dated 1871. $11\frac{5}{8} \times 15\frac{1}{2}$ in.	Miss Cowper Johnson.
117	Vase and fruit. Signed and dated 1877. $23\frac{1}{4} \times 17\frac{3}{8}$ in.	Mr. G. Attoe.
118	Marguerites Signed and dated 1890. $6\frac{5}{8} \times 9\frac{1}{2}$ in.	Mr. J. T. Havard.
119	Blue tits and fruit. Signed and dated 1879. Oval, $14\frac{1}{2} \times 17\frac{1}{2}$ in.	Mr. Walter Griffiths.
120	Partridge and poppies. Signed and dated 1878. Diameter, $17\frac{5}{8}$ in.	Exors. of Mr. Frank Hill.
121	Pineapple and tomatoes. Signed and dated 1889. $10\frac{5}{8} \times 12\frac{1}{2}$ in.	Mr. G. Attoe.
122	Carnations and fruit. Signed and dated 1881. $14\frac{5}{8} \times 17\frac{5}{8}$ in	Mr. C. R. Oury.
123	Bullfinches and fruit. Signed and dated 1876. $21\frac{3}{8} \times 17\frac{1}{2}$ in.	Mr. G. Attoe.
124	Peaches and grapes. Signed and dated 1887. $15\frac{1}{2} \times 13\frac{3}{4}$ in.	Mr. W. H. Wright.
125	Lowestoft china. $11\frac{3}{8} \times 13\frac{7}{8}$ in.	Mrs. Spashett.
126	Chrysanthemums and vases. Signed and dated 1889. $10\frac{1}{2} \times 12\frac{3}{8}$ in.	Mr. G. Attoe.
127	Honeysuckle and fruit. Signed and dated 1878. $24\frac{1}{2} \times 29\frac{1}{2}$ in.	Mr. H. J. Hannent.
128	Pears and grapes. 11×15 in.	Mr. Frank Hill.
129	Grapes and raspberries. Signed and dated 1883. $13\frac{1}{2} \times 16$ in.	Mr. W. Browne.

No.	*Subject*	*Lent by*
130	Cut melon and knife. Signed and dated 1884. $23\frac{1}{2} \times 19$ in.	Mr. G. Attoe.
131	Raspberries in cabbage leaf. Signed and dated 1884. $12\frac{1}{2} \times 10\frac{1}{2}$ in.	Colonel S. Garerd Hill, V.D.
132	Fruit and hollyhock. Signed and dated 1885. $13\frac{3}{4} \times 16\frac{3}{4}$ in.	Mr. Bernard Boswell.
133	Grapes in silver bowl. Signed and dated 1884. $16\frac{1}{2} \times 13\frac{5}{8}$ in.	Mr. G. Attoe.
134	Poppies and white lilac. Signed and dated 1890. $10\frac{3}{4} \times 15\frac{3}{4}$ in.	Dr. L. B. Mills.
135	Norwich Civic plate and fruit. Signed and dated 1886. $23\frac{1}{2} \times 19\frac{1}{2}$ in.	Mr. G. H. Gowing.
156	Convolvulus and fruit. Signed and dated 1890. $12\frac{5}{8} \times 10\frac{5}{8}$ in.	Mr. G. Attoe.
137	Apricots and raspberries. Signed. $10\frac{1}{4} \times 14\frac{1}{4}$ in.	Mr. Stanley Waller.
138	Basket with fruit. Signed and dated 1884. $19\frac{5}{8} \times 13\frac{5}{8}$ in.	Mr. G. Attoe.
139	Poppies and white lilac. Signed and dated 1891. $19\frac{1}{2} \times 16\frac{1}{2}$ in.	Mrs. Mealing Mills.
140	Full ripe. Signed and dated 1893. $20\frac{1}{2} \times 17\frac{1}{8}$ in.	Tolhouse Museum, Great Yarmouth.
141	Strawberries and roses. Signed. $11\frac{1}{2} \times 14\frac{1}{2}$ in.	Mr. Stanley Waller.
142	Russett apples and basket. 12×15 in.	Mr. E. E. Palmer.
143	Basket of Apples. Signed. 12×16 in.	Mr. Frank Perry.
144	White grapes. Signed and dated 1894. $9\frac{3}{8} \times 13\frac{1}{2}$ in.	Miss M. Gardiner.

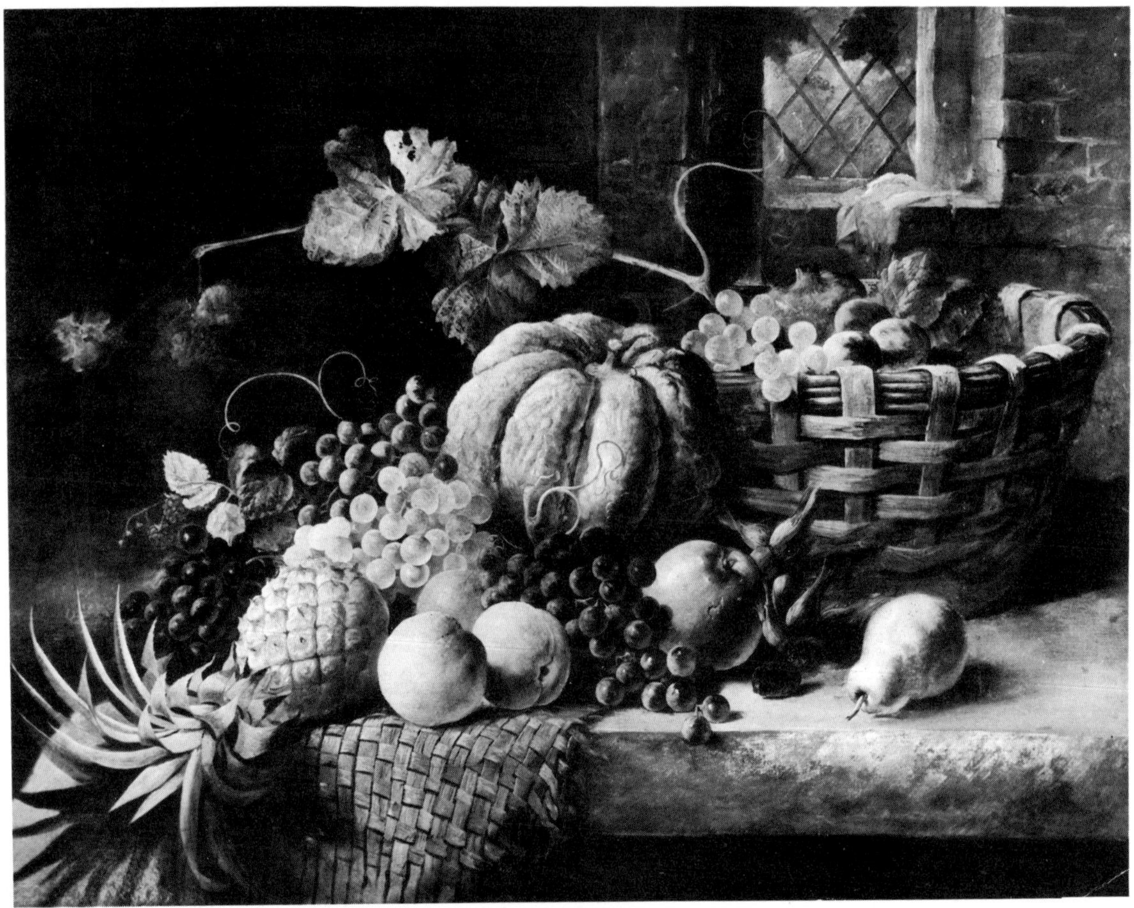

Eloise Harriet Stannard — *In the Outhouse* — *Oil on canvas* 28 × 36 *in.*

Exhibited at the Royal Academy, 1865

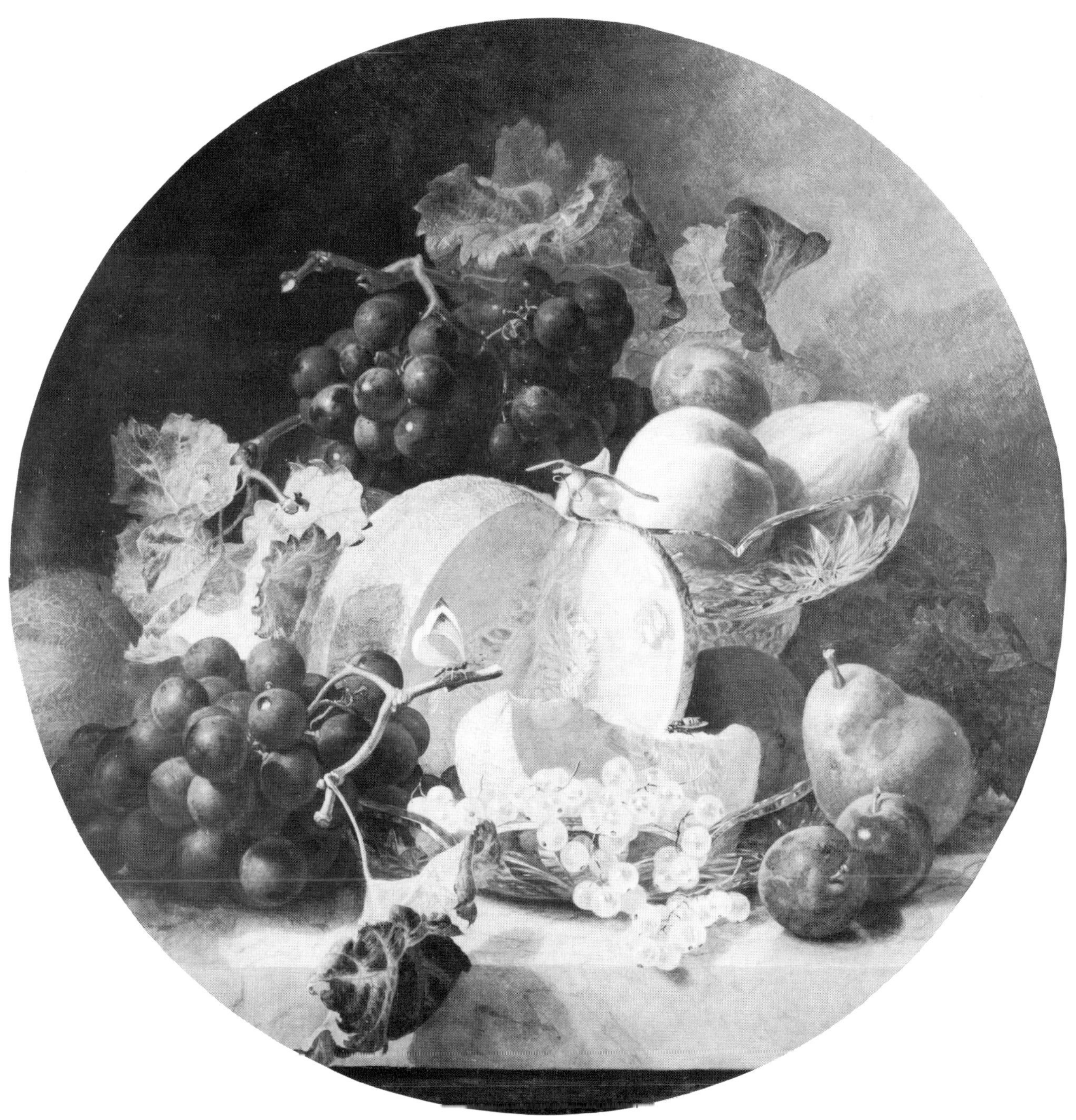

Eloise Harriet Stannard *Oil on canvas 20 in. dia.*

No.	*Subject*	*Lent by*
145	Strawberries and roses. Signed and dated 1905. $19\frac{5}{8} \times 14\frac{1}{2}$ in.	Mr. Frank Perry.
146	Partridges and barley. Signed and dated 1898. $11\frac{1}{2} \times 14\frac{1}{2}$ in.	Mr. G. Attoe.
147	Red currants. $8\frac{3}{8} \times 8\frac{1}{2}$ in.	Mr. Frank Perry.
148	Apricots. Signed and dated 1894. $8 \times 11\frac{1}{2}$ in.	Mr. R. G. Belson.
149	Strawberries. Signed and dated 1908. $10\frac{5}{8} \times 12\frac{5}{8}$ in.	Mrs. C. E. Davison.
150	Tomatoes. 8×12 in.	Mr. Frank Hill.
151	Plums. Signed and dated 1892. $8\frac{1}{8} \times 10\frac{5}{8}$ in.	Mr. H. Copeman.
152	Raspberries. Signed and dated 1894. $8\frac{1}{4} \times 11\frac{3}{4}$ in.	Mr. Madoc Powell.
153	Strawberries. Signed and dated 1888. $8\frac{3}{8} \times 10$ in.	Mr. W. H. Wright.
154	Russet apples. $9\frac{5}{8} \times 11\frac{5}{8}$ in.	Mr. E. E. Palmer.
155	Nasturtiums. $12\frac{1}{2} \times 18\frac{1}{4}$ in.	
156	Marguerites. Signed. $18\frac{1}{2} \times 12\frac{1}{2}$ in.	
157	Hawthorn. $13\frac{1}{2} \times 17\frac{1}{2}$ in.	Mr. Frank Hill.

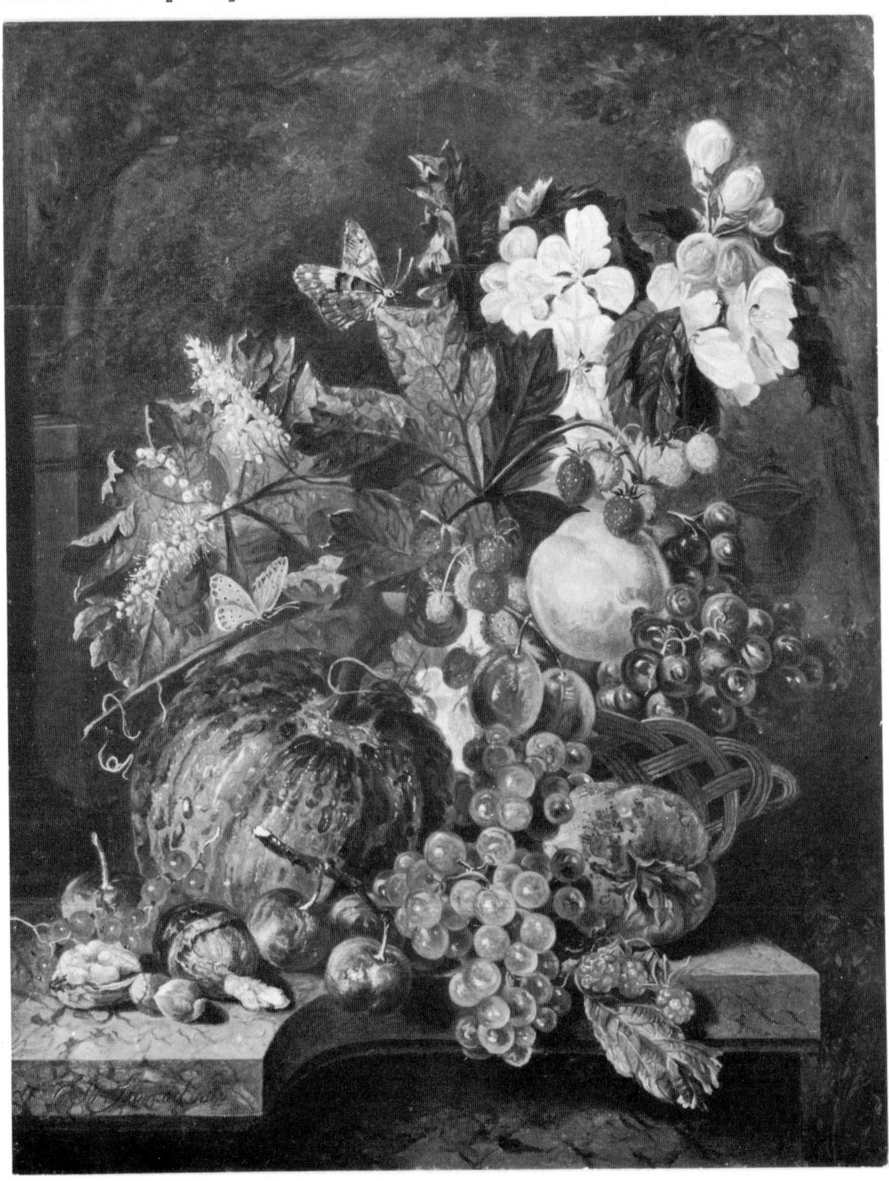

Emily Stannard (Mrs. Joseph Stannard), 1849 — *Oil on panel* 12×10 *in.* *(one of pair)*

EMILY STANNARD

(Mrs. Joseph Stannard)

(1803-1885)

1803 Emily Stannard was born in 1803, her father being Daniel Coppin, a friend of John Crome, and one of the original members of the Norwich Society, indeed, he was elected President in 1816. Her mother was a still life painter who visited the Rijksmuseum in Amsterdam to copy.

Little is known of her childhood apart from the fact that she was instructed in art by her parents.

1820 By 1820 such was the quality of her work that she was awarded the large gold medal of the Society of Arts, for an original flower painting. She also visited Holland at this time to copy works by Van Huysum.

1821 In 1821 the large gold medal was awarded to her for an original painting of fruit.

It was at the meeting of the Norwich Society that she met Joseph Stannard and it was probably due to her influence that he visited Holland. The love between them culminated in their marriage at St. George's, Tombland, Norwich, on the 3rd January,
1826 1826. They took a house, No. 5, St. Giles Terrace, Norwich.

1827 In 1827 her one and only child, Emily* was born. The arrival of the daughter brought great happiness to both Emily and Joseph, both painting some of their finest works
1828 about this time. In 1828 Emily was awarded the Isis Gold Medal for a painting of game. However, her husband's health was giving cause for alarm. Despite much care and visits to the coast he became seriously ill and passed away at 1 p.m. on the 7th December, 1830.

After Joseph's death Emily was referred to as Mrs. Joseph Stannard. Due to Joseph's success he left his wife with a certain income; presumably this was supplemented by the sale of her own works.

It would appear that Emily left the house in St. Giles shortly after Joseph's death and took a house in Rose Lane, King Street, Norwich, or she may have gone to live with her family.

Over the years she continued to paint, sending pictures to the British Institution and the Suffolk Street Exhibitions in London. From the painting (illustrated page 224)
1849 executed in 1849 we can see that she maintained a high standard of work.

Her daughter was also brought up to the Arts and spent most of her life teaching. Indeed, she may possibly have assisted her mother in the studio.

Whenever there were Loan Exhibitions in Norwich, Emily Stannard would readily
1885 lend her works. However, before the Loan Exhibition of 1886 could take place she had departed this life.

THE PAINTINGS

Emily Stannard's work is known for the strong Dutch influence. In fact, many of her works have been sold as being by eminent Dutch artists. Perhaps for this reason there are few of her signed works to be seen, although it is quite possible she signed only certain of her works. Her

---

*See "Further Painters"

earlier works have crisp impasto touches and sharp contrasting colours. The later works are softer and perhaps not of such high quality. She likes to introduce a marble slab and often signs on the slab, either with her initials, the "E" joined to the "S", or written in full "Emily Stannard or Ey. Stannard. I believe at one time she signed "Mrs. Joseph Stannard". It would appear that neither of the 1927 Exhibition works were signed. Her paintings of game compare favourably with the earlier masters. The painting of fish (illustrated page 227) is signed and dated E. Stannard 1854.

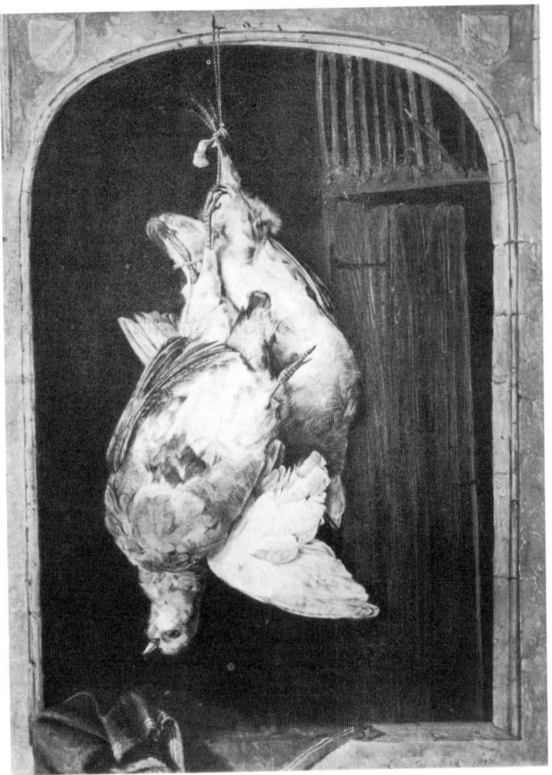

Emily Stannard (Mrs. Joseph Stannard)

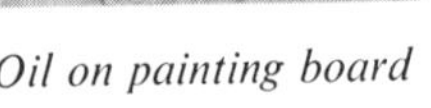

Oil on painting board

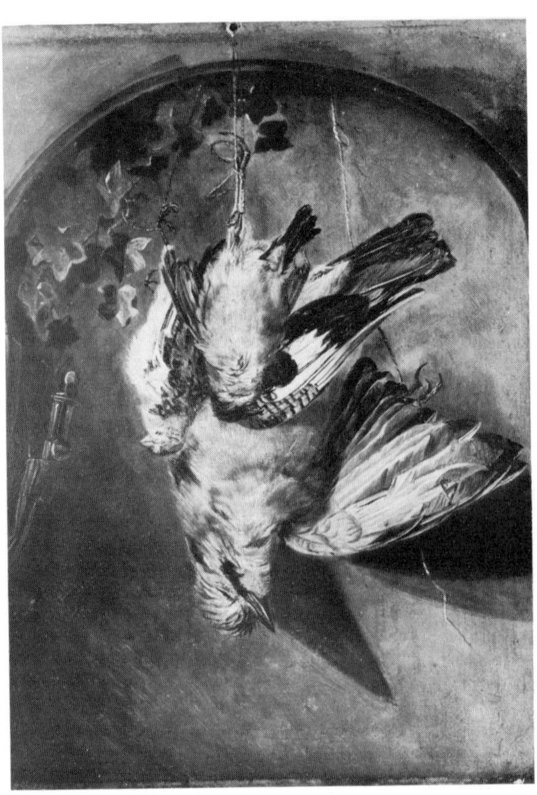

Emily Stannard (Mrs. Joseph Stannard) *Oil on board* $12 \times 9\frac{1}{2}$ *in.*

EXHIBITS AT BRITISH INSTITUTE

Year	*No.*	*Subject*
1832	361	Dead game. 22×17 in.
	583	A vase of flowers. 41×36 in.
1833	281	Dead hare. 15×17 in.
	328	Pigeons and small birds. 22×18 in.

FIRST EXHIBITION OF THE NORFOLK AND NORWICH ART UNION, 1839

No.	*Subject*
7	Group of fancy birds, from nature.
12	Fruit and flowers.
22	Partridge, from nature.
29	Hare with wood pigeons.

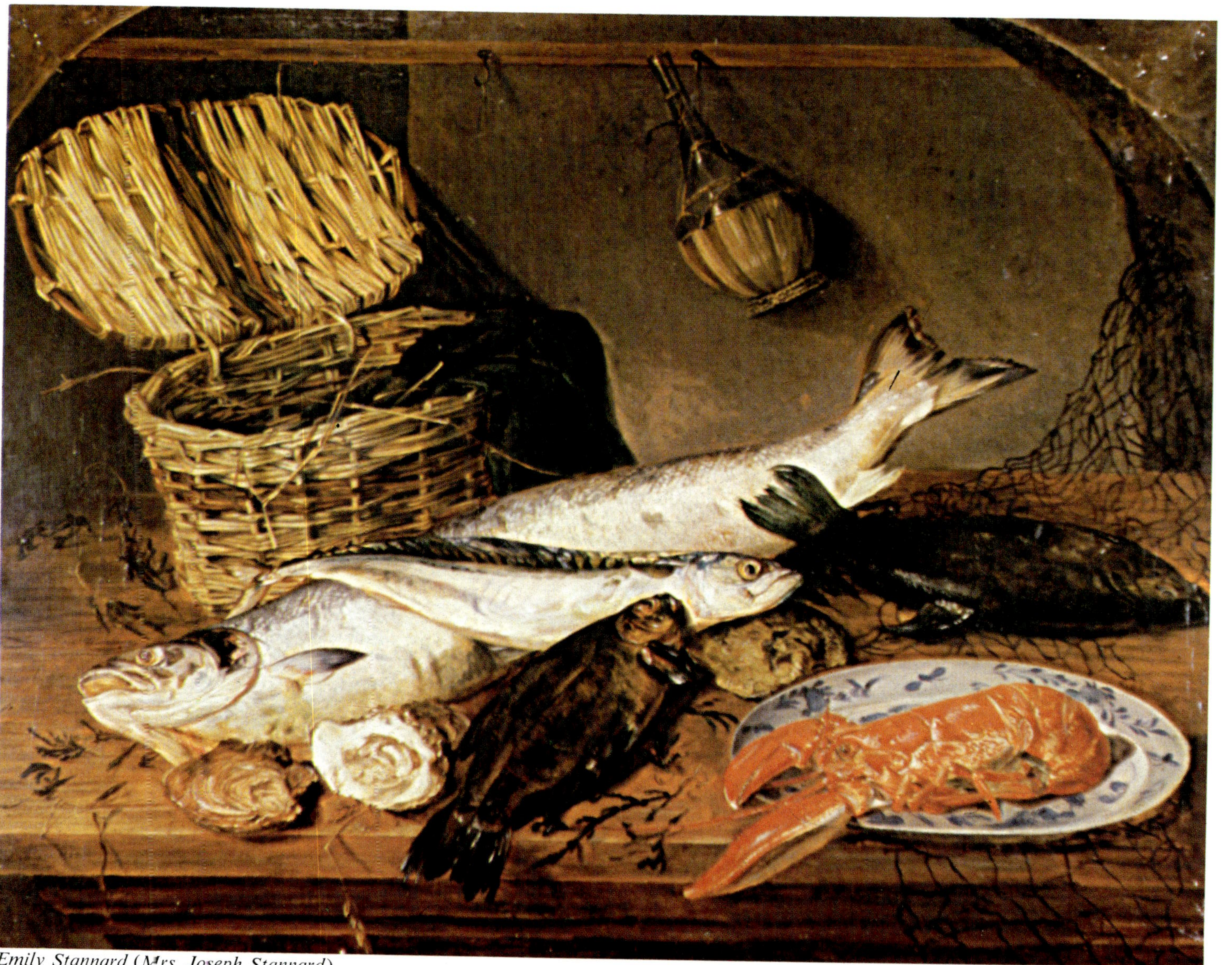

Emily Stannard (Mrs. Joseph Stannard) *Oil on Canvas* 25 × 30 *in.*

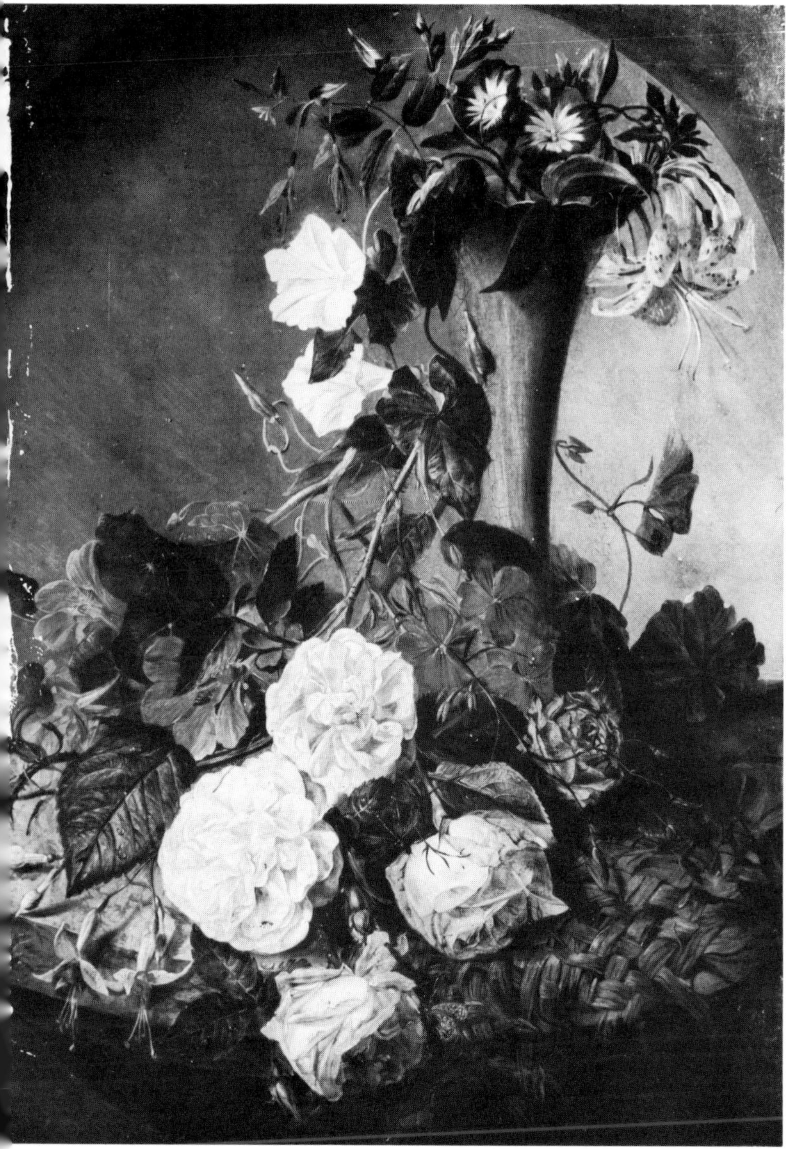
nily Stannard (Mrs. Joseph Stannard) — Oil on canvas

No.	*Subject*
174	Pheasant and wood pigeon.
195	Pheasant.
208	A vase of flowers.

FIRST EXHIBITION OF THE NORFOLK AND NORWICH ASSOCIATION FOR THE PROMOTION OF THE FINE ARTS, 1848

No.	*Subject*
28	Flowers.
59	Fruit and flowers.
195	Dead game.

SECOND EXHIBITION OF THE NORFOLK AND NORWICH ASSOCIATION FOR THE PROMOTION OF THE FINE ARTS, 1849

No.	*Subject*
43	Group of flowers.
238	Dead game.
258	Fruit and flowers.
279	Fruit and game, with a gold cup, in the possession of the Corporation of Norwich during the Mayoralty of Sir Thos. Glene.
314	Flowers.

THIRD EXHIBITION OF THE NORFOLK AND NORWICH ASSOCIATION FOR THE PROMOTION OF THE FINE ARTS, 1852

No.	*Subject*
37	The dead heron.
45	Flowers.
131	Flowers.

FOURTH EXHIBITION OF THE NORFOLK AND NORWICH ASSOCIATION FOR THE PROMOTION OF THE FINE ARTS, 1853

No.	*Subject*
9	Marsh birds.
107	Basket of flowers.

EXHIBITION OF THE NORFOLK AND NORWICH ASSOCIATION FOR THE PROMOTION OF THE FINE ARTS, 1855

Year	*Subject*	£ s. d.
19	Dead game.	
133	Dead birds.	
261	A day's sport.	15 0 0

EXHIBITION OF THE NORFOLK AND NORWICH FINE ARTS ASSOCIATION AND OF THE PHOTOGRAPHIC SOCIETY, 1856

No.	*Subject*	£	s.	d.
249	The bittern.	15	0	0
294	Autumn.	10	0	0

NORFOLK AND NORWICH FINE ARTS ASSOCIATION
Exhibition of the Works of Modern Artists, 1860

No.	*Subject*	£	s.	d.
2	Game.	—		
25	Autumn friends.	10	0	0
94	Jack and Jill—pets.	5	0	0
100	Flowers.	—		
187	Game.	—		
268	Flowers.	—		

NORWICH AND EASTERN COUNTIES WORKING CLASSES INDUSTRIAL EXHIBITION, 1867

No.	*Subject*	*Lent by*
851	Original painting—flowers.	
763	Dead game.	Wm. Dixon, Mount Pleasant.
891	Flowers.	Mr. T. G. Bayfield.
892	Game.	Mr. T. G. Bayfield.

NORWICH FINE ART ASSOCIATION
Exhibition of Works of Art by Modern Artists, 1868

No.	*Subject*	£	s.	d.
397	Flowers, from nature.	11	0	0

EAST ANGLIAN ART UNION, AND CITY OF NORWICH FINE ART ASSOCIATION
Exhibition of Works of Art by Modern Artists, 1870

No.	*Subject*	£	s.	d.
154	Birds. "Time was—we sipped the diamond dew And through the fields of ether flew, Loving and loved together! But man, who envied us our bliss, Cut short our joys and left but this Of dying thus together."	15	15	0
168	Gloxinias.	20	0	0

BRITISH MEDICAL ASSOCIATION LOAN COLLECTION
of the Works of Norfolk and Suffolk Artists, 1874

OIL PAINTINGS

No.	*Subject*	Lent by
221	Flowers.	Mrs. Stannard.
225	Dead bittern.	Mrs. J. Stannard.

EXHIBITION OF PICTURES BY LIVING ARTISTS
at the Victoria Hall Gallery, 1878

No.	*Subject*	£ s. d.
2	Flowers from my friends' gardens.	21 0 0 (in ink in margin)

NORWICH ART LOAN EXHIBITION
in aid of the Fund for the Restoration of the Church of St. Peter Mancroft, 1878

No.	*Subject*	*Lent by*
363	A dead hare.	Henry Stevenson, Esq.
406	Autumn flowers.	Lent by the Artist.

FINE ART EXHIBITION
in aid of the new Norfolk and Norwich Hospital, 1883

No.	*Subject*	*Lent by*
11	Flowers and fruit.	Mr. James Stowers.
12	Dead game.	Mr. Henry Stevenson.
25	Flowers and fruit.	Mr. James Stowers.
5	Flowers.	Mr. John Gunn.

ART LOAN EXHIBITION
in aid of the Fund for the Restoration of St. Peter Mancroft Church, 1885

No.	*Subject*	*Lent by*
104	Dead game—"Original"	Miss E. H. Stannard.

EXHIBITION OF NORWICH SCHOOL PICTURES
Norwich Museum and Art Galleries, October, 1927

OIL PAINTINGS

No.	*Subject*
108	Still life—fruit, vase, etc. $7\frac{1}{4} \times 9\frac{1}{4}$ in.
109	Still life—study of wild duck. $11\frac{1}{2} \times 13\frac{1}{2}$ in.

STANNARD EXHIBITION, 1934

No.	*Subject*	*Lent by*
39	Still life—an early study. Panel, $7\frac{1}{4} \times 9\frac{1}{8}$ in.	Mr. R. Lee Barber.
40	Still life—wild duck. Panel, $11\frac{1}{2} \times 13\frac{1}{2}$ in.	Mr. H. C. Townshend.
41	Still life—birds and crab. Panel, $9 \times 7\frac{5}{8}$ in.	Mr. G. A. Smith.
42	Flowers. Signed and dated 1861. $32 \times 25\frac{1}{8}$ in.	Mr. L. R. Nightingale.
43	Flowers. Panel, $14\frac{1}{2} \times 10\frac{3}{8}$ in.	Mrs. Ivan Spain.
44	Flowers. Signed and dated 1838. $13\frac{3}{4} \times 11\frac{3}{4}$ in.	Dr. R. J. Mills.
45	Children at breakfast, by Mrs. D. Coppin (mother of Mrs. Joseph Stannard). $19\frac{1}{2} \times 15\frac{1}{4}$ in.	Mr. W. Browne.
46	Flowers. Signed and dated 1878. $19\frac{1}{2} \times 15\frac{1}{2}$ in.	Mr. W. Browne.
47	Flowers. Panel, $14\frac{1}{2} \times 10\frac{3}{8}$ in.	Mrs. Ivan Spain.
48	Flowers. Signed and dated 1838. Panel, $13\frac{3}{4} \times 11\frac{5}{8}$ in.	Dr. R. J. Mills.

No.	*Subject*	*Lent by*
49	Still life—dead game. $33 \times 27\frac{1}{2}$ in.	Tolhouse Museum, Great Yarmouth.
50	Duck. Signed. Panel, $10\frac{1}{2} \times 14$ in.	Mr. Wm. Hubbard.
51	Dead game. $16\frac{1}{2} \times 19\frac{1}{2}$ in.	Miss A. Kitton.
52	Landscape with mill. Water-colour, 7×10 in.	Mr. G. J. Burton.
53	Landscape with figures. Water-colour, $8 \times 6\frac{1}{2}$ in.	Mr. G. J. Burton.
54	Studies of heads. Signed and dated 1854. Crayon, 10×15 in.	Mr. W. Browne.

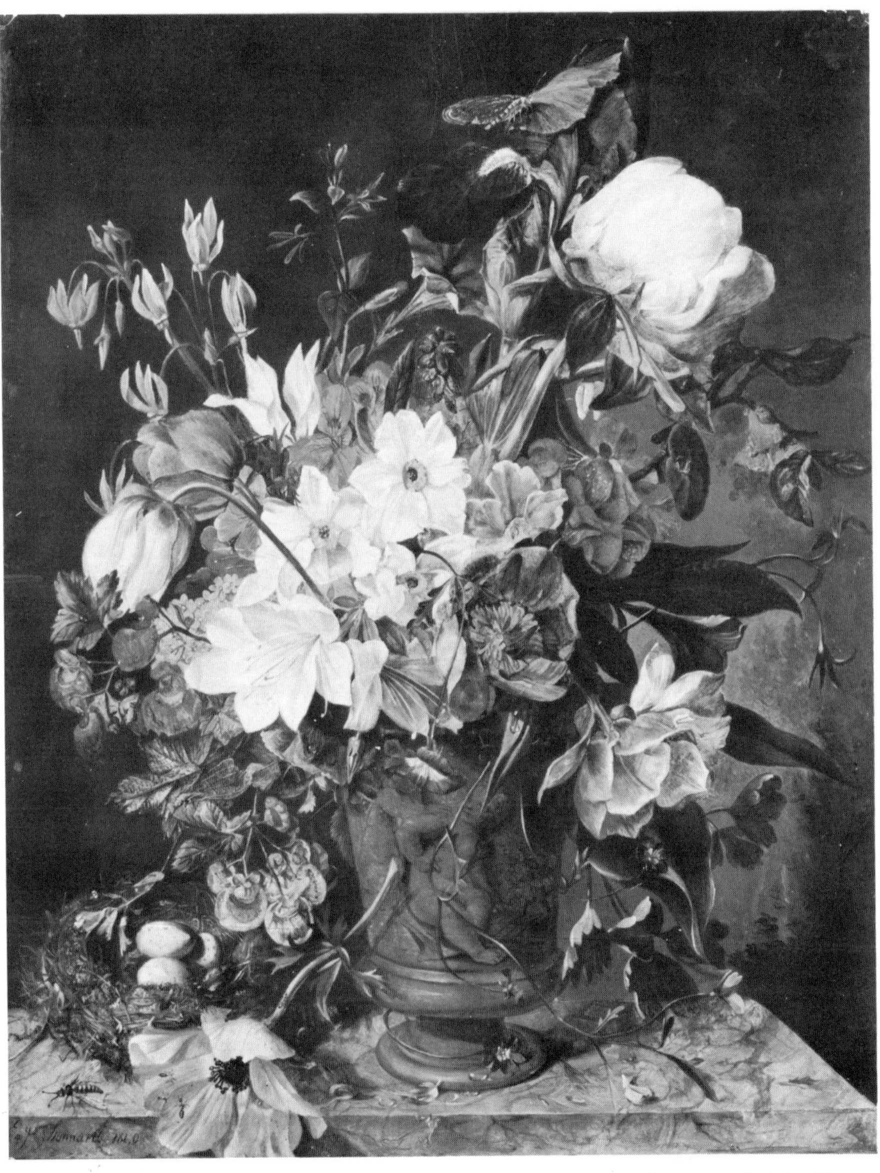

Emily Stannard (Mrs. Joseph Stannard), 1849 *Oil on panel* 12 × 10 *in.* *(one of pair)*

Portraits of members of the

NORWICH SCHOOL OF PAINTERS

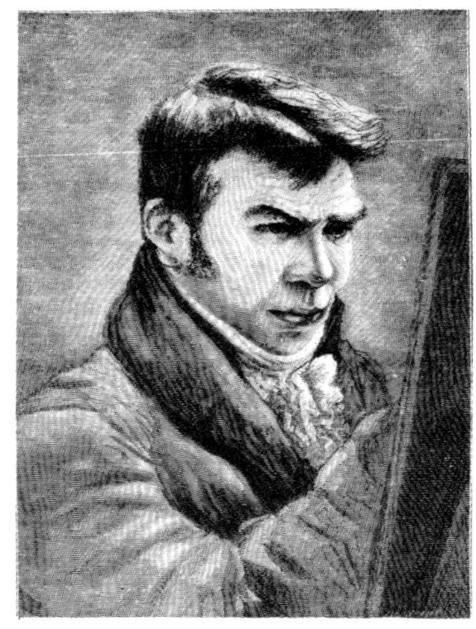

John Crome

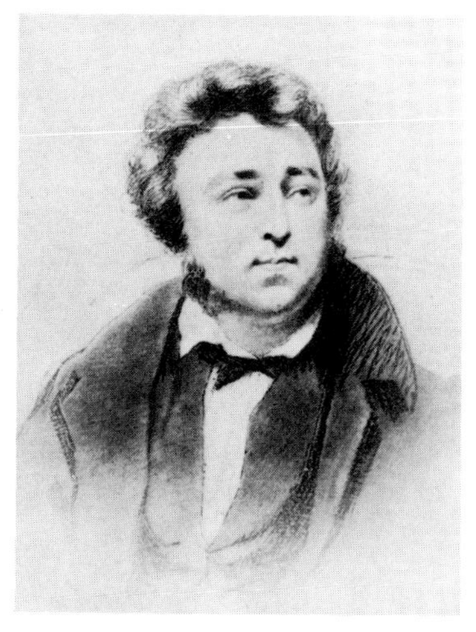

John Berney Crome

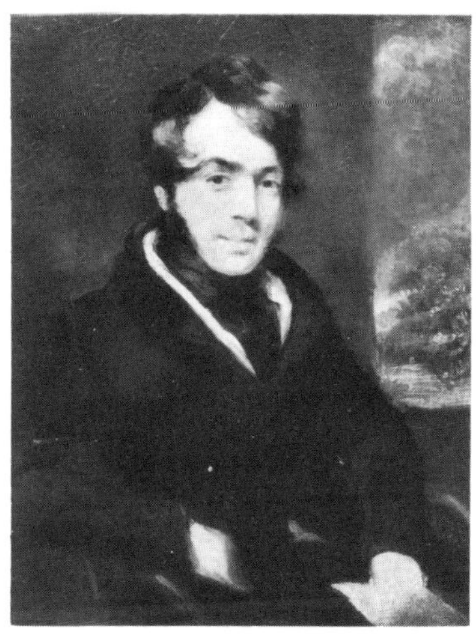

William Henry Crome

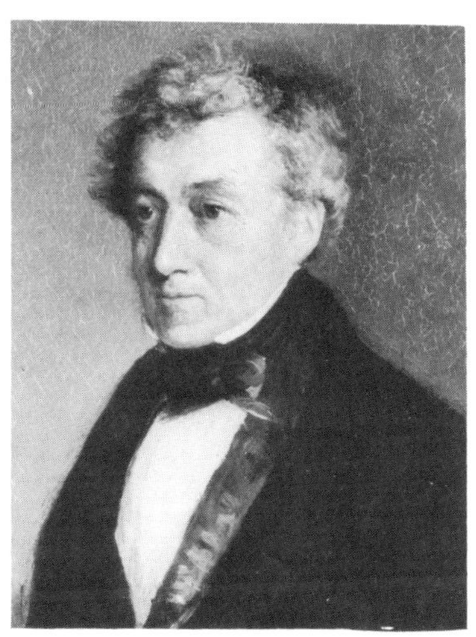

James Stark

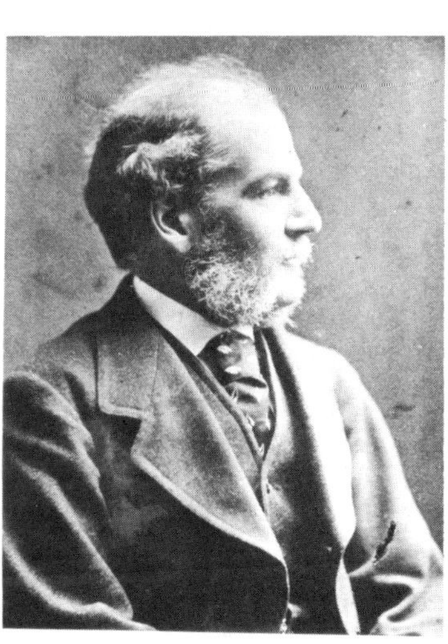

Arthur James Stark

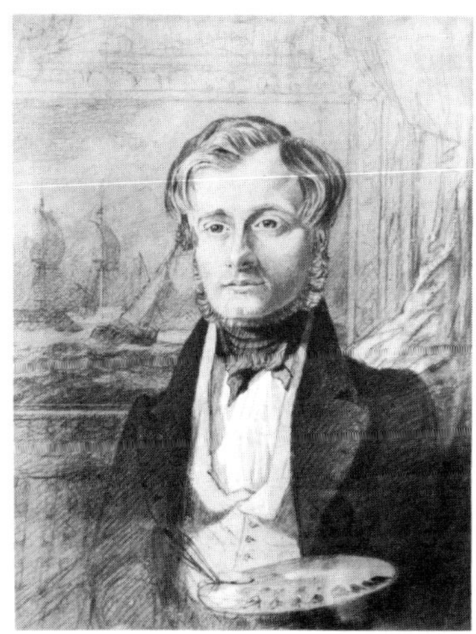

Alfred Priest

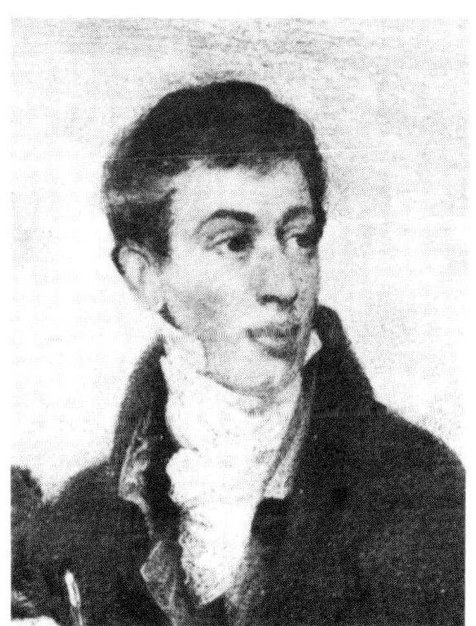

George Vincent

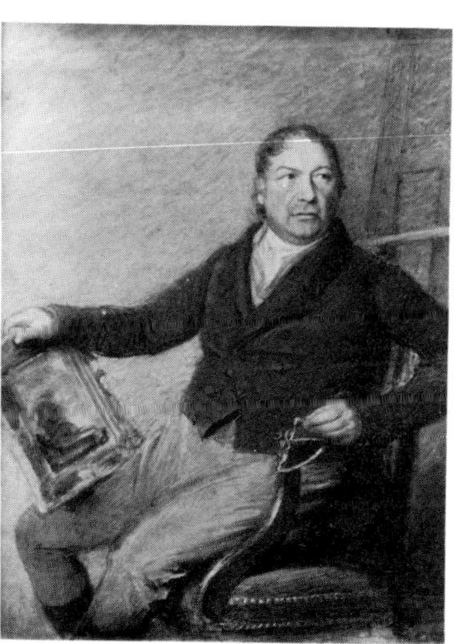

Robert Ladbrooke

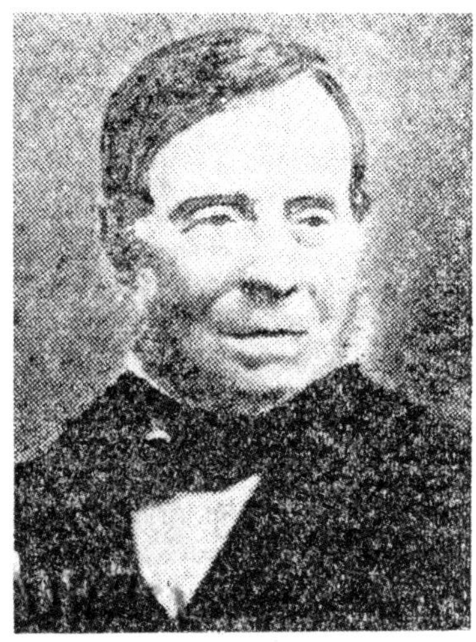
Henry Ladbrooke

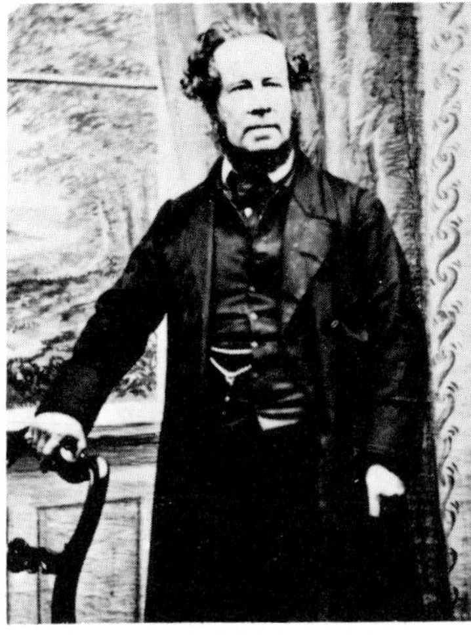
John Berney Ladbrooke

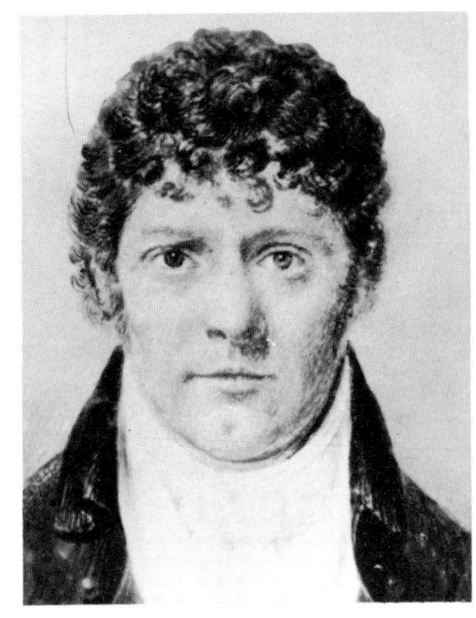
James Sillett

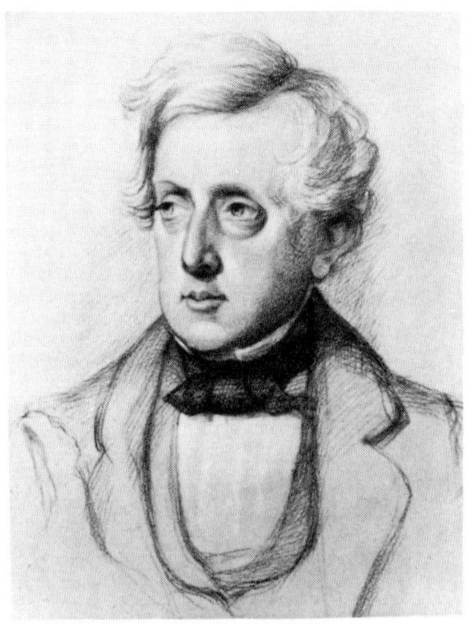
Henry Ninham

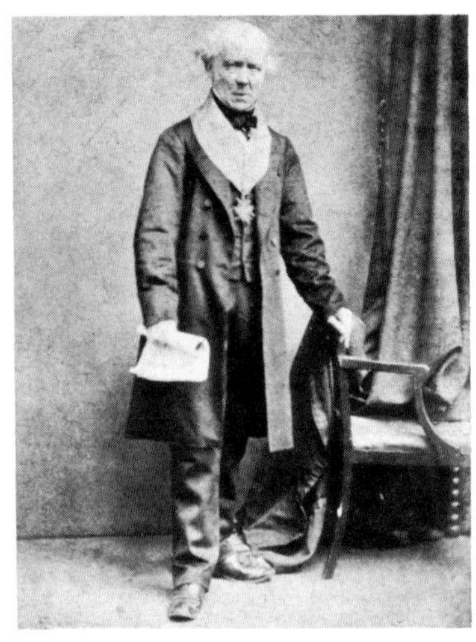
David Hodgson

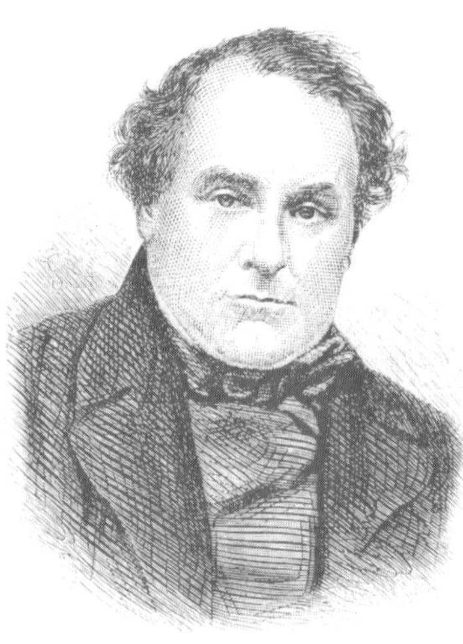
Henry Bright

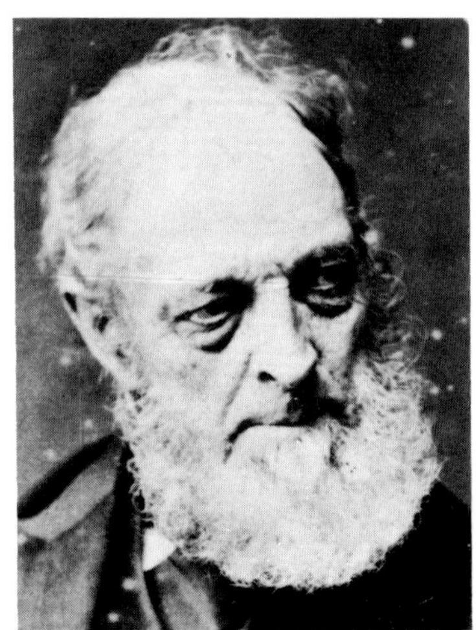
Obadiah Short

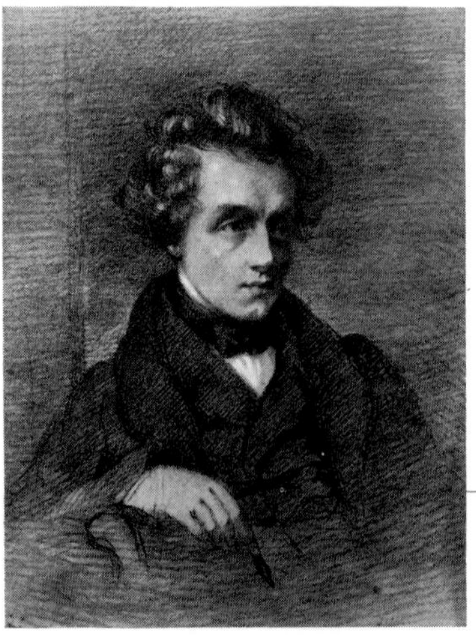
John Sell Cotman

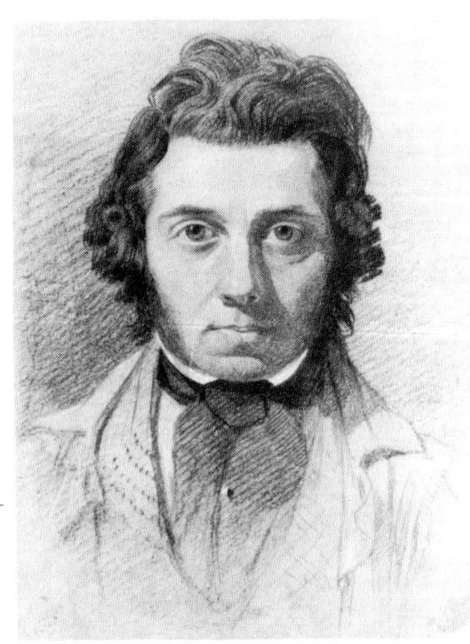
Miles Edmund Cotman

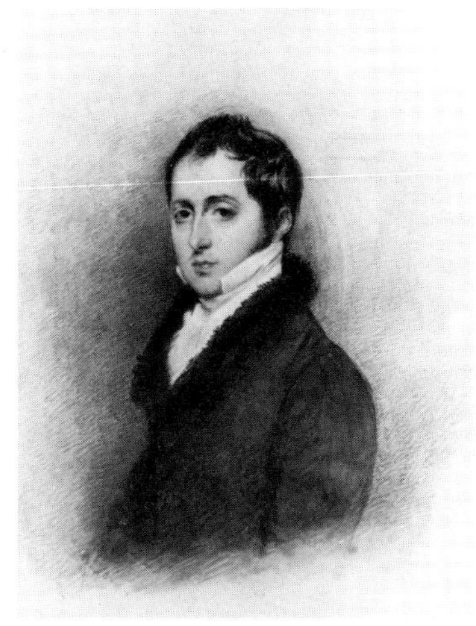

John Joseph Cotman

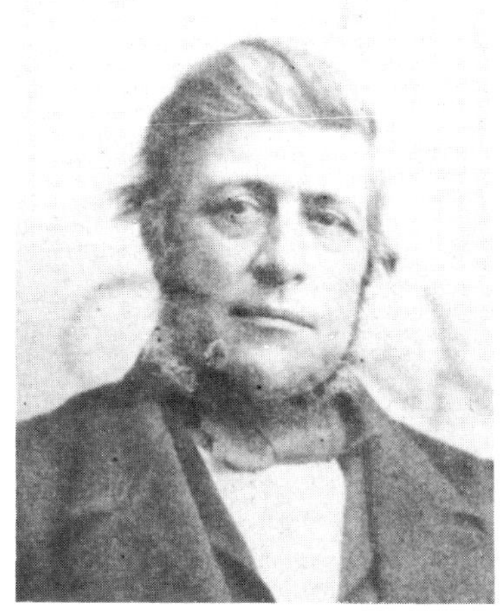

Thomas Lound

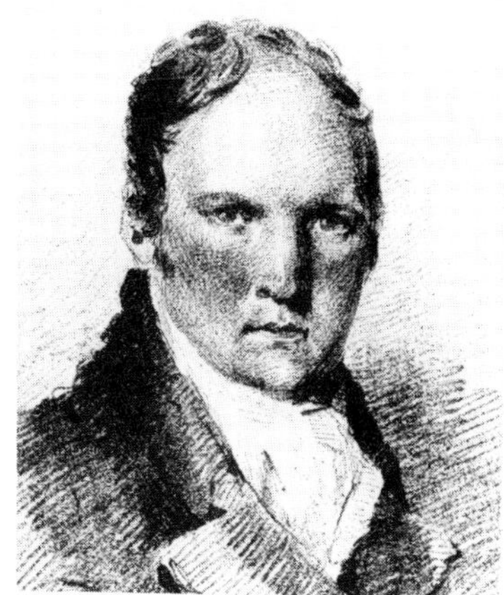

John Thirtle

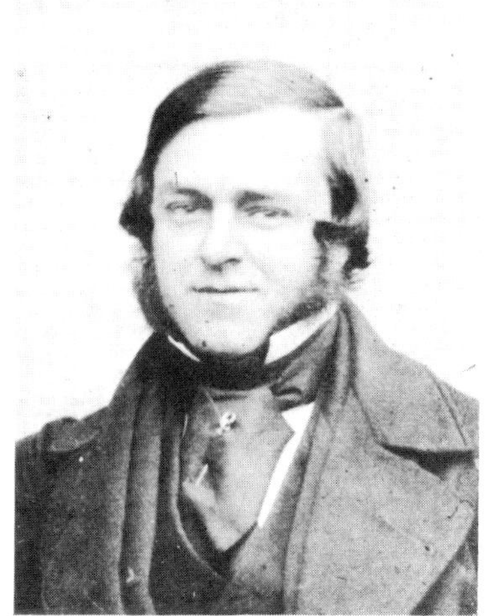

John Middleton

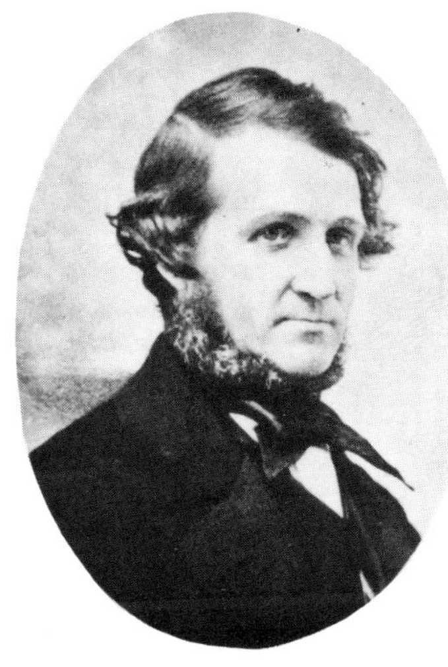

Robert Leman

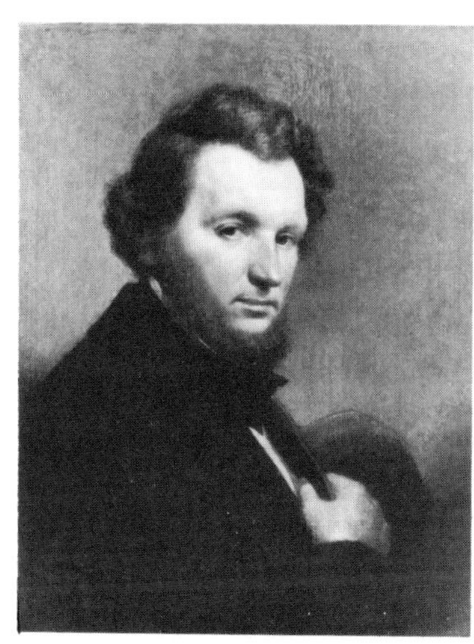

Anthony Sandys

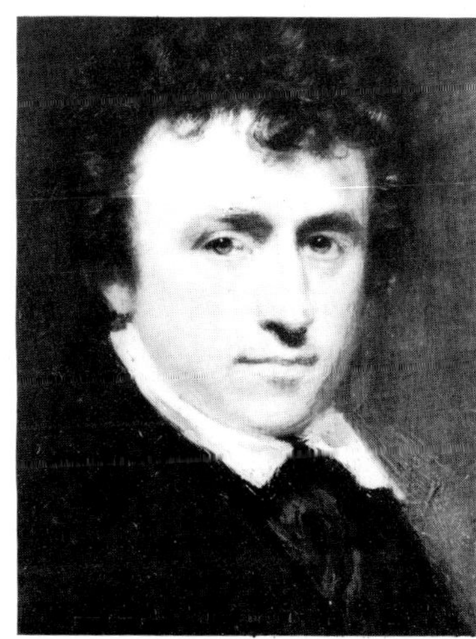

Joseph Stannard

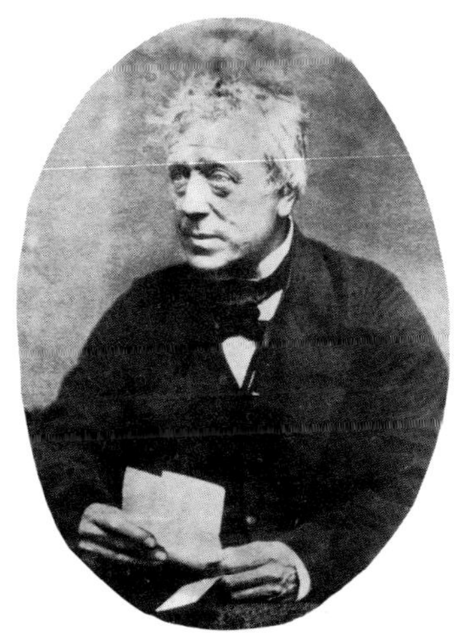

Alfred Stannard

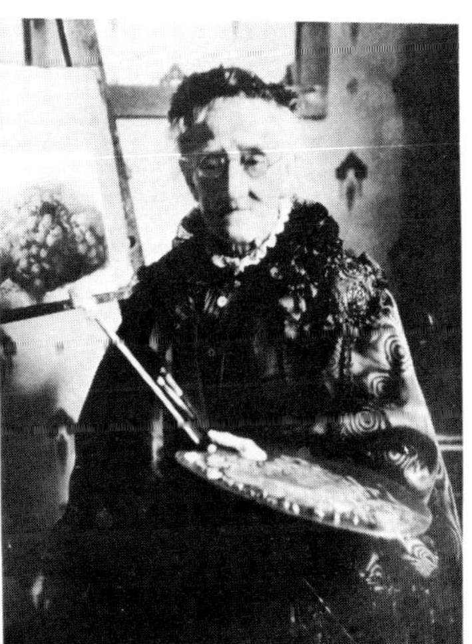

Eloise Harriet Stannard

Index

ACKNOWLEDGMENTS

I am indebted to the following Institutions for permission to publish the following plates:

Norfolk Museums Service:

Tintern Abbey, J. Crome
Portrait of J. B. Crome
Moonlight, J. B. Crome
Portrait of W. H. Crome
View near Norwich, W. H. Crome
Portrait of J. Stark
The Forest Gate, J. Stark
Sheep Washing
Beech Trees, A. Priest
Godstone Bridge, A. Priest
Valley of the Yare, G. Vincent
Fish Auction, G. Vincent
Portrait of Robert Ladbrooke
Foundry Bridge, R. Ladbrooke
Beach Scene, Mundesley, R. Ladbrooke
Bolton Abbey, H. Ladbrooke
Portrait of J. B. Ladbrooke
Water Lane, J. B. Ladbrooke
Landscape, F. Ladbrooke
Landscape, F. Ladbrooke
Moonlight, J. Sillett
Lifeboat going to a vessel in distress, W. Joy
Yarmouth Jetty, W. Joy
Beach Scene, J. Ninham
Portrait of Henry Ninham, A. Sandys
Whitefriars, Norwich
On the Wensum, Norwich
On the Wensum, Norwich, H. Ninham
Landscape, C. Hodgson
Portrait of David Hodgson
Old Fish Market, Norwich, D. Hodgson
Old Barn, Suffolk, H. Bright
Portrait of O. Short
Landscape, O. Short
Study of Horse, E. Cooper
The Buxton Family, H. Walton
Old Yarmouth Jetty, Alfred Stannard
Caistor Castle, Alfred Stannard
Ely Cathedral, Alfred George Stannard
Birds (to left), Mrs. Joseph Stannard
Dutch Fishing Boats, J. S. Cotman
St. Benet's Abbey, 1831, J. S. Cotman
Dutch Boats off Yarmouth, J. S. Cotman
Marine View, M. E. Cotman
Sea Piece—Unloading Timber, M. E. Cotman
Bishop Bridge, Norwich, 1875, J. J. Cotman
Lane near Carrow, J. J. Cotman
View near Norwich, J. J. Cotman
At Lakenham, Thomas Lound
View of Norwich, Thomas Lound
St. Benet's Abbey, Thomas Lound
Riverside Scene near Norwich, John Thirtle
St. Benet's Abbey, John Thirtle
King Street, Norwich, John Thirtle
Tombland, Norwich, John Thirtle
Portrait, John Middleton
Road Scene with Felled Timber, John Middleton
Cantley Beck, John Middleton
Tonbridge (Kent), John Middleton
Dock Leaves, John Middleton
Landscape with Pollards, John Middleton
Portrait of Crisp Brown, Joseph Clover
Whitlingham, Joseph Clover
Portrait of Artist, Robert Leman
Cossey Park, Robert Leman
Heath Scene, Robert Leman
Portrait of Artist, Anthony Sandys
Mill at Cromer, Robert Dixon
Portrait of Joseph Stannard, George Clint, R.A.
Herring Fishing at Yarmouth, Joseph Stannard
Thorpe Water Frolic, Joseph Stannard
Fresh Breeze off Lowestoft, Joseph Stannard
Portrait (photograph), Alfred Stannard
The Black Mill, Alfred Stannard

British Museum — *View of Norwich Castle* (chalk drawing), J. S. Cotman
Nottingham Art Gallery — *The Willow*, J. Crome
The Tate, London — *The Poringland Oak*, J. Crome
Kenwood House, London — *The Water Frolic*, J. and J. B. Crome
Yarmouth Museum — *Yarmouth Jetty*
National Gallery of Scotland — *The Beaters*, J. Crome

Printed and bound in Great Britain by
R. J. Acford Ltd., Industrial Estate, Chichester, Sussex